# MARYLAND MARRIAGES, 1634-1777

Compiled by
Robert Barnes

# CONTENTS

# FOREWORD

This book is a compilation of all marriages recorded from 1634 to 1777 in church records and other documents which are on deposit at the Maryland Historical Society in Baltimore or the Hall of Records in Annapolis. No attempt has been made to contact churches whose records are not on deposit at either of these two repositories or even to see if their marriage books are still in existence, for this would have been a task far beyond the scope of a single compiler and may have postponed the publication of this book indefinitely. It is hoped that this book will complement other collections of state-wide marriage records such as Frederick Bailey's *Early Massachusetts Marriages* and *Early Connecticut Marriages*, William Clemens' *North and South Carolina Marriage Records*, and the two collections for Pennsylvania by John Linn and William Henry Egle, all of which have been published by the Genealogical Publishing Company.

Prior to the establishment of the Anglican Church in 1692, the Maryland Assembly was concerned that accurate registers of marriages be kept. In 1640 the Assembly enacted a law requiring that banns be posted three days prior to the ceremony.[1] In October 1640 a law was passed stating that the names of "all that shall be borne, Married or burried within the province shall be exhibited to the Clarke of Every Court," who was to keep a "just register" and was to be allowed five pounds for every registration.[2] Four years later the law was amended so that anyone who neglected to register any such birth, marriage, or burial was to be fined twenty pounds of tobacco. This law was re-enacted in 1678.[3] After the Anglican Church was established as the official church of the colony, it was ordered that each parish keep a register of births, deaths,

[1] *Archives of Maryland,* I, 97.
[2] *Ibid.,* I, 345.
[3] *Ibid.,* I, 373; VII, 76.

and marriages within the parish, except for negroes and mulattos.[4]

A number of churches are known to have been established prior to 1777, but while portions of their registers have survived, their marriage records have not been preserved in any state repository. A cursory examination of the lists of Maryland's Protestant Episcopal parishes as given in Percy G. Skirven's *First Parishes of the Province of Maryland* shows that perhaps dozens of parishes do not have extant early records. For example, on the Eastern Shore of Maryland, in the area made up roughly of Kent, Queen Anne's, Talbot, Caroline, and Dorchester Counties, Skirven shows the following parishes established prior to 1777: St. Paul's, Chester, and Shrewsbury in Kent County; St. Paul's, St. Luke's, and Christ Church in Queen Anne's County; St. Michael's and St. Peter's in Talbot County; Great Choptank and Dorchester Parishes in Dorchester County; and St. John's in Caroline County. Of these eleven parishes, only St. Paul's and Shrewsbury in Kent, St. Luke's in Queen Anne's, St. Peter's in Talbot, and St. John's in Caroline have extant portions of their marriage records for the period covered by this book. Moreover, many Catholic, Baptist, Lutheran, and Presbyterian records do not appear to have been preserved. Nevertheless, this book contains close to twelve thousand marriages for the period 1634-1777.

The marriages in this book have been drawn from several sources. Of primary importance are the parish registers at the Hall of Records in Annapolis and the Maryland Historical Society in Baltimore. Many of the records at the latter institution are copies of the original registers made in the 1890s and early 1900s by that indefatigable copyist, Miss Lucy H. Harrison. The lists of marriage licenses issued by clerks of the various county courts up through 1777 constitute a second

[4]Percy G. Skirven, *First Parishes of the Province of Maryland* (Baltimore: 1923), p. 81.

important source. Licenses issued prior to 1777 in Anne Arundel, Talbot, and Caroline Counties, as well as licenses issued in 1777 in several other counties, have also been included in this work. In addition, marriages taken from various published sources, such as Kenneth Carroll's list of Nicholite marriages, and marriages performed by Father James Walton, S.J., have been drawn upon. These were originally published in the *Maryland Historical Magazine*. Finally, since church records were not kept until the last quarter of the seventeenth century, a number of marriage records and marriage references taken from the *Archives of Maryland* for the period immediately after 1634 up through 1670 have been included in an appendix.

Marriage notices in early Maryland newspapers have not been included, as they were considered outside the scope of this work; nonetheless, early newspapers should not be neglected by the student as an alternative source in locating marriages. Two sets of church records have not been included because they have been so recently published and because this author has not had the opportunity to examine the original records. These are: *Records of Marriages and Burials in the Monocacy Church in Frederick County, Maryland, and in the Evangelical Lutheran Congregation in the City of Frederick, Maryland, 1743-1811*, transcribed and edited by Frederick S. Weiser (Washington: The National Genealogical Society, 1972).

In this book the marriages are arranged alphabetically by the groom's last name. Following the groom's name is the date of the marriage and the name of the bride. Additional biographical information such as place of origin of either party, parentage of either party, or prior marriage has been included wherever possible. A code designation is given in the last column for each source, followed by a dash and then the page number on which the marriage is found. A list of code numbers explaining the title of the source and its location immediately precedes the list of marriages. A surname index of brides is given at the end of the book.

Every attempt has been made to spell the name exactly as it appeared in the register, so variations in spelling should be checked. One exception to this rule is the entry under the name Eyams, which was recorded under Ijams. When two different sources gave different dates or different spellings of names, or even two pages of the same source gave different data for the same marriage, the discrepancies have been noted.

This book would not have been possible without the help and cooperation of a number of persons. First of all thanks are due to the Maryland Historical Society and the Hall of Records for permission to use their records. The Maryland Genealogical Society and Pastor Frederick Weiser have graciously allowed me to use their transcriptions of certain church records described more completely in the List of Sources. Mary K. Meyer of the Maryland Historical Society and Bettie Carothers have been helpful in checking for the answers to last-minute questions. Work on the index has been expedited by the assistance of my son, Robert Barnes, Jr.

# LIST OF SOURCES CONSULTED

In the following list the initials MHS are used to designate records at the Maryland Historical Society in Baltimore, while the letters HR are used for records at the Hall of Records in Annapolis. All denominations are Protestant Episcopal unless otherwise noted.

## ANNE ARUNDEL COUNTY

1 AA - All Hallows Parish; copy made in 1888 by Lucy H. Harrison, at MHS.

2 AA - St. James' Parish; copy made in 1891 by Harrison, at MHS.

3 AA - St. Margaret's Parish; copy made in 1890 by Harrison, at MHS.

4 AA - St. Ann's Parish, Volume I; copy made in 1889 by Harrison, at MHS.

5 AA - ——————————, Volume II; copy made in 1889 by Harrison, at MHS.

6 AA - Christ Church Queen Caroline Parish (now in Howard County); copy made in 1892/3 by Harrison, at MHS.

7 AA - Anne Arundel County Marriage Licenses for 1777; original records at HR.

8 AA - Marriages performed by various ministers in 1777; in Leisenring, "Record of Maryland Marriages, 1777-1804," ms. at MHS.

9 AA - List of marriage licenses issued by Governors Ogle and Sharpe to All Hallows Parish, 1738-1768; found in Leisenring, at MHS.

## BALTIMORE COUNTY

1 BA - St. George's Parish; copy made by Harrison, at MHS.

2 BA - St. John's and St. George's Parish; copy made by Harrison, at MHS. (Despite the title of the manuscript, the records are chiefly those of St. John's Parish.)

3 BA - St. Paul's Parish; copy made by Harrison, at MHS.

4 BA - St. Thomas' Parish; copy made by Harrison, at MHS.

5 BA - First Presbyterian Church Register, Baltimore; copy made in 1906, at MHS.

6 BA(1) - St. John's Parish; original register, 1696–1798, at
HR, loose papers found with register.

7 BA(1) - St. John's Parish, original register, 1768-1861, at
HR, loose papers found with register.

8 BA - First German Reformed Church, Baltimore; two volumes of
handwritten copy, at MHS; marriages begin in Volume I,
p. 176.

9 BA - Baltimore County Marriage Licenses for 1777; original
records at HR.

10 BA - Marriages performed by various ministers in 1777; in
Leisenring, at MHS.

## CALVERT COUNTY

1 CA - Christ Church Parish; typed copy in ms. collection of
Dr. Christopher Johnston, at MHS.

2 CA - Christ Church Parish; original register, at HR.

3 CA - Marriage Certificates, 1778-1779 (contains some marriages
for 1777); MS. 1999, at MHS.

## CAROLINE COUNTY

1 CR - Caroline County Marriage Licenses for 1774–1777; copied
from original records at HR (Caroline County Land Commis-
sions, Liber G. F. # A, 1774-1793). On folio 6, the
marriage licenses are grouped under two dates, 9 August
1775 and 30 October 1775, but it is not possible to tell
whether the marriages were performed before or after each
date. Caroline County researchers may also wish to con-
sult Sara Seth Clark and Raymond B. Clark, Jr., Caroline
County Marriage Licenses, 1774-1825, and a Short History
of Caroline County (St. Michael's, Md.: 1969).

2 CR - St. John's Parish; copy made in 1893 by Harrison, at MHS.

## CECIL COUNTY

1 CE - St. Mary Ann's (North Elk) Parish; copy made in 1891 by
Harrison, at MHS.

2 CE - Cecil County, Maryland, Marriage Licenses, 1777–1840,
copied by the Captain Jeremiah Baker Chapter, Daughters
of the American Revolution, 1928 (repr. Baltimore:
Genealogical Publishing Co., 1974).

3 CE - St. Stephen's Parish; copy made in 1892 by Harrison, at
MHS.

4 CE - List of Marriages for Cecil County, Maryland, and Lewes,
Delaware; found by Rev. C. H. B. Turner in Marriage
Bonds of Dover, Delaware; in Leisenring, at MHS.

## CHARLES COUNTY

1 CH - Trinity Parish; copy of register, at MHS.

2 CH - Charles County Marriage License Returns, 1777–1801;
MS. 1999, at MHS.
    2 CH(1) - list returned 10 Nov. 1777 by Rev. Thomas

Thornton.

2 CH(2) - list returned 24 Nov. 1778 by Rev. John McPherson.

2 CH(3) - list returned 11 Nov. 1777 by Rev. Henry Fendall.

2 CH(4) - list returned by Rev. John McPherson.

2 CH(5) - list returned by Rev. Henry Fendall.

3 CH - Births, Deaths, and Marriages in Charles County, 1654–1726; typescript at MHS, taken from Court Libers P No. 1 and Q No. 1.

## FREDERICK COUNTY

1 FR - All Saints' Parish; copy made in 1901, by Harrison, at MHS.

2 FR - Prince George's Parish, Rock Creek; copy made in 1889 by Harrison, at MHS; also original register at HR.

3 FR - Grace Evangelical Lutheran Church (formerly St. Peter's, Rocky Hill), near Woodsboro; typescript copy of original register, translated by Pastor Frederick S. Weiser, Archivist, Lutheran Theological Seminary, Gettysburg, who has graciously allowed the marriages to be included; copy at MHS.

4 FR - First German Evangelical Reformed Church, Frederick; copy made in 1903, at MHS; marriages begin in Volume III, pp. 1103-1187.

5 FR - Moravian Church, Graceham; transcript of records prepared in 1942 by Henry James Young from the original records, at MHS.

## HARFORD COUNTY

1 HA - List of marriages performed by various ministers in 1777; found in Leisenring, at MHS.

## KENT COUNTY

1 KE - Marriages from Kent County Court Records; published in Archives of Maryland, LIV.

2 KE - Shrewsbury Parish; copy made in 1898 by Harrison, at MHS.

3 KE - St. Paul's Parish; copy at MHS.

4 KE - Chester Parish; original register at HR.

## MONTGOMERY COUNTY

1 MO - Lists of marriages performed by various ministers; published in Gaius M. Brumbaugh, Maryland Records, 2 vols., 1915–1928 (repr. Baltimore: Genealogical Pub. Co., 1975).

## PRINCE GEORGE'S COUNTY

1 PG - St. John's (King George's or Piscataway) Parish; copy made in 1884 by Harrison, at MHS.

2 PG - Queen Anne Parish; original register, 1686–1777, at HR.

3 PG - Prince George's County Marriage Licenses for 1777, published in Brumbaugh, Maryland Records, I, 93-172.

QUEEN ANNE'S COUNTY

1 QA - St. Luke's Parish; copy made in 1904/5, at MHS.

SAINT MARY'S COUNTY

1 SM - Marriages recorded in the diary of Rev. James Walton, S.
J., while at Newtown, St. Mary's County, from File 6.3,
Woodstock Archives; published in Edwin W. Beitzell, "Newtown Hundred," Maryland Historical Magazine, LI (June
1956), 125-139.

2 SM - St. Andrew's Parish; copy of register made in 1907 by
Harrison, at MHS.

3 SM - Lists of marriages performed by various ministers in 1777;
found in Leisenring, at MHS.

4 SM - Marriages for congregation at St. Inigo's Roman Catholic
Church, 1768-1769; published in Edwin M. Beitzell, The
Jesuit Missions of St. Mary's County, Maryland (N. p.,
N. d., ca. 1960), pp. 71-72.

SOMERSET COUNTY

1 SO - Manokin Presbyterian Church; original register, 1737-
1964, at HR.

2 SO - Coventry Parish; copy made in 1899/1900 by Harrison, at
MHS.

3 SO - Somerset Parish; abstracts of parish register in Turner
Genealogical Collection, at MHS.

4 SO - Marriages from Somerset County Court Records; published
in Archives of Maryland, LIV.

5 SO - Marriages found in Liber IKL; published in Clayton Torrence, Old Somerset on the Eastern Shore of Maryland,
1935 (repr. Baltimore: Genealogical Pub. Co., 1973),
pp. 396-400.

6 SO - Marriages found in Land Record Liber O # 1; published
in Torrence, p. 400.

7 SO - Marriages found in Liber DT # 7; published in Torrence,
p. 401.

8 SO - Marriages found in Liber AZ # 8; published in Torrence,
p. 401.

9 SO - Marriages found in Liber O # 7; published in Torrence,
pp. 401-402.

TALBOT COUNTY

1 TA - Marriages from Talbot County Court Records; published in
Archives of Maryland, LIV.

2 TA - St. Peter's Parish; copy made in 1895 by Harrison, at MHS.

3 TA - Leeds' List of Marriage Licenses; handwritten copy in
MS. 801 at MHS.

## WASHINGTON COUNTY

1 WA - Marriages performed by various ministers in 1777; published in Brumbaugh, II, 522-534.

## WICOMICO COUNTY

1 WI - Stepney Parish; original register, 1738-1838, at HR.

## WORCESTER COUNTY

1 WO - Worcester Parish; photocopy of original register, at MHS.

## SOCIETY OF FRIENDS

Friends' records usually indicate the month by a number, as 5th day, 3rd month, 1743. This is the form used in recording the marriages in this book unless the register also gave the name of month, in which case that was used.

1 SF - Cecil Monthly Meeting; photocopy of original register at MHS. See also Kenneth Carroll, Quakerism on the Eastern Shore (Baltimore: 1970), which contains a transcription of these records.

2 SF - Nicholite Marriage Records; published in Kenneth Carroll, "More About the Nicholites," Maryland Historical Magazine, XLVI (1951), 278-289.

3 SF - Pipe Creek Monthly Meeting; microfilm of original records at HR; abstracts of records prepared by Bliss Forbush on cards, at MHS.

4 SF - Gunpowder Monthly Meeting; microfilm of original records at HR; abstracts on cards at MHS.

5 SF - Clifts Monthly Meeting; published serially in Bulletin of the Maryland Genealogical Society; marriages begin in Vol. XVI, No. 1.

6 SF - West River Monthly Meeting; published serially in the Bulletin of the Maryland Genealogical Society, beginning Vol. XIV, No. 2.

7 SF - Deer Creek Monthly Meeting; microfilm of original register at HR.

8 SF - Third Haven Monthly Meeting; copy of records at MHS; marriages begin Vol. V, pp. 314-454, and continue in Vol. VI, pp. 1ff.; also transcribed in Carroll, Quakerism on the Eastern Shore.

9 SF - Nottingham Monthly Meeting; abstracts of records on cards at MHS.

# MARYLAND MARRIAGES,

## 1634-1777

| | |
|---|---|
| (?), (?), 27 March (?), Jane West | 2 TA-287 |
| (?), (?), 7 April 1713, Susannah Dryor | 1 AA-267 |
| (?), (?), 24 Jan. 1721/2, Ann Burgess | 1 AA-90 |
| (?), (?), 10 Dec. 1722, Ann Holt | 3 KE-245 |
| (?), (?), 1727, Hannah York | 2 BA-2 |
| (?), (?), 15 April 1746, Mary Frampton | 3 TA-58 |
| —iggan, 13 June 1769, Mary Gordon | 2 BA-258 |
| (?), Anthony, son Degue, 23 May 1753, Eliz. Downs | 2 BA-208 |
| (?), George, June 1691, Elizabeth Bayley | 1 AA-38 |
| (?), Hebijah, 7 July 1774, Rebecca Floyd | 1 CR |
| (?), Joseph, Dec. 1742, Rachel Ratcliff | 3 TA-41 |
| (?), Richard, 17 Feb. 1738, Johannah Arrowood | 3 TA-16 |
| (?), Thomas, 25 Dec. 1700, Mary Marshall | 1 AA-246 |
| (?), Thomas, 13 April 1704, (?) (?) | 4 AA-389 |
| (?), Thomas, 1714, Elizabeth Howard | 4 AA-392 |
| (?), William, 8 Jan. 1695, Ann (?) | 1 AA-33 |
| (?), William, 4 Aug. 1734, Jane Stevens | 1 CE-328 |
| Abbess, Edward, 24 Nov. 1734, Katherine Worton | 3 BA-152 |
| Abbett, William, 7 May 1731, Mary Freeman | 3 CE-18 |
| Abbit, John, 11 July 1745, Mary Nicholson | 1 QA-50 |
| Abbott, John, 10 Sept. 1718, Elizabeth Norris | 2 TA-88 |
| Abbott, Sam'l, Sr., 3 Dec. 1701, Elinor (?) | 2 TA-22 |
| Abbott, Samuell, 30 Jan. 1709, Margrett Shannahane | 2 TA-65 |
| Abbott, Samuel, Jr., Sarah Herbert | 2 TA-134 |
| Abbott, Samuel, 17 Aug. 1740, Priscilla Bishop | 3 TA-24 |
| Abbott, Samuel, 18 Aug. 1740, Priscilla Barnett | 2 TA-170 & 276 |
| Abbott, Silvester, 10 Feb. 1700, Elizabeth (?) | 2 TA-13 |
| Abbott, Silvester, 22 July 1731, Marg't Shaw | 2 TA-150 |
| Abbott, Thomas, 23 June 1713, Elizabeth Gilbord | 2 TA-71 |
| Abbott, Wm., 29 Dec. 1735, Ann Megrah | 2 TA-160 |
| Abel, Ignatius, 8 Nov. 1773, Mary Abel | 1 SM-136 |
| Abell, Caleb, 29 Dec. 1763, Mary Williams | 2 SM-57 |
| Abell, Robert, 3 Nov. 1777, Margarita Miles | 1 SM-137 |
| Abell, Zacharia, 15 Oct. 1772, Mary Strong | 1 SM-136 |
| Abercromby, Robert, 6 Aug. 1756, Ann Hatten | 2 BA-213 |
| Abington, John, 20 Oct. 1715, Mary Hutchison | 1 PG-269 |
| Abitt, Sillvester, 3 March 1727/8, Rebeckah Sanders | 2 TA-117 |
| Abrahams, Jacob, 28 May 1685, Isabel Omeli | 8 SF-338 |
| Abrahams, Richard, 27 Jan. 1714, Anne Clark | 2 TA-75 |
| Accars, James, 15 Nov. 1716, Elizabeth Abbott | 2 TA-78 |
| Acklind, John, 30 March 1741, Anne Lattemore | 1 QA-46 |
| Ackworth, Richard, 6 Dec. 1683, Sarah Hardy | 5 SO-396 |
| Acres, James, 24 Sept. 1741, Elizabeth Thompson | 2 TA-175 |
| Acton, Richard, 11 Dec. 1707, Ann Sewell | 4 AA-372 |
| Adam, Anterens, 26 Sept. 1764, Cath. Delater | 4 FR-1105 |
| Adam, John, 15 Feb. 1761, Margaret Weiss | 4 FR-1105 |
| Adams, Alexander, Jr., 19 May 1745, Sarah (Jones?) | 1 WI-34 |
| Adams, Andrew, 25 Feb. 1759, Mary Whittington | 1 WI-46 |

```
Adams, Gabriel, 20 Feb. 1704, Ann Morton              2 AA-326
Adams, Hance, 19 Dec. 1777, Philis Westlick           7 AA-2
Adams, John, 19 June 1729, Sarah Wilson               3 KE-238
Adams, John, 14 Feb. 1760, Sarah Dashiell, widow      1 WI-52
                                                      & 57
Adams, John, 24 Aug. 1777, Margaret Swing            10 BA-69
Adams, Joseph, 19 Dec. 1737, Eliz. Salsbury           1 QA-43
Adams, Josephus, 24 Oct. 1777, Eliza Watson           3 PG-164
Adams, Philip, 9 July 1670, Ann Crew                  5 SO-396
Adams, Philip, 1 Sept. 1691, Mary Barry               5 SO-396
Adams, Samuel, 1 May 1756, Rebecka Whittingham        1 WI-74
Adams, Samuel, 28 Dec. 1777, Sarah Nelson             2 CH (5)
Adcock, James, 13 Aug. 1752, Sarah Ridgers            1 QA-58
Adcock, William, 15 May 1757, Ann Wright              1 QA-62
Addams, Collins, 21 Oct. 1734, Tabbitha Quinton       2 SO-1
Addams, David, 20 Feb. 1766, Margit Tilghman          2 SO-100
Addams, Eli, 19 Nov. 1770, Sephiah Addams             2 SO-102
Addams, George, 4 Aug. 1774, Sarah Moor               2 SO-192
Addams, Hope, 26 Nov. 1772, Anne Maddux               2 SO-102
Addams, Isaac, 18 Sept. 1736, Elizabeth Addams        2 SO-191
Addams, Isaac, 10 Dec. 1764, Mary Cearsley            2 SO-100
Addams, Jacob, 24 Jan. 1760, Anne Addams              2 SO-99
Addams, Jess, 2 Sept. 1756, Sarah Howard              2 SO-98
Addams, Levi, 11 March 1773, Betty Potter             2 SO-192
Addams, Phillip, 7 June 1759, Rachel Potter           2 SO-2
Addams, Philip, 27 May 1767, Ann Hall                 2 SO-192
Addams, Samuell, 8 March 1735/6, Sarah Quinton        2 SO-193
Addams, Samuel, 1 April 1773, Nanne Mitchel           2 SO-102
Addams, Thomas, 28 March 1725, Margaret Cambel        3 BA-148
Addams, Thomas, 22 Dec. 1735, Rachell Addams          2 SO-190
Addams, (Wm.?), 20 April 1746, Tabytha Addams         2 SO-191
Addams, William, 23 July 1754, Leah Hath              2 SO-99
Addams, William, 23 March 1761, Sarah Taylor          2 SO-101
Addams, William, 14 Nov. 1765, Sarah Gunby            2 SO-100
Addams, William, son of Wm. of Condockway, 3 April 1776,
  Leah Bozman                                         2 SO-193
Addeson, Arter, 26 Dec. 1765, Keziah Jones            2 SO-100
Addison, Andrew, 4 Nov. 1708, Elizabeth Brittaine     1 AA-76
Addison, Rev. Henry, M. A., third son of the late Hon.
  Thomas Addison, 1 Aug. 1751, Rachel Dulany, dau. of
  Hon. Daniel Dulany and relict of William Knight, late
  of Cecil Co.                                        1 PG-317
Addison, Col. John, 21 April 1701, Eliza Tasker, dau.
  of Thomas Tasker, age 15                            1 PG-264
Addison, Col. Thomas, 17 June 1709, Elinor Smith, dau.
  of Col. Walter Smith, age c.19 years                1 PG-264
Adgate, Abel, 11 June 1734, Joneacre Cook             2 PG-6
Adkin, Charles, Nov. 1758, Rachel Makeby              4 FR-1104
Adkins, John, 20 Nov. 1716, Mary Murray               3 KE-238
Adkinson, James, 11 May 1749, Mary Lambden            2 TA-1
Adkinson, John, 11 Feb. 1734, Ann Shepard             1 BA-281
Adkinson, Nathan, 2 Feb. 1773, Susanna Salley         3 AA-113
Ady, Jonathan, 27 March 1743, Rebeccah York           2 BA-238
Aghen, Francis, 8 Sept. 1745, Lydia Price             3 BA-157
Ahern, Daniell, 13 Jan. 1707/8, Elizabeth Walker      4 AA-372
Ahern, Partrick (sic), 31 Aug. 1707, Sarah Dimond     4 AA-372
Airs, Abraham, 31 May 1772, Billy Drue Andrew         2 BA-264
Airs, George, 23 March 1774, Amelia Jones             1 WI-112
Airs, Jeremiah, 11 Feb. 1768, Sarah Deason            2 BA-231
Airs, Stephen, 29 Dec. 1767, Eliz. Wation             2 BA-231
Akeridge, William, 3 July 1726, Eliza Symmons         1 AA-103
Albudd, Thomas, 28 March 1772  Dinah Parker           2 BA-264
Alby, Edward, 26 (?) 1769, Lydia Shackells            2 AA-409
Alderton, Joseph, 6 April, 1749, Anne White           3 TA-73
Aldridge, Thomas, 15 July 1703, Elizabeth Purdy(e)    1 AA-64
                                                      & 255
```

| | |
|---|---|
| Aldridge, Thomas, 6 March 1728 (?) (?) | 1 AA-107 |
| Aldrutt, Joseph, 17 Nov. 1772, Jemima Says | 2 BA-265 |
| Alecksander, Thomas, 23 Jan. 1728, Susannah Foard | 2 TA-119 |
| Aleward, John, 14 Nov. 1676, Mary Dixon | 9 SO-402 |
| Alexander, Ebenezer, 13 June 1742, Catherine Tibbalds | 2 TA-267 |
| Alexander, Jacob, 24 April 1747, Rebecca Booth | 4 CE-261 |
| Alexander, Js. (sic), 14 Dec. 1757, Lydia Jones | 1 BA-373 |
| Alexander, John, 28 Nov. 1723, Alce Sulivant | 2 TA-105 |
| Alexander, John, 26 Jan. 1730, Amey Mackey | 2 TA-150 |
| Alexander, Thos., 28 May 1702, Mary (?) | 2 TA-25 |
| Alexander, Valentine, 23 Feb. 1762, Elizab. Dailin(r) | 4 FR-1105 |
| Alexander, Wm., 26 May 1740, Amey Alexander | 3 TA-22 |
|   2 TA-169 gives date as 3 June 1740. | |
| Alford, Edward, 23 April 1715, Mary Dawson | 2 TA-77 |
| Alford, George, 3 May 1725, Elizabeth Wilson | 3 KE-238 |
| Alford, Maccabees, 6 Aug. 1774, Rachael Bozman | 1 CR |
| Alford, Mosess, 25 May 1704, Mary Staple | 3 KE-237 |
| Alkin, Thomas, 2 March 1767, Ellen Middleton | 5 AA-2 |
| All, James, 6 July 1755, Mary Berwick | 1 QA-59 |
| Allain, Jacob, 12 Nov. 1765, Sarah Run | 2 BA-228 |
| Allein, Prindowell, 7 June 1766, Elizabeth Brown | 1 AA-149 |
| Allen, Adam, 11 May 1775, Henrietta Gott | 2 AA-412 |
| Allen, Benj'n, 31 Dec. 1724, Mary Prindowell | 4 AA-424 |
| Allen, George, 17 Dec. 1733, Rebecka Giles | 2 AA-368 |
| Allen, George, 5 Nov. 1754, Eliz. Dimsdale | 2 BA-211 |
| Allen, George, 9 Dec. 1754, Susannah Wood | 2 BA-211 |
| Allen, John, 12 Oct. 1710, Jone Cox | 1 AA-77 |
| Allen, John, 24 Nov. 1740, Ann Rhoades | 2 BA-119 |
| Allen, John, 15 Dec. 1763, Eleanor Brewer | 1 AA-150 |
| Allen, John, 4 Feb. 1770, Jemima Stansbury | 2 BA-259 |
| Allen, Joseph, 8 Dec. 1715, Eliza Peck | 2 AA-356 |
| Allen, Joseph, 2 Nov. 1743, Susanna Davis | 1 CH-177 |
| Allen, Joseph, 9 Sept. 1748, Betty Davis | 1 WI-38 |
| Allen, Rich'd, 14 May 1723, Elizabeth Miller | 1 AA-96 |
| Allen, Thomas, 28 Aug. 1734, Ann Bradley | 2 TA-156 |
| Allen, Wm., 30 June 1700, Elizabeth (?) | 2 TA-12 |
| Allen, William, July 1730, Sarah Turnmarcy | 3 AA-107 |
| Allen, William, 13 Oct. 1752, Elizabeth Jones | 1 BA-354 |
| Allen, William, 5 Oct. 1756, Elizabeth Wright | 2 BA-214 |
| Allen, William, 15 Dec. 1776, Elizabeth Crosby | 2 AA-413 |
| Allender, John, 27 March 1749, Lucina Roberts | 2 BA-157 |
| Alleycock, Anthony, 10 April 1765, Eliz. Fish | 2 BA-228 |
| Allin, Daniel, 9 Feb. 1719, Rebecca Newman | 3 CE-10 |
| Allin, John, 4 Feb. 1770, Jemima Stansbury | 2 BA-259 |
| Allin, William, 5 Oct. 1756, Eliz. Wright | 2 BA-214 |
| Allingsworth, Richard, 22 Oct. 1672, Margaret Covington | 5 SO-396 |
| Allis, John, Oct. 1705, Jane Blaksham | 3 AA-98 |
| Allison, John, 3 Nov. 1768, Eliaabeth Wilkins | 5 BA-1 |
| Allison, Richard, 26 June 1777, Anne Ramsey | 5 BA-1 |
| Allwell, Jacob, 11 July 1738, Sarah Gray | 3 AA-106 |
| Allwell, Jno., 30 Nov. 1704, Eliz. Jeff, widow | 4 AA-389 |
| Alman, Abram, 13 Jan. 1717, Margret Deane | 3 CE-9 |
| Almaney, John, (no date given), Eliz. Warhorn | 2 BA-242 |
| Almeny, Jno., 6 Feb. 1753, Eliz. Waddham | 2 BA-207 |
| Almoney, John, 6 Feb. 1770, Mary Watson | 2 BA-260 |
| Alon, William, 9 July 1773, (?) (?) | 1 CE-301 |
| Alpen, James, 27 Dec. 1704, Joan Poor | 3 KE-237 |
| Alquire, Abraham 10 Dec. 1745, Mary Kemp | 1 QA-51 |
| Alridge, John, 1 April 1719, Susannah Jones | 1 AA-291 |
| Alston, Ralph, 8 June 1739, Sarah Grason | 3 TA-17 |
| Altin, Jno., 7 Feb. 1704, Joan Moore | 2 TA-43 |
| Altried, Geo. M., 24 May 1768, Mary Marg. Messmor | 4 FR-1105 |
| Ambler, Thos., Jan. 1733, Mary Burton Shaw | 1 CA-114 |
| Ambrose, Abraham, 27 Aug. 1704, Elinor Mason | 3 KE-237 |
| Ambrose, Abram, 31 Aug. 1763, Frances Blackston | 3 KE-240 |

| | |
|---|---|
| Ambrose, John, 19 June 1729, Mary Sutton | 3 KE-238 |
| Amery, Samuel, 14 Feb. 1773, Catharine Matthews | 3 BA-207 |
| Amey, John, 31 May 17-(?), Mary Armstrong | 3 KE-238 |
| Amies, Edward, 12 Nov. 1770, Jane Cottman | 1 AA-150 |
| Amos, Benjamin, 19 Dec. 1752, Sarah Lyon | 2 BA-206 |
| Amos, Ludigate, 2 March 1711, Mary Orange | 1 AA-78 |
| Amos, Louldin, 3 June 1770, Rachael Bull | 2 BA-260 |
| Amos, Newdigate, 4 Jan. 1708/9, Honnor Fitzgerald | 4 AA-372 |
| Amos, Thomas, 25 Dec. 1735, Elizabeth Day | 2 BA-67 |
| Amos, William, son of Wm., dec., 4 day, 7 mo., 1765, Martha M. Bull, dau. of Luke Wiley | 1 SF-253 |
| Amos, William, Jr., son of Wm., 1 day, 7 mo., 1773, Susanna Howard, dau. of Benjamin | 1 SF-262 |
| Amoss, Benjamin, 19 Dec. 1752, Sarah Lyon | 2 BA-206 |
| Amoss, James, 29 Jan. 1739, Hannah Clark | 1 BA-275 |
| Amoss, James, 1 June 1773, Catheran Ristau | 2 BA-266 |
| Amoss, Jno., 17 Sept. 1749, Eliz. Stileve | 2 BA-199 |
| Amoss, Jos., 20 Nov. 1750, Martha Bradford | 2 BA-202 |
| Amoss, Mordicai, 16 Feb. 1748, Mary Scott | 2 BA-198 |
| Amoss, Nich's Day, 29 Oct. 1761, Christiana Ditto | 2 BA-222 |
| Amoss, Rob't., 22 Dec. 1765, Martha M'Comas | 2 BA-228 |
| Amoss, Thomas, Oct. 1772, Mary Miles | 2 BA-265 |
| Anctill, Francis, 19 Aug. 1708, Elizabeth Evans | 2 AA-335 |
| Anderson, Abra., 10 Feb. 1763, Ruth Merrideth | 2 BA-224 |
| Anderson, Ben., 2 Nov. 1752, Rozanna Little | 2 BA-206 |
| Anderson, Charles, 2 Nov. 1726, Grace Preston | 1 BA-248 |
| Anderson, James, 4 Nov. 1733, Anne Resho | 2 TA-105 |
| Anderson, Dr. James, 23 Nov. 1744, Sarah Thompson | 1 QA-50 |
| Anderson, James, 3 Jan. 1775, Mary Clark | 5 BA-1 |
| Anderson, John, 21 Aug. 1711, Ann Brookson | 3 KE-237 |
| Anderson, John, 15 Jan. 1723, Eliza Hannahane | 2 TA-106 |
| Anderson, John, 1 Sept. 1729, Elizabeth Bagnal | 6 AA-192 |
| Anderson, John, 13 Aug. 1733, Martha Holley | 2 TA-153 |
| Anderson, John, 1 Nov. 1747, Mary Dixson | 4 AA-449 |
| Anderson, John, 27 Sept. 1749, Sarah Shermon | 1 WI-55 |
| Anderson, John, 28 March 1763, Lydda Richards | 3 BA-167 |
| Anderson, John, 13 July 1769, Isbell Carr | 2 BA-259 |
| Anderson, John, c.Aug. 1775, Elizabeth Horney | 1 CR-6 |
| Anderson, Thomas, 10 Jan. 1721, Sarah Hollinshurst | 2 TA-98 |
| Anderson, Thomas, 18 March 1744, Mary Perdue | 2 BA-239 |
| 2 BA-190 gives 26 March 1744, as date. | |
| Anderson, William, 6 March 1696, Sarah (?) | 2 TA-3 |
| Anderson, Wm., 2 Sept. 1704, Margery Prise | 2 TA-41 |
| Anderson, Wm., 23 June 1709, Elizabeth Kilburn | 4 AA-378 |
| Anderson, William, 4 June 1715, Martha Carr | 2 TA-75 |
| Andersnn, William, April 1727, Sarah Thornbury | 1 AA-104 |
| Anderson, Wm., Jr., 31 Dec. 1739, Priscilla Mecotter | 2 TA-167 |
| Anderson, Wm., 24 July 1740, Mary Megrah | 2 TA-169 |
| Anderson, William, 21 Dec. 1740, Rebecca Lloyd | 1 QA-46 |
| Anderson, William, 7 July,1748, Margaret Surman | 1 WI-71 |
| Anderson, William, July 1749, Catherine Wardlowe | 2 TA-282 |
| Anderson, William, 19 Dec. 1751, Jane Little | 2 BA-204 |
| Anderson, William, 21 Aug. 1755, Mary Harrard | 2 BA-212 |
| Anderson, William, 22 Jan. 1769, Mary Hooper | 2 BA-257 |
| Andrew, Abraham, 22 Oct. 1747, Margret Lynch | 2 BA-194 |
| Andrew, George, 22 Sept. 1672, Thomason Hurt | 5 SO-396 |
| Andrew, Patrick, 30 June 1715, Mrs. Ann Bigger | 1 CA-113 |
| Andrews, John, 14 May 1723, Alice Greening | 4 AA-420 |
| Andrews, Thomas, 25 July 1708, Dorithy Edwards | 4 AA-378 |
| Andrews, Thomas, 2 Aug. 1715, Elizebeth Gutteridge | 4 AA-392 |
| Andrews, William, 14 Feb. 1732, Mary Bond | 2 BA-74 |
| Andss (sic), William, 7 Nov. 1771, Sarah Morris | 2 BA-263 |
| Anger, James, 1 Jan. 1756, Mary James | 2 BA-213 |
| Angley, John, 29 May 1736, Mary Welch | 2 TA-161 |
| Anglin, William, 22 July 1725, Elisab. Taylor, widow | 4 AA-425 |

Angling, John, 2 May 1724, Mary Uneth                        1 AA-328
  1 AA-98 gives date as 21 May, to Mary Unett.
Annuss, William, 26 Dec. 1734, Ruth Kerksey                  1 BA-277
Ansell, Benj., 7 Nov. 1763, Eliz. Johnson                    2 BA-225
Aphord, Matthias, 25 Nov. 1703, Ellin Grundy                 2 TA-38
Applebee, William, 13 Nov. 1750, Mary Jones                  2 BA-202
Appleby, Conrad, 19 Jan. 1773, Ann Creague                   3 BA-169
Archer, Jacob, 4 Oct. 1713, Mary Freeman                     3 CE-5
Archer, James, 8 Jan. 1752, Kathrine Mortimer                2 BA-204
Ardy, Francis, Jan. 1733, Margrett Mitchell                  2 BA-87
Ares, John, 25 Oct. 1702, Eliz. (?)                          2 TA-28
Ares, Jno., 9 Dec. 1704, Jane Hobbs                          2 TA-42
Ares, William, 16 Oct. 1710, Elizabeth Chaplin               2 TA-68
Arey, David, 1 Jan. 1695, Hannah Jadwin, dau. of John
  and Hannah Jadwin.                               8 SF-368
Arey, David, 12 Nov. 1707, Elizabeth Cook                    8 SF-435
Arey, Joseph, 10 Nov. 1708, Mary Baynard                     8 SF-452
Argrass, John, 7 Sept. 1703, Margret Jones                   2 TA-37
Arington, William, 18 Dec. 1727, Mary Haregrass              2 TA-117
Arlett, Francis, 23 May 1743, Mary Pullman                   2 TA-174
Armitage, John, 15 Dec. 1777, Mary Fulhart                  10 BA-69
Armitage, John, 15 Dec. 1777, Mary Fullhart                  9 BA
Armstrong, (?), 8 Oct. 1752, Mary Askins                     1 PG-293
Armstrong, Da'd, 5 Sept. 1765, Isabella Brierly              2 BA-228
Armstrong, Foster, 23 Nov. 1747, Eliza Spence                3 TA-67
Armstrong, Francis, Jr., 6 Aug. 1740, Rebecca Kirby          3 TA-24
Armstrong, George, 4 Feb. 1754, Mary Grimes                  2 BA-209
Armstrong, James, 2 Feb. 1772, Martha H-(?)                  2 BA-264
Armstrong, John, 26 Aug. 1714, Rebecca Hicks                 2 BA-6
Armstrong, Joshua, 20 Feb. 1757, Marg't Barns                1 BA-352
Armstrong, Nathaniel Shippard, 14 May 1769, Hannah
  Norris Lee                                       2 BA-258
Armstrong, Sol., July 1750, Susanah Roberts                  3 TA-78
Armstrong, Solomon, 2 Aug. 1744, Sarah Standiford            2 BA-191
Armstrong, Solomon, 25 Feb. 1749, Elizabeth Barns            1 BA-353
Armstrong, Thos., 11 Jan. 1735, Mary Berry                   2 TA-160
Armstrong, Thomas, 1749, Mary Carter                         2 BA-244
Armstrong, Thomas, 28 Dec. 1752, Sarah Dallerhyde            2 BA-206
                                                        & 242

Armstrong, William, 3 (?) 1735, Eliz. Shepherd               2 BA-77
Arner, John, 27 July 1752, Susanna Burn                      1 QA-59
Arnhold, Frederick, 11 June 1764, Martha Schauer             4 FR-1105
Arnold, Armania, 16 Jan. 1706, Eliz'th Baswassick            3 KE-237
Arnold, George, 2 Sept. 1733, (?) Timbleton                  3 BA-151
Arnold, James, 2 Oct. 1751, Providence Denton                2 BA-204
Arnold, John, 10 June 1736, Hannah Debrular                  3 KE-239
Arnold, Joseph, 20 July 1736, Susannah Chapman               3 BA-155
Arnold, Thomas, 15 Sept. 1742, Sarah Smith                   1 BA-329
                                                        & 333

Arnold, William, 23 Nov. 1722, Elizabeth Gilbert             1 BA-259
Arnold, William, 10 July 1747, Comfort Courtney              1 BA-361
Arnold, William, 26 Dec. 1747, Sarah Lee                     3 BA-161
Arnold, William, 1 Sept. 1775, Elizabeth Taylor              2 AA-412
Arpe, Jno., 29 July 1704, Rebecca (?)                        4 AA-389
Arpin, Francis, 21 March 1735, Ann Macfarlan                 1 BA-287
Arrants, Johannes, 25 Nov. 1745, Sarah Phillips              1 CE-294
Arrants, Johannes, 12 March 1752, Elizabeth Veazey,
  dau. of James                                    1 CE-295
Arrington, William, 5 Aug. 1740, Mary Donnelling             2 TA-170
Arthur, Alexander, 21 May 1704, Mary Smith                   2 AA-323
Ash, John, 8 Feb. 1763, Sabre Milhughs                       2 BA-224
Ashbrooke, John, 1687 (?) (?)                                3 CH
Ashbury, Joseph, 11 May 1749, Rebecca Vandeford              1 QA-55
Ashby, Joseph, 27 Dec. 1730, Ann Pew                         1 AA-111
Ashcom, Nathaniel, 26 Dec. 1706, Margret Bigger              1 CA-112

Ashcroft, Thomas, 20 Oct. 1742, Jane Horney          3 TA-40
Asher, Anthony, 26 Nov. 1749, Sarah Bevan            2 BA-244
  2 BA-199 gives 19 Dec. 1749 as date.
Ashew, Donnole, Feb. 1773, Eliz. Holt                2 BA-265
Ashford, Thomas, 1 June 1735, Mary Cox               1 BA-285
Ashly, (?), 14 Aug. 1714, Martha Wroth               3 KE-239
Ashly, Isaac, 9 July 1714, Mary Wroth                3 KE-238
Ashly, John, 3 Aug. 1714, Martha Wroth               3 KE-238
Ashly, John, 21 Feb. 1744, Anna Grimes               3 AA-106
Ashly, Wm., 25 Jan. 1718, Sarah ffuller              3 AA-100
Ashman, George, 9 Dec. 1736, Jemima Murray           3 BA-156
Ashmead, Joseph, 25 Dec. 1777, Ann Johnson           9 BA
Ashmore, Frederick, 8 Feb. 1759, Bridget Ayres       1 BA-368
Ashmore, William, son of Walter and Margaret, 19 July
  1756, Susannah O'Neal, widow of Daniel O'Neal      1 BA-365
Askins, William, 13 July 1777, Mary O'Neale         10 BA-68
Aspey, Thomas, 5 June 1757, Martha Morehead          2 BA-215
Asquith, William, 2 May 1762, Elizabeth Connell      3 BA-192
Assel, Nathaniel, 18 Sept. 1754, Sarah Jackson       1 BA-356
Atherton, Richard, 1 Nov. 1729, Susanna Norris       2 BA-17
Athey, John, 4 June 1711, Margratt Lewis             1 PG-279
Athorp, Thos., 27 Feb. 1727, Eliza Shaw              1 AA-106
Atkins, John, 20 Oct. 1713, Mary Haynes              3 KE-238
Atkins, Joshua, 28 Aug. 1718, Mary Lyon              2 TA-88
Atkinson, Aaron, 4 Nov. 1771 Ann Dixon               8 SF-141
Atkinson, Isaac, 7 May 1757, Elizabeth Nelson        1 WI-120
Atkinson, John, 23 Nov. 1729, Cornelia Young         1 QA-37
Atkinson, John, 7 Sept. 1738, Joan Tillotson         1 QA-44
Atkinson, John, 14 April 1752, Mary Elliott          1 QA-58
Atkinson, John, Jr., 23 April 1752, Sarah Elliott    1 QA-58
Atkinson, Joseph, 2 April 1699, Naomy Wright         8 SF-449
Atkinson, Joseph, 4 Dec. 1735, Elizabeth Dixon       8 SF-71
Atkinson, Joseph, 9 Sept. 1741, Eliza Clayland       3 TA-32
Atkinson, Joseph, 1 July 1763, Elizabeth Neal, Jr.   8 SF-118
Atkinson, Obadiah, 27 day, 11 mo., 1753, Elizabeth
  Harwood                                            8 SF-101
Atkinson, Samuell, 11 May 1757, Sarah Selbe          2 SO-99
Atkinson, Thomas, 24 Nov. 1775, Polley Bard          2 TA-3
Atkison, Richard, 23 Jan. 1705, Margaret Pickeren    1 AA-72
Atticks, John, 4 Feb. 1713, Elizabeth Barney         3 KE-238
Attkins, Robert, 10 June 1711, Eliza Highway         1 WI-28
Attwell, Benjamin, 6 Feb. 1776, Pricilla Crutchly    2 AA-412
Attwell, Joseph, 24 Jan. 1775, Rachel Phipps         2 AA-412
Attwell, Robert, 25 Jan. 1773, Mary Huyes            2 AA-411
Atwell, John, 11 Dec. 1707, Margaret Horn            2 AA-333
Atwell, William, 1770, Sarah Randall                 2 AA-409
Atwood, Henry, 9 Feb. 1718/9, Jane Pratt             2 AA-360
Atwood, James, 19 Jan. 1768, Henrietta Jarboe        4 SM-72
Aucher, Lawrence, 1 Sept. 1737, Alce Batts           1 BA-297
Audrey, William, 1 Sept. 1726, Rachell Barron        2 TA-113
Auger, James, 1 Jan. 1756, Mary James                2 BA-213
Aulder, George, 16 Dec. 1729, Elizebeth Keech        1 PG-285
Auren, Thomas, 5 Sept. 1776, Keesy Clark             1 CE-325
Aurkhutt, Alexander, 9 April 1705, Ann Barton        1 CA-112
Auron Thomas, 5 Sept. 1776, Keesy Clark              1 CE-295
Austin, Absolum, 8 Feb. 1745, Sarah Lambert          1 QA-51
Austin, Absolum, 24 Feb. 1746, Jane Leet             1 QA-53
Austin, Absolom, 29 March 1758, Sarah Graham         1 QA-63
Austin, Henry, 7 Oct. 1736, Priscilla Pierce         2 AA-379
Austin, Jacob, 19 July 1740, Rachal Hines            1 QA-46
Austin, John, 6 Jan. 1712, Jane Sparks               1 CA-114
Austin, John, 24 Nov. 1735, Catherine Bailey         1 QA-41
Austin, John, 11 May 1777, Ann Beeden                7 AA-1
Austin, Rich'd, 18 July 1746, Susan Eubanks          3 TA-60
Austin, Samuel, 1 Jan. 1743, Mary Green              1 QA-48

```
Austin, William, 3 July 1732, Martha McCannley          1 QA-39
Austin, Wm., 7 July 1735, Mary Mills                    2 TA-159
Austin, William, 13 Aug. 1735, Mary Cleaves             1 QA-41
Austin, William, 10 April 1744, Anne Hendrix            3 TA-48
  2 TA-197 gives date as 12 April 1744.
Avery, Samuel, 14 Feb. 1773, Catherine Matthews         1 CH-207
Avis, James, 19 April 1735, Mary Stevens                3 BA-153
Avren, Benedictes, 7 Nov. 1738, Sarah Kitely, dau. of
  John Kitely                                           1 CE-294
Avren, Rev. Jones, 16 May 1709, Keady Justice, dau.
  of Wm. and Mary Justice                               1 CE-294
Aydelot, John, 2 Dec. 1761, Hannah Wise                 1 WO-10
Ayers, Jeremiah, 2 April 1738, Mary Franklin            3 BA-156
Ayres, Harrison, 13 Aug. 1753, Rachel Ironshere         1 WO-11
Ayres, Jas., 25 Oct. 1774, Ann Griffin                  1 CR
Ayres, Thomas, 22 Jan. (?), Sarah Ingram                3 KE-238
Ayler, John, 28 Nov. 1743, Mary Seaverton               1 QA-48
Ayrris, Ambrose, 18 Feb. 1704, Margrett Bell            3 KE-237
Ayton, Henry, 9 July 1726, Jane Dorsey, widow           4 AA-427
B-(?), Thomas, Aug. (?), Prudence Faslett               3 KE-241
Baal, George, 9 May 1766, Sarah Blew                    1 CE-297
Bachelor, John, 5 day, 4 mo., 1769, Eleanor Addams      2 SF-288
Back, Nicholas, 9 Aug. 1763, Magd. Gullman              4 FR-1107
Backly, Mr. Thomas, 23 Jan. 1746/7, Mrs. Isabella
  Wethered                                              2 KE-264
Bacon, John, 1 March 1714, Beatrice Cruchly             1 AA-79
Bacon, John, 25 Aug. 1771, Temparance Hunt              2 BA-262
Badwell, Jas., 6 Oct. 1765, Ann White                   2 BA-228
Baear, Andrew, 12 Feb. 1739, Kath. Rosear               1 QA-45
Baechtly, Martin, 2 Dec. 1764, Veronica Schnebel        4 FR-1107
Baggs, Isaac, 29 April 1752, Elizabeth Merrick          1 QA-58
Baggs, John, 5 Jan. 1721, Mary Winchester,              2 TA-98
Baggs, John, 24 Dec. 1741, Rachal Tibbles               1 QA-47
Baggs, John, 12 Oct. 1752, Elizabeth Roe                1 QA-59
Baher, Morris, 15 Dec. 1777, Mary Allender              1 WA-526
Bailey, James, 23 Jan. 1734, Rebecca Synnot             1 QA-40
Bailey, Joseph, 27 Dec. 1748, Margaret Osborn           1 BA-362
Baily, Nehemiah, 27 July 1777, Mary Hobbard             1 HA-200
Bailey, William, 1 Jan. 1733, Eliza Mitchell            1 AA-117
Baily, William, 29 Jan. 1737, Elis. West                1 QA-43
Baker, Andrew, 18 June 1719, Marg't Anderson            2 AA-361
Baker, Anthony, 27 Oct. 1714, Eliz'th Cassadey          3 KE-244
Baker, Charles, 9 Jan. 1749, Eliz. Cockey               2 BA-200
Baker, Cha., Jr., 16 Dec. 1762, Eliz. Wheeler           2 BA-224
Baker, Cha., son of Morris, 6 March 1764, Eliz. Ditto   2 BA-226
Baker, Charles, 28 April 1771, Dinah Hendon             2 BA-262
Baker, Demuell, 22 April 1738, Sarah Downs              2 BA-129
Baker, Giles, 14 Oct. 1771, Eliz. Clarke                2 BA-263
Baker, James, 25 Sept. 1742, Catherine Smith            2 BA-124
Baker, Jeremiah, 14 Dec. 1769, Hannah Thackey           1 CE-320
Baker, John, 18 May 1710, Hannah Williams               1 CA-113
Baker, John, 16 April 1734, Mary Hilliard               3 BA-152
Baker, Lemuel, 5 March 1739, Sophia Meade               2 BA-137
Baker, Maurice, Jan. 1704, Sarah Nickels                3 AA-98
Baker, Morris, 9 Jan. 1704, Sarah Nicholson             4 AA-389
Baker, Nathan, 12 Jan. 1736/7, Joyce Yardley            1 CE-283
Baker, Nicholas, 4 Jan. 1741, Martha Wood               1 BA-324
Baker, Nicholas, 18 Jan. 1749/50, Mary Stevens          3 BA-163
Baker, Norton Grover, 23 day, 1 mo., 1742, Mary
  Rawlings                                              4 SF
Baker, Solomon, 4 June 1741, Mary (Dale ?)              1 WO-9
Baker, Theo's, 6 Oct. 1748, Eliz. Beldem                2 BA-197
Baker, Thomans, 1763, Margret Pheland                   1 CE-317
Baker, Thomas, 14 April 1734, Mary Crawford             1 BA-270
Baker, Thos., 20 Dec. 1762, Ann Pocock                  2 BA-224
```

Baker, Will'm, 10 Jan. 1704, Eliza Floyd                          4 AA-389
Baker, William, 16 Sept. 1737, Elizabeth Cannon                  1 BA-290
Baker, Wm., 3 May 1767, Eliz. Nichols                            2 BA-230
Baker, William, 2 June 1772, Roxannah Whiley                     2 BA-264
Baker, Zebediah, 28 Jan. 1749/50, Hannah Baker                  3 BA-163
Balch, Hezekiah James, 27 (Oct. 1768?), Martha
   McKinley                                                     2 BA-257
Balch, James, 19 Jan. 1737, Ann Goodwin                         1 BA-290
Baldwin, James, 20 Jan. 1714, Mary Tyler                        2 PG-1
Baley, David, 11 May 1741, Anne Tolson                          1 QA-46
Baley, James, 22 July 1736, Rachel Cleve                        1 QA-42
Baley, James, 21 Aug. 1746, Mary Collins                        1 QA-52
Baley, James, 10 Nov. 1748, Ann Honey                           1 QA-55
Baley, Matthew, 9 April 1751, Rachel White                     1 QA-57
Baley, Thomas, 19 April 1744, Hanah Cleaves                    1 QA-49
Baley, William, 24 Oct. 1737, Mary Riddle                      1 QA-43
Ball, Benj., of Kent Island, 5 mo., 8 day., 1714,
   Elizabeth Richardson, dau. of William and
   Margaret Richardson                                          6 SF-49
Ball, Daniel, 11 Aug. 1718, Eleanor Gardner                    2 AA-359
Ball, George, 9 May 1766, Sarah Blue                            1 CE-324
Ball, George, 1 Dec. 1776, Ann Kely                            1 CE-297
Ball, George, 1 Dec. 1777, Ann Keely                           1 CE-324
Ball, John, 19 Feb. 17-(?), Sarah Johnston                     1 PG-291
Ball, John, 14 Nov. 1711, Anne Sash                            1 AA-78
Ball, John, 11 Nov. 1725, Rebecca Pitt                         1 SF-58
Ball, John, 1 June 1747, Mary Rainey                           3 TA-65
Ball, Thomas, 6 April 1741, Mable Dawson                       3 TA-29
Ball, William, 8 Jan. 1776, Sally Townsend                     2 SO-198
Ballinger, William, son of Henry and Hannah, 3 Oct.
   1751, Cassandra Plummer, dau. of Samuel and Sarah.          3 SF
Baly, Robert, Aug. 1714, Sarah Smith                           3 AA-100
Baly, William, 28 Oct. 1746, Eliza Rathel                      3 TA-62
Balzel, Henry, 2 Nov. 1760, Marg. Alexander                    4 FR-1107
Balzel, Jacob, 30 Nov. 1766, Marg. Schley, widow               4 FR-1107
Balzel, Peter, 23 Feb. 1762, Catherine Ruesel                  4 FR-1107
Bambergern, John, 16 Jan. 1763, Elisab. Ulmann                 4 FR-1107
Banckes, William, 14 Jan. 1744, Deborah Hawkins                2 CR-269
Bande, Andrew, 25 April 1728, Debroah Dudly                    2 TA-118
Bane, Wm., 14 Oct. 1761, Lydia Johnson                         2 BA-222
Banes, William, 26 Dec. 1684, Anne Phesey                      5 SO-396
Bangall, Alexander, (no date given), Elizabeth Viney           3 KE-241
Baning, Charles, 9 Jan. 1739, Rachel Humphreys                 2 TA-168
Baning, Richard, 30 Nov. 1737, Esther Millson                  2 TA-164
Banks, Henery, 29 April 1716, Elizabeth Wickes                 3 KE-244
Banks, John, 18 Sept. 1756, Mary Kelley                        3 BA-72
Banks, William, 14 Jan. 1743, Debra Hawkins                    1 QA-49
Bankson, Andrew, 8 Sept. 1726, Rachel Artcher                  2 TA-113
Bankson, Joseph, 16 Jan. 1752, Elizabeth Slemaker,
   widow of James Slemaker.                                     3 BA-166
Bankstor, John, 29 June 1735, Marg't Kent                      2 TA-159
Banning, Charles, 5 Feb. 1721, Jane Marshell                   2 TA-98
                                                               & 100
Banning, William, 21 June 1774, Rebecca Cheezum                1 CR
Barber, (?), 20 July 1729, Francis Moll                        3 KE-245
Barber, Elias, 14 Dec. 1777, Elizab. Wainwright                3 SM-535
Barber, James, 18 July 1682, Mary Gush                         8 SF-410
Barber, John, 31 Aug. 1680, Anne (Winne ?)                     5 SO-396
Barber, John, 23 April 1710, Sarah Pingstone, als.
   James (1 AA-259 gives her name as Pringston)                1 AA-77
Barclay, Rev. John, Rector of St. Peter's, son of
   David and Christian of Co. Kingcarden, Scotland,
   4 May 1768, Rachel Goldsborough, dau. of Nicholas
   and Sarah                                                   2 TA-290
Barclay, Thomas, 26 March 1763, Margaret Cole                  3 BA-167

Barham, Joseph, 1753, Sarah Demmett                    2 BA-242
Barker, Charles, 13 Jan. 1707/8, Anne Jones            4 AA-372
Barker, Richard, 24 Sept. 1761, Mary Whorton           1 WO-15
Barker, Sam'll, 15 Nov. 1715, Mary Balard              1 PG-263
Barkhurst, Charles, 19 July 1744, Jane Carman          1 QA-49
Barkhurst, George, 16 May 1745, Amy Satterfield        1 QA-50
Barkhurst, George, 14 Aug. 1750, Mary Carrer           1 QA-57
Barkhurst, William, 2 March 1730, Hanah Burris         1 QA-36
Barkhurst, William, 5 Aug. 1735, Susanna Bown (sic)    1 QA-41
Barkley, Arch'd, 25 Aug. 1768, Martha Sheldon          2 BA-232
Barkley, Thomas, 17 June 1709, Margrit Blaylock        1 WI-23
Barleigh, Pasque, 21 Aug. 1684, Hannah Keene           5 SO-396
Barloe, John, 12 Feb. 1737, Elizabeth Keith            6 AA-202
Barnaby, Edward, 22 Sept. 1745, Elisabeth Farmer       2 BA-240
Barnard, Thomas, son of Richard and Ann, 8 day, 9 mo.
  1750, Sarah Miller, dau. of James and Ann            9 SF
Barnes, Ford, 21 Sept. 1721, Margaret Farmer           1 BA-228
Barnes, James, 27 May 1726, Bethia Loney               1 BA-258
Barnes, James, 14 Jan. 1728, Elizabeth Dawson          4 AA-431
Barnes, James, 12 Sept. 1733, Ann Brown                2 TA-154
Barnes, Job, 11 Oct. 1722, Constance West              1 BA-230
Barnes, Richard, 1 Feb. 1672, Susana Searle            5 SO-396
Barnes, Richard, 28 July 1716, Sarah Stevens           4 AA-398
Barnes, Rober (sic), 11 Feb. 1728, Loias Porter        4 AA-431
Barnes, William, 18 Sept. 1718, Susanna Davis          4 AA-406
Barnes, Zachar., 20 Jan. 1770, Susan Thompson          1 SM-135
Barnet, John, 26 July 1777, Elizabeth Hill             1 HA-200
Barnet, Thomas, 6 Feb. 1729, Ann Mattison              2 TA-148
Barnet, Thomas, Jr., 17 Aug. 1740, Rachel Connolly     3 TA-24
Barnet, Thomas, 18 Nov. 1746, Margritt Gregg           1 QA-52
Barnett, James, 9 Nov. 1737, Susannah Frith            2 TA-162
Barnett, John, 13 Nov. 1683, Alce Taylor               9 SO-402
Barnett, John, 30 Dec. 1746, Eliza Stevens             3 TA-64
  2 TA-281 gives date as 5 Jan. 1746/7.
Barnett, John, 17 Nov. 1748, Mary Hindsley             1 QA-55
Barnett, Thomas, Jr., 24 Aug. 1740, Rachel Connolly,
  widow                                                2 TA-169
                                                         & 277
Barnett, Thomas, 1 May 1744, Phebe Giles               3 TA-49
  2 TA-196 gives date as 3 May 1744.
Barnett, Thomas, 17 Aug. 1748, Eliza Bishop            1 QA-64
Barney, Benj., 23 April 1758, Delilah Bozley           2 BA-217
Barney, Francess, 3 Aug. 1714, Ruth Alford             3 KE-244
Barney, Moses, 5 April 1758, Sarah Bond                4 BA-73
Barney, William, 26 Jan. 1743, Frances Holland Watts   3 BA-167
Barnhart, Benjamin, 3 April 1773, Rachael Wood, dau.
  of Jos. and Catherine                                1 FR-10
Barns, Ford, 20 Oct. 1743, Ruth Garrett                1 BA-234
Barns, Grigory, 30 Nov. 1758, Elizabeth Mitchel        1 BA-382
Barns, Henry, 27 Oct. 1654, Eliz. Green                2 BA-211
Barns, Job, 2 Feb. 1749, Mary Crawford                 1 BA-353
Barns, Jno., 10 Aug. 1749, Eliz. Scott                 2 BA-198
Barns, William, 2 Nov. 1758, Margret Schott            1 CE-296
Barnwell, James, 31 July 1709, Elizabeth Slater        2 TA-61
Barnwell, James, Jr., 1 March 1742/3, Sarah Dudley     3 TA-42
Barnwell, James, Jr., 10 March 1742, Mary Dudley       2 TA-173
Barnwill, James, Jr., c. Aug. 1775, Sarah Charshe      1 CR-6
Barny, William, 22 June 1777, Mary Hinson              7 AA-1
  His name might be read as Barry.
Barrat, Dennis, 18 Jan. 1746, Xtan (sic) Manson        1 QA-52
Barrat, Phillip, 3 May 1713, Kathrine Terry            3 CE-5
Barrat, Philip, 8 June 1719, Mary Burnham              3 CE-9
Barrat, Philip, 20 Feb. 1720, Jane Merrit              3 CE-11
Barrat, Thomas, 7 Aug. 1748, Sarah Roberts             1 QA-54
Barratt, Darbey, 21 Feb. 1709, Catherine Vinton        2 TA-65

| | |
|---|---|
| Barratt, John, 26 Sept. 1750, Margrett Newell | 3 BA-164 |
| Barratt, William, 13 Jan. (?), Mary Clark | 3 KE-240 |
| Barret, Joseph, 24 Oct. 1773, Mary Outten | 2 SO-195 |
| Barrett, Andrew, 11 Dec. 1749, Mary Shepperd, dau. of Thomas and Ann | 1 CE-296 |
| Barrett, Arthur, 13 day, 6 mo., 1705, Lydia Chambers | 9 SF |
| Barrett, Arthur, son of Arthur and Lydia, 17 Dec. 1734, Hannah Brown, dau. of Messer and Jane | 9 SF |
| Barrett, Arthur, son of Arthur and Lydia, 11 day, 10 mo., 1735, Mary Pugh, dau. of John | 9 SF |
| Barrett, Joseph, 30 Jan. 1752, Rebecca Smith | 1 QA-58 |
| Barrett, Thomas, 5 Feb. 1708, Mary Fossett | 3 KE-242 |
| Barrett, Thomas, son of Arthur and Lydia, 29 Nov. 1739, Hannah Oldham, dau. of Thomas and Susanna | 9 SF |
| Barrett, William, (?) Jan. (?), Jane Rawlinson | 3 KE-241 |
| Barreymore, James, 25 Sept. 1719, Mary Frigs | 1 WI-1 |
| Barreymore, James, widower, 31 Jan. 1724/5, Eliz. Shehee (?) (sic) | 1 WI-1 |
| Barron, James, 9 Jan. 1721, Sarah Stacey | 2 TA-98 |
| Barrow, Ri., 4 Feb. 1743/4, Jane Kinnamont | 3 TA-47 |
| Barrow, Thomas, 29 Oct. 1744, Anne Davis | 3 TA-50 |
| Barry, John, 10 June 1712, Sarah Ridgely | 1 AA-78 |
| Bartlet, Daniel, 10 Aug. 1748, Rebeca Tompson | 3 TA-70 |
| Bartlet, Solomon, 10 day, 12 mo., 1775, Mary Victor | 2 SF-288 |
| Bartlet, James, son of Thomas, 2 day, 10 mo., 1731, Sarah Hopkins, dau. of Dennis | 8 SF-65 |
| Bartlett, John, 14 Oct. 1731, Elizabeth Chance | 2 TA-151 |
| Bartlett, John, 4 Jan. 1745/6, Sarah Rennolds | 3 TA-56 |
| Bartlett, Joseph, 11 Dec. 1735, Martha Milton, dau. of Abraham | 1 SF-73 |
| Bartlett, Nicholas, 15 July 1752, Rebecca Gilbert | 1 QA-58 |
| Bartlett, Thomas, Jr., 14 April 1731, Mary Regester | 8 SF-64 |
| Bartley, Jas., 25 May 1761, Mary Sheldon | 2 BA-221 |
| Barton, Azel, 29 Aug. 1769, Ann Holt | 2 BA-259 |
| Barton, James, 8 Oct. 1730, Temperance Rollo | 2 BA-68 |
| Barton, James, 19 Dec. 1756, Sarah Everett | 2 BA-214 |
| Barton, John, 1 June 1703, Hester Holmes | 1 CA-111 |
| Barton, John, 23 May 1738, Ann Hitchcock | 2 BA-104 |
| Barton, John, 20 Dec. 1770, Ruthe Gorsuch | 2 BA-261 |
| Barton, Lewes, 30 June 1757, Johannah Simmons | 2 BA-215 |
| Barton, Richard, 26 Dec. 1705, Elizabeth Lyllingame | 1 AA-72 |
| Barton, Richard, 11 Jan. 1721/2, Eliza Leeke | 1 AA-89 |
| Barton, Selah, 27 Dec. 1730, Rebecca Beddeson | 3 BA-150 |
| Barton, Selah, 24 Jan. 1733, Comfort Roberts | 3 BA-151 |
| Barton, Thomas, 24 Feb. 1733, Eliz. Ward | 2 BA-76 |
| Barton, Thomas, Jr., 16 April 1761, Phebe Cammell | 2 BA-221 |
| Barton, Wm., 9 April 1705, Catherine Place | 1 CA-112 |
| Barton, William, 25 Oct. 1731, Sarah Savory | 1 AA-113 |
| Barwick, James, 20 Dec. 1757, Elizabeth Swift | 1 QA-63 |
| Barwick, James, c. Oct. 1775, Rebekah Roberts | 1 CR-6 |
| Bashet, Richard, 29 Jan. 1744, Afria Boyd | 2 BA-239 |
| Bashiere, John, Dec. 1726, Mary Macdowel | 1 AA-104 |
| Bashiere, Robert, 2 Feb. 1726, Charity Macdowell | 1 AA-104 |
| Bashteen, William, March 1699, Lydia Allgood | 1 BA-191 |
| Basinby, Edward, 4 Sept. 1720, Sarah Evans | 2 PG-2 |
| Basket, Richard, 31 Jan. 1743, Adfire Boyd | 2 BA-190 |
| Basnett, Robart, 8 Oct. 1745, Sus. Maner | 1 QA-51 |
| Bassil, Ralph, 23 Sept. 1697, Rose Hopper | 1 AA-38 |
| Batcheldor, John, 6 April 1739, Eliza Burgess | 2 TA-165 |
| Batchelor, William, 27 Dec. 1714, Elizabeth Henricks | 2 TA-75 |
| Batchelor, Wm., 12 Dec. 1774, Margaret M'Can | 1 CR |
| Bateman, Christopher, 23 May 1758, Mary Wilkinson | 1 QA-63 |
| Bateman, Henry, 22 Dec. 1707, Sarah Powel | 4 AA-372 |
| Bateman, Henry, 31 July 1722, Mehitabel Holland | 4 AA-419 |
| Bateman, Michael, 12 May 1757, Mary Rush | 1 QA-62 |

| | |
|---|---|
| Bateman, William, 28 Jan. 1696, Sary Wells | 1 AA-35 |
| Bateman, William, 14 Sept. 1704, Elizabeth Westmycutt | 3 KE-241 |
| Bathershall, Henry, (?) Dec. (?), Rachell Rush | 3 KE-241 |
| Baton, Jno., 1 Sept. 1763, Reb. Armstrong | 2 BA-225 |
| Batsey, John, Dec. 1743, Eliza Larimore | 3 TA-46 |
| Battee, Benj., Aug. 1717, Ann Evans | 2 AA-358 |
| Battee, Ferdinando, 11 Dec. 1718, Elisabeth Wooden | 1 AA-288 |
| Battie, John, 1771, Agness Gott | 2 AA-411 |
| Batts, George, 3 Jan. 1740/1, Mary Courtney | 1 QA-46 |
| Batts, Humphrey, 6 April 1727, Mary Tyler | 1 PG-279 |
| Baughen, Stephen, 7 Dec. 1777, Barbara Shaffner | 10 BA-69 |
| Baughon, Stephen, 4 Dec. 1777, Barbara Shaffron | 9 BA |
| Baulch, John, 24 March 1735, Mary Cannon | 1 BA-289 |
| Bauman, John Jac., 25 Nov. 1767, Elizab. Keller | 4 FR-1107 |
| Baxster, Roger, 6 day, 11 mo., 1655, Mary Croutch | 1 KE-38 |
| Baxter, Francis, 9 June 1720, Susanna Ray | 2 PG-2 |
| Baxter, Thomas, 19 Dec. 1668, Hannah Fordah | 1 KE-187 |
| Bay, John, 8 Jan. 1722, Mary Vale | 2 TA-104 |
| Bayard, Samuel, 3 July 1729, Fransinah Malding, dau. of Mr. Francis Malding | 3 CE-19 |
| Bayfield, George, 29 April 1777, Mary Tasker | 2 AA-413 |
| Bayley, Groome Bright, 5 Oct. 1757, Mary Moore | 2 BA-216 |
| Bayley, John, 19 Jan. 1735, Ann Welch | 3 BA-154 |
| Bayley, Jno., 23 Dec. 1759, Ann Copland | 2 BA-219 |
| Bayley, Thomas, Jr., 26 Dec. 1758, Rachel Towson | 2 BA-49 |
| Bayley, William, 21 Oct. 1705, Elizabeth Gill | 1 AA-71 |
| Bayly, Henry, 21 July (?), Martha Harrel | 1 PG-295 |
| Bayly, Henry, 24 Dec. 1726, Lidia Skillington | 2 TA-114 |
| Bayly, Thomas, 30 Jan. 1707/8, Catherine Mack-(?) | 4 AA-372 |
| Baynard, George, 4 day, 10 mo., 1734, Susanna Powell | 8 SF-69 |
| Baynard, George, 30 Dec. 1746, Eliz'h Baynard | 1 QA-52 |
| Baynard, George, 20 Oct. 1751, Ann Wright | 1 QA-58 |
| Baynard, George, son of George and Ann, 12 Feb. 1775, Catherine Thompson, dau. of Dowdle and Hester | 2 CR-269 |
| Baynard, James, son of Nathan and Sarah, 7 Feb. 1775, Henrietta Pratt, dau. of Wm. and Mary | 2 CR-269 |
| Baynard, Thomas, 19 April 1704, Esther Pratt | 8 SF-420 |
| Baynard, Thomas, 7 Nov. 1746, Hannah Nickerson | 3 TA-62 |
| Baynard, Thomas, son of John, 19 Jan. 1747, Hannah Clarke | 2 CR-269 |
| Bayne, Jno., 30 Aug. 1753, Mary Webber | 2 BA-208 |
| Baynes, John, late of Popescastle, near Cockermouth, Cumberland, Eng. (born 23 March 1726 son of Daniel and Mary), 20 Aug. 1749, Mary Noble | 1 PG-289 |
| Bayne, William, 4 Nov. 1753, Mary Fenley | 1 PG-303 |
| Bays, John, 12 Sept. 1748, Eleanor Harryman | 3 BA-161 |
| Bazeman, Joseph, 13 July 1707, Mary Persias | 2 AA-332 |
| Bazill, John, 25 June 1724, Mary Purde | 1 AA-99 |
| Beachamp, Daniel, 31 Dec. 1759, Sarah Lannard | 2 SO-107 |
| Beadle, William, 23 Dec. 1703, Mary Williams | 1 AA-64 |
| Beadle, William, 16 Aug. 1751, Jane Barnaby, dau. of John | 3 CE-26 |
| Beaird, Thomas, 14 Nov. 1762, Sarah Boardman The name may also be read as Beairs. | 1 WI-81 |
| Beal, Thomas, 6 March 1769, Sarah Prisley | 2 BA-258 |
| Beal, William, 11 Feb. 1723, Elisabeth Stockett | 1 AA-98 |
| Beale, John, 19 Aug. 1708, Mrs. Elizabeth Norwood | 4 AA-378 |
| Beale, John, 9 Feb. 1729, Mary Roe | 1 QA-37 |
| Beale, John, 5 Oct. 1732, Anne Merredith | 1 QA-39 |
| Beall, George, 22 Jan. 1757, Elizabeth Turner | 4 FR-1103 |
| Beall, John Fendall, 27 Sept. (?), Mary Wilkinson | 1 PG-361 |
| Beall, Patrick, 2 March 1756, Elinor Goddard | 1 PG-312 |
| Beals, John, son of John and Mary, 20 day, 4 mo., 1714, Mary Brooke, dau. of John | 9 SF |
| Bean, Rob't, 14 Jan. 1722, Ann Roberts | 1 AA-227 |

| | | |
|---|---|---|
| Beard, Andrew, 11 April 1762, Mary Vivill | 9 AA-247 |
| Beard, Richard, 22 April 1740, Ruth Phelps | 9 AA-246 |
| Beard, Samuel, 16 Sept. 1777, Lehemiah Taylor | 1 HA-200 |
| Beasley, Edward, 1766, Elizabeth Beasley | 1 CE-301 |
| Beasley, Thomas, 29 Oct. 1720, Elizabeth Ives | 4 AA-412 |
| Beaswasicks, William, (no date given), Elizabeth Midland | 3 KE-241 |
| Beauchamp, Edward, 11 July 1762, Tabitha Lenard | 2 SO-111 |
| Beauchamp, Fountain, 11 Feb. 1748, Rhody Addams | 2 SO-4 |
| Beauchamp, Handy, 17 Feb. 1765, Mary Davis | 2 SO-111 |
| Beauchamp, Joshua, 28 March 1773, Mary Beauchamp | 2 SO-195 |
| Beauchamp, Levin, 1 May 1765, Tabitha Davis | 2 SO-111 |
| Beauchamp, Levin, 10 June 1777, Mary Beauchamp | 2 SO-200 |
| Beauchamp, Thomas, 12 Nov. 1769, Sarah Addams | 2 SO-103 |
| Beauchamp, William, (no date given), Anne Tilman | 2 SO-4 |
| Beaven, Joseph, 1753, Rachel Ashen | 2 BA-242 |
| Beavens, Roling, 22 Jan. 1746/7, Elizabeth Burn | 2 SO-8 |
| Beavens, Rowland, 22 Sept. 1765, Tabitha Dennis | 2 SO-195 |
| Beaver, Francis, (?) Feb. (?), Eliz'th Sharby | 3 KE-241 |
| Beaver, Jno., 19 Sept. 1749, Sarah Hawkins | 2 BA-199 |
| Beaver, William, Jr., Oct. 1740, Blanch Duly | 1 BA-320 |
| Beazley, Edward, 19 May 1774, Ann (?) | 1 CE-302 |
| Beck, (?), 14 Sept. 1713, Mary Ashly | 3 KE-243 |
| Beck, (Aquilla?), 31 July 1730, Jane Meeks | 3 KE-246 |
| Beck, Edward, 1 day, 7 mo., 1770, Araminti Wilson | 2 SF-288 |
| Beck, Elijah, 19 Nov. 1752, Martha Greenleefe | 2 BA-206 |
| Beck, Elisha, 31 July 1742, Sarah Baker | 2 BA-133 |
| Beck, James, 1 April 1733, Sarah Duvall | 2 PG-6 |
| Beck, James, Jr., 23 June 1761, Rebekah Walker | 2 PG-7 |
| Beck, Joshua, 12 June 1722, Martha Green | 3 KE-245 |
| Beck, Matthew, 10 Feb. 1740, Ann Horner | 2 BA-134 |
| Beck, Osborn, 8 Sept. 1763, Mary Welsh | 2 PG-7 |
| Beck, Samuel, 19 June 1729, Elizabeth Wilkinson | 1 QA-37 |
| Beck, Samuel, 5 Dec. 1753, Mary Groves | 2 BA-209 & 242 |
| Beck, Sam'll, 23 Dec. 1759, Sarah Davis | 3 KE-249 |
| Beck, Samuel Duvall, 29 March 1767, Susanna Tyler | 2 PG-7 |
| Beck, Vivean, 6 Sept. (?), Sarah Randal | 3 KE-240 |
| Becker, John Fred'k, 6 Aug. 1758, Mary Doroth. Dureman | 4 FR-1104 |
| Becker, Peter, 15 Sept. 1761, Anna Mary Nicol | 4 FR-1107 |
| Becker, Philip, 5 April 1762, Elizab. Baecker | 4 FR-1107 |
| Becket, Humphrey, 28 Aug. 1712, Dorcas Brown | 1 AA-271 |
| Becket ? , John, 17 Nov. 1724, Ann Drayne | 2 PG-3 |
| Beckett, Humphrey, 31 Oct. 1777, Lydia Sunderland | 1 CA-111a |
| Beckett, John, 18 Nov. 1723, Mary Nicholls | 2 PG-3 |
| Beckingham, William, of Annapolis, attorney at law, 25 May 1726, Elizabeth Piper | 4 AA-426 |
| Beckwith, Nehemiah, 10 July 1712, Frances Taylor | 8 SF-3 |
| Becraft, Abraham, 29 July 1731, Ann Spurrier | 4 AA-434 |
| Beddingfield, Anthony, 12 Feb. 1701, Mary Throgden, widow | 1 AA-58 |
| Beddoe, Griffith, 31 July 1728, Hannah Calder | 4 AA-430 |
| Beddoe, John, 3 Dec. 1724, Sarah Litton | 1 BA-238 |
| Bedle, John, Jr., 2 Feb. 1715, Mary Moance ? | 3 CE-11 |
| Bedle, Thomas, 1 Jan. 1717, Elizabeth Boulding | 3 CE-9 |
| Beecham, John, 16 Sept. 1735, Ann Burton | 1 BA-286 |
| Beedle, Henry, 19 Jan. 1768, Mary Bunkerd | 1 CE-297 |
| Beedle, John, Jr., son of John, 6 Nov. 1737, Rachael Penington, dau. of John, Sr. | 3 CE-20 |
| Beer, Henry, 28 June 1768, Margaret Winter | 4 FR-1107 |
| Beesley, Abraham, 22 Aug. 1717, Mary Neal | 2 TA-80 |
| Beesley, John, 14 Nov. 1727, Mary Marchall | 2 TA-116 |
| Beeston, William, 19 Dec. 1706, Sarah Chisups | 3 CE-5 |
| Beetle, Richard, 6 Aug. 1741, Augustine Bavington, dau. of John | 3 CE-23 |

Beezley, John, 19 Feb. 1739, Sarah Nuttell          2 TA-168
Beker, Thomas, 10 Aug. 1726, Mary Cox               3 CE-13
Belamy, David, 27 Feb. 1749/50, Mary Hanns          3 BA-163
Belcher, John, Feb. 1706, Mary Perkins, widow       1 BA-201
Bell, Andrew, 30 Oct. 1703, Mary Boucher            2 AA-322
Bell, Anthony, 25 Dec. 1687, Abigaill Roatch        5 SO-396
Bell, Rev. Hamilton, 30 March 1749, Mrs. Mary Robert-
  son, widow                                        3 SO-4
Bell, Henry, 12 Jan. 1743/4, Sarah Eason            3 TA-47
Bell, Jacob, 18 Feb. 1727, Elizabeth Rowles         3 BA-149
Bell, John, 2 April 1703, Susanna Higgdon           2 TA-32
Bell, Joseph, 21 Nov. 1729, Rachel Staicy           2 TA-121
Bell, Richard, 28 April 1704, Jane Denboe           3 CE-9
Bell, William, 14 April 1755, Ann Hardcastle        2 CR-269
Bellhook, Jeremiah, June 1727, Grace Richardson     2 TA-115
Bellows, Francis, 13 Nov. (?), Margrett Ayres       3 KE-242
Bellroes, Christopher, 25 Sept. 1719, Anna Thompson 1 BA-223
Belt, Jeremiah, 21 June 1746, Mary Sprigg           2 PG-7
Belt, John, 10 Feb. 1701, Lucy Lawrence; "married at
  a Quakers Meeting conivingly...which sd. Lucy
  Lawrence was then and now at the time of this regis-
  tring is the betrothed wife of Joseph Tilly...
  which accon is contra'ry to the law of God and
  man."                                             1 AA-58
Belt, John, son of Col. Joseph, 4 March 1727,
  Margaret Queen                                    2 PG-5
Belt, Osborn, 14 Dec. 1765, Dorothy Lucas           9 AA-250
Benfield, Abraham, 15 April 1737, Mary (?)          2 PG-7
Benham, John, 5 Feb. 1732, Elizabeth Millis         1 QA-39
Benkin, Jno., 9 Feb. 1765, Mary Fell                2 BA-227
Bennet, Charles, 1753, Martha Collins               2 BA-242
Bennet, Edward, 13 Oct. 1756, Priscilla Coventon    1 WI-59
Bennet, Edward, Jr., 30 March 1759, Jane Tully      1 WI-67
Bennet, John, 5 Feb. 1740, Sarah Morris             2 KE-244
Bennet, Richard, 4 Dec. 1769, Eliz. Jarom           2 BA-259
Bennet, William, 30 May 1754, Dorothy (Pully?)      1 WI-54
Bennett, Charles, 11 Sept. 1753, Martha Collins     2 BA-208
Bennett, Disboro, 21 April 1676, Mary Wells         1 KE-318
Bennett, George, 1 Dec. 1735, Eliza Briley          1 QA-41
Bennett, Isaac, 5 Nov. 1734, Eliz. Kersey           3 BA-152
Bennett, James, 12 Sept. 1708, Mary (?)             2 KE-177
Bennett, James, 15 Nov. 1769, Jane Weer             5 BA-1
Bennett, John, 6 Feb. 1683, Sarah Furnis            5 SO-396
Bennett, John, 8 Jan. 1683/4, Mary Furnis           9 SO-402
Bennett, John, 21 Sept. 1729, Margaret Steel        1 QA-37
Bennett, William, 10 Jan. 1709, Joan Leatherwood    4 AA-379
Bennett, Will'm, 6 Nov. 1713, Mrs. Ann Chintos      4 AA-380
Bennett, William, Feb. 1753, Mary Parker            2 BA-207
                                                    & 242
Bennington, Henry, 26 Dec. 1726, Sarah Harris       1 BA-248
Bennit, George, 13 Dec. 1733, Jane Linch            1 WI-22
Benny, James, 19 April 1746, Mable Chapman          3 TA-58
Benny, William, 1 Sept. 1760, Mary Hart             2 TA-286
Benson, Edward, 15 (?) 1714, Hannah, widow of
  Charles Hamonde                                   4 AA-393
Benson, George, May 1682, Anne Roberts              5 SO-396
Benson, James, 9 Aug. 1748, Hannah Ratcliff         3 TA-70
Benson, Philip, 23 Sept. 1708, Ann Ditto            3 KE-242
Benson, Thomas, 1752, Isabell Brown                 2 BA-242
Benson, Thomas, 23 Jan. 1753, Esabellah Brown       2 BA-207
Benson, William Thomas, 2 Feb. 1741, Ann Green      9 AA-247
Benston, Benjamin, 1 Jan. 1759, Elizabeth Dickeson  2 SO-110
Benston, Thomas, 14 July 1753, Sarah Dreaden        2 SO-108
Benston, William, 28 Oct. 1746, Sarah Riggin        2 SO-105
Bentham, Richard, 24 Feb. 1730, Elizabeth Severson  3 CE-16

Bentley, William, 30 July 1738, Elizabeth Butler          1 BA-290
Benton, Vincent, 30 Oct. 1735, Sarah Holms               1 QA-41
Berg, John, 17 Oct. 1762, Elizabeth Grumm                4 FR-1107
Berkum, Roger, 10 Dec. 1681, Lucia Jones                 5 SO-396
Berrett, John, c1769, Eliz. Anderson                     2 BA-258
Berrey, Jno., 14 Jan. 1762, Eliz. Berry                  2 BA-223
Berridge, (?), 30 (?) 1773, Grace Macmahan               2 TA-290
Berry, Daniel, 21 March 1734, Sarah Connor               2 TA-157
Berry, Dan'l, Feb. 1749/50, Jane Delaha                  3 TA-76
Berry, Edward, 23 Nov. 1708, Mary Procter                2 TA-51
Berry, George, 6 Feb. 1714, Mary Cox                     2 BA-4
Berry, George, April 1745, Hanah Pararah                 1 QA-50
Berry, Henry, 2 June 1700, Susannah Clements; they
     were servants to Joseph Hanslap                     1 AA-56
Berry, James, 14 April 1686, Sarah Woolchurch            8 SF-341
Berry, James, 11 Feb. 1691, Elizabeth Pitt               8 SF-356
Berry, James, 12 Nov. 1724, Sarah Skillington            8 SF-41
Berry, James, 29 day, 3 mo., 1768, Susanna Maxfield      8 SF-131
Berry, James, son of James, 15 day, 2 mo., 1776, Mary
     Bonsal, dau. of Joseph, late of Darby, Pa.          8 SF-154
Berry, John, 10 Oct. 1711, Ann Pratt                     8 SF-1
Berry, John, 27 Dec. 1711, Esther Foster                 3 KE-242
Berry, John, 11 July 1731, Susannah Lee                  3 BA-150
Berry, John, son of Samuel and Margaret, 20 day, 12
     mo., 1753, Patience Gregg, dau. of David and Lydia  9 SF
Berry, John, son of Joseph, 14 day, 6 mo., 1775,
     Margaret Milton, dau. of Abraham                    1 SF-106
Berry, Joseph, 27 Jan. 1752, Sarah Cockayne "the
     younger"                                            8 SF-96
Berry, Nathaniell, 8 July (?), Jane Hern                 3 KE-241
Berry, Samuel, 28 Oct. 1708, Martha Griffith             3 KE-242
Berry, Thomas, 4 May 1699, Sarah Godard                  8 SF-411
Berry, Thomas, 5 Nov. 1741, Esther Norman                2 KE-250
Besson, Nicholas, 3 Sept. 1722, Diana Hale               3 AA-102
Betsworth, John, 18 May 1749, Mary Revill Miles          2 SO-5
Betts, George, 7 Nov. 1669, Bridgett Bossman             5 SO-396
Betts, Solomon, 15 March 1759, Mary Finley               1 QA-65
Betty, Wm., 1 March 1757, Mary Dorothy Crush             4 FR-1103
Bevan, James, June 1769, Mary Ricket                     2 BA-258
Bevan, John, 17 July 1743, Anne Turner                   2 BA-239
Beven, Jno., 2 Jan. 1755, Ruth Jerman                    2 BA-211
Beven, Jno., 5 Oct. 1760, Eliz. Freeman                  2 BA-220
Bevend, Rowland, 27 Dec. 1670, Margaret Price            7 SO-401
Bevens, Rowland, 4 Aug. 1672, Mary Bewry                 5 SO-396
Bevin, Joseph, 15 Jan. 1754, Rachael Asher               2 BA-209
Bexley, Simon, 3 Sept. 1722, Ann Jones                   2 TA-103
Beyne, Epsworth, 26 May 1717, Kenrik Rumney              1 AA-79
                                                         & 277
Bickardike, Richard, 16 Oct. 1704, Ann Smith             4 AA-389
Bickerdike, Richard, 6 June 1728, Anne (?)               1 AA-147
Bickerton, John; request to pub. banns, no date
     given, Ann Peaiters?                                7 BA(1)
Bicklin, Joseph, 21 July 1759, Mary Taylor               1 QA-65
Biddeson, Thos., 17 July 1747, Ann Buegain               2 BA-196
     Her name might be read as Burgan.
Biddingsfield, Anthony, 12 Feb. 1701, Mary Hogdon        1 AA-249
Biddle, Benn, 22 Feb. 1770, Katheran Happuck Barton      2 BA-260
Biddy, John, 12 Nov. (?), Joan Mackarthy                 3 KE-241
Bidison, Jarvis, 13 Feb. 1770, Ruthe Robison             2 BA-260
Bier, Philip, 8 Oct. 1764, Eva Cath. Schley              4 FR-1107
Biggs, Benjamin, 26 Sept. 1745, Hennaretta Prudense
     Deborah Margretta Munday, dau. of Henry             1 FR-10
Bigland, Ralph, of Whitehaven, Co. Cumberland, Eng.,
     22 March 1749/50, Mary Kibble                       1 WI-41
                                                         & 58

Biles, Jonathan, 1 Sept. 1756, Mary Pitman                       1 QA-61
Bill, John, 7 May 1771, Mary Edwards                             2 BA-262
Billingsley, Baz'l, 29 Jan. 1767, Ruth Smithson                 2 BA-230
Billingsley, Chas., 23 Oct. 1760, Ann Barton                    2 BA-220
Billingsley, Jas., 16 June 1767, Ruth Gilbert                   2 BA-230
Billinsley, Walter, 13 Feb. 1772, Ruth Clarke                   2 BA-264
Billinsly, Walter, 27 Aug. 1742, Sarah Love                     1 BA-325
Billion, Francis Stephen, 25 April 1736, Susanna
     Lloyd                                                       1 QA-42
Billiter, Thomas, 14 Aug. 1715, Sarah King                      2 TA-76
Billy, negro man, 15 Oct. 1743, Hanah Sakman, mulatto
     woman, both belonging to Rich'd Scotton                    1 QA-48
Binks, Jacob, 20 April 1725, Mary Lasswell                      1 AA-100
Birch, Francis, 20 July 1720, Alie Owin                         1 PG-269
Birch, James, 14 July 1757, Sarah Shepherd                      1 QA-62
Birckhead, John, 12 mo., 6 day, 1745/6, Christian
     Harris                                                     6 SF-114
Birckhead, Nehemiah, 6 mo., 24 day, 1712, Margaret
     Johns                                                      6 SF-66
Bird, Francis, 5 Nov. 1724, Jane Littleton                      1 PG-278
Bird, Richard, 20 Sept. 1736, Mary Bird                         1 QA-42
Bird, Solomon, 29 Nov. 1753, Jemima Tylor                       2 SO-108
Bird, Thomas, 18 April 1764, Jemima Ward                        2 SO-112
Bird, Thomas, 2 (?) 1769, Dorothy Brown                         2 AA-409
Bird, William, 23 Nov. 1735, Sarah Gill                         1 QA-41
Birk, John, 19 June 1704, Rebecca Coleman                       2 AA-323
Birk, Tobias, 2 May 1708, Ann Bromigan                          4 AA-378
Birkhead, John, Jan. 1777, Debbora Simmons                      2 AA-413
Birkhead, Matthew, 25 June 1776, Elizabeth Gibson              2 AA-413
Birkhead, Nehemiah, 1682, Elizabeth Sloper                      6 SF-2
Birmey, Edward, 5 Dec. 1733, Sarah Mecotter                     2 TA-154
Birum, William, (?) July (?), Hannah Chandler                   3 KE-241
Bishop, David, 8 Aug. 1671, Sarah Persill                       7 SO-401
Bishop, Emanuell, 30 May 1705, Sarah (?)                        4 AA-390
Bishop, John, 31 Dec. 1672, Mary Bowen                          5 SO-396
Bishop, John, 28 Jan. 1748, Ruth Charlton                       4 AA-449
Bishop, Rich'd, 16 March 1737, Mary More                        1 QA-44
Bishop, Robert, 22 Sept. 1742, Elizabeth Day                    2 BA-124
Bishop, Roger, 9 April 1735, Avis Ginkins                       1 BA-281
Bishop, Thomas, 25 May 1730, Eliza Barber                       1 AA-110
Bishop, William, 24 (?) 1729, Anne McGuire                      1 QA-37
Bishop, William, 22 July 1742, Mary Harris                      4 AA-444
Bisit, Maj. David, 30 Jan. 1755, Mrs. Ann Adkinson             1 BA-350
Biven, William, 16 Feb. 1725, Ann Brushier                      2 PG-4
Black, Peter, 20 April 1735, Eliz'th Wilson                     1 BA-281
Black, William, 22 Sept. 1744, Esther Banneker                 3 BA-168
Blackiston, (?), 27 July 1729, Martha Dunn                      3 KE-245
Blackiston, Ebenezer, 14 April 1737, Mary Maxwell              3 KE-247
Blackiston, Elijah, 29 Nov. 1772, Avarilla Garrettson          1 BA-388
Blackiston, Michaell, 8 Dec. 17-(?), Ann Bradshaw              3 KE-247
Blackiston, (William?), 5 Feb. 1735, Ann Gleen                 3 KE-247
Blacklock, Thomas, 15 (?) 1738, Charity Lanham                 1 PG-286
Blackmore, Richard, 12 April 1758, Eliz'a Baley                1 QA-63
Blackston, Joseph, 21 Aug. 1738, Frances Lloyd                 1 QA-44
Blackstone, Capt. Peter, 1 March 1701, Eliz'th (?)             2 TA-24
Blades, James, 17 Feb. 1748/9, Mary Eaton                      3 TA-72
Blades, James Tucker, 18 Aug. 1755, Eliz'th Rouse             1 QA-59
Blades, Joseph, 9 Nov. 1743, Mary Hadaway                      3 TA-45
Blades, Joseph, 27 July 1745, Esther Eaton                     3 TA-54
Blades, Levin, 28 Jan. 1775, Betsy Newnam                      1 CR
Blades, Samuell, 21 Dec. 1748, Amela Barns                     2 SO-107
Blades, Samuel, 23 Dec. 1766, Mary Piltchard                   2 SO-194
Blake, John, 27 Aug. 1739, Frances Collison                    3 TA-18
Blake, Thomas, 2 Oct. 1775, Elisebeth Grumbels                2 SO-197
Blandel, Laurence, 27 April 1712, Elizabeth Hesket            2 AA-344

Blange, Jacob, of Kent in Tal. Co., 27 May 1703,
   Elizabeth Merriken, dau. of Joshua Merriken, Sr.     3 AA-96
Blay, James, 10 Aug. 1777, Elizabeth Day          10 BA-69
Bleamer, John, 2 Aug. 1718, Jane Colter          2 TA-87
Blessett, William, 6 Nov. 1738, Esther Norris      2 TA-166
Bley, John, 20 Nov. 1757, Mary Eliz'th Apple       4 FR-1103
Blinco, Uhlence, 6 Oct. 1777, Elizabeth Mires      10 BA-69
Bloyth, Stephen, 27 Aug. 1763, Rachel Lord        2 SO-103
Blunden, James, 1 Dec. 1759, Sarah Eights        2 BA-219
Board, James, 6 Jan. 1730, Ann Keightly         3 AA-103
Board, John, 13 Jan. 1733, Jemima Henderson       3 BA-151
Bob, Anthony, 18 June 1713, Anne Plummer         1 BA-216
Bob, John, 22 Feb. 1761, Magdalen Heckedorn       4 FR-1107
Bodien, Henry, 9 day, 1 mo., 1766, Margaret Wallis   1 SF-98
Body, Peter, 28 Dec. 1686, Frances Cannon, dau. of
   Stephen                                 5 SO-396
Body, Peter, 25 Aug. 1757, Mary Allinder        2 BA-216
Body, Stephen, 3 April 1722, Susanna Long       2 BA-147
Body, Stephen, 10 Feb. 1728, Elizabeth (?)       3 BA-147
Bogan, George, 12 Dec. 1771, Eliz. Amoss        2 BA-263
Boggs, Archibald, 4 Nov. 1777, Sarah Sutton      2 CE-1
Bogs, William, 24 (?) 1746, Margaret Blair       1 CE-320
Bohanin, Nathaniel, 6 Dec. 1742, Eleanor Vansandt,
   dau. of Garriot                      3 CE-24
Bohedeen, Mr. Henry, 17 Dec. 1747, Mrs. Sarah Wilson  2 KE-269
Bohon, Edw'd, 19 March 1761, Eliz. Jones        2 BA-221
Bohring(er), Andreas, c. Nov. 1760, Eva Rosina Kertscher,
   dau. of Andreas and Dorothea            5 FR-6
Bold, (?)-ariah, 13 Nov. 1750, Rachel Worron     1 WO-5
Bolton, Charles, 30 Dec. (?), Eleanor Dougherty   4 KE-18(R)
Bolton, Charles Mathias, July 1739, Ann Higginson   2 BA-137
Bolton, George, 3 Dec. 1747, Ann Walker        1 QA-53
Bolton, John, 16 Oct. 1755, Mary Hinesley       1 QA-60
Bolton, William, 19 Feb. 1746, Rachel Carman     1 QA-53
Bolton, William, 5 Sept. 1758, Sophia Daley      1 QA-64
Bond, Benjamin, 28 May 1737, Clemency Taylor    2 BA-92
Bond, Buckley, 17 April 1770, Charity Bond      2 BA-260
Bond, Daniel, 1 Nov. 1759, Patience Bozley      2 BA-219
Bond, Edward, 23 March 1769, Ruth Sampson      2 BA-258
Bond, Francis, 2 June 1747, Katherine Murphy     3 TA-65
Bond, Jacob, 28 Dec. 1747, Frances Partridge     3 BA-161
Bond, John, 21 Feb. 1733, Esabella Robinson     2 BA-82
Bond, John, son of Thomas, 26 day, 1 mo. (March),
   1734, Elizanna Webster, dau. of John        9 SF
Bond, John, 25 July 1755, Sarah Potter         1 QA-59
Bond, Jos., 13 Nov. 1764, Ann Watters         2 BA-227
Bond, Luke, 18 July 1762, Frances Webster      2 BA-223
Bond, Nicodemus, 1 Jan. 1765, Rachel Stevenson    4 BA-73
Bond, Peter, 1 Aug. 1735, Susannah Butler      3 BA-153
Bond, Peter, 25 Feb. 1772, Eliz. Scott         2 BA-264
Bond, Richard, 24 day, 7 mo., 1702, Elizabeth Chew  6 SF-38
Bond, Richard, 5 Aug. 1731, Mary Jones        3 BA-152
Bond, Samuel, son of Peter, 9 Feb. 1766, Charity Clark 4 BA-73
Bond, Stephen, 6 June 1673, Jane Sewell        5 SO-396
Bond, Thomas, 20 Sept. 1700, Ann Robison or Robinson
   of Balto. Co.                     1 AA-56
                                      & 245
Bond, Thomas, 13 April 1725, Elizabeth Scott     2 BA-36
Bond, Thomas, 9 May 1736, Phebe Thomas       3 BA-155
Bond, Thomas, "the 3rd," 3 Feb. 1765, Cathrine Fell  2 BA-227
Bond, Thos., son of Barnet, Feb. 1768, Sarah Bond   2 BA-231
Bond, Thomas, 21 Nov. 1771, Ruth Morrow       2 BA-263
Bond, Thomas, 19 Dec. 1771, Rebeckah Stansbury    2 BA-263
Bond, Uriah, 26 Dec. 1742, Anne Moon         2 BA-238
Bond, Uriah, 23 April 1748, Penillipie Coleman    2 BA-196

```
Bond, William, 16 Nov. 1771, Sarah Wrongs             2 BA-263
Bond, William, 28 Feb. 1777, Mary Nevison             3 SM-535
Bone, Sam'l, 25 Feb. 1759, Sarah Harryman             2 BA-218
Boney, Thomas, 20 Oct. 1771, Jean Davidson            2 SM-58
Bonner, John, 28 Feb. 1754, Christian Ingram          1 BA-381
Boohman, George, 22 Nov. 1777, Eve Breheri            1 WA-526
Booker, Joseph, 15 Sept. 1734, Eliz'th Herman         2 TA-157
Booker, Lambert, 27 July 1734, Elean'r Botfield       2 TA-156
Booker, Richard, 5 Dec. 1700, Sarah (?)               2 TA-11
Booker, Thomas, 3 Jan. 1696, Ellinor Orem, dau. of
  Andrew                                              8 SF-372
Boon, Benj., 9 Jan. 1745, Estr. Fawlinn               1 QA-51
Boon, Charles, 11 Sept. 1773, Elizabeth Stansbury     3 AA-113
Boon, Humphry, 2 Feb. 1743, Anna Burley               3 AA-107
Boon, Isaac, 9 Sept. 1736, Elis. Young                1 QA-42
Boon, Jacob, 21 Dec. 1758, Hannah Fisher              1 QA-64
Boon, James, c. Oct. 1775, Mary Toalson               1 CR-6
Boon, John, 17 Feb. 1731, Mary Burle                  3 AA-102
Boon, Joseph, 1 Nov. 1743, Ans. Young                 1 QA-49
Boon, William, 31 Jan. 1759, Rebeckah Chance          1 QA-64
Boone, John, 24 Sept. 1762, Elizabeth Williams        3 AA-114
Boone, Nicholas, 9 Feb. 1752, Wethay Ann Hammond      3 AA-111
Boone, Nicholis, 5 Feb. 1760, Susanah Jacobs          3 AA-111
Boone, Capt. Richard, 14 Dec. 1752, Hamutal
  Stinchecombe                                        3 AA-111
Boone, Robert, 17 Sept. 1702, Elizabeth (?)           3 AA-97
Booth, Antony, 23 Nov. 1727, Sarrah Phrampton         2 TA-117
Booth, Henry, 13 Feb. 1726/7, Jean Dolingon           2 TA-115
Booth, John, 18 Sept. 1712, Margret Gilberd           2 TA-72
Booth, John, 2 Nov. 1736, Mary Haynes                 3 KE-247
Booth, Robert (no date given), Sarah Filmoore         1 PG-262
Booth, Sam'l, 30 Oct. 1739, Rebecca Register          3 TA-19
Booth, William, 8 Dec. 1777, Rosannah Dougherty       2 CE-1
Boots, William, 1 June 1729, Ann Oxford               2 KE-269
Boram, Joseph, 7 Aug. 1753, Sarah Demmet              2 BA-208
Bordley, Stephen, 14 Oct. 1702, Ann Hynson            3 KE-240
Bordley, Stephen, 22 April 1731, Priscilla Murphy     3 KE-245
Bordley, Mr. Thomas, 26 Dec. 1708, Mrs. Rachel Beard  4 AA-378
Bordley, Thomas, 19 Dec. 1727, Mary Smithers          3 KE-245
Bordley, Thomas, 21 Feb. 1731, Ann Miller             3 KE-245
Bordley, William, son of Thomas, 14 Nov. 1755, Sarah
  Pearce, dau. of Col. Benjamin                       3 CE-26
Boreing, James, 5 Aug. 1734, Rebekah Gain, widow      3 BA-152
Boreing, James, 25 Dec. 1736, Martha Wheeler          3 BA-155
Boreing, Thomas, 21 Jan. 1730, Mary Haile             3 BA-150
Boreing, Thomas, 3 Feb. 1734, Elizabeth Welch         3 BA-153
Borer, Peter, 31 Jan. 1768, Magd. Schenkmayer         4 FR-1107
Borewell, Charles, 1750; note that the banns were
  "forbid" to Mary Hammond                            2 BA-241
Borns, Rob't, 21 July 1766, Morra Brian               2 BA-229
Boroughs, Abraham, March 1752, Elinor Barsnett        1 QA-58
Boroughs, Valentine, 22 May 1750, Rebecca White       1 QA-57
Borows, William, 6 Oct. 1757, Mary Borows             1 QA-63
Borris, William, 21 Feb. 1703, Mary Walker            2 AA-322
Bosick, William, 5 Aug. 1770, Mary Philpot            2 BA-260
Bosley, Gidion, 9 Jan. 1772, Sarah Cole               2 BA-263
Bosley, James, 16 Sept. 1770, Temperance Marsh        2 BA-260
Bosley, Thomas, 13 Dec. 1770, Mary Richards           2 BA-261
Bosline, James, 26 Nov. 1730, Elisabeth Parish        3 BA-150
Bosman, Edward, 1750, Rose Lyon                       2 BA-244
Bosman, Edward, 25 March 1773, Frances Saunders       2 BA-266
Bostock, James, 11 Sept. 1731, Ruth Wyet              1 QA-38
Bostock, James, 21 Feb. 1737/8, Lydia Burrows         1 QA-43
Bostock, Samuel, 14 Jan. 1730, Preciosia Crump        1 QA-38
Boston, (?), 14 Oct. 1751, Grace Mathews              2 SO-5
```

```
Boston, Esau, 26 July 1751, Rachel Doughety              2 SO-7
Boston, Henry, 19 May 1673, Elizabeth Rogerson          5 SO-396
Boston, Jacob, 29 Oct. 1747, Nelly Benston              2 SO-6
Boston, James, negro, 22 May 1735, Katherine Banneker,
   negro                                                3 BA-153
Boston, Marthews, 5 Feb. 1753, Martha Benston           2 SO-106
Boston, Matthews, 6 July 1761, Marget Sommors           2 SO-109
Boston, Richard, 21 April 1754, Mary Porter             2 SO-105
Boswell, John, 17 Nov. 1745, Mary Jennings              2 BA-240
Boswell, Thomas, 20 Nov. 1708, Mary Marcey              3 KE-242
Boswell, Thos., May 1752, Mary Chanley                  2 BA-241
Botcher, James, 1 April 1731, Jane Presbery             1 AA-112
Botfield, Michael, July 1746, Sarah Grayson             3 TA-60
Botfield, Shadrack, 19 Dec. 1740, Eleanor Greenwood     2 TA-171
Botfield, Shadrack, 14 Sept. 1743, Grace Ferrall        2 TA-196
Botfield, Zadock, 24 Dec. 1740, Sarah Merrick           3 TA-27
   2 TA-171 gives date as 27 Dec. 1740.
Bott, Richard, son of Richard, 24 Feb. 1760, Ketura
   Price, dau. of John                                  4 SF-248
Botts, John, 9 Dec. 1730, Sarah Wood                    1 BA-253
Boualch, Hezekiah, 30 July 1707, Matthew Brewenton      4 AA-372
Bouchell,, Peter, 28 Dec. 1737, Catherine Herman, dau.
   of Col. Eph'a Aug't Herman                           3 CE-23
Bouchell, Sluyter, 25 May 1738, Mary Bayard, dau.
   of Samuel                                            3 CE-24
Bouchelle, Peter, 28 March 1716, Mary Heyatt            3 CE-14
Bouldin, Richard, 17 Jan. 1716, Mary Hews               3 CE-10
Boulding, Thomas, 29 Jan. 1733/4, Ann Clark             3 CE-18
Boulson, John, 1750, Elizab. Steward                    2 BA-241
Boulting, John, merchant of Chestertown, 30 Dec. 1771,
   Mrs. Eleanor Dougherty, dau. of Edward Doughty       1 CE-296
Boulton, Charles, 4 July 1739, Ann Higginson            1 BA-308
Boulton, Henry, 6 Nov. 1728, Susanna Mobberly           2 PG-5
Bounds, Richard Stephens, 10 Aug. 1752, Mary Stevens    1 WI-55
Bourn, John, 11 Oct. 1744, Barbara Burke                2 BA-191
Bourn, Thomas, 15 Nov. 1741, Mica Copes                 1 QA-47
Bowdie, John, 2 Nov. 1730, Sarah Bowdie                 3 KE-246
Bowdle, Henry, 23 June 1720, Mary Gouldsborough         2 TA-93
Bowdle, Henry, 29 Nov. 1736, Judith Armstrong           2 TA-158
Bowdle, John, 20 Sept. 1748, Eliza Delaha               3 TA-70
Bowdle, Joseph, 16 Feb. 1731, Elizabeth Boyce           2 TA-151
Bowdle, Loftus, 27 Feb. 1716, Anne Thomas               2 TA-79
Bowdle, Thomas, 6 Dec. 1709, Sarah Gorsuch              2 TA-64
Bowdle, Thomas, 19 Nov. 1724, Mary Withgott             2 TA-110
Bowdle, Thomas, 27 May 1740, Mary Mears                 2 TA-169
Bowdy, Solomon, 13 April 170-(?), Kather. Eads          3 KE-242
Bowen, Benjamin, 4 day, 8 mo., 1744, Mary Carr          4 SF
Bowen, George, 27 March 1706, Elizabeth Gibbs           2 AA-329
Bowen, John, Jr., 7 Oct. 1699, Milcah Claxton           2 AA-297
Bowen, John, 11 Oct. 1744, Barbara Burke                2 BA-191
Bowen, Jonas, 14 Feb. 1750/1, Elizabeth Whith           3 BA-165
Bowen, Solomon, 28 Nov. 1751, Temperance Ensor          4 BA-71
Bowen, Thomas, 13 March 1717, Elizabeth Swillowen       1 AA-282
Bowen, Thomas, son of William and Mary, 5 day, 3 mo.,
   1742, Jane Edwards, dau. of Jonathan and Isabell     9 SF
Bowen, William, 16 Sept. 1753, Elizabeth Moss           2 BA-208
Bowers, James, 9 Nov.1697, Margrett Cock                3 CE-2
Bowers, John, son of John, of Kent Co., Del., 29 May
   1773, Mary Ann Powell, dau. of Howell                8 SF-147
Bowers, William, 21 April 1731, Jane Canaday            3 KE-247
Bowes, George, 11 Aug. 1720, Frances Everett            1 SF-55
Bowie, John, 18 Dec. (1735?), Eliz'h Pottinger          2 PG-6
Bowin, George, 27 March 1706, Elizabeth Gibbs           2 AA-329
Bowing, William, 1753, Elizabeth Moss                   2 BA-242
Bowles, Ignatius, 21 Jan. 1777, Catherine Gough         1 SM-137
```

```
Bowles, Isaac, 20 Sept. (?), Mary Kease               3 KE-241
Bowles, John, 4 Sept. 170-(?), Margrett McNeill       3 KE-241
Bowles, John, 11 Jan. 1776, Eliz. Payn                1 SM-137
Bowles, Nicholas, 21 Jan. 1728, Rachel Norris         2 BA-37
Bowlin, Thomas, 6 Jan. 1731/2, Margery Ruock          1 WI-19
Bowman, Samuel, 30 Nov. 1751, Ann Dickinson           2 TA-288
Box, Edward, 18 Feb. 1739, Eliz'h Roe                 1 QA-45
Boyard, Dan'l, 30 Jan. 1721, Ellinor Dodds            2 TA-99
Boyce, Alexander, 30 March 1733, Phebe Martin         2 TA-153
Boyce, James, 22 July 1713, Mary Week                 4 AA-380
Boyce, John, 30 Nov. 1721, Elizabeth Jephs            2 BA-19
Boyd, Abraham, 16 Oct. 1705, Mary Grey                1 AA-71
Boyd, Abraham, 8 Nov. 1728, Deborah Walley            2 PG-5
Boyd, Abraham, 5 Dec. 1737, Hester Butterworth        1 BA-299
Boyd, Archibald, 24 Nov. 1770, Margaret Dundass       1 AA-148
Boyd, Archibald, 9 Nov. 1777, Ann Scott               3 PG-101
Boyd, Benjamin, 27 Feb. 1758, Elinor Williams         2 PG-7
Boyd, Isaac, 18 March 1727, Susanna Noble             1 AA-106
Boyd, Jno., 28 March 1706, Elinour Fitchedmuns        1 AA-72
Boyd, John, 8 May 1734, Susan Baldwin                 2 PG-6
Boyd, John, 8 May 1777, Anne Little                   5 BA-1
Boyde, Benjamin, 30 Oct. 1733, Eliz'h Harwood         2 PG-6
Boyde, Thomas, 24 March 1757, Charity Duckett         2 PG-7
Boyer, Isaac, 1 Oct. 1746, Rebecca McCay              2 KE-262
Boyer, John, 24 Feb. 1744/5, Sarah Smythers           2 KE-256
Boyer, William, 26 Dec. 1688, Phillis Holeoger        3 CE-2
Boyes, James, 6 Aug. 1721, Anne Peirce                1 AA-307
Boyle, John, 21 Aug. 1701, Mary Jolly                 1 AA-57
                                                      & 247
Boys, Charles, 15 April 1759, Eliz. Verry             1 QA-65
Boyton, Jonathan, 15 July 1740, Elizabeth Genkins     1 BA-312
Bozewell, John, 17 Nov. 1745, Mary Jennings           2 BA-193
Bozley, Calib, 27 Feb. 1772, Eliz. Wheeler            2 BA-264
Bozley, Elisha, 29 June 1769, Eliz. Merryman          2 BA-259
Bozley, Ezekiel, 21 Oct. 1760, Eliz. Norris           2 BA-220
Bozley, James, 18 Sept. 1760, Rach'l Gorsuch          2 BA-220
Bozley, John, 18 Oct. 1759, Hannah Bull               2 BA-219
Bozley, Vincent, 28 March 1771, Wheelamina Norris     2 BA-262
Bozman, Edw., 27 Feb. 1749, Rozannah Lyon             2 BA-201
Bozman, John, June 1754, Lucretia Leeds               2 TA-289
Bozman, Thomas, 27 May 1715, Mrs. Mary Glen           2 TA-75
Bozman, Col. Thomas, 10 Jan. 1735, Elizabeth Taylor   2 TA-161
Bozwell, John, 17 Nov. 1745, Mary Jenings             2 BA-193
Brabant, Wm., 24 April 1706, Mary Gyatt               1 CA-112
Brace, Wm., 30 June 1715, Ann Lam                     2 KE-190
Bradbury, Jacob, 19 Feb. 1692, Ann Jadwin             8 SF-361
Bradbury, Roger, 16 Sept. 1704, Mary Marr             2 TA-41
Bradbury, Roger, 13 June 1731, Tomasin Martingale,    2 TA-150
Bradcutt, Richard, 24 Feb. 1715, Eliza Cook           2 PG-1
Braddis, Thomas, (?) Jan. (?), Sarah Baker            3 KE-241
Braden, Robert, 23 June 1772, Eliz. Wilkinson         2 BA-264
Bradfoord, James, 26 Sept. 1728, Martha Cornish       2 TA-118
Bradford, George, 3 Dec. 1746, Margaret Bonfield      2 BA-157
Bradford, Wm., 16 Feb. 1764, Sarah McComas            2 BA-226
Bradin, Thomas, 17 June 1722, Jane Worrall            2 TA-102
Bradley, John, 28 Nov. 1698, Ann Stiffin              1 AA-42
Bradley, John, 4 Dec. 1733, Margaret (?)              1 WI-5
Bradley, John, 2 Oct. 1743, Anne Evans                2 BA-126
                                                      & 239
Bradley, John, 15 Dec. 1746, Elizabeth Jones          3 BA-160
Bradley, Joseph, 1775, Betsy Richards                 1 CR
Bradley, Thomas, 5 Oct. 1769, Eliz. Harwood           2 BA-259
Bradly, Thomas, 28 Nov. 1698, Ann Stiffin             1 AA-43
Bradshaw, John, 20 June 1719, Mary Callmack           2 BA-17
Bradshaw, Thomas, 8 June 1732, Edith Price            2 TA-152
```

Brady, Solomon, 11 April 1774, Margaret Baily          1 CR
Brady, Terrence, Dec. 1740, Sarah Hilliard             1 BA-323
Braham, James, 1 Jan. 1773, Ellis Cooke                2 BA-265
Bramble, Giles, 10 July 1736, Elis. Pennington         1 QA-42
Bramble, John, 29 July 1755, Mary Belcher              1 QA-59
Bramwell, George, 7 March 1750, Susanna Fort           4 BA-71
Branford, Daniel, 17 April 1745, Mary Groshare         3 TA-52
Branford, Thomas, 26 Sept. 1719, Margaret Barton       1 AA-295
Brannan, Patrick, 11 Aug. 1769, Eliz. Johnston         2 BA-259
Brashear, William, 11 June 1734, Priscilla Prather     2 PG-6
Brashears, Charles, 1771, Margaret Cooly               2 AA-410
Brashears, Jonathan, June 1775, Susannah Welsh         2 AA-412
Brashears, Otho, 6 Jan. 1736, Mary Holmes              2 PG-7
Brashears, Waymacke, 14 Aug. 1764, Mary Mullican       9 AA-248
Brashears, Zedock, 16 Aug. 1773, Elizabeth Sparrow     2 AA-411
Brashier, Thomas, 13 Oct. 1726, Sarah Constance        1 BA-262
Bratten, Nicolas, 21 Feb. 1709, Mary Wood              1 AA-77
                                                       & 258
Braun, Stoffel, 9 Sept. 1761, Magdalen Maen            4 FR-1107
Brawner, Henry, 2 Jan. 1726/7, Elizabeth Barton        1 PG-269
Brawner, John, 8 Jan. 1716, Mary Downing               1 PG-281
  1 PG-262 gives her name as Mary Dunning.
Brengle, Jacob, 30 June 1761, Gertrude Bull            4 FR-1107
Brent, Robert, 6 May 1729, Mary Wharton                1 CH-174
Brereton, William, 16 Oct. 1727, Mary Walker           1 AA-105
Breward, Thomas, 1761, Hannah Creiger                  4 CE-261
Brewer, Henry, (no date given), Eleanor Welsh          1 AA-149
Brewer, John, 14 Feb. 1704, Dinah Battee               1 AA-65
Brewer, Joseph, 18 Dec. 1715, Jane Rutland             1 AA-79
Brewer, Joseph, son of Joseph, 30 May 1769, Jane
  Brewer, dau. of John                                 1 AA-149
Brewer, Nicholas, 14 Jan. 1745, Elizabeth Jacob        1 AA-125
Brewer, Thomas, 27 Sept. 1773, Minta Dawsey            1 SM-136
Brewer, William, 14 Feb. 1715, Martha Skeys            1 AA-79
Brewer, William, son of John Brewer IV and Eleanor,
  3 Dec. 1765, Rebekah Newton, dau. of Joseph and
  Ann of P. G. Co.                                     1 AA-152
Brewster, William, 26 June 1716, Jane Banister         2 PG-1
Brian, James, 4 July 1754, Mary Reaven                 2 BA-210
Brian, William, 5 May 1746, Hannah Wallis              2 BA-195
Brice, Jacob, May 1775, Christian Lewin                2 AA-412
Brice, James, 6 Jan. 1742, Mary Johnson                1 BA-327
Brice, John, 9 Sept. 1730, Mrs. Sarah Frisby           4 AA-433
Brice, John, 30 Oct. 1766, Mary Maccubbin, eldest dau.
  of Nicholas                                          5 AA-2
Brice, Richard, 22 Jan. 1740, Juda Grant               3 KE-248
Brice, Thomas, 24 Jan. 1739, Elizabeth Anhousin        1 BA-315
Brickman, Frederick Moses, 21 Feb. 1725, Mary Short    1 AA-102
Brierly, Thomas, 11 Feb. 1752, Ann Leat                2 BA-204
Brigdel, Daniel, 25 Aug. 1752, Rachel Johnston         3 AA-112
Briggs, Charity (sic), 20 April 1704, Bridgett Johns   1 AA-64
Bright, Francis, 7 Nov. 1719, Susanna Tozer; both were
  of Christ Church Parish, Kent Island                 4 AA-410
Bright, Thomas, 11 May 1662, Elizabeth Cripes          1 KE-186
Bright, William, 6 June 170-(?), Sarah Thorn           3 KE-241
Brimer, Will'm, 16 Sept. 1712, Katherine Campbell      4 AA-380
Brin, John, 28 April 1709, Anne Abbott                 2 TA-59
Brindley, Nathaniel, 1 April 1762, Rachel Spencer      1 BA-374
Brinn, William, 28 July 1741, Catharine Gaskin         3 TA-31
Brinton, Joseph, son of William and Jane, 14 April
  1748, Mary, widow of Joseph Elgar                    9 SF
Brisbane, John, 22 June 1756, Elianor Adcock           1 QA-61
Brisco, John, 23 July 1739, Hannah Corse               2 KE-230
Brisco, William, 29 April 1739, Mary Ann Jones         2 KE-230
Briscoe, John, 27 Nov. 1746, Anne Wood                 1 CH-184

Briscoe, Philip, 1 Nov. 1748, Cassandra Chunn          1 CH-184
Briscoe, Walter, 13 May 1762, Elizabeth Compton        1 CH-198
Brise, John, 16 Dec. 1701, Sarah Worthington           3 AA-96
  This name is usually rendered Brice.
Britt, Francis, 22 Nov. 1775, Easther Townsend         2 SO-197
Brittingham, Levi, 8 Nov. 1759, Orpha Long             2 SO-109
Broadly, George, 6 Dec. 1698, Joane Killinsworth       2 AA-295
Broadway, Joseph, 2 July 1759, Maryiny Devereux        1 QA-65
Brodaway, James, 8 Dec. 1737, Juliana Campbell         2 TA-271
Brogden, Rev. William, 24 Dec. 1741, Mrs. Elizabeth
  Chapman                                     1 AA-124
Broidered, John, 4 May 1742, Sophia Conner             4 AA-444
Bromfield, Peter, 25 Dec. 1718, Barbara Bennet         2 PG-2
Bromfield, Peter, 5 July 1731, Jane Tucker             2 PG-5
Bromwell, Robert, 9 April 1750, Mary Sherwood          3 TA-77
Brooke, Basil, 5 mo., 1 day, 1764, Elizabeth Hopkins,
  dau. of Gerrard                             6 SF-146
Brooke, Roger, 3 Dec. 1770, Maria Brooke               1 SM-135
  Both parties were third cousins.
Brookes, James, 1 June 1725, Deborah Snowden, dau.
  of Richard                                  6 SF-83
Brooks, Christopher, Jan. 1728/9, Rebecca Pryor        1 QA-36
Brooks, Henery, 22 Jan. 1711, Ellinor Fitchwaters      3 KE-242
Brooks, James, 15 Feb. 1774, Mary Kinnerly             6 BA(1)
Brooks, Joseph, 19 Nov. 1705, Anne Rice                1 AA-65
Brooks, Joseph, 28 May 1747, Elizabeth Phillips        2 BA-241
  2 BA-196 gives date as 1 June 1747.
Brooks, Mosely, 14 Aug. 1732, Jane Fleetwood           1 AA-114
Brooks, Philip, 29 March 1748, Mrs. Mary Johnson       2 KE-281
Brooks, Thomas, 4 April 1713, Mary Currey, widow       3 CE-7
Brooks, Will'm, 10 Dec. 1734, Sarah Jones              3 BA-152
Brooks, William, 28 April 1755, Bethia Stephens        2 BA-212
Brooksby, Cornelius, 29 March 1719, Anne Shahan        4 AA-407
Broom, Robert, 7 June 1756, Frances Jacobs             1 CE-296
Broome, John, 24 Nov. 1774, Betty Heighe Gantt         2 CA-53
Broomfield, Francis, (?) Oct. (?), Eliz'th Ward        3 KE-241
Broomwell, Abraham, 4 July 1746, Anne Spencer          3 TA-59
Brotherhood, Henry, 14 Feb. 1704, Joan Lester          1 AA-65
Broughton, John, 26 Feb. 1684, Elizabeth Bradshaw,
  dau. of William                            5 SO-396
Broughton, John, 3 March 1760, Mary Purkins            2 SO-109
Broughton, William, 20 Oct. 1745, Jemima Kellem        2 SO-7
Brown, (?), 22 June 1712, Eliz'th Slayfoot             3 KE-243
Brown, Absolom, 19 Jan. 1728/9, Sarah Shepherd         1 BA-246
Brown, Absolom, 18 Jan. 1734, Mary Cord                1 BA-282
Brown, Absolom, 5 Dec. 1752, Marg't Hanson             1 BA-354
Brown, Adam, 11 Feb. 1730, Sarah Long                  2 TA-150
Brown, Adam, 29 Dec. 1726, Elizabeth Needles           2 TA-114
Brown, Andrew, 26 Dec. 1733, Ann Sales                 2 TA-154
Brown, Anton, 31 Jan. 1774, Ann Brewer                 1 SM-136
Brown, Augustus, 22 April 1729, Ann Cutchen            1 BA-269
Brown, Basil, 20 June 1777, Ann Mattingly              1 SM-137
Brown, Christopher, 15 Aug. 1731, Abigal Fisher        2 TA-150
Brown, Daniel, son of William, 11 Nov. 1736, Susanna
  Oldham, dau. of Thomas                      9 SF
Brown, Daniel, son of William, 3 May 1753, Susannah
  Elgar, dau. of Joseph                       9 SF
Brown, Daniel, son of Messer, 3 day, 7 mo., 1757,
  Sarah Brown, dau. of Joshua                 9 SF
Brown, Daniel, Jr., son of Daniel and Elizabeth (Kirk),
  Miriam Gregg, dau. of David and Lydia       9 SF
Brown, David, son of Thomas and Frances, 29 day, 2 mo.,
  1776, Elizabeth Matthews, dau. of George and
  Dorothy                                     9 SF
Brown, Dickson, 17 June 1746, Elizabeth Trotten        3 BA-159

| | |
|---|---|
| Brown, Dixon, 7 Aug. 1777, Sarah Kingsbury | 10 BA-68 |
| Brown, Edward, Feb. 1745, Meremiah Hawkins | 1 QA-52 |
| Brown, Gabriel, 10 Feb. 1730, Mary Kean | 1 BA-256 |
| Brown, Hugh, 15 Aug. 1771, Ruth Barney | 2 BA-262 |
| Brown, Isaac, son of Jeremiah, 3 Nov. 1743, Lyddia Slatter, dau. of George | 9 SF |
| Brown, Isaac, son of Daniel and Susanna, 14 day, 8 mo., 1777, Sarah Ballinger, dau. of William and Cassandra | 3 SF |
| Brown, Isack, 13 July 1713, Elinor Campbell | 2 BA-2 |
| Brown, Isaiah, 7 April 1729, Mary Burras | 1 AA-108 |
| Brown, Jack, 13 July 1713, Elinor Campbell | 2 BA-2 |
| Brown, Jacob, son of William, 25 day, 11 mo., 1772, Elizabeth Cook, dau. of John and Rebecca | 9 SF |
| Brown, James, 8 day, 6 mo., 1679, Honour Clayton, dau. of William and Prudence | 9 SF |
| Brown, James, 22 Sept. 1745, Frances Chartres | 3 BA-157 |
| Brown, James, 2 April 1746, Sarah Johnson | 1 BA-342 |
| Brown, James, 22 June 1748, Sarah Johnson | 4 AA-450 |
| Brown, James, Jr., son of Thomas, 16 Feb. 1758, Elizabeth Morgan | 1 BA-374 |
| Brown, James, 16 Jan. 1758, Eliza Morgan | 1 BA-363 |
| Brown, James, 31 May 1767, Reb'a Wood | 2 BA-230 |
| Brown, Jeremiah, Jr., son of Jeremiah and Mary, 31 May 1739, Esther Gatchell, dau. of Elisha | 9 SF |
| Brown, Jeremiah, son of Daniel and Elizabeth, 14 day, 11 mo., 1765, Anna Wilson, dau. of Samuel and Katherine | 9 SF |
| Brown, Jeremiah, son of Joshua and Hannah, 15 day, 11 mo., 1770, Hannah England, dau. of Samuel and Sarah | 9 SF |
| Brown, John, 10 Feb. 1704, Mary Wilson | 2 TA-43 |
| Brown, John, 18 Nov. 1705, Elizabeth Sicklemore | 1 BA-206 |
| Brown, John, 17 Nov. 1709, Sarah Herrington | 2 AA-339 |
| Brown, John, 31 Aug. 1710, Easter Cook | 2 TA-67 |
| Brown, John, 10 April 1716, (wife not given) | 2 AA-357 |
| Brown, John, mariner, 14 April 1718, Anne Sanderson, widow | 4 AA-404 |
| Brown, John, of England, 28 Oct. 1726, Mrs. Rachel Scott, widow of Col. Edward Scott | 2 KE-219 |
| Brown, John, 29 Nov. 1730, Anne Turner | 3 BA-150 |
| Brown, John, 31 Jan. 1731, Sarah Sunderland | 4 AA-434 |
| Brown, John, (24?) April 1732, Elizabeth Harper | 2 PG-5 |
| Brown, John, 30 Sept. 1736, Jane Got | 2 AA-378 |
| Brown, John, 21 Feb. 1747, Comfort White | 2 BA-196 |
| Brown, John, 12 Aug. 1747, Eliz'h Ferril | 1 QA-53 |
| Brown, John, 1748, Comfort White | 2 BA-242 |
| Brown, John, son of Messer, 25 Nov. 1751, Jane Pugh, dau. of John | 9 SF |
| Brown, Capt. John, 23 Jan. 1752, Mrs. Jane Thompson, widow of Mr. John Thompson | 3 CE-25 |
| Brown, John, 17 Oct. 1753, Eliz. Bond | 2 BA-209 |
| Brown, John, 13 Jan. 1757, Cath. Carmichall | 1 QA-62 |
| Brown, John, 28 Aug. 1759, Sarah Kersey | 1 QA-65 |
| Brown, John, Sept. 1772, Margret O'Donil | 2 BA-265 |
| Brown, John, 25 Dec. 1777, Mary Macarty | 1 HA-201 |
| Brown, John Eliot, 17 Jan. 1720, Elisabeth Simson | 1 AA-302 |
| Brown, Jonas, 5 Aug. 1734, Elizabeth Paine | 1 CE-328 |
| Brown, Joseph, Jr., 17 Aug. 1727, Rebecca Simmons | 2 PG-4 |
| Brown, Joseph, 20 Jan. 1738, Susanna Miles | 9 AA-246 |
| Brown, Joseph, 3 June 1761, Avarilla Osborne | 1 BA-368 |
| Brown, Joshua, 14 Aug. 1777, Mary Weatherall | 1 HA-200 |
| Brown, Mark, 8 Nov. 1716, Susanna Fowler | 2 PG-1 |
| Brown, Messer (or Mercer), son of William, 13 Nov. 1710, Jane Richards | 9 SF |

Brown, Messer, son of William, 11 April 1728, Dinah
  Churchman, dau. of John and Hannah          9 SF
Brown, Messer, son of Messer and Jane, 5 Dec. 1739,
  Hannah Slater, dau. of George          9 SF
Brown, Morgan, 7 Dec. 1715, Rebechah Durden    8 SF-12
Brown, Morgan, 15 Jan. 1758, Welthy Collins    1 QA-63
Brown, Pelham, 21 Dec. 1773, Susan Low       1 SM-136
Brown, Rich'd, 31 Dec. 1704, Grace ffairbrooke   4 AA-389
Brown, Richard, son of William and Ann, 6 day, 9 mo.,
  1717, Hannah Reynolds, dau. of Henry and Prudence  9 SF
Brown, Richard, son of William and Ann, 9 Feb. 1730,
  Rachel Beeson, dau. of Edward          9 SF
Brown, Richard, son of William and Ann, 24 day, 8 mo.,
  1733, Mary Norton, dau. of Edward       9 SF
Brown, Robert, 27 Jan. 1700, Mary Tyndall     2 AA-314
Brown, Robert, 18 June 1702, Katherine Parnall, widow
  of James Parnall             1 AA-58
                              & 251
Brown, Robert, 11 Dec. 1732, Elizabeth Swan    2 PG-6
Brown, Rob't, 26 Dec. 1777, Mary Ireland     3 SM-535
Brown, Samuel, 2 Jan. 1709/10, Mary Skelton    1 BA-208
Brown, Samuel, son of William and Katherine, 8 day,
  3 mo., 1734, Elizabeth Harris, dau. of William  9 SF
Brown, Sam'l, 30 Oct. 1746, Milicent Hitchcock   1 CE-291
Brown, Samuel, son of Joshua and Hannah, 8 day, 2 mo.,
  1770, Ann Stedman, dau. of Richard and Ann   9 SF
Brown, Thomas, 13 Feb. 1704, Eliz. Stephens, widow  4 AA-390
Brown, Thomas, 24 Dec. 1712, Neomi Ladmore    2 TA-72
Brown, Thomas, 20 Feb. 1731/2, Ann Brushier    2 PG-5
Brown, Thomas, 7 Feb. 1739, Juliana Howard    2 TA-168
Brown, Thomas, 19 June 1739, Susanna Higginson   1 BA-308
Brown, Thomas, 26 April 1741, Mary Edmondson    2 TA-171
Brown, Thomas, 25 July 1758, Eliz'th Courtney   1 BA-361
Brown, Thos., 13 April 1760, Kezia Phraisher    2 BA-220
Brown, Thomas, 29 June 1777, Sarah Taylor     3 SM-103
Brown, William, 31 Aug. 1710, Margery Jones    1 AA-77
Brown, William, son of William and Ann, 1715, Eliza-
  beth Cowgill, dau. of John          9 SF
Brown, William, 20 June 1721, Esther Bester    1 AA-305
Brown, William, son of William and Ann, 15 March
  1721/2, Margaret Davis           9 SF
Brown, William, 5 Sept. 1723, Susanna Carmichael,
  widow                     1 WI-9
Brown, William, son of William and Esther, 11 day,
  2 mo., 1728, Susanna Churchman, dau. of John and
  Hannah                   9 SF
Brown, William, 2 Oct. 1738, Elizabeth Haines, dau.
  of William                9 SF
Brown, William, 31 Dec. 1740, Margaret Constance  1 BA-316
Brown, William, 12 Feb. 1775, Mary Scrivener    2 AA-412
Brown, William, son of Joseph and Hannah of Bucks Co.,
  Pa., 23 day, 2 mo., 1775, Elizabeth Lacie, dau. of
  Thomas and Esther            4 SF-265
Brown, Wilson, 10 May 1772, Mary Richards     2 SO-196
Browne, Daniel, 9 June 1698, Sarah Tucker     2 AA-294
Browne, Edward, 28 Oct. 1668, Sarah Williams    1 KE-187
Browne, Henry, 18 April 1705, Hannah Moss     3 AA-97
Browne, John, 16 Sept. 1668, Sarah Minard     5 SO-396
Browne, Thomas, 26 July 1692, Alice Horton     3 CH
Browne, Tho. (?), 23 Jan. 1700, Mary (?)      2 TA-12
Browning, George, 19 June 1701, Mary Kennard    3 CE-3
Browning, George, 30 day, 1 mo., 1767, Margaret Neal 8 SF-127
Browning, Ritson, 9 day, 5 mo., 1753, Sarah VanSant 1 SF-89
Browning, Thomas, 19 April 1708, Mary Ward     3 KE-242
Browning, William, 27 April 1729, Sarah Gooding   3 KE-246

Brownly, Arthur, 24 Sept. 1771, Nancy Norris            2 BA-263
Broxson, Wm., 18 Nov. 1697, Elizabeth Nicholson, widow  3 CE-2
Brucebanks, Abraham, 3 Dec. 1750, Mary Jackson          1 BA-356
Bruder, Jacob, 1 Jan. 1759, Eva Marg. Huber             4 FR-1104
Bruff, John, 31 Jan. 1749, Ann Allen                    2 BA-200
                                                        & 244
Bruff, Thomas, 28 Jan. (?), Alse Wickes                 3 KE-240
Bruff, Thomas, 8 June 1705, Catherine (?)               4 AA-390
Bruff, Thomas, 23 Aug. 1761, Bettey White               2 SO-109
Brumfield, Francis, 9 March (?), (?) (?)                1 CE-300
Brumfield, John, Aug. 1767, Elizabeth Gibson            1 CE-300
Brumfield, Nathan, 5 Dec. 1774, Ann Foster              1 CE-302
Brumfield, William, 25 Dec. 1765, Mary Brumfield        1 CE-300
Brunner, Jacob, 1 April 1759, Mary Barb. Kaufer         4 FR-1104
Brunner, Jacob, 5 July 1761, Margaret Geister           4 FR-1107
Brunner, Peter, son of George and Appolonia, 16 April
   1764, Dorothea Loehman, dau. of Jacob and Elizabeth
   (Haffner)                                            5 FR-10
Brusbanks, Edward, 19 June 1743, Bridget Baker          2 BA-238
Brushier, Benjamin, Jr., 24 Jan. 1720/1, Rebecca
   Walker, dau. of Charles                              2 PG-2
Brushier, John, 13 Aug. 1723, Ruth Walker               2 PG-3
Brushier, Samuel, Jr., 17 Dec. 1717, Eliza Brushier,
   dau. of Benjamin Brushier, Sr.                       2 PG-2
Brushier, Thomas, 11 Sept. 1711, Ann Venman             2 PG-1
Brushier, Thomas, 1 Feb. 1728/9, Ann Hyatt              2 PG-5
Bryan, Daniel, 28 Nov. 1703, Ann Veare                  1 BA-200
Bryan, Edward, 3 Dec. 1697, Mary Vickers, widow of
   Francis Vickers                                      2 TA-8
Bryan, James, 26 Jan. 1726/7, Rachel Cheney             4 AA-427
Bryan, James, 13 July 1777, Phoebe Bond                 10 BA-68
Bryan, John, 24 Sept. 1721, Elinor Jackson, widow       2 BA-17
Bryan, John, 28 June 1777, Lydia M'Donald               7 AA-1
Bryan, Rich'd, 30 Jan. 1757, Rachel Lanham              1 PG-317
Bryan, Thomas, 1 Dec. 1777, Maria Mattingly             1 SM-137
Bryan, William, 13 April 1746, Hannah Wallace           2 BA-240
Bryan, Wm., 4 May 1750, Diana Gutteridge                1 PG-289
Bryant, Arthur, 2 May 1750, Mary McDermut               2 KE-286
Buchanan, Andrew, barber in Annapolis, 12 Sept. 1751,
   Elizabeth Marshall                                   4 AA-454
Buchanan, Andrew, 20 July 1760, Susannah Lawson         3 BA-168
Buchanan, Archibald, Jr., 28 April 1729, Anne Robert    1 BA-250
Buchanan, Arch'd, 10 March 1768, Sarah Lee              2 BA-231
Buchanan, Jno., 5 July 1763, Mary Ramsey                2 BA-225
Buck, Benj., 10 Feb. 1763, Darkes Sutton                2 BA-224
Buck, James, 20 Jan. 1773, Cloe Crook                   2 BA-265
Buck, John, 20 Dec. 1705, Penelope Martain              3 AA-101
   4 AA-372 gives her name as Martin.
Buck, John, 11 Feb. 1742, Susanna Ingram                2 BA-143
Buck, Redman, 27 July 177, Eleanor Buck                 10 BA-68
Buckingham, Henry, 3 Dec. 1730, Elizabeth Lowe          8 SF-59
Buckingham, Henry, 3 Aug. 1740, Elizabeth Nicks         8 SF-79
Buckingham, Jno., Jan. 1697, Frances Hooper             3 AA-99
Buckingham, John, 31 Jan. 1720, Hannah Craws            3 AA-100
   4 AA-413 gives her name as Hannah Cross, widow.
Buckingham, John, 31 Jan. 1776, Sarah Cullember, dau.
   of Thomas and Mary                                   1 CA-113
Buckingham, Thomas, 3 Feb. 1697, Catharine Parratt      8 SF-412
Buckinham, Henry, 15 Sept. 1746, Elizb'th Price         3 TA-61
Buckley, James, 25 Feb. 1733, Elizabeth Rogers          2 TA-154
Buckley, John, Oct. 1772, Ann Gouldsmith                2 BA-265
Buckley, John, 19 Oct. 1777, Frances Hanby              1 HA-200
Buckley, Rich'd, 4 April 1748, Catharine Hindesley      1 QA-47
Buckley, Robert, 11 June 1730, Anne West                2 TA-148
Buckley, Thomas, 14 Jan. 1759, Rachel Flemming          2 TA-286

Buckley, William, 23 Dec. 1721, Elizabeth Wilkinson      2 TA-97
Buckly, Nicholas, 26 Jan. 1727, Eliz. Anderson           1 WI-25
Bucknal, Francis, 11 Nov. 1729, Blanch Brown             1 BA-258
Bucknal, Thomas, July 1701, Elizabeth Griffis            1 BA-192
  Banns were published at this time.
Bucknam, Batslian, 7 Oct. 1777, Sarah Mattox            10 BA-69
Bucknam, Zebediah, 7 Oct. 1777, Rachel Mattox           10 BA-69
Bucknell, John, 1719, Cathrine Lang                      3 AA-106
Buckner, William, 20 Sept. 1724, Mrs. Patience
  Colegate                                               3 BA-147
Budd, George, 12 May 1720, Sarah Young                   4 AA-411
Budd, Henry, 15 Nov. 1742, Elianer Howell                3 AA-109
Budd, Samuel, 27 Sept. 1747, Milcah Young                1 BA-387
Bugden, Tobias, 15 May 1749, Margaret Gassett            4 AA-451
Bull, Abraham, 1 June 1749, Mary Wyle                    2 BA-198
Bull, Edmund, 19 Nov. 1752, Susana Lyon                  1 BA-389
Bull, Isaac, 23 Jan. 1749, Hannah Robertson              2 BA-200
Bull, Isaac, 26 May 1761, Betty Ann Slade                2 BA-222
Bull, Jacob, Jr., 17 Oct. 1752, Ranrice Bussey           2 BA-206
Bull, John, 20 Feb. 1739, Hannah Ruff                    2 BA-143
Bull, Samuel, 1 Aug. 1734, Eliz'h Swearingen             2 PG-6
Bull, Wm., 16 June 1761, Sarah Billingsley               2 BA-222
Bullen, Aaron, 28 Feb. 1749/50, Sarah Catrope            3 TA-76
Bullen, Mr. John, 13 May 1703, Mrs. Margaret Knowles     2 TA-35
Bullen, John, 2 March 1741/2, Sarah Guida                4 AA-443
Bullen, Joseph, 27 Nov. 1721, Mary Turnner               2 TA-97
Bullen, Mr. Thomas, 31 Jan. 1726/7, Elizabeth Foard      2 TA-114
Bullen, Thomas, 8 May 1735, Rachel Turbutt, the
  younger dau. of Mr. Foster Turbutt                     2 TA-157
Bullevent, Joshua, 7 Feb. 1735, Mary Buttler             3 BA-155
Bullin, Henry, 14 Dec. 1704, Mary Clemence               2 TA-42
Bullock, Henry, 25 April 1696, Mary (?)                  2 TA-6
Bullock, James, 4 Jan. 1724, Mary Job                    1 BA-238
Bullock, John, 24 Nov. 1704, Ann Mackey                  2 TA-42
Bumnalley, Andrew, 6 May 1707, Elizabeth Blackett        1 CA-112
Bungey, Samuel, widower, 22 Aug. 1773, Mary Mull,
  widow                                                  3 BA-170
Bunker, John, 15 May 1765, Lydia Dillahunt               9 AA-250
Bunnall, John, 29 June 1722, Mary Hannahane              2 TA-103
Bunting, Abraham, son of Joseph and Rebeckah, 6 day,
  12 mo., 1753, Margaret Berry, dau. of Samuel and
  Margaret                                               9 SF
Bunton, Thomas, 2 Dec. 1735, Rebecca Nix                 2 TA-158
Burad, Darby, 7 Oct. 1701, Grizell (?)                   2 TA-21
Burbridge, Thomas, 10 March 1731, Deborah Terrin         1 QA-38
Burch, Benjamin, 9 Dec. 1773, Mary Matthews              1 CH-200
Burch, Jonathan, Jr., 15 Jan. 1764, Ann Newton, dau.
  of Joseph                                              1 PG-366
Burch, Joseph, 16 Nov. 1749, Sarah Jones                 1 QA-56
Burchfield, Adam, 2 Oct. 1753, Ann Nelson                1 BA-377
Burchfield, Robert, 4 Dec. 1735, Ann Clark               1 BA-286
Burchfield, Thomas, 30 June 1709, Mary Wilson            1 BA-208
Burchfield, Thomas, 4 Aug. 1721, Joanna Cantwell         1 BA-229
Burchfield, Thomas, 21 Feb. 1725, Elizabeth Macarley,
  widow                                                  1 BA-235
Burchfield, Thomas, 10 Aug. 1727, Mary Johnson           1 BA-243
Burchfield, Thomas, Jr., 13 July 1736, Sarah Gash        1 BA-292
Burchfield, Thomas, 20 March 1755, Elizabeth Turner      1 BA-359
Burchinal, Jeremiah, 6 Aug. 1741, Elizabeth Woodhal      2 KE-247
Burden, John, 20 June 1703, Rosannah Haines              2 TA-36
Burdet, William, 6 May 1777, Rachel Mobberly             7 AA-1
Burdit, William, 8 May 1777, Rachel Moberly              8 AA-15
Burdus, Richard, 21 March 1741/2, Mary Thorp             4 AA-443
Burgan, Philip, 24 Feb. 1746, Rebecca Green              2 BA-196
Burgan, Sutton, 6 Jan. 1708, Susannah Merris             3 KE-242

| | |
|---|---|
| Burges, Basil, 8 Feb. 1759, Anna Smith | 2 PG-7 |
| Burges, James, 12 Nov. 1716, Rebeka Buck | 1 AA-274 |
| Burges, Richard, 13 May 1703, Mary Slater | 2 TA-35 |
| Burges, Rich'd, Oct. 1749, Sarah Castle | 2 BA-199 |
| Burges, Wm., 30 Oct. 1750, Ra'l Virgin | 3 TA-79 |
| Burgess, Basil, 8 Feb. 1759, Anna (?) | 6 AA-216 |
| Burgess, Charles, 26 Oct. 1703, Elizabeth Hanslap, widow of Jos. Hanslap | 1 AA-64 |
| Burgess, Edward, 12 Jan. 1713, Sarah (?), widow | 4 AA-380 |
| Burgess, Hugh, 1 Feb. 1764, Alice Moore | 4 SF-251 |
| Burgess, John, 15 Dec. 1720, Jane Mockelfresh | 1 AA-302 |
| Burgess, John, 27 Jan. 1733, Matilda Sparrow | 1 AA-119 |
| Burgess, Joseph, 31 day, 10 mo., 1770, Mary Moore, dau. of William and Mary | 4 SF-257 |
| Burgess, Richard, 18 Aug. 1720, Elizabeth Williams | 2 TA-94 |
| Burgess, Richard, 20 Aug. 1749, Sarah Caswell | 2 BA-244 |
| 2 BA-199 gives date as Oct. 1749. | |
| Burgess, Samuell, 19 April 1716, Elizabeth Durdain | 1 AA-79 |
| Burgess, Stephen, 1 Feb. 1733, Isable Wafford | 2 TA-154 |
| Burgess, West, 31 Oct. 1765, Elisabeth Warfield | 6 AA-187 |
| Burgin, James, 16 Jan. 1766, Rebecca Smith | 2 KE-305 |
| Burgis, William, 13 Aug. 1697, Ann Watkins | 1 AA-37 |
| Burgiss, Jno., 12 May 1740, Hannah Bullock | 2 TA-168 |
| Burk, Barthallume, 12 April 1748, Mahanny (?) | 1 QA-54 |
| Burk, Edward, 4 May 1739, Anne Steward | 1 QA-45 |
| Burk, Henry, 6 Jan. 1706/7, Easter Pine | 1 BA-201 |
| Burk, John, 18 April 17-(?), Elizabeth Pearse | 3 KE-240 |
| Burk, John, 29 Dec. 1712, Eliz'th Booth | 3 KE-244 |
| Burk, John, 25 Dec. 1735, Hanna Tarbouton | 1 QA-41 |
| Burk, John, Sept. 1743, Sarah Young | 1 QA-49 |
| Burk, Richard, 28 Jan. 1723, Ellinor Saxton | 2 TA-106 |
| Burk, Rich'd, 10 Aug. 1766, Grace Farrier | 1 CE-325 |
| Burk, Thomas, 14 April 1737, Sarah Sicklemore | 2 BA-84 |
| Burk, Thomas, 21 June 1772, Deliah Peacock | 2 BA-264 |
| Burk, Tobias, 14 June 1774, Sarah Stainer | 1 CR |
| Burk, Ulick, 14 May 1732, Mary Leekings | 2 BA-41 |
| Burk, William, 2 Sept. 1730, Mary Sturgess | 3 KE-247 |
| Burk, William, 6 Oct. 1746, Rachel Sweatman | 1 QA-52 |
| Burk, W., 8 Nov. 1764, Mary Lemmon | 2 BA-227 |
| Burke, William, 16 June 1774, Jean Campbell | 1 CE-302 |
| Burkeloo, Abell Van, 7 June 1715, Cathrin Herman | 3 CE-13 |
| Burkhead, Christopher, 1 March 1729, Ann Harrison | 8 SF-54 |
| Burkit, Robert, 1 Oct. 1716, Mary Wharton | 2 BA-8 |
| Burle, Jno., 9 Oct. 1711, Elizebeth Hammond | 3 AA-98 |
| Burle, John, 22 Dec. 1730, Ann Hawkins | 3 AA-103 |
| Burle, Stephen, 14 Feb. 1709, Sarah Gosling | 3 AA-98 |
| Burley, John, 23 June 1743, Margrett Mortimore | 2 AA-108 |
| Burley, Jonas, 30 Oct. 1729, Elizabeth Reaves | 2 PG-5 |
| Burley, Richard, 27 Jan. 1737, Sarah Lindsey | 4 AA-439 |
| Burlin, Richard, 9 June 1772, Ann Hill | 3 AA-113 |
| Burn, James, 21 Dec. 1758, Sarah Robinson | 1 QA-64 |
| Burn, Joseph, 1 Sept. 1726, Margrett Carry | 2 TA-113 |
| Burnall, Thomas, 20 Aug. 1742, Martha Vickers | 3 TA-39 |
| Burne, Sollomon, 14 Feb. 1737, Jane Maiden | 2 TA-164 |
| Burnett, Peter, 3 Jan. 1769, Elisabeth Solomon | 2 BA-257 |
| Burnham, Thomas, 21 Aug. 1729, Mary Nurner | 3 CE-13 |
| Burns, Isaac, 31 March 1761, (?) Duwaull | 2 BA-221 |
| Burns, Thomas, 20 May 1777, Eleanor Doudle | 7 AA-1 |
| Burrell, Alexander (no date), Eleanor Dent | 1 PG-334 |
| Burrill, Samuell, 16 April 1704, Anne Tooly | 1 AA-64 |
| Burris, George, 2 March 1730, Rachel Barkhust | 1 QA-36 |
| Burroughs, Abraham, 17 Jan. 1744, Mary Barkhurst | 1 QA-50 |
| Burroughs, John, 17 March 1760, Priscila Reed | 1 FR-10 |
| Burroughs, William, 25 Nov. 1700, Mary Cox | 1 AA-56 |
| | & 246 |

```
Burrows, James, 25 July 1718, Mary Brown               2 PG-2
Burrows, John, 13 Aug. 1737, Elizabeth Barkhurst       1 QA-43
Burt, Henry, Jr., 7 June 1757, Cornelia Boon           1 QA-62
Burton, John, 15 Jan. 1743, Mary Hargas                1 BA-333
Burton, Joseph, 29 July 1703, Sarah Westall            1 AA-64
                                                       & 255
Burton, Joseph, 13 (Oct. 1768?), Constant Legatt       2 BA-257
Burton, Samuell, 29 March 1725, Jane Clark             1 AA-100
Burton, Wm., 17 Feb. 1763, Sarah Legatt                2 BA-224
Buryal, Jeremiah, 16 Oct. 1738, Mary McDaniel          2 TA-166
Busey, Paul, 1771, Sarah Crandel                       2 AA-411
Busey, Samuel, 13 July 1777, Sarah Roberts             3 PG-104
Bush, John, 11 Sept. 1715, Mary Hurlett                2 TA-76
Bush, John, 3 Nov. 1756, Rachell Curtiss               2 CR-269
Bush, Stephen, 24 Nov. 1736, Marg't White              2 TA-158
Bush, Thorny, 24 Aug. 1745, Elisa Pike                 3 BA-157
Bushnal, Edward, 6 Nov. 1755, Mary Peavey              1 QA-60
Bushup, William, 15 Sept. 1742, Mary Harrice           3 AA-110
Bussells, William, 18 Feb. 1750, Susannah Howard       1 QA-57
Bussey, Edward, 10 Aug. 1701, Martha Evans             1 CA-111
Buswell, Thos., 30 Aug. 1752, Mary Chamney             2 BA-206
Butall, Thomas, 12 Aug. 1705, Elizabeth Merritt        1 AA-65
Butcher, James, 16 May 1740, Eliz'th Estwood           1 BA-323
Butcher, James, 15 May 1741, Elizabeth Eastwood        1 BA-317
Butcher, William, 29 June 1741, Sarah Randel           2 KE-242
Butlar, Benjamin, 1728, Catherine Evans                3 KE-245
Butlar, Solomon, 22 Aug. 1758, Cata Colles             2 SO-197
Butler, Amon, 12 May 1745, Elizabeth Hawkins           4 BA-72
Butler, Daniel, 23 Aug. 1747, Mary Whitaker            2 BA-241
    2 BA-194 gives date as 4 Oct. 1747.
Butler, James, 13 June 1706, Joyce Carroll             4 AA-372
Butler, John, 24 Jan. 1751, Ann Allen                  2 BA-203
Butler, John, 18 Feb. 1751, Mary Perryman              2 BA-203
Butler, Moses, 3 Dec. 1774, Eleanar Plummer            1 CR
Butler, Nathan, 7 Oct. 1754, Rachael Denbow            2 BA-211
Butler, Richard, 13 Oct. 1755, Rebeckah Fields         1 QA-60
Butler, Rupert, 3 July 1711, Ann Harris                2 PG-1
Butler, Samuel, 2 Aug. 1772, Alice Burgess, widow
    of Hugh Burgess                                    3 BA-170
Butlers, Thomas, 23 Jan. 1696, Mary Burthel            1 BA-178
Butlin, James, 10 Sept. 1772, Sarah Brock              2 BA-265
Butteram, Isaac, 26 Dec. 1743, Ann Lyal                1 BA-341
Butteram, John, 8 Sept. 1714, Jane Mayer               2 BA-6
Butterfield, John, son of Thomas, 9 April 1731, Mary
    Brown, dau. of James and Honour                    9 SF
Butterfield, John, son of John and Mary, 8 day, 4 mo.,
    1756, Hannah Johnson, dau. of James                9 SF
Butters, James, 27 May 1736, Mary Burk                 3 KE-247
Butters, Thomas, 23 Jan. 1696, Mary Burthel            1 BA-178
Butterworth, Isaac, 18 Dec. 1728, Jane Wheeler         1 BA-340
Buttler, Thomas, 2 May 1734, Sarah White               1 AA-117
Byer, John, 3 April 1743, Ann Arnold                   1 FR-10
Byfoot, Moses, 27 Aug. 1749, Sarah Tayman              2 BA-244
    2 BA-199 gives date as 5 Sept. 1749.
Byle, Michael, 20 Jan. 1771, Margaret Gohon            2 BA-261
Byrd, Jese, 3 Oct. 1771, Mary Ricords                  1 WI-109
Byrn, Arthur, 2 May 1757, Rachel Brockson              1 QA-62
Bywaters, Thomas, 2 June 1734, Eddy Wood               3 BA-152
Cable, Rob't, 3 Nov. 1746, Eliz. Bradfield             2 BA-195
Cade, Robert, 18 Jan. 1748/9 Sarah Nowlman             3 TA-71
Cadle, James, 26 Aug. 1726, Frances Ridgely            1 AA-103
Caffrey, Anthony, 26 Nov. 1735, Johannah Hearn         3 BA-154
Cage, William, 18 Dec. 1777, Mary Mayhew               3 PG-104
Cain, Hugh, 15 Aug. 1777, Ann Reynolds                 1 WA-530
Cain, James, 25 Dec. 1744, Eliz'th Doyle               2 BA-240
    2 BA-191 gives date as 30 Dec. 1741.
```

```
Cain, James, 15 April 1746, Ann Spicer                    1 BA-342
Cain, John, 11 Sept. 1757, Ann White                      2 BA-216
Cain, John, 4 June 1769, Cathern Gibson                   2 BA-258
Caine, George, 28 Oct. 1743, Elizabeth Barrott            2 TA-196
Calahan, Darby, 29 Jan. 1719/20, Mary Packett, widow      4 AA-411
Calgin, Edward, 22 Feb. 1746, Frances Wood                1 QA-53
Calhoon, James, 18 Nov. 1766, Ann Gist                    4 BA-73
Calinder, William, 29 Dec. 1726, Rebeckah Hutton          2 TA-114
Calk, James, 26 Jan. 1739/40, Judith Tibbles              3 TA-21
Calk, Laurence, 6 Oct. 1744, Mary Camper                  3 TA-50
Calk, Peter, 2 Dec. 1740, Eliza Porter                    3 TA-27
Calk, Peter, 2 May 1747, Anne Davis                       3 TA-64
Calk, Peter, 11 Feb. 1748/9, Marg't Dawson                3 TA-72
Callaway, John, Jr., 25 Dec. 1709, Mary Gould             1 WI-4
Callaway, Samuel, 12 April 1762, Mary Price               1 WI-75
Callender, William, 26 Jan. 1724/5, Mary Mitchel          2 PG-4
Callingswood, Danniel, 17 Sept. 1723, Ester Field         1 AA-97
Calloway, Antho:, 10 Sept. 1658, Martha Thomas            1 KE-129
Calloway, William, 1 Dec. 1734, Margret More (?)          1 WI-11
Callowaye, Peter, 26 March 1667, Elyzabeth Johnson        4 SO-666
Calver, William, 1 Aug. 1754, Sarah Ray                   2 FR-255
  His name might be Calvin.
Calvert, Alexander, 14 May 1744, Mary Whealer             2 SO-10
Calvert, Hon. Benedict, Collector of H. M. Customs
  for Patuxent District, 21 April 1748, Elizabeth
  Calvert, only surviving dau. of the late Hon.
  Charles Calvert, Gov. of this Province                  4 AA-450
Calvert, Hon. Charles, 21 Nov. 1722, Rebecca Gerrard,
  dau. of John Gerrard, late of P. G. Co., dec.,
  and his wife Eliza; the groom was Gov. of Md.          2 PG-2
Calvin, William, 25 May 1735, Eliza Newnam                1 QA-41
Calwill, Sam'l, 13 Nov. 1764, Ann Richardson              2 BA-227
Cambden, John, 8 Oct. 1724, Katherine Hall                2 PG-3
Cambden, Joseph; 1771, "by lic., Cal. Co.," Mary
  Scrivener                                               2 AA-410
Cambol, William, 15 July 1703, Sarah Harper               1 AA-255
Camden, John, 28 Dec. 1718, Ester Wood                    2 PG-2
Cameron, John, 12 Dec. 1716, Marget Macckelltons          2 BA-9
Cameron, John, 21 June 1720, Sarah Crofford               2 BA-17
Cameron, Jno., 8 Dec. 1761, Mary Brown                    2 BA-222
Cammall, John, 17 March 1769, Margret Meds (?)            2 BA-258
Cammel, John, 1 Jan. 1734, Ann Johnson                    1 BA-278
Cammell, John, 7 April 1751, Ann Stevens                  2 BA-203
Cammell, Leven Roberts, 3 Aug. 1751, Mary Mainer          2 BA-203
Camoran, Absolum, 30 Dec. 1764, Sarah Beamer              2 BA-227
Campbell, Duncan, 12 Jan. 1729, Ann Higgins               2 TA-121
Campbell, Enoch, 30 Dec. 1771, Eliz. Hall                 1 SM-136
Campbell, James, born 16 March 1748, son of John and
  Jane Campbell, in Smithsborough, Co. Monaghan,
  Ireland, 11 Jan. 1764, Sarah Rutter                     1 CE-318
Campbell, John, 1751, Anne Stevens                        2 BA-241
Campbell, Mosess, June 1751, Rebecca Hughson              2 BA-217
Campbell, William, 3 Aug. 1777, Rebecca Curlew            7 AA-1
Camper, John, 28 Jan. 1744/5, Sarah Cuming                3 TA-52
Camper, William, 11 June 1727, Elizabeth Carter           2 TA-115
Campison, Leonard, 26 Dec. 1677, Margaret Morgan          5 SO-397
Canaday, John, 31 May 1701, Elizabeth Douze               3 KE-251
Canaday, John, 17 Aug. 1727, Marget Sumers                2 TA-116
Canaday, Wm., 27 Jan. 1761, Mary Stewart                  2 BA-221
Cann, James, 4 Dec. 1736, Rebeckah Lamb                   2 KE-225
Cann, John, 2 Jan. 1740, Rac'ell Dormett                  3 CE-23
Cannaday, John, 2 Dec. 1729, Mary Arnald                  1 BA-259
Cannaday, Roger, 6 Nov. 1709, Jane Dane                   3 KE-253
Cannan, Roger, 18 Nov. 1736, Anne Gibson                  2 BA-84
Canneday, William, 26 April 1668, Anne Fissher            4 SO-708
```

Cannel, Jerome, 1 Jan. 1733, Elizabeth (?)          2 KE-224
Cannon, Clement, 14 Dec. 1777, Mary Murphey          9 BA &
                                                    10 BA-69
Cannon, Elijah, c.Aug. 1775, Nancy (?)              1 CR-6
Cannon, James, 24 Dec. 1724, Mary Boren             1 BA-257
Cannon, John, 18 Oct. 1743, Elizabeth Sailes        2 TA-196
Cannon, Nath'll, 10 Jan. 1742/3, Margaret Auld      3 TA-41
Cannon, Thomas, 14 May 1712, Betty Cox              8 SF-7
Cannon, Thomas, 11 Oct. 1743, Elizabeth Sail        3 TA-44
Cannon, William, 18 Feb. 1695, Mary Willing         1 BA-177
Cannon, William, 28 Dec. 1721, Frances Johnson      1 BA-260
Canon, Robert, 8 July 1725, Sophia Johnson          1 BA-258
Canter, Trueman, 24 Nov. 1774, Elizabeth Heccky     1 CH-199
Cantwell, Edward, 5 Dec. 1699, Joan Chattum         1 BA-189
Cantwell, Edward, 5 Jan. 1744, Blanch Jackson       1 BA-337
Cantwell, Edw'd, 11 June 1761, Mary Vincent         2 BA-222
Cantwell, John, 4 Feb. 1732, Mary Burchfield        1 BA-265
Cantwell, Nicholls, 23 May 1762, Elizabeth McKim    2 BA-368
Cantwell, Wm., 23 May 1768, Mary Baxton             2 BA-231
Cape, John, 8 April 1696, Ellinor (?)               2 TA-6
Capel, Robert, 11 Feb. 1737, Anna Cox               3 AA-108
Car, John, 17 Dec. 1724, Judith Fish                2 TA-111
Carback, John Martin, 14 July 1734, Frances Mahorn  3 BA-152
Carback, John Valentine, 19 Dec. 1736, Mary Harryman 3 BA-156
Carback, Valentine, 14 Sept. 1769, Rachael Colls    2 BA-259
Carbery, Thomas, 29 May 1772, Monica Reily          1 SM-136
Carboo, John, 27 Aug. 1755, Ann Philips             1 QA-60
Cardel, James, 17 Feb. 1760, Eliz. Greaves          2 BA-219
Carey, Edward, 10 Dec. 1680, Katherine Ferrill      5 SO-397
Carey, Edw'd, 15 Jan. 1722, Mary Alexander          2 TA-104
Carey, Henry, 1746, Eliza Waller                    2 BA-240
Carlile, Alexander, 6 Sept. 1720, Margrit Macloster 1 WI-5
Carmady, Daniel, 13 Feb. 1739, Mary Vinton          2 TA-168
Carmain, Josias, 6 Nov. 1715, Sarah Brown           2 TA-76
Carman, Hezekiah, 24 July 1763, Elinor Talbott      2 BA-225
Carman, John, 24 Jan. 1735, Rachel Burton           1 QA-41
Carman, John, 18 Aug. 1750, Sarah Baley             1 QA-57
Carman, Thos., 17 Jan. 1744, Catherin Collins       1 QA-50
Carman, William, Jr., April 1729, Margaret Kersy    1 QA-36
Carnan, Christopher, 13 June 1751, Eliza North      3 BA-165
Carnan, John, 7 Sept. 1727, Margaret Rumsey, widow
   of Charles Rumsey                                3 CE-16
Carnan, John, 17 Oct. 1742, Rachel Alman, dau. of
   Abraham                                          3 CE-24
Carnes, Thomas, 29 Dec. 1740, Marg'tt Noble         2 TA-170
Carney, Daniel, 1 Nov. 1777, Alice Lovelace         2 CH(1)
Carpenter, George, 14 July 1777, Catharine Maddox   3 SM-535
Carpenter, John, 27 Jan. 1734, Mary Matthews        3 BA-153
Carr, Aquila, 21 day, 2 mo., 1745, Susanna Parrish  4 SF
Carr, Benjamin, Feb. 1773, Margaret Smith           2 AA-411
Carr, Benjamin, 22 Jan. 1775, Ruth Sheckels         2 AA-412
Carr, David, (May?) 1769, Mary Steel                2 BA-258
Carr, George, 20 Jan. 1715, Julian Harrison         2 TA-77
Carr, Hugh, 12 May 1767, Eleanor Weer               5 BA-3
Carr, James, 7 June 1747, Mary Ann Stone            1 QA-53
Carr, John, 9 March 1744/5, Mary McLachlan          4 AA-447
Carr, John, 12 Jan. 1776, Araminta Carr             1 CE-298
Carr, Richard, 1771, Sarah McSeney                  2 AA-410
Carr, Thomas, son of Walter and Lartha, 22 day, 9 mo.,
   1705, Elizabeth Price, dau. of Mordecai and Mary 6 SF-34
Carr, Thomas, 22 Dec. 1736, Elizabeth Thackrell     4 AA-438
Carravan, Richard, 1 Jan. 1723, Eliza Williams      2 TA-106
Carrman, Thomas, 9 May 1706, Frances Bright         1 AA-72
Carrol, Peter, 7 Oct. 1770, Martha Clarke           2 BA-261
Carroll, Daniel, 8 Nov. 1733, Elisabeth Purdy       1 AA-116

Carroll, Dominick, 3 Dec. 1725, Mary Frisby, widow
    of William Frisby                                     3 CE-17
Carroll, Ignatius, 5 Aug. 1771, Winifred Contsidur       1 SM-136
Carroll, James, 12 Jan. 1707, Margrett Miller            3 KE-252
Carroll, James, 24 Nov. 1736, Ann Bond                   2 BA-153
Carroll, John, 7 Feb. 1748, Mary Weathersby              1 QA-55
Carroll, Jno., 24 Dec. 1760, Cas. Welch                  2 BA-221
Carroll, Peter, 4 May 1710, Mary Renshaw                 1 BA-209
Carroll, Peter, 8 June 1739, Anne Hitchcock              2 BA-110
Carroll, Peter, 2 Oct. 1766, Eliz. Kitely               2 BA-229
Carroll, Peter, 7 Oct. 1770, Martha Clarke               2 BA-261
Carroll, Thomas, Jr., 19 Oct. 1686, Rebecca Walton       5 SO-397
Carrothus, Geo., 18 Feb. 1768, Jane Mitch'l              2 BA-231
Carsey, Edward, 23 Nov. 1738, Hanah Walker               2 TA-165
Carsey, Samuel, 25 Jan. (?), Mary Cottingham             2 SO-10
Carsey, William, 29 Sept. 1741, Elizabeth Marthews       2 SO-10
Carslake, John, 1 Dec. 1740, Sarah Kinnamont             3 TA-26
Carslake, John, 25 Nov. 1746, Henrietta Trippe           3 TA-62
Carslake, Thomas, 3 Feb. 1743/4, Eliza Grayson           3 TA-47
Carsley, Robert, 21 Dec. 1743, Mary Killam               2 SO-14
Carsly, Peter, 30 June 1772, Cateron Collings            2 SO-203
Cart, Lorny (?), 9 Dec. 1776, (?) Clapper                3 BA-669
Cartee, Brian, 2 Jan. 1750,Frances Leshordie             2 BA-202
Cartee, Darby, 14 Nov. 1756, Susannah Woolling           2 BA-214
Carter, Aaron, 30 Dec. 1751, Mary Waller                 1 WI-60
Carter, Benjamin, 9 Oct. 1777, Catharine Sturgen         1 HA-196
Carter, Benn, 16 May 1770, Martha Garison                2 BA-260
Carter, Daniel, 17 June 1719, Ruth Warfield, widow       4 AA-408
Carter, Daniel, 21 July 1734, Catherine Chandler         6 AA-201
Carter, Edward, 17 Nov. 1709, Issabella Hamilton         2 TA-63
Carter, Francis, 26 Jan. 1773, Ruth Bassett              3 AA-113
Carter, George, 14 Aug. 1677, Mary Nicholson             9 SO-402
    5 SO-397 gives date as 4 Sept. 1677.
Carter, Jeremiah, son of Ninevah, 12 day, 10 mo.,
    1757, Rachel Brown, dau. of Thomas and Elinor        9 SF
Carter, John, 9 Aug. 1710, Mary Lisbey                   1 AA-77
Carter, Robert, 8 Aug. 1745, Mary Welch                  2 BA-193
Carter, Samuel, son of John and Hannah, 1 day, 12
    mo., 1773, Sarah Sidwell, dau. of Henry and Helen    9 SF
Carter, Sparrow, 18 May 1716, Eliz. Saunders             1 AA-79
Carter, William, 19 May 1727, Elizabeth Tilden           3 KE-255
Carter, William, 18 Sept. 1735, Ann Haile                3 BA-154
Carter, William, 24 June 1759, Mary Day                  2 BA-218
Cartwright, Abram, 8 Nov. 17-?, Mary Ayres               3 KE-260
Cartwright, Jesse, 13 Dec. 1753, Margaret Amery          1 CH-188
Carty, Arthur, 4 Dec. 1770, Mary Murphey                 2 BA-261
Carvill, Alexander, 1 March 1714, Mary Haley             1 AA-79
Carvill, John, 25 Nov. 1732, Jane Harris                 3 KE-257
Cary, Christopher, 14 Jan. 1719/20, Mary Slade           2 AA-362
Cary, James, 12 Jan. 1776, Mary Stevenson                3 BA-670
Cary, Jno., 30 Dec. 1705, Eliz. Haly                     4 AA-372
Cary, Robert, 10 April 1710, Elisabeth Ingrum            1 AA-77
Case, John, 3 April 1711, Grace Young                    1 AA-78
Casley, John, 3 May 1712, Elizabeth Heborn               2 KE-183
Cassey, James, 17 Aug. 1758, Mary Brading                1 QA-64
Casson, Henry, 18 Oct. 1739, Esther Baynard              3 TA-18
Casson, John, 10 Feb. 1766, Sarah Green                  2 CR-270
Cater, John, 7 Feb. 1724, Anne Sporgen                   4 AA-425
Catlin, Fenton, 21 Aug. 1760, Catheron Dreaden           2 SO-115
Catlin, Robert, 9 Jan. 1676/7, Elizabeth Curtis          9 SO-402
    5 SO-397 gives date as 15 Feb. 1676.
Catlin, Thomas, 13 May 1731, Rebecca Wilson              3 KE-257
Catrick, Robert, 1 Jan. 1696, Mary Mose                  1 AA-36
Catrop, Stephen, 16 July 1746, Sarah Dudley              3 TA-59
Catrope, William, 28 Feb. 1738, Marg't Baker             2 TA-166

```
Cattenhead, John, Sept. 1744, Rachel Benit              1 QA-49
Cattenhead, John, 14 April 1752, Sarah Mansell          1 QA-58
Catton, William, 6 June 1717, Mary Strahan, alias
   Storton; both parties were of Westminster Parish.    4 AA-401
Caulk, Jacob, 7 Feb. 1713, Sarah Joce                   3 KE-254
Cavender, Charles, 19 July 1741, Sarah Scotton          1 QA-47
Cavindire, Patrick, 5 Jan. 1769, Mary Potee             2 BA-257
Cavy, Robert, 10 April 1710, Elizabeth Ingrum           1 AA-259
Cawthrey, John, 27 Aug. 1731, Isabel Allen              1 BA-252
Cazier, Richard, 15 April 1760, Susannah Kirkpatrick    1 CE-299
Cecill, John, 1718, Elizabeth Sallars                   2 PG-2
Cederson, Jack, 24 Nov. 1726, Mary Bush                 2 TA-114
Cendington, Roger, 24 Nov. 1718, Dinah Simons           2 AA-360
Ceney, William, 15 Jan. 1727/8, Elizabeth Johnson       2 TA-117
Chaffinch, John, 10 Oct. 1719, Dorcas Hall, widow       4 AA-410
Chain, John, 31 July 1777, Ann Tucker                   7 AA-1
Chaires, Benjamin, 1 Dec. 1730, Mary Salisbury          1 QA-37
Chairs, Benj., 24 Oct. 1752, Mary Wright Goodwin        1 QA-59
Chairs, Charles, 20 Feb. 1759, Ann Thomas               1 QA-64
Chairs, James, 24 April 1757, Esther Roe                1 QA-62
Chairs, Joseph, 27 July 1755, Catherine Godwin          1 QA-59
Chairs, Nathaniel, 8 Aug. 1759, Sarah Thomas            1 QA-65
Chalke, George, 9 April 1771, Eliz. Hughs               2 BA-262
Chalmer, Alixander, 4 Dec. 1739, Margaret Roberson      1 QA-45
Chalson, Da'd, 14 Feb. 1765, Mary York                  2 BA-227
Chamberlain, John, 31 Oct. 1737, Margaret Gittings      2 BA-120
Chamberlaine, Samuel, 24 Oct. 1771, Eliz. Pak't         2 BA-263
Chamberlaine, Thomas, 9 Dec. 1764, Eliz. Welkinson      2 BA-227
Chamberlin, John, 6 Feb. 1713, Jane Ashford             3 CE-5
Chambers, James, 6 July 1735, Ann Dean                  2 TA-159
Chambers, John, 28 Dec. 1729, Rebecca Dobson            2 TA-121
Chambers, Richard, 14 March 1675/6, Mary Ivery          9 SO-401
Chambers, Samuell, 23 July 1700, Mrs. Anne Gassaway,
   widow of Capt. Nicholas Gassaway                     1 AA-56
                                                        & 245

Chambers, Samuel, 10 Feb. 1736/6, Sophia Steward        1 AA-120
Chambers, Thomas, 28 June 1739, Mary Joyce              2 TA-167
Chambers, Thomas, 1748, Mary Cox                        2 BA-243
Chambers, Thomas, 6 Aug. 1748, Mary Fox                 2 BA-197
Chambers, Wm., 11 Feb. 1768, Mary Jewel                 2 BA-231
Chambly, John, 1 Oct. 1708, Margery Cheek; banns
   were published on this date                          1 BA-207
Chamier, Daniel, 25 Feb. 1768, Achsah Carnan            5 BA-3
Chamnis, Anthony, 24 Nov. 1735, Sarah Coale             3 BA-154
Chance, Bachelor, 25 Sept. 1755, Elizabeth Boggs        1 QA-60
Chance, Bartholomew, 7 July 1743, Deborah Oldfield      2 TA-196
Chance, Elijah, 8 Feb. 1739, Rebecca Atwell             3 TA-21
Chance, Jeremiah, 25 Nov. 1752, Wealthy Ann Milldews    2 BA-168
Chance, Rich'd, 10 June 1704, Ellen Pierceson           2 TA-40
Chancellour, John, 24 Oct. 1676, Abigail Harringdon     9 SO-402
Chancy, George, 22 June 1706, Mrs. Sarah Smith          1 BA-201
Chandlee, Benjamin, son of William, of Kilmore, Co.
   Kildare, Ireland, 25 day, 3 mo., 1710, Sarah Cotty   9 SF
Chandlee, Benjamin, Jr., son of Benjamin and Sarah,
   24 day, 1 mo., 1749/50, Mary Follwell, dau. of
   Edward                                               9 SF
Chandlee, William, son of Benjamin and Sarah, 10
   Nov. 1748, Mary Elgar, dau. of Joseph and Mary       9 SF
Chandler, Robert, 5 May 1713, Elizabeth Bryon           4 AA-380
Chandler, Will'm, 8 Feb. 1713, Ann Laswell              4 AA-392
Chaney, George, 28 Nov. 1734, Susannah Ogg              1 BA-276
Channell, Henery, 2 Feb. 1706, Margrett Ryley           3 KE-252
Chaplain, Francis, 18 Dec. 1742, Mary Webb              2 TA-173
Chaplain, John, 19 Sept. 1758, Rebecah Chaney           2 PG-7
Chaplin, Francis, 14 Dec. 1742, Mary Webb               3 TA-41
```

Chaplin, James, 20 Feb. 1704, Elizabeth (?)                    2 TA-44
Chapline, Joseph, 22 Oct. 1741, Ruhamah Williams, dau.
  of Rev. William Williams                                     1 FR-10
Chapman, Isaac, 27 Oct. 1734, Mary Fitchpatrick               3 BA-152
Chapman, James, 29 Nov. 1723, Mary Miles                      2 PG-3
Chapman, John, 18 June 1733, Sarah Durity                     3 KE-258
Chapman, John, 17 July 1746, Mary Hall                        3 BA-159
Chapman, Robert, 30 June 1736, Elizabeth Tayler              3 BA-155
Chapman, Thomas, 27 Dec. 1733, Ann Sheepard                   3 AA-104
                                                               & 107
Chapman, Thomas, 6 Oct. 1750, Hannah Large                   3 AA-110
Chapman, William, 21 Jan. 1719, Rebecca Chambers             1 AA-297
Charles, Elijah, 7 June 1775, Hebe Moore                     1 CR
Charles, Isaac, 21 day, 9 mo., 1766, Nancy Payne             2 SF-288
Charles, Solomon, 25 day, 3 mo., 1773, Sarah Addams          2 SF-288
Charles, William, 13 day, 5 mo., 1770, Leah Bartlett         2 SF-288
Charleson, Charles, 14 Nov. 1689, Dorothy Musgrove,
  widow                                                       3 CH
Charlton, Arthur, 14 July 1742, Elenor Harrison              1 FR-10
Charlton, Thomas, 13 Feb. 1715/6, Mary Fowler                4 AA-397
Charnock, Anthony, 14 May 1717, Hannah Hollingsworth         4 AA-400
Chase, Rev. Thomas, 19 July 1763, Ann Birch, eld. dau.
  of Thomas Birch, chirurgeon and man midwife in the
  town of Warwick in the county of Warwick, England          3 BA-167
Chase, Walter, 26 June 1766, Lucy Barber                     3 AA-113
Cheeck, Richard, 22 April 1710, Lydia Harpper                2 KE-196
Cheesclett, John, c.Oct. 1775, Eliza Hill                    1 CR-6
Cheesman, John, 25 June 1733, Mary Thorn                     1 QA-40
Cheesman, Samuell, 12 Jan. 1725/6, Anne Buckingham           2 TA-112
Cheevers, John, c.Oct. 1775, Sarah Chalaghene                1 CR-6
Cheiney, Charles, 2 Nov. 1777, Lucretia Gardiner             8 AA-13
Cheney, Andrew Francis, chirurgeon, son of James
  Cheney of Mount Cheney, Co. Cork, Ireland, 15
  July 1755, Mary Day Scott, dau. of Day Scott               1 WI-42
  3 SO-4 records the same marriage.
Cheney, Benjamin, 23 June 1719, Ruth Cheney                  1 AA-294
Cheney, Charles, 15 July 1701, Anne Pattison                 1 AA-57
                                                               & 247
Cheney, Charles, 13 April 1721, Mary Powell                  1 AA-303
Cheney, Charles, 12 Nov. 1723, Elisabeth Green               1 AA-97
                                                               & 324
Cheney, Greenbury, 16 Nov. 1725, Elizabeth Cheney            1 AA-101
Cheney, Isaiah, 27 May 1764, Rachel Phelps                   9 AA-248
Cheney, Jesse, 29 Nov. 1764, Ann Burgey                      9 AA-248
Cheney, John, 3 Jan. 1705, Mary Beadle                       1 AA-72
Cheney, John, 22 Sept. 1709, Elizabeth Tilly                 1 AA-257
  1 AA-77 gives her name as Tylley.
Cheney, John, 24 July 1718, Anne Burgess                     1 AA-284
Cheney, Lewis, 16 Feb. 1745, Mary Donaldson                  1 AA-125
Cheney, Richard, 11 Dec. 1707, Rachell Nicholson             1 AA-76
Cheney, Rich'd, 11 Sept. 1722, Mary Penn                     1 AA-92
                                                               & 314
Cheney, Thomas, 19 Aug. 1697, Sary Westall                   1 AA-37
Cheney, Thomas, 7 June 1716, Susanah Hoper                   1 AA-79
  1 AA-273 gives her name as Hopper.
Chenneworth, John, 26 Nov. 1730/1, Mary Smith                2 BA-40
Chenowith, Thomas, 14 Sept. 1766, Rachel Moore               2 BA-229
Chenowith, Thomas, 10 Aug. 1777, Anne Carroll               10 BA-77
Cherry, Oliver, 5 July 1718, Rebekah Holland                 4 AA-405
Cheshere, John, 18 July 1706, Hannah Gott                    2 AA-330
Chesley, Charles, 17 May 1752, Rebecca Vanderford            1 QA-58
Chester, Samuel, 18 Nov. 1776, Mary Coursy                   3 BA-669
Cheston, Daniel, 3 May 1742, Frances Augustina Steven-
  son                                                         4 AA-444
Cheston, James, 31 Aug. 1775, Ann Galloway                   2 AA-412

```
Chettle, Mahalaleel, 20 Aug. 1734, Ann Robertson        1 AA-118
Chew, Benjamin, 8 day, 10 mo., 1692, Elizabeth Benson,
  dau.-in-law of Richard Harrison                       6 SF-37
Chew, Benjamin, son of Benjamin, 1 May 1750, Cassandra
  Johns, dau. of Richard and Ann                        9 SF
Chew, John, 5 Jan. 1775, Elizabeth Gott                 2 AA-412
Chew, Joseph, 23 Jan. 1710, Mary Ford                   2 AA-342
Chew, Nathaniel, 12 Dec. 1775, Elizabeth Norris         2 AA-412
Chew, Samuel, son of Benjamin and Elizabeth, 7 day,
  8 mo., 1715, Mary Galloway, dau. of Sam'l and
  Ann                                                   6 SF-57
Chew, Samuel Lloyd, 28 June 1777, Dorothy Harrison      7 AA-1
  8 AA-13 gives date as 1 July 1777; see also
  2 AA-414.
Chew, William, son of Samuel and Anne,20 day, 10 mo.,
  1690, Sydney Wynn, dau. of Thomas and Martha Wynn
  of Pa.                                                6 SF
Chickly, James, 29 Jan. (?), Sary Cheney                1 AA-33
Chiffen, William, 21 May 1719, Rachel Mariarte          1 AA-292
Chilcoat, Humphrey, 3 March 1772, Sarah Ensor           2 BA-264
Chilcoate, John, 24 Dec. 1771, Providence Ensor         2 BA-263
Chilcott, James, 1698, Mary Tindale                     2 AA-295
Child, John, 1 Dec. 1730, Elizabeth Du Moulin           2 PG-5
Child, Samuel, 1770, Sarah Child                        2 AA-409
Childs, Benjamin, 26 Dec. 1733, Martty Bellows          3 CE-18
Childs, George, Nov. 1736, Martha Smithson              2 BA-138
Childs, Henry, 14 July 1732, Hannah Clark               3 CE-16
Childs, Henry, 1770, Sarah Scrivener                    2 AA-410
Childs, John, 4 Dec. 1743, Elizab. Meads                2 BA-239
  Banns were pub. three times: 2 BA-134.
Childs, John, 1752, Mary Groves                         2 BA-241
Childs, John, 22 July 1752, Sarah Groves                2 BA-205
Childs, Nathaniel, 25 Oct. 1704, Elinor Sturton         3 KE-252
Childs, Nathaniel, 23 Aug. 1737, Mary Hungard           3 CE-21
Childs, William, 9 Feb. 1715/6, Mary Cook               4 AA-397
Chillahon, Timothy, 7 June 1730, Mary Hungerford        1 AA-110
Chilton, Cuthbert, 29 July 1703, Mary Baker             1 CA-111
Chilton, Mathew, Jr., 9 May 1751, Rebecca Bull          2 CR-269
Chilton, William, 14 Sept. 1774, Rebecca Talbot         1 CR
Ching, John, 8 Jan. 1700, Ann Skidmore                  3 AA-96
Ching, John, 9 July 1738, Mary Farr                     1 CH-181
Chinworth, John, 16 Dec. 1736, Jane Wood                3 BA-156
Chinwoth, Thos., 14 Sept. 1766, Rach'l Moore            2 BA-229
Chipley, Joshua, May 1777, Mary Hunter                  1 CR-10
Chisholm, Archibald, 22 Sept. 1777, Elizabeth Waters    7 AA-2
  8 AA-13 gives date as 23 Sept. 1777.
Chissam, John, 31 Aug. 1678, Abigaile Bell              5 SO-397
Chittim, George, 22 Nov. 1705, Sarah Mallbey            2 AA-328
Choate, Edward, 22 May 1735, Ellinor Savage             3 BA-153
Chocke, John, 14 Oct. 1703, Margaret Tudor              2 AA-322
Chplin (sic), James, 5 June 1728, Elizabeth Martin      2 TA-118
Christ, Michael, 29 Dec. 1763, Elizab. Storm            4 FR-1117
Christian, Christian, 16 April 1707, Margrett Wissells  3 KE-252
Christian, James, 2 Feb. 1726, Margarett Symmons        1 AA-104
Christian, John, 12 Sept. 1745, Margret Hammelton       2 BA-193
Christie, Charles, 21 July 1754, Cordelia Stokes        2 BA-210
  1 BA-351 gives date as 22 July 1754.
Christmas, Charles, 9 Feb. 1742, Barbary Welsh          1 PG-290
Christopher, John, 26 Feb. 1759, Sarah Stanford         1 WI-46
Christopher, Jno., 31 Jan. 1764, Susan Saddon           2 BA-226
Chunn, John Thomas, 13 Oct. 1757, Martha Turner         1 CH-194
Chunn, Lancelot, 4 May 1753, Judith Cartwright          1 CH-185
Chunn, Samuel, 20 Jan. 1731, Susanna Love               1 CH-181
Chunn, Zachariah, 23 Dec. 1762, Charity Courts          1 CH-193
Chunn, Zachariah, 30 May 1764, Deborah Turner           1 CH-193
  1 CH-196 gives date as 31 May 1764.
```

| | |
|---|---|
| Church, John, 5 July 1734, Anis Austin | 4 AA-436 |
| Church, Thomas, 6 Dec. 1777, Eliza Bryan | 3 PG-106 |
| Churchman, George, son of John and Margaret, 28 May 1752, Hannah James, dau. of Mordecai and Gaynor | 9 SF |
| Churchman, John, of Saffron Waldo, Essex, Eng., 1696, Hannah Cerie, dau. of Thomas Cerie, late of Oxfordshire | 9 SF |
| Churchman, John, son of John and Hannah, 27 Jan. 1729/30, Margaret Brown, dau. of William and Esther | 9 SF |
| Churchman, Thomas, son of John and Hannah, 5 June 1745, Rachel Piggott, widow of John Piggott and dau. of Henry and Hannah Reynolds | 9 SF |
| Churchman, Thomas, son of John and Hannah, 18 Oct. 1770, Katherine Jones, dau. of John and Mary | 9 SF |
| Churchman, William, son of John and Hannah, 8 Dec. 1743, Abigail Brown, dau. of Daniel and Elizabeth | 9 SF |
| Clagitt, Thomas, son of John and Sarah of Fred. Co., 11 Oct. 1768, Mary Meek Magruder, dau. of Enoch and Meek | 1 PG-374 |
| Claney, Timothy, 19 Aug. 1725, Anne Stafford | 2 TA-112 |
| Clapham, John, 21 Dec. 1757, Rebecca Green, dau. of Jonas | 4 AA-456 |
| Clark, Aq'a, 8 April 1760, Mary Bull | 2 BA-219 |
| Clark, Benjamin, 1729, Jane Gray | 3 KE-256 |
| Clark, Caleb, 5 April 1721, Rebeckah Webb, widow | 8 SF-32 |
| Clark, Cuthbert, 19 June 1774, Mary Ann Brown | 1 SM-136 |
| Clark, Da'd, 23 Nov. 1767, Salley Lewes | 2 BA-231 |
| Clark, Edward, 28 Aug. 1750, Joanna Allcock | 8 SF-94 |
| Clark, Francis, 10 April 1775, Eleanor Hase | 3 BA-171 |
| Clark, George, 2 May 1711, Margaret Screech | 2 TA-69 |
| Clark, Henry, 21 April 1708, Sarah Parratt | 8 SF-438 |
| Clark, Henry, 21 Dec. 1732, Eliza Winters | 1 AA-115 |
| Clark, Henry, 12 April 1738, Rebecca Hutchings | 2 TA-164 |
| Clark, Henry, 5 Nov. 1746, Rebecca Cox | 8 SF-88 |
| Clark, Henry, 1 Jan. 1754, Jane Atkinson | 8 SF-98 |
| Clark, Henry, 20 Dec. 1777, Easter Beckett | 3 PG-106 |
| Clark, Hezekiah, 21 April 1719, Elizabeth Burton | 1 AA-292 |
| Clark, Isaac, 1 May 1738, Margaret Gordon | 3 AA-109 |
| Clark, James, 26 Nov. 1744, Eliz'h Buly | 1 QA-50 |
| Clark, James, 22 June 1755, Annah Mariah Passine | 2 BA-212 |
| Clark, James, (no date given), Rachel Rock | 6 BA(1) |
| Request to publish banns made. | |
| Clark, John, 24 Nov. 1704, Martha Shepard | 2 TA-42 |
| Clark, John, 2 Dec. 1708, Alce Withers | 1 AA-76 |
| Clark, John, 16 Oct. 1714, Elizabeth Draper | 1 BA-217 |
| 1 BA-213 gives date as 1713. | |
| Clark, John, 21 Oct. 1724, Rebeccah Henrix | 2 TA-110 |
| Clark, John, 6 Aug. 1737, Marg't Bevens | 2 TA-163 |
| Clark, John, 1 Feb. 1749, Mary Stuard | 3 AA-110 |
| Clark, Jno., 26 Aug. 1764, Eliz. Grates | 2 BA-226 |
| Clark, John, 4 April 1769, Sophia Lester | 1 BA-386 |
| Clark, Jos., 6 Nov. 1777, Bell Ferguson | 8 AA-13 |
| Clark, Joshua, 27 July 1730, Eliz'th Bandy | 2 TA-149 |
| Clark, Joshua, 16 Sept. 1772, Mary Bowles | 1 SM-136 |
| Clark, Richard, 11 Aug. 1713, Ruth Selman | 1 AA-268 |
| Clark, Robert, 18 Feb. 1718, Sillinah Smith | 1 BA-274 |
| Clark, Robert, 5 Dec. 1729, Elizabeth Smithson | 1 BA-272 |
| Clark, Rob't, 15 Nov. 1759, Kezia Barton | 2 BA-219 |
| Clark, Stepto, 8 Feb. 1736, Elizabeth Anderson | 3 BA-156 |
| Clark, Thom's, 4 Jan. 1727, Amy Rivers | 4 AA-429 |
| Clark, Thos., 14 Sept. 1734, Mary Madera | 1 AA-118 |
| Clark, Thomas, 18 Feb. 1748, Ann Culy | 3 AA-110 |
| Clark, Thos., 21 Nov. 1749, Cathrine Britain | 2 BA-199 |
| Clark, William, 24 April 1728, Susannah Dodson | 2 TA-118 |
| Clark, Wm., 19 Nov. 1731, Mary Atwell | 2 AA-367 |

```
Clark, William, 3 Nov. 1748, Mary Hollingsworth        1 QA-48
Clark, William, Jr., 18 May 1749, Martha Primrose      1 QA-55
Clark, William, 7 Dec. 1749, Tamer Low                 2 BA-199
Clark, William, 19 Sept. 1752, Alice Hollinsworth      1 QA-59
Clarke, James, 1753, Margaret Plant                    2 BA-242
Clarke, James, 28 May 1769, Rachael Rock               2 BA-258
Clarke, Joseph, 3 Nov. 1772, Bell Ferguson             7 AA-2
Clarke, Neal, 17 Oct. 1699, Jane Jones                 1 AA-49
Clarke, Robert, Dec. 1770, Eliz. Rigdon                2 BA-201
Clarke, William, 19 Nov. 1731, Mary Atwell             2 AA-367
Clarkson, Henry, 11 Feb. 1772, Darias Dyson            1 CH-198
Clarkson, William, 22 Nov. 1713, Elizabeth Hagian      1 PG-262
Clausy, John, 29 Dec. 1736, Mary Sing                  3 BA-156
Clayland, Lambert, 29 Dec. 1736, Eliz. Kirby           2 TA-158
Clayland, Moses, 16 June 1743, Rebecca Kirby           2 TA-198
Clayland, Will'm, 24 Aug. 1774, Sarah Vanderford       1 CR
Claymore, Francis, c.9 Aug. 1775, Nancy Clift          1 CR-6
Clayton, David, 8 June 1717, Elizabeth Selby           4 AA-400
Clayton, Edward, 26 April 1752, Hannah Chetham         1 QA-58
Clayton, Henry, 7 Nov. 1748, Mary Powell               1 QA-55
Clayton, Solomon, 27 Nov. 1729, Mary Chaires           1 QA-37
Cleark, Henry, 5 Dec. 1706, Katherine Brion            1 AA-73
Cleaver, Walter, 26 Dec. 1731, Sarah Vain              2 TA-151
Clebedints, Mich'l, 27 March 1765, Cath. Rozomister    2 BA-224
Cleggett, Nicho's, 11 Feb. 1768, Reb'a Young           2 BA-231
Cleland, Harris, 25 April 1739, Eliza Elbert           3 TA-16
Clements, Andrew, 20 Nov. 1718, Kathrin Jefferson      3 CE-11
Clements, Lambert, 24 July 1715, Sarah Dawson          2 TA-76
Clements, Mich'll, 1 Nov. 1713, Elizabeth Jonson       3 CE-5
Clemons, Calib, 9 Feb. 1752, Rebeccah Emory            1 QA-58
Clerk, John, 1732, Elizabeth (?)                       1 CE-332
Clerk, Thomas, 1749, Kathrine Breton                   2 BA-244
Cleynard, Emanuel, 2 March 1756, Sarah Thrift          2 BA-213
Cliff, Samuel, 24 Nov. 1715, Catherine Hues            2 TA-76
Clifft, Henry, 27 Nov. 1734, Eliza Dudley              2 TA-156
Clift, John, 28 Aug. 1701, Elizabeth (?)               2 TA-20
Clift, Joseph, 12 Jan. 1740, Mary Noble                2 TA-171
Clift, Matthew, 6 Feb. 1732, Mary Hilliard             1 AA-115
Climer, Charles, 1 Jan. 1709, Johannah Neal            2 TA-65
Climer, William, 20 Nov. 1722, Sarah Hayles            1 AA-94
Clinton, William, 14 Sept. 1774, Rebecca Talbot        1 CR-6
Cloather, Lewis, 4 Sept. 1765, Elizabeth Willson       9 SF
Cloather, Lewis, 13 day, 11 mo., 1768, Eleanor Coles
  Brown, widow of Thomas Brown                         9 SF
Cloather, Robert, 12 day, 1 mo., 1758, Rebeckah
  Simmons                                              1 SF-95
Close, Thos., 25 Dec. 1737, Hanna Clark                1 QA-43
Clother (?), Robert, 12 April 1732, Elizabeth Hamer    1 SF-63
Clough, James, 22 May 1739, Marey Burns                1 QA-45
Clove, John, 15 July 1714, Hannah Blackleah            3 KE-254
Cluff, Johnathan, 18 March 1765, Bettey Givens         2 SO-119
Cluff, Michael, 14 Aug. 1755, Sarah Killam             2 BA-15
Clumps, Thomas, 13 Jan. 1701, Mary Dollin              3 AA-96
Clutterbuck, Joseph, 7 June 1736, Mary Walker          3 BA-155
Coale, George, 26 Oct. 1735, Elizabeth Baker           3 BA-153
Coale, George, 20 Feb. 1736, Ann Jones                 3 BA-156
Coale, Philip, 6 day, 2 mo., 1697, Cassandra Skipwith  6 SF-24
Coale, Richard, 15 May 1735, Subbiner Haile            3 BA-153
Coale, Samuel, son of Skipwith and Margaret, 17 day,
  10 mo., 1776, Lydia Pusey, dau. of Joshua and Mary
  of Chester Co., Pa.                                  7 SF-36
Coale, Skipwith, son of Skipwith, 25 day, 9 mo., 1759,
  Sarah Hopkins, dau. of Joseph and Ann                9 SF
Coale, Thomas, 3 Dec. 1730, Mary Richardson, dau. of
  Joseph                                               6 SF
```

```
Coale, William, 19 Aug. 1735, Sarah Giles            9 SF
Coale, William, son of Thos., 5 Dec. 1752, Anne
  Stringer, dau. of Dr. Samuel Stringer             6 AA-218
Coale, William, 30 day, 12 mo., 1756, Sarah Robertson  6 SF-127
Coale, William, son of Skipwith, 7 day, 4 mo., 1761,
  Sarah Webster, dau. of Isaac                      7 SF-4
Coale, William, son of Skipwith, 18 day, 5 mo., 1769,
  Elizabeth Rigbie, dau. of James                   7 SF-16
Coate, John, 14 April 1707, Mary Daveridge          3 KE-252
Coats, Benj'n, 13 Oct. 1763, Mary Bellance          2 BA-225
Cobb, James, 30 Oct. 1709, Rebecca Emson            1 BA-208
Cobb, James, 21 Jan. 1734, Ruth Elledge             3 BA-153
Cobb, James, 18 March 1741, Mary Poge               1 BA-326
Coblenz, Peter, 6 May 1759, Susanna Keller          4 FR-1104
Cochran, Patrick, 8 Aug. 177, Mary Bland            7 AA-1
Cock, Israel, 24 Oct. 1721, Mary Robinson           2 TA-96
Cock, William, 18 June 1752, Susanhah Harriott      2 BA-205
Cockayne, Samuel, 6 June 1738, Sarah Sales          2 TA-165
Cockayne, Thomas, 5 day, 7 mo., 1764, Sarah Kemp    8 SF-117
Cockee, William, 29 Sept. 1668, Francis Vincent     4 SO-729
Cockey, Edward, of St. Marg't's, Westminster, 1 Aug.
  1717, Rhoda Harris of Kent Island, widow          4 AA-402
Cockey, Edward, 19 June 1753, Eleanor Pindell       4 BA-71
Cockey, Thomas, 15 May 1753, Prudence Gill          4 BA-71
Cockham, Carter, 7 Sept. 1774, Rebecca Clough       1 CR
Cockin, John, 22 May 1722, Alice Wells              2 BA-19
Cocklin, Sam'l, 6 Jan. 1740/1, Eliz'h Wyatt         1 QA-46
Cockran, Thomas, 31 Jan. 1735, Mary Barnett         3 BA-154
Cockrell, John, 4 March 1728, Mary Newman           3 CE-12
Cockrell, John, 1 June 1732, Tabitha Severson       3 CE-14
Cockrill, William, 29 June 1758, Mary Foreman       1 QA-63
Cocks, Jacob, 22 Feb. 1757, Mary Roberts            1 QA-62
Cocks, Jno., 23 April 1740, Mary Jemison            2 KE-233
Codd, Saint Leager, 18 Oct. 1700, Mary Francis      3 KE-251
Coe, Job, 2 March 1741/2, Sarah Norris              2 KE-245
Coghlan, Dennis, 18 July 1777, Rebecca Smith        3 PG-107
Cohee, John, 18 Nov. 1777, Celia Clark              1 CR-10
Cohee, Nicholas, 11 Dec. 1701, Sarah (?)            2 TA-22
Cohoon, Henry, 7 Oct. 1745, Rachel Matthews         2 SO-118
Cohhon, John, 15 Jan. 1749, Leah Mathas             2 SO-11
Cohhon, Samuel, 25 Oct. 1748, Margrett Adams        2 SO-12
Colbourne, Francis, 9 May 1708, Deborah Beamish     1 AA-76
Colbreath, William, 19 Oct. 1758, Eliza Smith       1 QA-64
Colbron, Joseph, 21 Dec. 1710, Mary Stone           2 PG-1
Cole, Cha.: 7 Feb. 1748, Ruth Samson                2 BA-198
Cole, Daniel, 24 April 1743, Mary Mansfield         2 KE-252
Cole, George, 2 March 1732, Martha Litten           1 BA-261
Cole, James, 19 July 1748, Jane Poloke              1 BA-360
Cole, James, 28 Nov. 1777, Ann Wilkins              7 AA-2
Cole, John, 17 Dec. 1728, Margaret Wright           3 CE-16
Cole, John, 25 Dec. 1730, Mary Charfinch            3 BA-150
Cole, John, 20 July 1738, Anne Starkey              1 QA-44
Cole, Matthew, 12 Nov. 1738, Mary Collins, dau. of
  James                                             3 CE-21
Cole, John, 27 Oct. 1777, Eleanor Hall              7 AA-2
  8 AA-13 gives date as 1 Nov. 1777.
Cole, Thomas, 23 day, 2 mo., 1747, Sarah Price      4 SF
Cole, Vincent, 24 July 1777, Anne Orum             10 BA-77
Cole, William, Jr., 30 day, 5 mo., 1689, Elizabeth
  Sparrow of the Clifts                             6 SF-39
Cole, William, 19 Aug. 1735, Sarah Giles            1 BA-284
Cole, William, 14 Dec. 1741, Ann Beck               2 KE-244
Cole, William, 21 Nov. 1742, Mary Stevens           2 BA-238
Cole, William, 20 April 1769, Eliz. Hardisty        2 BA-258
Cole, William, 6 Sept. 1772, Roxana Hilton          2 BA-265
```

Colegate, Thomas, 3 April 1770, Eliz. Clarke          2 BA-260
Colehoune, John, 16 June 1676, Jane Carter            9 SO-401
Coleman, James, 8 Jan. 1733, Susanna Bucker           2 TA-154
Coleman, John, 25 May 1738, Mary Farrow               1 QA-44
Coleman, John, 11 Feb. 1741/2, Margarit Ayres         1 QA-47
Coleman, John, 25 Sept. 1744, Elliner Ponder          1 QA-49
Coleman, Joseph, 31 day, 6 mo., 1712, Mary Thomas     6 SF-45
Coleman, R'd, 22 Aug. 1765, Mary Hatten               2 BA-228
Coleman, William, 29 Dec. 1748, Ann Pouder            1 QA-55
Coles, William, son of William, 16 June 1730, Prudence
  Shaw, dau. of Thomas                                9 SF
Colescott, William, c.Aug. 1775, Mary Wheatley        1 CR-6
Colgan, John, 18 May 1750, Elizabeth Flowers          1 QA-57
Colier, Nicholas Evans, 5 March 1746/7, Ann Collier   1 WI-39
Coligan, Mathew, 19 Jan. 1772, Sarah Neale            2 BA-264
Collacutt, John, 29 Dec. 1744, Barbara Robinson       1 QA-50
Collard, Samuel, 31 Oct. 1762, Agnus Ouchterloney     1 PG-319
Collen, Cornelius, 3 March 1700, Sarah (?)            2 TA-13
Collett, Daniel, 14 May 1749, Susanna McKenly         2 BA-243
  2 BA-198 gives date as 1 Aug. 1749.
Collett, Moses, 12 Jan. 1743, Elizabeth Wyle          2 BA-189
Collett, Robert, 12 May 1765, Mary Stewart            9 AA-250
Collier, Danby, 9 April 1737, Prisilah Nichols        1 WI-22
Collier, John, 29 Dec. 1765, Ann Jones                3 SO-1
Collier, Kindall, son of Potter and Elizabeth, 6 April
  1758, Sarah Fassett, dau. of John and Mary          1 WO-13
Collier, Nicholas Evans, 6 March 1758, Rebecka Evans  1 WI-56
Collier, Robert, 2 March 1675, Elizabeth Dashiell     5 SO-397
Collings, Edward, 17 Nov. 1739, Eliz'h Marley         1 QA-45
Collings, John, 29 Nov. 1720, Dorothy Robinson        2 TA-95
Collings, John, 18 June 1747, Mary Walker             1 QA-53
Collings, John, 2 March 1759, Ibigal (sic) Addams     2 SO-114
Collings, John Offley, 10 Feb. 1746, Sarah Sparks     1 QA-53
Collings, Robert, 1 Jan. 1704/5, Mary Watson          1 CA-113
Collins, Charles, 3 Dec. 1728, Elizabeth Griffith     3 KE-256
Collins, Edmund, 16 Nov. 1692, Honora (?)             5 SO-397
Collins, Edward, 4 Oct. 1748, Elizabeth Bennett       1 QA-54
Collins, George, 21 Dec. 1770, Ann Lucas              1 SM-135
Collins, James, 1 Aug. 1717, Ellinor Ozey, widow      3 CE-11
Collins, James, 14 July 1723, Mary Lankford           1 WI-22
Collins, John, 17 Feb. 1719, Juliana Penninton        3 CE-11
Collins, John, 12 Dec. 1745, Margret McDaniel         2 KE-260
Collins, John, 10 July 1748, Mary Hughes              3 BA-161
Collins, Moses, 6 Jan. 1750, Patience Powell          1 BA-363
Collins, Robert, 8 Aug. 1737, Jemima Joy              1 BA-299
Collins, Rob't, 12 Feb. 1757, Alice Bonaday           2 BA-215
Collins, Samuel, 3 Sept. 1680, Margaret Hodson        5 SO-397
Colins, Thos., 31 March 1737, Mary Sartain            1 QA-43
Collins, Thomas, 28 Dec. 1741, Rebecca Stevens        1 WI-54
Collins, William, 12 Oct. 1699, Martha Pratt          3 KE-251
Collins, William, 10 day, 6 mo., 1732, Ann Hales      1 SF-64
Collins, William, 11 Nov. 1736, Sarah Roberts         3 KE-258
Collins, William, 7 Nov. 1751, Johanna Cantwell       1 BA-363
Collins, William, 15 Dec. 1757, Rachell Beal          1 QA-63
Collison, William, 3 Dec. 1713, Susanna Adams         2 BA-4
Collison, Wm., 18 Feb. 1744/5, Mary Calk              3 TA-52
Collister, Henry, 11 June 1748, Sarah Trippe          3 TA-70
Colson, Henry, 22 May 1746, Marg't Pamphillon         3 TA-58
Colston, James, 26 Nov. 1743, Alice Orem              3 TA-46
Colton, Gervas, 27 Aug. 1749, Elenor Weathersby       1 QA-56
Comagis, Edward, 17 Nov. 1717, Mary Harwood           4 AA-402
Comberford, George, 4 Nov. 1717, Eliza Marsh, widow   4 AA-402
Comberford, George, 6 Feb. 1718/9, Mary Harwood; both
  of Kent Island                                      4 AA-407
Combes, Edw'd, 28 July 1697, Judith (?)               2 TA-18

| | |
|---|---|
| Combest, Ettie, 28 July 1767, Eliza Gilbert | 1 BA-389 |
| Combest, Israel, 2 Jan. 1765, Susanna Perryman | 1 BA-387 |
| Combest, Jacob, 2 June 1743, Mary Solovan | 1 BA-331 |
| Combest, Jacob, 2 Sept. 1770, Sarah Collins | 1 BA-389 |
| Combest, John, 25 Feb. 1741, Mary Bowdey | 1 BA-328 |
| Combs, Tho., 31 July 1765, Ann Nowland | 2 BA-228 |
| Comegyes, Jessey, 8 Dec. 1777, Mary Everyt | 2 CE-1 |
| Comegys, Edward, 15 day, 10 mo., 1737, Mary Thraul | 1 SF-72 |
| Comegys, John, 13 Oct. 1757, Sarah Spencer | 2 KE-295 |
| Comegys, William, 14 Dec. 1709, Mary (?) | 2 KE-180 |
| Comegys, William, Jr., 20 Nov. 17-(?), Ann Cosden | 2 KE-249 |
| Comegys, William, of Edward, 11 April 1758, Mary Forester | 2 KE-296 |
| Comes, John, 17 Jan. 1716, Sarah Newman | 3 CE-9 |
| Commagis, Edward, 22 March 1731, (?) Woodhall | 1 QA-38 |
| Commagis, John, 27 Nov. 1733, (?) Rochester | 1 QA-40 |
| Commegys, John, 23 Oct. 1757, Rhoda Seward | 1 QA-63 |
| Commegys, Wm., 4 March 1735, Charity Rochester | 1 QA-42 |
| Commegys, William, 7 Sept. 1756, Sarah Pinder | 1 QA-61 |
| Compton, William, 19 Nov. 1758, Susanna Briscoe, widow of Hezekiah Briscoe | 1 CH-198 |
| Conant, Rob'rt, 9 May 1705, Sophia Herrington | 2 AA-327 |
| Conaway, Charles, 8 Nov. 1743, Dianah Owly | 3 AA-107 |
| Conaway, James, 11 May 1714, Sarah Chappell | 3 AA-99 |
| Conaway, John, 14 May 1744, Anne Norwood | 3 BA-166 |
| Conaway, Joseph, 30 Jan. 1728, Mary ffloyd | 3 AA-102 |
| Condal, David, 30 Dec. 1733, Eliz'h Warner | 2 PG-6 |
| Condon, James, 17 April 1765, Mary Macnamara | 2 BA-217 |
| Conelly, Artura, 28 Oct. 1770, Eliz. Parker | 2 BA-261 |
| Conelly, William, 21 Dec. 1727, Racheell Baley | 2 TA-117 |
| Conery, John, 17 July 1774, Elizabeth Anderson | 1 CE-310 |
| Coney, Jeremiah, 23 Dec. 1766, Mary Coleman | 2 BA-230 |
| Congreve, James, 1 Dec. 1764, Mary Smith | 9 AA-247 |
| Connalle, James, 6 Jan. 1725, Ruth Maurice | 1 AA-101 |
| Connar, James, 30 Nov. 1777, Elizabeth McDonald | 10 BA-69 |
| Connard, Philip, 17 Dec. 1677, Mary Dance | 5 SO-397 |
| Connaway, Charles 17 Dec. 1747, Sophia Wooden | 3 BA-160 |
| Connaway, John, 15 July 1729, Catherine Pitts | 1 AA-109 |
| Connell, William, 2 April 1721, Mary Robinson | 3 BA-146 |
| Conner, Arthur, 4 Oct. 1710, Margaret Pollard | 2 TA-67 |
| Conner, Elijah, 12 Feb. 1756, Isabella Lankfoot | 2 SO-113 |
| Conner, John, 26 Dec. 1727, Ann Richardson | 1 AA-106 & 377 |
| Conner, John, Aug. 1744, Susanna Burgess | 2 BA-153 |
| Conniew (?), John, 18 Sept. 1673, Dorothy Bundick | 5 SO-397 |
| Connolly, Christopher, 14 Nov. 1734, Margaret Stapleford | 2 TA-156 |
| Connolly, Terrence, 12 April 1738, Mary Mullikin | 2 TA-165 |
| Connor, Dan'l, 7 Aug. 1734, Jemima Alexander | 2 TA-160 |
| Connor, James, 1 Jan. 1705, Elinor Flanagan | 3 KE-252 |
| Connor, John, 26 April 1739, Rachel Parrott | 2 TA-165 |
| Connor, Phillip, 4 March 1700, Jane Harris | 3 KE-251 |
| Connoway, John, 17 Aug. 1714, Ann Aegillston | 4 AA-392 |
| Constable, Robert, 7 June 1736, Judeth Cook | 3 BA-155 |
| Constantine, Patrick, 29 Sept. 1760, Anne Bond | 4 BA-72 |
| Conway, John, 9 Feb. 1741, Sarah Stoker | 3 TA-36 |
| Conway, Morgan, 12 Aug. 1761, Hannah Ruse | 2 BA-222 |
| Cook, Charles, 30 March 1741, Hannah Sweatman | 1 QA-46 |
| Cook, Cornelius, 16 Oct. 1729, Ann Jacobs | 3 CE-18 |
| Cook, Francis, 2 Nov. 1724, Mary Earl | 2 TA-110 |
| Cook, George, 31 Jan. 1726/7, Elizabeth Reynolds | 2 PG-4 |
| Cook, Jeames (sic), 2 Dec. 1725, Mary Hurluck | 2 TA-112 |
| Cook, Jeremiah, 9 Nov. 1758, Ann Brucebanks | 1 BA-359 |
| Cook, John, 17 Aug. 1702, Catherine (?) | 2 TA-27 |
| Cook, John, 31 Oct. 1706, Catherine Squibb | 4 AA-372 |

```
Cook, Jno., 12 May 1716, Eliza Westcote                    1 AA-88
Cook, John, 30 Dec. 1726, Sarah West                       1 BA-243
Cook, John, 29 Jan. 1748, Mary Price                       3 BA-162
Cook, John, son of John and Ellener, 13 April 1752,
    Rebecca Kirk, dau. of Roger and Elizabeth              9 SF
Cook, Richard, 9 Nov. 1769, Rebecca Murrey                 2 BA-259
Cook, Samuel, 11 Feb. 1734, Hannah Winn                    1 QA-40
Cook, Stephen, son of John and Eleanor, 3 day, 12
    mo. (n.s.), 1755, Hannah Reynolds, dau. of William
    and Mary                                               9 SF
Cook, Thomas, 3 Oct. 1739, Anne Wheeler                    3 BA-165
Cook, Thomas, 24 Dec. 1757, Ann Vasey                      1 QA-63
Cook, Thomas, 18 March 1759, Mary Ann Elliot               1 QA-65
Cook, William, 12 Aug. 1712, Eliza Anderson                2 PG-1
Cook, William, 27 Aug. 1713, Sarah Garrett                 1 BA-212
Cook, William, 27 Dec. 1728, Sarah Wright                  3 KE-256
Cook, William, 3 Feb. 1752, Ann Benham                     1 QA-58
Cooke, John, 16 May 1723, Theophilius Wilson               1 AA-96
Cooke, Thomas, 15 July 1728, Elizabeth Cooley              2 BA-27
Cooke, William, 28 Aug. 1777, Henrietta Beaven             3 PG-98
Cooksey, Thomas Reed, 12 March 1757, Elizabeth
    Matthews                                               1 CH-191
Cookson, Samuel, 20 day, 1 mo., 1773, Mary Haines          3 SF
Cookson, William, 31 May (?), Margrett Patterson           3 KE-244
Cooley, Daniell, 23 Oct. 1704, Elizabeth Watson            3 KE-252
Cooley, Nathaniell, 31 March 1729, Ann Rogers              3 KE-259
Cooley, William, 22 Dec. 1777, Anne Harwood                7 AA-2
Cooly, Matthew, 1771, Elisabeth Drury                      2 AA-410
Cooly, Matthew, 21 April 1776, Margaret Seirs              2 AA-413
Cooly, Thomas, 1 Dec. 1771, Sarah Collins                  2 BA-263
Cooly, William, 23 Dec. 1777, Ann Henwood                  2 AA-414
    8 AA-13 gives her name as Hinwood.
Coombs, William, 16 Dec. 1725, Margret Ogle                2 TA-112
Coop, Richard, 6 Dec. 1747, Hannah Stansbury               2 BA-242
Cooper, Benj., 5 May 1747, Marg't Haddaway                 3 TA-65
Cooper, George, 11 May 1721, Jane Ford                     2 TA-96
Cooper, George, 16 June 1777, Ann Southern                 3 BA-173
Cooper, Isaac, 22 Feb. 1731, Tabitha Millby                1 WI-21
Cooper, Jas., 6 Sept. 1764, Keziah Leach                   2 BA-226
Cooper, Jas., 14 April 1765, Ann Price                     2 BA-228
Cooper, John, 28 May 1667, Susanna Brayfeeld               4 SO-671
Cooper, John, 23 Oct. 1722, Alice Gill                     1 BA-270
Cooper, John, 26 Sept. 1739, Sarah Christian               2 TA-167
Cooper, John, 27 April 1774, Elizabeth Lucas               1 CR
Cooper, Richard, 12 Feb. 1701, Mary (?)                    2 TA-23
Cooper, Rich'd, Jr., 30 Dec. 1746, Anne Broadway           3 TA-64
Cooper, Samuel, 3 April 1722, Sarah Willson                1 WI-12
Cooper, Samuel, 20 June 1741, Cathrin Shockley             2 SO-15
Cooper, William, 25 Aug. 1745, Mary Harrison               3 TA-54
Coots, Robert, 25 Nov. 1734, Mary (?)                      2 PG-6
Copass, John, 16 Jan. 1742/3, Manerlin Wright              2 BA-238
Cope, David, son of John and Grace, 17 July 1777,
    Margaret Brown, dau. of Jacob and Betty                9 SF
Cope, John, 5 Feb. 1748, Mary Bush                         2 BA-194
                                                           & 242
Cope, John, Nov. 1752, Bridget Tafe or Tate                2 BA-241
Cope, Jno., 5 Feb. 1753, Brigitt Leate                     2 BA-207
Cope, Robert, 20 Jan. 1735, Mical Slade                    1 QA-41
Copeland, Lawrence, 22 Jan. 1737/8, Elis. Morris           1 QA-43
Copland, David, 27 Aug. 1747, Eliz. Duglas                 2 BA-196
Copland, John, 10 Nov. 1726, Mary Fowler                   2 PG-4
Copland, William, 12 Sept. 1720, Jane Jamson               1 AA-301
Coplin, William, c.Oct. 1775, Elizabeth Shaw               1 CR-6
Copper, George, 31 Dec. 1700, Mary Moss                    3 KE-252
Copping, John, 13 May 1703, Angelico Atkey, dau. of
    John                                                   3 CE-3
```

```
Coppock, John, son of Aaron, 16 March 1730/1,
    Margaret Coulson, dau. of Joseph and Margaret        9 SF
Coppock, Joseph, son of John and Margaret, 4
    May 1769, Jane Wilson, dau. of John                  9 SF
Coppock, Samuel, son of John and Margaret, 7 day,
    12 mo., 1775, Ellen Sidwell, dau. of Isaac
    and Ann                                              9 SF
Corback, Valentine, 14 Sept. 1769, Rachael Colls      2 BA-259
Corbat, Patrick, 13 Dec. 1777, Mary Cunningham       10 BA-69
Corbel, Patrick, 13 Dec. 1777, Mary Cunningham        9 BA
Corbin, Abraham, 4 Dec. 1766, Rachael Marshall        2 BA-230
Corbin, Benj., 9 Dec. 1755, Sarah Sye (or Lye)        2 BA-212
Corbin, Nath'l, 16 Oct. 1758, Sarah James             2 BA-217
Corbin, Peter, 12 Aug. 1750, Bettey Sheldron          2 SO-115
Corbin, William, 11 Aug. 1745, Rachel Wright          2 BA-240
Corbit, David, 12 June 1770, Ester Corbit (sic)       1 CE-319
Cord, Abraham, 19 Feb., 1733, Mary Pritchard          1 BA-270
Cord, Amos, 13 Nov. 1763, Susannah Kimbel             1 BA-387
Cord, Jacob, 20 June 1750, Elizabeth Cook             1 BA-362
Cord, Thomas, 4 Aug. 1698, Hannah Matthews            1 BA-178
Cord, Thomas, 10 Feb. 1730, Mary Williams             1 BA-252
Cordiman, Philip, 5 Feb. 1735, Ann Sampson            3 BA-155
Cordrey, Abraham, 16 July 1752, Elizabeth Furnis      2 SO-14
Cordsman, Philip, 1753, Anne Brooks                   2 BA-242
Cork, Peter, 28 Jan. 1724, Mary Sockwel               2 TA-111
Cork, William, 4 Aug. 1705, Anne Whitehead            3 KE-252
Corker, Dennis, 4 Feb. 1739, Jane Bennit              1 QA-45
Corkeran, James, 23 Sept. 1746, Hanah Merlin          1 QA-52
Corkerin, James, 22 Dec. 1715, Susannah Baley         2 TA-26
Corkrin, John, 12 Jan. 1737, Rachel Barnett           2 TA-164
Corkrin, William, 6 Feb. 1732, Judith Gass            2 TA-152
Cornelius, John, 27 Nov. 1751, Elenor Little          4 BA-70
Cornelius, Robert, 21 Dec. 1719, Mary Downy           1 AA-297
Cornell, John, 19 Feb. 171-?, Eda Holland             1 WO-6
Corner, Noah, 13 Aug. 1740, Rachel Holms              3 TA-24
    2 TA-271 gives date as 29 Aug. 1740, and her
    name as Holmes.
Cornih (sic), Noah, 5 July 1735, Elz'a Twille         2 TA-159
Cornish, Noah, 19 Aug. 1740, Rachel Homes             2 TA-169
Cornish, Solomon, 10 Oct. 1736, Tomoson Matthews      2 TA-159
Cornthwait, John, son of Thomas and Elizabeth of
    Bucks Co., Penna., 17 day, 4 mo., 1771, Mary
    Matthews, dau. of Oliver and Hannah               4 SF-261
Cornthwait, Robert, son of Thomas and Elizabeth,
    16 Nov. 1775, Grace Rogers, dau. of William
    and Grace                                          9 SF
Corse, David, 9 day, 11 mo., 1757, Mary Bowers        1 SF-93
Corse, David, 31 day, 8 mo., 1765, Elizabeth
    Fairbank, Jr.                                      8 SF-120
Corse, James, Jr., 23 day, 3 mo., 1710, Ann Beck      1 SF-53
Corte, Joseph, 25 Sept. 1741, Margrett Ricketts       1 CE-290
Corwin, William, 15 Aug. 1745, Rach'l Wright          2 BA-193
Cosley, James, 3 Jan. 1744, Mary Hill                 2 BA-192
Cosley, Rich'd, 7 July 1752, Eliz. Rhodes             2 BA-205
Costen, Isaac, 16 Jan. 1755, Sarah McCuddy            2 SO-15
Costin, John, 7 Aug. 1722, Rose Smith                 3 KE-255
Costley, James, 2 Aug. 1714, Elinor Chisnold          1 BA-215
Costly, James, 25 Dec. 1744, Mary Hill                2 BA-240
Costly, William, 26 Dec. 1709, Mary Ellis             1 BA-208
Coston, Henry, 21 Jan. 1760, Lydia Clarke             2 CR-269
Coston, Matthias, 29 Dec. 1745, Elizabeth Riggin      2 SO-15
Coston, Mathias, 24 May 1770, Sarah Persons           2 SO-16
Coston, Richard, 26 Feb. 1759, Sarah Meredith         1 QA-64
Cotrall, John, 1752, Anne Wood                        2 BA-241
Cotter, John, 24 Jan. 1730, Elean'r Ogle              2 TA-150
```

```
Cotter, John, 6 March 1736, Margery Matthews          2 TA-162
Cotterel, Jno., 10 March 1763, Sarah Reaven           2 BA-224
Cotterel, Thomas, 4 Aug. 1743, Frances Millhughes     2 BA-163
    2 BA-126 & 239 give date as 31 July 1743.
Cotterrel, John, 14 Jan. 1752, Ann Wood               2 BA-205
Cotterrell, Peter, 4 Feb. 1747, Precilla Gallaway     2 BA-194
Cottingham, Charles, 7 Nov. 1762, Elennor Toadvine    2 SO-118
Cottingham, Daniel, 24 Feb. 1753, Anne Cooper         2 SO-14
Cottingham, John, 27 Oct. 1745, Mary Boston           2 SO-118
Cottingham, John, 23 Feb. 1749, Ester Hopkins         2 SO-14
Cottingham, Stephen, 17 Jan. 1762, Martha Carsly      2 SO-203
Cottingham, Thomas, 8 July 1666, Mary Dixon, dau.
    of Ambrose                                        5 SO-397
Cottingham, Thomas, 16 Nov. 1769, Susanna Watts       2 SO-201
Cottingham, William, 11 Sept. 1754, Ruth Mills        2 SO-15
Cottingham, William, 28 May 1761, Bettey Toadvine     2 SO-117
Cottingham, William, 27 Nov. 1766, Martha Cottingham  2 SO-119
Cottingham, William, son of John of Wor. Co., 13
    March 1773, Leach Nicholson                       2 SO-204
Cottner, Alexander, 10 Aug. 1738, Mary Kiningmont     2 TA-165
Cottrall, Thomas, 31 July 1743, Frances Milhaus       2 BA-239
Couch, Joseph, 20 Feb. 1736, Phebe Morgan             2 TA-162
Coulbourn, Benjamin, 16 Dec. 1750, Elizabeth Tilman   2 SO-13
Coulbourn, Elijah, 2 May 1762, Rachel Tull            2 SO-202
Coulbourn, Mr. Isaac, 18 April 1769, Comfort Miller   2 SO-202
Coulbourn, James, 18 Nov. 1720, Mary Brown            2 TA-95
Coulbourn, Robert, 11 March 1776, Leah Holland        2 SO-205
Coulbourn, William, 19 Jan. 1735/6, Sarah Handy       2 SO-205
Coulbourn, William, 22 Sept. 1749, Elizabeth Cox      2 SO-12
Coulbourne, William, 15 June 1678, Anne Revell        5 SO-397
Coulson, James, 14 Sept. 1714, Elizabeth Bayley       2 TA-74
Coulter, Andrew, 20 Feb. 1750, Hannah Killpatrick     1 CE-299
Coulton, Jervis, 7 Nov. 1736, Anne Deverix            1 QA-42
Coup, Rich'd, 10 Dec. 1747, Hannah Stansbury          2 BA-194
Coursey, Thomas, 17 Oct. 1699, Ann Harris             3 KE-251
Courtney, John, 16 Aug. 1739, Frances Greenfield      1 BA-305
Courtney, Jonas, 15 Jan. 1738, Comfort Cole           1 BA-304
Courtney, Robert, 2 Oct. 1740, Hannah Cook            1 BA-315
Cousins, Edward, 27 April 1707, Eliz'th Fisher        3 KE-252
Couzens, John, son of John and Elizabeth, 19 day,
    5 mo., 1763, Sarah Pearson, dau. of John and Marga-
    ret                                               9 SF
Covan, John, 8 March 1680, Elizabeth Carr             5 SO-397
Covell, Jonathan, 14 Dec. 1707, Mary Caine            1 AA-76
Coventon, Henry, 19 day, 1 mo., 1738, Rachel Roe      1 SF-74
Coventon, James, 23 Nov. 1752, Mary Scott             1 QA-59
Covey, Noble, 3 day, 4 mo., 1775, Mary Bickham of
    Kent Co., Del.                                    2 SF-288
Covington, Jeremiah, 19 Sept. 1737, Cassandra Hyath   3 KE-259
Covington, John, 13 July 1731, Mary Airey             1 QA-38
Covington, John, Jr., 8 Oct. 1758, Hannah Dockery     1 QA-64
Covington, Nehemiah, July 1667, Anne Ingram           5 SO-397
Covington, Nehemiah, 5 Dec. 1733, Rachell Mariartee   1 AA-117
Covington, Peter, 8 Jan. 1741, Sophia Scott           3 TA-36
Covington, Thomas, 30 June 1668, Susana Cooper        4 SO-712
Covington, Thomas, 20 Aug. 1731, Mary Fillit          1 WI-21
Covinton, William, 1742, Sarah Newnam                 1 QA-47
Cowan, Alexander, 2 May 1771, Elionora Boyce          2 BA-262
Cowan, Dunham, 21 (Sept. 1768 ?), Mary Taylor         2 BA-257
Cowan, James, 30 Nov. 1777, Elizabeth McDonald        9 BA
Cowan, John, 25 Sept. 1712, Susanna Teage             1 BA-216
Coward, John, 17 Sept. 1742, Bridget Kenney           2 TA-173
    3 TA-39 gives date as 15 Sept. 1742.
Cowarden, Abraham, 2 Nov. 1738, Mary Joce             2 KE-277
    3 KE-259 gives same information.
```

Cowarden, Peter, 11 Sept. 1753, Anne Coppen, dau. of
  John and Angelico                                        3 CE-27
Cowarden, Thomas, 12 April 1716, Frances Ambrose           3 KE-254
Cowdray, James, Sept. 1723, Anne Green                     2 BA-30
Cowdry, John, 8 Jan. 1683/4, Mary Nuttley                  9 SO-402
Cowen, John, 22 April 1743, Elizabeth Bond                 1 BA-328
Cowen, John, 9 March 1745, Eliz'th Wood                    1 BA-345
Cowgill, Clayton, of Kent Co., Del., 27 day, 5 mo.,
  1763, Martha Neal                                        8 SF-112
Cowles, William, 29 July 1777, Ann Earlie                  3 PG-108
Cowley, John, 8 Nov. 1743, Eleanor Lowry                   3 TA-45
Cowley, John, 10 Nov. 1744, Eleanor Lowry                  2 TA-196
Cowley, Joseph, 3 Jan. 1734, Martha Cornish                2 TA-156
Cowley, Joseph, 3 Jan. 1734, Martha Corner                 2 TA-266
Cowman, Joseph, of London, mariner, 15 day, 1 mo.,
  1723/4, Sarah Hill, widow                                6 SF-109
Cowman, Joseph, 4 day, 4 mo., 1754, Eliza Snowden,
  dau. of Richard                                          6 SF
Cowman, Jno., (no date given), dau. of Gerard Hopkins      6 SF
Cowman, Richard, 28 Dec. 1775, Ann Dare                    2 AA-412
Cowman, William, 12 Dec. 1732, Mary Gelly                  1 QA-39
Cox, Abraham, 15 Nov. 1735, Ann Maclan                     3 CE-20
Cox, Abraham, 29 June 1769, Eliz. Merrydeth                2 BA-259
Cox, Arthur, 24 Dec. 1744, Rebecca Lane                    1 QA-50
Cox, Charles, 13 Sept. 1702, Mary Preston, dau. of
  John                                                     2 TA-27
Cox, Daniel, 3 March 1725, Ann Powell                      8 SF-45
Cox, Daniel, 22 April 1759, Sarah Mayne                    2 CR-270
Cox, Gessery, 21 July 1709, Shusannah Melleway             2 TA-61
Cox, Hill, 5 Jan. 1735/6, Charrety Seady                   1 WI-10
Cox, Isaac, 2 Sept. 1749, Sarah Turner                     3 TA-74
Cox, Isaac, 1 day, 7 mo., 1756, Rachel Atkinson            8 SF-124
Cox, Jacob, 25 Sept. 1722, Elizabeth Merriman              3 BA-147
Cox, Jacob, 13 Dec. 1744, Eliz'th Gain                     2 BA-239
Cox, James, 15 Aug. 1760, Mary White, widow, nee
  Alexander                                                3 BA-168
Cox, Jeremiah, 1770, Elizabeth Jones; by license,
  from Calvert Co.                                         2 AA-410
Cox, John, 20 April 1717, Rose Davis                       3 CE-8
Cox, John, 21 Feb. 1733, Elizabeth Lee                     2 TA-155
Cox, John, 30 Nov. 1742, Eliz. Simpson                     2 BA-124
Cox, John, 9 May 1748, Hannah Whittington                  2 SO-13
Cox, John, son of William and Mary, 7 April 1768,
  Sarah Stedman, dau. of Richard and Ann                   9 SF
Cox, Joseph, 22 May 1738, Eliza Vaughn                     2 TA-165
Cox, Merryman, 26 Dec. 1745, Honour Hall                   3 BA-158
Cox, Nathaniel, 13 May 1737, Ann Lee                       2 TA-163
Cox, Powel, 10 day, 6 mo., 1749, Mary Hull                 1 SF-85
Cox, Thomas, 8 Nov. 1706, Johannah Clark                   2 TA-45
Cox, Thomas, 4 Dec. 1714, Eliz. Clarkson                   1 WI-4
Cox, Thomas, 15 Jan. 1740, Sarah Rumsey, dau. of
  Charles and Margaret                                     3 CE-22
Cox, Thomas, Jr., 19 Jan. 1743, Margret Hendrickson,
  dau. of Henry                                            3 CE-24
Cox, Thos., 13 Dec. 1744, Eliz'th Gaine                    2 BA-191
Cox, William, son of William and Mary, 19 day, 5 mo.,
  1774, Rachel Gover, dau. of Ephraim and Eliz.            7 SF-26
Coxill, Hezekiah, 31 Oct. 1774, Eliza Carter               1 CR
Cozens, Geo., 13 March 1766, Marg'rt Whitely               2 BA-229
Cozine, George, 30 Jan. 1696, Ann Johnson                  3 CE-1
Crabb, Ralph, 22 Aug. 1716, Priscilla Sprigg, dau.
  of Col. Thomas                                           2 PG-2
Crabbin, Alexander, 4 Aug. 1758, Marcy Hynson, dau.
  of Nathaniel and Marcy                                   3 KE-262
Crabbin, Alex'r, 10 June 1767, Elizabeth Ayres, dau.
  of Abram and Sarah                                       3 KE-262

| | |
|---|---|
| Crabtree, Jno., 22 April 1755, Hannah Butcher | 2 BA-212 |
| Crabtree, Thos., 23 Oct. 1760, Eliz. Barton | 2 BA-220 |
| Crabtree, William, 17 Feb. 1725, Mary Pyke | 2 BA-36 |
| Crabtree, William, 27 May 1746, Hannah Whitaker | 2 BA-195 |
| Crabtree, Will'm, 25 April 1754, Ann Kiley | 2 BA-209 |
| Craddock, Rev. Thomas, 31 March 1746, Katherine | |
| Risteau, dau. of John and Katherine | 4 BA-70 |
| 3 BA-159 gives same date of marriage. | |
| Crafford, James, 12 Feb. 1712, Frances Ringgold | 3 KE-253 |
| Crafford, Richard, 17 Sept. 1709, Mary Covene | 1 CA-112 |
| Craft, Lawrance, 28 Dec. 1769, Mary Lymes | 2 BA-259 |
| Crafton, John, 24 May 1755, Rebeckah Carman | 1 QA-59 |
| Cragghead, Robert, 24 June 1736, Katherine Ward | 3 BA-155 |
| Crandall, Francis, 27 Dec. 1733, Jane Atwood | 2 AA-380 |
| Crandall, George, 12 Oct. 1768, Mary Phips | 9 AA-250 |
| Crandall, Joseph, 9 Oct. 1753, Wilelme (?) | 2 AA-392 |
| Crandall, William, 1771, Elizabeth Chaulk | 2 AA-410 |
| Crandell, Francis, 25 Sept. 1707, Esther Hill | 1 AA-76 |
| Crane, Thomas, 16 Sept. 1707, Elizabeth Ensor | 1 AA-76 |
| Cranfield, Joseph, 3 June 1723, Barbary Bright | 2 TA-104 |
| Crans, Robert, 25 July 1710, Ann Board | 3 AA-99 |
| Crans, Robert, 28 Nov. 1712, Hanah Gosnell | 3 AA-99 |
| Crawford, Adam, 16 April 1714, Mary (?) | 2 KE-189 |
| Crawford, James, 26 Dec. 1723, Mary Anderson | 2 PG-3 |
| Crawford, Mordecai, 16 Sept. 1750, Suhanna Tucker | 2 BA-201 |
| Crawford, Rob't, 27 July 1767, Alice Sattle | 2 BA-230 |
| Crawford, Robert, 7 May 1776, Ann Wells | 5 BA-3 |
| Cribb, Richard, 11 Feb. 1701, Ann Estell | 8 SF-388 |
| Crisup, Thomas, 30 April 1727, Hannah Johnson | 1 BA-247 |
| Criswell, Richard, 28 May 1746, Mary Wooden | 3 BA-159 |
| Criswell, Wm., 10 Oct. 1754, Margret Criswell | 2 BA-211 |
| Crockett, Dr. Benjamin, 30 June 1750, Elizabeth Chew; | |
| the marriage was performed in Cecil Co. by Rev. | |
| John Hambleton | 1 BA-350 |
| Crockett, Gilbert, 1727, Mary Chew | 9 SF |
| Crockett, John, 25 Dec. 1744; Ann Fixson | 2 BA-191 |
| Fol. 27 of the original register gives bride's | |
| name as Hixson. | |
| Crockett, John, 1747, Mary Richardson, dau. of Joseph | 9 SF |
| Crofts, Robert, 5 Jan. 1729, Macy Giles | 1 AA-110 |
| Crokat, John, 25 Dec. 1744, Anne Hickson | 2 BA-239 |
| Cromp, Thomas, 6 April 1703, Elizabeth Boughton | 1 AA-64 |
| Crompton, Joseph, 19 Oct. 1703, Mary Costly | 1 BA-199 |
| Cromwell, Alexander, 17 April 1733, Sarah Dorcey | 3 AA-109 |
| Cromwell, John, 1 Dec. 1728, Comfort Robosson | 3 AA-107 |
| Cromwell, John, 10 June 1770, Mary Dorsey | 2 BA-260 |
| Cromwell, Joshua, 26 Feb. 1767, Hellen Gray | 3 AA-112 |
| Cromwell, Oneal, 17 Dec. 1773, Sarah Ashley | 3 AA-113 |
| Cromwell, Weelgist, 10 Feb. 1740, Venesha Dorsey | 3 AA-109 |
| Cromwell, Wm., 10 June 1768, Eliz. Risteau | 2 BA-232 |
| Cronagam, Will'm, 25 Aug. 1741, Francis Jenins | 1 CE-291 |
| Cronagan, Will'm, 9 Feb. 1745, Jane Swann | 1 CE-291 |
| Croney (?), Jeremiah, 23 Dec. 1766, Mary Coleman | 2 BA-230 |
| Croney, Paul, 12 Aug. 1751, Elizabeth Carson | 1 BA-353 |
| Crook, James, 27 Dec. 1716, Sarah Burgess, widow | 4 AA-398 |
| Crook, Joseph, 24 April 1757, Prisilla Gallaway | 2 BA-215 |
| Crookshanks, Robert, 6 Oct. 1772, Ann Day | 2 BA-265 |
| Cross, Asael, 24 Aug. 1760, Mary Demmett | 2 BA-220 |
| Cross, Benjamin, 20 Jan. 1754, Eliz. Cole | 2 BA-209 |
| Cross, Henry, 19 June 1759, Margret Hicks | 2 BA-218 |
| Cross, Jeremiah, 18 Feb. 1762, Eleanor Wheeler | 9 AA-247 |
| Cross, John, 7 July 1715, Mary (?) | 4 AA-392 |
| Cross, John, 25 April 1745, Sarah Willkinson | 1 QA-50 |
| Cross, John, 28 Aug. 1753, Philliszana Hicks | 2 BA-208 |
| Cross, John, 1 (?) 1764, Henny Evins | 9 AA-249 |

Cross, Joseph, 13 Sept. 1730, Elisabeth Merryman          3 BA-149
Cross, Joshua, 25 April 1742, Mary Lusby                  4 AA-443
Cross, Rich'd, 1 Jan. 1761, Tab. Hix                      2 BA-221
Cross, Robert, 20 July 1710, Anne Bourd                   1 AA-77
Cross, Robert, 13 March 1744, Jemima Gosnell              4 BA-72
Cross, Robert, 8 Aug. 1751, Ann Davis                     1 QA-58
Cross, Sam'l, 28 March 1765, Susannah Presbury            1 BA-383
Cross, Sollomon, 8 Feb. 1754, Mary Keith                  2 BA-209
Cross, William, 24 Dec. 1738, Dorcus Croscomb             3 AA-105
Cross, William, 24 April 1753, Alice Cole                 2 BA-207
Crossley, Abraham, 1 Jan. 1741/2, Sarah Nicholson         1 QA-47
Crouch, Isaac, 3 May 1760, Ann Johnson                    1 CE-299
Crouch, James, 22 Sept. 1757, Hannah Starkey              2 BA-216
Crouch, John, 24 Feb. 1744/5, Elisabeth Evans             2 BA-45
Crouch, John, 20 Nov. 1777, Sarah Hull                    2 CE-1
Crouch, Joseph, 3 Jan. 1719, Mary Lynch                   3 BA-147
Crouch, Joseph, 27 July 1732, Elianer Penington           3 AA-103
Crouch, Joseph, 6 April 1745, Mary Rockhold               3 AA-107
Crouch, Thomas, 11 May 1754, Mary Ambross                 3 KE-259
Crouch, Wedge, 24 Dec. 1713, Mary Huitt                   3 KE-253
Crouch, William, 16 March 1702, Susannah Howard           3 AA-98
Crouch, William, 14 Jan. 1723, Kathrin Hopkins            3 AA-102
Crouch, William, 1 Aug. 1727, Anne Abrahams               2 TA-116
Crouley, David, 15 March 1699, Mary Everett; both of
   Cecil Co.; see also 1 SF.                              2 KE-43
Crow, James, 16 Nov. 1738, Hannah Simpson                 1 BA-304
Crow, James, 7 Feb. 1743, Grace Denson                    1 BA-333
Crow, John; on the Monday before Ash Monday, no
   year given, Judith Mage                                1 BA-271
Crow, John, 18 Oct. 1713, Martha Newman                   3 CE-7
Crow, John, 6 April 1719, Margaret Crompton               1 BA-227
Crow, Peter, 27 July 1765, Eliz. Brown                    2 BA-228
Crow, William, 24 May 1702, Mary Unick                    3 KE-251
Crowley, David, March 1729, Sarah Whitehead               3 KE-256
Crowly, David, 22 Sept. 1711, Mary Beck                   3 KE-253
Croxal, Richard, 1 May 1770, Hannah Jennings              2 BA-260
Croxall, Charles, 23 July 1746, Rebecca Moale             3 BA-159
Croxall, Richard, 12 Dec. 1748, Eleanor Buchanan          3 BA-162
Cruikshanks, Robert, 6 Oct. 1772, Ann Day                 2 BA-265
Crumbach, Conrad, 22 Nov. 1767, Margretha Silliman        3 FR-107
Crump, Michel, 3 Jan. 1739/40, Susannah Ducksbury         3 TA-20
Crump, Robert, 28 May 1731, Jane Lazonby                  1 QA-38
Crump, Thos., 6 April 1703, Elizabeth Boulton             1 AA-254
Crumpton, John, son of John Bartholomew, 31 Oct.
   1739, Elizabeth Piggott, dau. of John and Margery      9 SF
Crupper, Thomas, 25 May 1732, Anne Hines                  1 QA-39
Crusa, Timothy, 25 Jan. 1737/8, Mary Tarbutton            1 QA-43
Cruse, Timothy, 2 Jan. 1736, Marg't. Mab                  1 QA-42
Crutchinton, Geo., 16 June 1768, Ann Bak'r                2 BA-232
Crute, Robert, 18 Aug. 1751, Rachel Barns                 1 BA-382
Culbreth, John, 2 Aug. 1750, Jane Newnam                  1 QA-57
Culbreth, Jona., Aug. 1774, Sarah Broady                  1 CR
Culins, Jonathan, 14 April 1722, Elianer ffinks           3 AA-104
   3 AA-100 gives date as 15 April 1723 and bride's
   name as ffincks.
Cullen, Daniel, 2 Jan. 1756, Winnefort Miles              2 SO-119
Cullen, George, 1 Oct. 1673, Avis Grottin                 5 SO-397
Cullen, John, 12 Oct. 1694, Mary (?)                      5 SO-397
Cullen, John, 8 June 1769, Hannah Starling                2 SO-121
Culling, Jacob, 20 Aug. 1737, Mary Stafford               2 SO-114
Cullison, Joseph, 21 April 1772, Sarah Walker             2 BA-264
Cullum, William, 19 Aug. 1758, Mary Nichols               2 BA-217
Cullum, Wm., 30 Oct. 1760, Marg'rt. Gott                  2 BA-220
Cully, Henery, 29 Aug. 1723, Christian Beck               3 KE-255
Culpepper, John, 31 Jan. 1732, Mary Mitchell              1 AA-115

| | |
|---|---|
| Culpeper, Michael, 14 Jan. 1705, Ellinor Fidgarrill | 1 CA-112 |
| Culver, Benj., 16 Feb. 1732, Ann Dutton | 1 CE-282 |
| Culver, John, 2 Dec. 1711, Martha Coppinger | 1 AA-78 |
| Cumberford, Peter, 3 Nov. 1747, Eliza Horney | 3 TA-67 |
| Cumerford, Peter, 13 March 1743/4, Rebecca Darden | 3 TA-48 |
| Cumings, Nichols, 27 Aug. 1746, Mary Blackwell | 3 TA-60 |
| Cumming, Robert, carpenter, 14 Sept. 1731, Magdalen Wolf | 4 AA-434 |
| Cumming, Wm., 21 Jan. 1719/20, Elizabeth Coursey | 4 AA-411 |
| Cummings, Daniel, 7 Sept. 1756, Frances Wells | 1 QA-61 |
| Cummings, David, son of David and Sarah, of Phila., 24 day, 8 mo., 1774, Rachel Miller, dau. of Solomon and Sarah | 3 SF |
| Cummins, Robert, 15 Oct. 1732, Elizabeth Baker | 1 CE-334 |
| Cuninghame, Hugh, 1749, Mary Acre | 2 BA-243 |
| Cuningham, John, 2 Oct. 1716, Sarah Pinckney | 4 BA-398 |
| Cuningham, Wm., (29 Dec.?) 1761, Margarett Brierly | 2 BA-223 |
| Cunningham, James, Aug. 1773, Pathiah Standiford | 2 BA-266 |
| Cunningham, John, 11 June 1769, Eliz. Young | 2 BA-258 |
| Cunningham, John, 18 Nov. 1777, Elizabeth Caldwell | 2 CE-1 |
| Cunningham, Samuell, 15 April 1736, Mary Higginbothom | 3 KE-258 |
| Curier, William Colebourne, June 1683, Elizabeth Ellis, dau. of John Ellis, Jr. | 5 SO-397 |
| Curle, William; banns were requested to be posted on 10 Aug. 1775, Elizabeth Ward | 6 BA(1) |
| Curnelius, John, 27 Feb. 1717, Sarah White | 3 AA-107 |
| Curr, John, 16 April 1733, Jane Bourton | 1 AA-118 |
| Currer, John, 16 June 1740, Millicent Johnson | 1 CE-287 |
| Currey, Jno., 16 Oct. 1739, Kath'n Ruth | 1 QA-45 |
| Currier, Daniel Larke, 19 May 1710, Milliscent Fletcher, widow | 1 AA-77 & 259 |
| Currier, William, 26 Dec. 1713, Mary George | 1 CE-334 |
| Currier, William, 17 July 1774, Mary Bird, dau. of Empson and Susanna | 1 CE-322 |
| Curry, John, 1770, Ann Sheckels | 2 AA-409 |
| Curry, John, 4 Nov. 1775, Elizabeth Wilson | 3 BA-172 |
| Curry, Samuel, 13 March 1745/6, Mary Corse | 1 SF-78 |
| Currypool, John, 10 Oct. 1755, Elizabeth Bostock | 1 QA-60 |
| Curtis, Daniel, 1 July 1666, Mary Greene | 5 SO-397 |
| Curtis, Daniel, 5 Nov. 1758, Rachel Pearce | 4 BA-72 |
| Curtis, James, 2 Feb. 1685, Sarah Hall, dau. of Charles | 5 SO-397 |
| Curtis, James, 25 Feb. 1754, Sinah Holland | 2 SO-16 |
| Curtis, Nathaniel, 3 Oct. 1745, Sus'h Thomas | 1 QA-51 |
| Curtis, Samuell, 16 June 1762, Priscilla Williams | 2 SO-117 |
| Cusack, Ben, 22 July 1771, Ann Jones | 1 SM-136 |
| Cusdary, John, 23 Jan. 1728, Deborah Buckley | 4 AA-430 |
| Cutchin, Robert, 20 April 1731, Winiford Brewenton | 2 BA-82 |
| Cutchin, Thomas, 28 Oct. 1713, Jane Hicks | 2 BA-3 |
| Cutchin, Thomas, 5 Dec. 1743, Mary Gott | 2 BA-189 |
| Cuthart, Robt., 10 Dec. 1724, Mary Higgens | 2 TA-110 |
| Cutler, Francis, 30 Jan. 1745, Eleanor Wooden | 3 BA-158 |
| Dabbs, John, 8 mo. 1655, Nan Evans | 1 KE-38 |
| Dadd, Emmanuel, 29 (?) 1769, Elizabeth Harvey | 2 AA-409 |
| Daffin, Charles, 1775, (?) Bozman | 1 CR |
| Daffin, George, 13 Feb. 1773, Mary Bankson | 3 BA-170 |
| Daffin, Joseph, c.Aug. 1775, Eleonar Ennalls | 1 CR-6 |
| Dail, James, 28 March 1771, Ann McGaberon | 2 BA-262 |
| Daintrey, Richard, 23 Nov. 1727, Elizabeth Mason | 2 PG-4 |
| Dakes, George, 28 Nov. 1762, Mary Addams | 2 SO-124 |
| Dakes, James, 14 April 1748, Edeliah Addams | 2 SO-17 |
| Dakes, Robert, 13 Dec. 1749, Elizabeth Lows | 2 SO-18 |
| Dale, Dr. John, 21 April 1767, Mary Colegate, dau. of Richard Colegate, Jr. | 2 BA-98 |

Daley, James, 21 Dec. 1749, Mary Tippins                    1 QA-56
Daley, James, 20 April 1758, Araminta Sparks               1 QA-63
Dallam, Josias Middlemore, 25 Jan. 1770, Sarah Smith       1 BA-387
Dallam, R'd., 16 May 1765, Fra. Paca                       2 BA-228
Dallam, William, 10 Jan. 1737, Eliz. Johnson               2 BA-110
Dallam, Maj. William, 23 July 1754, Ann Matthews           1 BA-350
Dallam, Winston Smith, son of Richard and Frances,
   9 day, 1 mo., 1772, Margaret Gover, dau. of
   Ephraim and Elizabeth                                   7 SF-23
Dalowin, John, 29 March 1733, Ann Trayman                  2 TA-153
Dalton, Richard, 17 June 1736, Ann Maccaully               4 AA-438
Dancer, William, 8 Oct. 1777, Sarah Nutbrown               10 BA-69
Dande, Ralph, 23 Sept. 1714, Mary Fox                      1 BA-214
Dandridg, John, Nov. 1703, Joanna Hall                     3 AA-98
Daniell, Edward, 11 Oct. 1703, Ruth Sacurn                 3 KE-264
Danielson, Zochoriah, 29 Dec. 1777, Sarah Benson           3 PG-99
Dannelson, Thomas, 22 Jan. 1721/2, Susannah Cannon         1 AA-89
                                                           & 309
Dannely, Jeremiah, 24 Oct. 1771, Eliz. York                2 BA-263
Dannock, John, 16 Jan. 1743, Mary Palmore                  2 BA-125
Danson, Isaac, 12 Feb. 1745, Sarah Addams                  2 SO-19
Darby, John, 3 Dec. 1733, Ailce Gay                        3 BA-151
Darby, Nathaniel, 10 April 1721, Eliz. Demitt, widow       3 BA-146
Darden, Jo:, 12 June 1745, Mary Porter                     3 TA-53
Dare, Nath'l, 29 Aug. 1747, Ann Tongue                     2 AA-388
Dare, Patrick, 10 April 1705, Sarah Todd                   4 AA-390
Dariel, Emanuel, 18 Feb. 1739, Judieth Tennant             1 QA-45
Darlington, William, 4 June 1745, Ann Hind                 3 BA-157
Darnal, Francis, 12 Sept. 1756, Margrt Hernly              2 BA-214
Darnall, Henry, 5 June 1756, Sarah Golt                    1 QA-61
Darumple, (?), (no date given), Sarah Braser; the
   marriage took place "in the forest."                    2 BA-249
Dasheel, Benjamin, 25 Dec. 1777, Ann Yoe                   1 CA-111a
Dashiel, Capt. Joseph, 18 May 1757, Martha Bluett          1 WI-44
Dashiel, Thomas, 8 May 1757, Anne Guibert                  1 WI-44
Dashiell, Charles, 1 Jan. 1732/3, Elizabeth Ballard        1 WI-14
Dashiell, Capt. Clement, 5 Jan. 1740/1, Sarah Piper,
   dau. of William                                         1 WI-30
Dashiell, George, 6 Aug. 1760, Arosey (?) Fisher           1 WI-57
Dashiell, Henry, 1 Jan. 1755, Sarah Renshaw                1 WI-49
Dashiell, Isaac, 13 Aug. 1747, Henrietta Scarburgh         1 WI-56
Dashiell, James, 14 Sept. 1763, Sarah Evans                1 WI-100
Dashiell, Jesse, 9 Aug. 1739, Susanna Townsend             1 WI-47
Dashiell, Lowther (?), 19 Nov. 1743, Anna Piper,
   dau. of William                                         1 WI-39
Dashiell, Mathias, 25 Jan. 1775, Mary Hopkins              1 WI-107
Dashiell, Robert, 16 Sept. 1735, Esther Handy              1 WI-4
Dashiell, Thomas, 29 Oct. 1747, Jane Renshaw               1 WI-51
Dashiell, William, 25 Sept. 1768, Mary Fountain            1 WI-84
Dashiell, William F., 24 Aug. 1777, Prise (?) Evans        1 WI-107
Dashiells, Mitchell, son of Thomas, 16 Oct. 1743,
   Margit Collins (?)                                      1 WI-80
Daugherty, Obed, 20 June 1773, Rhoda Addams                2 SO-207
Daugherty, William, 2 Oct. 1737, Mary Bartle               1 BA-306
Davice, Jacob, 6 Feb. 1745, Eliz. Greer                    2 BA-193
Davice, John, 31 Jan. 1749, Martha Bull                    2 BA-200
Davice, Thos., 31 Jan. 1758, Eliz. Carback                 2 BA-217
Davice, Wm., 7 Feb. 1739, Mary Leech                       1 QA-45
Davice, Wm., 27 March 1763, Sarah Andrews                  2 BA-224
Davidge, Capt. John, 7 Nov. 1723, Mary Docwray             4 AA-421
Davidge, Robert, 12 May 1726, Rachel Warfield              4 AA-426
Davidson, Benjamin, 16 Oct. 1774, Elizabeth Baker          3 BA-171
Davidson, John, 2 July 1733, Mary Burk                     2 TA-153
Davidson, John, 14 Sept. 1769, Eleanor Strachan            1 AA-148
Davies, Isaac, 12 June 1701, Mary, widow of Robert
   Hopper                                                  1 AA-32

| | |
|---|---|
| Davies, Thomas, 7 April 1708, Anne Gross or Groce | 1 AA-76 |
| Davies, William, 19 Feb. 1659, Sarah Coming | 1 KE-129 |
| Davinn, Thomas, 10 Sept. 1771, Ann Harryman | 2 BA-263 |
| Davis, Beauchamp, 13 Feb. 1764, Naoma Beauchamp | 2 SO-125 |
| Davis, Benjamin, 25 Dec. 1738, Mary (?) | 1 WO-88 |
| Davis, Benjamin, 26 May 1757, Mary Cawood | 1 CH-197 |
| Davis, Benj., 26 Dec. 176-(?), Mary (?) | 1 WO-2 |
| Davis, Benjamin, 1 Jan. 1770, Maria Ritterin | 8 BA-176 |
| Davis, Charles, 11 May 1762, Sarah Moreland | 1 CH-193 |
| Davis, Christian, 2 Jan. 1749/50, Frances Coleman | 3 BA-163 |
| Davis, Christopher, 10 Dec. 1728, Frances Hill | 2 BA-30 |
| Davis, Daniel, 27 July 1725, Bridget Jones | 2 TA-111 |
| Davis, Daniel, 14 Feb. 1765, Ann Johnson | 1 AA-155 |
| 9 AA-249 gives same information. | |
| Davis, Mr. David, 2 Jan. 1726/7, Elizabeth Oldham | 2 TA-114 |
| Davis, David, 23 Jan. 1763, Elizabeth Dooley | 1 BA-374 |
| Davis, Edward, 14 May 1711, Mary Young | 3 KE-265 |
| Davis, Edward, 4 June 1735, Susannah Cope | 3 BA-153 |
| Davis, Francis, 2 Dec. 1764, Lydia Dent | 1 CH-198 |
| Davis, Henery, 24 Aug. 1711, Ann Foxen | 3 KE-265 |
| Davis, James, 26 April 1668, Ann Marckum | 6 SO-400 |
| Davis, James, 27 Jan. 1709, Panelipa Reed | 3 KE-265 |
| Davis, James, 2 Aug. 1741, Eliz'h Corker | 1 QA-47 |
| Davis, John, 6 June 1703, Eleoner Spicer | 2 AA-321 |
| Davis, John, 2 June 1730, Elizabeth Clark | 4 AA-432 |
| Davis, John, 19 Nov. 1732, Jane Anderson | 2 TA-152 |
| Davis, John, 22 July 1740, Jane Greenhough | 3 TA-24 |
| Davis, John, 3 April 1746, Anne Tribbles | 3 TA-57 |
| Davis, John, 15 Dec. 1757, Margaret Richardson | 1 QA-63 |
| Davis, John, son of Richard, 1758, Ariana Worthington | 3 AA-112 |
| Davis, John, 10 Sept. 1761, Mary Marschand, widow | 4 FR-1122 |
| Davis, John, 27 Dec. 1768, Margaret Atweel | 9 AA-250 |
| Davis, John, son of Thomas, 12 June 1770, Frances | |
| Mercer, dau. of Robert | 3 CE-28 |
| Davis, John Eberhard, 1 July 1764, Anna Reitenauer | 4 FR-1122 |
| Davis, Jonas, 26 April 1668, Anne Marckum | 4 SO-708 |
| Davis, Joseph, 2 Oct. 1744, Mary Barker | 1 CH-177 |
| Davis, Luke, 26 Feb. 1737/8, Anne Hunt | 1 CH-180 |
| Davis, Mathias, 16 Dec. 1764, Martha Powell | 1 WO-14 |
| | & 88 |
| Davis, Nicholas, 15 Oct. 1707, Martha Fitchgerald | 3 KE-264 |
| Davis, Peter, 19 Aug. 1749, Rebecca Bunting | 3 TA-74 |
| Davis, Philemon, 9 June 1757, Mary Wright | 1 QA-62 |
| Davis, Phillip, 19 Dec. 1703, Tabitha Norreist | 3 KE-264 |
| Davis, Philip, 16 Feb. 1770, Cloe Paston | 1 CH-200 |
| Davis, Phillip, 29 Dec. 1734, Elizabeth Wells | 1 QA-40 |
| Davis, Phillip, 23 Sept. 1745, Ann Austin | 1 QA-51 |
| Davis, Richard, c.1675, Elizabeth Barry | 5 SO-397 |
| Davis, Richard, 14 March 1675/6, Elizabeth Berre | 9 SO-401 |
| Davis, Richard, 15 Sept. 1719, Ruth Warfield | 4 AA-409 |
| Davis, Richard, 19 April 1724, Mary Jackson | 3 KE-267 |
| Davis, Richard, son of Richard, 26 March 1746, Sophia | |
| Symson, dau. of Amos | 6 AA-212 |
| Davis, Robert Pain, 10 March 1771, Mary Toogood | |
| Collins | 1 AA-153 |
| Davis, Thomas, 8 Nov. 1670, Judith Best | 7 SO-401 |
| Davis, Thomas, Sept. 1671, Judith Bloyes | 5 SO-397 |
| Davis, Thomas, 1676, Mary Nicholson | 9 SO-401 |
| Davis, Thomas, 7 May 1687, Sarah Guy | 5 SO-397 |
| Davis, Thomas, tailor, 1693, Elizabeth Clouder, dau. | |
| of Richard and Temperance | 3 CH |
| Davis, Thomas, 18 Aug. 1719, Eliza Ryder | 2 PG-2 |
| Davis, Thomas, 7 April 1732, Rachell Oyzer | 3 CE-14 |
| Davis, Thomas, 9 Jan. 1734/5, Rebecka Gregory | 3 CE-19 |
| Davis, William, 26 March 1667, Anne Hooper | 4 SO-666 |

Davis, William, 26 March 1667, Elizabeth Hooper          6 SO-400
Davis, William, Aug. 1667, Anne Hooper                   5 SO-397
Davis, William, 17 June 1705, Joanna Everitt             3 AA-97
Davis, William, 27 April 1718, Jane Robinson             3 KE-266
Davis, William, 22 Aug. 1736, Ann Lovegrove              3 KE-268
Davis, Zaccheus, 15 April 1759, Margaret Stone           1 CH-195
Davise, Soll., 20 Nov. 1760, Kesie Tudor                 2 BA-220
Davison, Charles, 6 July 1755, Elizabeth Adams           1 QA-59
Davison, John, July 1740, Rachal Bliss                   1 QA-46
Davity, Robert, 25 April 1771, Margaret Ellison          2 BA-262
Dawdredge, Wm., 3 Sept. 1749, Margaret Murphy            2 BA-244
Dawkins, Richard, 10 Feb. 1733, Jane Thornton            1 BA-269
Dawkins, William, 9 Aug. 1720, Mary Mackall              1 CA-114
Dawley, Thomas, 6 Oct. 1742, Mercy Abbott                2 TA-173
Dawney, James, 20 Nov. 1743, Mary Yeats                  2 BA-239
Dawney, John, March 1716, Lydia Swift                    2 BA-14
Dawney, Thomas, 1730, Anne Cowdrey                       2 BA-39
Dawson, Edward, Jr., 24 Jan. 1720/1, Marg't Allum        2 PG-2
Dawson, Enoch, 17 Sept. 1769, Eliz. Legat                2 BA-259
Dawson, John, 16 Sept. 1692, Elizabeth Thirst            3 CH
Dawson, John, 29 Dec. 1735, Ann Megrah                   2 TA-160
Dawson, John, 24 Nov. 1746, Marg't Dawson                3 TA-62
Dawson, Ralph, 14 April 1741, Anne Dawson                3 TA-30
Dawson, Ralph, 13 Sept. 1746, Eliza Harrington           3 TA-61
Dawson, Richard, 23 day, 8 mo., 1698, Susanna Foster     8 SF-379
Dawson, Solomon, son of Benjamin, of Kent Co., Del.,
  1 day, 2 mo., 1777, Lydia Bartlett, dau. of Joseph     8 SF-157
Dawson, Thomas, 2 Jan. 1700, Sarah ffuller               3 AA-96
Dawson, William, 30 June 1740, Alice Sutton              3 TA-23
Day, Edward, April 1681, Jane Walker                     5 SO-397
Day, Edward, 22 May 1722, Abarilla Taylor                2 BA-19
Day, Edw., 8 Feb. 1749, Ann Fell                         2 BA-200
Day, Edward, 19 Sept. 1771, Rebecca Clagett              2 BA-263
Day, Francis, 16 Nov. 1710, Elizabeth Simson             1 AA-77
Day, Francis, 5 Feb. 1732, Avis Ward                     1 AA-115
Day, George, 10 June 1669, Ellianor Ditty                5 SO-397
Day, Hezekiah, 12 July 1713, Alce Bonney                 2 BA-2
Day, John, of Edward, 20 July 1742, Philizanna Maxwell   2 BA-127
Day, John, of Edward, 30 Dec. 1764, Sarah York           2 BA-227
                                                           & 264
Day, John, son of Stephen Day of Bacon Fields in
  Buckinghamshire, Eng., 26 June 1765, Mary Evans        3 BA-169
Day, John, 30 Nov. 1775, Mary Gouldsmith Presbury        2 BA-264
Day, Joseph, son of John and Lydia, c.1762, Katherine
  (?) (last name not given)                              9 SF
Day, Nicholas, 14 July 1709, Elizabeth Cox               2 BA-42
Day, Sam'll, 14 Jan. 1722, Elizabeth Grey                1 WI-94
Day, Samuel, 17 Feb. 1723, Mary Ann Jordan               2 TA-106
Daye, John, 21 June 1733, Lydia Ross, dau. of Alex-
  ander and Katherine                                    9 SF
Deadman, Edm'd, 30 Jan. 1753, Eliz. Corbin               2 BA-207
  2 BA-242 gives her name as Corben.
Deadman, Thomas, 24 Sept. 1749, Sarah Griffin            2 BA-244
  2 BA-199 gives date as 2 Oct. 1749, and her name
  as Griffith.
Deal, James, 14 Feb. 1726/7, Eliza Wells                 2 AA-376
Deal, James, 12 Jan. 1731/2, Rachel Giles                2 AA-376
Deal, John, Jr., 25 Feb. (?), Hannah Heve-(?)            1 WO-4
Deale, John, Aug. 1776, Elizabeth Galwith                2 AA-413
Deale, William, 2 June 1777, Ann Norris                  7 AA-1
  8 AA-13 gives date as 5 June 1777; see also
  2 AA-413.
Dean, John, 12 Sept. 1774, Mary More                     1 SM-136
Dean, Jos., 4 Dec. 1770, Joan Stone                      1 SM-135
Dean, Richard, 3 Jan. 1739, Elizabeth Marsh              3 BA-156

| | |
|---|---|
| Deane, James, 31 Jan. 1773, Ann Lavy | 2 AA-411 |
| Deane, James, Feb. 1773, Sarah Lowey | 2 AA-411 |
| Dear, Finniss, 26 May 1757, Ellis Benston | 2 SO-122 |
| Deason, Benjamin, 21 Nov. 1742, (?) Shepard | 2 BA-238 |
| Deason, Benjamin, 9 Dec. 1742, Tarrisha Shepherd | 2 BA-124 |
| Deason, John, 1 May 1749, Mary Hall | 2 BA-198 |
| | & 243 |
| Deason, Joseph, 27 Nov. 1746, Ketura Hall | 2 BA-195 |
| | & 240 |
| Deason, Samuel, Sept. 1737, Mary Johnson | 2 BA-93 |
| Deason, William, 9 Feb. 1739, Anne Shepperd | 2 BA-103 |
| Death, Randall, 1733, Honour Kersy | 1 CE-334 |
| Deaver, Basil, 25 day, 11 mo., 1748, Chew Pierpoint | 4 SF |
| Deaver, John, 21 Oct. 1742, Perina Greenfield | 1 BA-325 |
| Deaver, John, 11 May 1756, Ann Bond | 1 BA-352 |
| 2 BA-213 gives same information. | |
| Deaver, Jno., 19 July 1759, Susannah Rigbie | 2 BA-218 |
| Deaver, Richard, Jr., 1 March 1732, Sarah Pritchard | 1 BA-263 |
| Deaver, Thomas, 9 June 1730, Deborah Hartley | 1 BA-282 |
| Deaver, William, 16 Dec. 1754, Susannah Birchfield | 1 BA-372 |
| Deavor, John, 12 July 1707, Hannah Bell | 2 AA-332 |
| Deavor, Stephen, 7 Jan. 1710, Mary Smith | 2 AA-341 |
| Debarway, Hugus, 10 June 1740, Cathe Dawley | 2 TA-160 |
| Debrula, John, 12 April 1704, Mary Drunkord | 1 BA-201 |
| Debrular, George, 20 Oct. 1713, Esther Lewis | 3 KE-266 |
| Debrular, John, 14 May 1743, Frances Burridge | 1 BA-337 |
| Debrular, Peter, 22 Dec. 1712, Margrett Skidmore | 3 KE-265 |
| Debruler, Benj., 25 Feb. 1756, Semele Jackson | 2 BA-213 |
| Debruler, John, 14 May 1744, Frances Buredy | 2 BA-190 |
| Debruler, William, 23 March 1743, Diana Greenfield | 2 BA-46 |
| | & 137 |
| Debruler, Wm., 9 Feb. 1764, Sarah Watters | 2 BA-226 |
| Debson, William, 16 Dec. 1737, Sarah Dunn | 1 QA-43 |
| Decausse, Leonard, 31 March 1746, Mary Hawkins | 3 BA-159 |
| Dedman, Thomas, (no date given), (wife's name not | |
| given) | 2 AA-354 |
| Deepup, John, 1 Jan. 1724, Marg't Smith | 2 TA-111 |
| Deere, John, 22 Aug. 1658, Eliz. Robinson | 1 KE-129 |
| Deford, Isac, 22 Dec. 1741, Eliz'h Johnson | 1 QA-47 |
| Deford, John, 21 Dec. 1732, Anne Tombins | 1 QA-39 |
| Deford, John Tomlin, 21 Sept. 1755, Eliz'th Bolton | 1 QA-60 |
| Deford, Lewis, 10 April 1735, Alice Wickes | 1 QA-40 |
| Deford, Luis, 3 Dec. 1745, Est'r Weeks | 1 QA-51 |
| Deford, Thomas, 19 May 1757, Mary Beal | 1 QA-62 |
| Deford, Thomas Lewis, 4 Sept. 1750, Mary Ann Austin | 1 QA-57 |
| Deford, William, 20 Nov. 1755, Mary Matthews | 1 QA-60 |
| Degen, George, 8 Jan. 1770, Catharina Seersin (?) | 8 BA-176 |
| Degroate, Aron, 10 Nov. 1697, Mary Collens | 3 CE-2 |
| Dehay, David, 13 Jan. 1736, Sarah Tilbury | 3 BA-156 |
| Delaha, Thomas, 26 June 1743, Sarah Withgott | 3 TA-43 |
| Delahanty, Edmond, 28 Feb. 1748/9, Mary Carvin | 3 TA-72 |
| Delahauntee, John, 2 June 1747, Hannah Neal | 3 TA-65 |
| Delahay, Henry, 3 Nov. 1742, Mary Combs | 3 TA-40 |
| Delahay, James, 12 Nov. 1719, Cornelia Fromiller | 2 TA-91 |
| Delahay, John Mullikin, 31 Jan. 1738, Eliza Ogle | 2 TA-166 |
| Delahay, Thomas, 9 July 1681, Eve Rich, dau. of | |
| William | 1 TA-602 |
| Delahay, Thomas, 22 June 1729, Elizabeth Abbott | 2 TA-120 |
| Delahuntee, Edmond, 10 July 1750, Sarah Prouse | 3 TA-78 |
| Delannaway, Thomas, 18 May 1749, Elizabeth Evans | 1 QA-55 |
| Delehay, Henry, 10 Nov. 1742, Marg't Combes | 2 TA-173 |
| Delehay, James, 20 Aug. (?), Sarah Prichard | 2 TA-263 |
| Delehay, James, 24 Aug. 1730, Sarah Prichard | 2 TA-149 |
| Delehay, Thomas, 29 June 1743, Sarah Withgott | 2 TA-198 |
| Delimere, Dávid, 27 Feb. 1701, Elizabeth Mauldin | 1 CA-111 |

Delinham, Robert, 8 March 1708, Jane Baxter                1 AA-256
Dement, William, son of John, 27 Aug. 1775, Elizabeth
  Bryan                                                    1 CH-203
Demett, James, 22 Sept. 1757, Rachel Sinclare             2 BA-216
Demett, William, 3 Oct. 1744, Sarah Smithers              2 BA-191
Demilliane, Gabriel, minister, 31 Jan. 1704, Ann
  Young                                                    1 CA-111
Demitt, James, 27 March 1723, Barbara Broad               2 BA-77
Demmett, Jno., 10 Jan. 1765, Rhoda Sinkler                2 BA-227
Demmett, Thomas, 26 Dec. 1734, Sophia Stansbury           3 BA-153
Demmett, Wm., 13 Dec. 1764, Dorothy Swann                 2 BA-227
Demmett, William, Jr., 13 May 1736, Cathrene Wardin
  Bull                                                     2 BA-77
Demmitt, Jno., 5 Aug. 1759, Frances Waits                 2 BA-219
Demorse, John, 2 Feb. 1743, Susannah Ramsey               2 BA-190
  2 BA-239 gives date as 1 Jan. 1744.
Demorse, Lewis, 6 Jan. 1743, Margrett Ramsey              2 BA-189
  2 BA-239 gives date as 1 Jan. 1744.
Dempster, David, 14 Nov. 1745, Rachel Seward              1 QA-51
Dempster, John, 27 June 1722, Jane (?)                    1 QA-36
Denaven, Dennis, 3 Oct. 1711, Rebecca Howard              1 AA-78
Denes, William, 30 Dec. 1733, Sarah Bennet                2 PG-6
Denham, Edward, 20 April 1726, Middleton Derrumple        1 BA-243
Denis, Jeames, 29 Aug. 1725, Abigall Nicols               2 TA-112
Denison, Thomas, 6 Feb. 1723, Elinor Readin               2 KE-191
Denning, John, 23 Nov. 173-(?), Mary Hackert              2 KE-225
Denning, John, 24 Dec. 1737, Mary Harper                  2 KE-220
Denning, Stephen, Jan. (?), Mary Greenwood                3 KE-264
Dennis, John, 16 June 1765, Eliaabeth Bateman             9 AA-249
Dennis, Samuel, 24 Nov. 1734, Alice Carragan              1 BA-282
Denny, James, 24 Dec. 1742, Mary Aldren                   3 TA-41
Denny, Joseph, 2 Jan. 1739, Rebecca Turner                2 TA-168
  3 TA-20 gives date as 26 Nov. 1739.
Denny, Peter, 10 Nov. 1747, Lucy Richardson               3 TA-67
Denson, John, 22 Dec. 1737, Eliz'th Cowen                 1 BA-299
Denston, William, 25 Oct. 1750, Esbal Townsand            2 SO-21
Dent, Hezekiah, 9 Nov. 1769, Catherine Poston             1 CH-199
Dent, Hezekiah, 13 Feb. 1774, Martha Burch                1 CH-204
Dent, John, 3 Feb. 1757, Margaret Dyson                   1 CH-194
Dent, John, 19 Jan. 1777, Eleanor Cecil                   2 AA-413
Dent, Peter, 6 May 1753, Mary Elinor Hawkins              1 PG-303
Dent, William, 8 Feb. 1684, Elizabeth Fowke, dau. of
  Mrs. Anne Fowke of Port Tobacco                         3 CH
Denton, John, 3 Feb. 1739, Rachel Down                    2 BA-122
Denton, Jno., 15 April 1765, Sarah Starkey                2 BA-228
Denton, Vachel, 23 Nov. 1721, Mrs. Anne Brice             4 AA-416
Denton, William, 17 Feb. 1725, Sarah Dallahide            2 BA-24
Denton, William, Jr., 1735, Rosanna Standton              2 BA-103
Denton, William, March 1739, Ann Wooden                   2 BA-106
Denton, William, Jr., 2 Feb. 1744, Mary Roberts           2 BA-156
Denton, William, 14 Dec. 1756, Mary Roberts               2 BA-214
Denune, William, 24 Dec. 1728, Elizabeth Duvall, dau.
  of Mareen                                                2 PG-5
Denune, William, 23 March 1762, Elizabeth Forest          9 AA-247
Denwood, Wilson, 31 Aug. 1758, Margaret Skirvin           1 SO-161
Depost, Martin, 16 Jan. 1697, Tammeson Holt               1 BA-178
Depost, Martin, Dec. 1729, Martha Anderson                1 BA-250
Derickson, Benj., 13 Feb. 1730, Lisha Whorton             1 WO-3
Derickson, Joseph, 27 Oct. 1730, Mary Vaples              1 WO-7
Derrick, John, 17 Dec. 1713, Susannah Richard             3 KE-266
Derrumple, John, Feb. 1734, Ellinor Allen                 1 CA-113
Derrumple, John, 10 July 1718, Grace Constable            1 CA-113
Deshroun, John, 7 Oct. 1728, Frances Hill                 1 WI-13
Desney, William, 20 Nov. 1756, Cathrine Loge              2 BA-214
Dessorne, Jasper, 19 Oct. 1732, Rebecca Short             1 AA-114

| | |
|---|---|
| Detter, William, 6 Oct. 1736, Jane Quine | 2 BA-77 |
| Dever, John, 5 Nov. 1776, Rebecca Talbot | 3 BA-669 |
| Devereux, Joseph, 25 April 1732, Anne Smith | 1 QA-38 |
| Devilbiss, George, 1772, at Wilmington, Del., Elizabeth Ogle | 5 FR-18 |
| Devinish, Robert, 25 April 1705, Elizabeth Whitehead | 3 KE-264 |
| Devonish, Robert, 22 April 1741, Hannah Devonish | 3 KE-268 |
| Devor, Richard, 23 Nov. 1703, Mary (?) | 2 AA-328 |
| Devor, Richard, 16 Dec. 1711, Mary Shierbott | 2 AA-344 |
| Dew, Robert. 3 Oct. 1754, Easther Reaven | 2 BA-211 |
| Dewley, William, 21 Oct. 1725, Blanch Jones | 1 BA-259 |
| Diamond, John, June 1743, Alis Hollingsworth | 1 QA-48 |
| Dias, Thomas, Sept. 1674, Jane Pelingham | 5 SO-397 |
| Dicas, Edward, 30 Sept. 1734, Ann Phillips | 3 KE-268 |
| Dicas, William, 25 Dec. 1707, Elizabeth Ambrose | 3 KE-264 |
| Dick, William, 1 Jan. 1773, Sarah Belt | 3 AA-113 |
| Dickenson, James, son of Wm. and Elizabeth, of Tal. Co., 21 day, 9 mo., 1717, Hannah Coale, dau. of Wm. and Eliza | 6 SF |
| Dickerson, Leven, 25 July 1753, Susannah Milbourn | 2 SO-20 |
| Dickeson, Charles, 2 Aug. 1739, Elizabeth Coston | 2 SO-17 |
| Dickeson, Edmond, 6 Jan. 1763, Mary Taylor | 2 SO-124 |
| Dickeson, Joshua, 2 Feb. 1758, Eliner Mitchell | 2 SO-23 |
| Dickeson, Josiah, 1 Feb. 1762, Bettey Redden | 2 SO-124 |
| Dickford, Isaac, 15 Aug. 1747, Mart Swift | 1 QA-53 |
| Dickin, Thomas, 30 May 1769, Mary Purdue | 2 BA-258 |
| Dickinson, Charles, 8 day, 5 mo., 1725, Sophyah Richardson | 8 SF-43 |
| Dickinson, Daniel, son of John, 13 day, 9 mo., 1746, Mary Hosier, dau. of Henry | 8 SF-106 |
| Dickinson, Henry (date not given), Sushanah Saratt | 1 PG-266 |
| Dickinson, James, 10 Aug. 1748, Rachel Taylor | 2 TA-283 |
| Dickinson, John, 23 Sept. 1692, Rebechah Thomas | 8 SF-9 |
| Dickinson, John, 11 June 1724, Rebekah Powell, dau. of Daniel | 8 SF-39 |
| Dickinson, John, 29 May 1730, Elizabeth Harrison | 8 SF-55 |
| Dickinson, John, 30 March 1758, Ann Trippe | 2 TA-287 |
| Dickinson, John, of Kent Co., Del., 27 June 1772, Lydia Powell, dau. of Thomas | 8 SF-147 |
| Dickinson, Samuel, 4 Jan. 1710, Judith Troth | 8 SF-454 |
| Dickinson, William, 16 Dec. 1680, Elizabeth Powell | 8 SF-328 |
| Dickinson, Wm., 8 Aug. 1743, Anne Bozman | 3 TA-44 |
| 2 TA-283 gives date as 24 Aug. 1743. | |
| Dickinson, William, 12 Jan. 1759, Laurana Richardson | 2 TA-286 |
| Dickson, Christopher, 11 April 1746, Mary Gardner | 3 AA-109 |
| Dickson, Henry, 5 Oct. 1758, Eliz. Tate | 2 BA-217 |
| Dickson, Peter, 24 May 1760, Margaret Peckoo | 1 BA-368 |
| Dickson, William, 26 Aug. 1701, Marack Care | 3 CE-3 |
| Dicus, William, 21 Dec. 1710, Mary Smith | 3 KE-265 |
| Digges, Jos., 30 Sept. 1770, Anne (Digges ?) | 1 SM-135 |
| Dikes, Henry, 24 Dec. 1756, Ann Allexander | 2 BA-214 |
| Dill, John, 7 April 1702, Sarah (?) | 2 TA-24 |
| Dill, John, 17 June 1732, Mary Early | 1 QA-39 |
| Dilling, William, 22 June 1729, Mary Willis | 3 KE-267 |
| Dillingham, Robert, 8 March 1708, Jane Bagster | 1 AA-77 |
| Dillon, Henry, 14 Feb. 1739, Mary Bannen | 3 TA-22 |
| Dillon, William, 30 May 1757, (?) Barrat | 1 QA-62 |
| Dimmitt, James, 27 March 1733, Barbary Broad | 3 BA-151 |
| Dingle, William, 12 April 1739, Ann Cook | 3 TA-16 |
| Dirickson, William, 7 March 1752, Arcadah Hazzard | 1 WO-10 |
| Dirrickson, Joseph, 7 Feb. 1768, Comfort Tunnell | 1 WO-16 |
| Dise, Stephen, 9 Nov. 1758, Mary Culling | 2 SO-122 |
| Disharoon, James, 29 Nov. 1775, Sarah Dority | 1 WI-115 |
| Disheroon, John, Jr., 21 Dec. 1732, Mary (?) | 1 WI-17 |
| Disheroon, William, 22 Sept. 1736, Mary Bullett | 1 WI-43 |

Dishroon, Lewis, Sr., 20 Nov. 1703, Jane Cox                      1 WI-21
Disney, Richard, 11 Feb. 1752, Elizabeth Guinn                    1 AA-132
Disny, Thomas, 29 June 1721, Anne Leffels                         1 AA-306
Dison, Edward, 28 April 1702, Anne Collett                        2 AA-317
Distance, Ralph, 13 May 1711, Sarah Whetston                      3 KE-265
Distance, Ralph, 21 April 1712, Elizabeth Frahill                3 KE-265
Ditto, William, 5 Dec. 1769, Leah Legoe                          2 BA-259
Dives, Chris., 24 June 1762, Sarah Nixion                        2 BA-223
Dives, Christopher, Aug. 1736, Sarah Arnell                      2 BA-112
Dives, Francis, 21 Nov. 1753, Mary Watters                       2 BA-209
Dives, Jno., 10 June 1766, Mary Greer                            2 BA-229
Divine, Charles, (date not given), Tamer Horner;
    last dated entry on page is 1 Aug. 1773                      2 BA-266
Dixon, Ambros, 13 March 1738, Martha Horsey                      2 SO-19
Dixon, David, 17 Dec. 1766, Mary Quinton                         2 SO-124
Dixon, George, 22 Jan. 1708, Mary Betty                          1 PG-273
Dixon, Isaac, 13 Aug. 1754, Sarah Lane                           2 SO-20
Dixon, John, 15 Dec. 1746, Mary Cox                              3 TA-63
    2 TA-279 gives date as 18 Dec. 1746.
Dixon, Nathaniel, 31 Dec. 1769, Ann Piper                        1 WI-91
Dixon, Peter, 24 May 1760, Margaret Peckoo                       1 BA-368
Dixon, Rich., 5 Jan. 1711, Alce Mackelfresh                      1 AA-78
Dixon, Robert, 20 April 1703, Ruth Manning                       1 CA-111
Dixon, Thomas, 12 Aug. 1672, Christiana Potter                   5 SO-397
Dixon, Thomas, 27 Feb. 1750, Grace Todvine                       2 SO-18
Dixon, William, 8 day, 4 mo., 1680, Elizabeth Crister-
    son                                                          8 SF-325
Dixon, William, 26 Aug. 1770, Anna Dasheal                       2 SO-125
    2 SO-126 gives her name as Dashiell.
Dixson, Henry, 6 Feb. 1764, Sarah Dallerhyde                     2 BA-226
Diz (Dietz), John Ad'm, 25 Sept. 1757, Mary Magd.
    Thom (or Thorn)                                              4 FR-1103
Doally, John, 25 Oct. 1755, Sueannah Mattox                      3 AA-111
Dobson, Charles, 27 Aug. 1751, Rachel Fitzhugh                   1 QA-58
Dobson, Isaac, 26 July 1730, Eliza Kerby                         2 TA-149
Dobson, Isaac, Jr., 20 June 1737, Hannah Powell,
    widow; 2 TA-163 gives date as 20 May 1737.                  2 TA-161
Dobson, James, 23 June 1745, Jane Montgomery                     2 BA-240
    2 BA-193 gives date as 1 July 1745 and the bride's
    name as Mongumry.
Dobson, James, 2 March 1749, Mary Wyatt                          1 QA-56
Dobson, James, 15 May 1759, Mary Linch                           1 QA-65
Dobson, William, 23 Aug. 1757, Rachel Cockling                   1 QA-62
Doce, John, 26 Nov. 1759, Eliz. Taylor                           2 BA-219
Docwra, Matthew, 17 Feb. 1729, Hannah Bourn                      1 QA-37
Dodd, Edmond, 11 Feb. 1730, Sarah MacKneat                       2 TA-150
Dodd, Jacob, 29 Jan. 1748, Mary Ayres                            1 QA-55
Dodson, Robert, 18 Aug. 1727, Mary Brumell                       2 TA-116
Doerry, Balthasar, 27 March 1759, Barb. Heinkely                4 FR-1104
Doerry, Peter, 5 May 1761, Cath. Feldman                        4 FR-1122
Dofler, Peter, 21 Dec. 1766, Margaret Schley                    4 FR-1122
Dolan, James, 13 Feb. 1745, Rebecca Thompson                     1 QA-51
Doley, John, 21 Oct. 1705, Margaret Hard                         1 AA-72
Doll, Conrad, 20 Sept. 1761, Ann M. Schisler                    4 FR-1122
Dolphin, Thomas, 1698, Elizabeth Edwards                        2 AA-295
Dommohay, Alex'd'r, 28 Feb. 1750, Mary Pamphillion              3 TA-82
Donahea, Daniel, 23 Sept. 1777, Sarah Swiny                    10 BA-69
Donahoe, John, 25 June 1704, Mary Conner                        3 KE-264
Donahue, Roger, 16 Jan. 1734, Elizabeth Thompson               1 BA-279
Donaldson, Jas., of Annap., merchant, 25 Feb. 1733/4,
    Mrs. Bridget Baxley                                         4 AA-436
Donallan, Thomas, 5 Feb. 1718, Elizabeth Dean                   2 TA-89
Donallin, John, 19 Sept. 1723, Suesannah Langley               2 TA-105
Donawin, Daniel, 27 July 1748, Johanna Arnold                   1 BA-48
Donawin, Thomas, 6 March 1731, Frances Hall                     1 BA-257

Donney, John, Nov. 1705, Hannah Dart                        3 AA-98
Donovan, Thomas, 6 March 1731, Frances Hall                 1 BA-257
Dooley, William, 15 Oct. 1725, Blanche Jones                1 BA-237
  1 BA-259 gives date as 21 Oct. 1725.
Door, Wm., 21 Sept. 1766, Bathsheba Green                   2 BA-229
Dorcey, John, 18 Dec. 1770, Marth. Woodland                 2 BA-261
Dorden, Stephen, 29 Nov. 1715, Rebechah Hosher, dau.
  of Henry                                                  8 SF-10
Dorden, Stephen, 1 Jan. 1695, Rebeckah Anderson,
  relict of Thomas Anderson                                 8 SF-366
Dorging, Patrick, 12 Sept. 1756, Mary Davis                 1 QA-61
Dorman, John, 31 Dec. 1672, Sarah Percell                   5 SO-397
Dorman, John, 1 Jan. 1750, Cathrin Tillmon                  2 SO-22
Dorman, Matthew, 19 Aug. 1672, Phillipa Gillman             5 SO-397
Dorman, Robert, 27 Nov. 1666, Elizabeth Knight              6 SO-400
Dorman, Samuel, 23 Dec. 1743, Rachel Tilman                 2 SO-18
Dorman, William, 15 Nov. 1764, Sarah Byrd                   1 WI-90
Dormon, Levin, 10 May 1772, Leah Dormon                     2 SO-127
Dorney, Jas., 14 Dec. 1743, Mary Yeats                      2 BA-189
Dorney, James, 14 May 1749, Anne Caddle                     2 BA-243
  2 BA-198 gives date as 9 Aug. 1749 and the bride's
  name as Ann Cadle.
Dorney, Jno., son of James, 19 Dec. 1771, Martha
  Woodland                                                  2 BA-78
Dorrington, Joseph, 18 Sept. 1705, Mary Shield              3 KE-264
Dorrington, Phillip, 2 Aug. 1708, Eliz'th Hutchins          3 KE-264
Dorsey, Caleb, son of John, (no date given), Sophia
  Dorsey, dau. of John                                      6 AA-216
Dorsey, Caleb, widower of Sophia, (no date given),
  Rebeckah Hammond                                          6 AA-216
Dorsey, Caleb, 24 Aug. 1704, Elinor Wharfield              4 AA-389
Dorsey, Elie, 24 Jan. 1744, Mary Crockett                   2 BA-192
Dorsey, Elisha, 15 Dec. (1768 ?), Mary Slade                2 BA-257
Dorsey, Henry, 31 July 1735, Elizabeth Worthington          6 AA-199
Dorsey, John, Jr., 22 Aug. 1702, Comfort Stimson            1 AA-58
                                                            & 251
Dorsey, John, 8 April 1708, Honor St-(?)                    4 AA-372
Dorsey, John, 2 Aug. 1724, Silvia Heathcoat                 1 CE-330
Dorsey, John Hammond, 16 Feb. 1743, Frances Watkins         2 BA-42
Dorsey, John Hammond, 20 Jan. 1772, Ann Maxwell             2 BA-264
Dorsey, Joshua, May 1711, Ann (?)                           6 AA-193
Dorsey, Joshua, 3 Nov. 1734, Flora Fitzsimmons              3 AA-108
  3 BA-152 gives same information.
Dorsey, Nicholas, 20 Dec. 1709, Frances Hughs               4 AA-379
Dorsey, Philemon, 19 Feb. 1738/9, Katherine Ridgely         6 AA-206
Dorsey, Vincent, 26 Oct. 1742, Sarah Day                    2 BA-124
                                                            & 149
Dortridge, Wm., 19 Oct. 1749, Margret Murphy                2 BA-199
Dottridge, William, 18 Sept. 1717, Lettice Taylor           2 BA-11
Doubtfy, Thos., 2 Nov. 1760, Luraner Poulson                2 BA-220
Dougety, Isaac, 7 Feb. 1758, Marth Ward                     2 SO-123
Dougherty, Nathaniel, 31 Oct. 1752, Rebeckah Marthews       2 SO-19
Dougherty, William, 2 Oct. 1737, Mary Bartle                1 BA-306
Douglas, William, 27 Sept. 1758, Mary Anderson              1 WI-72
Douglass, Benjamin, 16 Feb. 1775, Ann Middleton             1 PG-377
Douglass, Joseph Hamilton, 4 April 1768, Rachel Bayard      3 BA-170
Dove, Rich'd, 19 Jan. 1724, Martha Philips                  2 TA-111
Dove, Richard, 26 Aug. 1744, Mary Sisk                      2 TA-184
Dowd, Charles, 9 July 1777, Anne Sprauel                    7 AA-1
Dowdell, John, 9 May 1767, Catherine Buttler                2 TA-7
Dowell, Philip, 11 June 1702, Mary Tydings                  2 AA-318
Downes, Aaron, 11 Nov. 1756, Elizabeth Oxenham              2 CR-270
Downes, Charles, son of Charles, 25 Dec. 1775, Martha
  Russum, dau. of Edward                                    2 CR-270
Downs, Darby, March 1712, Ann Westbrook                     3 AA-99

| | |
|---|---|
| Downes, George, 12 June 1677, Anne Bossman | 9 SO-402 |
| Downes, George, 9 Aug. 1777, Ann Hall | 1 CR-10 |
| Downes, Nathan, 1 June 1774, Ann Cooper | 1 CR |
| Downes, Solomon, 29 Oct. 1754, Nancy Baning | 2 CR-270 |
| Downey, Ellixander, 21 Jan. 1747, Catherin Johnson | 1 QA-54 |
| Downing, Abednego, 30 June 1776, Millicent Waters | 1 CH-203 |
| Downs, Charles, 1 Jan. 1739, Mary Clayton | 1 QA-45 |
| Downs, Isaac, 25 April 1726, Eliza Vannasco | 1 AA-103 |
| Downs, Thomas, 15 Aug. 1738, Gulielmus Gooden | 1 BA-306 |
| Downs, Thomas, 5 Feb. 1754, Mary Clark | 2 BA-209 |
| Doyhaty, Morgan, 7 Aug. 1736, Mary Story | 1 QA-42 |
| Doyle, John, 7 April 1700, Jane Blaisdale | 3 KE-263 |
| Dozen, Peter, 25 Nov. 1711, Eliz'th Noble | 3 KE-265 |
| Drain, James, 14 Aug. 1733, Easter Hall | 3 AA-103 |
| Draper, John, 17 Nov. 1709, Abigal Symmons | 2 AA-339 |
| Draper, John, Jr., 9 Feb. 1734, Mary Rees | 1 BA-280 |
| Draper, Lawrence, 24 Dec. 1713, Mary Drew | 1 BA-213 |
| Draper, William, 11 Feb. 1703, Rose Hopper | 1 AA-64 |
| Drapper, William, 18 Feb. 1723, Abigal Brian | 1 AA-98 |
| Dreaden, Joshua, 3 Nov. 1771, Sarah Bowlva (?) | 2 SO-207 |
| Dreddin, David, 4 Sept. 1729, Hannah Noble | 2 SO-21 |
| Dreddin, Jonathan, 8 Nov. 1753, Rachel Weatherly | 2 SO-22 |
| Drew, Anthony, 17 May 1709, Margaret Brown | 1 BA-208 |
| Drew, George (date not given), Johannah Phillips | 1 BA-287 |
| Drew, George, 26 July 1722, Hannah Lusby | 4 AA-419 |
|   1 BA-246 gives her name as Hannah Lisbey. | |
| Driskell, Moses, 4 Feb. 1713, Katherine Elgin | 1 WI-6 |
| Driver, Christopher, c.Oct. 1775, Sarah Ringgold | 1 CR-6 |
| Drivett, Tidius, 9 April 1773, Ann Webster | 2 BA-266 |
| Druce, John, 11 Dec. 1746, Eleanor Maccalley | 4 AA-448 |
| Drudge, Jos., 12 July 1774, Ann Howard | 1 SM-136 |
| Drury, Charles, 2 June 1773, (?) Child | 2 AA-411 |
| Drury, Charles, 16 June 1733, Alice Adney, widow of | |
|   Mr. Moses Adney | 4 AA-435 |
| Drury, Ignatius, 11 Dec. 1769, Anastasia French | 1 SM-135 |
| Drury, Michael, 3 Nov. 1770, Ann Yets or Yates | 1 SM-135 |
| Drury, Philip, 4 Sept. 1770, Ann Newton | 1 SM-135 |
| Drury, Robert, 22 Aug. 1725, Mary (?) | 4 AA-425 |
| Duberly, William, 10 Oct. 1730, Mary Hill | 2 TA-149 |
| Ducke, William, 22 Feb. 1770, Jane Thompson | 2 BA-260 |
| Ducker, William, 21 Aug. 1721, Mary ffield | 2 PG-2 |
| Duckett, John, 3 March 1738, Sarah Haddock Waring | 9 AA-246 |
| Duckett, John, 9 Aug. 1759, Ann Raitt, dau. of John | |
|   and Ann Raitt | 2 PG-7 |
| Duckett, Richard, 13 Nov. 1729, Mary Nutwell | 2 PG-5 |
| Duckett, Richard, 2 June 173-(?), Eliz'h Williams (?) | 2 PG-6 |
| Duckitt, Richard, 26 Jan. 1698/9, Charity Jacob, dau. | |
|   of John and Ann | 1 AA-43 |
| Ducondry, Francis, 31 March 1703, Hellin Councill | 3 KE-264 |
| Duddin, William, 5 Feb. 1705, Elliner Ducondry | 3 KE-264 |
| Dudley, Abner, 27 April 1742, Rachel Clark | 3 TA-37 |
|   2 TA-172 gives date as 4 May 1742. | |
| Dudley, Joshua, 9 April 1777, Catherine Stewart | 3 BA-174 |
| Dudley, Richard, 4 Feb. 1718, Daborah Wilson | 2 TA-90 |
| Dudley, Richard, 16 Aug. 1774, Mary Manship | 1 CR |
| Dudley, Samuel, 2 Dec. 1720, Mary Needles | 2 TA-94 |
| Dudley, Thomas, 3 Nov. 1734, Eleanor Callender | 2 TA-157 |
| Dudley, William, c.Oct. 1775, Sarah Nicolls | 1 CR-6 |
| Dudly, James, 26 April 1728, Elizabeth Dobson | 2 TA-118 |
| Dudney, Roger, 10 Sept. 1708, Jane Leek | 1 BA-207 |
| Due, Samuel, 28 Jan. 1723, Jane Blamer | 2 TA-106 |
| Duell, Francis, 26 March 1750, Mary Eubanks | 3 TA-82 |
| Duerty, William, 13 Oct. 1704, Johannah Peurisably | 3 KE-264 |
| Duff, Simon, 28 Sept. 1728, Johana, widow of Saledine | |
|   Eagle | 3 AA-103 |

```
Duffey, Daniell, 25 June 1713, Elizabeth Rogers        3 KE-265
Duffy, Patrick, 27 Feb. 1737, Martha McHon             1 CH-174
Dugging, Alexander, 30 June 1750, Ann Miller           1 CE-292
Dugin, James, 11 Jan. 1775, Sarah Auren                1 CE-323
Duglis, Patriarch, 26 Dec. 1707, Margaret Bruer        2 AA-333
Duhamell, John, 26 Feb. 1759, Damsell Wilcox           1 QA-65
Duhataway, Jacob, son of Jacob and Marg't, 16 day,
   9 mo., 1712, Elizabeth Parrish, dau. of Edward
   and Mary                                            6 SF
Duke, Richard, 15 April 1729, Elianor Reves            1 AA-108
Dukes, John, April 1765, Mary Ann Townsend             2 SO-206
Dukes, Robert, April 1674, Elizabeth Dixon             5 SO-397
Dulany, Daniel, 2 Dec. 1754, Elizabeth Bradley         1 BA-373
Dulany, Dennis, 1734, Judah Odunoho                    1 WI-33
Dulany, Dennis, 23 Jan. 1749, Easter Fugate            2 BA-200
Dulany, John, 7 Sept. 1718, Mary Wilkinson             3 KE-267
Dulany, Lloyd, 15 June 1773, Elizabeth Brice           5 AA-4
Dulany, William, 1736, Mary Anderson                   2 BA-97
Duley, John, 9 Jan. 1717, Elizabeth Barnet             2 TA-82
Duley, James, 1771, Deborah Sheckel                    2 AA-410
Dulreple, Henry, 27 Oct. 1757, Mary Smith              2 BA-216
Dumbrill, Edw'd, 6 Feb. 1731, Anne Watts               1 AA-113
Dumillion, Benjamin, 14 Oct. 1777, Tabitha Burch       2 CH (1)
Dun, Dennis, 15 June 1746, Jane Crump                  3 BA-159
Dun, William, 31 July 1722, Mary Stokely               4 AA-419
Dunahoe, Cornelius, 23 July 1733, Mary Owens           3 KE-267
Dunahoe, John, 11 Aug. 1709, Elinor Sullovan           3 KE-264
Dunahoe, Thomas, 22 April 1747, Catherin Manson        1 QA-53
Dunbar, Govane, 29 June 1749, Sarah Lawrence           1 QA-55
Duncan, John, 25 May 1776, Margery Corner              2 TA-297
Dunford, John, 2 Nov. 1712, Honour Coffin              3 KE-265
Dunkan, George, 18 day, 4 mo., 1724, Mary Large        1 SF-56
Dunkan, George, 21 Jan. 1735, Margret Kinsey           1 SF-70
Dunkin, Robert, 3 Jan. 1749, Rosanna Hollinsworth      1 QA-56
Dunman, Henery, 23 Oct. 1712, Elizabeth Willis         3 KE-265
Dunn, Arthur, 2 June 1736, Margrett Fishpaw            3 BA-155
Dunn, David, 23 Dec. 1710, Sarah Lee                   3 KE-265
Dunn, Henry, 19 May 1755, Frances Williams             1 QA-59
Dunn, John, 2 June 1716, Mary Walker                   4 AA-397
Dunn, Robert, 9 May 1762, Sarah Wakeman or Pritchard   1 BA-367
Dunnick, John, 5 Dec. 1742, Mary Pasmore               2 BA-238
Dunning, James, 24 Jan. 1720, Anne Acton               1 PG-275
Dunnock, John, Dec. 1771, Casander Sutton              2 BA-263
Dunnowan, Darby, 24 May 1735, Eliza Buck               2 TA-159
Durbin, Daniel, 11 Aug. 1746, Ann Mitchel              1 BA-346
Durbin, Daniel, 12 Jan. 1764, Mary Johns, dau. of
   Richard and Anne                                    1 BA-381
Durbin, John, 20 Aug. 1715, Abarillah Scott            2 BA-7
Durbin, John, Jr., 16 Oct. 1740, Mary Hawkins          1 BA-314
Durbin, John, 13 Dec. 1743, Elioner Odan               2 BA-125
Durbin, John, 16 Sept. 1755, Rachel Childs             2 BA-212
Durbin, Jno., 2 Jan. 1759, Eliz. Smithson              2 BA-218
Durbin, Samuell, 4 July 1723, Ann Logden               3 BA-146
Durbin, Thos., 4 Oct. 1744, Margrett Stephens          2 BA-191
Durbin, Thomas, 28 May 1772, Frances sener Carty (sic) 2 BA-264
Durden, John, 7 Jan. 1713, Elisabeth Fowler            1 AA-269
Durden, Steven, 19 Aug. 1719, Mary Cox, dau. of
   Daniel                                              8 SF-21
Durdinn, John, 26 Aug. 1703, Anne White                1 AA-64
Durham, Da'd, 14 Nov. 1765, Sarah Smithson             2 BA-228
Durham, Edward, 28 Feb. 1728, Mary Gerish              1 BA-246
Durham, James, 12 Feb. 1720, Rebecca Anderson          2 BA-17
Durham, James, 30 Nov. 1729, Martha Booth              3 KE-267
Durham, Joshua, 10 Jan. 1754, Sarah Thompson           2 BA-209
Durham, Samuel, 15 Jan. 1723, Eleanor Smithson         2 BA-21
```

| | |
|---|---|
| Durham, Staley, 18 Feb. 1734/5, Mary Parlett | 3 BA-163 |
| Dushan, Phillip, 28 Oct. 1769, Eliz. Mallett | 2 BA-259 |
| Duskin, Michael, 6 June 1751, Sarah Johnson | 2 BA-203 |
| Duson, William, 31 Dec. 1700, Katherine Botham | 1 AA-56 |
| Dutenhoffer, Michael, 3 Jan. 1764, Rachel Wilkens | 4 FR-1122 |
| Dutton, David, 17 Sept. 1766, Bethui (sic) Bibbons | 1 WI-88 |
| Dutton, Isaac, 13 Oct. 1763, Elizabeth Hill; both were free mullatoes | 1 WI-73 |
| Dutton, Robert, son of John and Mary, 13 Nov. 1707, Ann Brown, dau. of William and Ann | 9 SF |
| Dutton, Rob't, 11 Dec. 1744, Mary Merriken | 2 BA-191 |
| Dutton, Robert, 24 Feb. 1757, Susanna Howard | 2 BA-177 |
| 4 SF-236 gives the year of marriage as 1755 and states that Robert was a son of Robert Dutton of Cecil Co., and that Susanna was a dau. of Lemuel Howard. | |
| Dutton, Robert, Jr., son of John and Mary, 24 day, 2 mo., 1757, Susanna Howard, dau. of Lemuel and Ann | 9 SF |
| Duval, Mareen, 1 Oct. 1724, Ruth Howard | 1 AA-99 |
| Duvall, Benj., 5 June 1738, Mary Wells | 9 AA-246 |
| Duvall, Charles, 16 Dec. 1764, Rebecca Beckett | 9 AA-248 |
| Duvall, John, 23 Oct. 1738, Ann Fowler | 9 AA-246 |
| Duvall, John, 16 Oct. 1768, Sarah Hiet | 9 AA-250 |
| Duvall, Lewis, 5 March 1699, Martha Ridgely | 1 AA-57 |
| Duvall, Lewis, 26 Nov. (1722 ?), Ellinor Farmer, dau. of Samuel | 2 PG-2 |
| Duvall, Lewis, 3 Oct. 1777, Elizabeth Wheeler | 1 AA-2 |
| Duvall, Mareen, 21 Oct. 1701, Elizabeth Jacob | 1 AA-57 & 248 |
| Duvall, Samuel, 18 June 1697, Elizabeth Clarke | 1 AA-37 |
| Duvall, Samuel, 16 (May ?), 1732, Elizabeth Mullikin | 2 PG-5 |
| Duzan, Peter, 24 July 1777, Keziah (?) | 1 HA-200 |
| Dwyer, Darby, 13 Oct. 1730, Mary Edgett | 2 TA-149 |
| Dyall, William, 7 Jan. 1728, Joannah Cannon | 2 TA-119 |
| Dyer, Nathaniell, 17 Feb. 1703, Elizabeth Staying | 3 KE-264 |
| Dyer, Patrick, 12 Oct. 1702, Comfort Barnes | 1 PG-263 |
| Dyer, Santelo (?), 7 Nov. 1723, Margaret Ryley | 2 PG-3 |
| Dyne, Jac., 16 March 1777, Eleanora More | 1 SM-137 |
| Dyson, Bennett, 27 Jan. 1765, Winifred Chunn | 1 CH-193 |
| Dyson, James, 17 Jan. 1744/5, Abigail Swann | 1 CH-183 |
| Dyson, Joseph, 17 April 1752, Elizabeth Chunn | 1 CH-186 |
| Dyson, Thomas, 17 Feb. 1760, Esther Dent | 1 CH-195 |
| Dyson, William, 31 Dec. 1700, Kath. Botham | 1 AA-246 |
| Eades, Henry, 17 Sept. 1696, Elizabeth Ware | 3 CE-1 |
| Eads, Joseph, 21 July 1745, Margaret Mansil | 1 QA-51 |
| Eads, Thomas, 19 Dec. 1704, Katherine Layton | 3 KE-269 |
| Eads, Thomas, 5 Jan. 1705, Mary Steal | 3 KE-269 |
| Eager, Thomas, 24 Aug. 1705, Hannah Pennington | 4 AA-390 |
| Eagle, Ralph, 13 Aug. 1722, Amy Gwillim | 1 AA-92 & 314 |
| Eagle, Ralph, 28 June 1729, Marg'tt Pew | 4 AA-431 |
| Eagle, Saladine, 19 May 1719, Joanna Mersey | 4 AA-408 |
| Eaglestone, Abraham, 20 Dec. 1730, Charity Johnes | 3 BA-150 |
| Earl, Thomas, 25 Nov. 1717, Welthan Wiggins | 2 TA-81 |
| Earl, Thomas, 29 Jan. 1718, Mary Taylor | 2 TA-89 |
| Earle, James, 11 Nov. 1737, Anne Scot | 1 QA-43 |
| Earle, John, April 1729, Martha Ringgold | 3 KE-270 |
| Earnshaw, John, 25 Nov. 1701, Elizabeth Clerk | 3 AA-96 |
| Earnshaw, John, 17 Feb. 1731, Rachel Locket | 3 AA-103 |
| Eason, Samuel, 20 Dec. 1716, Sarah Johnson | 2 TA-79 |
| Eaton, Anderton, 18 Nov. 1745, Sarah Stanton | 3 TA-55 |
| Eaves, George, 1 Sept. 1714, Mary Costley | 1 BA-215 |
| Eberhard, Rev. Nicholas Henry, 21 Feb. 1764, Sarah Van Vleck; marr. at Bethlehem (Penna.?) | 5 FR-22 |

```
Eberly, Valentine, 28 Feb. 1767, Ann. Barb. Schmid,
  widow                                                 4 FR-1126
Ebert, Michael, 6 Aug. 1761, Mary Clara Kappel          4 FR-1126
Eberz, Mathew, 7 April 1761, Cath. Magd. Mans           4 FR-1126
Ebtharp, Thomas, 18 Nov. 1733, Elizabeth Number         3 CE-17
Eddrington, Thomas, 30 Jan. 1732/3, Ann Oliver          3 CE-15
Eby, John, 12 Feb. 1765, Anna Mary Banz                 4 FR-1126
Eddee, Jonathan, 4 April 1743, Rebecca York             2 BA-125
Edelen, Christopher, 1707, Jane Jones                   1 PG-276
Edelen, Thomas, son of Richard, 9 Feb. 1719, Mary
  Blanford                                              1 PG-268
Edelin, Christopher, 24 July 1757, Rebecca Johnson,
  dau. of Dr. George                                    1 FR-11
Edens, Johns, 1771, Anne Vincent                        2 AA-411
Edgar, John, 18 Feb. 1740, Mary Wales                   3 TA-29
Edge, Aaron, 28 Aug. 1703, Ann Pew                      2 TA-37
Edge, James, 6 Feb. 1739/40, Hannah Davis               3 TA-21
Edmondson, Caleb, son of William, 16 June 1736,
  Esther Underhill, dau. of John                        9 SF
Edmondson, James, 18 Dec. 1691, Magdalen Stevens        8 SF-355
Edmondson, James, 31 day, 12 mo., 1773, Martha
  Bartlett                                              8 SF-148
Edmondson, John, 28 May 1685, Susannah Omeli            8 SF-339
Edmondson, John, 3 day, 7 mo., 1730, Mary Neal          8 SF-57
Edmondson, John, Jr., 28 Jan. 1763, Mary Neal,
  dau. of Edward                                        8 SF-107
Edmondson, John, 1 May 1772, Esther Bartlett            8 SF-143
Edmondson, Samuel, son of William, 10 Nov. 1736,
  Isabel Underhill, dau. of John                        9 SF
Edmondson, Solomon, 3 day, 8 mo., 1723, Esther
  Kennerly                                              8 SF-37
Edmondson, Thomas, 7 Aug. 1699, Mary Grasum, relict
  of Robert Grasum                                      8 SF-397
Edmondson, William, 25 Feb. 1692, Sarah Sharp           8 SF-363
Edmondson, William, 3 day, 11 mo., 1716, Margaret
  Berry, dau. of James                                  8 SF-14
Edmondson, William, 29 March 1720, Priscilla Cole       8 SF-29
Edmondson, William, 1 day, 10 mo., 1730, Elizabeth
  Troth, Jr.                                            8 SF-58
Edmondson, Wm., 2 Sept. 1746, Marg't Neighbours         3 TA-60
Edmondson, William, 6 day, 12 mo., 1769, Sarah Smith    8 SF-136
Edmonson, John, 20 April 1727, Mary Williams            2 TA-115
Edmundson, Archibald, 11 Dec. 1777, Blandey Sheen       1 WA-531
Edmundson, John, son of Caleb and Esther, 11 Oct.
  1764, Sarah Mendenhall, dau. of Joseph and Rachel     9 SF
Edmundson, Pollard, 5 March 1738, Mary Dickinson        2 TA-166
Edney, Thomas, 3 Dec. 1747, Constant Peningtone         3 BA-160
Edward, John, 23 Nov. 1769, Unity Legatt                2 BA-259
Edwards, Cadwallader, 12 April 1710, Mrs. Catherine
  Bourn                                                 4 AA-379
Edwards, Edward, Jan. 1734, Jemima Welsh                1 AA-119
Edwards, Edward, 18 Nov. 1742, Eliza Chilton            4 AA-444
Edwards, Edw'd, 1 April 1762, Cas. Beard                2 BA-223
Edwards, Isaac, 9 Oct. 1740, Rachel Banning             2 TA-170
Edwards, James, 9 March 1775, Ruth Stansbury            3 BA-171
Edwards, John, 15 Dec. 1709, Sarah Beetle               3 KE-270
Edwards, John, 23 Jan. 1727, Mary Merryman              3 BA-148
Edwards, Jonathan, son of Jonathan and Isabel, 1 June
  1763, Rachel Huff, dau. of Michael and Janet          9 SF
Edwards, Mosess, 1 May 1753, Ann Pickett                2 BA-208
Edwards, Steph., 21 July 1739, Hannah Clear             1 QA-45
Edwards, Walter, 18 Nov. 1749, Mary Small               1 QA-56
Edwards, William, 21 Aug. 1705, Susanna Piaripin        3 KE-269
Edwards, Wm., 17 Sept. 1748, Jane Broad                 2 BA-197
                                                        & 243
```

Edwards, William, 12 April 1760, Mary Manes            2 BA-220
Edwards, William, 30 April 1771, Susan Airs            2 BA-262
Edwin, William, 14 Dec. 1714, Mary Lewis              3 KE-270
Edy, William, 15 May 1759, Sarah Hilton              2 BA-218
Edye, William, 22 Nov. 1770, Cloe Standiford          2 BA-261
Eg (Ely?), John Henry, 18 Aug. 1761, Rosina Schmitt   4 FR-1126
Egle, Thomas, 6 Nov. 1763, Mary Bay                  2 BA-225
Egleston, Benj'n, 18 Aug. 1764, Sarah Dallas          2 BA-226
Egleston, Thos., 15 Sept. 1764, Cloe Dallas           2 BA-227
Eigenbrod, John Yost, 1756, Eva Maria Schorer        5 FR-24
Ekhart, Adam, 16 Aug. 1757, Eva Reisz (Rice)         4 FR-1103
Elder, Angel Bartenstin, 26 Dec. 1763, Mary Shelvey  2 BA-226
Elder, Charles, 14 Feb. 1769, Ruth Howard            4 BA-74
Elder, John, 19 Oct. 1708, Mary Morris               4 AA-378
Elder, Owen, 10 April 1766, Nancy Dorsey             4 BA-74
Eldrake, James, 29 June 1745, Sarah Raddle           3 TA-54
Eldrake, John Adam, 29 Sept. 1734, Anne Fairbanks    2 TA-157
Elenor, Andrew, 5 day, 3 mo., 1656, Anicake Hanson   1 KE-38
Ellcott, Phill Lock, 3 Sept. 1762, Sarah Sparks      2 BA-223
Elledge, Joseph, 4 Sept. 1733, Mary Rhoades, dau.
   of Richard and Magdalen                           2 BA-41,
                                                       & 75
Elliot, George, 20 June 1769, Theresa Anderson       2 BA-258
Elliot, James, 9 March 1759, Mary Atkins             2 BA-258
Elliot, Joseph, 18 Sept. 1748, Hannah Williams       1 QA-54
Elliot, Matthew, 30 Jan. 1721/2, Mary Richardson     1 AA-89
Elliot, Thomas, 1753, Rebecca Norris                 2 BA-242
Elliot, William, 7 May 1741, Karen Johnson           1 BA-318
Elliott, George, 12 Jan. 1732, Patience Buckner      3 BA-151
Elliott, George, 26 March 1756, Lucretia Bartlett    1 QA-61
Elliott, James, 29 Dec. 1736, Mary Weecks            2 BA-155
Elliott, James, 8 May 1753, Temperance Armstrong     2 BA-208
Elliott, James, 29 Dec. 1757, Agnes Harris           2 BA-216
Elliott, Jno., 23 Dec. 1761, Eliz. Wright            2 BA-222
Elliott, Marberril, 13 Jan. 1756, Jemima Standeford  2 BA-213
Elliott, Phillip, 22 Dec. 1752, Sarah Wright         2 BA-206
Elliott, Thomas, Nov. 1736, Eliz. Barton             2 BA-75
Elliott, Thomas, 14 April 1748, Ann Robinson         2 BA-196
Elliott, Thomas, Jr., 30 Jan. 1753, Rebecca Norris   2 BA-207
Elliott, Thomas, son of Thomas and Elizabeth, 29
   July 1765, Mary Chew, dau. of Benjamin and Sarah  1 CE-300
Elliott, William, 22 Jan. 1729, Tabitha Cleave       1 QA-36
Elliott, William, 17 May 1740, Karran Johnson        2 BA-205
Ellis, Jeofry, 11 June 1736, Martha Roe              1 QA-42
Ellis, John, Jr., Sept. 1686, Mary, widow of Thomas
   Shiletto                                           5 SO-397
Ellis, John, 2 April 1703, Margaret Coflin           3 KE-269
Ellis, Thomas, 25 Feb. 1733, Mary Carr               2 TA-155
Ellsby, Thomas, 31 Jan. 1726/7, Elizabeth Long       2 TA-115
Ellsom, Robert, 15 Dec. 1735, Jane Taylor            3 BA-154
Ellt, Henry, 21 June 1703, Elizabeth Topin           1 CA-113
Ellwood, Rich'd, 9 Oct. 1748, Mary Linzey            2 BA-197
   2 BA-243 gives her name as Lindsay.
Elms, Mabry, 6 Feb. 1734, Ann Puntany                3 BA-153
Elmsworth, Israel, 5 April 1777, Prisila Elleott     1 WI-114
Elmsworth, William, 25 March 1750, Rachel Beard      1 WI-87
Elson, John, 1 Feb. 1728/9, Joanna Bradcutt          2 PG-5
Elson, William, 2 Sept. 1764, Sarah Peach            9 AA-248
Elston, Ralph, Jr., 24 Nov. 1681, Elizabeth Bridges,
   dau. of Richard                                   1 TA-604
Elston, Ralph, 12 June 1739, Sarah Greason           2 TA-167
Elston, Rob't, 1 Aug. 1721, Eliz'th Parker           1 BA-254
Elton, William, 10 Oct. 1748, Dorothy Steel, widow   4 AA-451
Ely, Thomas, 24 day, 1 mo., 1776, Hannah Warner,
   dau. of Crosedale                                 7 SF-34

```
Elzey, Arnold, 8 Nov. 1750, Margaret Lindew            3 SO-4
Elzey, John, 19 May 1736, Major (sic) Shiles           1 WI-68
Elzey, John, 20 Feb. 1758, Mary Collins                1 WI-68
Emersent, Jonathan, 3 May 1721, Allice Grimes, widow   4 AA-414
Emerton, John, 21 Jan. 1698, Mary Herrington           2 AA-296
Emery, Daniell, 28 Nov. 1703, Mary Smith               1 AA-64
Emes, John, Sept. 1749, Elizabeth Stiles               2 BA-244
Emmerson, Woolman, c.Oct. 1775, Esther McGregory       1 CR-6
Emmerton, Jno., 15 Jan. 1712, Sarah Armstrong          2 AA-346
Emmit, Nathanel, 7 (March?) 1740, Hanna Davice         1 QA-45
Emory, Arthur, 25 July 1745, Rachal Curtis             1 QA-51
Emory, John, 14 Sept. 1758, Juliana Hawkins            1 QA-64
Emory, Thomas, 9 day, 6 mo., 1749, Sarah Bartlett      1 SF-86
Endsworth, Benjamin, 2 March 1741/2, Mary Willson      1 QA-47
England, Isaac, of Duck Creek, Newcastle Co., Del.,
   12 Aug. 1714, Elizabeth Hoodt, of Sassafras R.      1 SF-52
England, Isaac, 13 March 1741, Ann Corse               1 SF-76
England, Jno., 16 day, 3 mo., 1727, Marg't Birckhead   6 SF
England, John, son of John and Mary, 16 day, 11 mo.,
   1768, Sarah Swayne, dau. of Edward and Sarah        9 SF
England, John, 10 May 1727, Margaret Birckhead         9 SF
England, Joseph, son of Lewis, 20 April 1742,
   Elizabeth Dutton, dau. of Robert and Ann            9 SF
England, Joseph, son of Samuel and Sarah, 15 Jan.
   Jan. 1767, Deborah Haines, dau. of Joseph and
   Elizabeth                                           9 SF
England, Samuel, son of Joseph and Margaret, 11 Nov.
   1740, Sarah Slater, dau. of George and Sarah        9 SF
England, Thomas, 7 Aug. 1757, Annenal Saunders         1 QA-62
English, James, Sept. 1681, Sarah Bee                  5 SO-397
English, James, 10 Feb. 1743/4, Amey (?) Waller        1 WI-37
English, Thomas, 23 Dec. 1730, Hannah Cloak            1 QA-37
Enloes, Abraham, 1730, Mary Deason                     2 BA-99
Enloes, Abra., 28 Nov. 1754, Jemima Elliott            2 BA-211
Enloes, Henry, 26 May 1763, Mary Ellcott               2 BA-225
Enloes, Thos., 2 June 1754, Sarah James                2 BA-210
Enloes, Wm., 2 Feb. 1761, Avarilla Beck                2 BA-221
Ensor, Abraham, 30 Jan. 1750, Mary Merriman            3 BA-164
Ensor, George, 24 Dec. 1739, Elizabeth Reeves          2 BA-113
Ensor, John, 14 May 1700, Elizabeth Hines              1 AA-50
   1 AA-57 gives her name as Elizabeth Evans, widow.
Ensor, John, Jr., 6 March 1753, Eleanor Todd           3 BA-167
Ensor, John, 2 July 1772, Dorcas Gorsich               2 BA-264
Ensor, Thomas, 27 Jan. 1739, Mary Costley              2 BA-123
Ensor, Thomas, 22 Nov. 1770, Mary Talbott              2 BA-181
                                                       & 261
Enzor, Wm., 4 Sept. 1766, Martha Costley               2 BA-229
Ephernon, Robert, c.Oct. 1775, Rachel Santee           1 CR-6
Ereckson, John, 24 Feb. 1714, Elizabeth Trew           3 KE-270
Erickson, Erick, 27 July 1745, Eliz. Baker             2 BA-193
Ervine, David, 30 June 1751, Constant Sears            2 BA-203
Erwin, John, 2 Sept. 1733, Ann Dobson                  2 TA-153
Eskridge, George, 12 Jan. 1770, Elisabeth Coulbourne   2 SO-129
Ettland, William, 19 Nov. 1705, Mary Gore              3 KE-269
Eubanks, Thomas, Jr., 11 July 1717, Jean Clother,
   widow                                               8 SF-17
Eubanks, William, 9 Aug. 1704, Hannah Hall             8 SF-426
Eustis, John, 6 Jan. 1728, Margret Lowder              2 TA-119
Evall, Samuell, 25 Oct. 1713, Sarah Randall            3 KE-270
Evan, Jones, 6 Oct. 1709, Ann Drincall                 2 AA-338
Evans, (?), (?) Feb. (?), Elizabeth (?)                1 WO-4
Evans, (?), 4 Nov. (?), Sarah Hook                     1 WO-5
Evans, David, bricklayer, June 1743, Sarah Long        4 AA-445
Evans, David, 23 Nov. 1760, Elizabeth Marican          1 AA-139
Evans, David, 3 Dec. 1772, Eliz. Chance                2 BA-265
```

```
Evans, Edward, 22 May 1677, Mary Daniell            5 SO-397
Evans, Edward, 3 Dec. 1724, Rachel Johnson          1 BA-236
Evans, Evan, 15 Sept. 1713, Sarah Ambrose           3 KE-270
Evans, Gammag, 6 Oct. (?), Rachel Lockwood          1 WO-4
Evans, Isaac, 13 Sept. 1777, Mary Sboiwd (sic)      1 WA-527
Evans, John, 7 July 1713, Rebecca Comagys           3 KE-270
Evans, John, Jan. 1722/3, Martha Evans, dau. of John 2 PG-3
Evans, John, 22 Feb. 1727, Sarah Campbell           1 WO-6
Evans, John, Jr., March 1738/9, Mary Evains         1 WI-37
Evans, John, 7 Sept. 1755, Mary Forkner             2 BA-212
Evans, John, 16 Nov. 1756, Mary Collins             1 WO-10
Evans, John, Jr., 29 May 1773, Sarah Dashiell       1 WI-97
Evans, Joseph, 17 June 1776, Anne Ellicott          5 BA-5
Evans, Nicholas, 27 July 1749, Priscilla Gillis     1 WI-40
Evans, Richard, 14 March 1704, Hester Dunton        1 AA-65
Evans, Richard, 24 April 1720, Mary Rice            1 AA-299
Evans, Rowland, 2 Jan. 1716, Joan Washfield         2 TA-79
Evans, Samuel, 7 Dec. 1738, Priscilla Moore         9 AA-246
Evans, Thomas, 15 Dec. 1777, Sarah Husk             7 AA-2
Evans, Walter, 9 Aug. 1748, Ann Truitt              1 WO-9
Evans, William, 11 Oct. 1754, Mary Knotts           2 CR-270
Evans, William, 22 May 1755, Susanna Hines          1 QA-59
Evans, William, 27 July 1777, Mary Driskill         10 BA-68
Eveans, Joseph, 25 Oct. 1764, Philothis Francis     9 AA-247
Evens, Griffith, 17 Feb. 1704, Eliz. Curtis         2 TA-43
Evens, John, 19 Dec. 1731, Catherine Cook           3 BA-150
Evens, John, 21 Aug. 1745, Hannah Mister            2 SO-129
Evens, Leven, 7 Nov. 1767, Mary Bird                2 SO-128
Evens, Thomas, 13 Jan. 1714, Patience Jackson       2 TA-75
Evens, William, 28 May 1744, Scarbrough Corbin      2 SO-23
Everard, Lawrence, 1714, Sarah Slyng                4 AA-392
Everat, John, 5 May 1771, Eliz. Jackman             2 BA-262
Everdson, Everd, 1731, Annacart Plow                3 CE-16
Everdson, Jacob, 30 Dec. 1742, Hester Vanhorn, dau. of
  Nicholas                                          3 CE-23
Everet, James, 27 Dec. 1777, Mary Brown             10 BA-70
Everet, Samuel, 9 Dec. 1755, Hannah White           2 BA-212
Everett, Jas., 27 Dec. 1777, Mary Brown             9 BA
Everett, John, 31 Oct. 1728, Rebecca Poteet         2 BA-67
Everett, John, Aug. 1739, Comford Pearson           2 BA-109
Everett, John, 5 May 1771, Eliz. Jackman            2 BA-262
Everett, Wm., 25 Dec. 1764, Sarah Bord              2 BA-227
Everit, Larrance, 15 Oct. 1747, Phillip Ewbank      1 QA-53
Everitt, Hales, 23 June 1771, Priscilla Beck        4 KE-18
Everitt, Joseph, 26 day, 10 mo., 1774, Sarah Hewett 3 SF
Everitt, Samuel, 7 Aug. 1759, Mary Hutchinson       1 QA-65
Everitt, Thomas, 20 Dec. 1747, Margarett Price      1 BA-344
Everson, Everd, 29 July 1731, Elizabeth Harper      3 CE-15
Everton, Jeremiah, 21 March 1702, Hannah Irish      1 AA-64
                                                    & 254
Everton, Thomas, April 1686, Ann Wood               5 SO-397
Eves, Edw'd, 17 Feb. 1752, Lucy Ann Pine            2 BA-204
Evins, Robert, 22 Aug. 1771, Ann Bartinn            2 BA-262
Evitt, Arthur, 26 April 1668, Mary Grey             4 SO-708
Ewbanks, William, 15 Sept. 1757, Esther Countis     1 QA-62
Ewen, John, 29 April 1759, Mary Pratt               1 QA-65
Eyams.  See Ijams.
Eyles, Samuel, 27 March 1749, Elizabeth Swift       1 QA-55
Fabs, John, 30 Nov. 1708, Ann Snow                  2 TA-52
Fairbairn, Benjamin, 29 April 1777, Mary Ann Williams 5 AA-6
Fairbank, John, 14 Jan. 1700, Mary (?)              2 TA-12
Fairbanks, Thomas, 12 Jan. 1742/3, Mary Bridges     3 TA-41
Fairchild, Edw'd, 6 Dec. 1761, Margery Brittingham  2 BA-222
Fairebrother, Thomas, 5 June 1712, Mary Fuller      1 AA-78
Falcom, Thomas, 30 Jan. 1757, Sarah Emory           1 QA-62
```

```
Falconar, Alexander, 9 Feb. 1719, Susanna Duvall        2 PG-2
Falkner, Abraham, 17 Aug. 1738, Eliza Kemp              2 TA-165
Fallowfield, Wharton, 8 Nov. 1706, Catherine Hughs      2 TA-45
Fankake, Thomas, 26 Aug. 1733, Sarah Adams              3 CE-16
Fanning, John, Dec. 1702, Mary Davis                    3 KE-271
Fanning, Richard, 27 Jan. 1708, Alse Welsh              3 KE-271
Farebrother, Nathaniell, 13 Feb. 1723, Marg't Alce      1 AA-326
  1 AA-98 gives her name as Mary Alce.
Farley, John, 29 Oct. 1737, Mary Weeks                  1 BA-290
Farlow, Thomas, 8 Feb. 1734, Elizabeth Little           1 BA-282
Farmer, Gregory, 27 Aug. 1703, Sarah Hughes             1 BA-199
Farmer, Gregory, 14 June 1723, Rachel Emson             1 BA-231
Farmer, John, 3 June 1735, Sophia Jones                 1 BA-285
Farmer, Peter, 22 Nov. 1737, Mary Wood                  1 BA-299
Farmer, Thomas, 21 Jan. 1741, Elizabeth Ross            1 BA-324
Farnan, Joseph, 15 Dec. 1777, Alice Sutton             10 BA-70
Farnell, Isaac, 24 Nov. 1769, Rebeca Sweeting           2 BA-259
Farquhar, Allen, son of William and Ann, 11 day, 4 mo.,
  1765, Phebe Hibberd, dau. of Benjamin and Phebe       3 SF
Farquhar, Moses, son of William and Ann, (date not
  given), Sarah Poultney, dau. of John and Eleanor      3 SF
Farran, Joseph, 15 Dec. 1777, Alice Sutton              9 BA
Farrand, John, 2 May 1743, Mary Stonestreet             1 CH-181
Farrand, John, son of John, 13 Dec. 1772, Elizabeth
  Broady                                                1 CH-206
Farrell, Ezekiel, 14 Dec. 1758, Sarah Honey             1 QA-64
Farrell, John, 5 Feb. 1718, Elisabeth Hinton            1 AA-289
Farrow, George, 30 Oct. 1715, Sarah Carroll             3 KE-273
Faurnan (?), Thos., 4 Aug. 1761, Sarah Chapman          2 BA-222
ffeaston, John, 17 Jan. 1722, Eve Withgott              2 TA-104
Feddeman, Bartholomew, 11 Nov. 1756, Esther Downes      2 CR-270
Fedderman, Richard, 12 March 1738, Jane Maynadier       2 TA-166
Fell, Edward, 8 Oct. 1730, Ann Thomas, dau. of
  Samuel                                                6 SF
Fell, Edw'd, 2 Nov. 1758, Ann Bond                      2 BA-218
Fell, William, 8 Jan. 1732, Sarah Bond                  3 BA-151
Fellows, Matthias, 1720, Honnor Price                   3 CE-16
ffenaly, Charles, 11 April 1711, Elizabeth Harris       1 PG-283
Fend, James, 18 March 1704, Ann Dunn                    2 AA-326
Fenden, Jos., 27 Jan. 1743/4, Catharine Mahan           3 TA-47
Fenwick, Jacob, 12 June 1776, Henrietta Howard          1 SM-137
Fenwick, John, 11 Nov. 1772, Mary Thompson              1 SM-136
Fenwick, Philip, 3 Sept. 1770, Rebecca Greenwell        1 SM-135
Fenwick, Thomas, 3 July 1774, Eliz. Thomas              1 SM-136
Ferguson, Benjamin, 1 April 1761, Mary Rutter           1 CE-301
Ferguson, John, 29 Nov. 1715, Mary Williams             2 PG-2
Ferill, John, 3 April 1716, Margret Wright              1 AA-79
Ferrall, James, 21 April 1728, Grace Fish               2 TA-270
Ferrill, Daniel, 19 Dec. 1703, Agnis Scott              3 KE-271
Feston, John, 19 Jan. 1729, Eleanor Welch               2 TA-121
Few, Isaac, 15 Aug. 1754, Jennet Fell                   2 BA-211
Fiddis, John, 7 Jan. 170(?), Elizabeth Mitchell         3 KE-271
Fidrack, Jacob, 14 Nov. 1757, Eliz. Blackwalldren       2 BA-216
Field, John, 23 Dec. 1729, Catherine Hogg               1 BA-252
ffield, Thomas, Sept. 1696, Ann Douglas                 1 AA-34
Fields, Christopher, 23 July 1746, Rebecca Hull         2 KE-261
Fields, William, Aug. 1777, (?) Clare Poor              2 CH (3)
Fillengan, John, 12 March 1733/4, Margaret Money        3 CE-19
Finall, John, 22 Sept. 1762, Hamutal Davis              9 AA-247
Findley, James, 2 March 1740/1, Sarah Rochister         1 QA-46
Findley, John, 17 March 1740/1, Margarit Muntz          1 QA-46
Findly, James, 7 Jan. 1741/2, Margaret Reed             1 QA-47
Finecan, Peter, 4 June 17-(?), Mary Bateman             3 KE-271
ffinicomb, William, 24 (March?) 1714/5, Jane Wells      4 AA-392
Finicum, William, 6 March 1753, Isabella Fisher         2 KE-280
```

```
Finley, Peter, 12 June 1774, Eleanor Murphy              6 BA(1)
Finley, Thomas, 22 July 1747, Althea Kidd               3 BA-160
Finly, Rob't, 21 Feb. 1754, Mary Tiller                 3 KE-274
Firor (or Vierhur), Leonard, (date not given), Maria
   Barbara Wilhide                                       5 FR-32
Firribl (sic), James, 22 April 1728, Grace Fish         2 TA-118
Firth, William, 23 Dec. 1731, Dorothy Hollinsworth      1 QA-38
Fish, Edmund, 4 Feb. 1734, Mary Bowdle                  2 TA-157
Fish, Jac., 22 Aug. 1777, Ann Wheatley                  1 SM-137
Fish, William, 24 May 1720, Lucretia Day                1 AA-299
Fishborn, Ralph, 9 day 9 mo., 1673, Sarah Lewis         8 SF-316
Fisher, Edward, 1 day, 8 mo., 1699, Frances Willis,
   relict of Richard Willis                             8 SF-383
Fisher, James, 21 July 1777, Mary Hollon                1 CR-10
Fisher, John, 20 Feb. 1717, Sarah Bryney                2 TA-83
Fisher, John Pritchett, 6 April 1774, Ruth Thomas       1 CR
Fisher, Jonathan, 28 June 1722, Christian Moll          3 KE-273
Fisher, Michael, 12 Oct. 1721, Abigail Snow             2 TA-96
Fisher, Obediah, 23 April 1727, Margrit Bengerfield     2 KE-221
Fisher, Risdon, 1775, Mary Parker                       1 CR
ffisher, Simon, 8 Aug. 1698, Elizabeth (?)              2 TA-10
Fisher, Simon, 22 April 1728, Mary Bryne                2 TA-117
Fisher, Stephen, 26 Jan. 1741, Elizabeth Goodwin        1 BA-330
Fisher, Thomas, 27 March 1722, Sarah Dudley             2 TA-102
Fisher, Thomas, 18 Feb. 1761, Amelia Whiteacre, widow
   of Peter                                             1 BA-369
Fisher, Wm., 7 Feb. 1732/3, Sarah Deal                  2 AA-369
Fisher, William, 4 July 1776, Elizabeth Child           2 AA-413
Fitch, Henry, 28 Feb. 1758, Ruth Bayley                 2 BA-217
Fitchew, Wm., 11 June 1736, Rachel Coleman              1 QA-42
Fitzgerald, Maurice, 13 May 1735, Mary Keys             1 QA-40
Fitzjarrall, Edmond, 20 Nov. 1715, Margret Clark        2 TA-76
Fitzpatrick, Charles, 20 Oct. 1742, Jane Fairbourn      1 BA-325
Fitzpatrick, David, 9 Oct. 1740, Eleanor Oram           3 TA-25
Fitzpatrick, Owen, 9 Feb. 1720, Deborah Rawlings        4 AA-413
Fitzsimmons, Jas., 10 Sept. 1761, Mary Conner           2 BA-222
Fizzee, Will'm, 21 June 1777, Sarah Dematt              1 HA-200
Flannagen, Bartholomew, Sept. 1750, Eliz. Clarage       2 BA-214
Flannel, Francis, 1748, Sarah Whaland                   2 BA-243
Flannen, Francis, 2 Oct. 1748, Sarah Whealand           2 BA-197
Fleehartee, John, 7 April 1735, Hannah Penick           1 BA-280
Fleming, William, 26 Oct. 1752, Jean Handy              2 SO-25
Fleming, William, 5 Nov. 1759, Mary Jane (?)            2 BA-219
Flemman, David, 22 Nov. 1777, Mary McNeal              10 BA-69
Flemman, John, 18 Jan. 1735, Rachel Barnett             2 TA-161
Flemming, John, 20 Nov. 1777, Anne Hopkins              1 MO-518
Flemming, Joshua, 29 Jan. 1753, Rachel Atkinson         2 SO-25
Fletcher, George, 23 Nov. 1727, Elizabeth Stamp         2 PG-4
Fletcher, John, 3 April 1757, Rachel Parramore, widow   1 WI-66
Fletcher, Levin, 15 Dec. 1764, Mary Maddux              1 WI-88
Fletcher, Thomas, 23 June 1751, Elizabeth Moor          1 WI-61
Fletcher, Wm., June 1742, Mary Christian                3 TA-38
Fletcher, William, 26 Aug. 1742, Mary Christian         2 TA-172
Flick, Andrew, 12 June 1768, Ann Magd. Reichardt        4 FR-1128
Flin, Cornelius, 30 Jan. 1710, Anne Lowe                2 TA-69
Flin, Cornelius, 18 May 1721, Sarah Mecotter            2 TA-96
Flin, Edward, 1748, Mary Linsey                         2 BA-242
Fling, Michael, 24 May 1729, Elizabeth Wilkinson        1 QA-36
fflitcher, Joseph, 10 Feb. 1701, Elizabeth (?)          2 TA-24
Flood, William, 26 March 1733, Jane French              1 BA-264
Flory, John, 26 Dec. 1769, Anna Maria Segesterin        8 BA-176
Flower, Ralph, 20 Oct. 1709, Mary Harris                2 AA-338
fflower, William, 10 Dec. 1732, Mary Brace              2 PG-6
Flowers, William, 8 Feb. 1734, Mary Killey              3 BA-153
Floyd, Jeremiah, 30 Dec. 1735, Sarah Dwiggins           2 TA-160
```

| | |
|---|---|
| Floyd, Jesse, 5 Nov. 1774, Eliz. Swailes | 1 SM-137 |
| Floyd, Jesse, 18 March 1777, Mary Carey Reed | 1 SM-137 |
| Floyd, Moses, c.Oct. 1775, Drucilla Rumbly | 1 CR-6 |
| Floyd, Rowland, 1 Dec. 1726, Sarah Knobs | 2 TA-114 |
| Floyd, Thomas, 15 Jan. 1724, Anna Dawson | 3 AA-101 |
| Floyd, Thomas, 23 day, 4 mo., 1755, Rachel Daughaday | 4 SF-49 |
| Floyd, William, 13 Jan. 1714, Magdilene Johnson | 3 KE-272 |
| Flutcher, William, 16 Nov. 1672, Mary King | 5 SO-397 |
| ffoard, James, 15 July 1711, Elizabeth Preston | 3 AA-100 |
| Foard, Thomas, 24 Feb. 1727/8, Briggett Grifith | 2 TA-117 |
| Foard, William, Jr., 9 July 1740, Margret Neavil | 1 QA-46 |
| Focher, John, 20 Dec. 1744, Jane Pearman | 2 KE-254 |
| Fogg, Amus, 15 July 1742, Elenor Young | 1 CE-290 |
| Folcome, Volentine, 14 Jan. 1735, Eliza Mackmayhan | 2 TA-161 |
| Fontaine, Marcey, son of Nicholas, 28 Nov. 1745, Betty Gillis, dau. of Thomas | 3 SO-4 |
| Fookes, James, 3 day, 5 mo., 1720, Elizabeth Kennerly | 8 SF-25 |
| Fooks, John, 8 Nov. 1743, Mary Welling | 3 TA-45 |
| Foord, Allison, 27 March 1760, Winnifred Wheeler | 1 PG-319 |
| Ford, Ambrose, 3 Jan. 1722, Elizabeth Combs | 2 TA-104 |
| Ford, Daniel, 10 Feb. 1745, Sarah Maud | 1 QA-51 |
| Ford, Geo., 4 Jan. 1773, Dominica Plowden | 1 SM-136 |
| Ford, Isaac, 18 Dec. 1735, Mary Powell | 1 QA-41 |
| Ford, Isaac, 29 June 1748, Mary Corker | 1 QA-54 |
| Ford, John, 16 Feb. 1727, Mary Pane | 1 AA-106 |
| Ford, John, 8 Nov. 1744, Mary Sewel | 2 KE-257 |
| Ford, John, 2 June 1755, Sarah Murphy | 1 BA-355 |
| Ford, Philip, 30 Sept. 1775, Eliz. Spalden | 1 SM-137 |
| Ford, Raphael, 20 Jan. 1771, Anne Spalden | 1 SM-135 |
| Ford, Richard, 20 May 1736, Rachel Devenish | 1 QA-42 |
| Ford, Thomas, 1 Jan. 1711, Leah Price | 1 AA-78 |
| Ford, Thomas, 28 Feb. 1727, Bridget Griffin | 2 TA-270 |
| Ford, Thomas, 20 Nov. 1735, Rebecca Burrough | 1 QA-41 |
| Ford, Thomas, son of John, 29 Nov. 1764, Elizabeth Ford | 4 BA-73 |
| Ford, William, 6 Dec. 1697, Elizabeth Groves | 3 KE-271 |
| Ford, William, 7 Feb. 1743, Winf'd Aaron | 1 QA-49 |
| Ford, William, 29 Oct. 1745, Mary Slay | 1 QA-51 |
| Ford, William, 10 Oct. 1749, Elizabeth Leet | 1 QA-56 |
| Forde, Robert, 7 April 1706, Rebeckah (?) | 2 KE-174 |
| Fordred, William, 27 July 1745, Rebeckah Williams | 2 SO-24 |
| Foreacres, John, 27 Jan. 1757, Jane Burk | 1 QA-62 |
| Foreasy, Peter, 4 Nov. 1758, Ann Axter | 2 BA-218 |
| Foreman, Arthur, 13 May 1700, Mary Reed | 3 KE-271 |
| Foreman, Arthur, 2 June 1715, Honour Miller | 3 KE-272 |
| Foreman, Ezikiah, 15 Jan. 1757, Mary Mills | 3 AA-111 |
| Foreman, Francis, 13 Feb. 1728, Eliz'th Chairs | 1 QA-36 |
| Foreman, Francis, 2 June 1740, Sarah Hammilton | 1 QA-46 |
| Foreman, Robert, son of John and Elizabeth, 18 day, 3 mo., 1766, Mary Naylor, dau. of John and Jane | 9 SF |
| Foresight, Joseph, 28 Dec. 1724, Mary Wilson | 2 BA-23 |
| Foresight, Joseph, 19 Aug. 1731, Mary Marshall | 1 BA-259 |
| Forester, Rev. George William, 30 Oct. 1746, Mrs. Mary Clay | 2 KE-263 |
| fforman, Joseph, 16 Feb. 1720, Anna Hurd | 3 AA-102 |
| Forman, Robert, son of John and Elizabeth of Bucks Co., Penna., 17 day, 3 mo., 1766, Mary Naylor, dau. of John and Jane | 4 SF-254 |
| Fornal, John, 26 June 1757, Ann Lewis | 1 QA-62 |
| Forrest, William, 1 July 1735, Lucy Duvall | 2 PG-6 |
| Forrester, Robert, 30 Sept. 1756, Mary Bennett | 1 QA-61 |
| Forsett, Henry, 10 Aug. 1771, Margret Beally | 2 BA-262 |
| Forster, Richard, 20 Aug. (?), Sarah Manely | 1 CE-330 |
| Forster, Thomas, 30 March 1738, Mary Hunter, dau. of William | 3 CE-23 |

```
Fortner, William, 26 Nov. 1759, Nelley Boring          1 WO-11
Forward, Jacob, 19 June 1764, Faithfull Webb           1 BA-388
Fositt, 25 Nov. 1669, (?) (?)                          1 TA-602
Fossett, John, 19 Nov. 1723, Jane Fletcher             2 PG-3
Foster, Bazaliel, 24 Dec. 1734, Mary Mead              3 BA-152
Foster, Bazil, 10 Dec. 1749, Mary Allender             2 BA-199
Foster, Francis, son of Francis, 20 day, 5 mo.,1762,
  Elizabeth Brown, dau. of Thomas and Elizabeth        9 SF
Foster, James, 25 July 1777, Sarah Johnson            10 BA-68
Foster, John, 15 Feb. 1703, Eliza Green                2 PG-1
Foster, John, 9 Jan. 1710, Alce Dixson                 2 TA-68
Foster, Richard, 11 March 1704, Eliz. Purnell          2 AA-326
Foster, Richard, 12 May 1715, Sarah Kare               3 CE-7
Foster, Rigby, 21 Oct. 1736, Eliza Tompson             2 TA-159
Foster, Rigby, 19 March 1745, Catherine Rennolds       2 TA-279
  3 TA-57 gives date as 14 March 1745/6 and the
  bride's name as Cath. Rennolds.
Foster, Sam'l, 26 Feb. 1749, Margrett Caton            2 BA-200
Foster, Samuel, 1750, Margaret Guiton                  2 BA-244
Foster, Thomas, 25 Nov. 17-(?), Sarah Cross            2 PG-6
Foster, Thomas, 3 Aug. 1729, Wealthy Ann Herrington    3 KE-273
ffoster, William, 15 April 1724, Mary Smith            3 CE-12
Foster, William, 2 Jan. 1735, Elener Poulson           1 CE-301
Fottrell, Edward, 10 May 1739, Acshah Woodward         9 AA-246
Foubert, Francis, 26 Dec. 1751, Mary Swift             1 QA-58
Foubert, Francis, 29 April 1756, Mary Downey           1 QA-61
ffoueller, Thomas, 15 Oct. 1696, Susan Ijams           1 AA-35
ffouler, Benjamin, 20 Sept. 1732, Hellen Mortimer      3 AA-107
Foulks, William, of Acamack Co., Va., 2 day, 6 mo.,
  1704, Mary Foster, Jr.                               8 SF-4
Fountain, Marcy, 14 Sept. 1686, Mary Bossman, dau.
  of John                                              5 SO-397
Fountain, Samuel, 17 Aug. 1774, Major (sic) Fountain   1 CR
Fouracres, John, 23 July 1735, Sarah Halts             1 QA-41
Fowke, Gerrard, 31 Dec. 1686, Sarah Burdett, youngest
  dau. of Mr. Thomas Burdett                           3 CH
ffowler, Benj., 4 Dec. 1729, Rachel Selby              4 AA-432
Fowler, Benoni, 24 Sept. 1734, Kezia Isaac             2 PG-6
Fowler, Daniel, 23 Dec. 1711, Anne Devor               2 AA-344
Fowler, Jeremiah, 10 Feb. 1738, Drusilla Isaac         9 AA-246
Fowler, John, 6 Oct. 1724, Mary Lynthicum              1 AA-99
Fowler, Patrick, 8 Feb. 1731, Eliz'th Lattimore        1 QA-38
Fowler, Peter, 10 Oct. 1704, Agnes Gray                1 CA-111
Fowler, Richard, 13 Sept. 1730, Honour Logsdon         3 BA-149
Fowler, Richard, 31 Dec. 1754, Mary Fitch              2 BA-211
Fowler, Robert, 18 April 1680, Mary Wheler, widow      1 TA-602
Fowler, Robert, 2 March 1730, Anne Lattemore           1 QA-36
Fowler, Samuel, 3 June 1736, Sarah MacCarty            1 BA-294
Fowler, Thomas, 3 Nov. 1726, Eliza Day                 1 AA-103
Fowler, Thos., 19 June 1766, Jane Taylor               2 BA-229
Fowlar, William, 25 Aug. 1724, Susanna Duvall          2 PG-3
Fowler, William, 19 Feb. 1776, Mary Mattingly          1 SM-137
Frampton, John, 23 Feb. 1720, Sarah Harris             2 TA-95
Frampton, Thomas, 30 Oct. 1732, Sarah Withbee          2 TA-152
Franchey, David, 29 July 1703, Elizabeth Powell        3 KE-271
Francis, George, 7 Dec. 1729, Martha Booker            1 AA-110
Francis, John, 14 Nov. 1703, Elizabeth Winck           3 KE-271
Francis, Tench, 29 Dec. 1724, Eliza Turbett            2 TA-111
Frankland, Thomas, 26 Oct. 1729, Ruth Willmott         3 BA-149
Franklin, Cha.:, 19 April 1756, Hannah Harsh           2 BA-213
Franklin, John, 30 May 1776, Elizabeth Ward            2 AA-413
Franklin, Jos., 15 Jan. 1756, Eliz. Oakley             2 BA-213
Franklin, Richard, 30 July 1777, Ann Duvall            7 AA-1
Franklin, Robt., 19 day, 8 mo., 1697, Arteridge Giles  6 SF
Franklin, Thomas, 27 May 1711, Grace Currant           1 CA-114
```

```
Franks, Mathias, 26 Nov. 1750, Mary Morris        2 BA-202
Frantham, William, 6 Jan. 1755, Ann Newnam        2 CR-270
Frantom, Joseph, 1775, Mary Ann Gannon            1 CR
Frantum, John, 27 Sept. 1774, Eliza Hopkins Shawnahan  1 CR
Fraser, Dr. Alexander, 27 July 1718, Elizabeth Thomas  4 AA-405
Fraser, Dr. Alexander, 19 March 1726, Mrs. Alison
  Roberson                                        4 AA-428
Fraser, John, 8 Jan. 1718, Mary Bowen             1 AA-289
Fraser, John T., 30 Aug. 1777, Cassandra Evans    3 PG-114
Frassiers, Robert, 30 Oct. 1704, Mary (?)         4 AA-389
Fray, Charles, 28 Oct. 1716, Mary Tibbals         2 TA-78
Fray, Philemon, 3 April 1738, Mary Cox            2 TA-164
ffrayzer, Alexander, 20 Aug. 1713, Mary Stoop, widow  3 CE-7
Freeman, Benjamin, 6 Jan. 1717, Mary Macclefresh  6 AA-281
Freeman, David, 23 Jan. 1740, Martha Briant       9 AA-246
Freeman, Francis, 17 June 1724, Eliz'th Pike      1 BA-254
Freeman, James, 28 Oct. 1742, Margaret Butram     2 BA-238
Freeman, John, 13 June 1671, Rachel Moody         7 SO-401
  5 SO-397 gives date as 7 July 1671.
Freeman, John, 7 Oct. 1713, Mary Smithers         4 AA-380
Freeman, Joseph, 14 Feb. 1673, Mary Robbins       5 SO-397
Freeman, Moses, 18 June (?), Luraner Evans        1 WO-2
French, Benjamin, 25 June 1775, (?) Gist          2 AA-412
French, Jac., 25 May 1773, Susan Melton           1 SM-136
French, James Ormsby, 9 Aug. 1777, Elizabeth
  Kennedy                                        10 BA-68
French, Otho, 30 July 1727, Emm Dowlin            1 AA-105
French, Zorobable, 4 Nov. 1740, Elizabeth Leger   2 KE-243
Fretwell, Thomas, 22 Oct. 1727, Ann Palmer        1 BA-258
Frew, William, 28 day, 9 mo., 1733, Hannah Bodien 1 SF-166
Frey, Nicholas, 20 Aug. 1767, Catharine Schmecter 4 FR-1128
Friend, Daniel, 8 Aug. 1775, Cloe Sayr            1 SM-137
Friley, Da'd, 17 March 1768, Eliz. Armstrong      2 BA-231
Frisby, Henry, 15 June 1722, Ellin Evans          2 TA-102
Frisby, Capt. James, 9 Feb. 1713/4, Ariana
  Vanderheyden                                    3 CE-4
Frisby, Capt. Peregrine, 26 Jan. 1738, Mrs. Mary
  Holland                                         1 BA-307
Frissel, Nathan, 18 April 1751, Marg't Deason     2 BA-203
Frissill, John, 25 Oct. 1722, Providence Dallahide 2 BA-19
  2 BA-14 gives date as Nov. 1721.
Frith, Amer, 25 Feb. 1738, Sarah Pamphilion       2 TA-166
Frith, John, 3 Nov. 1734, Mary Kirby              2 TA-157
Frizel, Charles, Dec. 1725, Elizabeth Drain       3 AA-108
Frizell, Nathan, 1751, Margaret Deason            2 BA-241
Froggitt, John, 25 July 1708, Ann Hoock           3 KE-271
Fromiller, Francis, 10 Oct. 1722, Alce Barnett    2 TA-105
Frost, Jos., 2 Oct. 1761, Mary Baker              2 BA-22-
Frost, Robert, Feb. 1732, Franceis Tye            3 BA-150
Frost, William, 17 Dec. 1744, Susanna Roberson    2 BA-244
Frost, William, 21 Dec. 1749, Suhannah Robertson  2 BA-199
Fry, William, 19 Dec. 1747, Rebeca Crouch         1 QA-53
Fryer, George, 22 May 1743, Mary Merrit           2 TA-11
Fugate, Edw'd, 12 Jan. 1758, Eliz. Bacon          2 BA-216
Fulks, John, 18 Feb. 1760, Alice Wood             2 BA-219
Fullar, William, 3 Feb. 1733, Jane Johnson        1 BA-272
Fuller, Edward, 21 July 1720, Elizabeth Hilliard  3 AA-101
Fuller, Henry, 27 Aug. 1738, Elizabeth Cox        2 BA-98
Fuller Henry, 18 Feb. 1762, Eliz. Greer           2 BA-223
Fuller, John, 10 Dec. 1736, Ruth Danby            2 BA-72
Fuller, Jno., 7 Jan. 1755, Sarah Gott             2 BA-211
Fuller, Jno., Jr., 24 Dec. 1762, Avarilla Barton  2 BA-224
Fuller, Mordecai, 28 April 1745, Mary James       2 BA-240
  2 BA-192 gives date as 16 May 1745.
Fuller, Nicho's, 17 Feb. 1767, Eliz. Brian        2 BA-230
```

| | |
|---|---|
| Fuller, William, 3 Feb. 1733, Jane Johnson | 1 BA-272 |
| Fulton, Francis, 17 March 1757, Ann Mathews | 1 BA-353 |
| Fulton, John, 4 Aug. 1754, Hannah Norris | 2 BA-211 |
| Furness, John, 10 Feb. 1744, Jane Green | 2 BA-192 |
| 2 BA-240 gives date as 10 Feb. 1745. | |
| Fuston, John, 21 Oct. 1703, Jane Jinkins | 3 KE-271 |
| Fyer, Joseph, 3 Aug. 1762, Anna M. Donner | 4 FR-1128 |
| Gadd, Absolem, 19 Oct. 1758, Eliz. Cullison | 2 BA-217 |
| Gadd, Thomas, 22 Jan. 1732, Christian Ditto | 2 BA-69 |
| 2 BA-75 gives date as 21 Jan. 1733. | |
| Gadd, William, 29 May 1734, Mary Standeford | 2 BA-81 |
| Gaddis, George, 10 Nov. 1777, Isabella Hays | 9 BA |
| Gahagan, John, 11 July 1777, Anne Mackey | 10 BA-68 |
| Gailles, Mark, 29 May 1707, Hannah Ryley | 1 AA-73 |
| Gain, William, 1 Aug. 1727, Rebecca Harkins | 3 BA-150 |
| Gaines, Robert, 12 Aug. 1777, Ann Bowen | 1 CA-111a |
| Gaither, Benjamin, 8 Sept. 1709, Sarah Burgess | 1 AA-77 |
| | & 257 |
| Gaither, Edward, 21 Feb. 1709, Mary Duval | 1 AA-77 |
| | & 258 |
| Gaither, Edward, 19 Aug. 1734, Marg't Williams | 1 AA-118 |
| Gaither, John, 21 Aug. 1701, Jane Buck | 1 AA-57 |
| | & 247 |
| Gale, George, 30 Jan. 1750, Elizabeth Airey | 1 WI-62 |
| Gale, John, 25 June 1713, Elisabeth Ashman | 1 AA-267 |
| Gale, John, 11 day, 10 mo., 1745, Barsheba Lamb | 1 SF-80 |
| Galhampton, Thomas, 10 Nov. 1720, Elizabeth Hill | 1 BA-265 |
| Gallaspie, Rob't, 6 Nov. 1753, Eliz. Maxwell | 2 BA-209 |
| Gallaway, Aq'a, 6 Jan. 1761, Bethiah Stansbury | 2 BA-221 |
| Gallaway, James, 22 Feb. 1718, Mary Beck, widow | 3 CE-10 |
| Gallaway, John, 27 May 1744, Isabella Benn | 2 BA-190 |
| Gallaway, Mosess, 6 April 1750, Mary Nicholson | 2 BA-201 |
| Gallaway, Salathiel, 28 Sept. 1753, Prissilla James | 2 BA-208 |
| Gallion, Jacob, 24 Feb. 1755, Elizabeth Arnold | 1 BA-358 |
| Gallion, Jacob, 10 Jan. 1769, Mary Hanson | 1 BA-388 |
| Gallion, James, 15 Aug. 1731, Pheby Johnson | 1 BA-255 |
| Gallion, James, Jr., 7 Sept. 1758, Rachel Mariarty | 1 BA-367 |
| Gallion, John, 29 May 1726, Elizabeth Evans | 1 BA-239 |
| Gallion, Joseph, 21 Jan. 1753, Sarah Auchard | 1 BA-371 |
| Gallion, Sam'l, 27 April 1768, Sarah Mitch'l, | 2 BA-231 |
| Gallion, Solomon, 17 April 1733, Martha Johnson | 1 BA-267 |
| Gallion, Thomas, 1 Oct. 1732, Mary Young | 1 BA-273 |
| Galloway, Benjamin, 5 Sept. 1775, Henrietta Maria Chew | 2 AA-412 |
| Galloway, James, 29 Aug. 1767, Mary Ann Gooch | 3 BA-168 |
| Galloway, John, son of Samuel and Ann, 31 day, 5 mo., 1718, Mary Thomas, dau. of Samuel and Mary | 6 SF |
| Galloway, Joseph, 8 day, 6 mo., 1749, Ann Harris | 6 SF |
| Galloway, Peter, son of Samuel and Ann, 19 day, 11 mo., 1715, Elizabeth Rigbie, dau. of John and Eliza | 6 SF |
| Galloway, Richard, 10 day, 10 mo., 1686, Elizabeth Lawrence, widow | 6 SF |
| Galloway, Richard, Jr., 29 day, 7 mo., 1715, Sophia Richardson, dau. of Wm. and Marg't. | 6 SF |
| Galloway, Richard, Sr., 30 day, 5 mo., 1719, Sarah Sparrow | 6 SF |
| Galloway, Samuel, 12 day, 2 mo., 1705, Sarah Pope | 1 SF-50 |
| Galloway, Joseph, 18 Oct. 1722, Mrs. Susanna Paca | 2 BA-19 |
| Galloway, William, 20 Feb. 1774, Mary Pocock | 6 BA(1) |
| Gallyhampton, Thos., 22 Oct. 1761, Ann Mary Moore | 2 BA-222 |
| Gambole, William, 15 July 1703, Sarah Harper | 1 AA-64 |
| Gambrill, Rezin, 31 Dec. 1777, Mary Gaither | 7 AA-3 |
| Gantt, Edward, 26 June 1768, Ann Houghton Sloss, dau. of Thomas and Mary | 3 SO-4 |

Gardener, Robert, 3 May 1757, Avarilla Enloes        2 BA-215
Gardiner, Thomas, 27 Sept. 1777, Henrietta Goodrum   3 SM-535
Gardiner, William, 7 Nov. 1698, Ann Archer           2 AA-372
Gardner, Benjamin, 19 Feb. 1705, Ann Hall            3 AA-98
Gardner, Benjamin, 27 Dec. 1714, Sarah Petebone      3 AA-99
Gardner, Benjamin, 23 Oct. 1733, Mary brinkle        3 AA-105
Gardner, Benjamin, 8 Jan. 1745, Mary Gordon          3 AA-108
Gardner, George, 1771, Margaret Attwell              2 AA-411
Gardner, James, 8 Jan. 1761, Jane Hissey             4 BA-71
Gardner, Jno., 7 Jan. 1704, Ann Buringham            1 CA-111
Gardner, Jno., 25 Feb. 1759, Mary Meeds              2 BA-218
Gardner, Jno., 23 Dec. 1761, Mary York               2 BA-223
Gardner, John Petteybone, 12 Jan. 1740, Elizabeth
   Loney                                             3 AA-105
Gardner, John Pettibone, 8 Oct. 1750, Milkey Hall    3 AA-111
Gardner, Robert, 5 Jan. 1728, Mary Angleing          3 BA-149
Garetson, Cornelius, 1 day, 10 mo., 1761, Prisiler
   Ruley                                             6 SF
Garey, John, 30 Nov. 1748, Susan Davis               3 TA-71
Garey, Michael, 10 Jan. 1737, Rathell Sailes         2 TA-164
Garey, Wm., 12 July 1743, Mary Anne Elbert           3 TA-44
Garey, William, 12 June 1777, Henney Garland         1 CR-10
Garish, William, 23 Dec. 1697, Ann Pitchford, widow  3 CE-2
Garit, Alexander, 17 Nov. 1709, Mary Hambleton       1 AA-258
Garland, Henry, 27 Jan. 1743, Sarah Herrington       1 BA-333
Garland, James, 3 Feb. 1761, Jane Gaddis             1 BA-368
Garland, William, 10 June 1728, Bethia Ogg           1 BA-245
Garner, John, 14 Oct. 1697, Mary Welsh               1 AA-38
Garner, Jno., 6 Feb. 1704, Sarah Rockhold            4 AA-389
Garrat, Jacob, 22 Sept. 1717, Margret Wisecarver     3 CE-9
Garretson, Edward, 21 Dec. 1749, Avarilla Hanson     1 BA-350
   2 BA-199 gives same information.
Garretson, Geo., 24 March 1768, Martha Presbury      2 BA-231
Garretson, Richard, 20 Jan. 1756, Priscila Nellson   1 BA-352
Garrett, Amoss, 23 Aug. 1744, Frances Drew           1 BA-337
Garrett, Bennet, 15 Dec. 1737, Martha Presbury       1 BA-300
Garrett, Henry, 19 Dec. 1728, Mary Butterworth       1 BA-247
                                                       & 340
Garrett, Jno., 22 Nov. 1759, Margrett Baker          2 BA-219
Garrett, Robt., 20 Feb. 1762, Mary Dunstone          2 BA-223
Garrettson, Garrett, 15 Dec. 1702, Elizabeth Freebone 1 BA-198
Garrettson, Garrett, 12 March 1760, Mrs. Susannah
   Robinson, widow of Capt. Daniel Robinson          1 BA-381
Garrettson, George, 1 Nov. 1744, Mrs. Martha Todd    1 BA-341
Garrettson, George, 24 March 1768, Martha Presbury   1 BA-386
Garrettson, James, 24 April 1746, Catherine Nelson   1 BA-342
Garrettson, John, 21 April 1742, Sarah Merryarter    1 BA-324
Garrison, Paul, 8 May 1735, Elizabeth Frazer         3 BA-155
Gartrell, Charles, 7 Dec. 1777, Sarah Barnes         1 MO-516
Gash, Jno. Cornel, 17 Oct. 1763, Eliz. Rogen         2 BA-225
Gash, Thomas, 22 Dec. 1715, Hannah Gilbert           1 BA-219
Gassaway, John, 5 Dec. 1727, Sarah Cotter            1 AA-106
Gassaway, Nicholas, 2 June 1719, Elisabeth Hawkins   1 AA-293
Gassaway, Nicholas, 4 day, 9 mo., 1747, Margaret
   Pierpoint                                         4 SF
Gassaway, Thomas, 18 Dec. 1701, Susanna Hanslap      1 AA-57
                                                       & 249
Gassaway, Thomas, Jr., 22 June 1732, Sarah Geist     1 AA-114
Gatchell, Joseph, son of Elisha and Mary, 1 Jan.
   1765, Hannah Churchman, dau. of Thomas and Rachel 9 SF
Gater, John, 20 Aug. 1719, Elizabeth Warfield, widow 4 AA-409
Gaterel, Francis, 22 Dec. 1720, Mary Carr            1 AA-302
Gather, Alexander, 23 Oct. 1729, Sarah Wells         2 PG-5
Gaton, Benj., 26 Oct. 1750, Eliz. Skinnoni (sic)     2 BA-202
Gatrill, Francis, 22 Dec. 1720, Mary Carr            1 AA-100

Gatten, Jeremy, 14 Feb. 1773, Eliz. Drury                    1 SM-136
Gatward, Thomas, 4 Nov. 1707, Rebekah Gott                   2 AA-334
Gatwort, John, 1771, Ann Lambeth                             2 AA-410
Gawthrop, John, son of Thomas and Isabel, 9 May 1771,
  Patience Allen, dau. of John and Esther                    9 SF
Gay, Nicho. Ruxton, 21 Sept. 1751, Ann Lux                   3 BA-165
Gebbs, John, 1 Jan. 1751, Hannah Palmer                      2 BA-202
Geddes, William, son of Robert and Susannah, 24 June
  1759, Mary Handy, dau. of Capt. John                       3 SO-4
Geddis, George, 11 Dec. 1777, Isabella Hayes                 5 BA-6
Geiniz, John Wm., 19 April 1758, Johanna Weiszman            4 FR-1103
Geist, Christian, 9 July 1730, Sarah Brewer                  1 AA-110
Geist, Richard, 7 day, 10 mo., 1704, Zipporah Murray         6 SF
George, Joshua, 24 May 1722, Allice Docwray                  4 AA-418
George, Joseph, 20 Nov. 1729, Sarah Bartlett, dau.
  of John                                                    8 SF-52
George, Robert, 20 day, 6 mo., 1699, Barbara Everett         1 SF-45
George, Robert, son of Robert, 1 day 1 mo., 1768,
  Ann Edmondson, dau. of William                             8 SF-128
German, Henry, 21 May 1741, Sarah Wantland                   3 TA-30
Gestwood, Michael, 30 June 1729, Elizabeth (?)               1 BA-279
Getzelman, Andrew, 28 Nov. 1776, Mary Steward                3 BA-669
Ghiselin, William, 29 June 1726, Naomi Lusby, dau. of
  Robert Lusby, Sr., and his wife Mary                       4 AA-426
Gibbins, Thos., 28 Sept. 1748, Mary Buckley                  2 BA-197
Gibbons, Thomas, 6 April 1735, Hannah Sharp                  3 BA-153
Gibbs, Abraham, 27 Jan. 1744, Elizabeth Godard               2 SO-27
Gibbs, John, 1751, Hannah Palmer                             2 BA-241
Gibbs, Silvester, 14 July 1743, Sarah Houlson                3 KE-278
Gibbs, Thomas, 30 March 17-(?), Eliza Davey                  1 AA-91
  1 AA-313 gives date as 11 June 1722.
Gibbs, William, 17 Oct. 1765, Ann Jenkins                    1 PG-357
Gibson, George, 28 Dec. 1750, Frances Dehorty                3 TA-80
Gibson, Gideon, 12 day, 12 mo., 1777, Hannah Unkles          3 SF
Gibson, Hugh, 21 Nov. 1726, Eliz'th Kelley                   3 BA-669
Gibson, John, 13 Sept. 1732, Eliza Candley                   2 TA-152
Gibson, John, Dec. 1750, Eliza Sherwood                      3 TA-80
Gibson, Jonathan, 21 May 1745, Anne Hull                     3 TA-53
Gibson, Joseph, 3 Aug. 1773, Eleanor Stone                   1 AA-153
Gibson, Richard, 19 Feb. 1725/6, Margret B. Dawson           2 TA-112
Gibson, Robert, 15 Dec. 1702, Mrs. Mary Goldsmith            1 BA-197
Gibson, Thos., 22 Dec. 1761, Katherine Demorce               2 BA-222
Gibson, Woolman, 18 April 1718, Sarah Clements               2 TA-86
Gibson, Woolman, 6 Aug. 1774, Rebecca Bruff                  1 CR
Giddes, William, Collector of the King's Customs of
  Patapsco and Chester, 1 June 1768, Mary Wilmer,
  dau. of Simon                                              2 KE-317
Gidens, Thomas, 3 April 1719, Elizabeth Redgrave,
  dau. of Abraham                                            2 KE-196
Gietzendanner, Balthasar, 11 May 1758, Anna Steiner          4 FR-1104
Giezendanner, Jacob, 3 April 1757, Catherine Kast            4 FR-1103
Gilbert, Aquilla, 17 Jan. 1749, Eliz. Butler                 2 BA-200
Gilbert, Charles, 27 Srpt. 1744, Elizabeth Hawkins           1 BA-338
Gilbert, Jarvis, 10 June 1735, Elizabeth Preston             1 BA-283
Gilbert, Martin Taylor, 11 Oct. 1764, Martha Gilbert         1 BA-384
Gilbert, Michael, 17 Dec. 1728, Sarah Preston                1 BA-254
Gilbert, Michael, 23 Nov. 1738, Mary Taylor                  1 BA-303
Gilbert, Samuel, 26 April 1733, Martha Webster               1 BA-262
Gilbert, Thomas, Jr., 27 May 1700, Sarah Bedford             1 BA-192
Gilbert, Thomas, 1 April 1703, Hannah Ashford                1 BA-200
Gilbert, Thomas, 25 Dec. 1727, Elizabeth Cole                1 BA-279
Gilbert, Thomas, 14 June 1745, Mary Fowler                   1 BA-361
Giles, Ishmael, 25 Dec. 1711, Anne Thornbury                 1 AA-78
Giles, Jacob, son of John and Mary, 8 day, 11 mo.,
  1701, Elizabeth Arnoll, dau. of Richard and Martha         6 SF

```
Giles, Jacob, 3 Jan. 1728/9, Hannah Webster          9 SF
Giles, James, 12 April 1770, Anne Fell               1 BA-395
Giles, John, 1 Oct. 1695, Sarah Welsh                2 AA-291
Giles, John, son of John, of Balto. Co., 8 day, 11
  mo., 1723, Cassandra Smith, dau. of Nathan, of
  Cal. Co.                                           6 SF
Giles, John, 16 Oct. 1734, Sarah Butterworth         1 BA-277
  3 BA-152 gives same information.
Giles, Nathaniel, 8 day, 1 mo. 1729, Elizabeth Welch,
  widow, of A. A. Co.                                6 SF
Giles, Mr. Nathaniel, 7 March 1762, Sarah Hammond    1 BA-383
Giles, Richard, 4 Feb. 1724, Phebey Martin           2 TA-111
Giles, Thomas, 12 March 1730, Ann Harris             1 WI-40
Giles, William, 24 May 1734, Mary Carroll            2 TA-155
Giles, William, "Secundus," 10 Aug. 1741, Sarah Piper 1 WI-31
Gill, George, 28 Feb. 1732, Mary Aldridge            3 AA-103
Gill, George, 10 Sept. 1768, Vinah Alman             3 AA-113
Gill, John, 26 Feb. 1730, Mary Rogers                4 BA-70
Gill, John, Jr., 20 July 1758, Sarah Gorsuch         2 BA-217
  4 BA-72 gives same information.
Gill, Robert, Jr., 19 Nov. 1749, Lydia Musgrove      1 CH-183
Gill, Stephen, 16 Dec. 1708, Elizabeth Hubbert       4 AA-378
Gill, Thomas, 30 Aug. 1777, Sarah Jones              3 PG-117
  2 CH(1) gives date as 3 Sept. 1777.
Gill, William, 27 Nov. 1760, Ruth Cromwell           4 BA-72
Gillcoat, John, 24 Dec. 1771, Providence Ensor       2 BA-263
Gillcoat. See also Chilcoat.
Gillet, Thomas, 17 Oct. 1685, Jane Blades            5 SO-397
Gillis, Benjamin, 12 Dec. 1765, Easther Byrd         1 WI-81
Gillis, Thomas, 22 Sept. 1720, Priscilla Denwood     1 WI-13
Gillis, Thos., 16 Jan. 1766, Jane Ross               2 BA-229
Gillitt, Jno., 22 Aug. 1762, Sarah Walton            2 BA-223
Gin, James, 16 Feb. 1758, Mary Andrews               1 QA-63
Ginkins, Francis, 15 June 1732, Mary Downs           1 BA-267
Girton, Notley, 27 March 1768, Mary Tewill           1 PG-369
Gist, Joseph, 30 Aug. 1759, Elizabeth Elder          4 BA-73
Gist, Thomas, 2 July 1735, Susannah Cockey           4 BA-70
Gist, William, 22 Oct. 1737, Violetta Howard         4 BA-70
Giyton, Benjamin, 13 Dec. 1753, Amelia Scarf         2 BA-209
Gladen, Jacob, 31 Jan. 1753, Sarah Rice              2 BA-207
Glanden, James, 17 Nov. 1737, Margaret Satterfield   1 QA-43
Glanden, Nathan, 6 Oct. 1748, Rebecca West           1 QA-54
Glandin, Thos., 2 Feb. 1739, Mary Sillevent          1 QA-45
Glanding, James, 22 Oct. 1752, Juliana Hadley        1 QA-59
Glanding, Solomon, 9 June 1748, Mary Silvester       1 QA-54
Glanding, Solomon, 19 June 1758, Alice Ray           1 QA-63
Glanding, Thos., 29 April 1745, Ann Walker           1 QA-50
Glanding, Thomas, 6 Nov. 1756, Juliana Pearson       1 QA-61
Glanding, William, 5 Dec. 1751, Susannah Mitchell    1 QA-58
Glann, James, 23 May 1717, Mary Newman, widow        3 CE-8
Glanvill, Stephen, 19 Jan. 1733, Mary Smith          3 KE-276
Glaspin, Wm., 21 Feb. 1729, Sarah Lowry              1 BA-262
Glassington, John, 1 Aug. 1734, Mary Jordan          3 BA-152
Gleaves, Joseph, 31 July 1736, Ruth Brooks           2 KE-221
Glede, William, 15 Nov. 1750, Jane Russel            2 BA-202
Glen, Nicho., Nov. 1739, Mary Wright                 3 TA-19
Glen, Rev. William, Rector of St. Peter's Parish,
  15 Aug. 1709, Mrs. Mary Allen                      2 TA-62
Glover, John, 29 July 1717, Eliz. Henricks           2 TA-80
Glover, John, 17 Oct. 1740, Elizabeth Elston         3 TA-25
  2 TA-170 gives date as 25 Oct. 1740.
Glover, John, 16 March 1762, Elisabeth Mungumry      2 SO-130
Glover, John, 1 Nov. 1767, Elizabeth Powel           1 AA-146
Glover, Mark, 31 Oct. 1706, Jane Wood                2 AA-330
Glover, Richard, 23 Nov. 1707, Mary Jones            1 CA-112
```

| | |
|---|---|
| Glover, Thomas, 24 July 1714, Mary Farrell | 1 AA-78 |
| Goddard, Ellias, 29 May 1692, Jane West | 8 SF-358 |
| Goddard, George, 4 July 1679, Judith Goodin | 5 SO-397 |
| Goddard, Ignatius, 23 Dec. 1772, Ann Payn | 1 SM-136 |
| Godfrey, Richard, 30 Jan. 1732, Jane Hart | 1 QA-39 |
| Godgrace, John, 27 Dec. 1713, Mary Grover | 1 CA-114 |
| Godman, Humphry, 10 Feb. 1710, Mary Kirkland | 1 AA-78 |
| Godwin, Edward, 4 Nov. 1732, Mary Murphey | 1 QA-39 |
| Godwin, Edward, 9 Oct. 1755, Sarah Pickarine | 1 QA-60 |
| Godwin, William, 26 Dec. 1729, Sarah Scot | 1 QA-37 |
| Goe, William, 24 Jan. 1725, Mary Bateman | 2 PG-4 |
| Goe, William, 1754, Dorcas Turner | 2 PG-7 |
| Goforth, John, 16 Feb. 1757, Sarah Holding | 1 QA-62 |
| Gold, John, 28 April 1723, Elizabeth Nuch (?) | 2 PG-3 |
| Gold, Joseph, 22 Dec. 1715, Margaret Danielson | 2 PG-2 |
| Golden, Peter, 1742, Eliz. Earl | 2 BA-238 |
| Golding, John, 22 July 1770, Rachael Demmit | 2 BA-260 |
| Goldsborough, Charles, 2 Aug. 1739, Elizabeth Dickinson | 2 TA-167 |
| Goldsborough, N., Jr., son of Robert, 7 April 1746, Jane Banning | 3 TA-58 |
| Goldsborough, Nicholas, 25 Jan. 1721, Mrs. Sarah Turbutt | 2 TA-99 |
| Goldsborough, Nicolas, c.Aug. 1775, Rebecca Myers | 1 CR-6 |
| Goldsborough, Robert, Jr., 5 Nov. 1739, Sarah Nicols | 3 TA-19 |
| Goldsborough, Rob't, Jr., 8 July 1742, Mrs. Mary Anne Robins | 3 TA-38 |
| Goldsborough, William, 23 Jan. 1734, Elizabeth Robins | 2 TA-157 |
| Goldsborough, William, son of Robert, 2 Sept. 1747, Henrietta Maria Tilghman, widow of George Robins | 3 TA-66 |
| Goldsmith, John, 28 Oct. 1730, Elinor Hambleton | 3 BA-150 |
| Gollohan, John, 16 Feb. 1723, Frances Peregoy | 3 BA-147 |
| Golt, Thomas, 23 May 1735, Reb'a Parmar | 1 QA-41 |
| Goodbie, Jesper, 25 May 1755, Ann Bosell | 2 BA-212 |
| Goodhand, Marmaduke, 18 Nov. 1725, Hannah Jones | 3 AA-101 |
| Goodin, Alexander, 11 Nov. 1708, Susannah Watkins | 2 TA-49 |
| Gooding, Henry, 15 June 1766, Murrun Swan | 2 BA-229 |
| Gooding, William, 17 June 1705, Grace Hearle | 1 AA-65 |
| Goodman, John, 4 Nov. 1714, Leah Davis | 2 PG-1 |
| Goodman, John, 8 Jan. 1738, Rachel Mullican | 9 AA-246 |
| Goodrum, James, 19 Nov. 1749, Susanna Pye Stonestreet | 1 CH-185 |
| Goodwin, Benjamin, 6 Feb. 1742, Hannah Urquhart | 1 BA-331 |
| Goodwin, Edward, 30 June 1735, Sarah Beach | 2 PG-6 |
| Goodwin, Sam, 26 Dec. 1755, Rebecca Breedin | 1 BA-371 |
| Goodwine, George, 29 March 1730, Anne Rutter | 3 BA-149 |
| Gording, John, 12 Feb. 1711, Joan Sanders | 2 TA-71 |
| Gordon, Charles, 9 Feb. 1752, Elizabeth Flint Original register checked. | 2 FR-251 |
| Gordon, Daniel, 23 Nov. 1729, Mary West | 1 BA-258 |
| Gordon, George, 27 Sept. 1747, Esther Harris | 3 TA-66 |
| Gordon, John, 7 July 1771, Cather'n Hunt | 2 BA-262 |
| Gordon, Joseph, 15 Feb. 1752, Ruth Chaney | 1 BA-359 |
| Gordon, Thomas, April 1777, Mary Burton | 5 AA-5 |
| Gordon, Thomas, 11 June 1777, Ann Hardy | 3 PG-118 |
| Gordon, Wm., 29 Jan. 1761, Johannah Price | 2 BA-221 |
| Gore, Jacob, 28 March 1733, Rebecca Walker | 2 TA-153 |
| Gorman, John, 24 Feb. 1777, Mary Shepherd | 3 BA-172 |
| Gorsuch, Benj'n, 17 July 1760, Kerenhappuck Johnson | 2 BA-220 |
| Gorsuch, Charles, 12 June (?), Sarah (?) | 2 TA-14 |
| Gorsuch, Chas., of Balto. Co., son of John and Ann of Eng., 15 day, 12 mo., 1690, Ann Hawkins, dau. of John and Mary | 6 SF |
| Gorsuch, Charles, 2 Dec. 1725, Mary Cornich | 2 TA-112 |
| Gorsuch, Char., 18 Oct. 1746, Mary Dodson | 3 TA-61 |

```
Gorsuch, Charles, son of John, 1 Sept. 1763, Eleanor
  Bond                                                    4 BA-73
Gorsuch, John, 4 March 1735, Mary Price                   3 BA-155
Gorsuch, John, 6 Aug. 1767, Mary Wright                   2 BA-231
Gorsuch, Loveles, 23 Oct. 1679, Rebechah Preston          8 SF-320
Gorsuch, Lovelace, 11 Aug. 1696, Hannah Walley, late
  of Penna.                                               8 SF-371
Gorsuch, Richard, 5 June 1732, Elizabeth Eason            2 TA-152
Gorsuch, Richard, 29 May 1739, Mary Wheeler               2 TA-166
Gosard, Anthony, 9 Feb. 1752, Frances Jones               2 BA-204
Goslee, Daniel, 2 July 1747, Elizabeth Tully, widow       1 WI-59
Goslee, John, 10 Sept. 1754, Hannah Tull                  1 WI-58
Gosley, John, 6 June 1734, Joanah Cheeseman               1 WI-14
Goslin, Ambrose, c.Oct. 1775, Eliz'th Brown               1 CR-6
Goslin, Ezekiel, 23 day, 11 mo., 1766, Peggy Bartlett     2 SF-288
Gosnell, Maurice, 29 Nov. 1722, Susana Wright             3 AA-100
Gossage, William, 6 Nov. 1729, Julian Benson              1 AA-109
Gossutch, Rich'd, 3 Dec. 1696, Eliza Martin               2 TA-5
Gostwick, Nicholas, Dec. 1720, Abarilla Yanstone          3 BA-147
Gostwick, Thomas, Sept. 1717, Elizabeth Yanstone          3 BA-147
Goswick, Aquila, 14 Jan. 1749/50, Eliz'th Stansbury       3 BA-163
Gott, Anthony, 10 March 1773, Ann Barker                  2 AA-411
Gott, Ezekiel, 12 Nov. 1761, Elizabeth (?)                2 AA-400
Gott, Richard, 30 April 1758, Ruth Bond                   4 BA-72
Gouff, Thomas, 27 Dec. 1724, Ann Brooksby                 4 AA-424
Gough, John, 4 Sept. 1732, Anne Dunn                      1 QA-39
Gough, Thomas, 23 May 1743, Sophia Dorsey, dau. of
  Caleb                                                   4 AA-445
Gould, Benjamin, 28 March 1749, Sarah Woodland            1 QA-55
Gould, Benjamin, 8 Jan. 1782 (sic), Esther Hall           1 QA-47
  This entry is out of place with the others, which
  are chronological; it may have been written instead
  of 1728.
Gould, James, 7 Jan. 1747, Meremy Brown                   1 QA-54
Gould, Richard, 10 Aug. 1739, Mary Woodland               1 QA-45
Gould, Thomas, 14 Sept. (?), Sarah Whaley                 2 KE-248
Gould, William, 1 Aug. 1729, Margit Williams              2 KE-213
Goult, George, 6 May 1691, Mary Sockwell                  8 SF-353
Goult, William, 30 Sept. 1720, Hannah Parratt, widow      8 SF-31
Govane, James, 4 Aug. 1711, Mrs. Mary Hornwood            3 AA-99
Govane, James, 15 July 1713, Mrs. Elizabeth Hammond       3 AA-99
Gover, John, 15 Dec. 1757, Elizabeth Duvall               2 PG-7
Gover, Philip, 11 day, 8 mo., 1761, Mary Hopkins,
  dau. of Gerard                                          6 SF
Gover, Robert, 5 Dec. 1695, Elizabeth Cotton              2 AA-292
Gover, Samuel, 11 Nov. 1742, Hannah Webster, dau.
  of Isaac                                                9 SF
Grace, Aaron, 27 Jan. 1758, Ann Boyer, dau. of Peter
  and Esther                                              1 CE-302
Grace, Abell, 14 July 1709, Lydia Eubanks                 8 SF-441
Grace, Abell, 1 Jan. 1738, Rachel Kemp                    2 TA-165
Grace, Edward, 9 Dec. 1735, Patience Foster               3 BA-154
Grace, William, 29 Dec. 1738, Mary Morgan                 2 TA-274
Grace, William, 15 Dec. 1709, Elizabeth Hearse            2 AA-339
Grace, William, 9 Feb. 1718/9, Mary Castle                2 AA-360
Grace, Will, 25 April 1747, Mary Keatly                   1 CE-292
Grace, William, 26 Feb. 1750, Honour Joyce                4 AA-452
Grace, William, 11 Sept. 1750, Lucy Skinner               3 TA-78
Gradde, Edmund, 10 March 1697, Jellen Dunawin             1 BA-178
Grady, Cornelius, 29 May 1749, Joan Needles               1 QA-55
Grady, Edmund, 10 March 1697, Leellen Dunawin             1 BA-178
Graffith, Thomas, 6 Feb. 1729, Mary Simpkins              2 TA-121
Graham, James, 25 Dec. 1753, Mary Vine                    2 BA-209
Graham, Thos., 22 Sept. 1736, Elis Tootle                 1 QA-42
Grahame, James, Nov. 1753, Mary Vine                      2 BA-242
```

| | |
|---|---|
| Grant, Alexander, 17 Nov. 1709, Mary Hambleton | 1 AA-77 |
| Grant, Alexander, 16 Feb. 1730, Elisabeth Cole | 3 BA-150 |
| Grant, George, 23 Dec. 1759, Margret Langwell | 3 KE-278 |
| Grant, James, 1 Feb. 1753, Elizabeth Morris | 1 BA-354 |
| Grant, John, 29 Oct. 1745, Eliz'th Richardson | 3 KE-278 |
| Grant, John, 21 Oct. 1777, Ephana Claud | 3 PG-107 |
| Grant, Marmaduke, 15 May 1776, Eleanor Reiley | 3 BA-174 |
| Grant, Richard, 28 Sept. 1738, Margaret Austin | 1 QA-44 |
| Grason, Joshua, 20 Dec. 1730, Sarah Johnson | 2 TA-149 |
| Graves, Jos., 26 July 1764, Tab. Reeves | 2 BA-226 |
| Graves, William, 15 June 1735, Sarah Beaver | 1 BA-282 |
| Gray, Alexander, 12 April 1759, Margret Galeher | 1 CE-302 |
| Gray, David, 14 Dec. 1703, Penelope Parsons | 1 AA-64 |
| Gray, George, 24 April 1711, Jane Velson | 2 TA-69 |
| Gray, George, 24 June 1759, Esther Knight | 1 QA-65 |
| Gray, James, 21 March 1696, Alce Wood | 3 CE-1 |
| Gray, John, 14 Feb. 1717, Ann Hopkins | 3 AA-102 |
| Gray, John, 1 Dec. 1731, Jane Abbott | 1 CA-113 |
| Gray, John, 28 Aug. 1739, Ann Hawkins | 3 AA-109 |
| Gray, John, 30 Sept. 1750, Blansh Cantwell | 2 BA-202 |
| Gray, Joshua, 25 Feb. 1727, Mary Burly | 3 AA-103 |
| Gray, Joshua, 11 April 1742, Ruth Grims | 3 AA-109 |
| Gray, Robert, April 1743, Elizabeth Jaccobs | 3 AA-109 |
| Gray, Thomas, 29 May 1774, Mary Leggat | 6 BA(1) |
| Gray, Wm., 16 Oct. 1706, Martha Duke | 1 CA-112 |
| Gray, William, 28 May 1743, Providence Ellingsworth, widow | 1 WI-41 |
| Gray, William, 16 Sept. 1756, Mary Tulb | 2 SO-28 |
| Gray, Zachariah, 19 Dec. 1719, Mary Demitt | 3 BA-147 |
| Gray, Zachariah, 22 Dec. 1748, Mary Linch | 3 BA-162 |
| Gray, Zachariah, 22 July 1777, Susanna Parker | 1 MO-516 |
| Graydon, Willwam, 4 Dec. 1739, Mary Ayres | 1 BA-311 |
| Grayham, Thomas, 18 Sept. 1722, Keziah Pennington | 3 AA-100 |
| Grear, Isaac, 22 Sept. 1777, Martha McCracken | 2 CE-1 |
| Greaves, Thomas, 23 July 1752, Sarah Hollinsworth | 1 QA-59 |
| Greely, James, 8 July 17-(?), Mary Roach | 1 CE-330 |
| Green, Abell, 17 Dec. 1770, Lydia Palmer | 2 BA-261 |
| Green, Abraham, 28 Jan. 1749/50, Eliz'th Baxter | 3 BA-163 |
| Green, Abraham, 25 June 1770, Ruth Carback | 2 BA-260 |
| Green, Benjamin, 12 Oct. 1726, Rachell Thomas | 3 KE-276 |
| Green, Charles, 5 June 1753, Mary Colleton | 2 BA-208 |
| Green, Charles, 14 Aug. 1755, Welthyan Hadley | 1 QA-59 |
| Green, Frederick, printer, of Annap., 18 May 1775, Anne Sanders | 5 AA-6 |
| Green, Henry, 3 March 1711, Alice Purdy | 1 AA-78 |
| Green, Henry, 8 April 1735, Rhoda Sullivan | 1 QA-40 |
| Green, Henry, 5 June 1740, Mary Baley | 1 QA-46 |
| Green, Henry, 10 Dec. 1758, Sarah Howard | 2 BA-218 |
| Green, Hugh, 18 July 1717, Susanna Holland | 2 PG-1 |
| Green, James, 12 Jan. 1769, Elizabeth Stevens | 2 BA-257 |
| Green, John, Dec. 1720, Mary Sampson | 3 BA-147 |
| Green, John, 7 Sept. 1730, Margarett Williams | 3 AA-104 |
| Green, John, 8 March 1753, Ann Hardisty | 2 BA-207 |
| Green, John, 27 March 1757, Cathrine Todd | 2 BA-215 |
| Green, Jno., 25 Aug. 1763, Eliz. Barton | 2 BA-225 |
| Green, Joseph, 25 Feb. 1744, Mary Bown | 2 BA-192 |
| 2 BA-240 gives date as 24 Feb. 1745, and the bride's name as Bowen. | |
| Green, Michael, Jr., 30 Jan. 1748, Mary Archibold | 1 QA-55 |
| Green, Moses, 25 March 1762, Eliza Harriman | 3 BA-167 |
| Green, Peter, 29 July 1732, Martha Rogers | 3 KE-277 |
| Green, Peter, 19 Feb. 1744, Hanah Phillips | 1 QA-50 |
| Green, Philemon, 9 Oct. 1750, Elizabeth Hackett | 1 QA-57 |
| Green, Philip, 25 Oct. 1711, Sarah Seaborn | 1 AA-78 |
| Green, Philip, 7 Nov. 1723, Eliza Burrows | 2 PG-3 |

Green, Richard, 19 Nov. 1719, Margaret Young           4 AA-410
Green, Richard, 31 July 1743, Elizabeth Flualler       2 BA-239
Green, Richard, 8 Dec. 1772, Ann Jones                 2 BA-265
Green, Robard, 10 Feb. 1745, Mary Merideth             1 QA-51
Green, Robert, 21 Sept. 1746, Unity Corbin             2 BA-240
  2 BA-195 gives date as 25 Sept. 1746.
Green, Thomas, 10 Aug. 1716, Elizabeth Walker          1 PG-274
                                                                  & 276
Green, Thomas, 11 Aug. 1732, Elisabeth Carter          3 BA-150
Green, Thos., 25 Aug. 1763, Mary Wright                2 BA-225
Green, Vincent, 15 Sept. 1777, Elizabeth Eaglestone   10 BA-69
Green, William, 21 Aug. 1729, Hannah Haile             3 BA-149
Green, William, 30 Oct. 1744, Margaret Johnson         1 QA-49
Green, William, 17 Feb. 1751, Mary Hammond             2 BA-203
Greene, James, 26 July 1727, Eliza Dyar                1 PG-286
Greene, Job, born in Newport, R. I., 13 July 1772,
  Christian Pierce                                    3 BA-171
Greene, Richard, 17 April 1704, Margery Standbridge    2 AA-323
Greene, William, 2 Feb. 1666, Elizabeth, widow of
  Mark Manlove                                        5 SO-397
  6 SO-400 gives date as 27 Nov. 1666.
Greenhall, Wm., 27 Nov. 1755, Ruth Harrinton           2 BA-212
Greenhough, Wm., 13 Nov. 1743, Mary Ray                3 TA-46
Greening, Albert, 2 Jan. 1710, Alce Moore              1 AA-77
  · 1 AA-261 gives her name as Alice Moore.
Greening, Samuel, 1 March 1714, Anne Twine             2 BA-5
Greenway, Joseph, 25 Jan. 1746, Eliz. Tilley           2 BA-196
Greenwell, Joshua, 31 Jan. 1774, Eliz. Newton          1 SM-136
Greenwell, Raphael, 10 April 1774, Cloe Tarleton       1 SM-136
Greenwood, Bartholomew, 5 Aug. 1709, Mary Brown        2 TA-61
Greenwood, Bartholomew, 1 Aug. 1722, Sarah Wallis      2 TA-103
Greenwood, James, 10 Feb. 1749, Rebecca Stavely        2 KE-279
Greenwood, John, 7 Feb. 1739/40, Mary Stavely          2 KE-241
Greenwood, Rob't, 3 Dec. 1746, Sarah Taylor            3 TA-63
Greer, Benjamin, 2 Jan. 1745, Rachael Low              2 BA-193
Greer, George, 6 Oct. 1748, Anne Jones                 2 SO-26
Greer, James, 28 May 1741, Elizabeth Wright            2 BA-119
Greer, James, 24 May 1768, Eliner Hughes               2 BA-231
Greer, Jos., 18 Aug. 1750, Ann Low                     2 BA-201
Greer, Jos., 24 March 1768, Eliner Hughes              2 BA-231
Greer, Mosess, Jan. 1737, Mary Bayley                  2 BA-208
Greeves, James, 8 April 1707, Catherine Barton         1 CA-112
Gregg (Grig), Aaron, son of David, 16 July 1767,
  Elizabeth Bonsall, dau. of Obadiah and Elizabeth   9 SF
Gregory, Edward, 3 Nov. 1737, Anne Friss               1 QA-43
Gregory, Jas., 16 Oct. 1774, Eliza Bush                1 CR
Gregory, John, 27 July 1746, Mary Parlet               3 BA-159
Gregory, John, 16 Oct. 1774, Ann Armstrong             1 CR
Gregory, William, 22 Dec. 1741, Ursley Sparks          1 QA-47
Gresingham, Jere., 18 March 1748/9, Fran. Elbert       3 TA-72
Greves, Robert, 7 Nov. 1707, Margrett Howe             1 CA-112
Grey, James, 27 May 170, Hino Kennington               3 CE-3
Grey, John, 9 Dec. 1701, Mary Hendry                   1 AA-57
Grey, John, 9 Dec. 1701, Mary Handy                    1 AA-249
Grey, William, 10 Aug. 1775, Ann Permer                1 QA-59
Grice, Cesar, 1 Aug. 1728, Alice Handcock              1 AA-107
Griffen, Richard, Nov. 1749, Jean Lord                 2 BA-244
Griffeth, Timothey, 20 June 1745, Ann Baker            1 QA-50
Griffin, Charles, 25 Nov. 1740, Mary Sherwin           2 TA-195
  2 TA-170 gives date as 27 Nov. 1740.
Griffin, John, 3 Aug. 1695, Sarah Fowler               2 AA-291
Griffin, Jno., 4 March 1753, Ann Harp                  2 BA-207
Griffin, Peter, 9 June 1774, Sarah Scarf               6 BA(1)
Griffin, Rich'd, 21 Dec. 1749, Jane Loyd               2 BA-199
Griffin, Rich'd, 14 Sept. 1756, Ann White              2 BA-214

Griffis, John, 23 Jan. 1776, Rebecca Wood                        2 AA-412
Griffith, Benj., 27 Nov. 1755, Mary Riggs                       6 AA-215
Griffith, Charles, 29 Aug. 1717, Mary Mercer, widow            4 AA-402
Griffith, Edward, 12 Jan. 1720, Sarah Docwray                  4 AA-413
Griffith, Greenberry, 20 Jan. 1752, Ruth Riggs                 6 AA-185
Griffith, Henry, 9 April 1741, Elizabeth Dorsey, dau.
  of Edward                                                     6 AA-214
Griffith, Henry, 4 June 1751, Ruth Hammond                     6 AA-214
Griffith, Henry, son of Henry, 13 Nov. 1766, Sarah
  Warfield, dau. of John and Rachel                             6 AA-188
Griffith, Jackson, 26 Jan. 1738, Ann Blackiston                3 KE-277
Griffith, John, 7 Dec. 1746, Eliz. Bond                        2 BA-195
Griffith, Lewis, 5 Aug. 1739, Mary Johnson                     1 BA-308
Griffith, Lewis, 5 Dec. 1769, Susannah Stewart                 1 AA-148
Griffith, Luke, 13 Jan. 1757, Mrs. Blansh Hall, widow
  of Parker Hall                                                1 BA-378
Griffith, Orlando, 6 June 1717, Catherine Howard               4 AA-401
Griffith, Richard, son of William, 16 Dec. 1738, Mary
  Sidewell, dau. of John                                        9 SF
Griffith, Richard, 22 Nov. 1743, Jane Rees                     1 BA-333
Griffith, Salathiel, 10 March 1760, Nancy Owens                1 WI-76
Griffith, Samuel, 26 Nov. 1702, Sarah Evens                    2 AA-319
Griffith, Samuel, 24 Nov. 1726, Susannah Evans                 4 AA-427
Griffith, Sam'l, 15 March 1764, Freenettah Garrettson          1 BA-380
Griffith, William, 18 June 1747, Eliza Lowe                    3 TA-65
Griffiths, John, 29 July 1750, Henrietta Hollinsworth          1 QA-57
Griggory, Anthony, 5 June 1734, Lidia Grace                    2 TA-155
Grimes, John (date not given), Elizabeth Fosters               4 AA-393
Grimes, John, 1 May 1740, Margrett Huttson                     2 KE-233
Grimes, Nicholas, 1714/5, Elizabeth Toole                      4 AA-392
Grimes, Patrick, 11 April 1741, Mary Colthurst                 3 AA-106
Grimes, Sheppard, 26 Nov. 1741, Ruth Hall                      3 AA-107
Grimes, Vinson, 7 July 1772, Rebecca Todd                      3 AA-113
Grimes, Wm., 27 Oct. 1719, Elenor Drain                        4 AA-410
Grimes, William, 1 Jan. 1743, Elizabeth Bell                   3 AA-106
Grommi (sic), Andrew, 10 Jan. 1759, Anna Elizab. (?)           4 FR-1104
Groom, Peter, 3 July 1736, Elis. Earle                         1 QA-42
Groombridge, Jas., 15 Jan. 1765, Sarah Wyle                    2 BA-227
Groome, Richard, 13 Feb. 1739, Margaret Norton                 2 BA-121
Grosier, John, 31 Aug. 1727, Elizabeth Hawkins                 2 TA-116
Gross, Jacob, 9 Jan. 1745, Mary Richards                       3 BA-158
Grove, George, 17 Oct. 1763, Bethia Pines                      2 BA-225
Grover, George, Sr., July 1727, Magdalen Kelly                 2 BA-38
Grover, Josias, 25 Dec. 1754, Mary Anderson                    2 BA-211
Grover, William, Nov. 1746, Anne Harrod                        2 BA-240
Grover, William, 2 Dec. 1746, Ann Harwood                      2 BA-195
Grover, William, 14 Jan. 1752, Eliz. Enloes                    2 BA-204
Grover, William, 18 Dec. 1760, Ann Harrod                      2 BA-221
Groves, George, 26 Aug. 1752, Johannah Rigbie                  2 BA-206
Groves, Geo., 8 Jan. 1761, Mary Lax                            2 BA-221
Groves, Robert, 17 Sept. 1734, Elean'r Miller                  2 TA-157
Groves, William, 27 Sept. 1705, Isitt Rouse                    1 AA-65
Groves, Wm., 15 Jan. 1712, Mary Trot                           2 AA-346
Groves, William, Jan. 1721, Sarah Dallahide                    2 BA-31
Groves, Wm., 15 Jan. 1761, Sarah Dorney                        2 BA-221
Grudgings, Sutton, 13 Nov. 1770, Mary McGrevey                 2 BA-261
Grund, John Ad., 7 Feb. 1765, M. Chr. Hoffman                  4 FR-1131
Grundy, Robert, 6 Jan. 1703, Margret Pemberton                 2 TA-38
Grundy, Thomas, 2 May 1762, Eliz. Price                        2 BA-223
Gudgeon, William, 17 day, 3 mo., 1760, Mary Snow               1 SF-97
Gudgins, Thomas, 27 Nov. 1743, Mary Gott                       2 BA-239
Guest, Job, 23 July 1739, Bridget Wilcocks                     2 TA-165
Guida, John, 19 Jan. 1768, Jane Brooke                         4 SM-72
Guilder, Guilbert, 11 Aug. 1728, Elizabeth Casine             1 CE-329
Guilder, Hukill, 30 Dec. 1733/4, Eney Simpers                  1 CE-334

```
Gullam, Thomas, 27 Jan. 1770, Mary Green              2 BA-258
Gullett, William, 1 Nov. 1674, Susanna Mills          5 SO-397
Gulliver, Thomas, 4 April 1770, Jane Clinerown        2 BA-260
Gumley, John, of Newcastle Co., Penna., 29 day, 4 mo.,
   1704, Deborah Barber, of Cecil Co.                 1 SF-48
Gump(f), George (date not given), Rosina Mack         5 FR-43
Gump, John, 2 Feb. 1762, Elizabeth Juliana Weller     5 FR-43
Gunby, Francis, 14 Nov. 1676, Sarah Kirke             9 SO-402
Gunby, James, 26 Nov. 1744, Sarah White               2 SO-27
Gunby, John, 27 Jan. 1756, Sarah Melton               2 SO-129
Gunby, Kirk, 25 Dec. 1766, Elizabeth Cracket          2 SO-28
Gunby, Levin, 15 May 1763, Sabra Roach                2 SO-130
Gunterman, George, 1 April 1765, Rachel Milhaus       4 FR-1131
Gupton, John, 17 April 1747, Ann Langford             1 WI-63
Gurnill, Francis, 22 March 1772, Judith Carthy        2 BA-264
Gushard, Sam'l, 2 Nov. 1704, Ann Gongo                2 AA-354
Gutteredge, Edw'd, 24 Oct. 1759, Mary Scarf           2 BA-219
Guy, John, 26 Oct. 1743, Rachell Ward                 2 TA-198
Guy, John, 13 July 1766, Margarett Taylor             3 BA-168
Guyshard, Anthony, Nov. 1751, Frances Jones           2 BA-241
Guyton, Benjamin, 13 Dec. 1753, Amelia Scarf          2 BA-209
Guyton, Benj., 26 Sept. 1765, Cathrine Adams          2 BA-228
Guyton, Henry, 17 April 1738, Sarah Holt              2 BA-217
Guyton, Jos., 12 Dec. 1754, Hannah Whitaker           2 BA-211
Guyton, Underwood, 12 Aug. 1762, Prissilla Jackson    2 BA-223
Gwin, William, 3 Aug. 1697, Sarah (?)                 2 TA-8
Gwin, William, 28 June 1721, Sarah Ginkins            1 BA-265
Gwyn, Edward, 15 Nov. 1728, Easter Field              3 BA-149
Gyles, Wm., 12 Nov. 1740, Mary Connor                 2 TA-169
Gynn, Wm., 10 Oct. 1754, Mary Hill                    2 BA-211
Gyrling, Richard, 22 March 1667, Elizabeth Moorey     1 TA-602
Haberdine, John, 23 Dec. 1706, Elizabeth Barrington   1 AA-73
Hacket, Michael, 1749, Anne Sharp                     3 TA-73
Hacket, Thomas, 19 June 1735, Mary Ratcliffe          1 QA-41
Hacket, Thomas, 6 May 1744, Margarit Gould            1 QA-49
Hackett, John, 13 Feb. 1711, Anne Evins               3 CE-4
Hackett, Lawrance, 15 Nov. 1704, Ann Potts            2 TA-42
Hackett, Michaell, 28 July 1709, Mary Bowles          3 KE-282
Hackett, Oliver, Jr., 18 July 1777, Ann Wilson        1 CR-10
Hackett, Thomas, 8 June 1756, Mary Bateman            1 QA-61
Hackitt, Thos., 6 May 1744, Margarit Gould            1 QA-47
Hackney, John, 11 April 1726, Hanah (?)               2 TA-113
Hackney, John, 28 Sept. 1735, Phebe (?)               1 CE-283
Hadaway, Thos., Jr., 15 April 1749, Mary Lowe         3 TA-72
Hadaway, Wm., 9 Feb. 1740, Mary Lamdin                3 TA-29
Hadden, John, 24 Feb. 1717, Amy Short                 1 AA-281
Hadden, John, 1 Feb. 1721/2, Sarah Lerey              1 AA-89
Hadden, William, 27 Sept. 1733, Mary Ann Lemar        1 QA-40
Hadder, Anthony, 7 Sept. 1749, Mary Spears            1 QA-56
Haddinton, Laban, 27 Jan. 1763, Ann James             2 BA-224
Hader, Warin, 5 Sept. 1746, Tamar Thomasman           1 QA-52
Hadeway, Rowland, 25 Feb. 1741, Eliza Hunt            3 TA-37
Hadlebrook, Samuell, 9 Dec. 1722, Elinor Roach        3 KE-286
Hadley, John, 13 Jan. 1731, Rachel (Tate?)            1 QA-38
Hadley, John, 1 Sept. 1741, Mary Voies                1 QA-47
Hadley, John, 17 April 1750, Rebecca Bostock          1 QA-57
Hadley, Robert, 12 Feb. 1752, Rebeccah Satterfield    1 QA-58
Hadmington, William, 1769, Eliz. Bosley               2 BA-258
Hadock, John, 20 Sept. 1756, Rachel Kelly             2 SO-130
Hager, John Michael, 2 May 1765, Hanna Keller         4 FR-1134
Hail, Henry, 10 Sept. 1741, Mary Bradley              1 BA-319
Hail, Jno., 4 Sept. 1762, Hannah Poteet               2 BA-223
Haile, George, 17 Jan. 1735, Elizabeth Chawfinch      3 BA-154
Hailes, John, 23 May 1725, Hannah White               3 KE-286
Haines, Daniel, son of Joseph and Elizabeth, 25 day,
   3 mo., 1762, Mary Price, dau. of Mordecai and Eliz. 9 SF
```

Haines, Isaac, son of Joseph and Elizabeth, 24 day,
  11 mo., 1762, Mary England, dau. of John and Eliz.     9 SF
Haines, Jacob, son of William, 22 April 1725, Mary
  Coles, dau. of William                                 9 SF
Haines, Jacob, c.1768, Mary Marshall, dau. of
  Humphrey and Sarah                                     9 SF
Haines, Job, son of Joseph and Elizabeth, 6 Feb.
  1766, Esther Kirk, dau. of Timothy and Anne            9 SF
Hains, Daniel, son of Joseph and Elizabeth of West
  Nottingham, Chester Co., Penna., 25 day, 3 mo.,
  1762, Mary Price, dau. of Mordecai                     4 SF-248
Hains, Nathan, son of Joseph, of West Nottingham,
  of Chester Co., Penna., 23 day, 10 mo., 1755,
  Sophia Price, dau. of Mordecai                         6 SF-238
Hale, George, 10 May 1660, Margrett Hill                 1 KE-186
Hale, Nicholas, 25 Dec. 1723, Ann Long                   3 BA-148
Hale, Patrick, 17 Dec. 1709, (wife not given)            1 BA-208
Hale, William, 27 Feb. 1718, Mary Hippy                  4 AA-403
Haley, William, 23 Oct. 1755, Mrs. Elizabeth Henrietta
  Forrester                                              2 KE-290
Halfpenny, Bingham, 18 Feb. 1734, Mary Austin            1 QA-40
Halfpeny, Robert, 10 Nov. 1732, Eliza White              1 AA-115
Hall, Capt. Alexander, 3 July 1709, Mrs. Mabel
  Knowles                                                2 TA-61
Hall, Andrew, 3 Sept. 1750, Esther Brown                 1 QA-57
Hall, Andrew, 16 Feb. 1769, Jane Kelley                  2 BA-257
Hall, Aquilla, 17 Dec. 1720, Johanna Kemp, widow         1 BA-230
Hall, Aquila, 14 Feb. 1750, Sophia White                 1 BA-48
Hall, Aquilla, 22 Dec. 1772, Mary Davis                  1 SM-136
Hall, (Benjamin?), 19 (Dec.?), 1731, Sophia Welsh        2 PG-5
  The entries are faded.
Hall, Charles, Jr., 31 Oct. 1693, Martha Davis           5 SO-398
Hall, Charles, 5 Jan. 1700, Elizabeth Smithers           2 AA-314
Hall, Christopher, 18 May 1759, Arraminta Massy          2 KE-298
Hall, Cuthbert, 4 Aug. 174-(?), Rosetta Holman           2 KE-254
Hall, David, Jan. or Feb. 1747/8, Sarah Clark            3 TA-68
Hall, Edward, 17 Nov. 1709, Deranira Everit              4 AA-379
Hall, Edward, 9 Feb. 1713, Sarah Wood                    4 AA-392
Hall, Edward, 31 Oct. 1717, Avarilla Carvill             1 BA-227
Hall, Edward, 24 July 1718, Elizabeth Topping            4 AA-405
Hall, Edward, 10 Oct. 1738, Mary Belt                    9 AA-246
Hall, Edward, 2 Sept. 1756, Sarah Phillips               1 BA-364
Hall, Edward, 14 June 1764, Martha Odell                 2 PG-7
Hall, Elisha, 13 May 1762, Mary Nicholson                3 BA-167
Hall, George, 12 Feb. 1746/7, Martha Redgrave            2 KE-265
Hall, George, 13 Feb. 1757, Mary Meeds                   2 CR-271
Hall, Henry, minister of St. James' Parish, 5 Feb.
  1701, Mary Duvall                                      1 AA-57
                                                         & 249
Hall, Henry, 25 Sept. 1723, Martha Bateman               2 PG-3
Hall, Henry (Nov.?) 1734, Elizabeth Lansdale             2 PG-6
Hall, Major Henry, 12 Nov. 1734, Mrs. Elizabeth
  Lansdale                                               1 AA-129
Hall, Henry, the son of Major Henry Hall, and grandson
  of Rev. Henry Hall, 27 Dec. 1748, Elizabeth Watkins    1 AA-159
Hall, Henry, son of Henry and Elizabeth, 27 Dec. 1774,
  Margery Howard                                         1 AA-159
Hall, Henry, 17 Aug. 1777, Elizab. Board                 1 MO-521
Hall, Hugh, 22 April 1756, Hannah Rogers                 3 KE-290
Hall, Isaac, 28 Aug. 1770, Anne Mease                    5 BA-7
Hall, James, May 1772, Sarah Burk                        2 BA-264
Hall, James, widower, 25 Sept. 1722, Elizabeth Rablin,
  widow                                                  4 AA-419
Hall, James, 27 March 1729, Ann Drapier                  1 AA-108
Hall, Jesse, 27 Aug. 1766, Mary Beauchamp                2 SO-133

```
Hall, John, 18 July 1693, Martha Gouldsmith        1 BA-178
Hall, John, 6 May 1697, Ann Hollis                 1 BA-178
Hall, John, 19 Oct. 1710, Hannah Everet            1 AA-77
Hall, John, 31 March 1730, Jane Pritchard          1 AA-110
   1 AA-111 giv-s date as 31 March 1731.
Hall, John, Jr., 26 Nov. 1734, Mrs. Hannah Johns   1 BA-286
Hall, John, 17 April 1737, Eleanor Clark           2 TA-163
Hall, John, 2 June 1742, Susanna Marshall          1 BA-326
Hall, John, 9 Aug. 1743, Mrs. Barthiah Stansbury   1 BA-341
Hall, Mr. John, 3 Nov. 1746, Mrs. Rachel Perse     2 KE-262
Hall, Mr. John, "of S'n, T'n" (i.e., Swan Town),
   2 March 1748, Mrs. Cordelia Holland             1 BA-346
Hall, John, 14 Aug. 1757, Mary Price               2 BA-216
Hall, Jno., 22 Dec. 1763, Eliz. Williamson         2 BA-225
Hall, John Beadle, son of John Hall of Cranbury,
   20 Jan. 1777, Sarah Hall, dau. of John Hall
   of Swan Town                                    1 BA-395
                                                   & 396
Hall, Jonathan, 24 Feb. 1759, Elizabeth Rochester  1 QA-65
   1 QA-64 gives date as 25 Feb. 1759.
Hall, Joseph, 30 April 1735, Mary Tippin           2 PG-6
Hall, Mordecai, 21 Feb. 1744, Sarah Vines          3 AA-106
Hall, Nathaniel, 23 Dec. 1777, Mary Hughes         3 PG-120
Hall, Philip, 2 June 1772, Sarah Frazier           3 BA-177
Hall, Phillip, 26 Dec. 1705, Margret Boyse         1 AA-72
Hall, Richard, 21 day, 2 mo., 1680, Sarah Rastoe   8 SF-323
Hall, Richard, 6 Aug. 1699, Jane Judkins, relict
   of Obadiah Judkins                              8 SF-380
Hall, Richard, son of Elisha and Sarah, 4 day,
   7 mo., 1712, Mary Johns, widow of Aquila        6 SF
Hall, Robert, 18 Oct. 1682, Elizabeth Mackettrick  5 SO-397
Hall, Samuel, 30 April 1732, Margrit Brady         1 WI-1
Hall, Samuel, 9 Feb. 1746, Anne King               2 BA-240
Hall, Thomas, 23 Sept. 1723, Ann Green             3 BA-148
Hall, Thomas, 3 July 1725, Butler Genera           1 AA-100
Hall, Thomas, 4 Nov. 1734, Margery Smith           2 TA-157
Hall, Thomas, 15 June 1736, Sarah Marler           3 BA-155
Hall, Thomas, 18 June 1752, Elizabeth Meeds        2 CR-271
Hall, William, 14 June 1716, Mary Edwin            3 KE-285
Hall, William, 7 Feb. 1726, Mary Gwinn             3 AA-104
Hall, William, 17 Dec. 1734, Mary Merryman         3 BA-152
Hall, William, 13 March 1764, Ann Duckett          9 AA-248
Hall, William, 14 Oct. 1767, Sarah Wood            2 SO-134
Hall, William, 3 Feb. 1773, Margaret Harwood       2 AA-411
Hallam, John, 18 Dec. 1755, Isabella Fell          2 BA-213
Hallam, Thomas, 10 Sept. 1733, Eliz. Deaton        2 BA-87
Hambilton, James, 5 Dec. 1745, Frances Bolton      1 QA-51
Hambilton, John, 16 Aug. 1744, Marg't Dunavan      1 QA-49
Hambleton, Edward, 27 Nov. 1701, Elizabeth (?)     2 TA-22
Hambleton, John, 18 May 1727, Mary Salegaw         2 TA-115
Hambleton, John, 10 March 1752, Sarah Dennis       2 SO-31
Hambleton, Phil, 5 Jan. 1744/5, Sarah Sherwood     3 TA-51
   2 TA-197 gives date as 6 Jan. 1744.
Hambleton, Robert, 15 Nov. 1733, Rebecca Bignall   1 BA-284
Hambleton, Sam'l, 24 Aug. 1740, Mary Dorsett       2 TA-169
Hambleton, Thos., 30 Jan. 1753, Easther Samson     2 BA-207
Hambleton, William, 10 Jan. 1739, Sarah Mourfitt   1 QA-45
Hamblin, Benjamin, 28 Feb. 1717, Sarah Dowlin      3 KE-285
Hamblin, George, 14 March 1670/1, Margaret Pepper  7 SO-401
Hamby, Francis, 20 June 1729, Alse Monday          1 BA-258
Hamby, Samuel, 20 Aug. 1737, Mary Sympson          1 BA-332
   1 BA-290 gives date as 18 Aug. 1738.
Hamby, William, 25 Dec. 1722, Martha Simpson       1 BA-231
Hamer, Collins, 6 July 1749, Mary Ann Warner       1 QA-55
Hamer, John, 19 Feb. 1742, Hanah Ratcliffe         1 QA-48
```

Hamer, Thomas, 27 Aug. 1746, Eliz'th Ratcliffe        1 QA-52
Hamill, George, 10 April 1671, dau. of John Pepper    7 SO-401
Hamilton, Edward, 18 Oct. 1764, Margaret Smith        2 BA-227
Hamilton, Jacob, 8 Nov. 1767, Mary Gibs; in Va.       4 FR-1134
Hamilton, John, 7 Dec. 1738, Sydney Brown             4 BA-70
Hamilton, Rev. John, late of Strabane, Co. Tyrone,
  7 Sept. 1757, Jane, dau. of Benj. Peck of N. Y.,
  and widow of Rev. Richard Currer                    1 CE-303
Hamilton, John, 7 Dec. 1758, Sarah Thrift             2 BA-218
Hamilton, John, 8 Oct. 1759, Eliz. Dickson            2 BA-219
Hamilton, John, 2 July 1772, Catherine Margaretta
  Forester, dau. of Rev. George Wm. Forester of
  Kent Co., Md.                                       1 CE-303
  2 KE-312 gives same information.
Hamm, John, 16 Nov. 1703, Helinor Hollins             3 CE-4
Hamm, John, 3 Jan. 1749, Ann Swift                    1 QA-56
Hamman?, William, 27 Oct. 1735, Mary Bayley           3 CE-20
Hammelton, Edw'd, 18 Oct. 1764, Margr't Smith         2 BA-227
Hammerstone, Richard, 17 Dec. 1777, Mary Wooster      3 PG-120
Hammet, John, 22 Sept. 1733, Rachel Dalby             1 QA-40
Hammett, John, 29 Dec. 1748, Mary Woodward            1 QA-55
Hammilton, Jno., 7 Dec. 1758, Sarah Thrift            2 BA-218
Hammilton, Jno., 8 Oct. 1759, Eliz. Dixson            2 BA-219
Hammond, Benjamin, 14 Sept. 1726, Sarah Eagle, dau. of
  Mr. Saladine Eagle                                  3 AA-101
Hammond, Benjamin, 6 April 1735, Margett Talbott      3 BA-153
Hammond, Charles, 24 Oct. 1715, Mrs. Rachel Greenberey 3 AA-99
Hammond, John, son of Thomas John Hammond, 14 June
  1748, Anne Gaither                                  4 AA-450
Hammond, John, 28 March 1773, Mary Humphreys          3 AA-113
Hammond, Lawrance, 26 May 1730, Ruth Grinise, dau.
  of John, a son James                                3 AA-105
Hammond, Laurance, 21 June 1734, Ebarilla Simpkins    3 BA-152
Hammond, Lawrence, 5 Dec. 1736, Margarett Hughes,
  dau. of Thomas and Mary                             3 AA-105
Hammond, Mordecai, 2 Sept. 1719, Frances Lilingston   3 AA-102
Hammond, Nathan, 30 Jan. 1731, Anne Welsh             1 AA-113
Hammond, Reazen, 2 Sept. 1760, Rebecca Hawkins        3 AA-112
Hammond, Thomas, son of William, 6 Jan. 1714, Jane
  Lillingston, dau. of Rev. John Lillingston of
  Q. A. Co.                                           3 AA-101
Hammond, Thomas, son of John, 28 June 1721, Ann
  Cockey                                              3 AA-101
Hammond, William, 3 Aug. 1732, Mary Merriken          3 AA-104
Hammond, William, 26 Aug. 1735, Eliza Raven           3 BA-154
Hammond, William, 9 March 1739, Sarah Sheredine       3 BA-156
Hampton, George, 8 Nov. 1733, Mary Hooten             3 CE-19
Hanan, William, 5 Jan. 1733, Eliza Cashon             1 AA-117
Hance, Addam, 25 Oct. 1744, Ruth Sutton               2 BA-191
Hancock, Stephen, 19 May 1741, Hellen Leshoday        3 AA-106
Hancock, William, Aug. 1724, Sarah Fincks             3 AA-105
Hancock, William, 29 Sept. 1750, Honour Stringer      3 BA-164
Hand, Joseph, 21 June 1774, Lydia Jones               1 CR
Hand, Peter, 12 Dec. 1750, Rachel Baley               1 QA-57
Handcock, Thomas, 1775, Celia Morris                  1 CR
Handerside, William, 18 Aug. 1771, Mary Williams      2 BA-262
Handland, John, 1749, Mary Cantwell                   2 BA-243
Handslap, Joseph, 10 Aug. 1699, Elizabeth Thomas      1 AA-49
Handy, George, eldest son of Isaac and Ann, 9 Feb.
  1755, Nelly Gillis                                  1 WI-98
Handy, John, 25 Dec. 1748, Ann Nutter                 1 WI-40
Handy, John, 3 Nov. 1768, Prise Long                  2 SO-136
Handy, Samuel, March 1679, Mary Sewell                5 SO-398
Handy, Samuel, 9 May 1736, Betty Bolithor             2 SO-30
Handy, Samuel, 15 Dec. 1737, Mary Dennis              2 SO-32

```
Handy, Saywell, 25 Feb. 1759, Mary Ann Sudler        2 SO-131
Handy, William, 25 Aug. 1768, Mary Robins            2 SO-134
Hankings, Jno., 7 Sept. 1708, Mrs. Eliz. Needles     2 TA-48
Hanks, Peter, 20 Aug. 1704, Mary Beez                4 AA-389
Hanks, Thos., 9 March 1748, Sarah Hewett             2 BA-198
Hannah, Wm., 3 Feb. 1763, Martha Meeks               2 BA-224
Hannah, Wm., 13 Dec. 1763, Ann Blood                 2 BA-225
Hannan, James, 29 Aug. 1756, Hannah Jackson          1 BA-358
Hannes, Miles, 24 Nov. 1698, Elizabeth Kelley        1 BA-186
Hanshaw, Charles, 23 Nov. 1746, Hannah Mattox        3 AA-110
Hanson, Frederick, 14 Feb. 1711, Mary Lowder         3 KE-283
Hanson, George, 22 Jan. 1711, Mary Hurtt             3 KE-283
Hanson, George, 17 Sept. 1713, Jane Hynson           3 KE-284
Hanson, Hance, 29 March 1679, Martha Wells Ward      3 KE-279
Hanson, Hanse, 29 May 1707, Ann Hamer                3 KE-282
Hanson, Hollis, 30 Dec. 1777, Avarilla Hollingsworth 1 HA-201
Hanson, Jacob, 8 Jan. 1723/4, Rebecca Miles          1 BA-243
Hanson, Jacob, 23 Jan. 1738, Margaret Hugs           1 BA-309
Hanson, John, 4 Aug. 1743, Semelia Garrettson        1 BA-332
Hanson, Jonathan, son of Timothy and Barbara of
   Philadelphia Co., 29 day, 5 mo., 1718, Mary Price,
   dau. of Mordecai and Mary                         6 SF
Hanson, Jonathan, 12 June 1733, Sarah Spicer         3 BA-151
Hanson, Samuel, Jr., 28 day, 10 mo., 1768, Lydia
   Berry                                             8 SF-133
Hanson, Timothy, Jr., of Kent, Penna., 20 day, 2 mo.,
   1743, Elizabeth Skillington                       8 SF-81
Harbaugh, George, 4 Oct. 1746, Catherine Williar     5 FR-49
Harbaugh, John (date not given), Maria Catherine
   Huber                                             5 FR-51
Harbaugh, John George, 27 Nov. 1770, Elizabeth Binkele 5 FR-52
Harbert, Charles, 21 Aug. 1718, Margret Tucker       2 TA-87
Harbert, Edward, 21 May 1724, Mary McNatt            2 TA-107
Harbett, John, 5 June 1718, Ann Bullock              2 TA-87
Harbutt, Jno., 21 July 1706, Rebecka Williams        1 CA-112
Hardaginn, Edmond, 30 Dec. 1714, Cathrine Jenkins    2 TA-75
Hardcastle, Robert, c. Oct. 1775, Mary Sylvester     1 CR-6
Harden, Henry, 6 Jan. 1713, Elizabeth Glover         2 TA-72
Harden, Joseph, 7 Aug. 1718, Martha Fromilier        2 TA-87
Harden, Joseph, 23 June 1743, Mary Eldrick           2 TA-198
Harden, Robert, 7 Nov. 1744, Rebecca Connor          2 TA-196
Harden, William, 25 Feb. 1733, Elizabeth Anderson    2 TA-155
Hardesty, Francis, 13 Jan. 1703, Ruth Gather         1 AA-64
Hardesty, Henry, 28 June 1777, Ann Selman (?)        7 AA-1
Hardesty, John, 25 July 1775, Catherine Thompson     1 SM-137
Hardesty, Joshua, 5 Oct. 1746, Keziah Taylor         2 BA-240
Hardey, George, 11 Feb. 1753, Lucy Dent              1 PG-316
Hardgrass, John, 1 Oct. 1724, Ann Scott              2 TA-109
Hardie, George, 4 Oct. 1719, Eliza Drayen            1 PG-262
Hardikin, Edward, 8 June 1718, Elizabeth Alford      2 TA-87
Hardin, Edward, 1 June 1732, Martha Oldham           2 TA-152
Hardin, John, 5 Dec. 1720, Elisabeth Miller          1 AA-302
Hardine, John, 17 Jan. 1711, Margaret Watts          1 AA-78
Harding, Benjamin, 18 Nov. 1739, Hannah Martin       2 TA-167
   3 TA-19 gives same information.
Harding, Edward, 2 June 1740, Rosannah Loud          2 TA-169
Harding, Edw'd, 21 June 1740, Rose Lowe              3 TA-23
Harding, Henry, 2 Dec. 1745, Eliza Dodson            3 TA-55
Harding, Robert, 7 April 1701, Elizabeth (?)         2 TA-24
Harding, Wm., 5 Feb. 1765, Mary Wiskitt              2 BA-227
Hardisty, Francis, 4 Feb. 1719, Dorcas Lincecom      1 AA-297
Hardman, Jefery, 21 Aug. 1692, Elizabeth Booker      8 SF-360
Hardson, John, 19 Nov. 1734, Mary Anne James         2 TA-156
Hardy, Henry, of Pyckawaxon, 21 Aug. 1694, Elinor,
   dau. of John Compton, of St. M. Co.               3 CH
```

Hardy, James, 8 May 1723, Eliz. Frond                          1 WI-2
Hardy?, James, 23 Feb. 1739/40, Winford Cornish               1 WI-32
Hardy, John, 7 Aug. 1757, Hannah Lanardy                      2 BA-216
Hargidon, Mark, 5 Aug. 1719, Jane Dias                        2 TA-90
Hargisty, Joshua, 6 Oct. 1746, Kezie Taylor                   2 BA-195
Hargrass, John, 31 Aug. 1721, Eliza Martindale               2 TA-96
Harkim, William, 14 April 1771, Christian Holland            2 BA-262
Harlan, Jacob, 27 July 1751, Deborah Barton                  1 FR-11
Harman, William, 24 June 1744, Sarah Powell                  2 BA-190
  2 BA-239 gives groom's name as Harmon, and the
  date as 17 June 1744.
Harnet, Michael, 9 Jan. 1763, Ann Hunt                       3 BA-167
Harper, Edward, 4 April 1682, Lydia Hudson                   5 SO-398
  5 SO-398 also gives date as 13 May 1682, and
  bride's name as Huttson.
Harper, John, Nov. 1740, Mary Weithers                       3 CE-22
Harper, John, 12 Dec. 1717, Anne Crawley                     4 AA-403
Harper, John, 1 Jan. 1760, Catheron Addams                   2 SO-130
Harper, Samuel, 27 Dec. 1744, Sarah MacCraree                1 BA-339
Harper, Thomas, 9 Oct. 1748, Mary Hawke                      1 QA-54
Harper, Thos., 19 June 1759, Mary Shields                    2 BA-218
Harr, William, 7 Feb. 1726, Mary Cash, dau. of John
  Cash                                                       2 PG-4
Harrice, Wm., 13 Jan. 1756, Mary Ginn                        2 BA-213
Harriman, George, 30 March 1725, Ann Wilkinson               3 BA-148
Harriman, Samuel, 18 Aug. 1723, Jane Smith                   3 BA-147
Harrington, Cornelius, 16 May 1710, Sarah Lee                3 KE-282
Harrington, David, 28 Feb. 1749/50, Mary Hunter             3 TA-77
Harrington, Nath'l, 16 Feb. 1764, Temperance Merryman       2 BA-226
Harrington, Philip, 5 July 1759, Rebeckah Morgan            1 QA-65
Harrington, William, 28 Feb. 1758, Ann Hughlett             1 QA-63
Harriott, Oliver, 13 Oct. 1717, Susanna Morrow             2 BA-10
Harris, Abraham, 22 Feb. 1754, Director Dickerson           2 SO-34
Harris, Amos, 31 Dec. 1730, Rebecca Scot                    2 TA-149
Harris, Charles, 23 Jan. 1772, Mary Green                   1 WI-94
Harris, Daniell, 23 May 1708, Elinor Fitchgerrald           3 KE-282
Harris, Edmund, 12 May 1706, Elizabeth Wright               2 AA-329
Harris, Edward, 19 June 1719, Frances Johnson               1 BA-230
Harris, George, 18 Feb. 1723, Rebecca Aldridge              1 AA-98
Harris, Henry, 30 May 1734, Mary Fisher                     2 TA-155
Harris, Henry, 4 Nov. 1740, Mary Witchot                    3 TA-25
  2 TA-169 gives date as 6 Nov. 1740 and the bride's
  name as Withgote.
Harris, James, 22 April 1701, Elizabeth Jones               3 KE-280
Harris, James, Dec. 1721, Dorothy Rogers                    2 BA-35
Harris, James, 30 Sept. 1746, Rebecca Baley                 1 QA-52
Harris, James, 2 March 1749/50, Sarah Dormon                2 SO-33
Harris, James, 4 June 1771, Cassandra James                 2 BA-262
Harris, John, 21 Oct. 1702, Mary (?)                        4 AA-380
Harris, John, 26 May 1757, Mary Marshel                     2 SO-130
Harris, John, of Va., 11 day, 3 mo., 1760, Rachel
  Plummer, dau. of Samuel of P. G. Co.                      6 SF
Harris, Lloyd, 4 July 1721, Eleanor Rogers, widow
  of Nicholas Rogers                                        3 BA-148
Harris, Moses, of Va., 3 day, 12 mo., 1761, Elizabeth
  Plummer                                                   6 SF
Harris, Richard, 17 Jan. 1682, Susanna Richardson           5 SO-398
Harris, Richard, 24 Sept. 1735, Margaret Giles              1 WI-67
Harris, Samuel, son of William, of Cal. Co., 2 day,
  4 mo., 1771, Rachel Wilson, dau. of Henry                 4 SF-256
Harris, Spencer, 26 Feb. 1749, Sinah McDannell              2 SO-35
Harris, Thomas, 20 July 1704, Mary Mitley                   2 AA-324
Harris, William, 5 March 1676, Alce Roberts                 5 SO-397
Harris, William, 8 Dec. 1702, Elizabeth Rose                2 AA-319
Harrison, Amos, 6 Nov. 1703, Jillion Botton                 2 TA-37

Harrison, Benjamin, 23 Feb. 1775, Sarah Steward    2 AA-412
Harrison, Edw'd, Feb. 1743/4, Fran. White    3 TA-47
   2 TA-196 gives date as 24 Feb. 1743 and the bride's
   name as Frances White.
Harrison, Ephraim, 27 May 1720, Mary Hutchison    1 AA-299
Harrison, Francis, 1716, Dorothy Lowe    2 TA-77
Harrison, George, 28 Aug. 1731, Rachell Matthews    1 QA-38
Harrison, George, 16 Dec. 1777, Sarah Dent    3 SM-536
Harrison, James, 25 Jan. 1741, Joanna Sherwood    3 TA-36
Harrison, John, 10 Jan. 1670/1, Judith Godfrey    7 SO-401
   5 SO-397 gives date as 18 Feb. 1670.
Harrison, John, 26 Dec. 1710, Sarah Gilbord    2 TA-68
Harrison, John, 4 Sept. 1733, Johanna Morris    3 BA-151
Harrison, John, 8 March 1735, Judith Pamphillion    2 TA-160
Harrison, John, 29 Aug. 1742, Lidia Ragon    2 TA-172
Harrison, John, 20 Oct. 1749, Fortune Neal    3 TA-75
Harrison, Jonathan, 4 Sept. 1733, Johannah Morris    3 BA-151
Harrison, Josias, 26 Dec. 1723, Mary Cornelius    1 AA-98
Harrison, Perry, Dec. 1750, Jane Fiddeman    3 TA-80
Harrison, Rich'd, 7 day, 3 mo., 1695, Elizabeth Hall    6 SF
Harrison, Richard, 23 April 1777, Mary Johns    2 AA-413
Harrison, Samuel, 18 Feb. 1776, Rachel Harrison    2 AA-412
Harrison, Thomas, 16 April 1777, Mary White    3 BA-172
Harrison, William, 20 April 1699, Elizabeth Dickinson    8 SF-451
Harrison, William, 2 Nov. 1710, Sarah Cook    2 TA-68
Harrison, William, 30 day, 8 mo., 1721, Elizabeth
Richardson    8 SF-33
Harrison, William, 10 Sept. 1730, Mary Bailey    1 QA-37
Harrison, William, 12 May 1740, Elizabeth Langain    3 BA-156
Harrison, William, 28 Aug. 1740, Isabel Mills    3 TA-25
   2 TA-169 gives date as 15 Sept. 1740 and the bride's
   name as Eliza Mills.
Harriss, Nehemiah, 25 Aug. 1777, Sarah Fletcher    1 WA-531
Harrisson, Cornelius, 16 Sept. 1727, Sarah White    1 AA-105
Harry, William, 12 Dec. 1710, Mary Peacock    3 KE-282
Harryman, Charles, 2 Feb. 1730, Milleson Haile    3 BA-150
Harryman, Charles, 6 Feb. 1752, Eliz. Reaven    2 BA-204
Harryman, George, 17 Oct. 1749, Sarah Reaven    2 BA-199
Harryman, Geo., 31 Jan. 1764, Sarah Merryman    2 BA-226
Harryman, John, 1 May 1752, Eliz. Clerk    2 BA-205
Harryman, Robert, 24 Jan. 1733, Elizabeth Simkins    3 BA-151
Harryman, Samuel, 3 June 1728, Comfort Taylor    3 BA-149
Harryman, Thomas, 1 March 1756, Ann Stansbury    2 BA-213
Hart, Edward, 17 May 1772, Mary Gaffin    2 BA-264
Hart, Samuel, 16 Aug. 1742, Catherin Gardner    3 AA-109
Hartegin, William, 9 April 1748, Mary Sawell    3 BA-161
Hartly, Joseph, 3 Sept. 1714, Ann Spiring    3 KE-284
Hartshorn, John, 20 Jan. 1731, Mabel Routh    1 QA-38
Hartshorn, John, 19 Nov. 1733, Elizabeth Spry    1 QA-39
Hartshorn, William, 26 Dec. 1735, Mary Oldson    1 QA-41
Hartway, Feiters, 27 July 1745, Elizabeth Parnetson    3 BA-157
Harvey, Alex'r, 13 June 1777, Eleanor McDaniel    1 HA-200
Harvey, Alexander, 19 July 1777, Rebecca McCauley    3 PG-121
Harvey, Thomas, 26 Dec. 1682, Elizabeth Greene    5 SO-398
Harvey, Samuel, 28 June 1720, Eliza Darby    4 AA-412
Harvey, Thomas, 16 Jan. 1757, Cassandra Gott    4 BA-71
Harvey, William, 14 Oct. 1721, Mary Horner    1 WI-8
Harvey, William, 2 Feb. 1726, Margaret Norman    1 AA-104
Harvey, William, 2 March 1730, Mary Sherbert    1 AA-111
Harvie, James, 12 April 1777, Eleanor Hodgkin    2 AA-413
Harvin, Joshua, 1 March 1753, Elizabeth Ray    2 FR-255
Harwood, Bozman, 6 Sept. 1774, Ann Harwood    1 CR
Harwood, Jno., 19 June 1707, Johanna Scorch    1 AA-73
Harwood, John, 5 Nov. 1742, Mary Perkins    3 TA-40
Harwood, Peter, 20 Sept. 1690, Elizabeth Taylor    8 SF-347

Harwood, Peter, Jr., 14 day, 12 mo., 1722, Grace
   Hopkins                                              8 SF-36
Harwood, Peter, 6 Sept. 1744, Susanna Steward         8 SF-87
Harwood, Richard, 9 Feb. 1737/8, Ann Watkins          1 AA-143
Harwood, Richard, Jr., 3 Feb. 1767, Margaret Hall     1 AA-144
Harwood, Robert, 13 April 1731, Mary Durden           8 SF-75
Harwood, Rob't, 22 Dec. 1744, Rachel Bozman           3 TA-51
   2 TA-197 gives date as 23 Dec. 1744.
Harwood, Sol., 15 Dec. 1746, Barbary Gibson           3 TA-63
Harwood, Thomas, 11 Sept. 1718, Sarah Belt            1 AA-287
Harwood, Thomas, 16 Jan. 1772, Margaret Strachan      1 AA-153
Haselupe, John, 30 March 1730, Blanch Jones           4 AA-432
Hasfurt, George, 8 Oct. 1674, Clements Kerne (or
   Keene)                                               5 SO-397
Hasfurt, George, 29 Nov. 1677, Elizabeth Hudson       5 SO-397
Hash, Darby, 27 April 1703, Dorathy Judar?            3 KE-281
Haslip, William, 12 May 1732, Ruth Enshaw             1 AA-114
Hassard, Edward, 8 Dec. 1671, Ann Carr                8 SO-401
   5 SO-397 gives date as Feb. 1671.
Hassell, John, 29 May 1739, Mary Willson              2 KE-239
Haste, Daniel, 2 Aug. 1680, Sarah Rogers              5 SO-397
Hastings, Isaac, 27 Oct. 1757, Sarah Brooks           1 QA-63
Hastings, Oliver, 19 Oct. 173-(?), Sarah Bell         2 KE-229
Hastins, George, 6 May 1714, Mary Higly               3 KE-284
Hatcheson, John, 21 Dec. 1758, Martha Ricaud          3 KE-291
Hatcheson, Nathan (date not given), Martha Miller     3 KE-290
Hatcheson, Robert, 10 Dec. 1749, Mary Ringgold        3 KE-289
Hatcheson, Vincent, 22 April 1716, Rachell Noleman    3 KE-285
Hatchman, Thomas, 8 Aug. 1718, Elisabeth Taylor       1 AA-284
Hatherly, John, 21 Dec. 1704, Elizabeth Ewynns        1 AA-65
Hatlew, Joseph, 4 Sept. 1713, Ann Spiring             3 KE-284
Hatlin, Thos., 29 Jan. 1767, Cathrine Bayley          2 BA-230
Hatten, Aq'a, 29 Dec. 1767, Eliz. Crook               2 BA-231
Hatten, Chainey, 31 Dec. 1761, Kez. Bailey            2 BA-223
Hatten, Jno., 16 Nov. 1765, Unity Welcher             2 BA-228
Hattfield, Mansfield, 7 Feb. 1765, Hannah Armstrong   2 BA-227
Hatton, John, 17 May 1733, Sarah Chieniey             2 BA-78
Hatton, Joseph, 17 Oct. 1710, Lucy Marbury, dau. of
   Francis                                              1 PG-259
Hatton, Joseph, 14 Oct. 1777, Martha Jones            3 PG-122
Hatton, Joseph, 5 Nov. 1777, Martha Jones             2 CH(1)
Hausen, William, 24 Oct. 1758, Sus. Freund            4 FR-1104
Hayward, Joseph, 9 day, 6 mo., 1757, Rebekah Scott,
   dau. of Jacob and Hannah                             9 SF
Haward, Job, 29 April 1704, Ann Howell                2 TA-40
Hawk, Greenville, 5 Aug. 1730, Mary Weeks             1 QA-36
Hawker, Robert, 26 Aug. 1764, Ann Waugh               9 AA-248
Hawker, William, 26 Jan. 1708, Sarah Price            1 AA-77
Hawkins, James, 22 Feb. 1773, Susannah Atlar          2 BA-265
Hawkins, John, Jr., 23 Dec. 1718, Rebecca Em(er)son   1 BA-222
Hawkins, John, son of John and Elizabeth, 17 Feb.
   1731, Susannah Fraser                                1 PG-261
Hawkins, John, 12 June 1733, Mary Simkins             3 BA-151
   4 BA-70 gives date as 13 June 1733.
Hawkins, John, 1 March 1741, Mary Wells               1 BA-327
Hawkins, John, 19 July 1761, Dorothy Wood             1 CH-190
Hawkins, Jos., 19 May 1744, Sarah Macdanile           2 BA-190
Hawkins, Mathew, 25 July, 1730, Rachel Burle          3 AA-109
Hiwkins, Mathew, 25 July 1746, Fran's Gould           1 QA-52
Hawkins, Nathan, 14 Feb. 1744, Ruth Cole              2 BA-192
Hawkins, Rich'd, 20 Nov. 1745, Rebecca Bradley        1 QA-51
Hawkins, Robert, 15 Nov. 1701, Anne Preble            1 BA-217
Hawkins, Robert, Jr., 13 Jan. 1742, Lydia Crutchley   1 BA-326
Hawkins, Rob't, 23 April 1764, Martha Davice          2 BA-226
Hawkins, Thos., son of John and Mary, 30 day, 5 mo.,
   1704, Eliza Giles, dau. of Richard and Marg't Arndell  6 SF

```
Hawkins, Thomas, 24 Jan. 1731, Eliz'th Farmer          1 BA-266
Hawkins, Thos., 22 June 1761, Rach'l Marsh             2 BA-222
Hawkins, William, 13 May (?), Sarah Noble              1 PG-284
Hawkridge, John, 24 Jan. 1743, Mary Richards           2 TA-196
Hawlines, Robert (19?) May 1772, Arebella Mitchel      2 BA-264
Hay, John, 2 Sept. 1777, Martha Andrews               10 BA-69
Haycraft, William, 18 July 1742, Mary Penington        3 AA-109
Hayes, William, Dec. 1775, Elizabeth Simmons           2 AA-412
Hayfield, James, 4 Dec. 1711, Anne Philpot             1 AA-265
  1 AA-78 gives date as 24 Dec. 1711.
Hayman, Henry, Jr., 24 Aug. 1687, Mathewe, dau. of
  Thomas Standridge                                    5 SO-398
Haymond, John, 22 Aug. 1723, Margaret Calder           2 PG-3
Haymore, John, 23 July 1705, Elizabeth Browne          3 KE-281
Haynes, Abraham, 21 Jan. 1773, Sarah Ricketts          4 KE-18r
Haynes, William, 4 Aug. (?), Mary Schooling            3 KE-282
Haynes, William, 27 April 1737, Mary Bennett           3 KE-288
Hays, Abraham, 21 Oct. 1744, Fanny Lytle               2 BA-239
  2 BA-92 gives groom's name as Edmund Hayes, and
  states that the banns were published three times
  by the above date.
Hays, Edmund, 8 Aug. 1751, Mary Bunnell                2 BA-203
Hays, John, 31 Oct. 1727, Mary Crabtree                1 BA-253
Hays, Lawrence, 22 Nov. 1716, Martha Sellman           1 AA-275
Hays, Thomas, 11 Aug. 1735, Mary Norrington            2 BA-149
Hayse, Mosses, 14 Nov. 1777, Sarah Daniel              1 MO-527
Hayward, Joseph, 9 day, 6 mo., 1757, Rebecca Scott,
  dau. of Joseph and Hannah                            4 SF-237
  9 SF gives the same information.
Hayward, Thomas, 4 Sept. 1753, Sarah Elzey, dau. of
  Major John                                           3 SO-4
Hayward, William, 29 day, 11 mo., 1757, Sydney Pier-
  point, dau. of Charles and Sydney                    4 SF-240
Hayward, William, 29 Nov. 1760, Marg't Robins          2 TA-287
Hazell, John, 7 Nov. 1704, Mary Nevitt                 1 CA-111
Hazenbiller, John, 26 Nov. 1767, Barb. Schnepf; in
  Va.                                                  4 FR-1134
Heairn, Jacob, 1 May 1765, Ginnit Gildcroy             2 SO-134
Heale, (?)-muel, 28 April (?), Elizabeth (?)           1 WO-2
Heard, William, 27 Nov. 1776, Susan Abell              1 SM-137
Heartlis, Joseph, 16 Dec. 1707, Mary Ann Fanton        3 KE-282
Heath, Mr. James, 25 Oct. 1759, Susannah Hall          1 BA-369
Heath, Robert, 13 April 1741, Mary Lamb                3 AA-106
Heath, Samuel, 29 Nov. 1771, Susan Lewis               2 BA-263
Heather, Richard, 29 Sept. 1757, Ann Gachell           1 QA-63
Heaven, John, 19 Aug. 1727, Elizabeth Fettyplace       4 AA-428
Hebedine, Thomas, 11 Aug. 1706, Elizabeth Raynire      1 CA-112
Hedge, Henry, banns were pub. Whitsunday, 1700, Máry
  Parker                                               1 BA-191
Hedington, Zebulon, 31 March 1771, Eliz. Lemmon        2 BA-262
Heickler, Nicholas, 20 Feb. 1759, An. Marg. Meyer      4 FR-1104
Heiner, John, 28 May 1761, Margaret Gebhard            4 FR-1134
Heir, John, 9 Oct. 1760, Eliz. Jones                   2 BA-220
Heirs, Jno., 7 Jan. 1762, Ann Welmoth                  2 BA-223
Heldebroad, Deowald, 8 July 1753, Mary Pickett         2 BA-208
Hellen, Peter, 24 Nov. 1726, Jan Parran                2 CA-23
Hellsby, Jeames, 19 Dec. 1727, Marget Slaughter        2 TA-117
Helm, Jno., 2 Sept. 1762, Cueler Bozley                2 BA-223
Helsby, James, 6 Jan. 1719, Elizabeth Harden           2 TA-92
Hely, John, 23 Dec. 1744, Sophia Rhodes                2 BA-191
                                                         & 239
Hen (Haine?), Lewis, 25 Sept. 1762, Susan Miller       4 FR-1134
Henderside, William, request dated 27 July 1771 to
  pub. banns, Mary Williams                            6 BA(1)
Henderside, William, 18 Aug. 1771, Mary Williams       2 BA-262
```

Henderson, Rev. Jacob, 2 Nov. 1746, Mrs. Mary Tyler    9 AA-246
Henderson, Jacob, 7 Aug. 1764, Edeth Henderson    2 SO-133
Henderson, Juron, 17 Nov. (1768?), Martha Wood    2 BA-257
Henderson, Phillip, 30 June 1768, Eliz. Smith    2 BA-232
Henderson, Richard, 3rd son of Rev. Richard Henderson
   of the parish of Blantyre, Lanarkshire, Scotland,
   by Janet Cleland, 19 Nov. 1761, Sarah Brice, dau.
   of John    1 PG-355
Henderson, Sam'l, 3 June 1751, Ede Outen    2 SO-31
   2 SO-132 gives bride's name as Edeth Outten.
Henderson, Thomas, 14 Aug. 1729, Mary ffrizbey    3 AA-103
Henderson, Thos. Frisby, 19 Sept. 1757, Hannah
   Hollandsworth, widow of George Hollandsworth    1 BA-380
Henderson, William, Aug. 1684, Sarah Bishop    5 SO-398
Henderson, William, 1748, Mary Traheren    2 SO-33
Henderson, William, 30 Oct. 1769, Elizabeth Coulbourn•    2 SO-135
Hendlen, Peter, 6 Aug. 1758, Mary Leek    1 BA-358
Hendon, Henry, 8 Aug. 1773, Mary Westfield    2 BA-266
Hendon, Isham, 27 Feb. 1749, Kezie Johnson    2 BA-200
Hendon, James, 7 Feb. 1754, Hannah Norris    2 BA-209
Hendon, Joseph, 31 July 1753, Mary Crudgents    2 BA-208
Hendon, William, 11 Nov. 1746, Lydie Hendon    2 BA-195
Hendress, Adam, 1744, Ruth Sutton    2 BA-239
Hendrickson, Henry, 5 June 1717, Elizabeth Etherinton    3 CE-10
Hendrickson, Peter, 9 Oct. 1728, Catherine Boushell    3 CE-16
Hendrix, Henry, 11 Feb. 1739, Esther Eubanks    3 TA-21
Hendrixson, Benj., 28 April 1763, Cathrine Haundrix    2 BA-225
Hendrixson, Garrett, 26 Feb. 1759, Mary Jackson    2 BA-218
Hendrixson, Jacob, 7 April 1763, Ann Low    2 BA-224
Hendrixson, Jno., 16 Oct. 1748, Ruth Sing    2 BA-197
Henley, Christopher, 28 Dec. 1704, Ezbett Smith    3 KE-281
Henley, Peter, 7 June 1761, Mary Wild    1 BA-371
Henly, John, 3 Feb. 1712, Esther Ricketts    3 KE-284
Henney, William, 9 May 1748, Constant Truelock    1 QA-54
Henrich, George, 21 Feb. 1762, Soph. Hoffman    4 FR-1134
Henrix, Henry, 14 Feb. 1739, Esther Eubanks    2 TA-168
Henrix, John, 30 July 1696, Rebecca Fortune, dau. of
   Robert    2 TA-4
Henry, John, 10 Feb. 1757, Mary Copeland    2 BA-214
Henwood, William, 26 Dec. 1727, Anne Ridgely    4 AA-429
Hepbourn, Richard, 12 Dec. 1732, Mary McCartey    1 QA-39
Herbert, James, 16 Dec. 1732, Anne Carr    2 TA-152
Herbert, William, 28 Nov. 1756, Eliz. Inchmore    2 BA-214
Herbert, William, 10 Jan. 1768, Anne Milbourne    4 SM-72
Hercium, James, 25 Jan. 1739, Rebecka Ayrs    1 QA-45
Herdester, Josua, 18 Sept. 1769, Isabella Williams
   "an der Catores; Beide Englishe"    8 BA-176
Herman, Edward, 7 Aug. 1731, Eliza Row    2 TA-150
Herman, James, 26 Jan. 1731, Sarah Frampton    2 TA-151
Herman, James, 24 Nov. 1734, Elizabeth Start    2 TA-156
Hern, William, 28 April 1738, Mary Trulock    2 KE-240
Herne, William, 31 Dec. 1672, Katherine Maltis    7 SO-401
   5 SO-397 gives bride's name as Mallis.
Hernly, Darby, Jr., 12 April 1757, Elizabeth
   Chamberlain    2 BA-215
Hernly, Edm'd, 17 Sept. 1759, Lattes Wetherall    2 BA-219
Heron, David, 9 Nov. 1752, Elisabeth Jones    1 QA-59
Heron, Elijah, 14 Nov. 1754, Sarah Johnson    1 WI-99
Heron, James, 23 April 1753, Mary Potter    2 BA-207
Herrick, William Williams, 25 May 1774, Ann Countess    1 CR
Herring, John, 2 Oct. 1777, Mary Strahan    1 MO-519
Herrington, Jacob, 26 Oct. 1720, Hannah Johnson    1 BA-237
Herrington, John, 2 Sept. 1712, Sarah Phillips    2 TA-72
Herrington, Nathan, 13 Dec. 1768, Elizabeth Herrington    2 CR-271
Hertzog, Engelberth, son of Peter, 29 Aug. 1769,
   Christina Spies, dau. of Ludwig    3 FR-105

Hervey, Samuell, 1715, Mary Watts                          4 AA-392
Heseltine, Charles, 7 Sept. 1720, Ebeanor Webb             1 CA-114
Hess, Jacob, 29 Sept. 1767, Rebec. Marg. Ohrndorf          4 FR-1134
Hestor, William, 24 Dec. 1728, Ziporah Duval, dau.
   of Mareen                                               2 PG-5
Hett, John, 12 July 1752, Rachell Jacobs                   1 AA-133
Heugh, Andrew, 14 Oct. 1751, Sarah Needham                 2 FR-276
   See also p. 280 of orig. register.
Heward, Jno., 6 Jan. 1704, Mary Milnes                     2 TA-43
Hewes, Edward, son of Joseph and Ann, 11 Oct. 1720,
   Mary Stubbs, dau. of Daniel and Ruth                    9 SF
Hewey, John, 13 Oct. 1750, Ra.: Ray                        3 TA-79
Hewit, John, 14 June 1773, Elizabeth Tucker                2 AA-411
Hewit, Joshua, 15 Jan. 1729, Mary Gilbert                  2 TA-121
Hewit, Richard, 28 July 1722, Elizabeth Fraser             4 AA-419
Hewitt, Charles, 6 Feb. 1749, Rachel Lewis                 1 QA-56
Hewitt, William, 15 May 1767, Jane Becker                  5 AA-3
Hewling, Jonas, 20 Dec. 1732, Ann Bowen                    3 BA-150
Hewston, William, 23 July 1777, Isabel Crookshanks         5 CE-1
   2 CE-1 gives same information.
Hewytt, Robert, 9 Jan. 1723, Elizabeth Chandler            4 AA-422
Heyall?, Edward, 1 July 1733, Amey Godfrey                 2 TA-153
Heyden, Samuel, 23 Jan. 1679, Ruth Miver?                  5 SO-398
Hichcock, William, 2 Feb. 1769, Cordelia Robison           2 BA-257
Hickcock, Richard, 8 July 1745, Mary Ann Hamer             1 QA-50
Hickman, John, 23 April 1728, Elizabeth Makan              2 KE-209
Hicks, Giles, 3 Dec. 1759, Mary Oxenham                    2 CR-271
Hicks, Henry, 30 April 1732, Anne Jenings                  1 QA-38
Hicks, Isaac, 24 Nov. 1748, Eliz. Miller                   2 BA-198
Hicks, Jacob, 2 March 1767, Ann Hitchcock                  2 BA-230
Hicks, James, 23 July 1710, Sarah Dowlin                   3 KE-282
Hicks, Jas., 23 April 1761, Mary Mothby                    2 BA-221
Hicks, Jo.:, 26 March 1748, Rebecca Carslake               3 TA-69
Hicks, Nehemiah, 12 June 1725, Phillisanna Hitchcock       2 BA-72
Hicks, Roger, 3 April 1733, Elizabeth Barkhurst            1 QA-40
Hicks, Thomas, 28 Sept. 1724, Mary Howard                  1 AA-99
Hicks, William, 24 Dec. 1747, Tabitha Stansbury            2 BA-194
                                                             & 242
Hicks, William, 12 Jan. 1748, Flora Cole                   2 BA-198
Higgans, John, 11 Nov. 1709, Mary Bullock                  2 TA-64
Higgenbothem, Richard, 14 Aug. 1677, Dennis Fountaine      9 SO-402
Higginbothom, Oliver, 3 Feb. 1708, Eliz'th Stevens         3 KE-282
Higgins, Andrew, 2 Sept. 1740, Mary Price                  3 TA-25
Higgins, Andrew, 6 May 1743, Elizabeth Kinnement           3 TA-43
Higgins, James, 25 Aug. 1777, Hannah James                 1 CR-10
Higgins, John, 4 Jan. 1727, Elizabeth Covey                2 TA-117
Higgins, John, 27 Sept. 1755, Ruth Philips                 1 QA-60
Higgins, Michael, 7 Feb. 1743, Isabel Powel                1 QA-49
Higgins, Nicholas, 25 Nov. 1714, Elizabeth Woolman         2 TA-75
Higgins, Richard, 27 Oct. 1765, Elizabeth Clark            9 AA-250
Higgins, William, 7 Nov. 1733, Margaret Lankford           2 TA-154
Higginson, Sam'l, 29 Jan. 1760, Darkes Barker              2 BA-219
Hildebrand, Adam, 23 Feb. 1761, A. M. Schaub               4 FR-1134
Hill, Abell, 10 July 1711, Susanna Gott                    1 AA-78
Hill, Alexander, 15 July 1731, Mary Redman                 1 BA-254
Hill, Alexander, 10 May 1744, Elioner Durbin               2 BA-190
Hill, Alexander, 10 March 1772, Eliz. Kelley               2 BA-264
Hill, Anthony, 18 Dec. 1732, Sarah Williams                1 AA-115
Hill, George, 6 Dec. 1711, Joan Britain                    3 KE-283
Hill, Hasidia, 26 April 1659, Ann Sheares                  1 KE-129
Hill, Henry, Jr., son of Henry and Mary, 9 day, 1 mo.,
   1720/1, Sarah Galloway, dau. of Sam'l and Ann           6 SF
Hill, Henry, 4 Nov. 1738, Sarah Galloway                   6 SF
Hill, Henry, 12 day, 3 mo., 1748, Mary Thomas              6 SF
Hill, Hope, 7 Feb. 1752, Rebecca Williams                  2 SO-35

```
Hill, James, 22 Oct. 1723, Eliza Clark              2 PG-3
Hill, James, 7 Dec. 1729, Mary Beale                7 AA-110
Hill, Jas., 23 Dec. 1762, Camilia Cadle             2 BA-224
Hill, Jas., 12 Feb. 1767, Hannah Wright             2 BA-230
Hill, Jas., 15 Oct. 1767, Sarah Alms                2 BA-231
Hill, John, Sept. 1674, Alce Brangeman              5 SO-397
Hill, John, 20 Nov. 1777, Sarah Naley               2 CE-1
Hill, Joseph, 17 day, 7 mo., 1724, Sarah Richardson 6 SF
Hill, Levin, son of Henry, 10 day, 11 mo., 1722/3,
   Eliza Hopkins, dau. of Gerrard                   6 SF
Hill, Richard, 5 Feb. 1771, Martha Chapman          2 BA-261
Hill, Samuel, 9 July 1727, Mary Dickson             2 TA-115
Hill, Samuel, 9 Feb. 1745, Ann King                 2 BA-194
Hill, Sam'l, 6 March 1760, Elizabeth Hopkins        1 BA-383
Hill, Samuel, son of John, 6 day, 3 mo., 1760,
   Elizabeth Hopkins, dau. of Joseph and Ann        9 SF
Hill, Thomas, Jr., 4 day, 1 mo., 1655, Margret Balie 1 KE-38
Hill, Thomas, 2 May 1742, Mary Stanton              1 QA-47
Hill, Thomas, 9 May 1749, Elizabeth Morgin          6 AA-210
Hill, Thomas, 23 July 1751, Dorcas Nelson           3 AA-110
Hill, Thomas, 19 Feb. 1757, Elizabeth Roe           2 CR-271
Hill, Thos., 25 Dec. 1763, Christian Meek           2 BA-226
Hill, William, 2 March 1701, Margaret Man           1 AA-250
   1 AA-58 gives her name as Margaret Marr.
Hill, William, Sept. 1724, Martha Green             2 BA-29
Hill, William, son of Stephen and Rebecka, 14 Sept.
   1768, Elizabeth Mitchell, dau. of Josiah and Sophia 1 WO-5
Hillary, Thomas, Jr., 9 Nov. 1727, Sarah Odill      2 PG-4
Hilleary, John, 18 Dec. 1735, Margaret King         2 PG-6
Hillen, Peter, 14 March 1746/7, Penelope Pattison   2 CA-46
Hillen, Solomon, 7 Oct. 1729, Elizabeth Raven       3 BA-149
Hilliard, Danill, 1703, Elizabeth Worrill           3 AA-99
Hilliard, Isaac, 14 Nov. 1676, Mary Thomas          9 SO-402
Hilliard, John, 14 Nov. 1676, Alce Roberts          9 SO-402
Hilliard, Thomas, 7 Feb. 1737, Susanna West         1 BA-299
Hills, William, June 1667, Elizabeth or Edith
   Headlowe                                         3 CH
Hilton, Joseph, 22 June 1769, Mary Troit            2 BA-258
Hind, William, June 1750, Henrietta Baker           1 QA-57
Hinderson, John, 1 July 1680, Elizabeth Barnabe     5 SO-398
Hindon, Jos., 9 Jan. 1766, Hannah Starkey           2 BA-229
Hindon, Richard, 8 June 1723, Sarah Garder          3 BA-148
Hinds, Thomas, 25 April 1730, Anne Wilson           1 QA-37
Hine, Jonathan, 20 Feb. 1730, Sarah Roberts         3 CE-13
Hines, Benj'n, 9 March 1742, Cornelia Warner        1 QA-48
Hines, Charles, 6 April 1735, Mary Rickets          1 QA-40
Hines, Nathaniel, 14 Feb. 1749, Mary Reed           1 QA-56
Hines, Thomas, 31 Jan. 1743, Anne Kemp              1 QA-49
Hines, Vincent, 10 Feb. 1731, Elizabeth Ponder      1 QA-38
Hinesly, Nathaniel, 21 Aug. 1733, Sophia Merredith  1 QA-39
Hinesly, Peter, 21 Aug. 1733, Mary James            1 QA-39
Hinesly, Thomas, 16 Nov. 1743, Rachel Olford        1 QA-48
Hinkes, Thomas, July 1746, Sarah Hewitt             2 BA-240
Hinks, William, 14 Feb. 1715/6, Elizabeth Bri-(?)   4 AA-397
Hinley, Timothy, 31 March 1746, Mary Adcock         1 QA-52
Hinsley, Charles, 11 June 1730, Catherine Foubert   1 QA-37
Hinsley, Peter, 14 Jan. 1745, Elliner Dawley        1 QA-51
Hinton, Jno., 22 June 1707, Elizabeth Cocksider     1 AA-73
Hinton, Thomas, 28 Aug. 1718, Rachel Howard         4 AA-405
Hinton, William, 24 Dec. 1721, Mary Durintune       4 AA-416
Hiscot, Benjamin, 28 Jan. 1741, Elizabeth Iiams     4 AA-443
Hitch, Robert, 14 Feb. 1751, Eve Hitch              1 WI-50
Hitch, William, 22 Oct. 1755, Ann Collins           1 WI-47
Hitchcock, Asael, 8 Oct. 1742, Sarah Norris         2 BA-130
   2 BA-133 gives date as 8 Oct. 1741.
```

```
Hitchcock, Isaac, 5 July 1764, Nancy Horne          2 BA-226
Hitchcock, Josiah, 10 July 1755, Susanna Garland    2 BA-47
Hitchcock, Nickles, 12 Oct. 1775, Sarah Polsen      1 CE-326
Hitchcock, William, 7 Sept. 1716, Anne Jones        2 BA-9
Hitchcock, William, Jr., 8 Nov. 1729, Susanna Slade 2 BA-74
Hitchcock, William, 2 Feb. 1769, Cordelia Robison   2 BA-257
Hix, James, 23 April 1761, Mary Mothby              2 BA-221
Hixson, John, 18 Jan. 1727/8, Hannah Sanders        2 TA-117
Hoany?, Thos., 28 Sept. 1736, Sarah Byrom           1 QA-42
Hobbs, James, 30 March 1742, Jane Brown             1 QA-47
Hobbs, James, 6 March 1745/6, Abigal Thomas         1 QA-52
Hobbs, Solomon, 27 Jan. 1757, Mary Ann Emory        1 QA-62
Hobeard, Thomas, 3 March 1771, Dinah Morel          2 BA-261
Hobs, John, 20 Aug. 1704, Mary Wilde                1 CA-111
Hocketty, Wm., 3 Aug. 1741, Mary Ann Worton         1 QA-47
Hocraft, Sylvanus, 16 Feb. 1772, Mary Goff          2 BA-264
Hodday, 7 Feb. 1769, Mary Byde                      2 BA-257
Hodder, Nehemiah, 26 June 17-(?), Cade (?)          1 WO-2
Hodg, George, 1712, Elizabeth Stanton               3 AA-100
Hodge, Philip, 13 March 1774, Jane Sutton           6 BA(1)
Hodges, Richard, 30 Dec. 1738, Mary Lucas           9 AA-246
Hodgess, John, 10 May 1699, Mary Newes              3 KE-280
Hodges, John, 18 Sept. 1746, Ann Bursels            1 QA-52
Hodges, William, 23 Dec. 1746, Frances Bradsha      3 KE-289
Hodgkin, Thomas Brooke, 24 Feb. 1757, Martha Evitts 4 AA-456
Hodgkins, Bennett, 20 April 1771, Susan Gatten      1 SM-136
Hodgskin, Jonas, 23 Dec. 1747, Rodey Driggs         2 SO-34
Hodskin, Joseph, 17 Oct. 1738, Catherine Carroll    1 BA-305
Hoff, Jacob, 17 Aug. 1762, Catharine Faut           4 FR-1134
Hoff, Lewis, 2 Oct. 1765, Catherine Fortune         4 FR-1134
Hoffman, Jacob, 26 June 1768, Barbara Brunner       4 FR-1134
Hoffman, Rudolph, 8 May 1758, Dorothy Weisz         4 FR-1104
Hoffmann, Geo. P., 6 Jan. 1767, M. Doroth. Len, widow 4 FR-1134
Hogan, James, 30 Jan. 1706, Elliner Dwyer          2 TA-46
Hogan, Patrick, 9 July 1775, Eliz. Engleton         1 SM-136
Hogan, Umphrey, 10 Jan. 1713, Rebekah Murphey       4 AA-380
Hogg, Laban, 22 Oct. 1751, Ruth Stansbury           2 BA-204
Hogins, William, 5 July 1754, Rachel Stavely        2 KE-288
Hogle, James, 19 Feb. 1738, Sarah Marshall          2 TA-166
Hognar, Jno., 6 Sept. 1763, Artelier Lowen          2 BA-225
Holoday, Francis, 16 Dec. 1736, Sarah Tompson       2 KE-222
Holbeucke, Joseph, 4 Feb. 1696/7, Temperance Ward   1 AA-36
Holbrook, John, 8 Feb. 1721/2, Ann Jones            1 AA-89
Holbrook, John, 8 Feb. 1721, Jane Jones             1 AA-309
Holbrook, Joseph, 8 Aug. 1711, Dorrothy Callingswood 1 AA-78
Holbrook, Joseph, 4 Oct. 1716, Mary Mont            1 AA-274
Holbrook, Joseph, 27 Dec. 1730, Mary Culver         1 AA-111
Holbrook, Thomas, 8 Aug. 1676, Alce Leverton        9 SO-401
Holburt, Samuel, 5 Oct. 1718, Jane Grey             4 AA-406
Holden, William, 8 June 1718, Rachel Ducktree       3 KE-285
Holding, Benj., 29 Oct. 1747, Sarah Betts           1 QA-53
Holdsworth, Thos., 1 Jan. 1712, Barbara Smith       1 CA-113
Holebank, Benjamin, 25 Nov. 1711, Mary Prise        3 KE-283
Holebrook, Roger, 3 April 1738, Mary Boston         3 BA-156
Holebrook, Thomas, 20 Aug. 1756, Sarah Hamilton,
   widow                                            2 BA-44
Holiday, William, 2 June 1694, Katherine Russell    2 AA-291
Holing, William, 3 Aug. 1709, Mary (?)              1 PG-259
Holland, (?)-muell, 1744, Tabitha Campbell          1 WO-9
Holland, Benjamin, 6 Jan. 1703, Mary Wilson         2 AA-322
Holland, Capell, 27 May 1718, Katherine Eldridge    2 AA-359
Holland, Edward, 14 June 1777, Jane Sullivan        7 AA-1
Holland, Francis, 7 June 1744, Cordela Night        1 BA-337
Holland, Gabriel, 5 May 1773, Sarah Harryman        2 BA-266
Holland, Jacob, 11 Nov. 1714, (?) Madcalf           2 AA-354
```

```
Holland, James, 9 Oct. 1729, Amy Simmons           2 PG-5
Holland, John, 11 Dec. 1701, Ann Spicer            2 AA-317
Holland, John, 8 June 1740, Sarah Wilabee          1 BA-305
Holland, John, 23 Dec. 1755, Eliz. Sicklemore      2 BA-213
Holland, Jno., 4 March 1766, Mary Wicks            2 BA-226
Holland, John, 14 Oct. 1770, Ann Baker             2 BA-261
Holland, Levi, 25 Oct. 1776, Sarah Cottingham      2 SO-137
Holland, Michael, 2 Feb. 1747, Mary Powell         2 SO-30
Holland, Otho, 9 Dec. 1718, Mary Howard, widow     4 AA-406
Holland, Richard, son of Thomas, dec., and Marg't,
  14 day, 10 mo., 1743, Ruth Plummer, dau. of Sam'l
  and Sarah                                        6 SF
Holland, Thomas, son of Anthony and Isabel, 3 day,
  2 mo., 1712, Marg't Waters, dau. of John         6 SF
Holland, Thos., 9 Sept. 1760, Margr't Riley        2 BA-220
Holland, Thos., 21 Dec. 1766, Ann Viteau           2 BA-230
Hollandsworth, George, 1 Dec. 1737, Hannah Nelson  1 BA-299
Hollice, Henry, 14 July 1711, Elizabeth Caudry     1 AA-78
Holliday, James, 30 Oct. 1721, Sarah Molton        1 BA-229
Holliday, John, 1770, Ann Carr                     2 AA-410
Hollingshead, Obadia, 5 Jan. 1704, Mary (?)        4 AA-389
Hollingsworth, George, son of Abraham, 19 Dec. 1734,
  Hanna McKay, dau. of Robert                      9 SF
Hollingsworth, James, 27 Feb. 1714, Anne Cutching  1 BA-215
Hollingsworth, James, 23 Dec. 1777, Mary McCracken 1 HA-200
Hollingsworth, Jno., 10 Nov. 1736, Elis. Carman    1 QA-42
Hollingsworth, John, Aug. 1741, Mary Deaver        1 BA-323
Hollingsworth, John, 1 Jan. 1743, Mary Devonshire  1 QA-48
Hollingsworth, Thomas, 14 Jan. 1741, Keziah Hollis 1 BA-321
Hollingsworth, Thomas, 4 June 1744, Eliz'h Jones   1 QA-49
Hollingsworth, William, 1 Jan. 1743, Sarah Robinson 1 QA-48
Hollingsworth, Zeb'n, 18 April 1727, Ann Mauldin   1 CE-285
Hollingsworth, Zeb, 21 July 1741, Mary Jacob       1 CE-288
  1 CE-289 gives date as 1 July 1741.
Hollins, John, Nov. 1709, Abigale Bateman, widow   3 CE-8
Hollinsworth, Charles, 4 Aug. 1730, Elisabeth Tyre 1 QA-36
Hollinsworth, John, 3 July 1730, Hannah Hacket     1 QA-37
Hollinsworth, John, Jr., March 1749, Mary Crupper  1 QA-56
Hollinworth, Isaac, 4 Dec. 1735, Rose Monsieur     1 QA-41
Hollinworth, Vincent, 31 Aug. 1733, Mary Herbert   1 QA-39
Hollis, Amos, 30 June 1761, Martha Everett, widow of
  John Everett                                     1 BA-369
Hollis, Henry, 14 July 1711, Elisabeth Coderey     1 AA-263
Hollis, James, 25 March 1706, Sarah Clarke         3 KE-281
Hollis, John, 30 July 1749, Mary Groom             2 BA-244
  2 BA-198 gives date as 12 Aug. 1749.
Hollis, Thomas, 11 Aug. 1715, Ann Green            3 KE-285
Hollis, William, 6 March 1708, Sarah Morgan        3 KE-282
Hollis, William, 13 March 1720, Ann Rhodes         1 BA-229
Hollis, William, 15 March 1748, Sarah Gallion      1 BA-359
Hollis, William, 1 Sept. 1763, Eliz'th Miller      3 KE-290
Hollister, Thomas, 8 Aug. 1723, Anne Allcock       1 AA-97
Holloway, John, 27 Jan. 17-(?), Fran... (?)-ford   1 WO-8
Holloway, R'd, 26 Dec. 1760, Eliz. George          2 BA-221
Holly, John, 4 March 1712, Hester Birch            1 PG-269
Hollyday, George, 13 July 1738, Mary Steward       1 QA-44
Hollyday, Henry, 9 Dec. 1749, Anna Maria Robins    2 TA-283
Hollyhock, Joseph, 5 Nov. (1704 ?), Elizabeth Saint 3 KE-281
Holmes, Richard, 21 Sept. 1703, Eve Delahay        2 TA-37
Holmes, Richard, 27 July 1725, Mary Attkins        2 TA-112
Holmes, Richard, 26 Jan. 1732, Sarah Mullican      2 TA-152
Holmes, Richard, 21 June 1739, Rachel Abbott       2 TA-167
Holmes, William, 8 May 1711, Mary Pottenger        1 AA-78
Holmoney, Jno., 30 Oct. 1760, Eliz. Billingsley    2 BA-220
Holms, Charles, 25 Dec. 1716, Barbary Williams     2 TA-79
```

```
Holms, John, 18 Aug. 1720, Ann Abbott              2 TA-94
Holms, Richard, 1 Dec. 1720, Sarah Abbott          2 TA-94
Holms, Richard, 15 June 1739, Rachel Abbott        3 TA-17
Holms, Thom's, 8 Jan. 1707, Mary Rosann            4 AA-380
Holms, Thomas, 8 Jan. 1707/8, Mary Rossier         4 AA-372
Holms, Walter, 3 Dec. 1725, Elizabeth Bradcut      1 AA-101
Holms, William, 15 Aug. 1738, (?) (?)              9 AA-246
Holsey, John, 11 Aug. 1737, Sarah Troth            2 TA-164
Holshot, Jno., 12 Aug. 1701, Dorothy Ireland       1 CA-111
Holt, Arnald, 11 Feb. 1744, Martha Boarding        2 BA-192
  2 BA-240 gives date as Feb. 1745.
Holt, George, 6 June 1763, Cathrine Price, dau. of
  William                                          3 CE-26
Holt, John, 7 Dec. 1721, Elizabeth Timmings        2 TA-97
Holton, George, 19 May 1726, Mary Money            3 CE-13
Holton, James, 6 Feb. 1734, Martha Harding         2 TA-157
Holton, Jessey, 16 Nov. 1734, Sarah Porter, dau. of
  (James ?) Porter                                 3 CE-19
Holywood, Christopher, 12 Jan. 1718/9, Margaret
  Sedgwick                                         4 AA-407
Holz, Jacob, 14 Sept. 1761, Catherine Haelt        4 FR-1134
Holzinger, Geo. M., 25 Nov. 1767, An. B. Schneider 4 FR-1134
Homewood, Thomas, 9 Jan. 1727, Rachell Meriken     3 AA-102
Homewood, Capt. Thomas, 16 Dec. 1731, Ann Hammond,
  dau. of Charles                                  3 AA-105
Honey, Thomas Valentine, 18 Jan. 1756, Rachel Ruth 1 QA-60
Honey, Thomas Vallintine, 10 July 1744, Sarah Sparks 1 QA-49
Honey, Valentine Thomas, 25 Jan. 1759, Mary Colbreath 1 QA-64
Honey, William, 3 March 1752, Jane Burcalow        1 QA-58
Hood, Charles, 15 Aug. 1765, Mary Mitchell         9 AA-249
Hood, Richard, 5 Feb. 1748, Mary Orford            3 BA-163
Hood, Thomas, 30 July 1707, Elizabeth Battee, widow 1 AA-76
Hood, William, 1 July 1728, Elizabeth Maccubbin    1 AA-107
Hook, Roger, 13 Feb. 1696, An (sic) Taylor         2 TA-5
Hook, Stephen, 6 Feb. 1757, Dorothy Barklett       1 QA-62
Hoolins, Nicholas, 24 Oct. 1710, Elliner Jones     2 TA-68
Hooper, Henry, 4 July 1669, Elizabeth Denwood      5 SO-397
Hooper, Isaac, 10 Nov. 1770, Elizabeth Hollyday    2 CA-58
Hooper, Jno., 19 Sept. 1765, Sara Jerues           2 BA-228
Hooper, Phillip, 28 April 1771, Eliz. Palmer       2 BA-262
Hooper, Thomas, 21 Oct. 1708, Susanna Nicholson    1 AA-76
Hope, George, 21 Dec. 1703, Dorcas Turner          1 AA-64
Hope, George, 27 May 1706, Judith Clark            1 AA-72
Hope, Jas., 24 May 1768, Eliner Demorce            2 BA-231
Hopkins, Andrew, 11 Nov. 1745, Eliza Skinner       3 TA-55
Hopkins, Ben:, 10 Nov. 1740, Mary Skinner          3 TA-26
Hopkins, Dennis, 28 June 1720, Sarah Edmondson     2 TA-93
Hopkins, Elisha, son of Gerrard, 27 day, 6 mo.,
  1777, Hannah Howell, dau. of Isaac and Patience,
  of Phila.                                        6 SF
Hopkins, Fran.:, 30 April 1745, Susannah Wats      3 TA-52
Hopkins, George Collair, 27 Aug. 1761, Betty
  Leatherbury                                      1 WI-118
Hopkins, Gerard, 1770, Eleanor Ward                2 AA-409
Hopkins, Gerrard, Jr., 7 day, 3 mo., 1730, Mary Hall,
  dau. of Richard Hall                             6 SF
Hopkins, Isaac, 18 April 1747, Margaret Nicholson  1 WI-52
Hopkins, John, 27 Dec. 1713, Ann Hickinbottom      2 BA-4
Hopkins, John, 19 Nov. 1717, Elizabeth Dunning     1 PG-268
Hopkins, John, 10 Feb. 1745/6, Eleanor Wrightson,
  widow of Francis Wrightson                       3 TA-56
Hopkins, John, son of Samuel and Sarah, 24 day, 11
  mo., 1768, Elizabeth Chew, dau. of Joseph and Sarah 7 SF-22
Hopkins, Johns, 16 day, 2 mo., 1758, Elizabeth Thomas,
  dau. of Samuel                                   6 SF
```

Hopkins, Johns, 14 day, 9 mo., 1749, Mary Crockett          6 SF
Hopkins, Johns, Jr., son of Johns, 30 day, 5 mo.,
  1775, Elizabeth Harris, dau. of William                  6 SF
Hopkins, Jona'n, 22 April 1750, Rachel Connakin            3 TA-77
Hopkins, Joseph, son of Gerrard and Marg't, 17 day,
  6 mo., 1727, Ann Chew, dau. of John and Elizabeth        6 SF
  9 SF gives same information.
Hopkins, Joseph, son of Joseph and Ann, 9 day, 2 mo.,
  1769, Elizabeth Gover, dau. of Ephraim and Eliza-
  beth                                                     7 SF-30
Hopkins, Joshua, 10 Aug. 1739, Sarah Watts                 3 TA-17
  2 TA-167 gives date as 16 Aug. 1739.
Hopkins, Levy, 8 Nov. 1772, Betty Nicholson                1 WI-98
Hopkins, Phillip, 24 March 1705, Johanna Priner            3 KE-281
Hopkins, Philip, 1771, Moore Cole                          2 AA-411
Hopkins, Philip, 13 March 1775, Catherine Evans            5 BA-7
Hopkins, Philip, 30 Oct. 1777, Mary Mobberly               7 AA-2
  8 AA-15 gives date as 31 Oct. 1777, and the bride's
  name as Moberly.
Hopkins, Richard, 12 Sept. 1723, Mary Resho                2 TA-105
Hopkins, Richard, 17 Sept. 1727, Mary Thrift               2 TA-116
Hopkins, Rich'd, 14 Oct. 1764, Eliz. Gellard               2 BA-227
Hopkins, Richard, son of Gerrard, 23 day, 12 mo.,
  1774, Ann Snowden, dau. of Samuel                        6 SF
Hopkins, Robert, 22 May 1738, Eliza Tunney                 2 TA-165
Hopkins, Rob't, 16 July 1767, Eliz. Talbott                2 BA-230
Hopkins, Rob't, 3 Oct. 1774, Dorcas Hooper                 1 CR
Hopkins, Samuell, 14 Dec. 1738, Sarah Robinson             2 TA-166
Hopkins, Samuel, 2 day, 7 mo., 1740, Sarah Giles           4 SF
Hopkins, Samuel, 25 Jan. 1741, Esther Rigbey               3 TA-36
Hopkins, Samuel, son of Philip and Elizabeth, 8 day,
  6 mo., 1769, Mary Gover, dau. of Ephraim and
  Elizabeth                                                7 SF-18
Hopkins, William, 31 March 1700, Dorathy Willis            3 KE-280
Hopper, Abraham, 8 Jan. 1764, Mary Hillen                  2 CA-48
Hopper, James, 5 May 1709, Elizabeth Pattison              1 AA-77
                                                           & 256
Hopper, John, 20 Aug. 1730, Rachell Nicholson              1 AA-111
Hopper, Robert, 16 April 1718, Deborah Lee                 1 AA-282
Hopper, William, 15 April 1776, Ann Cox                    2 CR-271
Horn, William, 28 Oct. 1697, Sarah Franklin                2 AA-294
Horne, Jno., 24 July 1764, Eleaner Ryley                   2 BA-226
Horner, Jas., 25 Dec. 1760, Tam'r Cameron                  2 BA-221
Horner, Nath'l, 26 April 1764, Jane Wiggfield              2 BA-226
Horner, Richard, 8 July 1745, Mary Hewet                   3 AA-109
Horner, Thomas, 27 Oct. 1741, Grace Anderson               1 BA-320
Horner, Vachel, 9 Dec. 1766, Sarah Jacobs                  3 AA-112
Horney, James, 11 Jan. 1741, Elizabeth Hopkins             3 TA-36
Horney, Jeffrey, 6 Oct. 1739, Deborah Baynard              3 TA-18
Horney, John, 11 June 1750, Sarah Wantling                 3 TA-78
Horney, Phil., 21 May 1745, Mary Wilson                    3 TA-53
Horney, Sol., 8 March 1748/9, Mary Gibson                  3 TA-72
Horrohone, John, 22 Dec. 1709, Mary Clifford               2 TA-64
Horsey, Isaac, 7 Aug. 1688, Sarah (?)                      5 SO-398
Horsey, James, 3 Feb. 1728/9, Mary Seward                  1 QA-36
Horsey, John, of John, 1 May 1776, Amelia Leatherbury      2 SO-138
Horsey, Outerbridge, 12 March 1738/9, Mary Dixon           2 SO-31
Horsey, Revel, 1 April 1759, Sarah Fosset                  2 SO-131
Horsey, Smith, 31 May 1746, Mary Coleman                   2 SO-30
Horsford, John, 30 March 1719, Anne Hayfield               1 AA-291
Horsley, Rich'd, 9 May 1697, Mary Vickery                  2 TA-7
Horssman, Thomas, 19 Sept. 1681, Jane Edgar                5 SO-397
Hort, John Andrews, 16 April 1750, Margarett Forbush       1 QA-56
Horton, Rich'd, 21 Aug. 1755, Eliz. Davice                 2 BA-212
Horton, William, 18 Dec. 1707, Mary Davis                  4 AA-372

Horton, William, 21 March 1759, Elizabeth Wakerman or
  Pritchard                                              1 BA-367
Horton, William, 3 Oct. 1769, Eliz. Jarrett              2 BA-185
Hoskins, Edward, 8 April 1705, Mary Prise               3 KE-281
Hoskinson, Elisha, 21 July 1777, Henrietta Brashears    3 PG-101
Houchins, William, 29 Nov. 1748, Hannah Gwin            3 BA-162
Hoult, Joseph, 27 March 1703, Ellin Abbott              2 TA-38
Houlton, James, 13 Feb. 1728/9, Mary Manton             2 TA-120
House, John, 1750, Penelope Bond                        2 BA-244
Householder, Hen., 16 Feb. 1769, Mary Jonas             2 BA-257
Householder, Jacob, 8 Nov. 1770, Eliza White            2 BA-261
Houston, Francis, 6 March 1769, Scarbrough Broadwaters  2 SO-130
Houston, John, 18 Oct. 1749, Mary Milbourn              2 SO-136
Houston, John, 10 Dec. 1771, Hannah Waltham             2 BA-263
Houston, John, 13 Nov. 1775, Ann Glastor                2 SO-137
Hovington, Jonathan, 10 Dec. 1729, Betty Cooper         1 WI-10
Hovington, Richard, 24 Aug. 1734, Ann Garrett           1 WI-5
Hovington, Thomas, 11 Aug. 1727, Margrit Evans          1 WI-22
How, William, 11 June 1761, Mary Lester                 1 BA-378
How, William, 27 Jan. 1771, Margaret Jackson            2 BA-261
Howard, Benjamin, 22 Jan. 1716, Cathrine Buck           3 AA-102
Howard, Benjamin, 7 Oct. 1755, Sarah Bond               2 BA-212
Howard, Benjamin, son of Lemuel, 4 Dec. 1766, Mary
  Dutton, dau. of Robert                               4 SF-252
  2 BA-229 gives same information.
Howard, Charles, 1 Aug. 1715, Mary Selby                4 AA-392
Howard, Cornelius, 24 Jan. 1738, Ruth Eager             4 BA-70
Howard, David, 22 July 1711, Catherine Barley           2 AA-343
Howard, Edmond, 27 Feb., 1728, Ruth Teale               3 BA-155
Howard, Edmund, 26 May 1681, Margaret Dent              5 SO-397
Howard, George, 18 Feb. 1762, Priscilla Lankford        2 SO-132
Howard, George, 21 July 1774, (?) Walker, of Q. A. Co.  1 CR
Howard, James, 8 Dec. 1720, Barbara Taylor              4 AA-413
Howard, James, son of Henry and Hannah, 12 day, 11 mo.,
  1761, Alice Passmore, dau. of Augustine and Judith   9 SF
Howard, John, 17 Sept. 1732, Elizabeth Gassaway         1 AA-114
Howard, John Beal, 18 April 1765, Blansh Hall, dau. of
  Parker                                               2 BA-187
Howard, John Griffith, 7 Dec. 1746, Eliz. Bond          2 BA-195
Howard, Joseph, 12 Dec. 1706, Anne Burrass              1 AA-73
Howard, Joseph, 28 Sept. 1708, Margery Keith            4 AA-378
Howard, Joseph, son of Joseph and Margaret, 4 July
  1771, Margaret Hall                                  1 AA-149
Howard, Lemuel, 11 Jan. 1730, Mrs. Anne Ward            2 BA-91
Howard, Lemuel, 7 Dec. 1760, Martha Scott               2 BA-220
Howard, Matthew, 26 Oct. 1714, Mary Browning, widow
  of George                                            2 KE-204
Howard, Nehemiah, 28 Oct. 170-(?), Sarah Collings       1 WO-4
Howard, Robert, 29 Dec. 1730, Tamer Smith               2 TA-149
Howard, Robert, Sept. 1772, Susan Holland               2 BA-265
Howard, Samuel, 29 Jan. 1740, Patience Dorsey           4 AA-442
Howard, Thomas, 15 Dec. 1720, Priscilla Selby           4 AA-413
Howard, Thomas, 4 July 1723, Cathrine Johnson           3 BA-146
Howard, Thomas Gassaway, 24 Feb. 1765, Frances Holland,
  dau. of Francis                                      2 BA-187
Howard, William, 4 Jan. 1673, Mary Hobday               5 SO-397
Howard, William, 6 Nov. 1712, Eliz'th Seeny             3 KE-283
Howard, William, 2 July 1728, Juliannah White           2 TA-118
Howard, William, 16 May 1730, Martha Burn               2 TA-148
Howard, William, 13 Jan. 1732, Grace Wood               1 AA-115
Howard, William, 1771, Hanna Ford                       2 AA-410
Howard, William, 4 July 1776, Eleanora Thompson         1 SM-137
Howarton, William, 19 Jan. 1695, Katherine Ridge        2 AA-292
Howel, James, 13 April 1748, Obedience Brookshire       1 QA-54
Howel, Samuel, 8 Dec. 1720, Priscilla Freeborn          1 BA-279

Howell, John, April 1740, Mary Hall                         2 KE-232
Howell, Samuel, 11 Sept. 1747, Sarah Durbin                1 BA-70
Howell, William, son of George and Mary, both from
    Co. Cork, Ireland, 9 Nov. 1755, Ruth Smith, dau. of
    William and Sarah                                      1 CE-305
Howerton, William, 24 Sept. 1724, Alice Hennis             2 PG-3
Howlet, Robert, undated request to publish banns,
    Elizabeth Boone                                        6 BA(1)
Hows, John, 22 July 1750, Penelipy Bond                    2 BA-201
Howsley, William, 2 April 1711, Eliz'th Ambey              3 KE-282
Huber, Jacob, 2 March 1761, Christina Kern                 4 FR-1134
Huchings, Thomas, 28 Nov. 1703, Mary Cox                   2 TA-38
Huchison, John, 27 June 1716, Mary Pirkins                 3 CE-9
Huck, Jacob, 26 Dec. 1769, Elisabeth Huckin                8 BA-176
Huckil, Henry, 16 Feb. 1729, Elioner Butcher               3 CE-18
Hudson, Henry, 26 May 1751, Rhoda Tingle                   1 WO-10
Hudson, Hugh, 5 Feb. 1709, Cathrine Donagan                2 TA-65
Hudson, Jonathan, 6 April 1772, Tabitha Tilghman           2 SO-138
Hudson, William, 3 Nov. 1742, Catherine Cary               4 AA-444
Hudson, William, 30 Jan. 1749, Sarah Deason                2 BA-200
                                                             & 244
Hues, George, 17 Feb. 1716, Eliz. Simmons                  2 TA-79
Hues, Robert, 3 Nov. 1721, Margret Nicholis                2 TA-97
Huet, Thomas, 25 May 1769, Ann Wyle                        2 BA-258
Huff, John, 25 Nov. 1706, Ann Morgan                       3 KE-282
Huff, John, 24 March 1771, Eliz. Ferguson                  2 BA-261
Huffington, Lazarus, 23 Nov. 1759, Mary Harris             1 WI-63
Huffington, Levin, 12 Nov. 1753, Mattilda Ackworth         1 WI-71
Hugg, William, 24 Sept. 1777, Mary Flintham                2 CE-1
Huggins, John, 27 April 1700, Elizabeth Morley             2 AA-298
Huggins, John, Jr., 7 Oct. 1742, Mary Downs                2 BA-144
                                                             & 238
Huggins, Wm., 19 Dec. 1754, Ann Talbee                     2 BA-211
Hughdell, William, 26 Jan. 1758, Mary Costley              2 BA-217
Hughdell, William, 9 July 1761, Hannah Beck                2 BA-222
Hughes, Felix, 1 Oct. 1743, Catherine Noble                1 BA-339
Hughes, James, 13 Aug. 1733, Alice Davis                   3 CE-17
Hughes, John, 20 Nov. 1710, Sarah Holland                  2 PG-1
Hughes, John, 14 March 1775, Agness Graham                 5 BA-7
Hughes, Jonathan, 10 Dec. 1728, Jane Shepherd              1 BA-249
Hughes, Samuel, 4 Nov. 1714, Jane Scott, widow of
    Francis Watkins                                        1 BA-215
Hughes, Thomas, 26 Oct. 1765, Ann Plummer                  9 AA-249
Hughes, Thomas, 16 May 1774, Frances Forrester, of
    Georgetown, Kent Co.                                   1 CE-313
Hughes, Thomas, 25 Aug. 1774, Frances Dorcas
    Forester                                               2 KE-312
Hughes, William, 24 June 1743, Ann Bellows                 2 BA-126
Hughs, Aron, 22 Nov. 1764, Eliz. Taylor                    2 BA-227
Hughs, James, 4 Feb. 1722, Eleanor Orange                  1 AA-94
                                                             & 318
Hughs, James, 6 April 1769, Eliz. Weeks                    2 BA-258
Hughs, John, 20 Jan. 1703, Elizabeth Wilson                2 TA-38
Hughs, John, 6 Feb. 1738, Aviss Hancok                     3 AA-109
Hughs, John, 11 Sept. 1740, Elizabeth Norris               1 BA-313
Hughs, Jno., Jr., 19 Feb. 1767, Sarah Day Wright           2 BA-230
Hughs, John, 23 May 1771, Tabitha Haryman                  2 BA-262
Hughs, John Hall, 26 Jan. 1769, Ann Everitt                1 BA-390
Hughs, Sollomon, 7 June 1772, Sophia Wright                2 BA-264
Hughs, Thomas, 21 Sept. 1703, Mary Whiborn                 2 AA-322
Hughs, Thomas, 5 Dec. 1731, Catherine Denice               3 BA-150
Hughs, Thomas, 4 Jan. 1770, Margret Talbott                2 BA-257
Hughs, William, 25 Nov. 1716, Elizabeth Croley             4 AA-398
Hughs, William, 11 Dec. 1735, Hannah Bankston              3 BA-154
Hughs, William, 5 Feb. 1769, Ann Beck                      2 BA 257

```
Hughston, John, 10 Dec. 1771, Hannah Waltham          2 BA-263
Hugins  John, 29 Aug. 1742, Mary Downes               2 BA-238
Hugs, Nerson, 29 Nov. 1770, Margret Little            2 BA-261
Hukill, John, 18 June 1733, Mary Husbands             3 CE-16
Hull, Daniel, 5 day, 8 mo., 1748, Martha Throul       1 SF-84
Hull, David, 11 day, 11 mo., 1730, Margaret Weather-
   hill                                               1 SF-62
Hull, Ferdinando, 29 Sept. 1742, Elizabeth Stavely    2 KE-249
Hull, Joseph, 28 Aug. 1712, Hannah Stapeley           3 KE-283
Hull, Nath'l, 20 Oct. 1739, Anne Franton              3 TA-18
Hull, Nathaniel, 22 Sept. 1741, Marg't Pattison       3 TA-33
   2 TA-191 gives date as 6 Oct. 1741.
Humperis, Joseph, 18 Jan. 1707/8, Ell-(?) Maskswell   4 AA-372
Humphrey, Joseph, 25 Sept. 1748, Anne Jenkins         1 PG-288
Humphrey, Thomas, 29 April 1674, Mary King            5 SO-397
Humphreys, Robert, 2 Sept. 1664, Elizabeth Bromton    1 KE-186
Humphreys, Thomas, 17 Feb. 1728/9, Rachel Moore       2 TA-120
Humphreys, Thomas, 1 July 1730, Elizabeth Powell      4 AA-433
Humphris, Joshua, 28 Aug. 1755, Esther Neale          1 WI-72
Humphris, Richard, 13 May 1703, Mary Barwell          3 AA-96
Humphris, Thomas, 23 April 1736, Temperance Morris    1 WI-48
Humphrys, William, 8 Nov. 1742, Cumfort Croker        3 AA-106
Hunn, Francis, 7 July 1754, Margrett James            2 BA-210
Hunt, Daniell, 11 Feb. 1731, Sarah Phillips           1 WI-7
Hunt, James, 6 Aug. 1742, Mary Murrin                 2 BA-238
Hunt, Roger, 24 May 1741, Susanna McKey               2 KE-247
Hunt, Samuel, 9 Feb. 1777, Willeyminah Gott           2 AA-413
Hunt, Simon, 31 Oct. 1771, Mary Noland                2 BA-263
Hunter, James, 28 Sept. 1761, Sarah Walch             1 CE-320
Hunter, Joseph, 30 July 1777, Elizab. Durham          1 HA-200
Hunter, Robert, 13 Feb. 1723, Margarett Linn          2 TA-106
Hunter, Samuel, clerk, 16 Feb. 1749, Mary Ann Carter,
   dau. of Richard Carter of Q. A. Co.                1 FR-11
Hunter, Samuel, 29 Sept. 1749, Elizabeth Knotts       1 QA-56
Hunter, William, 24 April 1747, Rebecca Williams      1 QA-53
Huntt, Daniell, 21 Jan. 1704, Rebecca Moss            3 KE-281
Hurd, John, 18 June 1739, Ruth Norwood                4 BA-70
Hurd, John, 24 Sept. 1749, Susanna Seymore            1 QA-56
Hurd, Robertt, 17 Dec. 1727, Elizabeth (?)            3 KE-286
Hurford, Joseph, son of John and Hannah, 20 day, 10
   mo., 1763, Naomi Greenland                         7 SF-12
Hurlack, James, 19 Dec. 1710, Sarah Foard             2 TA-68
Hurley, Joshua, 20 April 1747, Mary Barker            3 TA-64
Hurley, Timothy, 26 Jan. 1703, Mary Robinson          2 TA-38
Hurkey, Timothy, 16 Feb. 1734, Katherine Gayer        3 BA-153
Hurst, Charles, 22 Aug. 1756, Eliz'th Gaines          1 QA-61
Hurst, John, May 1718, Mary ffincks                   3 AA-100
Hurst, Jonathan, 29 Dec. 1729, Ann Gore               3 BA-149
Hurt, Dan'l, 19 Oct. 1774, Sarah Leddenham            1 CR
Hurt, John, 1 May 1729, Margit Wallis                 2 KE-216
Hurtt, Morgan, 2 Feb. 1714, Mary Prise                3 KE-284
Hurtt, Morgan, 27 Sept. 1771, Sarah Miller            3 KE-290
Husband, James, 1 Jan. 1717, Alice Parr, widow        3 CE-10
Husband, William, 20 May 1720, Mary Kinkey            3 CE-11
Husbands, William, 26 July 1733, Margaret Kennedy     3 CE-16
Hush, Joseph, 7 Feb. 1728, Mary Stevans               1 WI-26
Hussey, Michael, 20 May 1735, Marg't Shield           1 QA-41
Hussey, Thomas, 8 May 1738, Rachel Wilkinson          1 QA-44
Hutchens, Rich'd, 20 Jan. 1767, Philliszanner
   Standeford                                         2 BA-230
Hutchens, Thomas, 12 May 1736, Hannah Seemons         2 BA-98
Hutchenson, Simon, 25 Aug. 1746, Ann Newman           2 BA-195
Hutchenson, Simon, 12 Aug. 1750, Pennil Brooker       2 BA-201
   2 BA-244 gives bride's name as Brooke.
Hutcheson, Simon, 24 Aug. 1746, Anne Newman           2 BA-240
```

Hutchings, John, 9 May 1726, Eliz'th Wright          2 BA-38
Hutchings, Samuel, 4 Feb. 1741, Rebecca Dyas          2 TA-174
Hutchings, Thomas, 6 Jan. 1728, Percila Bradbery          2 TA-119
Hutchins, John, 12 April 1732, Leah Parrott          2 TA-135
Hutchins, Nich's, 4 Jan. 1763, Mary Standiford          2 BA-224
Hutchins, Thomas, 11 March 1773, Jemima Johnson          2 BA-266
Hutchinson, John, 13 Feb. 1738, Henrietta Lemar          1 QA-36
Hutchinson, John, 28 Sept. 1738, Alice Dorin          2 TA-166
Hutchinson, John, 30 July 1740, Elizabeth Buckley          2 TA-170
Hutchinson, Nathan, 2 June 1777, Tracy Tredwell          3 PG-126
Hutchinson, Richard, 22 Feb. 1749/50, Sarah Harrison          3 BA-163
Hutchinson, Thomas, 7 Oct. 1723, Ann Bennet          2 PG-3
Hutchison, Simon, 1750, Penelope Brooke          2 BA-244
Hutton, James, 25 (?) 1769, Susanna Davis          2 AA-409
Hutton, William, 1 Dec. 1722, Mary Bickerdike          4 AA-420
Hutton, William, 7 Jan. 1727, Catherine Randal          1 AA-106
Hutton, William, 22 June 1733, Elizabeth Malcoster          1 WI-2
Hutton, William, 30 March 1777, Margaret Hopkins          2 AA-413
Huxson, Jno., 26 Jan. 1764, Ann Wood          2 BA-226
Hyat, Christopher, 22 Feb. 1759, Eliz. Taylor          2 BA-218
Hyat, Peter, 1728, Alice Howerton          2 PG-5
Hyatt, Chris., 10 Sept. 1777, Lucy Peach          3 PG-126
Hyde, Thomas, 15 Sept. 1749, Elizabeth Bishop          4 AA-452
Hyland, John, 29 April 1739, Martha Tilden          1 CE-287
Hyland, Nicholas, son of Col. Nicholas, 2 Aug. 1764,
     Margery Kankey, dau. of John and Ann          1 CE-304
Hyland, Stephen, Dec. 1774, Rebecca Tilden          1 CE-305
Hyland, Stephen, 20 March 1777, Araminta Harmon or
     Hamm          1 CE-305
Hynesley, Nathaniel, 30 Sept. 1737, Mary Holford          1 QA-419
Hynson, Charles, 25 March 1687, Margarett Harris          3 KE-279
Hynson, Charles, 30 Nov. 1739, Phebe Carvill          3 KE-289
Hynson, Charles, 6 Nov. 176-(?), Sarah Woltham          3 KE-291
Hynson, Jno., 1 June 1693, Mary Stoop, dau. of John          3 CE-1
Hynson, Nathaniell, 6 Aug. 1714, Mary Kelley          3 KE-284
Hynson, Nathaniel, 29 Oct. 1735, Mary Smith          3 KE-288
Hynson, Nath'l, 11 April 1746, Susanna Keene          3 TA-58
Hynson, Richard, 15 June 1732, Anne Merredith          1 QA-39
Hynson, Thomas, 19 Oct. 1710, Wealthy Ann Tilden          3 KE-283
Hynton, John, 18 Sept. 1729, Mary Boyde          1 AA-168
Idol, Samuel, 1 Jan. 1716, Esther Walton          1 AA-275
Ijams (Eyams), Richard, 16 Jan. 1706, Anne Cheney          1 AA-73
Ijams, William, 27 Aug. 1696, Elizabeth Plummer          1 AA-34
Ijams (Jiams), William, 9 Oct. 1720, Elizabeth Jones          1 AA-301
Impey, Peter, 24 Oct. 1723, Margarett Lynsey          1 AA-97
Impey, Peter, 11 July 1725, Phillis Emerson; the groom
     was a "free mallatto;" the bride was a negro belong-
     ing to Thos. Gassaway          1 AA-100
Impey, Peter, 21 Jan. 1731, (?) (?)          1 AA-113
Inch, John, 6 July 1745, Jane Reynolds          4 AA-447
Ingram, Benjamin, 5 Jan. 1743, Susannah Coin          2 BA-189
Ingram, Francis, 8 Jan. 1756, Sarah White          2 BA-213
Ingram, James, Aug. 1682, Mary Askewe          5 SO-398
Ingram, James, 25 Aug. 1752, Catherine Young          2 BA-206
Ingram, James, 27 Nov. 1770, Mary Holt          2 BA-261
Ingram. John, 10 Aug. 1669, Hannah Jenkins          1 KE-186
Ingram, John, 20 Oct. 1680, Sarah Prince          5 SO-398
Ingram, John, 10 Jan. 1704, Mary Bruington          3 KE-293
Ingram, John, 3 Sept. 1705, Mary Homewood          3 AA-97
Ingram, Levin, 3 Feb. 1761, Hannah Legoe          2 BA-221
Ingram, Peesly, 25 June 1730, Ruth Hammond, dau. of
     Major Charles Hammond          4 AA-432
Ingram, William, 6 Nov. 1731, Phebe Whitehead          2 BA-73
Ireland, Gilbert, 28 Nov. 1775, Eleanor Liles          2 AA-412
Ireland, Joseph, 10 July 1761, Mrs. Alathea Comegys          2 KE-300

```
Ireland, Samuel, 1 Jan. 1715, Anne White               2 TA-77
Ireland, Samuel, 3 Feb. 1718, Sarah Bignal             2 TA-89
Ireland, William, 15 Oct. 1704, Aire (?)               2 TA-42
Ironsheare, Joseph, 8 July 1752, Esther Coller         1 WO-7
Ironside, John, 27 July 1749, Anne Bradshaw            3 TA-74
Irving, Thomas, 10 Feb. (1760 ?), Sarah Handy, widow
  of Samuel Handy                                      3 SO-1
Isaacs, Lazarus, 23 Oct. 1777, Sarah Fightmaster       1 MO-522
Isham, James (date not given), Elizabeth Robinson      2 BA-11
Isham, James, 1 June 1738, Mrs. Mary Warren            2 BA-91
Isham, James, 13 Oct. 1743, Jane Johnston              2 BA-90
Jackman, George, 22 June 1771, Eliz. Giles             2 BA-262
Jackman, Robert, 2 Dec. 1770, Sarah Whitaker           2 BA-261
Jacks, Thomas, 9 Nov. 1704, Elizabeth Walters          1 AA-65
Jackson, Edward, 26 Jan. 1768, Margret McMullen        1 CE-320
Jackson, Edward, 12 Jan. 1773, Sarah Greenland         1 CE-316
Jackson, George, 5 Oct. 1744, Dit Tippins              1 QA-49
Jackson, Henry, 3 April 17-6, Mary Bond                2 BA-229
Jackson, Isaac, 17 July 1733, Mary Hollingsworth       2 BA-69
Jackson, Jacob, 4 Oct. 1731, Frances Dallahide         2 BA-39
Jackson, John, 8 Aug. 1719, Mary White                 2 TA-90
Jackson, John, 17 March 1743/4, Catharine Finney       3 TA-48
Jackson, Joseph, 4 April 1752, Ann Seward              1 QA-58
Jackson, Moses, 20 Aug. 1756, Margaret Sutton          1 BA-365
Jackson, Richard, 5 May 1715, Ann Froggett             3 KE-294
Jackson, Robert, 24 Aug. 1699, Isabel Hooper           1 BA-188
Jackson, Robert, 25 Nov. 1765, Esther Mason            9 AA-249
Jackson, Robert, 1771, Lydia Phipps                    2 AA-410
Jackson, Samuel, 11 Dec. 1698, Sarah Mathews           1 BA-185
Jackson, Samuel, 24 April 1754, Alce Crockett          1 WI-101
Jackson, Samuel, 27 May 1762, Patience Wright          1 WI-101
Jackson, Thomas, 25 July 1703, Mary Kembal             1 BA-199
Jackson, Thomas, 12 Dec. 1709, Mary Blackiston         3 KE-293
Jackson, Thomas, Sept. 1724, Elizabeth Debruler        1 BA-249
Jackson, Thomas, 24 (?) 1729, Judith Wyet              1 QA-37
Jackson, Thomas, 7 Oct. 1735, Sarah Humphris           1 WI-24
Jackson, Thomas, 14 July 1757, Patience Harryman       2 BA-215
Jackson, William, 12 Nov. 1730, Mary Griffin           2 BA-80
Jackson, William John, 27 Feb. 1741, Elisabeth Mote    4 AA-443
Jacob, Benjamin, 1 May 1711, Alice Westale             1 AA-78
Jacob, Benjamin, 21 Feb. 1771, Elenor Odell            2 PG-7
Jacob, Daniel, 19 Aug. 1767, Salome Lueder             4 FR-1142
Jacob, Dorsey, son of Richard, 29 Aug. 1773, Ruth
  Merriken, dau. of Hugh                               3 AA-114
Jacob, Franz, 5 May 1761, M. Elizab. Holz              4 FR-1142
Jacob, Jeremiah, 29 Nov. 1736, Rachel Gaither          1 AA-120
Jacob, John, 4 July 1706, Mary Swanson                 1 AA-72
Jacob, John, 24 Aug. 1731, Alice Cheney, alias Jones   1 AA-112
Jacob, Jno., 29 March 1761, Mary Lynch                 2 BA-221
Jacob, John, 23 June 1761, Catherine Wenderoth         4 FR-1142
Jacob, Joseph, 1 Oct. 1706, Elizabeth Joanes           1 AA-72
Jacob, Mordecai, 10 Sept. 1741, Ruth Tyler             2 PG-7
Jacob, Mordecai, 7 Dec. 1745, Jemima Isaac             2 PG-7
Jacob, Richard, 1 Jan. 1717/8, Hannah Howard           4 AA-407
Jacob, Samuel, 19 Jan. 17-(?), Mary Davis              1 AA-147
Jacob, Samuel, 21 May 1719, Elisabeth Stewart          1 AA-293
Jacob, William, 5th son of Zachariah Jacob of A. A.
  Co., 19 July 1772, Mary Monk, dau. of Rinaldo Monk,
  late of London, by Rachel his wife, widow of Edward
  Riston of Rangers' Forest, Balto. Co.                3 BA-174
Jacobs, Bartholomew, 26 Jan. 1758, Eliz'th Register    1 QA-63
Jacobs, Benjamin, 17 July 1732, Ann Hope               3 AA-104
Jacobs, Henry, 12 May 1736, Anne Edwards               1 QA-42
Jacobs, Curtis, 1775, Polly Cannon                     1 CR
Jacobs, John, 6 Jan. 1732, Mary Hopper                 1 AA-115
```

```
Jacobs, John, 28 March 1776, Mary Davis                     1 AA-154
Jacobs, Joseph, 19 May 1743, Hannah Wright                  3 AA-108
Jacobs, Joshua, 6 March 1749, Jane Yee                      1 QA-56
Jacobs, William, c.Aug. 1775, Elizabeth Bowdle             1 CR-6
Jadwin, Bartholomew, 26 June 1680, Ann Estell              8 SF-325
Jadwin, Bartholomew, 21 Feb. 1744, Grace Swift             1 QA-50
Jadwin, Jeremiah, 9 Nov. 1701, Isabel Harrison             8 SF-408
Jadwin, Jeremiah, 29 June 1749, Rachel Davis               1 QA-55
Jadwin, John, 5 Dec. 1721, Mary Burn                       2 TA-97
Jadwin, Robert, 11 Feb. 1699, Martha Wootters              8 SF-399
Jadwin, Robert, 7 June 1715, Elizabeth Hill                2 TA-75
Jadwin, Solomon, 10 Dec. 1744, Mary West                   1 QA-50
James, Anthony, 13 May 1703, Sarah Pingstone               2 TA-35
James, Daniel, 7 Nov. 1777, Catherine Hayse                3 PG-122
James, Enoch, 10 June 1759, Temperance Rollo               2 BA-218
James, Henry, 26 June 1745, Mary Henley                    2 BA-179
                                                             & 193
James, Henry, 2 June 1771, Mary Smith                      2 BA-262
James, John, 17 June 1729, Martha Jervis                   3 KE-295
James, John, 1 Nov. 1731, Mary Alexander                   2 TA-151
James, Jno., 14 April 1761, Avarilla Standeford            2 BA-221
James, Joseph, 31 Aug. 1710, Elizabeth Shepherd            2 TA-67
James, Joseph, 11 Aug. 1737, Marg't Merrick                2 TA-163
James, Lawrance, 1 Aug. 1744, Eliza Horney                 3 TA-50
James, Mich'll, 20 Aug. 1736, Constant Shepherd            2 BA-73
James, Richard, a Manny Indian, 22 Aug. 1688, Honor
  (?)                                                      5 SO-398
James, Rich'd, 11 June 1702, Sarah Taylor                  2 TA-30
James, Richard, 4 April 1714, Elizabeth Roe                2 KE-186
James, Rob't, 2 July 1767, Sarah Jones                     2 BA-230
James, Solomon, 18 June 1760, Rach'l Corbin                2 BA-220
James, Thomas, 13 Jan. 173-(?), Elizabeth Lashle           2 PG-6
James, Thomas, 29 Nov. 1748, Jane Hicks                    2 BA-198
James, Thomas, 25 Sept. 1752, Mary Manning                 2 SM-57
James, Thomas, 27 day, 8 mo., 1761, Anne Amos, dau.
  of William and Hannah                                    4 SF-246
James, Thos., 4 Dec. 1764, Eliz. Clark                     2 BA-227
James, Walter, 29 Dec. 1736, Eliza Winford                 2 TA-158
James, Walt., 23 Dec. 1762, Cordelia Legoe                 2 BA-224
James, Watkins, 4 May 1758, Unity Green                    2 BA-217
Jameson, John, 6 Feb. 1727, Eliza Beal                     1 AA-106
Jameson, William, 25 Jan. 1759, Mary Martin                2 BA-218
Janes, John, 2 Jan. 1760, Elizabeth Welling                1 PG-316
Jans, Peter, 25 April 1769, Catharina Angst                5 FR-60
Jarboe, Charles, 19 Oct. 1772, Eliz. Stone                 1 SM-136
Jarboe, Rod, 17 Nov. 1772, Monica Williams                 1 SM-136
Jarboe, Thomas, 28 Nov. 1772, Ann Lucas                    1 SM-136
Jarman, Jno., 22 Jan. 1756, Mary Russell                   2 BA-213
Jarman, Joseph, 17 (Feb. ?) 1728, Anne Thomas              1 QA-36
Jarman, Thomas, 29 April 1733, Mary Rawley                 2 BA-108
Jarman, William, 17 Feb. 1739, Sarah Rutledge              2 BA-137
Jarves, Jno., 2 July 1761, Sarah Wright                    2 BA-222
Jarvis, Calib, 15 Aug. 1757, Mary Revel Betsworth          2 SO-37
Jarvis, Jno., 29 Dec. 1761, Mary Freeman                   2 BA-223
Jarviss, Philip, 9 July 1733, Mary Conaway                 3 AA-103
Javyr, Philip, 31 Sept. 1768, in New Castle, Del.,
  Lidia (?)                                                1 CE-320
Jay, William, 6 Dec. 1705, Sarah Wilder                    1 AA-72
Jeff, William, 12 Aug. 1697, Ruth Marthews                 1 BA-178
Jefferies, James, 21 June 1728, Jane Mitchell              1 AA-147
Jeffors, Simon, 16 Sept. 1734, Anne Hardgrass              2 TA-157
Jeffrey, John, 28 May 1749, Sarah Williams                 2 BA-243
Jeffriys, Jno., 14 Nov. 1749, Sarah Williams               2 BA-199
Jeminey, James, 25 Feb. 1717, Sarah Cox                    2 TA-83
Jenckins, Francis, 12 April 1672, the widow of Henry
  Weedon                                                   5 SO-398
```

Jeneons, Edward, 13 May 1711, Elizabeth Piscood            1 CA-114
Jenifer, Michael, 9 Jan. 1718, Mary Parker, dau. of
  George and Susanna                                        1 CA-113
Jenings, Edmund, son and heir of Edmund Jenings of
  the colony of Va., 2 July 1728, Ariana Bordley,
  widow of Thomas Bordley                                   4 AA-430
Jenings, Joseph, 23 May 1742, Mary Rider                   2 BA-126
Jenings, Thomas, son of Rev. Henry Jenings, late of
  St. M. Co., dec., 17 July 1732, Mrs. Rebecca Sanders,
  dau. of Robert Sanders of A. A. Co.                       4 AA-435
Jenkenson, Emanuel, 1 Nov. 1704, Elizabeth Jadwin          8 SF-428
Jenkings, John, 5 Nov. 1704, Frances Pollett, of P.
  G. Co.                                                    1 AA-65
Jenkins, Andrew, 12 Jan. 1743, Eliz. Boyd                  2 BA-189
Jenkins, Edmund, 26 May 1773, Eliz. Milborn                1 SM-136
Jenkins, Enoch, 26 Jan. 1718, Ann Clarno                   1 PG-268
Jenkins, Francis, 15 June 1732, Mary Downs                 1 BA-267
Jenkins, Henry, 25 Dec. 1743, Elizab. Boyd                 2 BA-239
Jenkins, Jarvis, 29 Jan. 1744/5, Sarah Kibble              1 WI-43
Jenkins, Jonathan, 5 Aug. 1761, Esther Hillman             1 WI-74
Jenkins, Joseph, 23 Jan. 1742, Mary (?)                    2 SM-57
Jenkins, Lewes, 14 Feb. 1768, Eliz. Harris                 2 BA-231
Jenkins, Thomas, 26 Jan. 1742/3, Eliza White               3 TA-42
  2 TA-175 gives date as 31 Jan. 1742.
Jenkins, William, 26 Aug. 1674, Ann Stadley                5 SO-398
Jenkins, William, 14 Aug. 1726, Rachel Balls               1 BA-255.
Jenkins, William, 25 March 1758, Mary Clark                1 BA-363
Jenkinson, Emanuel, 1 day, 10 mo., 1679, Elizabeth
  Morgain                                                   8 SF-321
Jenkinson, Emanuel, 14 day, 3 mo., 1759, Martha Bowers     1 SF-96
Jenkinson, John, 29 May 1761, Mary Coventon                8 SF-105
Jenkinson, Philip, 4 day, 12 mo., 1730, Sarah Webb,
  dau. of John                                              8 SF-61
Jenning, Thomas, 13 Jan. 1754, Charity Partee              1 PG-301
Jennings, Joseph, 24 April 1743, Mary Rider                2 BA-238
Jennings, Thos., 17 July 1732, Rebecca Sanders             1 AA-114
Jennings, William, 20 Aug. 1770, Hannah Rutlidge           2 BA-260
Jerman, Benjamin, 28 Nov. 1753, Eliz. Rutledge             2 BA-209
                                                             & 242
Jerman, John, 17 June 1756, Jane Hollinsworth              1 QA-61
Jerman, Joseph, 5 Nov. 1755, Ann Knotts                    1 QA-60
Jervis, Edward, 20 July 1708, Margrett Wade                3 KE-293
Jervis, James, 1 Sept. 1709, Sarah Smith                   3 KE-293
Jessop, William, 25 June 1748, Margaret Walker             3 BA-156
Jiams, Rich'd, 19 Jan. 1737, Mary Nicols                   4 AA-439
  See also Ijams.
Joaland, Robert, 2 Nov. 1704, Joan Butcher                 3 KE-293
Joanes, Phillip, 3 Jan. 1700, Mary Rowles                  3 AA-97
Joanes, William, 21 June 1702, Alse Smith                  3 AA-98
Joans, William, 24 day, 12 mo., 1679, Sarah Hall           8 SF-321
Jobson, John, 23 July 1711, Hester Holyday, widow          3 CE-6
Jobson, Phil., 21 Sept. 1736, An: Hamer                    1 QA-42
John, Benjamin, 16 June 1777, Elizabeth Scott              4 CE-261
Johnes, Hugh, 19 Feb. 1735, Sarah Kemp                     3 BA-155
Johns, Aquila, 16 day, 9 mo., 1704, Mary Hosier, of
  Kent Co.                                                  1 SF-49
Johns, Aquila, 27 Jan. 1757, Hannah Bond                   2 BA-214
Johns, Isaac, son of Richard and Elizabeth, 25 day,
  10 mo., 1712, Ann Galloway, dau. of Samuel and Anne      6 SF
Johns, Kinsey, 1 Dec. 1773, Betty Steward                  2 AA-411
Johns, Richard, 25 Nov. 1773, Sarah Weems                  2 AA-411
Johns, Richard, 11 Jan. 1776, Mary Franklin                2 AA-412
Johnson, Aaron, 8 Dec. 1726, Margarett Miles               1 AA-104
Johnson, Andrew, 15 Oct. 1724, Elizabeth Cotter            2 TA-110
Johnson, Aron, 26 Oct. 1758, Achsah Merrideth              2 BA-218

Johnson, Francis, 10 Feb. 1736, Elianor Hamilton        1 QA-43
Johnson, George, 23 July 1737, Mary Harrison            4 AA-439
Johnson, George, 23 Jan. 1755, Ann Shepard              1 CE-306
Johnson, Hans, 14 Sept. 1756, Mary Offley               1 QA-61
Johnson, Henry, 4 Nov. 1729, Mary Hamilton              1 QA-37
Johnson, Henry, 24 Sept. 1747, Ann Bone                 3 BA-160
Johnson, Isaac, 2 Nov. 1770, Sarah Dickson              1 CE-324
Johnson, Isaac, 28 July 1771, Jemima Ward               2 SO-139
Johnson, Israel, 12 Jan. 1742, Sarah Hutchens           2 BA-125
Johnson, Jacob, 5 April 1730, Eliz. Drake               1 CE-282
Johnson, Jacob, 23 Nov. 1743, Hannah Baker              2 BA-189
Johnson, Jacob, 25 Feb. 1749, Eliz. Hendon              2 BA-200
Johnson, James, 16 March 1769, Elizabeth Hall           2 BA-258
Johnson, Jno., 7 Feb. 1704, Shusannah Benstead          2 TA-43
Johnson, John, 27 May 1711, Mary Williams               1 AA-78
Johnson, John, 12 Jan. 1713, Sarah Jones                2 TA-73
Johnson, John, 24 Oct. 1728, Christian Coffin           4 AA-430
Johnson, John, 27 April 1731, Ann Hamilton              1 QA-38
Johnson, John, 4 Dec. 1732, Mary Needles                1 QA-39
Johnson, John, 1 Jan. 1733, Hannah Mitchell             1 BA-271
Johnson, John, 15 Jan. 1735, Mary Thompson              1 QA-41
Johnson, John, 5 June 1755, Mary Coward                 1 QA-59
Johnson, Joseph, 5 July 171-(?), Ann Todd               1 BA-212
Johnson, Leonard, 31 Jan. 1774, Mary Malohorn           1 SM-136
Johnson, Moses, 1 Feb. 1757, Prissilla Standeford       2 BA-214
Johnson, Nathan, 11 Feb. 1755, Eliz. Wright             2 BA-212
Johnson, Peter, 30 Nov. 1731, Mary Mayo                 1 AA-113
Johnson, Peter, 4 Aug. 1747, Mary Woodwal               1 QA-53
Johnson, Phillip, 26 Dec. 1769, Sophia Wathusd (sic)    2 BA-259
Johnson, Randal, 19 Sept. 1721, Elizabeth James         2 TA-96
Johnson, Roberd, 15 Feb. 1725, Sarah Fish               2 TA-113
Johnson, Robert, 13 Jan. 1716/7, Rebekah Ragg           4 AA-398
Johnson, Robert, 18 April 1756, Mary McMillin           1 QA-61
Johnson, Robert, 20 April 1765, Mary Fleming            2 BA-228
Johnson, Robert, 3 Sept. 1777, Alice Peterkin           3 BA-173
    10 BA-69 gives date as 23 Sept. 1777.
Johnson, Samuel, 17 Feb. 1708, Ann Nelson               4 AA-378
Johnson, Samuel, 21 June 1742, Susanna Lusby            4 AA-444
Johnson, Samuel, 12 Oct. 1777, Agnes Wilson             1 MO-516
Johnson, Simon, 4 Nov. 1738, Catherine Vandeveare       1 CE-289
Johnson, Thomas, 3 Sept. 1716, Mary Enlove or Enloes    2 BA-9
Johnson, Thomas, 1 July 1722, Milliscent Hyland         1 CE-333
Johnson, Thomas, 17 Oct. 1724, Alis Bond                1 BA-252
Johnson, Thomas, 21 Feb. 1738, Sarah Hyams              9 AA-246
Johnson, Thomas, 7 Feb. 1743, Eliz. Hutchens            2 BA-190
Johnson, Thomas, Jr., 29 Nov. 1748, Mary Clark          1 BA-346
Johnson, Thomas, 14 Feb. 1751, Ann Bradley              1 BA-373
Johnson, William, of Ratcliffe, Old Eng., 26 Dec.
    1682, Sarah Edmondson, dau. of John and Sarah       8 SF-329
Johnson, William, 22 Sept. 1733, Mary Ann Poaling       3 BA-151
Johnson, William, 30 March 1741, Elizabeth Massy        2 KE-239
Johnson, William, 11 Dec. 1746, Mary Pusey              2 SO-36
Johnson, William, 24 April 1747, Mrs. Beatrice Perse    2 KE-263
Johnson, William, 8 Sept. 1757, Rachael Bull            2 BA-216
Johnson, William, 3 Nov. 1765, Catherine Desney         2 BA-228
Johnston, Isral, 7 April 1743, Jeane Dossey             1 FR-11
Johnston, John, 25 Jan. 1730, Margaret Law              1 QA-38
Johnston, John, 5 June 1755, Mary Coward                2 KE-293
Johnston, John, July 1769, Eliz. Easton                 2 BA-259
Johnston, Mathias, 30 Oct. 1716, Magdalene Poulson      1 CE-331
Johnstone, Wm., 28 June 1767, Mary Griffin              2 BA-230
Joice, John, 3 July 1721, Sarah Brooks                  2 PG-2
Joice, Thomas, 22 April 1716, Eliza Cheeny              2 PG-1
Joiner, Joseph, 1770, Rebecca Mellove                   2 AA-409
Jolly, James, wireworker, 30 Sept. 1753, Susanna
    Ireland                                             4 AA-455

| | |
|---|---|
| Jones, Andrew, 13 Jan. 1680, Elizabeth Winder | 5 SO-398 |
| Jones, Aquila, 7 May 1741, Elizabeth Brice | 1 BA-322 |
| Jones, Benjamin, 29 Jan. 1734, Susanah Knock | 2 KE-227 |
| Jones, Benjamin, 5 Jan. 1737, Dinah Merriken | 2 BA-93 |
| Jones, Benjamin, 25 Sept. 1755, Mary Clark | 1 QA-60 |
| Jones, Benjamin, 23 March 1761, Honor Kelley | 4 BA-72 |
| Jones, Benjamin, son of Luke and Rachel, 16 Sept. 1773, Sarah Forrister, dau. of Wm. | 3 AA-114 |
| Jones, Benjamin, 31 Dec. 1777, Mary Ann Myers | 7 AA-3 |
| Jones, Cadwalladay, 30 April 1704, Mary Paywell | 1 BA-259 |
| Jones, Cadwallader, 23 April 1702, Mary Ellis | 1 BA-196 |
| Jones, Calib, 11 Feb. 1773, Mrs. Betty Wheatley | 2 SO-139 |
| Jones, Charles, 8 Dec. 1681, Grissegon Barre | 5 SO-398 |
| Jones, Charles, 26 Dec. 1727, Frances Cobb | 1 BA-257 |
| Jones, Charles, 26 Dec. 1752, Hannah Nichols | 2 BA-206 & 242 |
| Jones, Chas., 6 Feb. 1767, Mary Clark | 2 BA-230 |
| Jones, Daniel, 29 Sept. 1774, Elizabeth Mills | 2 SO-141 |
| Jones, David, 22 Oct. 1706, Margaret Morley | 2 AA-330 |
| Jones, David, 19 April 1734, Martha Hanson | 3 KE-295 |
| Jones, Edward, 1669, Mary Barnabe | 5 SO-398 |
| Jones, Edward, 29 Jan. 1710, Susannah Bell | 2 TA-69 |
| Jones, Edward, 24 Aug. 1719, Jane Slater | 2 TA-90 |
| Jones, Edward, 17 Aug. 1738, Phebe Williams | 1 QA-44 |
| Jones, Emanuel, 14 Aug. 1757, Martha Parkew | 2 BA-216 |
| Jones, Evan, 28 May 1713, Mary Bradford | 1 PG-259 |
| Jones, George, 3 Feb. 1740, Elizabeth Linley | 1 BA-317 |
| Jones, Griffin, 19 Sept. 1747, Mary Smith | 2 BA-193 |
| Jones, Griffith, 15 Dec. 1709, Frances Butler | 2 TA-64 |
| Jones, Griffith, 18 Dec. 1712, Sarah Porter | 3 KE-294 |
| Jones, Henry, 4 Oct. 1777, Rebecca Knighton | 7 AA-2 |
| Jones, Henry, 16 Oct. 1777, Reb'a Knighton | 8 AA-13 |
| Jones, Jacob, 9 Jan. 1676/7, Elizabeth Stevens | 9 SO-402 |
| Jones, Jacob, 10 Feb. 1742, Rachel Cottrell | 2 BA-125 |
| Jones, Jacob, 10 Feb. 1743, Sarah Collett | 2 BA-140 |
| Jones, James McMurray, 21 Dec. 1759, Prissey Dorman | 1 WI-96 |
| Jones, Jeremiah, 6 Dec. 1777, Sarah Harp | 9 BA |
| 10 BA-70 gives date as 25 Dec. 1777. | |
| Jones, John, 8 July 1695, Martha Loveill | 1 BA-177 |
| Jones, Jno., 13 Aug. 1695, Mary MacHadray | 3 CE-1 |
| Jones, John, 21 Oct. 1706, Mary Darby | 3 KE-293 |
| Jones, John, 10 July 1723, Ann Carter | 1 WI-17 |
| Jones, John, 1724, Hannah Dawson | 3 AA-110 |
| Jones, John, 26 Jan. 1726/7, Deborah Linchicom | 4 AA-427 |
| Jones, John, 31 Oct. 1728, Mary Lankford | 2 TA-118 |
| Jones, John, 17 Feb. 1728, Christian Lankford | 2 TA-269 |
| 2 TA-120 gives date as 17 Feb. 1728/9. | |
| Jones, John, Dec. 1732, Hannah Wooley | 2 BA-82 |
| Jones, John, 16 April 1733, (?)  (?) | 1 CE-332 |
| Jones, John, 3 May 1736, Elizabeth Townrow | 2 TA-269 |
| 2 TA-161 gives date as 23 June 1736, and the bride's name as Townroe. | |
| Jones, John, 11 July 1739, Mary Williams | 1 QA-45 |
| Jones, John, 15 Aug. 1741, Lurana Barron | 3 TA-32 |
| Jones, John, 20 April 1742, Rachel Higgins | 2 TA-175 |
| Jones, John, 1748, Sarah Poulson | 2 BA-243 |
| Jones, Jno., 28 March 1749, Sarah Morris | 2 BA-198 & 243 |
| Jones, John, 14 July 1749, Sarah Poulson | 2 BA-197 |
| Jones, John, 26 June 1753, Mary Starkey | 2 BA-208 |
| Jones, Jno., 17 April 1763, Mary Airs | 2 BA-225 |
| Jones, John, 30 May 1763, Margaret Jackson | 1 BA-379 |
| Jones, Jonas, 15 Jan. 1761, Ann Watts | 2 BA-221 |
| Jones, Jonas, 20 Sept. 1774, Eliza Sill | 1 CR |
| Jones, Jonathan, 10 Nov. 1736, Martha Farmer | 1 BA-294 |

Jones, Joseph, 16 Feb. 1703, Elizabeth Elder                     1 AA-64
Jones, Joseph, 10 Dec. 1704, Mary Pybern                         1 AA-65
Jones, Joseph, son of Griffith and Joane, of Phila-
     delphia Co., Penna., 8 day, 4 mo., 1704, Margaret
     Birckhead, dau. of Nehemiah, of A. A. Co.                   6 SF
Jones, Joseph, 22 Oct. 1712, Mary Harwood                        2 AA-345
Jones, Luke, 30 May 1751, Rachel Phillips                        3 AA-110
Jones, Morgan, 12 Oct. 1733, Susana Hill                         2 AA-369
Jones, Morgan, 20 Jan. 1757, Priscilla (?)                       2 AA-396
Jones, Moses, 14 Jan. 1766, Rebecca Ruten                        1 CE-319
Jones, Peter, 6 May 1739, Mrs. Mary Bellus                       2 KE-225
Jones, Philip, 18 Sept. 1719, Hannah Rattenbury                  3 AA-100
Jones, Philip, 29 May 1723, Jemima Eager, widow                  3 BA-146
Jones, Philip, 2 Oct. 1727, Ann Rattenbury, dau. of
     Dr. John and Margaret                                       3 BA-151
Jones, Picket, 14 Dec. 1746, Elizabeth James                     2 BA-240
     2 BA-196 gives date as 16 Dec. 1746.
Jones, Rice, 25 Oct. 1713, Sarah Hews                            3 KE-294
Jones, Richard, 18 Feb. 1717, Jane Sweringen                     2 PG-1
Jones, Richard, 15 July 1718, Elizabeth Clark                    1 AA-284
Jones, Richard, 26 Nov. 1734, Ann Bovin                          2 PG-6
Jones, Richard, 25 May 1758, Ann Fraisher                        2 BA-217
Jones, Richard, 27 Aug. 1758, Eliza Matthews                     1 QA-64
Jones, R'd, 7 June 1764, Sarah Wright                            2 BA-226
Jones, Robert, 27 June 1703, Anne Yates                          2 TA-37
Jones, Robert, 24 Nov. 1709, Ann Lewis                           8 SF-445
Jones, Roger, 24 June 1704, Mary Carr                            2 TA-40
Jones, Roger, 29 Feb. 1711, Elizabeth Dennis                     2 TA-71
Jones, Samuel, 14 Aug. 1677, Mary Davis                          9 SO-402
Jones, Samuel, Nov. 1691, Mary Flannakin                         5 SO-398
Jones, Samuel, 19 Feb. 1748, Isabella Douglas                    3 BA-163
Jones, Silvestine, Nov. 1719, Mary Hinton                        2 BA-16
Jones, Solomon, 31 Jan. 1743, Anne Bradley                       1 QA-49
Jones, Stephen, 26 Oct. 1707, Rebekah Darby                      1 AA-76
Jones, Thomas, 12 July 1702, Mary Willis                         3 KE-293
Jones, Thomas, 9 Dec. 1705, Mary Barker                          1 AA-72
Jones, Thomas, 18 April 1706, Dorothy Chittham                   1 CA-112
Jones, Thomas, 11 May 1708, Mary Tillard                         2 KE-183
Jones, Thomas, 14 Nov. 1733, Sarah Ford                          1 QA-40
Jones, Thomas, 10 Oct. 1750, Eliz. Shaw                          2 BA-202
Jones, Thomas, son of Capt. Thomas Jones of Liverpool,
     15 Oct. 1751, Elizabeth Guibert, dau. of Joshua
     Guibert of St. M. Co.                                       3 SO-4
Jones, Thomas, 20 June 1757, Mary Dooley                         1 BA-362
Jones, Thomas, 14 Dec. 1761, Elizabeth Baxter, dau. of
     Col. James and Elizabeth                                    1 CE-306
Jones, Thos., 14 Jan. 1766, Jane Russel                          2 BA-229
Jones, Thomas, 15 July 1775, Mary Beauchamp                      2 SO-38
Jones, William, (date not given), Hannah Norris                  2 AA-356
Jones, William, 5 Jan. 1700, Honora (?)                          2 TA-11
Jones, William, 13 Feb. 1710, Susan Jacob                        1 AA-78
Jones, William, 21 Nov. 1711, Mary Cooper                        2 TA-70
Jones, William, 20 Feb. 1720, Susannah Spruton                   2 TA-95
Jones, William, 31 Jan. 1737/8, Mary Pammer                      1 PG-282
Jones, William, 20 Dec. 1740, Mary Spencer                       2 KE-239
Jones, William, 30 March 1741, Ann Maccubbin                     2 BA-106
Jones, William, Dec. 1744, Katherine Brokley                     2 BA-239
     2 BA-191 gives date as 23 Dec. 1744.
Jones, William, 5 March 1745/6, Rebec. Clark                     3 TA-57
Jones, William, 14 April 1745, Anne Huggins                      2 BA-240
     2 BA-192 gives date as 2 May 1745.
Jones, William, 7 Nov. 1745, Mary Scotton                        1 QA-51
Jones, William, 22 Jan. 1751, Elizabeth Williams                2 BA-202
Jones, William, 1 March 1762, Sarah Lanham                       1 PG-320
Jones, William, 11 April 1771, Hannah Hynes                      2 BA-262

```
Jones, William, 5 June 1772, Eliz. King                 2 BA-264
Jones, William, 9 Aug. 1777, Sarah Williams            10 BA-68
Jonnes, Edward, 10 May 1661, Margrett Hale              1 KE-186
Jonson, Andrew, 25 Jan. 1707/8, Elizabeth Vetherall    3 AA-99
Jonson, Josiah, 26 March 1777, Hanah Merrall           1 CE-324
Jonson, Mark, 25 Nov. 1729, Elizabeth Cockey           3 AA-104
Jonson, Oneall, 3 Aug. 1738, Mary Fenell               3 AA-108
Jonson, Solomon, 17 May 1746, Mary Hancock             3 AA-110
Jonson, Thomas, 16 Oct. 1701, Rachel Robeson           3 AA-99
Jonson, Thomas, 3 Feb. 1731, Mary Earnshaw             3 AA-103
Jopson, Thomas, 23 April 1721, Susanna Allein          4 AA-414
Jordan, Absalom, 28 Dec. 1740, Eliz. Christian         3 TA-27
  2 TA-171 gives date as 1 Jan. 1740/1.
Jordan, John, 3 May 1752, Mary Ann Jackson             1 QA-58
Jordan, Michael, 10 Nov. 1776, Eliz'th Devines         3 BA-669
Jordeen, Aaron, 9 Dec. 1720, Margaret Dowlin           4 AA-413
Jourdan, John, April 1745, Mary Ann Buckley            1 QA-50
Jourdin, John, 11 Feb. 1745, Sarah Powel               1 QA-51
Joy, Joseph, 29 May 1770, Frances Dallam               1 BA-386
Joy, Thos., 16 Feb. 1775, Sara Fields                  1 SM-137
Joyce, Henry, 25 Dec. 1734, Mary Gibson                2 TA-156
Joyce, Richard, May 1759, Fanny Shaw                   3 AA-112
Joyce, Thomas, 1 Dec. 1747, Eleanor Thornton           3 BA-160
Joyce, William, 25 May 1760, Sarah Lee                 3 BA-167
Jub, Robert, 6 July 1704, Ellinor (?)                  3 AA-97
Jubes, James, 9 Oct. 1752, Sarah Dirickson             1 WO-13
Jubes, James, 19 Feb. 1754, Levinah Farwell            1 WO-13
Judg, Daniel, 19 Nov. 1736, Sarah Fowler               1 BA-294
Judkins, Obadiah, 11 day, 9 mo., 1669, Joan Davis      8 SF-315
Judkins, Obadiah, 4 day, 11 mo., 1681, Joan Huntington 8 SF-328
Judkins, Obadiah, Jr., 22 Sept. 1692, Elizabeth
  Parratt                                              8 SF-360
Judy, Da'd, 7 Feb. 1765, Eliz. Masters                 2 BA-227
Juet, Nathaniel, 15 Oct. 1759, Rebecca Mister          2 SO-140
Julian, Isaac, son of Stephen, 3 June 1770, Susannah
  Hedges, dau. of Charles                              1 FR-11
Julian, John, son of Stephen, 14 June 1770, Elizabeth
  Butler, dau. of Peter                                1 FR-11
Julien, Jacob, 2 Feb. 1743/4, Catherine Hedges         1 FR-11
Julien, Stephen, 14 July 1743, Ann Hedges              1 FR-11
Jung, Peter, 9 Aug. 1757, Barbara Begard               4 FR-1103
Justice, Moses, 18 Aug. 1734, Ann Wilds                1 CE-278
Justice, Moses, 4 Sept. 1737, Sarah Morgan             1 CE-278
Justice, Peter, 28 Jan. 1731, Catherine Crew           1 CE-286
Kankey, John, 6 June 1738, Rebecca Hyland              1 CE-306
Karson, William, 29 July 1744, Eliz. Johnson           2 BA-191
Kates, Michael, 26 June 1729, Sarah Brampton           2 TA-121
Kathen, William, 30 Sept. 1738, Martha Davis           2 KE-221
Kean, Timothy, 14 May 1709, Mary Moore                 1 BA-208
Kear, Benjamin, 4 Sept. 1747, Mary Grownoho            2 KE-286
Keare, Robert, 30 Oct. 1713, Rachel Hannah             3 KE-296
Kearnes, Arthur, 7 Oct. 1777, Mary Davidson            7 AA-2
Kearney, John, 27 Dec. 1744, Rachal Primrose           1 QA-50
Kearton, William, 17 April 1746, Mary Burn             2 KE-260
Keating, John, 21 Aug. 1713, Sarah Schooling           3 KE-296
Keatting, William, Sr., 30 July 1772, Darcus Massy     2 KE-311
Keeedly, John, 14 July 1734, Susannah Gray             1 CE-333
Keef, Cornelius, 16 Nov. 1707, Dianna Cockarill        3 KE-296
Keen, Vachel, of Balto. Co., Gent., 6 Sept. 1759,
  Penelope Boyer, widow                                2 KE-296
Keen, William, Jr., 14 July 1692, Sarah Ackworth       5 SO-398
Keen, William, 21 Nov. 1757, Sushannah Copperwhite     2 BA-216
Keene, William, 3 Feb. 1751/2, Sarah (?)               2 AA-390
Keets, John, c.Oct. 1775, Ann Chalaghane               1 CR-6
Keith, David, 12 Jan. 1743, Sarah Kitely               2 BA-189
  2 BA-239 gives date as 25 Dec. 1743.
```

```
Keith, Patrick, 9 Dec. 1776, Esther Redman          3 BA-172
                                                      & 669
Keive, Jno., 25 Nov. 1705, Catherine ffahee          4 AA-390
Kelke, Richard, 8 April 1708, Katherine (?)          4 AA-372
Kellam, Isaac, 7 July 1771, Sarah Moor               2 SO-41
Kellam, John, 24 Feb. 1762, Sarah Outten             2 SO-38
Kelle, Patrick, (date not given), Mary Mash          3 BA-149
Kellee, Benjamin, 16 day, 8 mo., 1724, Mary Boots    1 SF-57
Keller, Jacob, 28 May 1758, Elizabeth Leitert        4 FR-1104
Keller, Jacob, 19 Jan. 1768, Mary Humbert            4 FR-1143
Kelley, James, 28 April 1753, Mary Beamsley          2 BA-208
Kelley, Patrick, 13 Nov. 1701, Elizabeth Sumons      1 CA-111
Kelly, Barnaby, 25 Dec. 1753, Henewritta Athey       1 PG-301
Kelly, Cornelious, 7 July 1741, Alce Low             1 BA-322
Kelly, Jacob, 18 Nov. 1731, Margaret Hony            1 QA-38
Kelly, James, 20 May 1747, Rachel Buckley            1 QA-53
Kelly, Mordecai, 19 Nov. 1757, Mary Hines            2 BA-172
Kelly, Thomas, 31 Jan. 1733, (?) (?)                 1 CE-281
Kelly, Thomas, 4 June 1736, Mary Mushgrove           3 BA-155
Kelly, William, Jr., 26 Dec. 1777, Martha Loveall    9 BA
Kelsey, William, 8 Dec. 1761, Ann Hutchins           2 BA-222
Kembal, John, Jr., 16 April 1703, Elizabeth Gilbert  1 BA-200
Kembal, Robert, 12 Oct. 1738, Sarah Taylor           1 BA-290
Kembal, Rowland, 15 May 17-(?), Mary Jackson         1 BA-222
Kemp, James, 2 June 1749, Elizabeth Williams         8 SF-92
Kemp, John, son of Robert and Elizabeth, 1 Jan.
  1705, Mary Ball, dau. of Thomas and Susanna        8 SF-443
Kemp, Jonathan, 2 Dec. 1745, Margaret Barnet         3 BA-158
Kemp, Mathew, 1 Oct. 1724, Mary Mackeny              1 CE-277
Kemp, Rich'd, 24 Sept. 1745, Mary Green              1 QA-51
Kemp, Thos., 31 March 1741, Alice Hollingsworth      1 QA-46
Kemp, William, 27 May 1715, Hannah Warren            1 CA-114
Kemp, William, 11 July 1717, Martha Eubanks, Jr.     8 SF-16
Kemp, William, 8 Feb. 1742, Mary Scrivener           1 QA-48
Kendal, William, 9 Dec. 1751, Maryan Jacobs          3 KE-297
Kendall, William, 31 July 1722, Elinor Roach         3 KE-296
Kenderdine, John, 12 Nov. 1749, Ann Roberts          1 QA-56
Kenhan, Coleworth, 7 July 1744, Mary Tridge          2 BA-190
Kenly, Daniel, 6 Nov. 1739, Frances Wells            1 BA-330
Kennard, John, 6 March 1738/9, Mrs. Sarah Pearce     2 KE-223
Kennard, Phillip, 8 Dec. 1708, Mary Baily            3 KE-296
Kennard, Richard, c.Aug. 1775, Anne Carroll          1 CR-6
Kennedy, Hugh, 25 July 1745, Sarah Radish            1 WI-46
Kennedy, Patrick, 6 June 1772, Hannah French, widow  3 BA-169
Kennerly, Joseph, 14 Nov. 1711, Mary Stevens         8 SF-5
Kenton, Solomon, 7 Feb. 1733, Mary Powell, dau. of
  Howell                                             8 SF-62
Kensey, Thomas, 2 April 1730, Cathrin Porter         2 KE-216
Kent, Andrew, 9 Feb. 1725, Margaret Foy              1 AA-102
Kent, John, 6 July 1758, Elizabeth Clare             2 CA-48
Kent, Joseph, (date not given), Mary Dobson          1 QA-40
Kenton, William, of Lankepor Co., Va., 13 April 1687,
  Mary Parratt, relict of Henry Parratt              8 SF-342
Kenton, William, 1 May 1698, Rebeckah Dudley         8 SF-377
Ker, Rev. Jacob, 1767, Esther Wilson                 1 SO-161
Kerby, Nathanel, 3 June 1707, Elizabeth Deale        1 AA-73
Kerr, Daniel, 25 March 1773, Hamutal Bishop          3 AA-113
Kersey, (?), 30 Oct. 1757, Sarah Edwards             2 TA-290
Kersey, Fran:, 20 April 1750, Eliza Lamdin           3 TA-77
Kersey, Henry, 21 July 1746, Eliz. Whealand          2 BA-195
Kersey, James, 3 May 1732, Susanna Godwin            1 QA-38
Kersey, James, 26 Jan. 1752, Sarah Harris            1 QA-58
Kersey, Jno., 8 Nov. 1705, Elizabeth (?)             4 AA-390
Kersey, John, 5 Aug. 1740, Ann Lawson                2 TA-170
Kersey, John, Jr., 27 Feb. 1749, Suhannah Shaw       2 BA-201
```

Kersey, John, 18 April 1752, Kathrine Martin          2 BA-205
Kershaw, Francis, 12 Sept. 1756, Rebecca Brady          2 CA-39
Kershshaw, William, 24 Nov. 1756, Betty Dirickson          1 WO-11
Kersy, Henry, 21 July 1746, Eliz. Whealand          2 BA-195
Keys, John, 24 Sept. 1740, Jane Ayres          1 QA-46
Keys, John, 23 Oct. 1750, Elizabeth Daley          1 QA-57
Keys, John, 19 May 1751, Elisabeth McNemarr          1 QA-57
Kibble, John, 27 Feb. 1672, Abigail Horsey          5 SO-398
Kibble, William, March 1734, Mary Plowright          3 BA-152
Kibble, William, 20 April 1736, Hannah Stevens          1 WI-49
Kibble, William, 24 July 1763, Elizabeth Stewart          1 WI-74
Kilbreth, John, 7 April 1729, Mary Webb          1 QA-36
Kilburn, Charles, 18 April 1709, Elizabeth Welply          4 AA-378
Killam, John, 24 Nov. 1738, Sarah Macloster          1 WI-36
Killey, James, 2 Sept. 1735, Prudence Logsdon          3 BA-154
     The groom's name may be also read as Kelley.
Killiston, Robert, 2 Oct. 1734, Elizabeth Anderson          1 AA-118
Killom, William, 1 Dec. 1741, Rachel Hanko(ck?)          1 WO-7
Killpatrick, Samuel, 16 Nov. 1761, Jannet Good          1 CE-306
Killum, Edward, 20 Jan. 1772, Priscilla Taylor          1 WI-93
Kilpatrick, Samuel, 8 March 1775, "the late Elenor
     Foster, elias Kilpatrick"          1 CE-307
Kiltey, Will, 11 May 1769, Cristenah Hoshel          3 AA-113
Kimball, John, Jr., 6 Nov. 1717, Rebecca Atkins          3 CE-11
Kimball, Samuel, 19 Feb. 1747, Jamima Barns          1 BA-352
Kimball, Stephen, 22 March 1758, Margaret Daugherty,
     alias Barkey          1 BA-360
Kimball, William, 1 Jan. 1754, Sarah Hanson          1 BA-354
Kimber, John, 17 June 1731, Mary Etherinton          3 CE-17
Kimber, John, 23 Jan. 1740, Catherine Money, dau. of
     Robert          3 CE-22
Kimber, Joseph, 19 March 1769, Salley Willmot          2 BA-258
Kimber, William, 1749, Mary Jackson          2 BA-244
Kimble, John, 19 May 1743, Agness Beatty          1 FR-11
Kimble, Richard, 18 Oct. 1764, Jane Jemison          5 SO-398
Kimble, Titan Leeds, 22 Jan. 1765, Mary Avery          1 CE-308
     The groom was born 27 July 1747.
Kimler, Wm., 19 Aug. 1749, Mary Jackson          2 BA-199
King, Anthony, 20 Aug. 1722, Eliza Rakestraw          1 AA-92
King, Charles, 29 March 1741, Anne Green          2 BA-106
King, Daniel, 12 Jan. 1723, Ann Stanhope          1 AA-98
King, Elias, 24 Dec. 1699, Mary Tildon          3 KE-296
King, Elisha, 11 Dec. 1775, Lydia Webster          1 PG-392
King, Ephraim, 6 March 1757,.Anne Handy, widow          1 WI-49
King, Francis, 25 Sept. 1717, Marg't Sprigg, dau. of
     Col. Thomas Sprigg          2 PG-2
King, James, 2 Sept. 1708, Sarah Denny          3 KE-296
King, James, 28 April 1709, Isabella Pennell          9 SF
King, John, of Morumsco, 11 Feb. 1672, Elizabeth Crew          5 SO-398
King, John, 6 April 1687, Elizabeth Ballard          5 SO-398
King, John, 12 April 1766, Mary Horner          3 AA-112
King, John, Nov. 1777, Susannah Lynch          2 CH(5)
King, John, 25 Nov. 1777, Susannah Leach          3 PG-130
King, Joseph, 14 June 1756, Dradon Johnson          1 CH-200
King, Robert, 13 June 1777, Judith Wood          2 CH(4)
King, Robert Jenkins, 11 Feb. 1776, Mary Stevens          2 SO-41
King, Thomas, 6 Sept. 1739, Elinor Butler          4 AA-441
King, Thomas, 23 Oct. 1743, Elianor Hill          2 BA-239
     2 BA-133 gives date as 23 Oct. 1744.
King, Thomas, 25 Dec. 1744, Eliz'th Thomas          1 QA-50
King, Thomas, son of James and Isabel, 11 day, 12 mo.,
     1755, Anne Coppock, dau. of John and Margaret          9 SF
King, Vincent, son of James and Isabel, 12 Dec.
     1771, Mary Brown, dau. of Joshua and Hannah          9 SF
Kingstone, John, 29 April 17(54 ?), Catherine Cheshere          2 BA-209

| | |
|---|---|
| Kinington, Thomas, 15 June 1695, Hannah Trego | 1 BA-177 |
| Kinnament, Sam'l, 9 March 1747, Mary Nutwell | 3 TA-69 |
| Kinnamont, John, 17 Aug. 1748, Agness Hicks | 3 TA-70 |
| Kinsey, Francis, 14 Oct. 1708, Margrett Morris | 3 KE-296 |
| Kinsey, Robert, 1 Aug. 1710, Mary Wood | 1 BA-209 |
| Kirbey, John, 1775, Sarah Kirbey | 1 CR |
| Kirby, Benj'n, 28 Nov. 1744, Eliza Cumerford | 3 TA-51 |
| Kirby, William, 2 Feb. 1737, Anna Watters | 3 AA-105 |
| Kirchner, George, 1 July 1764, Anna M. Flenner | 4 FR-1143 |
| Kirk, Abner, son of William and Mary, 11 Oct. 1770, Anne Allen, dau. of William and Rachel | 9 SF |
| Kirk, Alphonsus, son of Roger and Elizabeth, 23 Feb. 1692/3, Abigail Sharply, dau. of Adam and Mary | 9 SF |
| Kirk, Garrett, 28 Dec. 1777, Sarah Wingate | 2 CE-1 |
| Kirk, George, 9 Dec. 1705, Mary Kilk | 2 AA-328 |
| Kirk, Joseph, son of William and Mary, 8 June 1769, Judith Knight, dau. of William and Elizabeth | 9 SF |
| Kirk, Roger, son of Alphonsus and Abigail, 9 Feb. 1726/7, Jean Bowen, dau. of Henry | 9 SF |
| Kirk, Roger, son of Timothy and Ann, 7 April 1774, Rachel Hughes, dau. of Elisha and Mary | 9 SF |
| Kirk, Thomas, 11 Feb. 1723, Anne Brown | 2 TA-106 |
| Kirk, Timothy, son of Roger and Elizabeth, 29 day, 8 mo., 1741, Anne Gatchell, dau. of Elisha | 9 SF |
| Kirk, Timothy, son of Roger and Jane, 18 March 1762, Lydia Barrett, dau. of Arthur and Hannah | 9 SF |
| Kirk, William, son of Samuel, 6 day, 3 mo., 1730, Margaret Davis Brown, widow of William Brown | 9 SF |
| Kirk, William, son of Samuel, 2 mo., 1747, Mary Norton Brown, widow of Richard Brown, and dau. of Edward Norton | 9 SF |
| Kirkham, James, 11 Aug. 1703, Affrica Dordon | 8 SF-415 |
| Kirkland, William, 19 Dec. 1723, Elisabeth Holiday | 1 AA-98 |
| Kirshaw, James, 21 Aug. 1725, Margett Maldin | 1 CA-114 |
| Kirsie, Phillip, 26 Dec. 1710, Mary Alexander | 2 TA-68 |
| Kirwan, Dominick, 20 Aug. 1724, Mary Shannahane | 2 TA-107 |
| Kitchen, William, 22 Dec. 1722, Ann Evans | 2 PG-3 |
| Kitely, Francis, 1751, Martha Thomas | 2 BA-241 |
|    2 BA-203 gives date as 12 May 1751, and the bride's name as Mary Thomas. | |
| Kitely, Thomas, 5 May 1726, Elian'r Finks | 1 AA-103 |
| Kitten, Thos., 7 April 1763, Mary Bood | 2 BA-224 |
| Klein, Jacob, 13 Jan. 1767, Anna Mary Seiler | 4 FR-1143 |
| Klein, John, 19 April 1759, Anna Baily | 4 FR-1104 |
| Klein, Nich., 4 April 1768, A. M. Hrueger | 4 FR-1143 |
| Knapp, Jno., 17 Jan. 1756, Ann Miller | 2 BA-213 |
| Knight, Benja., 6 Aug. 1723, Jane Merriman | 3 BA-146 |
| Knight, James, 15 July 1755, Pethena Glall | 2 SO-156 |
| Knight, John, 19 Dec. 1736, Eliza Anderson | 1 AA-120 |
| Knight, Dr. John, son of Stephen and Sarah, 15 May 1740, Mrs. Mary Thompson, dau. of John and Mary | 3 CE-25 |
| Knight, John, chirurgeon, son of Stephen Knight, 15 May 1743, Mary Thompson, dau. of Col. John | 3 CE-24 |
| Knight, Joshua, 23 April 1749, Margret Harris | 2 SO-40 |
| Knight, Light, 12 Oct. 1743, Rachel Ruse | 1 BA-382 |
| Knight, Rob't, 15 Dec. 1760, Ann Limb | 2 BA-220 |
| Knight, Stephen, 24 Feb. 1708, Sarah Robinson, widow | 3 CE-6 |
| Knight, Stephen, 30 Nov. 1731, Ann Seaton | 3 KE-296 |
| Knight, Thomas, 28 Nov. 1718, Susanna Simpson | 1 BA-222 |
| Knight, Thos., 18 July 1763, (?) Burns | 2 BA-225 |
| Knight, William, of Cecil Co., 2 Nov. 1741, Rachel Dulany, dau. of Daniel | 4 AA-442 |
|    9 AA-246 gives same information. | |
| Knight, William, 7 Feb. 1752, Sarah Cox | 2 BA-204 |
| Knighton, Keyser, 1734, Sarah Holliday | 1 AA-118 |

```
Knighton, Thomas, 3 Dec. 1700, Dorothy Wood          2 AA-313
Knighton, Thomas, 8 Oct. 1723, Mary Lockwood         1 AA-97
Knock, Daniel, 22 April 1731, Mary Dening            2 KE-218
Knock, Francis, 1 Sept. 1743, Ann Redgrave           2 KE-255
Knock, Henary, 21 Dec. 1727, Mary Boyer              2 KE-210
Knock, Henry, Sr., 14 Oct. 1739, Cathrine Masson     2 KE-230
Knock, Henry, 19 April 1747, Mary Berry              2 KE-264
Knock, John, 6 May 1755, Mary Denning                2 KE-285
Knoleman, Richard, 27 July 1729, Jane Hanson         3 KE-296
Knott, James, 23 June 1743, Anne Scott               1 QA-48
Knott, James, 26 Sept. 1743, Elis'th Jones           1 QA-48
Knotts, James, 1 Aug. 1745, Sarah Spry               1 QA-51
Knotts, John, 26 June 1738, Sophia Jones             1 QA-44
Knotts, Robard, Feb. 1745, Estr Dawley               1 QA-51
Knotts, Solomon, 11 Nov. 1755, Sarah Jerman          1 QA-60
Knotts, Solomon, 22 April 1759, Rebeckah Hynson      1 QA-65
Knotts, William, 27 Nov. 1745, Rachel Serton         1 QA-51
Knowele, Jno., 23 July 1748, Rebecca Blake           2 BA-197
Knowles, Joseph, 23 April 1742, Eliz'th Stapleford   2 TA-175
Knox, George, 25 Dec. 1755, Dinah Detter             2 BA-213
Kobelenz, Peter, 5 Nov. 1764, Elizab. Hesson         4 FR-1143
Kobell, Robert, 23 March 1746, Elizabeth Bradfield   2 BA-240
Kornmann, George, 25 March 1763, Sarah Harrison      4 FR-1143
Kraemer, George, 8 May 1763, Mary Magd. Holz         4 FR-1143
Krans, William, 16 March 1762, Catharine Rieser      4 FR-1143
Krieger, Lawrence, 30 Aug. 1774, Anna Maria Harbaugh 5 FR-67
Kunz, Jacob, 17 Jan. 1764, Marg. Haegel or Naegel    4 FR-1143
Kunz, John Nich., 18 Sept. 1764, Susan Haev-(?)      4 FR-1143
Kunz, Nicholas, 4 Jan. 1763, An. Mary Eckhard        4 FR-1143
L. or Beck, Christoph, 12 April 1759, Soph. Rosin
   Urbach                                            4 FR-1104
Labey, Thomas, 6 Aug. 1708, Sarah Pindell            1 AA-76
Lacecey, John, 25 March 1706, Mary Jackson           1 AA-72
Lacey, Thomas, 18 day, 12 mo., 1777, Elizabeth Hay-
   hurst                                             4 SF-273
Lackey, Alexander, 24 April 1724, Ann Nutter, widow
   of Matthew Nutter                                 1 WI-29
Laerthy, Phillip, 18 May 1703, Cathe. Loomey         3 KE-298
Laffwell, John, 20 Jan. 1719, Margaret Lee           1 AA-297
Lain, John, 31 Dec. 1728, Margery Slone              2 TA-119
Lain, Timothy, 30 Dec. 1740, Sarah Adkinson          1 QA-46
Lair, Joseph, 7 Jan. 1742, Mary Bishop               2 BA-125
Lake, Henry, 13 Nov. 1683, Mary Cooke                9 SO-402
   5 SO-398 gives date as 25 Dec. 1683.
Lake, John, 31 Jan. 1748, Mary Smith                 2 BA-242
Lakey?, Christopher, 15 Sept. 1724, Mary Huntly      2 PG-3
Laking, Abraham, 10 Oct. 1717, Martha Lee            2 PG-1
Lallin, Redmond, (date not given), Rachel Millis     1 QA-40
Lamb, Francis, 3 April 1714, Rosamond Beck           3 KE-298
Lamb, George, 10 day, 11 mo., 1756, Sarah George     1 SF-103
Lamb, John, 25 July 1701, Elizabeth Belt, widow of
   John Belt                                         1 AA-57
                                                     & 247
Lamb, John, 16 April 1703, Kathrein Galloway         3 AA-96
Lamb, Joshua, 8 day, 4 mo., 1752, Susannah Corse     1 SF-100
Lambard, John, 6 Feb. 1732, Mary Brown               2 AA-368
Lambe, John, 1 Oct. 1736, Elizabeth Hodge            3 AA-107
Lambe, John, 17 Oct. 1742, Sarah Gordon              3 AA-108
Lambert, Henry, 12 Nov. 1744, Rachel Leet            1 QA-50
Lambert, Richard, 10 July 1743, Frans. Phillips      1 QA-48
Lambeth, John, 1771, Lucy Varnall                    2 AA-410
Lambeth, William, 6 Oct. 1765, Mary Gutwood          9 AA-249
Lamdin, Daniel, 3 Aug. 1741, Eliza Hadaway           3 TA-32
Lamdin, John, 13 Aug. 1741, Anne Thomas              1 QA-47
Lamdin, Rob't, 3 Dec. 1748, Eliza Spry               3 TA-71
```

```
Lana-(?), (?), 20 Sept. 1724, Elizabeth                   1 AA-99
Lancaster, Tho., 25 Dec. 1777, Christian Gordin           1 HA-201
Lane, Denis, 21 May 1762, Honour (?)                      2 TA-25
Lane, Dennis, 26 April 1702, Honor (?)                    2 TA-24
Lane, Gallant, 19 June 1744, Sarah Ubanks                 1 QA-49
Lane, Gally, 14 Sept. 1774, Orninta Dial                  1 CR
Lane, George, 20 Oct. 1678, Dennis Fountaine              5 SO-398
Lane, James, Jr., 26 Nov. 1746, Rebecca Mason             1 QA-53
Lane, James, Sept. 1748, Juliana Young                    1 QA-54
Lane, John, Jr., 29 April 1752, Eliz'th Townsend          1 QA-58
Lane, John, 18 Sept. 1754, Avarilla Bozeley               2 BA-211
Lane, John, 6 Oct. 1768, Rebecca Dorsey                   2 BA-257
Lane, John, 21 May 1776, Rachel Brown                     2 AA-413
Lane, Nicholas, 7 Sept. 1738, Sarah Lord                  1 QA-44
Lane, Richard, Dec. 1776, Elizabeth Weems                 2 AA-413
Lane, Thomas, 3 Oct. 1755, Frances Roe                    1 QA-60
Lane, Thomas, 16 Nov. 1760, Eliz. Prushman                2 AA-220
Lane, Timothy, 11 April 1674, Mary Ball                   5 SO-398
Lane, Tydings, 9 May 1743, Hester Bobby                   1 FR-11
Lane, Walter, 16 April 1684, Sarah Gunby                  5 SO-398
Lane, Walter, 24 Sept. 1689, Sarah Wilson                 5 SO-398
Lane, Walter, 5 May 1762, Leah Dennis                     2 SO-193
Lang, John, 1 Jan. 1712, Cathirin Howard                  2 AA-346
Lang, William, 3 June 1759, Sabrew Swill Cassaway         1 QA-65
Langford, John, 24 Aug. 1714, Ann Ralph                   1 WI-6
Langford, Thomas, 14 July 1723, Mary Collins              1 WI-3
Langford, Thomas, 14 Dec. 1744, Sarah More               2 SO-44
Langley, Thomas, 24 (June ?), 1729, Alice Jackson         1 QA-37
Langreene, James, 1 Dec. 1684, Alce Primme                5 SO-398
Langsdall, William, 22 Aug. 1734, Judah Daw               1 WI-8
Lanham, John, Jr., 14 Feb. 1708, Mary Dickinson; the
    marriage was performed by Henry Acton, Justice of
    the Peace for the County                              1 PG-266
Lanham, John, the Third, 16 Jan. 1738/9, Mary Piles       1 PG-287
Lanham, Ralph, 21 Feb. 1720, Ellenor Jones                1 PG-270
Lanham, William, 15 Jan. 1720, Alce Tolburt               1 PG-280
Lankaster, Henry, 15 Jan. 1697, Anne Satchell, widow      3 CE-2
Lankford, David, 2 Jan. 1763, Martha Addams               2 SO-144
Lankford, Ezekel, 10 Nov. 1757, Martha Addams             2 SO-47
Lankford, John, 10 Sept. 1757, Jean Frazer                2 SO-47
Lankford, Killiam, 13 March 1753, Mary White              2 SO-47
Lankford, Lazarus, 2 Feb. 1757, Rachel Powel              2 SO-46
Lankford, Pusey, 21 Nov. 1746, Sarah Smith                2 SO-45
Lankford, Thomas, 15 Sept. 1754, Winney Martin            2 SO-47
Lankford, Thomas, 11 Sept. 1769, Leah Dukes               2 SO-146
Lankford, William, 6 Aug. 1728, Margrett Gillbird         2 TA-118
Lankford, William, 11 Aug. 1757, Rachel Wilson            2 SO-48
Lansdale, Charles, 19 April 1767, Cathorine Wheeler,
    dau. of Clement Wheeler                               1 PG-376
Lansdall, Charles, 20 April 1767, Catherine Wheeler       1 PG-287
Lanzey, Alexander, 20 Jan. 1704, Mary Parsons             2 AA-326
Laramore, Leavin, 28 Sept. 1762, Mary Oneale              1 WI-81
Laramore, Roger, 17 Feb. 1707, Margarett Dare             3 CE-4
Lare, Joseph, 19 Dec. 1742, Mary Bishop                   2 BA-238
Laremore, Thomas, 4 Aug. 1680, Katherine (?)              5 SO-398
Large, Joseph, 14 Dec. 1733, Hannah Gibbens               1 AA-117
Larider, Joseph, 19 April 1702, Susanna Webb              1 AA-250
Larimore, Elijah, 8 April 1766, Catherine Mezick          1 WI-86
Larimore, Thos., 25 April 1744, Esther Taylor             3 TA-48
Lark, Daniel, 20 May 1749, Henrietta Appleby              3 AA-110
Larke, Daniel.  See Currier, Daniel Larke.
Larkin, Jeremiah, 16 Aug. 1702, Margaret Brown            2 AA-318
Larkin, John, 31 Dec. 1746, Eliz'h Taylor                 1 QA-52
Larkin, Nicholas, 14 Feb. 1709, Margaret Gott             2 AA-340
Larkins, Jeremiah, 11 June 1733, Rachel Sinklar, widow    3 CE-16
```

```
Larkins, John, 6 March 1749, Miliner Herring        1 QA-56
Larkins, Thomas, 20 Sept. 1697, Margritt Gassaway   1 AA-38
Larone, Dennis, 7 Nov. 1709, Cathrine Waley         2 TA-63
Larramore, Rogar, 22 Dec. 1719, Augustin Frisby,
   widow                                            3 CE-10
Larrance, Samuel, 4 March 1746, Margaret Pinder     1 QA-53
Larring?, William, 14 Feb. 1737/8, Esther Hollings-
   worth                                            1 QA-43
Larwood, John, 28 July 1737, Mary Kenton            1 QA-43
Larwood, John, 20 Dec. 1739, Mary Hussley           1 QA-45
Lasewell, Jacob, 29 Oct. 1724, Rebecca Beecraft     1 AA-332
Lashle, Robert, 6 Jan. 173-(?), Eliz'th Soper       2 PG-6
Laster, John, 6 Aug. 1744, Ann Spencer              2 KE-253
Lasswell, Jacob, 29 Oct. 1724, Rebecca Beecraft     1 AA-99
Latamus, James, 21 Oct. 1727, Diana Severson        3 CE-13
Laten, Will, 13 March 1669, Sarah Shirtt, widow     1 TA-601
Latham, Joshua, 16 Feb. 1714/5, Anne Lawrance       3 CE-8
Latham, Joshua, 30 Aug. 1716, Mary Kare, widow      3 CE-8
Latimore, James, 20 Oct. 1747, Sarah Thompson       2 BA-241
Lattamore, Jno., 25 Dec. 1766, Ann Wright           2 BA-230
Lattemore, James, banns pub. on 20 Oct. 1747, Sarah
   Thompson                                         2 BA-241
Lattemore, James, 7 Dec. 1760, Hannah Bradley       2 BA-220
Lattymus, James, 21 Sept. 1740, Mary Hugg           3 CE-22
Lauracy, John, 26 Nov. 1738, Mary Denson            1 BA-290
Laurence, Joseph, 14 Dec. 1738, Hannah Turner       2 TA-166
Lavy, John, 1770, Mary Stovell                      2 AA-409
Law, John, 23 Aug. 1746, Isabell Low                1 QA-52
Law, John, 14 Nov. 1758, Elizabeth Lawson           2 BA-218
Lawe, Richard, 14 March 1675/6, Anne Smith          9 SO-401
Lawes, John, 13 June 1671, Katherine Nelson, widow  7 SO-401
Lawler, David, 1715, Elizabeth Polson               4 AA-393
Lawler, Henry, 6 July 1704, Bridgett Carmacker      3 KE-298
Lawler, Patrick, 8 Dec. 1776, Sarah Garner          3 BA-669
Lawrance, John, late of Liverpoole, Lancs., Eng.,
   28 Aug. 1749, Mary Plafay                        1 PG-288
Lawrance, Joseph, 5 Dec. 1759, Ann May              2 BA-219
Lawrance, Thos., 1 Nov. 1759, Sarah Briggs          2 BA-219
Lawrence, Benja., son of Benj. and Eliza, 6 day, 11
   mo., 1701/2, Rachel Marriartee, dau. of Edward and
   Honor                                            6 SF
Lawrence, Henry, April 1672, Elizabeth Williams     8 SO-401
   5 SO-398 gives date as 4 July 1672.
Lawrence, James, 26 May 1731, Mary Thomas           1 QA-38
Lawrence, John, 9 Sept. 1702, Martha Milsom         8 SF-414
Lawrence, John, 11 Sept. 1740, Elizabeth Stavely    2 KE-251
Lawrence, Joseph, 5 Dec. 1759, Ann May              2 BA-219
Larwence, Peter, 17 Jan. 1732, Sarah Hamilton       1 QA-39
Lawrence, Richard, 25 Dec. 1702, Constant Merry     3 KE-298
Lawrence, Richard, 24 Dec. 1704, Mary Wilson        3 KE-298
Larwence, Rob't, 25 Sept. 1740, Julin Savage        2 KE-236
Laws, Panter, 3 Feb. 1736, Catherine Jones          3 SO-4
Laws, Panter, 2 Feb. 1739, Mary Bozman              3 SO-4
Lawson, John, 14 July 1724, Rebecca Woodall         4 AA-423
Lawson, Jno., 15 Nov. 1764, Sarah Harratt           2 BA-227
Lawson, Thos., 20 July 1749, Ann Herrington         2 BA-198
Lawton, John, 23 July 1768, Elizabeth Hancock       3 AA-112
Lax, Thomas, 20 Dec. 1730, Martha Porter            3 BA-150
Lax, Thomas, 27 July 1766, Mary Groves              2 BA-229
Laxton, Thomas, 14 Srpt. 1708, Elizabeth Wilson, of
   P. G. Co.                                        2 AA-335
Layfield, George, 5 Nov. 1738, Betty Bozman         2 SO-43
Layhe, Joseph, 2 Jan. 1728/9, Sarah Booker          2 TA-119
Layhe, William, 29 Jan. 1728/9, Mary Macoter        2 TA-119
Layner, William, 20 Nov. 1707, Mary Joyner          3 KE-298
```

Lazby, Oliver, 19 Aug. 1759, Rachel Price                          1 QA-65
Lazell, Michaell, 26 Dec. 1705, Martha Cook                        3 KE-298
Lazzieur, Joseph, 19 April 1702, Susanna Webb                      1 AA-58
                                                                   & 250
Lea, Dennis, 15 July 1729, Eliza Cheney                            1 AA-109
Leach, Ambross, 5 July 1749, Eliz. Nearn                           2 BA-197
Leach, John, 27 Sept. 1770, Mary Johnson                           2 BA-261
Leach, Rich'd, 26 Dec. 1745, Rebecca Levil                         1 QA-51
Leach, Thos., 1 Dec. 1776, Eliz. Spalden                           1 SM-137
Leachman, Andrew, 8 May 1712, Ellinor Burk                         2 PG-1
Leage, John, 31 Oct. 1703, Elizabeth Millin                        2 AA-322
League, James, 2 May 1759, Eliner Enloes                           2 BA-218
Leak, Henry, 7 June 1705, Elizabeth Ward                           1 AA-65
Leake, Joseph, 9 Dec. 1740, Susanna Stuart                         9 AA-246
Leamers (?), Daniel, 1770, Elizabeth Coupler                       2 AA-409
Lear (?), Ignatius, 3 Nov. 1777, Ann Hudless                      10 BA-69
Leatch, James, 19 Feb. 1776, Margaret Ireland                      2 AA-412
Leatherbury, Thomas, 15 Jan. 1771, Ann Taylor                      1 WI-109
Leatum, John, 21 Feb. 1720/1, Elizabeth Blisset                    4 AA-414
Lecester, Jessey, 30 June 1772, Constantine Morioke                2 BA-264
LeCompte, Antho.:, 8 July 1745, Sarah Skinner                      3 TA-54
LeCompte, Peter, 2 July 1730, Elizabeth Abbott                     2 TA-148
LeCompte, Peter, 5 Sept. 1733, Rachel Stapleford                   2 TA-154
Ledermann, Frederick, 5 June 1764, Cath. Sailer                    4 FR-1148
Ledgley, Jno., 13 March 1766, Susan Foreacher                      2 BA-229
Lee, Alexander, 30 Oct. 1735, Eliza Pindar                         1 QA-41
Lee, Alexander, 6 April 1749, Rachel Graves                        1 QA-55
Lee, Charles, 28 July 1778, Marg't Leach                           1 CA-111a
Lee, Corbin, 31 Jan. 1754, Mrs. Eleanor Thornton                   2 BA-210
Lee, Edward, 2 Nov. 1701, Anne Vandobender                         1 AA-57
   1 AA-248 gives date as 2 Oct. 1701, and the bride's
   name as Ann Bendor.
Lee, Edward, 7 Feb. 1737, Susannah Bazil                           1 AA-121
Lee, James, 18 Sept. 1757, Margarett Collins                       1 QA-63
Lee, John, 24 Dec. 1704, Katherine Knight                          3 KE-298
Lee, John, 2 May 1706, Ann Green                                   3 KE-298
Lee, John, 28 April 1731, Isabella Mountsier                       1 QA-36
Lee, John, 4 April 1733, Alce Norris                               1 BA-266
Lee, John, 10 June 1735, Jane Hickson                              1 BA-285
Lee, John, 1 July 1737, Jennott Cornish                            2 TA-163
Lee, John, 23 Nov. 1746, Margaret Howard                           2 BA-240
Lee, John, 14 July 1777, Ann Williams                              7 AA-1
   8 AA-13 gives date as 15 July 1777.
Lee, Joseph, 12 June 1733, Eliz'th Ashmore                         1 BA-265
Lee, Lewis, 16 Nov. 1738, Sarah Gray                               9 AA-246
Lee, Oliver, 6 Feb. 1708, Elliner Barker                           2 TA-57
Lee, Oliver, 24 Dec. 1744, Sarah Parsons                           2 TA-196
Lee, Richard, 25 day, 8 mo., 1668, Joan Lippitt                    8 SF-314
Lee, Robert, 16 April 1704, Elizabeth Munday                       1 CA-111
Lee, Sheerwood, 3 Nov. 1729, Eliner Temple                         1 BA-254
Lee, Thomas, 1 Jan. 1744, Sarah Jackson                            1 QA-50
Lee, Thomas, 23 Feb. 1752, Margaret Ruth                           1 QA-58
Lee, Thomas, 9 Aug. 1757, Sarah Silvester                          1 QA-62
Lee, William, 4 Sept. 1740, Mary Waddell                           2 TA-170
Lee, William, 17 April 1744, Mary Pinder                           1 QA-49
Leech, Ambrose, 7 July 1748, Elizabeth Nairn                       2 BA-243
Leech, Philip, 1 June 1756, Sarah Nearn                            2 BA-213
Leeds, John, Jr., 14 day, 2 mo., 1726, Rachel Harrison             8 SF-47
Leek, Henry, 16 Dec. 1736, Cassandra Ijams                         1 AA-120
Leeley, Peter, 15 Sept. 1726, Margrett Hunter                      2 TA-113
Leeman, Jacob, 9 Aug. 1757, Ann Mary Jung                          4 FR-1103
Leemon, Eliz'th (sic: probably Alexius), Nov. 1771,
   Rachel Stansbury                                                2 BA-263
Lees, Thomas, 2 Jan. 1704, Mary Symmons                            2 AA-325
Leeth, John, 6 April 1758, Sarah Hutchinson                        1 QA-63

| | |
|---|---|
| Leff, William, 12 Aug. 1697, Ruth Matthews | 1 BA-178 |
| Lefue, Lewis, 8 May 1744, Sarah Low | 2 BA-134 |
| Legat, William, 1750, Martha Bracket | 2 BA-244 |
| Legate, Thomas, 15 April 1754, Mary Phurmey | 2 BA-209 |
| Legatt, Jno., 25 Oct. 1759, Ann James | 2 BA-219 |
| Legatt, Jos., 6 May 1766, Eliz. Burk | 2 BA-229 |
| Legatt, Sutton, 7 April 1763, Hannah Green | 2 BA-224 |
| Legg, Edward, 2 Feb. 1728/9, Mary Margin | 2 TA-120 |
| Leggett, Joshua, (date not given), Eliz. Burk | 2 BA-255 |
| Leggett, William, 13 July 1750, Ann Blackett | 2 BA-201 |
| Leggot, James, 25 June 1772, Eliz. Baker | 2 BA-264 |
| Leggott, James, 25 June 1772, Eliz. Baker | 2 BA-264 |
| Lego, Benjamin, 4 Nov. or 11 Dec. 1723, Jean Taylor, widow | 2 BA-22 & 31 |
| Lego, Luke, 18 Feb. 1766, Cloe Denton | 2 BA-229 |
| Legoe, Benedick, 7 Aug. 1770, Sally Hick | 2 BA-260 |
| Legoe, Benjamin, Jr., 25 Oct. 1740, Judeax Bruceton | 2 BA-116 |
| Legoe, Joseph, 20 Feb. 1770, Nancy Wilcher | 2 BA-260 |
| Legoe, Moses, 7 Jan. 1773, Catherine Hutton | 2 BA-265 |
| Legoe, Spencer, 16 Nov. 1762, Eliz. Jackson | 2 BA-224 |
| Legoe, Spencer, 26 May 1768, Eliz. Hicks | 2 BA-231 |
| Leidig, Gabriel, 18 March 1759, Cath. Delater | 4 FR-1104 |
| Leiper, Andrew, 23 Sept. 1775, Elizabeth Dorsey | 2 AA-412 |
| Leith, Alexander, 16 Feb. 1759, Rachel Neal | 2 TA-286 |
| Lemar, Charles, (date not given), Anne Young | 1 QA-40 |
| Lemar, Gallant, 27 Sept. 1733, Mary Wheeler | 1 QA-40 |
| Lemar, Luke, 1 Dec. 1748, Amy Sprawl | 1 QA-55 |
| Lemarr, John, 21 Jan. 1714, Susanna Tyler | 2 PG-1 |
| Lemmon, Alexis, 9 Dec. 1777, Rachael Jones | 9 BA |
| Lemmon, Eliz'th (sic: probably Alexius), 29 Nov. 1771, Rachel Stansbury | 2 BA-263 |
| Lendrum, Rev. Andrew, 18 Oct. 1749, Jane Burney; the marriage was performed in Newcastle on Delaware by the Rev. George Ross | 1 BA-366 |
| Lenix, R'd, 15 April 1764, Prissilla Carter | 2 BA-226 |
| Lensted, Richard, 9 April 1744, Hannah Acers | 3 AA-106 |
| Leonard, John, 1 Feb. 1781, Mary Watson | 2 SO-146 |
| Lester, George, 8 Dec. 1737, Alce Lee | 1 BA-299 |
| Lester, Peter, 8 May 1713, Anne (?) | 1 BA-214 |
| Letherland, George, 24 Dec. 1748, Margaret Thomas | 3 BA-162 |
| Letton, Richard, 18 April 1689, Honor Durdin | 6 SF |
| Letrote, James, 19 April 1742, Sarah Curseter | 2 TA-175 |
| Levenston, Dunkin, 29 Dec. 1758, Leah Collin | 2 SO-48 |
| Leverly, Thomas, 7 June 1736, Elizabeth Henderson | 3 BA-155 |
| Leverton, Isaac, 25 June 1745, Susanah Nots | 3 TA-53 |
| Leverton, Moses, 29 day, 5 mo., 1768, Nancy Addams | 2 SF-288 |
| Levett, William, 6 Oct. 1737, Marg't Langford | 2 TA-162 |
| Levly, George, 1 Jan. 1770, Chartine Mull | 3 BA-170 |
| Lewden (Lowden), John son of Josiah, 6 May 1762, Rachel Brown, dau. of Jeremiah and Esther | 9 SF |
| Lewen, Robert, 30 June 1668, Anne Nolton | 4 SO-712 |
| Lewes, Thomas, 3 June 1695, Anne Parsons | 5 SO-398 |
| Lewes, William, 31 Aug. 1726, Margett Batchellor | 2 TA-113 |
| Lewin, Robert. See Stewnes, William. | |
| Lewin, Samuel, 27 Aug. 1776, Mary Lane | 2 AA-413 |
| Lewis, Elijah, 3 April 1775, Mary Sullivan | 5 BA-9 |
| Lewis, George, 2 March 1742, Elizabeth Hamm, widow of Ephraim Hamm | 3 CA-24 |
| Lewis, Henry, of A. A. Co., 12 June 1677, Elizabeth Boston | 9 SO-402 |
| Lewis, Isaac, 24 Dec. 1765, Catherine Higginson | 9 AA-249 |
| Lewis, John, of Dor. Co., cooper, 2 April 1717, Elizabeth Winsley | 4 AA-398 & 400 |

```
Lewis, John, 10 Nov. 1727, Hesten Phillips            1 CE-277
Lewis, John, 18 Dec. 1733, Margaret Dawley            1 BA-276
Lewis, John, 22 Swpt. 1738, Margaret Moore            9 AA-246
Lewis, Joseph, 29 Aug. 1749, Mary Millburne           1 QA-56
Lewis, Nicholas, 14 April 1761, Hannah Small          3 AA-112
Lewis, Richard, Jan. 1718, Elisabeth Battee           1 AA-289
Lewis, Richard, of Balto. Co., son of Richard and
  Elizabeth, late of Eng., 15 day, 3 mo., 1723,
  Betty Giles, dau. of John and Sarah                 6 SF
Lewis, Richard, 9 Jan. 1745/6, Virlendah Wheeler      4 AA-447
Lewis, Samuel, 19 Dec. 1737, Sarah Marshall           1 BA-300
Lewis, Samuel, 29 Aug. 1745, Margaret Hughs           1 BA-341
Lewis, Thomas, 14 Feb. 1703, Eliner Stoaks            3 KE-298
Lewis, William, 26 May 1729, Eliza Wantland           1 AA-108
Lewis, William, 20 May 1730, Anna Stinchecomb         3 AA-102
Libbey, John, 1 Jan. 1712, Emy Elizabeth Cathrop      2 TA-70
License, Peter, 27 Dec. 1711, Elizabeth Wancy         1 AA-266
  1 AA-78 gives bride's name as Waney.
Liden, Shadrack, c.Oct. 1775, Rebekah Foxwell         1 CR-6
Lifely, Marke, (date not given), Sarah Hancock        4 AA-393
Light, John, 1680, Elizabeth Greene                   5 SO-398
Liles, Robert, 12 Dec. 1723, Priscilla Nutwell        2 PG-3
Limes, Robert, 22 June 1712, Margaret Steevens        2 AA-345
Limm?, Absolam, 18 Aug. 1748, Jane Vanderford         1 QA-54
Lin, Cha.:, 26 May 1768, Ann Howard                   2 BA-232
Linager, Isaac, 16 day, 4 mo., 1769, Rosannah (?)     2 SF-288
Linch, James, 25 June 1756, Rhoda Sparks              1 QA-61
Linch, John, 6 June 1723, Ellinor Hunter              2 TA-104
Linch, Patrick, 1722, Martha Bowen                    3 BA-148
Linch, Roebuck, 16 Aug. 1747, Jemima Stansbury        3 BA-160
Linch, William, 6 Sept. 1740, Elinor Todd             3 BA-164
Linchfield, William, 26 March 1749, Sarah Parks       2 BA-243
Linckhorn, John, 30 Sept. 1697, Elizabeth Browning    3 CE-2
Lindsay, Edmund, 20 Feb. 1725, Elizabeth Beasley      1 BA-235
  1 BA-260 gives date as 28 Feb. 1725, and the bride's
  name as Boozley.
Lindsey, David, 1676, Sarah Connard, dau. of Philip   9 SO-401
  5 SO-398 gives date as 5 Oct. 1676.
Lindsey, Patrick, 24 (?) 1729, Sarah Swift            1 QA-37
Lines, Thomas, 4 March 1702, Elizabeth Vincett        1 AA-64
Lingenfelder, Geo. B., 10 Feb. 1761, Barb. Brunner    4 FR-1148
Lingenfelder, Valent., 28 Sept. 1765, M. Elizabeth
  Daub                                                4 FR-1148
Lingum, Daniel, 14 Jan. 1723, (wife's name not
  given)                                              2 TA-106
Linley, John, 13 June 1708, Mary Webb                 3 KE-298
Linsicom, Ezikia, 5 Oct. 1697, Milkee Francis         1 AA-38
Linsicom, Thomas, 22 June 1698, Debora Wayman         1 AA-39
Lintch, James, 10 Sept. 1774, Rebecca Flaherty        1 CR
Linthicum, Francis, 28 Jan. 1755, Mary Mayo           1 AA-141
Linton, Henry, 24 Aug. 1725, Anne Waltho              1 AA-101
Linzey, Edmond, 28 Feb. 1725, Eliz'th Boozley         1 BA-260
Lippings, Henry, 18 May 1737, Abigail Sparks          1 QA-43
Liptrot, Jno., 2 Sept. 1704, Mary Lunt                2 TA-41
Lister, Jesse, 8 Dec. 1754, Betty Harris              2 SO-46
Lister, Thomas, Sept. 1682, Abigail London            5 SO-398
Litle, Guy, 25 March 1751, Eliza Ruff                 2 BA-171
Litle, John, 24 Nov. 1743, Ann Jobson                 1 QA-48
Litell, Nathaniel, 1 Nov. 1744, Mary Jackson          1 CE-298
Littell, Thomas, 13 June 1734, Elisabeth Hayfield     1 AA-118
Little, George, 3 July 1763, Catherine Robertson      1 BA-380
Little, James, 24 May 1777, Rachell Conoway           3 BA-173
Little, John, 29 Nov. 1744, Martha Massey             2 KE-255
Little, Jno., 19 May 1766, Eliz. Little               2 BA-229
Little, Robert, 9 July 1773, Mary Wamsley             3 AA-113
```

```
Little, Thomas, 27 June 1731, Mary Shepard          1 BA-257
Little, Thomas, 28 Feb. 1737, Avarilla Osborn       1 BA-295
Little, Walter, 11 July 1734, Jamima Hayfield       1 AA-118
Little, William, 14 July 1730, Elizabeth Leach      2 TA-149
Littlejohn, Thos., 19 Nov. 1751, Margrett Johnson   2 BA-204
Littler, Joshua, son of Samuel and Rachel, 9 Nov. 1733,
    Deborah Oldham, dau. of Thomas and Susannah     9 SF
Littler, Samuel, 31 July 1707, Rachel Minshall Taylor,
    widow of Thomas Taylor, dau. of John Minshall   9 SF
Littler, Samuel, Jr., son of Samuel and Rachel, 22
    Aug. 1735, Mary Brooks, dau. of Thomas          9 SF
Livermore, Thos., 23 June 1749, Anne Day            3 TA-74
Lizenby, Henry, 18 April 1745, Amy Powel            1 QA-50
Lloyd, Evan, 11 Feb. 1734, Sarah Deford             1 QA-40
Lloyd, Henry, 10 June 177, Rebecca Griffin          2 AA-413
Lloyd, John, 9 Aug. 1729, Jane (?)                  4 AA-431
Lloyd, John, 22 Dec. 1741, Susan Hickey             3 TA-34
    2 TA-174 gives date as 31 Dec. 1741.
Lloyd, John, 28 April 1768, Anne Ewing              5 BA-9
Lloyd, Philemon, 11 April 1709, Mrs. Margaret Freeman,
    "so called"                                     4 AA-378
Lloyd, Thomas, 6 day, 3 mo., 1766, Mary, widow of
    1) Joseph Elgar, and 2) Joseph Brinton          9 SF
Lloyd, William, 9 April 1707, Grisell Johnston      1 PG-261
Loader, Richard, 2 Feb. 1733, Sarah Elliott         1 BA-269
Loch, Dr. William, 18 Sept. 1710, Mary Biggs        2 AA-340
Lock, Daniel, 5 Aug. 1718, Mary Ducker              2 TA-87
Lock, Richard, 26 Dec. 1749, Lilley Wilkinson       1 QA-56
Lockard, John, 24 Oct. 1739, Christian Lippins      1 BA-308
Locker, John, 31 Aug. 1713, Magdlen Ray             1 PG-277
Locker, Phil, 9 June 1750, Eliz'h Evans             1 PG-289
Locker, Thomas, 13 Jan. 1716, Elliner Evans         1 PG-267
Locket, Robert, Nov. 1729, Rachel Haycraft          3 AA-102
Lockwell, Thomas, Sr., 11 July 1703, Mary Fortune   2 TA-36
Lockwood, Benj., 24 March 1746/7, Rebekah Morris    1 WO-5
Lockwood, John, 2 Jan. (1748/9 ?), Sarah Holland    1 WO-6
Lockwood, Samuel, 16 Dec. (?), Leah (?)             1 WO-2
Loderforrester, Peter, 30 Nov. 1704, Mary Nelson    1 AA-65
Lofferd, Jno., 14 April 1761, Isabella Ray          2 BA-221
Logan, John, 2 Dec. 1769, Eliz. Pustlay or Pristlay 2 BA-259
Logan, Thomas, born in Aberdeen, Scotland, 13 Feb.
    1774, Susanna Daly, late of Dublin, Ireland     3 BA-171
Logdin, Thos., 22 Nov. 1767, Ann Conner             2 BA-231
Loge, Manasseh, 27 Feb. 1734/5, Sarah Derrel        3 CE-20
Logon, Alexander, 12 May 1711, Christian Grant      4 AA-380
Logoz, Barnaby, 19 Nov. 1704, Mary (?)              4 AA-389
Logsdon, John, 9 Oct. 1735, Margrett Woolley        3 BA-154
Lomax, Thos., 11 Feb. 1755, Sarah Downey            2 BA-212
Loney, John, 22 Dec. 1737, Sarah Denson             1 BA-299
Long, Coalburn, 29 Oct. 1769, Abigal Harris         2 SO-143
Long, David, 22 Oct. 1759, Mary Boone               3 AA-111
Long, Geo., 9 Aug. 1768, Susannah Pollard           2 BA-232
Long, John, 8 March 1735, Elliner Owens             3 BA-155
Long, John, 12 July 1744, Ann Herington             1 QA-49
Long, John, 31 Jan. 1748, Blanch Whitaker           2 BA-198
Long, John, 16 Oct. 1760, Catherine Camoron         2 SO-145
Long, John, 8 Nov. 1768, Mary Addams                2 SO-144
Long, Mos., 13 Sept. 1764, Ann Brown                2 BA-226
Long, Moses, 30 March 1752, Marg'rt Grace Worbleton 2 BA-205
Long, Samuel, 15 Feb. 1667, Jane Michell or Minshall 5 SO-398
Long, Samuel, 22 Feb. 1693/4, Elizabeth King        5 SO-398
Long, Sewell, 28 May 1745, Mary Brooksby            4 AA-447
Long, Thomas, 29 Dec. 1709, Elizabeth Nun           2 TA-65
Longcake, Stephen, 27 Jan. 1745, Betty Harris       1 WI-52
Longe, (?)-vid, 20 May (?), Ann Lockwood            1 WO-3
```

Longley, Joseph, 27 Feb. 1708, Rachell Roberts                3 KE-298
Lony, Benjamin, 7 May 1745, Ann Norris                       2 BA-192
Loockerman, Jacob, 26 April 1711, Magdalen Edmondson         2 TA-69
Loockerman, Richard, c.Aug. 1775, Mary Darden                1 CR-6
Lookerman, Vin.: 3 Jan. 1741/2, Susan Berwick                3 TA-34
Loomy, John, 10 Nov. 1768, Sarah Gouldsmith                  2 BA-232
Lord, Potter, 20 Dec. 1748, Charrity Addams                  2 SO-44
Lord, Potter, 15 Jan. 1750/1, Rebeckah Wheler                2 SO-44
Lord, Thomas, Feb. 1767, Mary Wilson                         2 SO-147
Loud, Charles, 31 Dec. 1739, Priscilla Pickering             2 TA-167
Loud, Robert, 21 Dec. 1730, Rosaman Connelly                 2 TA-149
Loudridge, William, 20 March 1674, Katherine Jones           5 SO-398
Loughton, Joseph, 4 Aug. 1701, Mary Smith                    3 KE-298
Louis, John, 16 Sept. 1724, Allice Dixon                     4 AA-423
Love, Jno., 10 Feb. 1704, Mary (?)                           2 TA-43
Love, Jno., 26 June 1713, Anne Preston                       2 TA-71
Love, John, 1 Jan. 1718, Rebekah Stapleford                  2 TA-89
Love, Robert, 9 June 1729, Sarah Bond                        2 BA-63
Love, Samuel, Jr., 5 Dec. 1742, Mary Haw                     1 CH-184
Love, William, 27 April 1706, Arabella Walston               1 BA-201
Love, William, 2 Jan. 1710, Anne Bell                        2 TA-68
Love, William, 17 Nov. 1747, Elizabeth Scott                 1 CH-179
Loveday, Thomas, 27 March 1746, Grace Martin                 3 TA-57
Lovedie, John, 11 April 1703, Sarah Harden                   2 TA-34
Lovington, Richard, 14 June 1736, Martha Warren              3 BA-155
Lovly, Deliverance, 24 Aug. 1658, Eliz. Ward                 1 KE-129
Low, Hugh, 18 Sept. 1755, Pennellipie Harsh                  2 BA-212
Low, Ignatius, 20 Nov. 1777, Priscilla Norris                1 SM-137
Low, John, 29 March 1744, Susannah Cox                       2 BA-190
                                                             & 239
Low, Ralph, 15 Sept. 1755, Ann Renshaw                       1 WI-70
Low, Thos., 1753, Sarah Mainer                               2 BA-242
  2 BA-209 gives date as Jan. 1754.
Low, William, 30 Jan. 1746, Ann Davice                       2 BA-121
Lowd, Thomas, 18 April 1703, Cathrine Gilmer                 2 TA-39
Lowden, Thomas, (date not given), Eliza Walker               1 PG-263
Lowder, Charles, 2 March 1730, Anne Sutter                   1 QA-36
Lowder, Robert, 3 Jan. 1736, Elizabeth Eubanks               2 TA-162
Lowe, Charles, 30 Nov. 1739, Priscilla Blake                 3 TA-20
Lowe, George, 29 Dec. 1754, Sarah Cotman                     1 WI-62
Lowe, Henry, 20 Dec. 1753, Nancy Lindsey                     1 PG-301
Lowe, Hugh, 5 June 1729, Mary Freeman                        2 BA-37
Lowe, Isaac, 5 Nov. 1761, Sarah Mitchell                     2 BA-222
Lowe, John, 2 Feb. 1700, Mary Bartlett                       8 SF-406
Lowe, Thomas, 1728/9, Thamar Love                            2 BA-63
Lowe, William, 6 July 1710, Temperance Pickett               1 BA-209
Lowes, Henry, Jr., son of Henry and Esther, 21 July
  1759, Easther Dashiells                                    1 WI-79
Lowry, Edward, 16 Aug. 1722, Sarah Jenkins                   1 BA-262
Lowry, James, 27 April 1748, Mary Vezey                      1 CE-307
Lowry, Thomas, 17 Jan. 1774, Catherine Brian                 3 BA-181
Loyd, John, 31 Aug. 1730, Rebecca Knotts                     1 QA-37
Luars, Hans, 6 Nov. 1720, Mary Bedwell                       1 AA-301
Lucas, Barton, 28 Nov. 1762, Priscilla Sprigg                9 AA-247
Lucas, Charles, 20 Nov. 1718, Eliza Evans                    2 PG-2
Lucas, John, 27 April 1774, Keziah Morgan                    1 CR
Lucas, Thos., 2 March 1762, Mary Chamberlaine                2 BA-223
Lucas, William, 7 Jan. 1733, Eliza Roberts                   1 AA-117
Lucus, William, 27 July 1728, Mary Scorke                    4 AA-430
Ludlam, William, 13 Jan. 1703, Sarah Little                  2 AA-322
Ludlee, Wm., Jan. 1713, Eliz. Trott                          2 AA-348
Luellen, Samuel, 30 March 1684, Anne Kelly                   5 SO-398
Luellin, Mr., 2 July 1702, Mary (?)                          2 TA-26
Lum, Jonas, 4 Feb. (?), Mary Massy                           1 CE-329
Lum, Michael, 9 July 1739, Mary Makenne                      1 CE-286

Lurtey, Nicholas, 9 Dec. 1729, Esther Needles          1 QA-37
Lusby, John, 1 July 1702, Eleanor Cross                4 AA-372
Lusby, John, son of John and Eleanor, 25 July 1734,
  Magdalen Killman                                     4 AA-436
Lusby, John, 23 Sept. 1762, Catherine Edwards          9 AA-247
Lusby, Robert, 21 Aug. 1707, Mary Baldwyn              4 AA-372
Lusby, Robert, 30 May 1765, Eliz. Hughes               2 BA-228
Lusby, Samuel, 29 March 1752, Susanah Stewart          1 AA-132
Lusby, Thomas, son of Robert, 18 July 1736, Sarah
  Garey                                                4 AA-438
Lux, Darbe, 16 May 1722, Ann Sanders                   1 AA-90
Lux, William, 16 July 1752, Agnes Walker               3 BA-165
Lyal, John, 2 Feb. 1717, Ann Muture                    2 TA-258
Lyal, John, 16 Aug. 1736, Eliz't Farmer                1 BA-299
Lyder, James, 20 Jan. 1771, Ann Meedes                 2 BA-261
Lye, John, 11 Dec. 1735, Presotia Hitchcock            3 BA-154
Lyley, James, 14 Aug. 1738, Margaret Painter           1 BA-290
Lynch, Hugh, 25 Aug. 1733, Jane Mullican               2 TA-153
Lynch, James, 23 Nov. 1728, Mary Lee                   1 BA-260
Lynch, Jas., 18 Nov. 1762, Comfort Burton or Barton    2 BA-224
Lynch, Patrick, 20 April 1747, Averilla Day            2 BA-196
Lynch, Robert, 31 March 1730, Anne Crouch, widow
  of William Crouch                                    2 TA-261
Lynch, Thomas, 8 Feb. 1729/30, Priscila Willshare      2 KE-229
Lynch, William, 3 Feb. 1749, Margaret Lynch            2 BA-243
Lynchfield, Wm., 26 March 1749, Sarah Parks            2 BA-198
Lyndsey, William, son of William, 26 April 1772,
  Catherine Woodbury, dau. of Jonathan Woodbury,
  late of Bristol                                      3 CE-27
Lynes, Thomas, 4 March 1702, Eliz. Finsett             1 AA-254
Lynn, David, 24 Aug. 1746, Eliz. Copland               2 BA-195
Lynthicum, Francis, 15 Oct. 1732, Elianor Williams     1 AA-114
Lynthicum, Thomas, 28 April 1724, Sarah Burton         1 AA-98
Lyon, David, 30 Sept. 1708, Mary Rouse                 2 AA-335
Lyon, Jonathan, 1 Oct. 1747, Sarah Clark               2 BA-194
Lyon, Josiah, 16 Oct. 1763, Eliza Brown                1 BA-380
Lyon, Rob't, 31 Oct. 1765, Susan Rhodes                2 BA-228
Lysz, Andrew, 10 Feb. 1767, Catharine Wolf             4 FR-1148
McAlpine, Andrew, 24 Feb. 1718, Deliverance Pomfret    4 AA-403
McAy, George, 1770, Flora McQun                        2 AA-410
McBride, Thomas, 28 Nov. 1769, Mary Scotty             2 BA-259
M'Cabe, John, 14 June 1758, Eleanor Goodwin            1 BA-70
Macanun, Cornelius, 13 March 1708, Ann Thornton        2 AA-336
Maccan, Owen, 25 April 1735, Elizabeth Cullen          1 BA-286
McCarry, John, 14 Sept. 1735, Elizabeth Murphey        4 AA-437
Mccartee, John, 29 May 1718, Elizabeth Taylor          2 TA-92
McCarty, Daniel, 20 Jan. 1714, Sarah Norris            1 BA-217
Maccarty, John, 26 Feb. 1747/8, Mary Cooper            3 TA-68
MacCarty, Samuel, 16 Nov. 1739, Sarah Robinson         1 BA-309
MacCarty, Thos., 7 Aug. 1735, Rebecca Tucker           2 TA-159
MacCarty, William, 23 March 1739, Jane Smith           1 BA-311
MacCay, Daniel, 26 March 1722, Katherine Craigh        1 AA-90
McCay, Henry, 3 Feb. 1726, Rebecca Noble               3 CE-18
MacChaly, Thomas, 23 Dec. 1701, Elizabeth Ridgely      1 AA-57
                                                        & 249
MacClanhan, Nathaniell, 19 Oct. 1736, Mary Wiatt       2 KE-234
MacClannahan, Thomas, 23 May 1758, Margaret Hines      1 QA-63
MacClayland, Alexander, 30 May 1734, Mary Abbott       2 TA-155
McClean, Daniel, 30 Dec. 1735, Jane Hamilton           1 QA-41
McCleary, Samuel, 20 May 1740, Magdalen Bassett,
  dau. of Arnold                                       3 CE-24
McClemmy, Whitty, 4 Aug. 1751, Sarah Waters            3 SO-1
McCliston, Capt. George, 28 Feb. 1753, Mary Townsand   1 WI-95
McClogan, Daniel, 27 June 1772, Eliner Price           2 BA-264
McClong, Adam, 24 Dec. 1764, Letitia Richardson        2 BA-227

MacCloud, William, 18 Sept. 1737, Ruth Crawford          1 BA-298
M'Cloughon, Thomas, 10 July 1761, Deb. King              2 BA-222
McClure, Richard, 1727, Catherine Mackeve                1 CE-332
McCollum, Alexander, 12 Nov. 1745, Elizabeth Beeston     3 BA-158
McComas, Alexander, 15 Nov. 1713, Elizabeth Day          2 BA-3
McComas, Alexander, 23 Aug. 1728, Hannah Whitaker        2 BA-38
Maccomas, Aquilla, 2 Jan. 1752, Sarah Preston            2 BA-204
McComas, Daniel, 26 Dec. 1734, Martha Scott              2 BA-119
Maccomas, Daniel, Jr., 26 Jan. 1743, Tabitha Johnson     2 BA-189
Maccomas, Daniel, son of Elixander, Sr., 15 March 1753,
   Hannah Taylor                                         2 BA-207
Maccomas, Dan'l, 10 Oct. 1758, Ann Miles                 2 BA-217
McComas, Elecksander, 19 Nov. 1713, Elizabeth Day        2 BA-3
Maccomas, Jas., 15 Nov. 1761, Eliz. Hillin               2 BA-222
Maccomas, William, 22 Jan. 1760, Eliz. Scott             2 BA-219
MacComus, Alexander, 23 Aug. 1728, Hannah Wittacre       2 BA-38
MacComus, William, 27 July 1742, Hannah Deaver           1 BA-324
McConchie, William, 25 Sept. 1777, Eliza Muncaster       2 CH(3)
McConikin, John, 20 Sept. 1762, Eleonor Long             3 BA-168
McConnican, John, 26 Feb. 1753, Mary Darby               3 BA-168
Maccotter, John, 10 Feb. 1729, Margaret Allesby          2 TA-148
McCracken, John, 30 Nov. 1736, Judith Scidmore           3 KE-305
McCrady, Isaac, 13 April 1774, Hannah Cearsly            2 SO-148
Maccrah, Owen, 23 April 1676, Mary Benderwell            5 SO-398
McCray, Zepheniah, 21 Oct. 1777, Mary Gatton             1 MO-519
McCredy, Alexander, 21 July 1774, Sarah Randell          2 SO-147
McCubbin, Jno., 29 Jan. 1761, Sarah Holland              2 BA-221
Maccubbin, Nicholas, son of Zachariah Maccubbin and
   Susanna Maccubbin who was a dau. of Nicholas and
   Hester Nicholson, 21 July 1747, Mary Clare Carroll,
   dau. of Dr. Charles Carroll, and Dorothy his
   wife                                                  4 AA-448
Maccubbin, William, 22 Oct. 1772, (?) Wallingsford       3 AA-113
Maccubbin, Zachariah, 7 Nov. 1745, Sarah Norwood         3 BA-158
McCuddy, William, 9 April 1764, Elisabeth Carey          2 SO-210
M'Cullister, Edw'd M., 21 Oct. 1754, Mary Ryley          2 BA-211
McCulloch, David, merchant of Joppa, Balto. Co.,
   2nd son of John McCulloch of Torhousekey in the
   shire of Galloway, 4 July 1759, Mary Dick, eld.
   dau. of James and Margaret Dick                       1 AA-145
McCune, Andrew, 28 May 1772, Sarah Gist                  4 BA-74
McCurahon, Arthur, 29 June 1726, Rachel Gilbert          1 BA-240
McCutchon, John, 5 Aug. 1777, Elizabeth Hathorn          2 CE-1
Macdaniel, Dan'l, 10 Dec. 1724, Esther Mordick           2 TA-110
MacDaniel, Daniel, 30 June 1741, Eve McClayland          2 TA-172
MacDaniel, David, 1715, Sarah Jones                      2 PG-1
McDaniel, Edward, 27 April 1777, Ann Owens               2 AA-413
MacDaniel, James, 1 June 1739, Sarah Jones               1 BA-306
MackDaniel, Daniell, 4 March 1727, Mary Sallsbery        2 TA-117
Mackdaniell, Daniel, 17 Feb. 1728/9, Margret
   Sherodine                                             2 TA-120
McDaniel, Thomas, 14 June 1777, Ann Chattam              2 CH(1)
McDaniell, Zackariah, 12 June 1708, Bridgett Powell      3 KE-301
McDermont, Timothy, 10 April 1747, Mary Warden           1 QA-53
M'Donald, John, 15 Dec. 1777, Elizabeth Babington        7 AA-2
MacDonell, Arthur, 25 (?) 1705, Ellin Owins              2 TA-43
McDonnell, William, 16 June 1772, Mary Callaghan         5 BA-9
Macdowel, Phillip, 3 Nov. 1724, Mary Richardson          1 AA-103
M'Duggle, James M., 28 June 1747, Eliner Hammond         2 BA-196
McEven, Christopher, 6 Sept. 1747, Ann Walker            3 BA-160
McFarson, Alexander, 28 Nov. 1776, Mary Weems            2 AA-413
Macfee, Malcolm, banns posted, date not given,
   Elizabeth Franklin                                    6 BA(1)
McFeel, Markum, 14 Nov. 1771, Eliz. Franklin             2 BA-263
Macgall, Jno., 2 Dec. 1756, Jane Martin                  2 BA-214

Macgee, Jno., 15 July 1756, Marg'rt Little               2 BA-213
McGee, Ransey, 26 Nov. 1775, Elizabeth Gist              4 BA-74
MakGill, David, 6 March 1708/9, Grace Boon               1 CA-112
MacGill, Rev. James, 8 Oct. 1730, Sarah Hilleary,
  eld. dau. of Thomas, of P. G. Co.                      6 AA-198
MacGill, John, 4 Dec. 1759, Elizabeth Duvall             2 PG-7
Macgomery, William, 7 Nov. 1738, Mary Brierly            1 BA-322
McGraw, Edward, 7 April 1765, Margaret Bourke            2 CR-271
MacGregory, Daniel, 22 July 1727, Ann Henderson          1 AA-105
McGrigors, Dugil, 18 Oct. 1745, Estr Vanderford          1 QA-51
McGuire, John, 10 Feb. 1771, Mary Tipton                 2 BA-261
Mackey, Dan'll, 8 Jan. 1729, (?) (?)                     1 AA-110
McIlven, Thomas, 26 Jan. 1730, Mary Botfield             2 TA-150
Mackall, Benjamin, IV, 20 Nov. 1769, Rebecca Potts       5 AA-3
Mackall, John, 11 March 1758, Margaret Gough             2 CA-39
                                                           & 42
Mackarte, Daniel, 23 Jan. 1703/4, (?) Woolsher           1 BA-200
Mackarty, Daniell, 15 April 1707, Eliz'th Matthews       3 KE-301
McKay, Robert, Jr., son of Robert, 27 July 1735,
  Patience Job, dau. of Andrew and Elizabeth             9 SF
Mackelfish, David, 8 Oct. 1733, Martha Sellman           1 AA-116
Mackubbin, Samuel, 20 Oct. 1702, Elizabeth Prise         2 AA-318
Mackdermod, Hugh, 18 Aug. 1731, Eliza Fagon              2 TA-150
Mackean, Peter, 5 Aug. 1736, Clara Holmes                2 PG-7
MacKenley, Allen, 23 April 1745, Susanne Freziel         2 BA-192
McKenley, Roger, 1 June 1760, Mary Kelley                2 BA-200
MacKenney, Alexander, 4 Sept. 1710, Catherine Plunkitt   1 CA-113
M'Kennon, Daniel, 9 Dec. 1777, Maria Wilson              7 AA-2
Mackettrick, John, 28 May 1667, Mary Allen, widow        4 SO-671
Mackeway, Patrick, 29 Sept. 1705, Elizabeth Martin       2 TA-44
Mackey, (?), 13 Dec. 1763, Ann White                     1 CH-192
Mackey, Daniell, 9 Nov. 1704, Alice Goodwell             1 AA-65
Mackey, William, 12 Aug. 1701, Mary Prinse               3 KE-299
Mackgugin, Patrick, 21 Sept. 1735, Elizabeth
  Mackdaniel                                             3 BA-154
MacKinnie, John, 26 Dec. 1777, Mary Kirshaw              1 CA-111a
MacKinney, Timothy, 17 July 1709, Hannah Neal            2 TA-61
Macklane, John, 14 Jan. 1733, Margett Taylor             3 BA-151
Macklayland, Fenly?, 18 Nov. 1704, Ann Wadson            2 TA-42
Macklefish, Thomas, 11 Jan. 1727, Susanna Cheney         1 AA-106
Macklefresh, David, 3 Jan. 1722, Mary Leeke              1 AA-94
Mackmillion, George, Jan. 1669, Grace Carr               3 CH
McKnaughton, William, 23 Jan. 1777 (wife's name not
  given)                                                 2 AA-413
Mackness, John, 1751, Eliz'th Morris                     2 BA-241
McKnitt, John, 28 March 1693, Jane Wallis                5 SO-399
MacKown, Francis, 22 Jan. 1735, Sarah Falcom             1 QA-41
Mackubin, William, 11 Aug. 1735, Clara Phips             3 BA-154
McLander, Nicholas, 16 Aug. 1714, Elinor Hogin           3 KE-303
McLaughlin, Ralph, 10 Feb. 1748, Rachel Newnam           1 QA-55
McLellan, David, 30 April 1768, Janit Buchanan           5 BA-9
McLeod, Robert, 24 Feb. 1733/4, Elizabeth McLeod         4 AA-436
McLure, David, 25 March 1773, Elisabeth Crone            5 BA-9
Macmahan, Wm., c.Aug. 1775, Catherine Missen             1 CR-6
McManus, John, 12 Jan. 1734/5, Elizabeth Campbell        3 CE-21
McMayhan, Thomas, 27 Feb. 1735, Susannah Welch           2 TA-160
McMullan, Alexander, 1 June 1776, Hannah Stringhar       3 BA-172
McNaire, Thomas, 1 Oct. 1765, Ann Burgess                1 AA-151
McNamee, Barnabas, 8 April 1756, Mary Pearson, dau.
  of John and Margaret                                   9 SF
McNawhaun, Martin, 17 Dec. 1707, Mary Murfey             3 KE-301
McNeer, John, 16 June 1700, Joan Copinger                3 KE-299
Macolough, William, 18 April 1737, Katherine Macolough   3 AA-104
Macotter, Hezekiah, 1 June 1707, Elizabeth Price         2 TA-120
Macotter, Hezekiah, Jr., 10 Nov. 1736, Eliza Trayman     2 TA-159

McPherson, William, 13 Aug. 1737, Elioner Wilkinson    1 CH-191
McRea, Samuel, 12 Dec. 1770, Janet Weer                5 BA-9
Macutter, Samuel, 23 Nov. 1776, Margaret Pocock        3 BA-669
Macway, Patrick, 9 Feb. 1740, Mary Hunt                3 TA-29
Mace, Thomas, 27 Dec. 1775, Mary Neil                  2 AA-413
Mack, Edmon, 21 Feb. 1725/6, Sarah Flin                2 TA-113
Maddin, John, 21 Sept. 1707, Kather: Flanakin          3 KE-301
Maddin, John, 9 Feb. 1734, Anne Bennett                1 QA-40
Maddox, William, 17 Dec. 1720, Margaret Crorcombs      4 AA-413
Maddux, Alexander, 12 July 1754, Betty Powell          2 SO-53
Maddux, Bell, 1 April 1753, Margaret Marchant          2 SO-52
Maddux, Francis, 26 Aug. 1757, Elizabeth Bigland       1 WI-76
Made, William, 18 Dec. 1698, Jane Hambilton            3 KE-299
Magdahiell, Daniell, 23 May 1702, Ann (?)              2 TA-25
Magee, David, 31 Oct. 1745, Mary MacGlamery            1 WI-79
Magee, Peter, 23 Dec. 1736, Mary Noble                 1 WI-3
Maggers, Jno., 26 May 1756, Rebecca Polard             2 BA-213
Maggs, Daniel, 19 July 1703, Grace Canfield            3 KE-300
Maggs, Daniell, 15 Oct. 1713, Wealthy Ann Evans        3 KE-302
Magill, Rev. James, 8 Oct. 1730, Mrs. Sarah Hillary    2 PG-5
Magisson,RJohn, 9 May 1665, Janne Shears               1 KE-186
Maglavin, William, 4 April 1714, Elynor James          2 KE-185
Magnor, Edward, 17 May 1722, Mildrett Magnor           3 KE-304
Magruda, Robert, 5 Dec. 1734, Sarah Crabb              2 PG-6
Magruder, Alexander, 19 Feb. 1765, Susanna Lemar       9 AA-250
Magruder, John, 1 Dec. 1715, Susanna Smith             2 PG-1
Mahall, Timothy, 17 (?) 1745, Mary Stephens            1 PG-288
Mahone, John, 3 Sept. 1751, Mary Crews                 1 QA-58
Maid, Thomas, 13 Sept. 1724, Jane Pope                 2 PG-3
Maidagil?, John, 20 Feb. 1757, Charity Duvall          2 PG-7
Mainard, Laurance, 28 May 1732, Elizabeth Foster       1 AA-114
Mainard, R'd, 19 Feb. 1765, Ann Wright                 2 BA-227
Mainer, William, 14 Dec. 1729, Martha Tucker           3 BA-149
Mainly, William, 24 Sept. 1747, Rebecca George         1 CE-293
Mairer, Wm., 1 April 1766, Mary Armstrong              2 BA-229
Major, James, 18 Sept. 1775, Eva Greathouse            5 BA-9
Major, Peter, 27 Oct. 1730, Mary Slider                3 BA-149
Major, Thos., 22 Jan. 1761, Jemima Fuller              2 BA-221
Majors, Elias, 8 Sept. 1763, Diana Bozley              2 BA-225
Malcolm, John, 22 Aug. 1777, Mary Lawrence             1 CR-10
Mallence, Emanuel, 11 Feb. 1750, Margaret Reeves       2 BA-244
Mallane, Emanuel, 13 Feb. 1749, Margrett Reeves        2 BA-200
Mallane, Jno., 8 Nov. 1748, Edith Cole                 2 BA-198
    2 BA-243 gives groom's name as Mallanee, and the
    date as 6 Nov. 1748.
Mallaney, Michael, 31 Jan. 1771, Eliz. Collison        2 BA-261
Mallone, Robert, 12 Sept. 1728, Mary Harrison          1 WI-6
Malohone, Jac., 21 April 1771, Maria Langley           1 SM-136
Malone, Michael, 1 May 1719, Joan Allen                4 AA-408
Malone, Thomas, 16 Dec. 1777, Mary Harper              1 MO-519
Malooney, Michael, 2 Feb. 1749, Rebcca Antony          2 CR-271
Manaydier, Rev. Daniel, Rector of St. Peter's, 12 Jan.
    1720, Mrs. Hannah Parrott                          2 TA-95
Manby, Edw'd, 30 Aug. 1761, Mary Rice                  2 BA-222
Manchester, Thos., 18 June 1725, Sarah Morgin          2 TA-111
Mand, James, 27 Jan. 1736, Sarah Nevill                1 QA-42
Manders, William, 7 Oct. 1714, Ann Darley              4 AA-392
Manford, William, 26 Aug. 1734, Diana Skinner          2 TA-156
Mangran, Francis, 23 Nov. 1727, Mary Leey              2 TA-116
Maning, Francis, 30 Jan. 1774, Patience Grifes         3 BA-170
Maning, Richard, 7 April 1733, Elizabeth Smith         1 BA-266
Manley, Jacob, 15 Dec. 1768, Rebecca Lum               1 CE-308
Manlove, John, 9 Aug. 1672, Elizabeth Lee              5 SO-398
Manlove, Mark, 5 April 1672, Elizabeth Greene          8 SO-401
Manlove, Thomas, 1667, Jane Dillamas                   5 SO-398

```
Manlove, Thomas, 30 July 1667, Jane De Lamas           4 SO-679
Manlove, William, 8 Aug. 1676, Mary Robbins            9 SO-401
Manlove, William, 1 Nov. 1676, Alce Robins             5 SO-398
Manning, Richard, 7 April 1733, Eliz'th Lemmon         1 BA-266
Manor, Timothy, 2 April 1747, Mary Heather             1 QA-53
Mansell, George, of A. A. Co., Gent., 4 March 1714,
    Sarah Norwood                                      1 PG-260
Mansfield, Edward, 10 Feb. 1740/1, Sarah Alfree        1 QA-46
Mansfield, John, 10 Feb. 1740/1, Jane Lawson           1 QA-46
Mansfield, Rich'd, 29 Nov. 1736, Elis. Smith           1 QA-42
Mansfield, Robert, 13 Nov. 1740, Jemimah Coe           2 KE-237
Mansfield, Samuel, 16 June 174-(?), Mary Piner         2 KE-256
Manson, James, 17 (Feb.?) 1728, Sarah Loyd             1 QA-36
Manss?, Daniel, 10 Nov. 1767, Eva Spiegel              4 FR-1151
Manyard, Henry, 17 Feb. 1703, Sarah Hopkins            3 AA-98
Marbury, Francis, 14 Sept. 1714, Frances Head          1 PG-267
Marcer, John, 18 Sept. 1765, Rebecca Judah             6 BA(1)
March, John, 24 June 1703, Ellinor Anderson            3 KE-300
March, John, 8 Aug. 1744, Sarah Briscoe                2 KE-260
March, Thomas, 26 Feb. 1744, Sophia Corvin             2 BA-192
Marchent, Richard, 28 July 1723, Mary Sweeting         3 BA-146
Marchment, Samuel, 25 March 1685, Mary Wharton         5 SO-398
Marcy, Jonathan, 25 Nov. 1701, Mrs. Ann Collyer,
    "spinster"                                         1 BA-196
Mardary, William, 26 Dec. 1733, Catherine Lahay        2 TA-272
    2 TA-154 gives date as 27 Dec. 1733.
Mardurt, William, 12 Dec. 1727, Bridgett Cogklan       1 PG-272
Mariarte, Ninian, 8 May 1735, Jane Griffin             2 PG-6
Marine, James, 2 June 1719, Grace Sedgwicks            1 AA-293
Markgrave, Francis, 27 Dec. 1724, Elion'r Meginney     2 TA-111
Markland, William, 19 Nov. 1770, Orpha Edenfield,
    dau. of John Ensor, Sr.                            3 BA-169
Marlett, John, 28 May 1667, Hannah Manlove             4 SO-671
Marloy, Ralph, 22 May 1717, Anne Middleton, dau. of
    John and Mary                                      1 PG-276
Marr, James, 7 Jan. 1713, Eliz. Farmer                 2 AA-348
Marr, John, Jr., 21 (?) 1709, Elizabeth Peal           2 AA-409
Marrer, John, Jan. 1772, Rebecka Coligate              2 BA-263
Marriott, Augustine, 1 Jan. 1729, Mary Warfield, dau.
    of John and Ruth                                   4 AA-432
Marriott, Sylvanus, 8 Dec. 1730, Rachel Davis          4 AA-433
Marritt, John, 5 June 1667, Hannah Manlove             5 SO-398
    Another entry on the same page gives the date as
    25 June 1667.
Marrot, Jno., 19 April 1707, Mary Miller               2 TA-47
Marrly, William, 21 Oct. 1777, Sarah Barry            10 BA-69
Marsey, Samuel, 12 Oct. 1740, Sarah Farmer             1 QA-46
Marsh, Edmund, 21 Sept. 1711, Catherine Wiggins        2 TA-70
Marsh, Edmund, 2 Dec. 1735, Jane Sisk                  2 TA-192
Marsh, George, 15 Aug. 1681, Elizabeth Davis           5 SO-398
Marsh, Gilbert, 20 Feb. 1747, Lavina Bucknam           3 BA-161
Marsh, James, 14 July 1669, Alce Gale                  2 AA-296
Marsh, Jas., 11 Aug. 1756, (?) Taylor                  2 BA-213
Marsh, John, 13 Feb. 1756, Catherine Collins           1 QA-60
Marsh, Jno., 7 April 1763, Mary Rockhold               2 BA-224
Marsh, Josiah, 17 Nov. 1745, Sarah Breeset             3 BA-158
Marsh, Thomas, 6 July 1738, Mary Johnson               1 QA-44
Marsh, Thomas, 10 Feb. 1745, Sophia Corbin             2 BA-240
Marshal, Jacob, 5 June 1774, Mary Sandiford            6 BA(1)
Marshal, Thomas, 29 May 1720, Martha Messure           1 AA-299
Marshall, John, 1775, (?) Sherwood                     1 CR
Marshall, John D., 2 May 1776, Ann Wailes              2 SO-210
Marshall, Rich'd, 7 April 1748, Sarah Carroll          3 TA-69
Marshall, Robert, 5 Jan. 1739, Cristian Jenings        3 AA-105
Marshall, Thomas, negro, 25 Dec. 1700, Mary (?), negro 1 AA-56
```

| | |
|---|---|
| Marshall, Thomas, 3 Oct. 1740, Sarah Bull | 2 BA-154 |
| Marshall, William, 19 June 1718, Mrs. Mary Wells | 1 BA-221 |
| Marshel, Thomas, 25 March 1766, Easter Marshel | 2 SO-154 |
| Marshell, Isaac, 17 Feb. 1768, Sarah Tilghman | 2 SO-151 |
| Marshell, Stephen, 12 April 1770, Mary Gunby | 2 SO-152 |
| Marthews, Phillip, 26 Nov. 1747, Sophia Holland | 2 SO-49 |
| Martin, Charles, 25 Aug. 1701, Elizabeth (?) | 2 TA-20 |
| Martin, Francis, Nov. 1683, Mary Roatch | 5 SO-399 |
| Martin, George, 27 Dec. 1734, Elizabeth Curr | 1 AA-118 |
| Martin, Henry, 25 June 1743, Jane Robinson | 3 TA-43 |
| Martin, Henry, 31 June 1743, Jane Robinson | 2 TA-198 |
| Martin, John (date not given), Ann Dorsey | 6 AA-192 |
| Martin, John, 14 Aug. 1714, Mary Holloway | 4 AA-392 |
| Martin, John, 27 April 1741, Mary Carey | 3 TA-30 |
| Martin, Michael, March 1736, Mary Fling | 2 BA-150 |
| Martin, Phil, 3 April 1742, Phoebe Bowdle | 3 TA-37 |
|   2 TA-175 gives date as 15 April 1742. | |
| Martin, Robert, 4 April 1737, Mary Walker | 2 TA-163 |
| Martin, Sam'l, 17 Nov. 1742, Grace Stewart | 3 TA-40 |
|   2 TA-173 gives date as 18 Nov. 1742. | |
| Martin, Sam'l, 17 April 1754, Eleanor Williams | 2 BA-209 |
| Martin, Thos., Jr., 11 Feb. 1701, Ann (?) | 2 TA-23 |
| Martin, Thomas, 19 Dec. 1717, Jane Thomas | 2 TA-83 |
| Martin, Thomas, 14 Jan. 1734, Elizabeth Goldsborough | 2 TA-156 |
| Martin, Thos., Jr., 14 April 1743, Mary Ennalls | 3 TA-42 |
| Martin, William, 21 Oct. 1705, Elizabeth Chapple | 1 CA-112 |
| Martin, William, 9 June 1709, Phebe Bowdle | 2 TA-60 |
| Martin, William, 18 Oct. 1721, Penelope Peterson | 1 AA-308 |
| Martin, Wm., 12 Feb. 1736, Mary Kinspear | 1 QA-43 |
| Martin, William, 5 Aug. 1737, Ann Bowdle, widow | 2 TA-163 |
| Martin, Zenos, 5 Dec. 1744, Rachel Sutton | 2 TA-197 |
| Martindale, Daniel, 16 Dec. 1736, Eliza Greenwood | 2 TA-158 |
| Martindale, Perdue, 1775, Anne Andrew | 1 CR |
| Martindale, William, 27 June 1777, Esther Baynor | 1 CR-10 |
| Martingdale, Henry, 3 Feb. 1718, Eliz. Resho | 2 TA-89 |
| Martland, Charles, 25 July 1722, Mary Coward ? | 2 TA-103 |
| Marvell, Thomas, 16 June 1721, Elizabeth Hugins | 1 WI-10 |
| Maryartee, Edward, 5 Feb. 1705, Rachell Grey | 1 AA-72 |
| Mash, James, 25 Sept. 1737, Margrett Harris | 3 BA-156 |
| Masham, Philip, 3 June 1745, Mary Newman | 3 BA-157 |
| Maskel, Joseph, 8 Aug. 1755, Helen Henderton | 2 BA-212 |
| Maslin, Thomas, 4 Dec. 1711, Jane Britain | 3 KE-301 |
| Maslin, Thomas, 11 Dec. 1735, Mary Anne Lamb | 1 SF-68 |
| Mason, Henry, c.Oct. 1775, Esther Baggs | 1 CR-6 |
| Mason, James, 23 Nov. 1727, Susanna Tucker | 2 PG-4 |
| Mason, John, 20 Dec. 1733, Frances Allen | 2 BA-67 |
| Mason, John, 20 Aug. 1739, Eliza Ferrall | 2 TA-167 |
| Mason, John, Aug. 1749, Deborah Satterfield | 1 QA-56 |
| Mason, John, 13 Aug. 1751, Elizabeth Nevill | 1 QA-58 |
| Mason, John, seaman, 2 April 1762, Lydia Delahunt; | |
|   the marriage was performed by Rev. Samuel Keene at | |
|   the house of Wm. Woodward in Annapolis. The wit- | |
|   nesses were Elisha Fowler, Wm. Garrett Woodward, | |
|   and Hannah Hall. | 5 AA-1 |
| Mason, John, son of George and Jane, of Chester Co., | |
|   Penna., 3 day, 10 mo., 1776, Ann Howard, dau. | |
|   of Benjamin and Sarah | 4 SF-269 |
| Mason, Joseph, 10 April 1757, Mariah Grover | 1 BA-356 |
| Mason, Peter, 6 Oct. 1744, Mary Davis | 2 BA-191 |
| Mason, Solomon, 28 Nov. 1733, Sarah Stanton | 1 QA-40 |
| Mason, Solomon, 10 Feb. 1757, Mary Gudgeon | 1 QA-62 |
| Mason, Stephen, 22 April 1717, Jane Gregory | 4 AA-398 |
| | & 400 |
| Mason, Thomas, 17 June 1742, Edith Cook | 3 TA-38 |
| Mason, William, 18 Aug. 1680, Anne Deene | 5 SO-398 |

Mason, William, 5 May 1741, Prisalla Punney        1 QA-46
Mason, Wm. Winchester, 10 Dec. 1750, Tabitha Purnal  3 TA-80
Massey, Aquilla, son of Jonathan, 7 Jan. 1724/5, Sarah
  Coale, dau. of William                            6 SF
Massey, Jonathan, son of Aquilla, 6 day, 7 mo., 1763,
  Cassandra Webster, dau. of Isaac                  7 SF-10
Massy, James, Jr., 27 Aug. 1743, Jane Spry          1 QA-48
Massy, Peter, 2 Nov. 1736, Notly Wright             1 QA-42
Masters, Thomas, banns published on 28 April 1706,
  Margaret Jones                                    1 BA-201
Masterson, John, 18 Nov. 1725, Ann Peterson         1 AA-101
Mather, George, 14 Aug. 1708, Susanna Story         1 AA-76
Mathes, William, 29 Jan. 1701, Ann (?)              2 TA-23
Mathews, Charles, 8 Jan. 1739, Mary Ann Faulenen    1 QA-45
Mathews, James, 19 March 1771, Sophia Hall          1 BA-388
Mathews, Capt. John, 23 Feb. 1748, Milcah Lusby     1 BA-350
Mathews, Levin, 1 April 1761, Mary Hewlings         1 BA-366
Mathews, Leven, 29 Nov. 1764, Mary Day              2 BA-227
Mathews, Richard, 17 Aug. 1758, Margret King        2 BA-217
Mathews, Samuel, 22 Oct. 1756, Mary McCready        2 SO-54
Mathis, John, 18 June 1727, Ester Mordick           2 TA-115
Mathis, John, 17 Aug. 1727, Mary Bush               2 TA-116
Mathison, Alex'r, 2 Aug. 1756, Sarah Morris         1 BA-355
Matthews, Auriah, 7 Nov. 1703, Sarah Gannon         2 TA-37
Matthews, Bayly, 25 Jan. 1760, Elizabeth Carsly     2 SO-54
Mathhews, Baley, 10 Aug. 1765, Rebecca Wheeler      2 SO-147
Matthews, Boaz, 16 Dec. 1755, Sarah Potter          2 SO-54
Matthews, David, 14 May 1767, Sarah Cearsley        2 SO-151
Matthews, George, son of Oliver, 3 June 1731, Eliza-
  beth Wright, dau. of James and Mary               9 SF
Matthews, George, 3 day, 12 mo., 1777, Sarah Nailor  4 SF-274
Matthews, Jacob, 26 Sept. 1771, Rachel Viney        2 SO-211
Matthews, James, 11 Dec. 1726, Catherine Knott      1 AA-104
Matthews, John, 18 April 1737, Ann Maxwell          1 BA-295
Matthews, Leven, 29 Nov. 1764, Mary Day, dau. of
  John and Philizanna                               1 BA-384
Matthews, Patrick, 23 Jan. 1734/5, Mary Strough     3 CE-19
Matthews, Roger, 14 Nov. 1710, Mary Carvill         1 BA-215
Matthews, Roger, 13 May 1726, Elizabeth Garrett     1 BA-244
Matthews, Thomas, 20 Feb. 1731, Rebecca Henricks    2 TA-151
Matthews, Thomas, 7 Nov. 1736, Elizabeth Matthews   3 BA-156
Matthews, Thomas, 26 day, 11 mo., 1751, Rachel Price  4 SF
Matthews, Thomas. See Thomas McIlven. In the parish
  register the name was first entered Matthews,
  then McIlven, and the name Matthews was scratched
  out.
Matthews, William, 3 day, 8 mo., 1774, Ann Price, widow
  of Aquila Price                                   4 SF-276
Matthias, James, 11 Dec. 1776, Magdalen Button      3 BA-669
Mattingly, Luke, 11 Feb. 1772, Eliz. Thompson       1 SM-136
Mattocks, Edward, 12 Oct. 1714, Elizabeth Smith     3 AA-99
Mattox, Charles, 20 Oct. 1737, Hannah White         3 AA-105
Mattox, Jonas, 22 April 1711, Ann Bentley           3 CE-4
Mattox, William, Dec. 1720, Margeret Croscomb       3 AA-100
Mattucks, Jno., 17 May 1767, Mary Parwell           2 BA-230
Maud, Daniel, of the City of London, 17 Aug. 1710,
  Magdalen Stevens                                  8 SF-447
Maud, James, 25 Dec. 1740, Sarah Seward             1 QA-46
Maughan, Murty, 28 June 1733, Ann Leshly            1 CE-281
Maughlin, Richard, 25 Oct. 1711, Kath: Ferrill      3 KE-302
Mauhane, Thimithy, 7 April 1716, Sarah Macknew      1 PG-268
Mauhawn, Thomas, 12 April 1716, Mary Moore          3 KE-303
Mauhon, Edward, 1 Jan. 1704, Honour Alpen           3 KE-300
Maule, Daniel, son of Thomas and Zilla, 14 March
  1776, Hannah Brown, dau. of Joshua and Hannah     9 SF

| | |
|---|---|
| Maurice, Rich'd, 17 Feb. 1723, Elisabeth Holman | 1 AA-326 |
| Maurice, Robert, 17 Feb. 1723, Elizabeth Holman | 1 AA-98 |
| Maxfield, Joseph, 14 day, 9 mo., 1744?, Sarah Warner | 1 SF-91 |
| Maxfield, Robert, 20 Oct. 1702, Ann Park | 3 KE-300 |
| Maxfield, Robert, 1 Feb. 1728, Margrett Jarviss | 3 BA-149 |
| Maxwell, James, 7 Sept. 1755, Phebe Jackson | 2 BA-212 |
| May, Henry, 15 Sept. 1735, Mary Dun | 1 QA-41 |
| May, John, 23 May 1711, Eliz. Buckley | 2 BA-263 |
| May, Peter, 16 May 1728, Mary Davidson | 2 TA-118 |
| May, Peter, 26 June 1777, Elizabeth Guy | 10 BA-68 |
| Maybury, Francis, 11 May 1736, Rose Irwin | 1 CE-284 |
| Maynadier, Daniel, 11 May 1746, Mary Murray | 2 TA-283 |
| Maynard, Henry, 7 May 1741, Laraday Hammond | 3 AA-107 |
| Maynard, Thomas, 25 Aug. 1693, Ann Smith | 1 CA-113 |
| Mayner, James, 3 Nov. 1748, Elizabeth Parsons | 1 QA-54 |
| Mayner, Jno., 8 Jan. 1756, Mary Lawson | 2 BA-213 |
| Mayner, William, 7 April 1752, Sarah Hayse | 1 QA-58 |
| Maynor, James, 27 Dec. 1702, Mary Prise | 3 KE-300 |
| Mayo, Joseph, 10 July 1735, Sarah Stockett | 1 AA-119 |
| Mayo, Joshua, 10 July 1707, Hannah Searson | 1 AA-76 |
| Mayson, Phill., 10 Jan. 1713, Eliza Duning | 1 PG-275 |
| Meack, Morick, 7 Aug. 1726, Eleoner Warin | 3 BA-148 |
| Mead, Benj., 10 Nov. 1708, Elizabeth Dawdridge | 3 AA-98 |
| Mead, Benj'n, son of Benj., 6 May 1762, Mary Brannan | 2 BA-223 |
| Mead, Edward, 13 Oct. 1713, Darcass Evins | 2 AA-3 |
| Mead, James, 5 Dec. 1742, Elizabeth James | 2 BA-238 |
| Mead, James, son of Edward, 21 Dec. 1747, Ann Forrest | 2 BA-194 |
| Mead, John, 31 Dec. 1730, Mary Hewett | 3 AA-104 |
| Mead, John, 17 Oct. 1731, Rebecca Smith | 4 AA-434 |
| Mead, Joseph, 14 Dec. 1711, Eleanor Hackett | 1 AA-78 |
| Meade, Samuel, 14 Oct. 1756, Mary Duff | 3 AA-111 |
| Meads, James, 1747, Ann Forrest | 2 BA-242 |
| Meakins, Joshua, 29 Sept. 1728, Elizabeth Browning | 3 CE-20 |
| Meale, William, 7 Oct. 1759, Sarah Hill | 2 BA-219 |
| Mears, Abraham, 7 Sept. 1704, Martha Killinsworth | 2 AA-324 |
| Mears, Abraham, 31 Dec. 1752, Jane Slaughter | 2 BA-206 |
| Meccelpin, Robert, 4 Dec. 1732, Jane Johnson | 1 WI-61 |
| Mecombes, James, 12 Sept. 1773, Eloner Jones | 3 BA-170 |
| Medari, Chs. Fred'k, 2 Nov. 1756, Cath. Gerrson | 4 FR-1103 |
| Medcalf, John, 6 Aug. 1735, Mary Norris | 2 AA-377 |
| Medcalf, William, 7 Oct. 1733, Ann Lowther | 1 QA-40 |
| Medcalfe, Abraham, son of James and Margaret, 18 day, 6 mo., 1767, Mary Pyle, dau. of Moses and Mary | 9 SF |
| Medcluff, Thos., 28 Aug. 1735, Mary Holmes | 2 TA-160 |
| Medford, Balmor, 20 Jan. 1725, Sarah Unith | 2 KE-184 |
| Medlem, Henry, 5 Oct. 1706, Naomy Prentice | 1 AA-72 |
| Meed, Joseph, 10 Jan. 1737, Mary Lego | 2 BA-94 |
| Meed, Wm., 10 Jan. 1767, Sarah York | 2 BA-230 |
| Meeds, Abraham, 20 March 1737, Frances Glanden | 1 QA-44 |
| Meeds, Thomas, 12 Jan. 1756, Mary Rowings | 2 BA-213 |
| Meek, Jeremiah, 18 Sept. 1731, Sarah Lee | 4 AA-434 |
| Meek, John, 4 Dec. 1716, Hannah Brown | 4 AA-398 |
| Meek, Sam'll, 19 Sept. 1734, Alice Ridgely | 1 AA-118 |
| Meekins, James, 6 May 1756, Margaret Lang | 1 QA-61 |
| Meeks, Francis, 3 Jan. 1704, Mary Smith | 3 KE-300 |
| Meeks, Walter, 27 March 1700, Jane Reed | 3 KE-299 |
| Meerede, Isaac, 3 June 1751, Ellender Allen | 2 SO-52 |
| Meers, Jno., 8 Dec. 1715, Jane Gilberd | 2 TA-77 |
| Meers, William, 4 day, 1 mo., 1679, Elizabeth Webb | 8 SF-322 |
| Megay, Robert, 2 Feb. 1758, Sarah Lester | 1 BA-359 |
| Megeney, Arthur, 27 June 1722, (wife's name not given) | 2 TA-102 |
| Meglue, Peter, 19 Dec. 1756, Jemima Collins | 2 CR-271 |
| Megrah, Arthur, 2 Feb. 1738, Mary Sutton | 2 TA-166 |
| Megroy, James, 5 Feb. 1733, Mary Robinson | 2 TA-154 |
| Mekeney, Alexander, 3 June 1742, Susannah Foster | 1 CE-290 |

Mekeney, Garrit, 26 Jan. 1738/9, Margret Curyeur        1 CE-285
Melleway, Jno., 26 Dec. 1704, Shusannah Robinson        2 TA-43
Mellvin, Robert, 11 Nov. 1744, Edath Taylor             2 SO-50
Mellvin, William, 18 Dec. 1738, Mary Benston            2 SO-50
Meloy, William, 2 April 1772, Catherine Anglin          3 AA-113
Melson, John, 9 Jan. 1671/2, Elizabeth Painter          8 SO-401
    5 SO-398 gives date as 4 April 1672.
Melton, James, 27 Dec. 1737, Elizabeth Ward             2 TA-164
Melton, Joshua, 10 Nov. 1772, Sarah Molohorn            1 SM-136
Melvin, George, 3 Oct. 1767, Viana Roggers              2 SO-153
Melvin, Jonathan, 23 Dec. 1762, Leah Melton             2 SO-150
Melvin, Robert, 20 May 1773, Director Webb              2 SO-153
Melvin, Samuell, 28 Dec. 1763, Mary Benston             2 SO-150
Melvin, Smith, 20 Oct. 1763, Mary Walker                2 SO-151
Melvin, William, 11 March 1770, Leah Robertson          2 SO-153
Menson, R'd, 24 March 1763, Mary Ward                   2 BA-224
Mercer, Jno., 28 Feb. 1765, Reb. Judy                   2 BA-227
Mercer, Luke, 1 Aug. 1738, Barbara Jacks                6 AA-202
Mercer, Robert, 1 Aug.1727, Anne Mounce                 3 CE-15
Mercer, Thomas, 13 Dec. 1732, Jane Oliver               3 CE-15
Merchant, Benjamin, 18 June 1743, Ann Bidgood           2 TA-198
Merchant, Ja.:, 25 April 1709, Jean Stewart             2 TA-59
Merchant, James, Jr., 2 March 1738, Mary Walker         2 TA-166
Merchant, John, 27 Dec. 1736, Dorothy Catrop            2 TA-158
Merchant, William, 10 Jan. 1722, Mary Tucker            2 TA-104
Mercier, Franciss, 7 June 1713, Marg'tt Weldon          4 AA-380
Mercier, Richard, 9 May 1772, Cassandra Tevis           5 BA-9
Meredith, Benjamin, 4 Jan. 1758, Eliza Brown            1 QA-63
Meredith, John, 3 Aug. 1730, Elizabeth Griffith         1 QA-37
Meredith, Samuel, 3 Feb. 1735, Elizabeth Cook           3 BA-154
Meredith, Samuel, 2 Feb. 1748, Jemima Taylor            3 BA-162
Meredith, Thomas, 13 Feb. 1763, Hannah Hutchins         2 BA-224
Meredith, William, Jr., 9 Aug. 1748, Juliana Hutch-
    inson                                               1 QA-54
Meredith, William, 27 June 1755, Rebeckah Loyd          1 QA-59
Meredith, William, 8 Jan. 1756, Sarah Thomas            1 QA-60
Merekin, Jno., 26 Sept. 1710, Mary Stephens             3 AA-99
Merekin, John, Jr., 28 Oct. 1746, Ann Sadler            3 AA-110
Merick, Jacob, 23 Oct. 1734, Ann Willing                1 WI-24
Merideth, Charles, 14 May 1744, Ann Atkinson            1 QA-49
Merike, Hugh, 20 Nov. 1716, Sarah Burley                4 AA-398
Merredith, John, 5 Oct. 1731, Anne Griffith             1 QA-38
Merrell, John, 8 Dec. 1748, Comfort Henderson           2 SO-51
Merrell, Scarbrough, 17 June 1753, Sarah Chuff          2 SO-148
Merrell, Simpson, 19 Feb. 1758, Calte West              2 SO-155
Merriarter, Edward, 17 Feb. 1736, Sarah Hanson          1 BA-293
Merrick, Henry, 1 Nov. 1720, Jane Evans                 1 AA-301
Merrick, Isaac, 20 Sept. 1744, Mary Lane                1 QA-49
Merrick, James, 10 Dec. 1713, Elizabeth Barron          2 TA-72
Merrick, James, Jr., 14 Aug. 1740, Mary Connor          2 TA-170
Merrick, James, 1775, Zelpha or Tilpha Quatermus        1 CR
Merriday, Henry, 29 Oct. 1711, Sarah Aldridg            3 AA-100
Merrideth, Thomas, 22 May 1755, Susanna Cox             2 BA-212
Merrideth, Thos., 13 Feb. 1763, Hannah Hutchens         2 BA-224
Merriken, Hugh, Nov. 1719, Ann Westall                  3 AA-100
Merriken, Hugh, 26 Nov. 1719, Anne Weston               4 AA-410
Merriken, Jacob, 6 Feb. 1749, Constant Oley             3 AA-110
Merriken, John, 4 Nov. 1756, Elizabeth Moss             3 AA-111
Merriken, Joseph, 23 Oct. 1769, Ann Small               3 AA-114
Merriken, Joshua, 16 Feb. 1709/10, Elizabeth Ewins      1 BA-209
Merriken, Joshua, 24 June 1718, Dinah Day               2 BA-11
Merriken, Joshua, 13 Aug. 1751, Margaret Todd           3 AA-110
Merrill, Thomas, 11 Feb. 1753, Leah Hall                2 SO-52
Merriman, John, 30 Dec. 1725, Sarah Rogers              3 BA-148
Merriott, William, 27 May 1729, Dorothy Guyther         1 AA-108

| | |
|---|---|
| Merrit, Richard, 17 April 1745, Ann Hudson | 2 KE-256 |
| Merrit, Thomas, 6 May (?), Martha (?) | 3 CE-15 |
| Merrit, Thomas, 12 April 1703, Katherine Taylour | 1 AA-254 |
| Merritt, Samuel, 29 Nov. 1708, Phebe Milward | 3 KE-301 |
| Merritt, Thomas, 12 April 1703, Katherine Taylor | 1 AA-64 |
| Merryman, Benjamin, 2 Feb. 1762, Mary Bell | 2 BA-223 |
| Merryman, Charles, 27 Feb. 1730, Milleson Hailes | 3 BA-150 |
| Merryman, John, 8 Dec. 1777, Sarah Smith | 9 BA |
|    10 BA-69 gives same information. 3 BA-184 gives | |
|    date as 9 Dec. 1777, and adds that the bride was | |
|    the widow of Capt. John Addison Smith. | |
| Merryman, Nicholas, 1 May 1755, Avarilla Reaven | 2 BA-212 |
| Mersch, Bastian, 5 March 1762, Magd. Burghard | 4 FR-1151 |
| Mesex, Lewen (or Julien?), 29 April 1674, Sarah | |
|    Convention | 5 SO-398 |
| Messick, Jacob, 25 May 1772, Sarah Porter | 1 WI-122 |
| Metcalf, Thomas, 23 July 1726, Sarah Gott | 1 AA-103 |
| Metheny, William, 12 Jan. 1735, Eliz. Banberry | 2 BA-90 |
| Meyerer, John Joshua, 29 March 1757, Mary Kaempf | 4 FR-1103 |
| Mibbs, Thos., 5 Jan. 1764, Latita York | 2 BA-226 |
| Michael, Daniel, 15 May 1758, Mary Schober | 4 FR-1104 |
| Michael, George, 2 Aug. 1755, Barbary Rissard | 1 BA-354 |
| Michael, Peter, 28 Feb. 1764, Dorothy Schmitt | 4 FR-1151 |
| Michael, William, 13 May 1719, Elizabeth Herrington | 8 SF-22 |
| Michall, John, 2 Sept. 1704, Grace Billiler | 2 TA-41 |
| Michel, John, 8 Nov. 1702, Mary Sonson | 1 AA-252 |
| Michell, Wm., 12 Nov. 1702, Alice (?) | 2 TA-29 |
| Middlemore, Josias, 9 Oct. 1720, Mrs. Frances Bechley | 2 BA-33 |
| Middleton, Horatio, 25 May 1775, Susanna Stoddert | 1 PG-377 |
| Middleton, Lutener, 6 Aug. 1705, Elizabeth Miller | 3 KE-300 |
| Middleton, Thomas, 7 June 1743, Jane Perry | 1 BA-329 |
| Middleton, Thomas, 13 Sept. 1777, Winnifred Powell | 1 MO-522 |
| Midford, Jno., (date not given), Jaine Hyland, widow | 3 CE-1 |
| Midleton, Studley, 28 May 1740, Martha Wallis | 2 KE-234 |
| Mier, John Henry, 11 Jan. 1758, Eliza Cole | 3 BA-166 |
| Mifflin, Daniel, of Accomac Co., Va., 15 day, 9 mo., | |
|    1744, Mary Warner | 1 SF-92 |
| Mifflin, Southy, of Swan Gutt, Va., 15 day, 6 mo., | |
|    1753, Johannah Thom(as?) | 1 SF-90 |
| Migraugh, John, 26 Sept. 1708, Ann Lee | 4 AA-378 |
| Milard, Zeakel, 27 March 1744, Hannah Croker | 3 AA-106 |
| Milberry, Capt. Nathaniel, 23 June 1764, Jane Sing | 9 AA-248 |
| Milborn, Samuel, 27 May 1727, Mary Whalls | 2 KE-213 |
| Milbourn, William, 20 April 1750, Levinah Tomlinson | 2 SO-53 |
| Milburn, Robert, 25 Jan. 1736/7, Elinor (?) | 1 CE-283 |
| Miles, (?), 18 Feb. 1723, Alse Fanning | 3 KE-304 |
| Miles, Evan, 24 July 1726, Elizabeth Davis | 1 BA-244 |
| Miles, Henry, 28 Jan. 1667, Mary Barnebe | 4 SO-703 |
| Miles, Isaac, 28 Oct. 1742, Ann Preston | 2 BA-124 |
| Miles, Jacob, 10 Nov. 1748, Hannah MacComas | 2 BA-198 |
| | & 243 |
| Miles, John, 3 Oct. 1745, Mary Purnell | 2 AA-387 |
| Miles, Richard, 19 Sept. 1762, Ruth Simmons | 9 AA-247 |
| Miles, Thomas, 27 day, 4 mo., 1704, Ruth Jones, dau. | |
|    of Jos. and Elizabeth | 6 SF |
| Miles, Thomas, 23 day, 10 mo., 1714, Elizabeth White, | |
|    of P. G. Co., widow | 6 SF |
| Miles, Thos., Jr., 11 Oct. 1744, Margrett Taylor | 2 BA-191 |
| Miles, Thos., 7 Aug. 1768, Mary Coeing | 2 BA-232 |
| Miles, Thomas, Dec. 1771, Hannah Thompson | 2 BA-263 |
| Miles, William, 17 Dec. 1751, Elizabeth Juett | 2 SO-51 |
| Miles, William, 20 Dec. 1777, Fanny Smith | 7 AA-2 |
|    8 AA-13 gives date as 23 Dec. 1777. 2 AA-414 | |
|    gives date as 25 Dec. 1777. | |
| Milham, Joseph, 28 Nov. 1756, Jane Candle | 2 BA-214 |

| | | |
|---|---|---|
| Milhughs, Aquilla, 17 Dec. 1749, Eliz. Parkes | 2 | BA-199 |
| Milhuse, Aquila, 17 Dec. 1749, Elizabeth Parks | 2 | BA-244 |
| Mill, William, 15 Dec. 1726, Jane Maccrumb | 1 | AA-104 |
| Millaway, John, 1 Aug. 1727, Sarah Sumers | 2 | TA-116 |
| Millburn, Calib, 4 March 1760, Ann Collings | 2 | SO-149 |
| Millen, Henry, 5 July 1720, Mary Norris | 1 | BA-225 |
| Miller, Arthur, 23 July 1705, Sarah Jones | 3 | KE-300 |
| Miller, George, 9 Dec. 1725, Rachell Connoway | 1 | AA-101 |
| Miller, John, 11 Feb. 1725, Mary Gain | 3 | BA-150 |
| Miller, John, 10 Aug. 1738, Anne Kemp | 1 | QA-44 |
| Miller, John, 14 Dec. 1745, Eleanor Smith | 3 | BA-158 |
| Miller, John, 11 Oct. 1756, Rachel Paulson | 1 | CE-322 |
| Miller, Jno., 9 Sept. 1760, Eliz. Harris | 2 | BA-220 |
| Miller, John, son of John and Sarah, 2 Sept. 1762, Nanney Dirickson, dau. of Joseph and Mary | 1 | WO-12 |
| Miller, John, Sept. 1777, Mary Hill | 3 | BA-176 |
| Miller, John Price, 30 Oct. 1730, Elizabeth Taylor | 2 | TA-149 |
| Miller, Jonathan, 6 Nov. 1708, Mary Battom | 2 | TA-49 |
| Miller, Jonathan, 8 July 1736, Marg't Duly | 2 | TA-161 |
| Miller, Joseph, 11 Sept. 1759, Mary Oursler | 4 | BA-73 |
| Miller, Michael, 2 Sept. 17-(?), Martha Glanvill | 3 | KE-306 |
| Miller, Nicholas, 15 Dec. 1708, Ellinor Waterman | 3 | KE-301 |
| Miller, Patrick, son of Gayen and Margaret, 5 Nov. 1735, Patience Haines, dau. of Joseph | 9 | SF |
| Miller, Rich'd, 4 June 1752, Eliz. Hicks | 2 | BA-205 |
| Miller, Richard, 20 Nov. 1763, Martha Page | 3 | KE-307 |
| Miller, Solomon, son of Robert and Ruth of Chester Co., Penna., 26 day, 7 mo., 1751, Sarah Matthews, dau. of Thomas and Sarah | 4 | SF |
| Miller, Theophilus, 1748, Sarah Burk | 2 | BA-243 |
| Miller, Thos., 24 July 1748, Sarah Burk | 2 | BA-197 |
| Miller, Thomas, 15 Dec. 1757, Jane Groom | 3 | KE-306 |
| Miller, Warrick, son of Robert and Ruth, of Chester Co., Penna., 29 day, 4 mo., 1762, Elizabeth Price, dau. of Mordecai and Elizabeth | 4 | SF-249 |
| Miller, William, 21 Oct. 1707, Grace Young | 1 | CA-112 |
| Millert, Christopher, 14 Oct. 1705, Elizabeth Harris | 1 | AA-65 |
| Milligan, George, 23 March 1730/1, Catherine Baldwin, dau. of Col. John Baldwin | 3 | CE-25 |
| Millis, James, 18 Feb. 1734, Catherine Russam | 2 | TA-157 |
| Mills, Charles, 14 Dec. 173-(?), Ann Hammond | 2 | KE-247 |
| Mills, Cornelius, 6 Jan. 1775, Elizabeth Goldsmith | 5 | AA-5 |
| Mills, David, 24 Jan. 1716, Elizabeth Elston | 2 | TA-81 |
| Mills, Henry, 29 Jan. 1749/50, Mary Watts | 3 | TA-76 |
| Mills, James, 19 Oct. 1711, Sarah Slat'r | 2 | TA-70 |
| Mills, James, 12 May 1737, Jane Swift | 1 | QA-43 |
| Mills, Justinian, 26 Oct. 1751, Mary Dant | 2 | SM-57 |
| Mills, Leonard, 4 Dec. 1777, China Fraser | 1 | CA-111a |
| Mills, Ralph, 21 May 1728, Mary Pamer | 2 | TA-118 |
| Mills, Thomas, 18 April 1720, Cathrine Jones | 2 | TA-92 |
| Mills, Thomas, son of John, 18 day, 4 mo., 1730, Elizabeth Harrold | 9 | SF |
| Mills, William, 5 Oct. 1735, Mary Kent | 3 | BA-154 |
| Millson, Samuel, 1 May 1749, Priscilla Lemar | 1 | QA-55 |
| Milns, David, (date not given), Mary (?) | 2 | TA-47 |
| Milson, Samuell, 7 May 1703, Elizabeth Brady | 3 | KE-300 |
| Milton, Abraham, 10 June 1713, Barbary Everett | 3 | KE-302 |
| Milton, Abraham, Jr., 26 day, 8 mo., 1733, Mary Ball | 1 | SF-65 |
| Milton, Abraham, 12 day, 2 mo., 1752, Mary Jones | 1 | SF-88 |
| Milton, Isaac, 5 day, 2 mo., 1739, Ann Bartlett | 8 | SF-74 |
| Milton, James, 14 Oct. 1719, Catherine White | 4 | AA-410 |
| Minar, Thomas, 25 Jan. 1733/4, Margarett Wallace | 3 | CE-18 |
| Miner, William, 4 Sept. 1748, Isabella Fara | 2 | BA-243 |
| Minishal, Randolph, 169-(?), Alice Potter | 5 | SO-399 |
| Minner, Edward, 6 May 1774, Priscilla Collison | 1 | CR |

| | |
|---|---|
| Minskey, Samuel, 18 Aug. 1777, Sophia Fowler | 7 AA-1 |
| Mirik, Teall, 27 July 1726, Rachel Skinner | 2 TA-113 |
| Mirrell, William, 16 Jan. 1755, Comfort Marshell | 2 SO-53 |
| Mirrick, Daniell, 28 July 1726, Mary Ferel | 2 TA-113 |
| Miser, Wm., 4 Nov. 1758, Ruth Meeds | 2 BA-218 |
| Miser, Wm., 7 June 1763, Hannah Berry | 2 BA-225 |
| Mister, William, 16 Oct. 1749, Comfort Evens | 2 SO-50 |
| Mitchel, James, 2 Jan. 1769, Mary Hardwick | 2 BA-257 |
| Mitchel, Thomas, Jr., 24 Dec. 1742, Hannah Osborn | 1 BA-329 |
| Mitchel, Thomas, 14 Sept. 1777, Anne Hobson | 10 BA-69 |
| Mitchel, William, 11 June 1751, Sarah Osborn, dau. of Benj. | 1 BA-381 |
| Mitchell, Edward, 21 Nov. 1706, Grace Lewis | 1 AA-72 |
| Mitchell, Edward, 24 day, 10 mo. (Dec.), 1747, Elizabeth Gatchell Hughes, widow of Thomas Hughes, and dau. of Elisha and Rachel Gatchell | 9 SF |
| Mitchell, George, 29 Sept. 1668, Isabell Higgins | 4 SO-729 |
| Mitchell, Isaac, 23 Feb. 1748/9, Jeanett Gray | 2 SO-50 |
| Mitchell, Jno., 14 July 1700, Susanna Burgess, dau. of Col. Wm. and Ursula | 1 AA-56 |
| Mitchell, John, servant of Jos. Jones, 8 Nov. 1702, Mary Sonsom | 1 AA-64 |
| Mitchell, Jno., 13 May 1740, Mary Vain | 2 TA-160 |
| Mitchell, Jno. Pope, 5 May 1773, Polley Purnall | 1 WO-16 |
| Mitchell, Josiah, 7 March 1753, Sophia Hill | 1 WO-14 |
| Mitchell, Richard, 1 Jan. 1733, Eliz'th Williams | 1 BA-271 |
| Mitchell, Theodore, 27 Nov. 1777, Mary Wells | 3 PG-166 |
| Mitchell, William, 2 July 1721, Lucy Vandaule | 4 AA-415 |
| Mitchell, William, 30 Sept. 1736, Elizabeth Elliott | 2 BA-83 |
| 2 BA-121 gives the year as 1737. | & 101 |
| Mitchéller, Alexander, 14 Nov. 1676, Anne Surnam | 9 SO-402 |
| Mitchender, John, 8 Feb. 1729, Mary Chanlor | 3 BA-149 |
| Mitley, Christopher, 7 Jan. 1700, Mary Cashmore | 2 AA-314 |
| Mittelkauf, John, 19 July 1757, Mary Eliz'th Brunner | 4 FR-1103 |
| Miver, William, 4 Sept. 1748, Isabell Fara | 2 BA-243 |
| Miver, Wm., 10 Oct. 1748, Elizabeth Finer | 2 BA-197 |
| Moale, John, Esq., 25 May 1758, Ellin North, dau. of Capt. Robert North | 3 BA-192 |
| Mobberly, John, Jr., 12 Feb. 1711/2, Rachel Pindell | 2 PG-1 |
| Mobberly, John, Sr., 28 Feb. 1716, Susanna Scaggs, widow of Ann Scaggs | 2 PG-2 |
| Mock, James, 16 March 1771, Hannah Holebrook | 2 BA-258 |
| Mockbee, Brock, 22 Dec. 1715, Eliza Beckett | 2 PG-1 |
| Mockbee, Brock, 22 Jan. 1738, Rachel Gore | 9 AA-246 |
| Mockbee, John, 20 Aug. 1777, Mary Robinson | 3 PG-139 |
| Mockbee, John, 21 Aug. 1777, Marg't Robinson | 1 MO-522 |
| Moffitt, Richard, 7 Jan. 1744, Mary Haley | 2 KE-284 |
| Moll, John, 13 June 1711, Mary Whitworth | 3 KE-301 |
| Monah, Charles, 5 Feb. 1750, Elisabeth Nevill | 1 QA-57 |
| Monat, James, 10 Feb. 1706, Sarah Bateman | 1 AA-73 |
| Monday, Arthur, 26 Dec. 1730, Eliz'th Hamby | 1 BA-257 |
| Monday, James, May 1769, Elizabeth Little | 2 BA-258 |
| Monday, Robert, of St. Michael's Parish, 15 Dec. 1700, Catherine Hogill | 2 TA-11 |
| Money, John, 26 Oct. 1738, Rachel Ashley | 3 CE-21 |
| Money, Robert, 4 Oct. 1706, Margaret Dorrell | 3 CE-4 |
| Money, Thomas, 14 Aug. 1747, Elizabeth Chamberlain, widow of William | 3 CE-28 |
| Mongumry, Dennis, 14 Feb. 1769, Elisabeth Taws | 2 SO-151 |
| Monk, Gilbert, 12 Feb. 1703, Margrett Bullock | 3 KE-300 |
| Monk, Gilbert, 25 May 1708, Mary Kelly | 3 KE-301 |
| Monk, Henry, 2 Dec. 1708, Honour Connor | 3 KE-301 |
| Monk, Richard, 26 June 1756, Agnes Taylor | 1 BA-355 |
| Monk, Samuel, 21 Nov. 1698, Ann Skinner | 2 AA-372 |

Monk, William, 1728, Margrett Brooks                      3 KE-304
Monk, William, 3 Dec. 1736, Eliz. Fuller                  2 BA-74
Monnett, Isaac, 9 Feb. 1768, Ann Hillen                   2 CA-47
Monro, Alexander, 30 Sept. 1763, Ann Pattern              6 AA-186
Monsieur, Thomas, 19 July 1733, Elisabeth Newnam          1 QA-40
Monsieur, William, 4 Sept. 1729, Sarah Lowther            1 QA-37
Montague, Abraham, 10 June 1729, Mary Crump               1 QA-36
Montague, Jadwin, 12 Nov. 1777, Henrietta Hynson          1 CR-10
Montague, William, 24 Dec. 1746, Sarah Steed              1 QA-52
Montgomery, John, 19 Jan. 1777, Sarah Relp                5 BA-9
Montigue, Jeremiah, 21 Dec. 1758, Jane West               1 QA-64
Monts, Christian, 30 March 1755, Margaretta Miyon         2 BA-212
Moobrey, Robert, son of William and Barbara, 30 Jan.
    1752, Phebe Brown, widow of William Brown             9 SF
Moody, William, 14 April 1737, Ruth Marshall              2 TA-162
Moody, William, 13 Jan. 1740, Eliza Gaskin                3 TA-28
    2 TA-171 gives date as 16 Jan. 1740 and the bride's
    name as Elizabeth Gasken.
Mooles, Thomas, 13 Nov. (1768 ?), Mary Drake              2 BA-257
Moolson, Thomas, 1669, Ann Taylor                         5 SO-398
Moon, Thomas, 9 Nov. 1719, Elizabeth Wright, widow        4 AA-410
Mooney, Charles, 4 Jan. 1736, Margarett Brown             2 TA-162
Moonshaw, John, 22 May 1727, Eliza Fisher                 4 AA-428
Moony, Patrick, 19 Nov. 1746, Mary Ann Nevil              1 QA-52
Moor, Christian, 1 March 1737, Marg't Sanders             2 TA-275
Moor, Christopher, 6 Aug. 1722, Judith Lord               2 TA-103
Moor, Christopher, 5 Aug. 1724, Eliz. Shaw                2 TA-110
Moor, Xpher, 5 March 1738, Marg't Saunders                2 TA-166
Moor, Edward, 11 April 1757, Amey Ashley                  1 QA-62
Moor, Francis, 27 April 1705, Elizabeth Stogdon           2 AA-327
Moor, James, 8 Dec. 1747, Elizabeth Dement                1 CH-188
Moor, John, 7 Nov. 1706, Eliza Danielson                  2 PG-1
Moor, John, 25 June 1746, Sarah Sparks                    1 QA-52
Moor, John, 20 Jan. 1757, Eliza Cook                      1 QA-62
Moor, Joshua E., 22 Sept. 1768, Isabella Hickman          1 WI-113
Moor, Levin, 4 Sept. 1757, Mary Darby                     1 WI-64
Moor, Thomas, son of William, 7 July 1751, Ann Evans?,
    widow                                                 1 WI-39
Moor, Wm., 10 May 1716, Mary Gatrill                      1 AA-88
Moor, William, 4 Dec. 1744, Rachel Baning                2 TA-187
Moor, William, 10 Jan. 1770, Bettey Peacock              2 SO-151
Moore, Christopher, 17 Sept. 1728, Mary Mulikin           2 TA-118
Moore, Edward, 4 Dec. 1700, Alice Withers                 1 AA-56
Moore, James, 21 Sept. 1722, Bidgett Steward              2 TA-105
Moore, James, 9 Dec. 1728, Mary Blades                    2 TA-119
Moore, James, Jr., 28 Aug. 1744, Hannah Willmott          2 BA-133
Moore, James Francis, 18 Feb. 1773, Ann Standiford        2 BA-265
Moore, John, 25 Oct. 1685, Anne Mitchell                  5 SO-399
Moore, Joseph, 29 March 1703, Sarah Watts                 2 TA-33
Moore, Martin, 26 March 1667, Margarett Cornelius         4 SO-666
    5 SO-398 gives date as 13 April 1667.
Moore, Mich'l, 20 April 1758, Keziah Shipton              2 BA-217
Moore, Mordecai, son of Richard, 9 day, 8 mo., 1739,
    Elizabeth Coleman, dau. of Joseph Coleman of P. G.
    Co., who was a practitioner of physic                 6 SF
Moore, Mr. Richard, 29 March 1752, Mary Magdalen West     1 AA-132
Moore, Ryley, son of William, 16 Aug. 1726, Sarah
    Holland                                               2 PG-4
Moore, Samuell, 18 Nov. 1708, Katherine Collins           4 AA-378
Moore, Sam'l, 12 April 1762, Senea Futt                   1 BA-371
Moore, William, 20 Jan. 1723, Ann Stapleton               1 AA-98
Moore, William, 6 Jan. 1725, Margaret Smith               1 AA-101
Moore, William, 28 Jan. 1730, Mary Page                   1 QA-38
Moore, Wm., 16 Dec. 1760, Martha Mortimer                 2 BA-220
Morales, Saloader, 22 May 1725, Mary Preris?              4 AA-424

Mordant, William, 22 Dec. 1715, Ann Watts            2 PG-2
More, Benedict, 14 Dec. 1775, Susan Peacock          1 SM-137
More, Edward, 4 Dec. 1700, Alice Withers             1 AA-246
More, Henry, 20 Oct. 1733, Agnus Taylor              1 BA-268
More, Jacob, 4 May 1776, Ann Dorsey                  1 SM-136
More, Joseph, 15 July 1737, Kisiah Rutter            1 CE-285
More, Michael, 31 March 1777, Bridget Macartey       3 BA-173
More, Stephen, 18 May 1746, Alice Woien              1 QA-52
More, William, Jr., 7 March 1732, Rachell Ralph      1 WI-7
More, William, 19 April 1744, Martha Tate            1 QA-49
Morgain, Richard, 25 Feb. 1730, Phebe Skinner        2 TA-150
Morgan, Charles, 6 Jan. 1746, Margaret Pogue         1 BA-376
Morgan, David, 17 May 1744, Pydia Cooper             2 BA-190
Morgan, Edward, 14 Sept. 1733, Elioner Parsley       3 CE-19
Morgan, Enock, 3 day, 7 mo., 1742, Sarah Neal        8 SF-80
Morgan, George, 10 Feb. 1699/1700, Elizabeth Smith   1 BA-190
Morgan, Henry, 17 April (?), Ann Catherine Dehoes    1 CE-328
Morgan, Henry, 14 May 1744, Sarah Pike               2 BA-190
Morgan, James, 25 Feb. 1718, Mary Merikee            4 AA-403
Morgan, James, 13 Dec. 1728, Jane Brashier           1 BA-255
Morgan, James, 8 July 1737, Elizabeth Walker         1 BA-290
Morgan, James, 12 Nov. 1749, Mary Green              2 BA-199
                                                     & 244
Morgan, James, 18 July 1754, Mary Davis              1 BA-372
Morgan, James, 5 Jan. 1775, Sarah Bryon              5 BA-9
Morgan, John, 16 Jan. 1725, Dorithy Newbanks         3 CE-16
Morgan, Joseph, Sept. 1740, Constance Barns          1 BA-327
Morgan, Phillip, 18 Feb. 1707, Sarah Jadwin          8 SF-436
Morgan, Richard, 23 Dec. 1703, Alice Butterfield     1 AA-64
Morgan, Richard, 22 Dec. 1720, Mary Jarvis           1 AA-302
Morgan, Richard, 19 Jan. 1762, Susanah Jacobs        1 AA-139
Morgan, Thomas, 14 Dec. 1708, Margrit Ellt           1 CA-113
Morlin, Jacob, 19 Dec. 1710, Sarah Armstrong         2 TA-68
Moron, Edward, 1 May 1736, Eliz'th Lambeth           1 BA-296
Morrice, Jaccob, 30 Nov. 1745, Rachel Joyce          3 AA-108
Morris, (?), 8 Sept. 1722, Eliz. Truitt              1 WO-5
Morris, Abraham, 25 Dec. 1723, Sarah Murry           2 TA-106
Morris, Dennis, 11 Jan. 1724, Mary Fairbanks         2 TA-111
Morris, Edmund, 15 Oct. 1736, Mary Debruler          1 BA-292
Morris, Griffin, 23 July 1684, Sarah Vaus            5 SO-399
Morris, John, 18 Aug. 1733, Anne Condon              3 CE-16
Morris, John, 31 July 1743, Sarah Gilbert            2 BA-239
Morris, John, 1 Oct. 1744, Mary Shermon              1 WI-45
Morris, John, 15 April 1745, Mary Carman             1 QA-50
Morris, John, 17 May 1748, Sarah Deaver              2 BA-197
Morris, John, 26 May 1749, Hannah Burrows            1 QA-55
Morris, John, 25 May 1760, Mary Plummer              2 BA-220
Morris, Jno., son of Edward, 25 Feb. 1768, Mary Beaver  2 BA-231
Morris, Joseph, 20 Nov. 1739, Mary Stevens           1 WI-46
Morris, Joseph, 14 Dec. 1756, Elizabeth Mallone      1 WI-44
Morris, Manus, 23 April 1680, Elizabeth Ellis        5 SO-398
Morris, Richard, 29 July 1668, Jeane Putbery         1 KE-186
Morris, Richard, 25 Dec. 1734, Mary Murphew          1 BA-277
Morris, Samuel, 7 Nov. 1770, Rebecca Owen            5 BA-9
Morris, Samuel, 21 Aug. 1777, Mary Walmsley          2 CE-1
Morris, Thomas, 14 July 1698, Elizabeth Jackson      1 BA-178
Morris, Thomas, 25 Feb. 1708, Ann Bradley            3 KE-301
Morris, Thomas, 19 Jan. 1731, Mary Murphy            1 BA-259
Morris, Thos., 10 Oct. 1749, Frances Shaw            2 BA-199
                                                     & 244
Morris, William, 2 July 1709, Frances Merry          3 KE-301
Morriss, Hugh, 24 Nov. 1739, Jane Curley             1 QA-45
Morriss, James, 7 July 1728, Katherine Shaun         2 PG-5
Morriss, Thomas, 19 Jan. 1731, Mary Murphy           1 BA-259
Morriss, Thomas, 5 Feb. 1740/1, Rebecca Lemar        1 QA-46

| | |
|---|---|
| Morroe, Anguish, of Dor. Co., 8 Aug. 1676, Rose | |
| Daniel | 9 SO-401 |
| Mors, Ebenezer, 28 April 1735, Sarah Fox | 1 PG-284 |
| Morsel, Thomas, 16 Aug. 1745, Mary Collins | 2 KE-258 |
| Morton, John, 20 Feb. 1759, Mary Ann Wright | 2 CR-271 |
| Morton, John, 5 July 1771, Sarah Harlins | 2 BA-262 |
| Morton, Joseph, Feb. 1771, Molley Shelby | 2 BA-261 |
| Morton, Thomas, 22 Dec. 1776, Susannah Weems | 2 AA-413 |
| Mose, George, 3 Aug. 1707, Mary Sander of Kent Island | 1 AA-76 |
| Moss, James, 20 Jan. 1772, Mary Lamb | 3 AA-113 |
| Moss, Richard, 1719, Jeane Skidmore | 3 AA-104 |
| Moss, Richard, 1736, Rachel Robeson | 3 AA-105 |
| Moss, Thomas, 15 May 1755, Sarah Appleby | 3 AA-111 |
| Moss, Wm., 12 June 1739, Rebecca Price | 3 TA-17 |
| Motherby, Charles, 14 Dec. 1736, Rebekah Newman | 3 BA-156 |
| Mott, Edmund, 22 July 1728, Margaret Boor | 1 AA-107 |
| Mott, Gersham, Jr., of Penna., 8 day, 6 mo., 1750, | |
| Rachel Vansant | 1 SF-82 |
| Moulen, Robert, 15 Aug. 1718, Rachel James | 4 AA-405 |
| Moulins, John, 15 Jan. 1744, Sarah Brown | 2 BA-239 |
| Moulton, Walter, 4 Nov. 1704, Lydyah Bryant | 2 TA-42 |
| Mounce, Robert, Jr., 2 Feb. 1733/4, Ruth Mackdowell, | |
| widow | 3 CE-18 |
| Mount, Richard, 29 Aug. 1718, Sarah Davies | 1 AA-286 |
| Mueller, Abrah., 24 Feb. 1761, Marg. Huetzel | 4 FR-1151 |
| Mueller, Stephan, 16 March 1762, Rachel Bopp | 4 FR-1151 |
| Mull, Jacob, 8 July 1777, Anne Charter | 10 BA-68 |
| Mullakin, Thomas, Jr., 16 Jan. 1762, Mary Mears | 9 AA-247 |
| Mullen, John, 16 Jan. 1743, Sarah Brown | 2 BA-189 |
| Muller, John Geo., 25 April 1758, Magd. Maderi | 4 FR-1103 |
| Mullican, James, 24 Nov. 1720, Mary Holmes | 2 TA-96 |
| Mullican, Pattrick, 6 April 1671, Elizabeth Kindcade | 1 TA-602 |
| Mullican, Samuel, 1 May 1750, Ruth Parrot | 3 TA-77 |
| Mullikin, James, 31 Oct. 1734, Mary Pottinger | 2 PG-6 |
| Mullikin, Patrick, 28 Nov. 1736, Mary Lord | 2 TA-158 |
| Mullikin, Samuel, 24 Sept. 1722, Anne Holmes | 2 TA-104 |
| Mullikin, Thomas, 25 Oct. 1714, Eliza Wilson | 2 PG-1 |
| Mullikin, Thomas, Feb. 1761, Elizabeth Williams | 2 PG-7 |
| Mullikin, William, 6 June 1727, Margaret Turner | 2 PG-4 |
| Mullikin, William, 3 Nov. 1737, Eleanor Robinson | 2 TA-162 |
| Mulner, Charles, Jan. 1773, Casander Chamberlane | 2 BA-265 |
| Mumford, (?)-liam, 27 Aug. 174-(?), Meriday (?) | 1 WO-3 |
| Mummy, John, 7 Aug. 1777, Margaret Beam | 10 BA-68 |
| Mumpford, John, 20 April 1735, Mary Ailey | 1 QA-40 |
| Mumpford, John, 15 Oct. 1735, Rebecca Devnish | 1 QA-41 |
| Munday, Henry, 25 Nov. 1725, Susanna Temple | 1 BA-259 |
| Munfort, John, 2 Jan. 1706/7, Elliza Lee | 4 AA-372 |
| Munger, Edward, 28 July 1730, Mary Singdall | 3 BA-149 |
| Munger, Samuel, Dec. 1745, Eliz'h Briggs | 1 QA-51 |
| Mungumery, Robert, 12 Aug. 1718, Alice Smith, widow | 3 BA-147 |
| Munroe, Major, 22 April 1738, Sarah Smith | 4 AA-439 |
| Munttegue, Will, 12 Oct. 1668, Elizabeth Morgaine | 1 TA-601 |
| Murcot, John, 28 April 1709, Anne Norveill | 1 AA-77 |
| | & 256 |
| Murdagh, Daniel, 23 Oct. 1740, Martha Cowen | 1 BA-319 |
| Murfey, Andrew, 26 Nov. 1768, Anne Right | 1 WI-112 |
| Murfey, James, 1 Jan. 1712, Marg't Hynson | 3 KE-302 |
| Murfey, Roger, 11 Aug. 1715, Mary Green | 3 KE-303 |
| Murmet, Michael, 23 Dec. 1777, Mary Thomson | 1 MO-516 |
| Murphew, John, 7 March 1707, Mary Elliott | 1 BA-245 |
| Muryhey, Abraham, 10 Jan. 1758, Elizabeth Boswell | 1 CH-195 |
| Murphey, Charles, 1 Jan. 1714, Mary Thomson | 2 TA-75 |
| Murphey, Charles, 5 Aug. 1747, Eliz'h Martin | 1 QA-53 |
| Murphey, Garrett, 21 May 1773, Catherine Small | 2 BA-266 |
| Murphey, James, 5 June 1732, Eliza Mackway | 2 TA-152 |

| | |
|---|---|
| Murphey, James, 3 Sept. 1733, Mary Mason | 2 TA-153 |
| Murphey, James, 9 Nov. 1746, Sarah Cheyne | 2 BA-240 |
| Murphey, John, 19 Jan. 1700, Esther (?) | 2 TA-12 |
| Murphey, Martin, 15 Dec. 1754, Eliz. Collett | 2 BA-211 |
| Murphey, Patrick, 2 Sept. 1755, Eliz. Dunahue | 2 BA-212 |
| Murphey, Thomas, 25 Dec. 1728, Catherin Common | 2 TA-119 |
| Murphey, Wm., 23 Dec. 1777, Sophia West | 1 HA-200 |
| Murphy, Daniel, Jr., 17 Feb. 1757, Anne Moreton | 1 CH-197 |
| Murphy, Hezekiah, 15 Oct. 1767, Elizabeth Hill | 1 CH-194 |
| Murphy, James, 15 Dec. 1746, Sarah Chainy | 2 BA-195 |
| Murphy, James, 17 Sept. 1753, Phebe Skeerer | 2 BA-48 |
| Murphy, Thomas, 1 April 1706, Martha Royall | 3 KE-300 |
| Murphy, William, 2 Aug. 1751, Sarah Gissard | 1 BA-354 |
| Murphy, Zepheniah, 29 Dec. 1765, Margaret Hill | 1 CH-194 |
| Murray, Dr. William, 22 Jan. 1740, Ann Smith | 3 KE-306 |
| Murrein, Jack, 4 Dec. 1769, Mary Johnson | 1 SM-135 |
| Murrein, Thomas, 25 Dec. 1733, Mary Hadaway | 3 CE-18 |
| Murrey, Nath'l, 24 Jan. 1760, Racahel Bayley | 2 BA-219 |
| Murrey, Zachariah, 27 May 1767, Margr't Simmons | 2 BA-230 |
| Murry, Jeremiah, 5 March 1738/9, Mary Everit | 2 KE-225 |
| Murry, John, 30 May 1769, Weathy Ann Cotteral | 2 BA-258 |
| Murray, Mellchezadeck, son of James and Jemima, dec., 13 day, 9 mo., 1723, Sophia Giles, dau. of John and Sarah | 6 SF |
| Musgroves, Anthony, 25 Nov. 1707, Margaret Deavor | 2 AA-332 |
| Myers, Balcher, 18 April 1770, Margaret Wright | 5 BA-9 |
| Nabb, Charles, 20 April 1737, Elisabeth Wyat | 1 QA-43 |
| Nairne, Robert, 29 Oct. 1724, Ann Lerman | 2 BA-23 |
| Nash, Alexander, 20 Jan. 1662, Ruth Hill | 1 KE-186 |
| Nation, George, of St. Paul's Par., P. G. Co., 15 Oct. 1704, Ann White | 1 AA-65 |
| Neal, Charles, 1771, Elizabeth Jones | 2 AA-410 |
| Neal, Edward, 1 day, 10 mo., 1725, Elizabeth Jones | 8 SF-44 |
| Neal, Jeremiah, 10 April 1717, Elizabeth Lewis, dau. of Charles | 8 SF-17 |
| Neal, Jonathan, 2 day, 2 mo., 1763, Sarah Wilson, Jr. | 8 SF-109 |
| Neal, Samuel, 2 day, 2 mo., 1718, Hannah Webb | 8 SF-20 |
| Neale, Thomas, 23 July 1777, Martha Philpot | 7 AA-1 |
| Nearn, Benjamin, 11 Feb. 1752, Eliz. Keys | 2 BA-204 |
| Needham, William, 17 May 1736, Martha Throne | 1 PG-271 |
| Needle, Thomas, 25 Dec. 1722, Mary Thompson | 4 AA-420 |
| Needles, Edward, 18 May 1722, Mary Tonnard | 2 TA-102 |
| Needles, Edward, 18 Dec. 1723, Elizabeth Thomas | 2 TA-105 |
| Needles, William, 21 Nov. 1722, Eliza Tonnard | 2 TA-105 |
| Neelson, William, 21 Dec. 1746, Deborah Fairbrother | 3 AA-111 |
| Neigh, George, 15 Nov. 1777, Mary Sailor | 1 WA-533 |
| Neighbours, Thomas, Sept. 1743, Rebecca Tibbles | 3 TA-44 |
| Neil, Thomas, April 1748, Mary Wagstar | 2 BA-243 |
| Neil, Thomas, 24 July 1777, Martha Philpott | 2 AA-414 |
| 8 AA-13 gives same entry. | |
| Nellson, Ambross, 5 Feb. 1707/8, Sarah Du-(?) | 4 AA-372 |
| Nellson, Aquilla, 20 Jan. 1757, Sarah Chancey | 1 BA-358 |
| Nellson, John, 30 Jan. 1745, Dinah Mezick | 1 WI-63 |
| Nelman, Anthony, 1 Aug. 1773, Mary McCall | 2 BA-266 |
| Nelms, William, 21 Sept. 1749, Jane Webb | 1 QA-56 |
| Nelson, Ambross, 11 July 1745, Sarah Watterfall | 3 AA-107 |
| Nelson, Benjamin, shipwright, 8 Dec. 1763, Margaret Hedrick, real dau. of Elizabeth Elliott, and dau. in law to Thomas Elliott | 1 CE-309 |
| Nelson, Hancelip, 10 Aug. 1747, Dorcas Cross | 3 AA-108 |
| Nelson, John, 15 Nov. 1715, ffrances (?) | 2 BA-16 |
| Nelson, John, 12 Jan. 1718, Frances Rhodes | 2 BA-9 |
| Nelson, John, 17 Sept. 1731, Mary Loath | 1 CE-330 |
| Nesham, Benjamin, 10 May 1680, Elizabeth Jemison | 5 SO-399 |
| Netcomb, George, 5 June 1759, Sarah Gregory | 2 BA-218 |

Nevil, William, 7 Sept. 1731, Mary Harris          1 QA-38
Nevill, David, 28 Sept. 1758, Martha Wharton       1 QA-64
Nevill, John, 15 Dec. 1748, Catherine Nevill       1 QA-55
Nevill, John, 19 June 1759, Elizabeth Alsop        1 QA-65
Nevill, Walter, 12 Nov. 1731, Elizabeth Lambden    1 QA-38
Nevit, William, 26 Feb. 1735, Rachel Bailey        1 QA-41
Nevitt, James, 31 May 1777, Ruth Conn              3 PG-108
New, Timothy, 13 Dec. 1764, Sarah Beaver           2 BA-227
Newbee, Bernerd, 19 Oct. 1706, Lettice Ireland     1 AA-72
Newbold, John, 6 June 1754, Leah Brittingham       2 SO-56
Newcom, Robert, 10 June 1740, Margaret Benson      3 TA-23
Newcomb, Timothy, 19 Nov. 1747, Grace Jadwin       1 QA-53
Newel, John, 12 day, 2 mo., 1752, Marth. Collins   1 SF-87
Newell, John, 4 Feb. 1759, Eliza Wilkinson         1 QA-64
Newgent, Silvester, 5 Dec. 1756, (?) (?)           1 CE-310
Newill, John, 29 July 1711, Ellinor Loyd           3 KE-308
Newland, Thomas, 10 Jan. 1740, Frances Smith       1 BA-344
Newman, John, 9 April 1713, Elizabeth Malane       3 CE-7
Newman, John, 18 Jan. 1731, Catherine Ley          2 TA-151
Newman, Walter, Jr., 31 Oct. 1716, (?) (?)         3 CE-9
Newman, William, 25 July 1734, Mary Gain           3 BA-152
Newnam, Benjamin, 26 June 1732, Hanna Monsieur     1 QA-39
Newnam, Benjamin, 29 Feb. 1756, Mary Reiley        1 QA-60
Newnam, Edward, 11 Sept. 1729, Mary Ears           1 QA-36
Newnam, Edward, 11 Sept. 1729, Mary Ayres          1 QA-39
Newnam, Edward, 31 Oct. 1746, Deborah Ackres       2 TA-282
Newnam, Jno., 26 Oct. 1736, Elis. Swift            1 QA-42
Newnam, John, 16 Sept. 1756, Eliza Forakers        1 QA-61
Newnam, John, Jr., 21 Dec. 1758, Elinor Seward     1 QA-64
Newnam, Joseph, 17 Jan. 1723, Rebecca Skinner      2 TA-107
Newnam, Joseph, 18 Nov. 1736, Sarah Wells          1 QA-42
Newnam, Joeeph, 6 Oct. 1745, Sarah Cook            1 QA-51
Newnam, Joseph, 13 Dec. 1747, (?) Skibbow          1 QA-53
Newnam, Nathan'll, 26 Nov. 1741, Cathrin Woodwal   1 QA-47
Newnam, Skinner, c.Oct. 1775, Mary Bozman          1 CR-6
Newnam, Solomon, 14 Nov. 1743, Mary Woodwal        1 QA-48
Newnam, William, 2 Oct. 1729, Hannah Commages      1 QA-37
Newnam, William, 7 May 1750, Eliz'th Brown         1 QA-57
Newnham, John, 21 Aug. 1735, Rachel Sutton         1 QA-41
News, Timothy, 11 March 1741, Rebecca Rhodes       2 BA-134
Newsome, John, 16 Feb. 1715, Ann Stinchcomb        1 BA-220
Newster, Thos., 4 Feb. 1749/50, Ann Freeman        3 BA-163
Newton, Alban, 30 March 1773, Marion Pike          1 SM-136
Newton, Bernaar, 11 Dec. 1769, Mary Pain           1 SM-135
Newton, Bernard, 8 Feb. 1775, Mary Pike            1 SM-137
Newton, Charles, 6 Feb. 1752, Sarah Rice           2 BA-204
Newton, Gabriel, 24 Oct. 1775, Henrietta Wheatley  1 SM-137
Newton, Hugh, 27 Oct. 1744, Mary Hill              1 QA-49
Newton, James, 20 Aug. 1752, Margaret Chappell     1 QA-59
Newton, John, 11 Feb. 1719, Catherine Lovelet      1 AA-297
Newton, John, 20 Oct. 1733, Mary (?)               1 WI-5
Newton, Joseph, (date not given), Ann Odall        1 PG-285
Newton, Robert, 28 Aug. 1735, Eliz'h Smith         2 PG-6
Newton, Thomas, 9 Sept. 1731, Mary Gregory         1 QA-38
Newton, William, 26 Oct. 1777, Elizabeth Stubble   10 BA-69
Nicholls, James, 8 Aug. 1671, Martha Popley        7 SO-401
Nicholls, Thomas, 8 Oct. 1717, Ann Davis           2 PG-1
Nicholls, William, 9 Sept. 1711, Mary Mockby       2 PG-1
Nicholls, William, 13 Feb. 1715, Ann Burrows       2 PG-1
Nicholls, William, 23 Oct. 1718, Sarah Simons      2 AA-360
Nichols, Hugh, 26 Nov. 1745, Ann Cross             1 QA-51
Nichols, James, 10 Jan. 1723, Phillis Hardy        1 WI-23
Nichols, Thomas, 21 Aug. 1740, Frances James       2 BA-191
Nichols, Thos., 10 Feb. 1763, Prissella Back       2 BA-224
Nichols, William, 4 Nov. 1708, Elizabeth Sellman   1 AA-76

Nichols, William, 10 Nov. 1737, Sarah Green                     2 PG-7
Nicholson, Alexander, 23 Sept. 1777, Catherine Malone          10 BA-69
Nicholson, James, 1663, Mary Price                              5 SO-399
Nicholson, James, 4 Oct. 1722, Rebecca Ward                     1 AA-93
Nicholson, James, 24 Dec. 1757, Ducella Durbin                  2 BA-216
Nicholson, Jeremiah, 13 Oct. 1764, Rebeccah Jacobs              9 AA-247
Nicholson, John, 23 Dec. 1708, Esther Ijams                    1 AA-76
Nicholson, John, 27 Aug. 1758, Ann Wiggins                     1 QA-64
Nicholson, Nathan, 16 March 1749, Ruth Bond                    2 BA-201
Nicholson, Thomas, 31 Jan. 1750, Sarah Boroughs               1 QA-57
Nicholson, William, 22 May 1729, Elizabeth Beale               4 AA-431
Nicholus, John, 25 Jan. 1715, Mary Todd                       3 AA-102
Nickerson, Nathan, 29 Aug. 1774, Mable Grace                  1 CR
Nickoldson, William, 24 April 1750, Mary Connell              3 BA-164
Nicks, George, 24 Jan. 1738, Cath. Buckingham                 2 TA-166
Niclas, John Geo., 16 Nov. 1767, An. Barb. Hofman             4 FR-1157
Nicolls, Humphrey, 27 Dec. 1742, Anne McDoodle               2 TA-173
Nicols, Charles, 23 July 1754, Mary Smith                    2 CR-272
Nicols, Jere:, 29 May 1739, Deb. Lloyd                       3 TA-16
Nicols, John, 5 May 1736, Mary Noble                         2 TA-158
Nicols, Jonathan, 25 April 1743, Mary Knowles                3 TA-42
Nicols, Robert Lloyd, c.Aug. 1775, Susanna Chamber-
  laine                                                      1 CR-6
Nicols, William, 21 May 1760, Henrietta Maria Chamber-
  laine                                                      2 TA-286
Nicolson, Richard, 23 Nov. 1755, Sarah Ashley                1 QA-60
Niel, Thomas, April 1747, banns pub. three times;
  Mary Wagster                                               2 BA-243
Nilms, John, 29 Dec. 1768, Nancy Williams                    1 WI-89
Nixon, Jonathan, 29 July 1738, Mary Searitt; one or
  both parties were "late of Leek in the County of
  Staford Shire, Eng."                                      1 PG-357
Nixson, Richard, 12 Sept. 1722, Mary Gregg                   2 TA-103
Nixson, Thomas, 23 July 1747, Sarah Thompson                 2 BA-161
Noads, John, 6 Feb. 1704, Ann Shooter                        2 AA-326
Noah, Rich'd, 27 Nov. 1730, Mary Oxley                       1 AA-111
Noah, Richard, 9 June 1734, Martha Meads                     1 BA-271
Noble, George, Gent., 27 Jan. (?), Charity Wheeler,
  "Gent'w."                                                  1 PG-270
Noble, Isaac, Jan. 1675/6, Mary Robeson                      9 SO-401
  5 SO-399 gives the date as 9 May 1676 and the
  bride's name as Mary Robinson.
Noble, Joseph, son of Joseph and Catherine, born in
  Cockermouth, Cumberland, Eng., on 17 April 1689,
  2 Dec. 1708, Mary Wheeler                                 1 PG-272
Noble, Joseph, son of Joseph, 5 March 1738, Martha
  Tarvin, dau. of Richard                                   1 PG-273
Noble, Mark, 27 Nov. 1707, Elizabeth Heaburn                 3 KE-308
Noble, Mark, 16 Oct. 1708, Elizabeth Cooper                  2 TA-49
Noble, Robert, 30 Oct. 1741, Marg't Price                    3 TA-33
Noble, Robert, 17 Jan. 1758, Elizabeth Matthews             1 QA-63
Noble, William, 21 Feb. 1731, Ann Durbin                     2 BA-40
Nock, Ezekiel, of Kent Co., Del., 27 day, 9 mo., 1753,
  Sarah Maxfield                                             8 SF-142
Nock, Thomas, Jr., 13 day, 5 mo. (May), 1773, Mary
  Caulk                                                      1 SF-104
Nolen, Henery, 5 Nov. 1711, Sarah Cambell                   3 KE-308
Noles, John, 17 Nov. 1708, Susannah Grace                   3 KE-308
Nomberss, Peter, 9 Oct. 1711, Ann Pennington, widow         3 CE-4
Norcote, Thomas, 18 Oct. 1772, Judy Jones                   3 AA-113
Norly, Andrew, 8 Sept. 1708, Jane Hyssett                   3 KE-308
Norman, Benja., 19 Dec. 1764, Elizabeth (?)                 2 AA-398
Norman, George, 26 Oct. 1717, Mary Wood                     4 AA-402
Norman, Nicholas, 11 Aug. 1706, Elizabeth Howard            2 AA-330
Norman, Nicholas, 24 Dec. 1731, Eliza Carr                  2 AA-368

Norman, Thomas, 1771, Margaret Deale                    2 AA-410
Norrington, Francis, 19 Feb. 1749, Mary Everett         2 BA-200
  2 VA-244 gives date as 1750.
Norrington, John, 1 Aug. 1737, Mary Hays               2 BA-99
Norris, Abra., 4 Dec. 1762, Rebecca Kitely             2 BA-224
Norris, Benjamin, 8 Oct. 1719, Sarah (?)               2 BA-16
Norris, Benjamin, son of Ben, 7 March 1754, Mary
  Devoll                                               2 BA-209
Norris, Benj'n, 3 April 1768, Eliz. Richardson         2 BA-231
Norris, Dan'l, 28 Sept. 1762, Sarah Beaver             2 BA-224
Norris, Edw'd, son of Jos., 19 Sept. 1754, Mary Wyle   2 BA-211
Norris, Edward, 21 Nov. 1771, Eliz. Amoss              2 BA-263
Norris, Ignatius, 22 March 1770, Lucia Pike            1 SM-135
Norris, Jac., 6 March 1773, Monica Greenwell           1 SM-136
Norris, Jas., 1 Jan. 1744, Eliz. Davis                 2 BA-191
Norris, Jas., son of Edw., 2 Aug. 1750, Philiszana
  Barton                                               2 BA-201
Norris, Jas., 5 Dec. 1765, Mary Norris                 2 BA-228
Norris, John, (date not given), Clare Wells            2 AA-355
Norris, John, 3 April 1716, Mary Newman                2 AA-356
Norris, John, 24 Feb. 1733, Catherine Mullican         2 TA-155
Norris, John, 29 Nov. 1736, Sarah Steward              1 AA-120
Norris, John, 3 April 1744, Susannah Bradford          2 BA-190
Norris, John, 19 Jan. 1758, Mary Blond                 2 BA-216
Norris, John, 12 Nov. 1772, Marth. Long                2 BA-265
Norris, John Baptist, 18 Aug. 1770, M. Woodward        1 SM-135
Norris, Jos., 20 Nov. 1766, Christian Price            2 BA-230
Norris, Joseph, 25 Jan. 1770, Eliz. Cole               2 BA-259
Norris, Thomas, Jr., 26 Dec. 1736, Eliz. McComas       2 BA-76
Norris, Thomas, 10 Oct. 1738, Avarilla Scott           2 BA-120
Norris, Thos., 11 Sept. 1757, Rebecca Potter           2 BA-216
Norris, Thos., son of Benj., 20 July 1761, Ann Buck-
  ingham                                               2 BA-222
Norris, Thos., 4 May 1762, Hannah Norrington           2 BA-223
Norris, Thomas, 1 June 1776, Catherine Mattingly       1 SM-137
Norris, William, 24 Jan. 1751, Eliz. Horn              2 BA-203
Norris, William, 22 Sept. 1765, Sarah Waters           9 AA-250
Norriss, Eliz., "married Xber 1, 1704, Buried Xber
  3, 1704."                                            2 AA-354
North, Jas., 5 Dec. 1762, Margr't Richardson           2 BA-224
Northcoat, James, 16 July 1723, Hannah Smith           3 AA-104
Northerman, Jacob, 4 June 1753, Mary (?)               1 CE-309
Northing, William, 11 Nov. 1727, Hannah Godfrey        1 AA-106
Norton, Edward, son of Edward, of Co. Armagh, Ire.,
  16 Oct. 173-(?), Elizabeth Brown, dau. of William
  and Elizabeth                                        9 SF
Norton, George, 7 Nov. 1735, Margrett Wright           3 BA-154
Norton, Nehemiah, 20 Oct. 1765, Elizabeth Kennett      9 AA-249
Norton, Stephen, 11 day, 4 mo., 1776, Sophia Lay       7 SF-35
Norton, William, 1 Feb. 1722, Eliz'th Clark            1 BA-269
Norvil, John, 2 Feb. 1735, Mary Bayley                 1 BA-287
Norwood, Edward, 9 Nov. 1746, Mary Fitzsimmonds        3 BA-160
Norwood, Phillip, 2 Jan. 1704, Hannah (?)              4 AA-389
Norwood, Samuel, 21 April 1730, Mary Mullikin          1 AA-110
Nottingham, Basil, 31 Dec. 1774, Joanna Stone          1 SM-137
Noughton, William, 12 Dec. 1672, Katherine Newgent     5 SO-399
Nowland, Daniell, 6 Jan. 1713, Mary Hill, widow        3 CE-5
Nusewondon, Dan'l, 14 Nov. 1761, Sarah Asher           2 BA-222
Nuton, Thos., 3 March 1740/1, Sarah Saulsbury          1 QA-46
Nutter, John Huill, 13 Aug. 1727, Margrit Carlile      1 WI-28
Nutter, John Huill, 4 April 1735, Ann Nutter           1 WI-29
Nutter, Robert, c.Aug. 1775, Sarah Bagwell             1 CR-6
Nutter.  See also Hutton.
Nuttle, Elias, 1771, Sarah Sherbert                    2 AA-411
Oakdin, John, 23 Oct. 1748, Susannah Harps             2 BA-243

| | |
|---|---|
| Oakley, Esau, 15 Oct. 1774, Jane Smith | 3 BA-171 |
| Oberholdt, Abraham, 22 Aug. 1767, Anna Witmor | 4 FR-1158 |
| OBrian, Phillipe, 7 Jan. 1704, Mary Riley | 4 AA-389 |
| OBrian, Thomas, 14 June 1757, Amelia Wooling | 2 BA-215 |
| Obryan, John, c.Oct. 1775, Sarah McGinney | 1 CR-6 |
| O'Bryan, Terrance, 4 May 1720, Mary Lewill? | 1 PG-277 |
| O'Bryon, John, 4 Dec. 1756, Mary Chairs | 1 QA-61 |
| OBryon,Solomon, 23 Nov. 1758, Martha Roe | 1 QA-64 |
| OCain, Mannus, 26 Nov. 1750, Eliz. M'Kenly | 2 BA-202 |
| Ochs, John Adam, 7 Feb. 1757, Mary Appol. Hoffman | 4 FR-1103 |
| Odell, Rignal, 25 Aug. 1754, Martha Duckett | 2 PG-7 |
| Odett, John, 17 Sept. 1735, Mary Magdalen Goutey | 2 TA-266 |
| Offley, Michael, of Duck Creek, Newcastle Co., Del., 8 June 1743, Phebe Corse | 1 SF-77 |
| Offley, Robert, 16 Nov. 1731, Margaret Benton | 1 QA-38 |
| Ogg, George, Sr., 22 Aug. 1722, Mary Potee | 3 BA-155 |
| Oggdon, John, 19 Nov. 1748, Susanah Harps | 2 BA-198 |
| Ogle, Benjamin, 18 Sept. 1770, Henny Margaret Hill | 1 AA-152 |
| Ogle, Thomas, Dec. 1756, Sarah Ogle | 4 FR-1103 |
| Okee, John, 4 Sept. 1666, Mary Vincent | 6 SO-400 |
| 5 SO-399 gives date as 2 Oct. 1666 | |
| Oldfield, Henry, 15 July 1717, Sarah Barber | 2 TA-80 |
| Oldfield, John, 18 Aug. 1720, Sarah Moor | 2 TA-94 |
| Oldfield, William, 10 Nov. 1719, Sarah Turner | 2 TA-91 |
| Oldham, Edward, 29 May 1735, Mary Lowe | 2 TA-159 |
| Oldham, Nathan, 18 Nov. 1766, Elizabeth Giles | 4 CE-261 |
| Oldham, Thomas, 3 July 1728, Rachel Minshall Taylor Littler, widow of 1) Thomas Taylorm and 2) Samuel Littler | 9 SF |
| Oldham, William, son of Thomas and Susanna, 10 June 1736, Sarah Dix, dau. of Nathan | 9 SF |
| Oldham, William, 1 April 1754, Ruth Talbott | 2 BA-209 |
| Oldridg, Thomas, 10 June 1702, Rebecca Hancock | 3 AA-97 |
| Olephint, William, 23 Feb. 1736, Sarah Jones | 1 WI-11 |
| Oliver, John, 9 April 1716, Mary Isaac | 2 PG-1 |
| Oliver, John, 14 July 1720, Sarah Smith | 2 BA-16 |
| Oliver, John, 6 July 1745, Alice Twelves | 3 BA-157 |
| Olley, Sebastian, 28 April 1701, Dianagh Deverin | 3 AA-96 |
| Omelia, Bryan, 27 day, 6 mo., 1676, Mary Lewis | 8 SF-316 |
| O'Mullen, Edward, 23 Dec. 1733, Mary Maclegum | 1 CE-329 |
| O'Neal, Daniel, 1737, Mary Johnson | 2 AA-378 |
| O'Neal, John, 23 Dec. 1777, Mary Smith | 1 MO-516 |
| O'Neall, Daniel, 12 June 1743, Susanna Lacey | 2 BA-126 |
| Onion, Benjamin, 4 Nov. 1765, Ann Turner | 9 AA-248 |
| Onion, Zacheus, 2 Dec. 1757, Hannah Bond | 2 BA-175 |
| Onions, John, 18 June 1740, Susanah Cherson? | 1 WO-8 |
| Oram, Henry, 7 Nov. 1765, Sarah Dives | 2 BA-228 |
| Oram, John, 27 Sept. 1769, Rachel Wantland | 2 BA-259 |
| Oram, John, c.Oct. 1775, Mary Marshall | 1 CR-6 |
| Orange, John, 26 Nov. 1704, Mary Wright | 1 AA-65 |
| Orem, Andrew, 21 day, 12 mo., 1678, Eliner Morris | 8 SF-319 |
| Orem, Andrew, 11 Aug. 1747, Rachel Benson | 3 TA-66 |
| Organ, William, 20 April 1752, Esther Majors | 4 BA-72 |
| Orick, Will'm, Oct. 1704, Hannah (?) | 4 AA-389 |
| Orman, Joseph, 3 June 1734, Hannah Baily | 4 AA-436 |
| Ormes, Robert, 4 Feb. 1741, Dorcas Devor | 4 AA-443 |
| Ormond, Samuel, 19 May 1746, Ann Lambeth | 3 BA-159 |
| Orrell?, Thomas, 1 June 1774, Sarah Somman? | 1 CR |
| Orrick, James, 23 March 1709, Priscilla Ruley | 4 AA-379 |
| Orrick, John, 15 Dec. 1719, Susanah Hammond | 3 AA-102 |
| Orrick, John, 20 Feb. 1757, Caroline Hammond | 3 BA-166 |
| Orrick, William, 22 Oct. 1700, Katherine Duvall | 1 AA-56 & 246 |
| Orsler, Edward, 21 Nov. 1734, Ruth Owens | 3 BA-152 |
| Osbond, Edward, 16 Oct. 1749, Hannah Hurst | 3 AA-113 |

Osborn, Daniel, 2 Feb. 1715, Mary Lansey or Tansey 2 AA-356
Osborn, Jacob, 24 Feb. 1758, Sarah Fowler 1 BA-358
Osborn, James, 17 Sept. 1743, Jane Hughes 1 BA-332
Osborn, Thomas, 3 Aug. 1751, Elizabeth Simpson 1 BA-381
Osborn, William, 24 Jan. 1710, Avarilla (?) 1 BA-248
Osborn, William, 1 March 1727/8, Cathurinah Rhoades 1 BA-245
Osborn, William, 18 June 1745, Margaret Lyall 1 BA-358
Osborn, William, 3 Aug. 1762, Ann Bissett, widow of
 David Bisset 1 BA-70
Osborne, Joseph, 25 Jan. 1761, Urath Bond 4 BA-73
Osburn, Cyrus, 10 Oct. 1775, Susannah Robinson 1 BA-392
Osburn, John, 24 Dec. 1732, Mary Sullivan 3 BA-150
Osen, Daniel, 29 Dec. 1724, Alice Walton 2 TA-111
Osment, John, 15 Jan. 1739/40, Mary Floyd 3 TA-20
Osment, Thos., 21 May 1749, Pris. Dobson 3 TA-73
Othason, Robert, 28 Feb. 1737/8, Rebeckah Numbers 3 CE-21
Othneel, Philip, 30 Sept. 1708, Mary Dixon 2 AA-335
Ottaway, Thom's, 5 Aug. 1713, Sarah Mullaien 4 AA-380
Otterson, Otho, 21 Dec. 1704, Mary Matthiason, widow 3 CE-3
Ottwell, James, 4 Feb. 1753, Mary Quinton 2 SO-58
Otwell, James, 23 March 1761, Sarah Pusey 2 SO-57
Outten, Abraham, 3 Dec. 1747, Betty White 2 SO-58
Outten, Isaac, 11 Jan. 1770, Sarah Waggarman 2 SO-157
Outten, Punrell, 13 Sept. 1741, Mary Houston 2 SO-58
Outwell, James, Feb. 1776, Tabitha Matthews 2 SO-57
Overard, Peter, 6 April 1710, Mary Murphy 4 AA-379
Owe, Johan, 24 Oct. 1777, Susannah Windlass 1 WA-528
Owen, Edward, of Kent. Penna., 15 March 1684, Hannah
 Baxter 8 SF-335
Owen, Jno., 12 Nov. 1761, Permelie Cheyne 2 BA-222
Owen, Lewis, 19 June 1720, Eliza Quiney 4 AA-412
Owen, Peter, 30 March 1743, Elizabeth Dorman 2 SO-59
Owen, Thomas, 1669, Mary Turner 5 SO-399
Owens, Charles, Oct. 1777, Betty Burton 1 CA-111a
Owens, Henry, 6 June 1775, Sarah Gardner 2 AA-412
Owens, John, 4 Feb. 1705, Elizabeth Spicer 1 AA-72
Owens, Joseph, 10 Feb. 1718/9, Eliza Williams 2 AA-360
Owens, Thomas, 2 Feb. 1740, Mary Lankford 2 SO-60
Owens, William, 1775, Elizabeth Miffin 1 CR
Owing, Edw'd, 20 Jan. 1766, Ruth Carlile 2 BA-229
Owings, James, 1771, Elizabeth Owings 2 AA-410
Owings, James, 1771, Ann Pritchard 2 AA-410
Owings, Joshua, 9 March 1735, Mary Cockey 3 BA-155
Owings, Joshua, 4 Oct. 1777, Rachel Crook 10 BA-69
Owings, Robert, 23 Dec. 1730, Hannah Forquer 3 BA-150
Owings, Samuel, 1 Jan. 1729, Urath Randall, dau. of
 Thomas and Hannah 4 BA-70
 3 BA-150 gives date as 1 Jan. 1730.
Owings, Sam'l, Jr., 6 Oct. 1765, Deborah Lynch 4 BA-75
Owings, Thos., 30 April 1749, Mary Hicks 2 BA-198
Owings, Thomas, 27 Nov. 1760, Ruth Lawrence 4 BA-74
Owly, Sebastine, 9 Feb. 1725, Elizabeth Hall 3 AA-102
Oxenham, Richard, 21 Dec. 1777, Elizabeth Rathall 1 CR-10
Ozier, Francis, 7 Feb. 1736/7, Mary Wood, dau. of
 Catherine 3 CE-20
Paca, Aquila, 11 Sept. 1699, Martha Phillips 1 BA-189
Paca, Aq'a, 8 Dec. 1763, Eliz. Franklin 2 BA-225
Paca, John, 2 Nov. 1732, Elizabeth Smith 2 BA-148
Paca, John, Jr., 6 Feb. 1752, Margaret Lee 1 BA-349
Packer, William, 1776, Elenor Wright 3 BA-189
Packett, Daniel, 28 Dec. 1717, Mary Matthews 4 AA-403
Paden, John, 2 Sept. 1763, Betty Henderson 2 SO-65
Padisson, John, 4 June 1714, Sarah Long 2 TA-73
Page, Daniel, 16 Nov. 1777, Leonora Piles 1 CA-111a
 3 PG-143 gives same information.

Page, Geo., 8 April 1740, Letitia Brown                          3 TA-22
Page, John, son of Ralph and Elizabeth, 1 Jan. 1764,
  Milcah Groom, dau. of Samuel and Margaret                      3 KE-312
Page, John, 26 Jan. 1772, Deep Rose (sic)                        2 BA-264
Page, Jonathan, July (?), Hannah Pendar                          3 KE-310
Page, Ralph, 12 April 1732, Elizabeth Miller                     3 KE-312
Page, William, 3 Oct. 1748, Esther Miller                        3 BA-162
Pain, Beaver, 7 Feb. 1757, Eliz. Marshall                        2 BA-214
Pain, Jno., 21 April 1705, Cathrine Secum                        2 TA-43
Pairmain?, Henery, 4 June (?), Jane Brion                        3 KE-310
Palmer, Benjamin, 8 March 1753, Margaret Hall                    2 KE-301
Palmer, George, 15 July 1736, Mary Lowder                        2 TA-161
Palmer, Geo., 30 Aug. 1761, Mary Tipper                          2 BA-222
Palmer, John, 22 Feb. 1735, Mary Lanham                          1 PG-282
Palmer, John, 5 Nov. 1769, Lidie Collins                         2 BA-259
Palmer, Joseph, 30 April 1762, Mary Ford                         2 KE-302
Palmer, Nathaniel, 11 June 1721, Winifred Walter                 1 AA-305
Palmer, Nathan'l, 3 Dec. 1723, Esther Evans, widow              4 AA-422
Palmer, Sam'll, 14 July 1765, Sarah Fields                       2 BA-228
Palmer, Thomas, 25 Oct. 1727, Ann Scott                          1 AA-105
Palmer, Thomas, 28 Dec. 1732, Jude Elliott                       1 BA-75
Palmer, Thomas, 29 Oct. 1751, Hannah Norton                      1 CE-310
Palmer, Thomas, 23 May 1761, Mary Sommersell                     1 CE-310
  1 CE-311 gives date as 1 June 1761, and states
  that the bridegroom was a widower and that the
  bride was a widow.
Palmer, William, 24 Nov. 1734, Eliz'h Vernon                     2 PG-6
Panter, John, 26 March 1667, Mary Williams                       4 SO-666
Paragy, Joseph, 17 Feb. 1735, Flora Ryder                        3 BA-155
Pardo, Benjamin, 15 Oct. 1752, Ann Holins                        1 QA-59
Parish, Joseph, 12 July 1770, Charity Bosley                     2 BA-260
Parish, Rich'd, 4 Nov. 1776, Sarah Baker                         3 BA-669
Parker, (?), 22 June 1704, Mary Davis                            3 KE-309
Parker, Edw'd, 3 Sept. 1761, Eliz. Westcomb                      2 BA-222
Parker, John, 3 Nov. 1732, Sarah Amery                           1 CE-279
Parker, John, 1 Jan. 1739, Elizabeth Danbie                      2 BA-105
  2 BA-110 gives bride's name as Mary Danbe.
Parker, John, 6 Aug. 1749, Jane Campeon                          1 QA-56
Parker, Jno., 3 Jan. 1757, Eliz. Carback                         2 BA-214
Parker, Richard, 11 April 1711, Sarah Peton                      2 TA-69
Parker, Robert, 29 Nov. 1762, Mary Capas                         2 BA-224
Parker, Thomas, 17 Feb. 17-(?), Martha Woodland                  3 KE-310
Parker, Thomas, 13 Sept. 1730, Anne Crain                        3 BA-149
Parkes, Aquila, 13 Oct. 1777, Elizabeth Taylor                   10 BA-69
Parkison, Abraham, 16 Aug. 1777, Dianna Woodfield                7 AA-1
Parks, Edmund, 9 July 1764, Eliz. Sinkler                        2 BA-226
Parks, John, 11 Sept. 1743, Bridget Milhews                      2 BA-239
  2 BA-189 gives date as 29 Oct. 1743, and bride's
  surname as Millhughs.
Parks, John, 10 Sept. 1748, Sarah Linchfield                     3 BA-161
Parks, Jno., 3 Nov. 1761, Kezia Rutledge                         2 BA-222
Parks, Phillip, 22 Dec. 1746, Hannah Packow                      2 BA-196
  2 BA-241 gives bride's name as Hannah Peckon.
Parks, Robert, 19 Nov. 1761, Mary Fuller                         2 BA-222
Parland, Walter, 28 Dec. 1747, Prisalla Bishop                   1 QA-54
Parlet, Martin, 16 April 1723, Mary Burrows                      2 PG-3
Parlett, William, 1 Feb. 1773, Elizabeth Dew                     3 BA-169
Parmer, William, 5 June 1729, Catherine Hussey                   1 QA-36
Parnel, James, 1 Sept. 1701, Catherine Chaney                    1 AA-248
  1 AA-57 gives bride's name as Cheney.
Parramore, John, 28 Aug. 1743, Ellinor Walker                    1 WI-49
Parran, Alexander, 16 Feb. 1693, Mary Ashcom                     1 CA-112
Parratt, Benjamin, 21 Oct. 1680, Elizabeth Keen                  8 SF-327
Parratt, Benjamin, 6 April 1698, Elizabeth Estell                8 SF-376
Parratt, Benjamin, 9 July 1704, Jane Clark, Jr.                  8 SF-423

Parratt, Benjamin, 27 Sept. 1728, Deborah Arey          8 SF-48
Parratt, Benjamin, 5 March 1755, Mary Ann Wilson        8 SF-99
Parratt, George, 3 day, 11 mo., 1677, Elizabeth
   Bodwell                                              8 SF-317
Parratt, Henry, 25 July 1683, Mary Bates                8 SF-331
Parratt, Henry, 3 Feb. 1697, Sarah Taylor               8 SF-374
Parratt, Peter, 26 Nov. 1730, Ann Ledingham             2 TA-268
Parratt, Will, 30 Nov. 1669, Sarah Morgaine             1 TA-602
Parratt, William, 10 Jan. 1704, Susanna Silvester       8 SF-430
Parren, John, Jr., 19 July 1722, Esther Wilson          4 AA-418
Parrish, Alexander, 1 Feb. 1737, Jane Chatto            1 BA-295
Parrish, Edward, of A. A. Co., 10 Feb. 1722, Rachel
   Harwood                                              8 SF-35
Parrish, Edward, 3 May 1735, Elizabeth Gill             3 BA-153
Parrish, Jno., son of Edward and Clare, 23 day, 11
   mo., 1700, Sarah Horn, widow; dau. of Robert and
   Sarah Franklin                                       6 SF
Parrish, John, 2 Jan. 1733, Elizabeth Thomas            3 BA-151
Parrish, John, son of William, 6 day, 1 mo., 1744,
   Mary Price, dau. of John                             4 SF
Parrish, Joseph, 28 Aug. 1753, Cassandra Talbot         2 BA-208
Parrish, Mordecai, son of John and Mary, 28 day, 9
   mo., 1775, Rachel Malone, dau. of John and Edith     4 SF-267
Parrish, William, Jr., 25 day, 1 mo., 1742, Keturah
   Price                                                4 SF
Parrish, William, 14 Aug. 1774, Rachael Harwood?        1 CR
Parrot, James, 1 May 1750, Mary Mullican                3 TA-77
Parrot, John, 8 April 1751, Neomi Shepard               3 AA-110
Parrot, William, 4 Sept. 1777, Mary Stallions           2 AA-414
   8 AA-13 gives same information.
Parrott, Aaron, 31 day, 1 mo., 1763, Mary Neal          8 SF-115
Parrott, Abner, 9 Feb. 1740/1, Joanah Thomas            3 TA-28
Parrott, Abner, 11 Feb. 1740, Joanna Thomas             2 TA-171
Parrott, Francis, 27 May 1736, Rose Lord                2 TA-161
Parrott, Gabriel, Jr., 5 May 1698, (wife's name not
   given); buried 11 May 1698                           2 AA-294
Parrott, James, 1 Jan. 1740, Eleanor Homes              2 TA-170
   3 TA-27 gives date as 7 Jan. 1740.
Parrott, Peter, 26 Dec. 1730, Anne Leadingham           2 TA-149
Parrott, Samuel, 11 March 1764, Anne Sollers            9 AA-248
Parrott, William, 5 July 1734, Rosanna Clark            2 TA-155
Parrott, William, 2 Feb. 1748/9, Penelope Sherwood      3 TA-71
Parry, John, 17 Dec. 1704, Elizabeth Williams           1 AA-65
Parsley, Bartholomew, 17 Dec. 1741, Judith Roberts,
   dau. of Jno. Roberts, Sr.                            3 CE-23
Parsley, Israel, 5 Feb. 1743, Sarah Cheyrton            2 BA-190
Parsley, Richard, 5 Aug. 1716, Sarah Brace              3 CE-8
Parson, Thomas, 14 Jan. 1773, Mary Perdue               2 BA-265
Parsons, Benjamin, 25 Aug. 1730, Rachel Newnam          1 QA-37
Parsons, George, 1 Dec. 1732, Hanah Stevens             1 WI-77
Parsons, George, 14 Nov. 1736, Sarah Venson             2 PG-7
Parsons, George, 29 Jan. 1762, Temperance Shermon       1 WI-78
Parsons, Henry, son of Henry and Margaret, 3 Oct.
   1744, Elizabeth Berry, dau. of Samuel and Margaret   9 SF
Parsons, John, 3 April 1729, Mary Smith                 1 WI-12
Parsons, John, 3 April 1737, Elizabeth Falum            1 WI-1
Parsons, John, 11 May 1777, Hester Taylor               2 AA-413
Parsons, Jonathan, 31 Jan. 1759, Sarah Mills            1 WI-78
Parsons, Peter, 2 May 1703, Ursulla Jenkins             1 WI-77
Parsons, Thomas, 29 Sept. 1748, Jane Pitt               1 QA-54
Parsons, Thomas, 14 Jan. 1773, Mary Perdue              2 BA-265
Parsons, William, 6 Jan. 1733/4, Garturett Laurax       3 CE-18
Parsons, William, 6 Jan. 1757, Hannah Hearn             1 WI-78
Partridge, Richard, 18 Nov. 1671, Margaret Lee          5 SO-399
Partridge, Robert, 27 Nov. 1777, Rachel Lewis          10 BA-69

Parvin, Benjamin, son of Francis, 3 day 4 mo., 1770,
  Sarah Powell, dau. of Daniel                           8 SF-139
Parvis, John, 12 April 1737, Rachel Swift                1 QA-43
Pasley, Israel, 22 Jan. 1744, Sarah Cheverton            2 BA-239
Passifield, Samuel, 24 Dec. 1744, Rachel Gary            2 TA-273
Passmore, Augustine, son of John and Mary, 28 day,
  1 mo., 1754, Hannah Howard, dau. of Henry              9 SF
Paterson, James, 15 Nov. 1705, Mary Blancher             2 AA-329
Paterson, James, 13 Sept. 1777, Joanna Ford             10 BA-69
Patten, John, 7 Nov. 1706, Charity Cheney                1 AA-72
Patterson, James, 11 June 1761, Sarah Revel              2 SO-158
Patterson, William, 13 Nov. 1777, Phebe Daniel           1 WA-528
Patteson, Garrett, 4 July 1773, Cloe Dean                2 BA-266
Pattingal, Samuel, 17 Feb. 1741, Catherine Darby         4 AA-443
Pattinson, John, 15 July 1741, Marg't Sherwood           2 TA-172
Pattison, John, Jr., 3 July 1741, Margaret Sherwood      3 TA-31
Patton, Matthew, 9 May 1775, Rebecca May                 5 BA-11
Paul, Nicholas, 11 Sept. 1764, Elizab. Hermann           4 FR-1159
Paus, Christian (or Christoph), 1745, at Bethlehem,
  Magdalena Frey                                         5 FR-88
Pawson, Matthew, c.Aug. 1775, Mary Caulk                 1 CR-6
Payn, Jos., 11 Dec. 1769, Binnie Stuart                  1 SM-135
Payne, George, son of Josiah and Martha, 26 day,
  3 mo. (n.s.), 1752, Rachel Cowgill, dau. of Henry      9 SF
Payne, George, 25 April 1772, Elizabeth Smith, widow     3 BA-169
Payne, John, 23 Sept. 1667, Mary White                   3 CH
Payne, John, 25 Dec. 1721, Susanna Rose                  4 AA-416
Payne, Joseph, 1 June 1731, Mary Gibbs                   4 AA-434
Peach, Joseph, 17 Feb. 1725/6, Mary Isaac, dau. of
  Richard                                                2 PG-4
Peacock, Jacob, 30 April 1703, Jane Kindall              3 AA-97
Peacock, Jacob, 26 Oct. 1720, Honor Harden, widow        3 BA-147
Peacock, John, May 1747, Anne Higgins                    2 BA-241
Peacock, John, 29 Dec. 1747, Ann Wiggin                  2 BA-194
Peacock, Luke, 26 July 1753, Constant Sicklemore         2 BA-208
Peacock, Richard, 19 Oct. 1704, Ann Allen                3 KE-309
Peacock, Robert, 20 April 1729, Mary Brooks              2 KE-228
Peak, Jos., 11 Dec. 1769, Susan Yets (Yates?)            1 SM-135
Peak, Thomas, 23 Dec. 1777, Eliz. Keymer                 1 MO-516
Pearce, Benjamin, 31 July 1734, Margarett Ward, dau.
  of Henry                                               3 CE-19
Pearce, Daniel, son of Col. Benjamin, 4 May 1752,
  Sarah Alman, dau. of Abraham                           3 CE-25
Pearce, Henry Ward, son of Benjamin, 16 Jan. 1759,
  Mrs. Anna Statia Carroll, dau. of Dominick Carroll     3 CE-28
Pearce, James, 7 Aug. 1771, Catherine Susanah
  Shannon                                                2 KE-310
Pearce, John, 23 Jan. 1724, Catherine Harroll            4 AA-424
Pearce, Nathaniel, 20 Oct. 1715, Sarah (?)               2 KE-187
Pearce, William, 5 Sept. 1711, Elizabeth Anderson        1 AA-78
Pearce, William, 3 June 1735, Mary Crawford              3 BA-153
Pearce, William, 22 May 1768, Johanna French             1 AA-144
Pearck, John, 17 June 1697, Margarett Blake              3 CE-1
Pearkins, Ebenezer, 14 May 1740, Mrs. Sarah Barney       2 KE-233
Pearle, James, 2 April 1682, Mary Glover                 5 SO-399
Pearse, Daniell, 4 Feb. 1704, Mary Caulk                 3 KE-309
Pearse, Gideon, Jr., 6 June 1734, Beatrice Codd          3 KE-312
Pearson, Thomas, formerly of Eng., but now mariner
  of A. A. Co., 10 day, 8 mo., 1775, Mary Gassaway,
  widow                                                  6 SF
Pearsy, Danell, 10 (?) 16-(?), Ann Hopper                1 AA-33
Peck, Comfort, of Providence, R. I., 11 Dec. 1750,
  Priscilla Green                                        1 WI-51
Peck, John, 25 May 1729, Mary Noble                      2 TA-120
Pedder, John, 9 July 1738, Christian Williams            2 BA-91

```
Peddicoat, Nicholas, 23 Dec. 1735, Ann Jacks            3 BA-154
Pedington, Henry, 25 Aug. 1674, Margaret Griffith       5 SO-399
Peecock, Sam'l, 6 Jan. 1731, Eliz'a Ellt                1 CA-114
Peek, John Baptist, 16 Feb. 1768, Grace Craghill        4 SM-72
Peele, Charles, 12 Jan. 1762, Rachel Brewer             9 AA-247
Peerman, James, 14 Feb. 1726, Ann Maccubbin, dau. of
   John Maccubbin                                       4 AA-427
Peirce, John, 18 Nov. 17-(?), Mary Sympson              1 AA-97
Peirpoint, Larkin, 1730, Sarah Simmons                  2 PG-5
Peirpoint, Larking, 19 Nov. 1725, Charity Duckett       2 PG-4
Pell, Thomas, 14 June 1725, Mary Lennord                2 KE-194
Pemberton, Benjamin, 22 Dec. 1726, Mrs. Elizabeth
   Lurtey                                               2 TA-114
Pemberton, John, 11 June 1684, Margaret Matthews        8 SF-332
Pemberton, Joseph, son of Israel, of Phila., 2 day,
   6 mo., 1767, Ann Galloway, dau. of Joseph            6 SF
Penington, Charles, 12 Dec. 1772, Kiziah Abbett         3 AA-113
Penington, James, 21 Aug. 1729, Marian Jackson          1 QA-37
Penington, James, 11 Dec. 1742, Elizabeth Beastin, dau.
   of William                                           3 CE-24
Penington, John, 7 June 1733, Margaret Penington        3 CE-17
Penington, John, 25 Nov. 1733, Elizabeth Umberson       1 CE-281
Penington, John, son of John, 19 Oct. 1735, Alice
   Ward, dau. of John                                   3 CE-20
Penington, John, Sr., Oct. 1740, Mary Othoson, dau.
   of Garriot Othoson                                   3 CE-22
Penington, Josiah, 24 Feb. 1771, Jemima Hanson          3 BA-170
Penington, William, Jr., 15 Dec. 1706, Susannah Smart   3 AA-98
Penington, William Drake, 22 Dec. 1777, Mary Hutchison  2 CE-1
Peninton, Henry, Dec. 1708, Elizabeth Drake             3 CE-4
Peninton, John, 3 April 1716, Sarah Beadle              3 CE-7
Peninton, Richard, 4 Sept. 1711, Mary Wheeler           3 CE-6
Peninton, Robert, 13 Oct. 1716, Mary Ryland             3 CE-12
Peninton, William, 14 Sept. 1713, Mary Atkey            3 CE-5
Peninton, William, 2 March 1730/1, Ann Burgin           2 KE-218
Penman, John, 20 Sept. 1750, Margret Bayl               2 BA-201
Penn, Edward, 11 Feb. 1703, Judith Deavour              1 AA-64
Pennell, Caleb, son of John, 26 Oct. 1727, Sarah
   Whitaker, dau. of Mary                               9 SF
Pennick, Thomas, 15 March 1769, Ann Almon               2 BA-258
Pennington, Cesar, 2 July 1730, Rachel Langoe           2 TA-148
Pennington, Henry, Jr., 14 Dec. 1735, Ann Clements,
   widow of Cornelius Clements                          3 CE-20
Peoo, Stephen, 8 Sept. 1726, Sarah Doo                  3 AA-101
   3 AA-102 gives the bride's name as Deo.
Perdue, John, 31 Aug. 1701, Mary Jarvis                 1 AA-248
Perdue, Laban, 11 Feb. 1754, Sarah Allen                2 BA-209
Perdue, Walter, 3 Oct. 1776, Martha Watson              3 BA-172
Perdue, William, 4 Feb. 1747, Rebecca Low               2 BA-194
   2 BA-242 gives year as 1748 and the bride's name
   as Lowe.
Perdy, Henry, 8 Jan. 1700, Ann Sanders                  1 AA-246
Peregoy, Henry, 16 Feb. 1716, Amy Green                 3 BA-147
Peregoy, Joseph, 17 Feb. 1735, Flora Ryder              3 BA-155
Perigo, Nathan, 7 Dec. 1757, Rebecca Evans              3 BA-167
Perigo, Nicholas, 21 Nov. 1776, Eleanor Shermedine      3 BA-669
Perigoe, Henry, 24 Nov. 1745, Providence Corbin         2 BA-240
   2 BA-193 gives date as 14 Jan. 1745.
Perkins, Adam, 23 May 1743, Mary Walters                1 BA-330
Perkins, Daniell, 1 May 1715, Susannah Starton          3 KE-310
Perkins, David, 18 Feb. 1723, Sarah Reding              2 KE-200
Perkins, Elisha, 1 Dec. 1718, Margaret Servil           1 BA-227
Perkins, Isaac, May 1739, Mary Lee                      1 BA-305
Perkins, John, March 1683, Sarah Roatch                 5 SO-399
Perkins, John, 13 Jan. 1745/6, Mary Harris              2 SO-61
```

```
Perkins, Reuben, 5 Nov. 1748, Avarilla Durbin          1 BA-346
Perkins, Richard, Jr., 5 Jan. 1735, Eliz'th Cutchen    1 BA-288
Perkins, William, 3 Feb. 1703/4, Martha Miles          1 BA-200
Perkins, William, 17 June 1777, Susanna Clarke         3 PG-146
Permar, James, 13 Feb. 1737/8, Sarah Young             1 QA-43
Perrey, Edw'd, 10 May 1768, Frances Saunders           2 BA-231
Perrey, John, 15 Nov. 1739, Mary Clough                1 QA-45
Perrigoe, Andrew, Jr., 17 April 1750, Alice Edwards    2 BA-201
Perry, Edward, 12 July 1777, Lurana Clarke             3 PG-106
Perry, Hugh, 12 Jan. 1704, Elizabeth Devenish          3 KE-309
Perry, John, 20 Feb. 1720, Mary Bird                   1 AA-303
Perry, John, 11 July 1727, Eliza Millman               2 PG-4
Perry, John, 25 June 1731, Rebecca Crawley             1 QA-38
Perry, John, 9 Jan. 1735, Priscilla Ray                2 PG-7
Perry, Joseph, 30 Dec. 1756, Mary Wilson               9 AA-247
Perry, Robert, 5 June 1724, Elizabeth Davis            1 AA-99
Perry, William, 12 Dec. 1726, Sarah Maccarty           1 BA-258
Perry, William, 4 Dec. 1751, Elizabellaw Perkins       1 BA-361
Perryman, Roger, 15 July 1742, Martha Armstrong        1 BA-337
Perryman, Wm., 1 March 1735, Susanna Amosson           1 QA-42
Persons, John, 12 Aug. 1744, Catherin Ponder           1 QA-49
Peryman, Roger, 15 April 1728, Mary Burrage            1 CE-331
Peterson, Rozamus, 21 Oct. 1705, Penelope Kimball      1 AA-72
Petters, Edward, 8 Aug. 1715, Catherine Hanning        4 AA-392
Pettibone, Joseph, 19 Dec. 1717, Isabella Wilson       4 AA-403
Pettibone, Philip, 8 Sept. 1743, Anna Stinchcomb       3 AA-108
Petticoat, John, 27 Aug. 1771, Rebecca Boring          2 BA-262
Pettingall, Samuel, 11 April 1733, (wife's name not
   given)                                              1 AA-117
Pettit, Jacob, 5 Aug. 1777, Ann Green                  2 CE-1
Pewtery, James, 24 July 1730, Judith Dowlin            1 AA-110
Pharez, Thomas, 15 Nov. 1722, Sarah Mecoppy            2 TA-105
Phebus, George, 14 Oct. 1678, Ann Streete              5 SO-399
Phelps, Avinton, 23 April 1730, Rachel Muckelduroy     1 BA-251
Phelps, Charles, 19 Dec. 1723, Susanna Stephens        1 AA-97
Phelps, John, 16 Oct. 1718, Susan Meek                 1 AA-287
Phelps, John, 9 Aug. 1730, Sarah Bazill                1 AA-111
Phelps, Walter, Jr., 1 Dec. 1702, Mary Cheney, Jr.     1 AA-64
                                                         & 252
Phelps, Walter, 2 Jan. 1717, Rose Basil                1 AA-280
Phelps, Walter, Jr., 9 Jan. 1727, Mary Bazill          1 AA-106
Phelps, William, 8 Aug. 1706, Elizabeth Cheney         1 AA-72
Phelps, William, 11 Dec. 1718, Rachel (?)              1 AA-288
Phenix, William, 31 Dec. 1702, Bridget Linsey          2 AA-319
Philber, Jno., 11 Aug. 1768, Eliner Wordgworth         2 BA-232
Philips, John, 17 Feb. 1728, Jennet Lasswell           4 AA-431
Philips, Pawl, 17 Aug. 1729, Susana Gray               3 AA-103
Philips, Thomas, 17 Aug. 1756, Mary Lawrence           1 QA-61
Phillips, Bartholomew, 16 July 1696, Mary (?)          2 TA-4
Phillips, Daniel, 2 Nov. 1756, Ann (?)                 1 WI-104
Phillips, David, 1 May 1759, Sarah Swift               1 QA-65
Phillips, Edward, 20 May 1773, Mary Medcalf            2 BA-86
Phillips, George, 11 Jan. 1758, Betty Twilly, widow    1 WI-69
Phillips, Henry, 12 Aug. 1708, Jane Rawlinson          3 KE-310
Phillips, Henry, 3 July 1740, Mary Tinlock or Turlock  2 KE-239
Phillips, Isaac, May 1773, Prudence Sickelmore         2 BA-266
Phillips, James, 27 Sept. 1737, Mrs. Sarah Knight      1 BA-247
Phillips, James, 26 Dec. 1743, Sarah Lamdin            1 QA-48
Phillips, James, 2 Jan. 1746, Leah Henderson           2 SO-158
Phillips, James, 18 March 1762, Mary Acworth           1 WI-94
Phillips, Mr. James, 25 June 1767, Martha Paca, dau.
   of John                                             1 BA-385
   2 BA-230 has same information.
Phillips, Josiah, 23 Nov. 1761, Elizabeth Bennet       1 WI-64
Phillips, Nathan, 18 April 1733, Jane Simcoe           1 CE-331
```

```
Phillips, Nathan, 30 July 1777, Elizabeth Kankey      2 CE-1
Phillips, Paul, 1 July 1731, Sarah Wallas             4 AA-434
Phillips, Richard, 4 Jan. 1733/4, Anne Bennet         1 WI-66
Phillips, Robard, 30 Oct. 1744, Myrtilla Serton       1 QA-49
Phillips, Robard, 31 Dec. 1746, Ann Lambden           1 QA-52
Phillips, Robert, 1 March 1750, Hannah Cross          1 QA-57
Phillips, Roger, 22 Oct. 1672, Dorothy Clarke         5 SO-399
Phillips, Samuel, 19 March 1724, Elizabeth Brooks     1 CE-332
Phillips, Sam'l, 28 Sept. 1749, Solvolitte Bozwell    2 BA-199
Phillips, William, 22 Jan. 1744, Margaret Low         1 WI-65
Phillips, Zephaniah, 8 Jan. 1744, Catherine Scott     1 CH-175
Philpott, Robert, 27 Dec. 1700, Ann Banks             1 AA-56
                                                        & 246
Phillpot, Thomas, July 1686, Mary Goldsmith           5 SO-399
Phinnes, Isaac, 31 July 1722, Jane Spier              4 AA-419
Phipps, John, 28 Dec. 1719, Mary Wittis, widow        3 BA-148
Phipps, John, 30 Nov. 1765, Hannah Randall            9 AA-249
Phipps, Nathaniel, 1771, Susannah Tuckes              2 AA-410
Phipps, Roger, 1771, Artridge Franklin                2 AA-411
Phoebus, George, Jr., 8 Jan. 1727, Mary Hambley       3 SO-4
Phramton, Robert, 29 July 1731, Mary Cockoe           2 TA-150
Piborn, Richard, 11 Nov. 1718, Sarah Morrice          1 AA-288
Pibus, John, 25 July 1776, Eleanor Ward               2 AA-413
Pickerell, James, 8 May 1733, Elizabeth Simmons       2 AA-368
Pickering, Charles, 28 Feb. 1748/9, Mary Carvin       3 TA-72
Pickering, Francis, Jr., 22 July 1740, Mary Stewart   2 TA-169
Pickering, John, 8 March 1759, Sarah Cook             1 QA-65
Picket, William, 21 Nov. 1717, Mary Ruley             4 AA-402
Pickett, Geo., 16 Feb. 1751, Barbary Gorsuch          2 BA-203
Pickett, Heathcote, 26 Jan. 1742, Eliz. Wright        2 BA-125
Pickett, Jno., 3 Oct. 1756, Pemela Dukes              2 BA-214
Pickett, Matthew, 23 Dec. 1711, Cathrine (?)          2 TA-70
Pickett, William, 23 Dec. 1756, Mary Dukes            2 BA-214
Pickett, William, 13 Dec. 1777, Jemima Deaver         9 BA
Pickford, Mark, 27 Sept. 1745, Grace Legg             1 QA-51
Pickrell, Thomas, 15 Oct. 1712, Eliza Marloy          1 PG-276
Pickring, Francis, 18 July 1740, Mary Stewart         3 TA-23
Picot, Daniel, 17 May 1750, Elizabeth Brown           1 CE-292
Pierce, Daniel, 25 June 1722, Eliza Burgess           1 AA-91
                                                        & 313
Pierce, John, 8 Nov. 1723, Sarah Sympson              1 AA-324
Pierce, Thomas, 28 Dec. 1747, Mary Humphries          3 BA-161
Pierce, William, 9 Nov. 1714, Elizabeth Bettson       2 TA-75
Pierce, William, 8 Aug. 1722, Rebecca Love            2 TA-103
Pierpoint, Francis, 2 Oct. 1701, Elizabeth Mitchell   1 AA-57
   1 AA-248 gives bride's name as Elizabeth Michael.
Pierpoint, Francis, son of Charles, 19 day, 11 mo.,
   1737, Sarah Richardson, dau. of Joseph             6 SF
Pierpoint, John, son of Charles and Sydney, 10 day,
   6 mo., 1737, Ann Gassaway, dau. of Nicholas and
   Elizabeth                                          6 SF
Pierson, Symon, 25 July 1715, Sarah Schaw             2 BA-7
Piggot, John, 18 March 1713, Margery Brown            9 SF
Piggot, John, son of John and Margery, 25 Dec. 1737,
   Rachel Reynolds, dau. of Henry                     9 SF
Piggot, John, son of Samuel and Rebeckah, 3 Feb.
   1768, Phebe Harris, dau. of John and Phebe         9 SF
Piggot, Samuel, son of John and Margery, 8 Aug. 1744,
   Rebeckah Bowen                                     9 SF
Pigman, Ignatius, 3 Aug. 1777, Susanna Lamar          1 MO-516
Pike, John M., 1 Sept. 1747, Mary Poteet              2 BA-193
Pike, William, 16 July 1699, Mary Ousmore; both servants
   to Mr. Thomas Larkins                              1 AA-49
Pike, Wm., 9 June 1752, Mary Crabtree                 2 BA-205
Pile, William, 29 April 1723, Eliza Hutchinson        2 PG-3
```

Pilgrim, Amos, 25 June 1730, Rachel MacMahon                      1 BA-273
Pilketon, Richard, 28 Feb. 1775, Anna Hutchings                  1 SM-137
Pilles, Thomas, Sept. 1730, Margrett Finex                       3 BA-149
Pilly, John, 8 July 1736, Mary Wheeley                           3 BA-156
Pindel, John, 1770, Margaret Drury                               2 AA-410
Pindell, John, 6 Nov. 1757, Eleanor Gill                         4 BA-71
Pinder, William, 30 Jan. 1752, Sarah Barratt                    1 QA-58
Pindergist, Luke, 26 Jan. 1768, Rach'l Simmons                  2 BA-231
Pindle, Philip, 3 Aug. 1709, Elizabeth Holland                  1 AA-77
                                                                 & 257
Pine, Francis, 2 Feb. 1669, Mary Vicaris                         1 KE-285
   1 KE-187 gives date as 24 Feb. 1669.
Pine, John, 16 Nov. 1775, Mary Coats                             5 BA-11
Piner, Thomas, 11 Feb. 1706, Rachel Glanvill                    3 KE-310
Pines, Abra., 11 Sept. 1754, Phillis Beven                      2 BA-211
Pines, Charles, Aug. 1741, Eliz. Bays                           2 BA-129
Pinkham, Richard, 26 Nov. 1733, Phillis Noble                   3 BA-151
Pinkston, William, 4 March 1716/7, Martha Nellson               4 AA-398
   4 AA-400 gives date as 4 March 1717.
Pinkstone, William, Oct. 1743, Ann Lumon                        2 BA-149
Piper, John, son of William, 18 Feb. 1748, Ann Piper,
   dau. of Christopher                                          1 WI-75
Piper, John, son of William, 5 May 1758, Agnes
   Finney, dau. of William                                     1 WI-75
Piper, Tobias, 8 Aug. 1676, Mary Empson                        9 SO-401
Pippen, Joseph, 22 Jan. 1746, Margaret Maccoy                  1 QA-52
Pipper, William, 31 May 1730, Christian Murry                  2 KE-216
Pippin, Benjamin, 16 Dec. 1756, Charity Montegue               1 QA-61
Pippin, John, 11 April 1751, Elisabeth Mounticue               1 QA-57
Pitchfork, Thomas, 24 May 1735, Frances Domohoy                2 TA-159
Pitstow, Robert Love, 23 Sept. 1736, Ann Royston               3 BA-155
Pitt, John, 25 Aug. 1680, Sarah Thomas                         8 SF-326
Pitt, John, 6 Nov. 1706, Elizabeth Baynard                     8 SF-434
Pitts, Hillary, 5 Jan. 1776, Easther Powell                    1 WO-28
Pitts, John, 24 Sept. 1722, Catherine Milburn; both
   servants to Thos. Worthington                               4 AA-419
Pitts, John, 6 Feb. 1766, Susanna Bond                         4 BA-73
Pitts, Josia, 7 June 1770, Sarah Barton                        2 BA-260
Platt, Samuel, 12 Feb. 1714, Elizabeth King                    2 TA-75
Pleasants, Robert, son of John, 14 April 1748 (o.s.),
   Mary Webster, dau. of Isaac and Margaret                    9 SF
Pleasants, Robert, Jr., son of Thomas and Mary,
   24 day, 5 mo., 1759, Susannah Webster, dau. of
   Isaac and Margaret                                          9 SF
Pleasants, Robert, son of John, of Va., 7 day, 2 mo.,
   1760, Mary, widow of Henry Hill and dau. of Philip
   Thomas                                                      6 SF
Pleasants, Thomas, of Goochland Co., Va., 2 day, 6
   mo., 1761, Elizabeth Brookes, dau. of James                6 SF
Plowins, William, 8 Dec. 1777, Rachel Dawson                   1 CR-10
Plowman, John, 3 May 1736, Sarah Chambers                      3 BA-155
Plummer, Jerome, 7 June 1737, Margaret Child, Jr.              6 SF
Plummer, Jerom, 11 day, 12 mo., 1741/2, Mary Harris            6 SF
Plummer, John, son of Thomas, 18 day, 3 mo., 1736,
   Rachel Miles, dau. of Thomas                                6 SF
Plummer, Jno., 25 day, 12 mo., 1772, Johannah Hopkins,
   dau. of Gerard                                              6 SF
Plummer, John, 23 July 1777, Sarah Phillips                    1 CR-28
Plummer, Sam'l, son of Thomas and Elizabeth, 4 day,
   1 mo., 1723/4, Sarah Miles, dau. of Thomas                 6 SF
Plummer, Samuel, son of Thomas and Elizabeth, 4
   March 1723/4, at Indian Spring, Meeting, Sarah Miles,
   dau. of Thomas and Ruth                                     3 SF
Plummer, Thos., Jr., 6 Feb. 1715, Sarah Wilson                 2 PG-1
Plummer, Thomas, son of Robert, 15 day, 11 mo., 1758,
   Phebe Cook, dau. of John                                    9 SF

Plummer, Thomas, son of Samuel and Sarah, 29 day, 4
  mo., 1761, Eleanor Walker Poultney, widow of John
  Poultney and dau. of Wm. and Sarah Walker           3 SF
Plummer, Yates, 23 day, 12 mo., 1768, Artridge Waters,
  dau. of Samuel                                      6 SF
Plunket, James, 10 Feb. 1742/3, Eliza James           2 TA-173
  3 TA-41 gives date of license as 15 Dec. 1742.
Pocock, Dan'l, Jr., 26 June 1751, Sarah Jones         2 BA-203
Pocock, James, 20 Sept. 1756, Jemima Barton           2 BA-214
Pocock, John, 3 Nov. 1757, Ruth Gott                  2 BA-216
Poess, Rd. sister (sic), 4 Sept. 1763, Johannah
  Thomas                                              2 BA-225
Pogue, Joseph, 30 July 1752, Sarah Farmer             1 BA-375
Poily, Richard, 7 Feb. 1771, Susan Hayden             1 SM-135
Points, John, 27 Aug. 1777, Jean Slover               1 WA-533
Polk, Daniel, 1775, Margaret Nutter White             1 CR
Polk, Zephaniah, 1775, Lucretia Cawsey                1 CR
Pollard, William, 2 Oct. 1752, Rebecca Hayes          2 BA-206
Pollard, William, 13 Oct. 1753, Eliz. Smith           2 BA-209
Pollard, William, 19 May 1755, Mary Hildebrand        2 BA-212
Pollet, William, 1753, Elizabeth Hill                 2 BA-242
Pologue, Daniel, 25 Jan. 1737, Jane Antil             1 BA-300
Polson, Francis, 1748, Mary Dennick                   2 BA-243
Pond, John, 13 Nov. 1706, Margaret Powel              2 AA-330
Ponder, Jno., 27 Dec. 1736, Mary Newnam               1 QA-42
Ponder, Morgin, 14 Sept. 1743, Ann Hines              1 QA-48
Ponder, William, 15 July 1740, Judith Wyat            1 QA-46
Pontaney, William, 29 Sept. 1745, Sarah Wooden        3 BA-157
Pooer, Robert, 27 June 1710, Anne Lewis               1 PG-268
Pool, Jno., 25 May 1736, Mary Pelly                   1 QA-42
Pool, Richard, 12 Aug. 1703, Johannah Duval           1 AA-255
Poole, Basil, 24 Nov. 1724, Loys Shipley              4 AA-424
Poole, John Curry, 26 Sept. 1742, Sarah Thompson      2 TA-173
Poole, Richard, 12 Aug. 1703, Johanna Duvall          1 AA-64
Poole, Richard, 24 Feb. 1730, Mary Phelps             1 AA-111
Poole, Thomas, 27 June 1735, Sarah Irons              1 QA-41
Pooley, Matthias, 11 Dec. 1735, Sarah Jerrom          3 KE-311
Pooley, Nicholas, 9 Jan. 1709, Sarah Rynolds          3 CE-7
Poor, James, 1747, Sarah Elliot                       2 BA-242
Poor, John, 10 Aug. 1707, Mary Haggins                3 KE-310
Poor, Nicho's, 6 Jan. 1753, Eliz. Erickson            2 BA-207
Pope, Thos., 23 Feb. 1711, Elizabeth·Partridge        3 CE-4
Pope, William, Aug. (?), Martha Glanvill              3 KE-310
Popes, Mallakey, 18 Feb. 1758, Rozina Housten         2 BA-217
Porter, Aaron, 19 Aug. 1740, Jane MacKenny            1 BA-317
Porter, Alexander, 5 Dec. 1759, Ann Beachamp          2 SO-64
Porter, Benjamin, son of Robert and Elizabeth, 31
  Dec. 1775, Anne Money, dau. of John and Rachel      3 CE-28
Porter, James, 21 Jan. 1744/5, Anne Rippen            3 TA-51
Porter, James, Oct. 1747, Mary Bonyon                 1 QA-53
Porter, James, c.Aug. 1775, Sophia Parmare            1 CR-6
Porter, John, 25 Jan. 1688, Elizabeth Gray            5 SO-399
Porter, John, Jr., 7 Feb. 1740/1, Susanna Davis       3 TA-28
Porter, John, 1 April 1756, Margret Baird             2 SO-62
Porter, John, 3 Oct. 1774, Lydia Kinnemont            1 CR
Porter, Joseph, of Cecil Co., 10 day, 3 mo., 1699,
  Susanna Wetherill, of Cecil Co.                     2 KE-42
  1 SF has same information.
Porter, Matthew, 8 Jan. 1752, Mary Virdian            2 SO-64
Porter, Rich'd, Jr., 21 May 1741, Sarah Williamson    1 QA-47
Porter, Samuel, 12 July 1747, Katherine Herring       2 BA-241
Porter, Samuel, 6 June 1748, Catherine Herring        2 BA-197
Potee, John, 17 June 1755, Eliz. Ryley                2 BA-212
Potee, Lewes, 2 Dec. 1754, Sarah Meadows              2 BA-211
Potee, Thomas, 22 March 1741, Ann Potee               2 BA-141

Poteet, James, 20 Sept. 1748, Eliz. Crabtree            2 BA-197
Poteet, Jno., 20 April 1762, Ann M'Comas               2 BA-223
Poteet, Lewis, 12 June 1722, Catherine Green           2 BA-19
Poteet, Thos., 24 Dec. 1761, Eliz. Taylor              2 BA-223
Poteet, William, 12 June 1733, Jane Stewart            1 BA-268
Potelt, Peircey, 12 Oct. 1743, Jemima Hitchcock        2 BA-126
Potter, Henry, 26 Sept. 1750, Mary Wood                2 SO-61
Potter, Mr. Martin, 28 Aug. 1738,Mrs. Susanna Jonson   2 KE-234
Potter, Thomas, 2 May 1751, Sarah Cohoon               2 SO-63
Potter, Thomas Wood, 20 Jan. 1757, Sabrow Gunby        2 SO-63
Pottinger, Robert, 2 Dec. 1718, Ann Evans              2 PG-2
Pottinger, Samuel, 11 July 1717, Eliza Tyler, dau. of
  Robert                                               2 PG-2
Potts, (?), 4 June 1704, Martha Hanson                 3 KE-309
Poulson, Cornelius, 23 Dec. 1720, Ann Emson            1 BA-226
Poulson, Francis, 13 Feb. 1749, Mary Dennock           2 BA-200
Poulson, John, 8 April 1751, Eliz. Stewart             2 BA-203
Poulson, Joseph, 1739, Frances Allen                   2 BA-127
Poultney, Anthony, son of John and Eleanor, 22 day,
  5 mo., 1777, Susanna Plummer, dau. of Samuel and
  Sarah                                                3 SF
Pound, Jno., 20 July 1707, Elizabeth Francis; negroes
  belonging to Mr. Taylor and Mr. Stockett             1 AA-33
Povey, Benj'n, 16 June 1745, Mary Fitzgarrold          1 QA-50
Powel, Benjamin, 24 day, 1 mo., 1755, Mary Pierpoint   4 SF-49
Powel, Britain, 14 Jan. 1762, Sarah Long               2 SO-157
Powel, George, 6 Sept. 1744, Ann Ford                  1 QA-49
Powel, James, 27 June 1709, Mary Sanders               2 TA-61
Powel, John, 21 July 1720, Elisabeth Pierce            1 AA-300
Powel, John, 6 March 1743, Amy Andrews                 1 QA-49
Powel, Samuel, 3 Sept. 1746, Rachel Peary              1 WO-12
Powell, Daniel, 20 Sept. 1694, Susanna Pitt            8 SF-364
Powell, Daniel, 6 Jan. 1734, Mary Sherwood             8 SF-68
Powell, Howell, Jr., 6 Oct. 1698, Joanna Pryer         8 SF-392
Powell, Howell, Jr., 2 day, 2 mo., 1704, Esther
  Bartlett                                             8 SF-26
Powell, Howell, 2 Oct. 1718, Sarah Edmondson           2 TA-88
Powell, Howell, 2 Oct. 1718, Sarah Edmondson           8 SF-24
Powell, James, 21 Sept. 1729, Hannah Parratt           8 SF-49
Powell, John, 27 April 1703, Mary Dunstan              1 AA-254
Powell, Jno., 27 April 1703, Mary Dunstone             1 AA-64
Powell, John, 21 April 1707, Elizabeth Purner          4 AA-372
Powell, John, 14 Jan. 1722, Mary Haivil                1 AA-94
Powell, John, 17 Jan. 1722, Mary Carvill               1 AA-317
Powell, John, Sept. 1725, Philis Temple                2 BA-38
Powell, John, Jr., 8 Oct. 1731, Mary Knewstub, dau.
  of Robert Knewstub                                   2 PG-5
Powell, John, 26 April 1737, Rebecah Giles             1 WI-3
Powell, John, 26 May 1748, Mabil Smith                 1 QA-54
Powell, Rich'd, Oct. 1713, Dorothy Jones               2 AA-350
Powell, Richard, 2 Jan. 1723, Mary Croley              1 AA-98
Powell, Thomas, 10 Oct. 1737, Lucey Sherwood           2 TA-161
Powell, Thos., 15 Dec. 1740, Mary Hawk                 1 QA-46
Powell, Thomas, 15 Jan. 1741, Mary Needles             2 TA-174
Powell, Thomas, Nov. 1741, (Margaret) Needles          3 TA-33
Powell, Thos., 4 Jan. 1745/6, Mary Dudley              3 TA-56
Powell, Thos., Jan. 1750/1, Mary Ann Geddins           3 TA-81
Powell, William, 15 Dec. 1709, Alice Archur            2 AA-339
Power, Robert, 5 Oct. 1752, Mary Barker                1 PG-293
Poyer, Robert, 4 March 1687, Rose Bayley               5 SO-399
Prabal, Jacob, 2 Jan. 1733/4, Elizabeth Phillips       3 CE-17
Prat, Henry, 18 Dec. 1735, Ruth Bailey                 1 QA-41
Prather, Allen, 10 Oct. 1738, Jane Prather             9 AA-246
Prather, Baruch, 16 Nov. 1775, Sarah Higgins           2 FR-283
Prather, John Smith, 17 Feb. 1725/6, Elizabeth Nutwell 2 PG-4

```
Pratt, George, 2 July 1690, Mary Parratt              8 SF-349
Pratt, George, 19 Oct. 1692, Elizabeth Parratt, relict
  of Geo. Parratt                                     8 SF-351
Pratt, George, 12 May 1700, Sarah Broadway            8 SF-417
Pratt, Isaiah, 9 Nov. 1709, Hannah Clark              8 SF-446
Pratt, John, 28 July 1724, Ellinor Williams           2 PG-3
Pratt, Thomas, 2 Feb. 1755, Eleanor Magruder          2 PG-7
Prentice, William, 6 April 1678, Elizabeth Johnson    5 SO-399
Presbury, Goldsmith, 10 June 1756, Eliz. Tolley       2 BA-213
Presbury, James, 26 Feb. 1708, Martha Goldsmith       1 BA-207
Presbury, Joseph, 11 July 1723, Eleanor Carlisle      2 BA-20
Presbury, Joseph, 11 Jan. 1749, Sarah Pycraft         2 BA-200
Presbury, Thomas, 29 Dec. 1748, Ann Woodward          3 BA-162
Presbury, Thos., Dec. 1749, Ann Woodard               2 BA-202
Presbury, Wm., 16 Jan. 1757, Clemency Hughs           2 BA-214
Presbury, William, 3 Sept. 1771, Cordelia Debruler    2 BA-262
Presbury, William Robinson, 23 Feb. 1764, Martha Hall,
  dau. of Capt. John Hall of Cran'y                   1 BA-380
Presgraves, George, 30 Sept. 1750, Mary Holbrook      3 BA-164
Presgrove, George, 1 Jan. 1744, Hannah Nicholas       2 BA-140
Prestgrave, Jeremiah, 28 Sept. 1729, Sarah Kelley     1 AA-109
Preston, Barnett, 28 Dec. 1749, Sarah Ruff            2 BA-200
Preston, Bernard, 28 Dec. 1749, Sarah Ruff            1 BA-366
Preston, Daniel, 5 Jan. 1737, Ann Grafton             1 BA-290
Preston, Daniel, May 1772, Ann Rigdon                 2 BA-264
Preston, James, Oct. 1713, Elizabeth Pritchard        2 BA-32
Preston, James, 17 July 1726, Avarilla Nowell         2 BA-32
Preston, James, 15 May 1733, Sarah Putteet            1 BA-268
Preston, James, 30 March 1749, Clemency Bond          2 BA-198
Preston, James, Jr., 11 May 1756, Mary Bond           2 BA-49
Preston, Jas., Jr., 13 May 1762, Ann Lusby            2 BA-223
Preston, John, 29 Aug. 1743, Mary Garnet              1 BA-337
Preston, John, 30 March 1746, Mary Mayis              1 QA-52
Preston, John, 23 July 1747, Isabela Low              1 QA-53
Preston, John, 16 Aug. 1752, Elizabeth Brussells      1 QA-59
Preston, Martin, 25 Nov. 1770, Rebecca Scott          2 BA-261
Preston, Thomas, 9 Dec. 1721, Elizabeth Deaver        2 BA-20
Preston, William, 24 Jan. 1710, (wife's name not given) 2 AA-342
Pretty, William, 15 Jan. 1739, Sarah Praither         9 AA-246
Price, Alexander, 29 Jan. 1680, Rebecca Thomas, dau.
  of Alexander                                        5 SO-399
Price, Andrew, June 1725, Elizabeth Perry             3 CE-12
Price, Aquila, son of John and Rebecca, 27 day, 2
  mo., 1772, Anne Griffith, dau. of Isaac and Anne    4 SF-260
Price, Benjamin, 22 June 1730, Elizabeth Hewett       3 BA-150
Price, David, 31 Dec. 1715, Katherine fflin           3 CE-9
Price, David, 13 April 1738, Martha Roe               1 QA-44
Price, David, 18 Nov. 1755, Mary Ann Elliott          2 BA-212
Price, Edward, 29 Nov. 1698, Elizabeth Lun            2 AA-372
Price, James, 11 Aug. 1736, Sarah Reading             2 KE-226
Price, James, 18 Dec. 1740, Sarah Rickets, dau. of
  John Thomas Rickets                                 3 CE-22
Price, James, April 1770, Elinor Carroll              2 BA-260
Price, John, 23 Aug. 1702, Alce (?)                   2 TA-27
Price, John, Nov. 1714, Mary Davis                    3 CE-6
Price, John, 9 Nov. 1721, Hannah Brian                1 AA-308
Price, John, 19 Sept. 1723, Rebecca Pierce            2 TA-105
Price, John, 29 Dec. 1724, Edith Brown                2 TA-111
Price, John, 30 Sept. 1730, Elis'th Clark             1 QA-36
Price, John, 13 April 1737, Elizabeth Buckingham      2 TA-162
Price, John, Jr., 26 day, 6 mo., 1748, Mary Parrish   4 SF
Price, John, son of John, 26 day, 1 mo., 1753,
  Urith Cole                                          4 SF
Price, Joseph, 19 Nov. 1734, Jane Barrett, widow
  of Philip Barrett                                   3 CE-25
```

Price, Mordecai, of Balto. Co., 28 day, 2 mo., 1724,
   Elizabeth White, dau. of Guy and Elizabeth            6 SF
Price, Mordecia, son of John, 30 day, 8 mo., 1754,
   Mary Hyatt                                             4 SF-47
Price, Mordecai, son of Mordecai and Elizabeth,
   27 day, 12 mo., 1759, Rachel Moore, dau. of Walter
   and Anne                                               4 SF
Price, Mordecai, son of John and Rebecca, 1 day, 1 mo.,
   1772, Tabitha Tipton, dau. of William and Angeline     4 SF-258
Price, Richard, 27 July 1726, Sarah Clark                  3 CE-12
Price, Robert, 31 Dec. 1734, Eliz. Shepard                 2 BA-90
Price, Robert, 18 Sept. 1739, Elizabeth Miles              2 BA-127
Price, Samuel, son of Mordecai and Elizabeth, 28 day,
   12 mo., 1760, Ann Moore, dau. of Walter and Anne       4 SF-245
Price, Step'n, 20 April 1749, Rebecca Hicks                2 BA-198
Price, Thomas, of Kent Island, 21 April 1720, Ann
   Griffith                                               4 AA-411
Price, Thomas, 29 Jan. 1726, Martha Spencer                1 BA-247
Price, Thomas, 1 July 1732, Katurah Merryman               3 BA-151
Price, Thomas, 4 May 1743, Sarah Cross                     1 BA-331
Price, Thomas, 29 Oct. 1743, Martha Robinson               3 TA-45
Price, Thomas, 1749, Lyddia Lane                           3 TA-75
Price, Thomas, 22 Dec. 1756, Patience Kibble               1 WI-48
Price, Thomas, 11 June 1772, Mary Gatt                     2 BA-264
Price, Timothy, 29 Oct. 1774, Ann Dudley                   1 CR
Price, Vincent, 21 Dec. 1740, Africa Lane                  2 TA-170
Price, Vissey, 19 Oct. 1769, Sim. Barton                   2 BA-259
Price, William, 7 July 1707, Kathrin MacCandrick,
   widow                                                  3 CE-6
Price, William, 1 Aug. 1717, Sarah Wallis                  3 CE-8
Price, William, 7 Dec. 1729, Marg'tt Macom                 4 AA-432
Price, William, Jr., 12 Feb. 1737/8, Mary Roberts,
   dau. of John                                           3 CE-21
Price, William, 22 Nov. 1756, Mary Seymore                 1 QA-61
Price, William, 19 May 1771, Mary Noland                   2 BA-262
Price, William, 5 Nov. 1774, Mary Birkham                  1 CR
Price, William Archer, 7 Nov. 1758, Eliza Baker            1 QA-64
Prichard, Benjamin, 1 Sept. 1732, Mary Green               1 AA-114
Prichard, David, 14 Feb. 1750, Mary Heningman              1 WI-71
Prichard, John, 1 Oct. 1734, Jane Mullican                 2 TA-157
Prichard, Peter, 12 Oct. 1737, Elizabeth Abbott            2 TA-161
Prichitt, Samuell, 13 July 1727, Ane Caresey               2 TA-115
Prickett, Geo., 11 Feb. 1762, Mary Johnson                 2 BA-223
Prickett, Joseph, 21 May 1757, Sarah Talbott               2 BA-215
Prickett, Josiah, 10 Jan. 1764, Mary Elliott               2 BA-226
Pride, Abel, 17 June 1704, Margret (?)                     2 TA-40
Priestman, George, 31 July 1777, Frances Stokes            10 BA-68
Prigg, William, 27 Jan. 1745, Jane Carson                  2 BA-193
Prigg, William, 26 Jan. 1746, Jean Carsan                  2 BA-240
Prigg, William, 21 Nov. 1749, Martha Morgan                1 BA-364
Prigg, Wm., 22 Nov. 1749, Martha Morgan                    2 BA-199
Prim, Richard, 14 Aug. 1677, Alce Wilson                   9 SO-402
Primon, Peter, 7 Nov. 1767, Magd. Forsch                   4 FR-1159
Primrose, Archibald, 16 Feb. 1728, Prudence Morgan         1 QA-36
Primrose, Archibald, 27 July 1755, Sarah Borows            1 QA-59
Primrose, George, 10 Oct. 1725, Martha Woodall             3 KE-311
Primrose, George, 18 Nov. 1756, Hannah Hackett             1 QA-61
Primrose, John, 16 July 1751, Elisabeth Whitington         1 QA-58
Primrose, Violate (sic), 39 Jan. 1747, Sara Hart           1 QA-54
Primrose, Violet (sic), 28 Dec. 1737, Margaret
   Woodward                                               1 QA-43
Primrose, William, 15 March 1743, Bridgit Nevil            1 QA-49
Prine, James, 20 May 1773, Mary Stewart                    2 BA-266
Prine Simon, 3 Jan. 1768, Hannah Miles                     2 BA-231
Prine, William, Nov. 1771, Sophia Coleback                 2 BA-263

```
Pring, James, 1753, Rachel Riset                         2 BA-242
Print, John, 2 Jan. 1721, Elizabeth Helsby               2 TA-98
Prior, Randul, 23 Jan. 1759, Easter Cottingham           2 SO-65
Prise, John, 21 Jan. 1706, Mary Wroth                    3 KE-309
Prise, John, 14 Nov. 1710, Margaret Huebanks             2 TA-68
Prise, William, 8 April 1707, Mary Hodgess               3 KE-310
Prise, William, Jr., 1723, Anne Browning                 3 CE-12
Prisk, Morrice, 8 Sept. 1703, Mary Welch                 2 TA-37
Prisly, William, 22 Nov. 1740, Eliza Matthews            3 TA-26
Pritchard, Charles, 27 Nov. 1729, Sarah Neal             2 TA-121
Pritchard, James, 1 May 1735, Elizabeth Durbin           1 BA-283
Pritchard, James, 8 July 1768, Elizabeth Carr, dau.
    of Walter and Elizabeth                              1 CE-318
Pritchard, Obediah, 7 Feb. 1733, Eliz'th Litten          1 BA-269
Pritchard, Samuel, 13 July 1735, Isabella Cotrall        1 BA-283
Pritchett, John, son of Michael, born in Herburn
    Parish, Staffordshire, 2 March 1701, Eliza Bener,
    born in Sepney Parish, in Middlesex                  1 PG-259
Procter, Jonathan, 30 July 1772, Yorinth Pringion        2 BA-265
Procter, Joseph, 13 Feb. 1776, Ruth Cheney               2 AA-412
Proctor, John, 26 June 1777, Martha Smillet             10 BA-68
Proctor, William, 12 April 1726, Jane Partridge          2 PG-4
Pronce, George, 1 Aug. 1724, Mary Loveday                2 TA-110
    2 TA-190 gives date as 1 Oct. 1724.
Pronce, George, 22 April 1731, Jane Harding              2 TA-191
Pronce, George, 24 Dec. 1741, Marg't Miller              2 TA-175
Prosser, Charles, 1753, Margaret Simkine                 2 BA-242
    2 BA-208 gives date as 27 Sept. 1753, and the
    bride's name as Margrett Synkins.
Protharo, William, 29 Oct. 1746, Rachal Davis            1 QA-52
Protser, Charles, 20 Nov. 1738, Mary Jarves              2 BA-100
Protzman, Jacob, son of Lorenz and Maria Elizabeth
    (Hains), 10 May 1768, Johanna Leinbach, dau. of
    Frederick and Elizabeth                              5 FR-91
Prout, John, Sept. 1674, Mary Wilkinson                  5 SO-399
Prout, Joseph, 25 Feb. 1730, Anna Coward                 2 TA-150
Prynne, Peter, 13 Nov. 1760, Hannah Amoss                2 BA-220
Pryor, John, 24 Dec. 17-(?), Sarah Clark                 3 KE-310
Puckham, John, and Indian, 25 Feb. 1682, Jone John-
    son, a negro                                         5 SO-399
Pugh, John, son of John and Jane, 7 Oct. 1742, Sarah
    Littler, dau. of Samuel and Rachel                   9 SF
Pugh, John, son of John and Jane, 1 June 1769, Hannah
    Bennett, dau. of William and Catherine               9 SF
Pugh, John, son of William and Mary, 9 May 1771,
    Rachel Barrett, dau. of Thomas and Hannah            9 SF
Pugh, John, 18 July 1773, Mary Owen                      5 BA-11
Pugh, Joshua, son of John and Sarah, 19 Dec. 1765,
    Hannah Chandler, dau. of Jacob and Martha            9 SF
Pugh, Merriday, 27 Aug. 1733, Elizabeth Acres            2 TA-153
Pugh, William, son of John and Jane, 8 April 1742,
    Mary Brown, dau. of Messer and Jane                  9 SF
Pugh, William, son of John and Jane, 20 April 1758,
    Patience Brown Casner, widow of Jacob Casner and
    dau. of Daniel Brown                                 9 SF
Pumphrey, Timothy, 30 June 1730, Mary Peirce             4 AA-432
Punney, Thomas, 15 June 1739, Persilla Neadels           1 QA-45
Purdew, John, 13 Aug. 1701, Mary Jarvis, widow           1 AA-57
Purdy, Edmond, 13 Jan. 1755, Elizabeth Hunter            1 AA-135
Purdy, Henry, 8 Jan. 1700, Anne Saunders                 1 AA-57
                                                         & 246
Purdy, John, 30 Nov. 1704, Sarah Seamour                 1 AA-65
Purdy, William, 30 Aug. 1711, Anne Mackelfresh           1 AA-78
Purdy, William, 2 June 1729, Eliza Bennett               1 AA-108
Purere, William, 16 Jan. 1772, Eliz. Perdere             2 BA-263
```

Purkins, John, 27 Nov. 1772, Rachel Long                    2 SO-158
Purnall, Rich'd, Jr., 16 April 1751, Mary Pickering         2 AA-390
Purnall, Thomas, Jr., 27 June 1745, Susannah Vickers        3 TA-53
Purviance, Samuel, 18 April 1776, Catherine Stewart         5 BA-11
Pusey, David, 16 May 1777, Rachel Lankford                  2 SO-65
Pusey, George, son of John and Catherine of Penna.,
  7 day, 9 mo., 1769, Sarah Cox, dau. of William and
  Mary                                                      7 SF-20
Putmore, Benjamin, 25 Nov. 1777, Elizabeth Moles            7 AA-2
Puttee, Peter, 11 Feb. 1773, Eliz. Hughes                   2 BA-265
Puzey, John, 13 Feb. 1763, Nelley Otwell                    2 SO-157
Pybus, John, 3 Feb. 1729, Isabella Perry                    1 AA-110
Pycraft, Thomas, 5 Feb. 1731, Sarah Preston, widow          2 BA-40
  1 BA-254 gives date as 6 Feb. 1730.
Pye, Edward, 25 Feb. 1735, Sarah Queen                      1 PG-278
Pyle, Moses, son of John and Lydia, 29 day, 2 mo.
  (O.S.), 1736, Mary Darlington, dau. of Abraham and
  Elizabeth                                                 9 SF
Pyle, Moses, son of John and Lydia, 9 Dec. 1741,
  Mary Cook, dau. of John and Eleanor                       9 SF
Queen, Samuel, 17 Feb. 1723, Sarah Edelen                   1 PG-277
Quelling, Clement, 4 Jan. 1747, Sus. Miller                 1 QA-54
Quillen, Joseph, 9 Nov. 1735, Elizabeth Locham              1 WO-3
Quilline, Teague, 25 Feb. 1741/2, Mary Hering               1 QA-47
Quinley, Jas., 26 May 1761, Sarah Garritt                   2 BA-222
Quinny, Selathyell, 5 Aug. 1715, Elizabeth Jobson           4 AA-392
Quinton, Walter, 18 Nov. 1703, Alice Meglowin               2 TA-37
Rabbits, William, Feb. 1714/5, Rebeckah Morgan              4 AA-392
Rabling, John, 24 April 1728, Hannah Clark                  1 AA-147
Rabling, Joseph, 9 Nov. 1731, Mary Russell                  1 AA-113
Raddish, Huron, 10 Oct. 1753, Elizabeth Johnson,
  widow                                                     2 BA-45
Radford, Walter, 26 Sept. 1745, Mary Webb                   1 QA-51
Radford, William, 27 Dec. 1772, Jane Jones                  2 BA-265
Raey, James, of Annan, Co. Annandale, Scot., 11 June
  1761, Ellinor Stevens                                     1 WI-56
Raffe, Edward, 16 Nov. 1705, Usley Veale                    3 KE-313
Rage, John, Jr., 25 Dec. 1757, Eliza Primrose               1 QA-63
Ragen, Richard, 15 Aug. 1741, Lidia Golt                    3 TA-32
Ragless, James, 5 May 1702, Elizabeth (?)                   2 TA-25
Ragon, Daniel, 26 Dec. 1732, Sarah Lewis                    3 BA-150
Ragon, Timothy, 24 Nov. 1703, Mary Lary                     3 AA-96
Railey, Charles, 26 Nov. 1732, Jane Honey                   1 QA-39
Railey, John, 16 Nov. 1731, Patience Benton                 1 QA-38
Railey, William, 17 Sept. 1759, Margret Rhodes              2 BA-219
Raiman, Michael, 24 Nov. 1744, Sarah Ackland                2 KE-254
Raimon, John, 15 Feb. 1712, Susanna Duer                    4 AA-380
Rainey, Peter, June 1742, Mary Fairbanks                    3 TA-38
Rainsford, George, 21 Aug. 1757, Cath'n McCarty             1 QA-62
Raisin, Thomas, 30 Jan. 1713, Mary Warner                   3 KE-315
Rakestraw, Richard, 23 Sept. 1705, Elizabeth Ward           1 AA-65
Raley, Charles, 1 Jan. 1740/1, Damsin Hines                 1 QA-46
Ramage, Adam, 27 May 1762, Sus'h Horner                     2 BA-223
Ramsay, John, merchant, 11 April 1737, Mrs. Sarah
  Smith, an heiress                                         4 AA-438
Ramsden, George, 3 March 1722, Jane Knocker                 1 AA-95
Ramsey, James, 3 Jan. 1733, Elizabeth Milam                 3 BA-151
Ramsey, William, 21 Dec. 1730, Eliz'th Dau                  1 BA-262
Randal, Richard, 30 July 1776, Frances Stevens              2 AA-413
Randall, Roger, 26 Dec. 1742, Rachel Stevens                3 BA-156
Randall, William, 27 Aug. 1728, Catherine Lewis             1 AA-107
Randall, William, 15 Jan. 1758, Constant Cockey             4 BA-71
Rankin, George, born in Eng., 25 Feb. 1771, Mary
  Bull, dau. of Constantine Bull                            3 BA-173
Rantin, William, 7 Aug. 1709, Elizabeth Smith               3 AA-98

| | |
|---|---|
| Rapp, Jacob, 21 June 1768, Mary Barb. Brengel | 4 FR-1162 |
| Rasberry, Thomas, 16 Oct. 1700, Anne Lambeth | 1 AA-56 |
| | & 245 |
| Ratcliff, Charles, 7 Oct. 1777, Elizabeth Lybrant | 7 AA-2 |
| Ratcliff, James, 12 Jan. 1720, Sarah Warner | 8 SF-28 |
| Ratcliffe, Richard, 16 Feb. 1750, Mary Newton | 1 QA-57 |
| Ratcliffe, William, 3 June 1759, Susanna Curtis | 1 QA-65 |
| Ratclift, Richard, 13 May 1691, Mary Caterne | 8 SF-354 |
| Rattenbury, John, 3 Nov. 1745, Margret Jones | 3 BA-158 |
| Rau, Johannes, 30 July 1769, Catherine Hafner, | 3 FR-105 |
| Ravencroft, Benjamin, 21 Sept. 1722, Mary (?) | 2 TA-105 |
| Rawles, James, 29 March 1752, Sarah Butler | 1 AA-132 |
| Rawley, James, 15 Aug. 1685, Jane Wilson | 5 SO-399 |
| Rawlings, Aaron, 14 Dec. 1725, Susanna Beard | 1 AA-101 |
| Rawlings, Francis, 21 July 1772, Sarah Hall | 3 AA-113 |
| Rawlings, Jonathan, 28 March 1741, Elizabeth Watkins | 9 AA-247 |
| Rawlings, Loyd, 12 Dec. 1776, Elizabeth Brothers | 3 BA-670 |
| Rawlings, Richard, 13 Jan. 1708/9, Deborah Pinch | 1 AA-76 |
| Rawlings, William, 28 April 1734, Elizabeth Green | 3 BA-151 |
| Rawlins, Daniel, 12 July 1716, Mary Rumney | 1 AA-273 |
| Rawlins, John, 13 Jan. 1712, Eleanor Ridgly | 1 AA-272 |
| Rawlins, Joseph, 6 Jan. 1708, Jane Mitchell | 3 KE-313 |
| Rawlins, William, 28 April 1735, Elizabeth Green | 3 BA-154 |
| Ray, Nicholas, 7 (?) 1769, Susanna Shackels | 2 AA-409 |
| Ray, Thomas, 20 Jan. 1745/6, Sarah Edmondson | 3 TA-56 |
| Rayner, Peter, 14 Feb. 1754, Mary Perren | 2 BA-209 |
| Rea, John, chyrurgeon, 8 Aug. 1699, Anna Mary Powell, widow | 2 AA-297 |
| Read, Alexander, 27 Nov. 1777, Rebecca Stevens | 1 MO-520 |
| Read, Edward, request to pub. banns dated 15 Sept. 1771, Susanah Shelley | 7 BA(1) |
| Read, John, 12 April 1757, Eliza Jackson | 1 BA-355 |
| Read, Joseph, 28 March 1774, Agnes Miller | 6 BA(1) |
| Read, Will, 4 April 1671, Hellener Hurley | 1 TA-602 |
| Read, William, 10 May 1752, Sarah Mallone | 1 WI-73 |
| Reading, Rich'd, 31 March 1746, Mary Ann Powel | 1 QA-52 |
| Reading, Samuell, 22 Nov. 1733, Ann Reed | 3 KE-319 |
| Reading, Thomas, 11 Dec. 1705, the widow Gittings | 4 AA-390 |
| Reading, William, 14 Sept. 1704, Ann Rogers | 3 KE-313 |
| Readus, James, 15 Dec. 1741, Catherine Parsons, dau. of William | 3 CE-23 |
| Ready, Bryan, 12 Oct. 1735, Katherine Carr | 1 WI-10 |
| Reagan, John, 21 Jan. 1753, Mary Morrice | 3 BA-151 |
| Reams, Herod, 15 June 1746, Eliza Porter | 3 TA-59 |
| Reardon, James, 7 Aug. 1777, Mary Sutton | 1 HA-200 |
| Reardon, John, 24 Feb. 1733, Ann Whitehead | 3 KE-319 |
| Reasin, Mathew, 27 Dec. 1754, Mary Dickson | 1 BA-360 |
| Reaven, Luke, 20 Aug. 1765, Ann Rigbie | 2 BA-228 |
| Reaves, John, 30 Nov. 1707, Sarah Rawlins | 2 AA-333 |
| Reaves, William, (date not given), Martha Stevens | 2 BA-249 |
| Reber, Christopher, 10 Sept. 1762, Catherine Mack | 4 FR-1162 |
| Rechester, Robert, 1 Jan. 1698, Mary Booker, relict of Thomas Booker | 8 SF-395 |
| Records, Lemee, 9 April 1762, Sophia Byrd | 1 WI-110 |
| Redchester, Jeremiah, 23 July 1743, Eliz'th Baron | 2 TA-196 |
| Reddell, John, 23 April 1760, Eleanor Daugherty | 1 BA-366 |
| Redgrave, William, 11 July 1751, Elis'th Manson | 1 QA-57 |
| Redick, Robert, Aug. 1730, Catherine Eliason | 3 CE-15 |
| Redien, Claudius, 12 Sept. 1756, Elinor Arling | 1 QA-61 |
| Redish, Joseph, 21 Sept. 1741, Marg't Holly | 3 TA-33 |
| Redman, Christopher, 3 June 1737, Ann Bell | 1 BA-296 |
| Redmond, William, 23 April 1732, Elizabeth Williams | 1 QA-38 |
| Ree, James, March 1739, Mary Doyle | 1 BA-308 |
| Reed, David, 10 Oct. 1750, Ann Sparks | 1 QA-57 |
| Reed, George, 2 May 1709, Mary Tilton | 3 KE-314 |

Reed, Gilbert, 16 Jan. 1750, Hannah Betts                    1 QA-57
Reed, Jacob, 6 day, 10 mo., 1733, Anne Pierpoint, dau.
  of Charles and Johanna                                     4 SF-264
Reed, Jno., 29 Aug. 1736, Mary Armiger Gibs                  1 QA-42
Reed, John, 10 July 1775, Rebecca Latham                     1 SM-137
Reed, John, 1 May 1777, Mary Drew                            2 BA-189
Reed, Philip, 16 July 1776, Ann Smith                        1 SM-137
Reed, William, 25 Sept. 1755, Eliz'th Broadaway              1 QA-60
Rees, Daniel, 28 Dec. 1743, Elizabeth Night                  1 BA-339
Rees, David, son of Morris and Sarah, 25 May 1756,
  Martha Chandler, dau. of Jacob                             9 SF
Rees, Morris, 19 day, 1 mo. 1718, Sarah Butterfield,
  dau. of Thomas                                             9 SF
Rees, Solomon, 6 Nov. 1737, Mary Draper                      1 BA-299
Reese, William, 10 July 1746, Ann O'herd                     1 BA-353
Reeves, James, 10 Aug. 1749, Sarah Pouder or Ponder          1 QA-56
Reeves, John, 6 Jan. 1728, Elizabeth Fleet                   4 AA-430
Reeves, Josias, 11 Jan. 1756, Letita Reaven ·                2 BA-213
Reeves, Rog'r, 12 Sept. 1756, Phebe Progdon                  2 BA-213
Reeves, Thomas, 7 June 1770, Mary Connelly                   2 BA-260
Reeves, Thomas, 28 Sept. 1777, Mary Scroggan Oakley          2 CH(4)
Regan, Morris, 15 May 1716, Elizabeth Smith                  2 TA-77
Regester, Francis, 2 day, 10 mo., 1731, Margaret
  Bartlett                                                   8 SF-67
Regester, John, 14 Dec. 1738, Sarah Brodaway                 2 TA-166
Regester, John, 28 day, 2 mo., 1766, Esther Wilson           8 SF-126
Regester, Robert, 4 Jan. 1704, Sarah Neal                    8 SF-429
Regester, Samuel, 2 Oct. 1775, Ann Wilson                    8 SF-151
Regester, William, 2 Feb. 1700, Sarah Booker                 8 SF-405
Register, Jeremiah, 11 July 1743, Eliza Baron                3 TA-43
Reid, James, 11 Sept. 1768, Margaret Purdy                   5 AA-3
Reiley, John, 18 Jan. 1756, Sarah Crapper                    1 QA-60
Reives, John, 4 Feb. 1706, Elinour Murfee                    1 AA-73
Relfe, Thomas, 12 March 1680, Ann Hoston (Houston)           5 SO-399
Relph, Thomas, 12 Dec. 1751, Charity Callaway                1 WI-65
Remsperger, John, 8 April 1762, Anna M. Brunner              4 FR-1162
Rench, Ralph, 21 Dec. 1755, Margret Watkins                  2 BA-213
Rennells, Thomas, 13 March 1690, Ann Regester                8 SF-352
Renner, Philip, 17 April 1757, Anna Mary Einck               4 FR-1103
Rennesperger, Geo., 20 Dec. 1756, Maria Elizab.
  Brenner                                                    4 FR-1103
Rennolds, John, June 1743, Sarah Lenard                      3 TA-43
Renshaw, Abraham, 15 June 1738, Ann Hawkins                  1 BA-290
Renshaw, John, 27 March 1735, Mary Litten                    1 BA-281
Renshaw, John, 16 Aug. 1762, Mary Bishop                     1 BA-377
Renshaw, Joseph, 28 Oct. 1742, Eliz'th Wells                 1 BA-328
Renshaw, Thomas, 16 Dec. 1718, Anne Charvel                  4 AA-406
Renshaw, Thomas, 29 Jan. 1739, Frances Clark                 1 BA-275
Repose, Anthony, 24 Dec. 1739, Elizabeth Armstrong           3 CE-23
Resho, Steven, 26 Dec. 1719, Ann Dodd                        2 TA-92
Resting, Edward, 18 March 1715/6, Mary Chaffey               2 PG-1
Revell, Randall, Oct. 1682, Sarah Ballard                    5 SO-399
Reward, Patrick, 6 Jan. 1731, Ann Carliss                    1 BA-259
Reyley, Thomas, 5 July 1741, Elizabeth Daniell               2 TA-172
Reynalls, Richard, 18 Feb. 1723, Rachell Cook                2 TA-106
Reynard, Joseph, 23 June 1709, Mary Lusby                    4 AA-378
Reyner, Eben, 31 July 1746, Sarah Perkins                    2 KE-262
Reyner, Ebenezer, 28 June 1764, Elizabeth Perkins            2 KE-305
Reyner, Ebenezer, 5 Dec. 1771, Rachel Boyer                  2 KE-308
Reynolds, Edward, 18 May 1722, Mary Altmain                  3 CE-18
Reynolds, Henry, son of Henry, 23 May 1733, Ann Howell,
  widow of Wm. Howell, dau. of Henry and Mary Worley         9 SF
Reynolds, Henry, son of Henry, 23 June 1743, Mary
  Coles Haines, widow of Jacob Haines, dau. of Wm.
  Coles                                                      9 SF

Reynolds, Henry, son of Henry and Hannah, 29 April
  1747, Mary Haines, dau. of Jacob and Mary            9 SF
Reynolds, Jacob, son of Henry and Hannah, 10 Oct.
  1751, Rebeckah Daye, dau. of John and Lydia          9 SF
Reynolds, John, 27 May 1744, Eliz'th Tonker (or
  Turner)                                              1 QA-49
Reynolds, John, 11 Feb. 1746, Patience Anderson        1 QA-53
Reynolds, John, c.Aug. 1775, Elizabeth Pennington      1 CR-6
Reynolds, Joseph, son of Henry and Hannah, 27 Feb.
  1754, Sarah Haines, dau. of Jacob and Mary           9 SF
Reynolds, Robert, 1 Feb. 1720, Catherine Buckley       4 AA-413
Reynolds, Robert, 11 Feb. 1746, Margarit Burt          1 QA-53
Reynolds, Robert, son of William, 8 Sept. 1763,
  Mary Wright, dau. of Benjamin                        5 AA-2
Reynolds, Samuel, son of Henry and Hannah, 12 May
  1743 (o.s.), Sarah Haines, dau. of Joseph and
  Elizabeth                                            9 SF
Reynolds, Samuel, son of Henry and Hannah, 25 March
  1747 (o.s.), Susanna Sidwell, dau. of Richard
  and Joanna                                           9 SF
Reynolds, Samuel, son of Samuel and Susanna, 4 July
  1776, Isabel King, dau. of Thomas and Ann            9 SF
Reynolds, Thom's, 30 Nov. 1699, Sarah Griffith         4 AA-372
Reynolds, Thomas, Jr., 8 July 1722, Elizabeth (?)      4 AA-418
Reynolds, Thomas, son of Thomas, 26 June 1766,
  Catherine Wood, dau. of Joseph                       1 FR-12
Reynolds, William, 7 Feb. 1710, Elizabeth Lunn         1 AA-77
Reynolds, William, son of Henry and Prudence, 23 Jan.
  1723/4 (o.s.), Mary Brown, dau. of William           9 SF
Reynolds, William, 7 April 1735, Martha Jeofry         1 QA-40
Reynolds, William, 1 Dec. 1739, Mrs. Deborah Lyng,
  widow                                                4 AA-441
Reynolds, William, son of Henry and Prudence, 9 Dec.
  1739 (o.s.), Rachel John, dau. of Thomas             9 SF
Reynolds, William, son of Henry and Hannah, 5 May
  1743, Prudence Haines, dau. of Jacob and Mary        9 SF
Reynolds, William, 5 Dec. 1777, Ann Griffith           3 PG-119
Rhodes, Abraham, 6 Aug. 1772, Rox'a Standiford         2 BA-265
Rhodes, John, 21 Sept. 1735, Sarah Moore               1 WI-18
Rhodes, Jno., 17 Oct. 1754, Mary Keen                  2 BA-211
Rhodes, John, 25 Oct. 1768, Sarah Standiford           2 BA-257
Rhodes, Richard, 9 Feb. 1740, Sarah Whitaker           2 BA-111
Rhodes, Richard, 16 April 1769, Sarah Prosper          2 BA-258
Rhodes, Thomas, 23 June 1743, Margaret Allen           1 BA-330
Rhodes, William, 17 Jan. 1717, Mary (?)                2 BA-10
Rhodous, Joseph, June 1725, Ann Polion                 2 BA-61
Rhods, John, 30 Oct. 1777, Ann Sweeney                 7 AA-2
Rice, David, 16 Oct. 1729, Elizabeth Watts             3 CE-15
Rice, Hugh, 9 Nov. 1748, Katherine Skinner             3 TA-71
Rice, John, 29 Aug. 1774, Elizabeth Clark              1 CR
Rice, William, 20 Dec. 1746, Mary Merrick              3 TA-63
Rich, Jno., 2 Oct. 1759, Ann Massey                    2 BA-219
Rich, Joseph, son of Joseph, 27 April 1742 (o.s.),
  Sarah Coulson, dau. of Thomas                        9 SF
Rich, Peater, 26 June 1739, Susanna Nich's             1 QA-45
Rich, Peter, son of Joseph, 24 June 1742, Martha
  Robinson, dau. of John                               9 SF
Richards, David, 10 Nov. 1718, Anne Waters, widow      4 AA-408
Richards, Edward, 9 June 1745, Prisilla Stanton        1 QA-45
Richards, John, 14 March 1675/6, Grace Dixon           9 SO-401
Richards, Richard, 14 July 1754, Sarah Hooker          2 BA-211
Richards, Sam'll, 17 July 1733, Mary Wood              2 AA-367
Richards, Thomas, 25 Dec. 1707, Margrett Delaine       1 CA-112
Richards, Will, 27 Dec. 1658, Mary Short               1 KE-129
Richardson, Anthony, 19 Nov. 1737, Elizabeth Dickinson 2 TA-162

Richardson, Ben, 23 Nov. 1746, Mary Ringold            3 TA-62
Richardson, Benjamin, 5 March 1753, Jemima Standiford  2 BA-207
Richardson, Dan'l, son of William and Elizabeth, 4
    day, 12 mo., 1691, Elizabeth Welsh, dau. of John
    and Mary                                           6 SF
Richardson, Dan'l, 12 day, 11 mo., 1754, Margaret
    Hopkins, dau. of Gerrard                           6 SF
Richardson, Daniel son of Nathaniel, 1 day, 7 mo.,
    1774, Rebecca Dickinson, dau. of Daniel            8 SF-150
Richardson, James, 3 Jan. 1744, Sophia Standiford      2 BA-192
Richardson, James, 16 Jan. 1759, Rach'l Stone          2 BA-218
Richardson, James, a tailor, 31 May 1759, Mary Ruff,
    widow of Ric'd Ruff                                1 BA-367
Richardson, John, 2 Oct. 1706, Katherine Connaway      1 AA-72
Richardson, John, 21 Nov. 1742, Mary Walker            2 BA-46
Richardson, Joseph, son of William and Eliz., 25 day,
    8 mo., 1705, Sarah Thomas, dau. of Samuel and Mary 6 SF
Richardson, Joseph, son of Wm. and Margaret, 6 day,
    1 mo., 1722, Rebekah Johns, dau. of Aquila and Mary 6 SF
Richardson, Mark, 2 Oct. 1701, Mary Barrinton          1 AA-249
Richardson, Nathan, son of Wm. and Margaret, 30 day,
    8 mo., 1735, Elizabeth Crockett, dau. of John and
    Mary                                               6 SF
Richardson, Nathaniel, 10 May 1747, Elizabeth Gott     2 BA-241
Richardson, Nathan, 20 April 1749, Hannah Webster
    Gover, widow of Samuel Gover, and dau. of Isaac
    Webster                                            9 SF
Richardson, Richard, son of William and Margaret,
    26 day, 3 mo., 1730, Marg't Coale, dau. of Wm. and
    Elizabeth                                          6 SF
Richardson, Richard, 13 day, 8 mo., 1754, Elizabeth
    Thomas                                             6 SF
Richardson, Samuel, 30 Dec. 1755, Sarah Davis          1 BA-375
Richardson, Samuel, 30 Dec. 1756, Sarah Davice         2 BA-214
Richardson, Thomas, 15 Dec. 1709, Bridget Clark        2 AA-339
Richardson, Thomas, 20 May 1720, Sarah Standifor       2 BA-19
Richardson, Thomas, 26 May 1721, Sarah (?)             2 BA-20
Richardson, Thomas, of A. A. Co., 10 day, 9 mo.,
    1737, Ann Thomas                                   1 SF-71
Richardson, Thomas, 11 day, 2 mo., 1762, Milcah Giles  6 SF
Richardson, Thomas, 14 Nov. 1777, Katharin Calphone    8 AA-15
Richardson, Vincent, 6 Jan. 1771, Martha Norris        2 BA-261
Richardson, William, Jr., 16 day, 5 mo., 1689, Marga-
    ret Smith, dau. of Alece Smith                     6 SF
Richardson, William, 19 April 1724, Ellener Hall       2 KE-200
Richardson, William, 13 May 1740, Margaret Thompson    1 QA-46
Richardson, William, 27 Nov. 1757, Sarah Covington     1 QA-63
Richardson, William, 27 March 1759, Mary Davice        2 BA-218
Richardson, William, 21 Jan. 1773, Eliz. Norton        2 BA-265
Richie, Archibald, 10 April 1732, Elizabeth McCabe,
    widow                                              1 WI-14
Richie, Daniel, 27 June 1762, Deliah Mezick            1 WI-85
Richison, Mark, 2 Dec. 1701, Mary Barrington           1 AA-57
Richison, Richard, 3 Dec. 1707, Anne Aldridge          1 AA-76
Rick, William, 15 Aug. 1731, Eliz'th Buttum            1 BA-259
Rickard, Benjamin, 4 Feb. 1730, Jane Cooper            3 KE-319
Rickards, John, 8 Aug. 1676, Elizabeth Trevett         9 SO-401
Rickeots, Edw'd, 3 Feb. 1729, Mary Cheney              1 AA-110
Rickeots, John, 4 Feb. 1724, Elisa Bettenfield         1 AA-100
Rickeots, William, 2 Jan. 1732, Margarett Cheney       1 AA-115
Ricket, William, June 1743, Sarah Bolton               1 QA-48
Rickets, Sam'l, 24 Dec. 1753, Hannah Mead              2 BA-209
Rickets, Thomas, Jr., 10 Dec. 1702, Rebecca Nicholson  1 AA-252
Rickett, John, 7 Dec. 1741, Anne Richardson            1 QA-47
Ricketts, Benjamin, 18 Oct. 1746, Eliner Maxwell       2 BA-151

Ricketts, Benjamin, 2 June 1759, Mary Cutchin          2 BA-217
Ricketts, Evan, 2 March 1742, Rachel Ward, dau. of
  John Ward                                             3 CE-24
Ricketts, Jeremiah, 15 Jan. 1712, Ann Jones            3 KE-315
Ricketts, John, 2 June 1760, Sarah Penington           1 CE-313
Ricketts, Richard, 19 Aug. 1742, Rebecca Cheney        1 AA-123
Ricketts, Samuel, 24 Dec. 1753, Hannah Mead            2 BA-209
Ricketts, Thomas, 10 Dec. 1702, Rebecca Nicholson      1 AA-64
Ricketts, Thomas, Sr., 14 Aug. 1705, Sarah Rawlins     1 AA-65
Ricketts, William, 10 Dec. 1749, Frances Burn          1 QA-56
Rickits, Edward, 30 Jan. 1728/9, Mary Silivant         2 TA-120
Ricords, Thos., 20 April 1740, Sarah Lamee             1 WI-31
Riddell, Capt. James, 1 Jan. 1773, Ann Plumber         3 BA-169
Riddle, Andrew, 1 Jan. 1738, Ann Nicholoe              1 BA-306
Riddle, Andrew, 23 April 1753, Jane Venney             2 BA-207
Riddle, Benjamin, 7 April 1742, Jane McMurry           1 FR-12
Riddle, John, Jr., 9 Feb. 1729, Elizabeth Lentall      2 PG-5
Riddle, John, 31 May 1735, Eleanor Lee                 2 PG-6
Riddlesden, Mr. Vanhaesdenck, "the convict," 7 Feb.
  1720, Mrs. Sarah Herbert, "the convict;" above his
  name is written "William Wrigglesden"               4 AA-413
Rider, Francis, 7 Aug. 1750, Frances Hopham            2 BA-201
Ridgely, Greenbury, son of Henry, 26 Oct. 1752, Lucy
  Stringer, dau. of Dr. Samuel                         6 AA-212
Ridgely, Henry, 2 Oct. 1722, Eliza Warfield, dau. of
  Benj. Warfield                                       4 AA-420
  6 AA-204 gives same information.
Ridgely, Henry, Jr., 12 Jan. 1729, Catherine Lusby,
  dau. of Robert Lusby, Jr., and his wife Mary         4 AA-432
Ridgely, Henry, son of Henry, 11 Nov. 1750, Anne
  Dorsey, dau. of Joshua                               6 AA-189
Ridgely, Jehosaphat, 16 Nov. 1721, Frances Ruley       4 AA-416
Ridgely, John, 1 Nov. 1736, Eliza Mayo                 1 AA-120
Ridgely, William, 4 March 1702, Jane Westall           1 AA-64
Ridgely, William, 14 April 1726, Mary Orrick           1 AA-102
Ridger, William, 18 Jan. 1732, Margaret Perry          1 QA-39
Ridgly, Nicholas, 26 Dec. 1711, Sarah Worthington      3 AA-98
Ridgly, William, 4 March 1702, Jane Westhall           1 AA-253
Ridgway, William, 19 Nov. 1724, Sarah Gorsuch          2 TA-110
Ridgway, William, 11 May 1749, Mary Ferrill            1 QA-55
Ridgway, William, 30 Jan. 1752, Mary Bostick           1 QA-58
Ridley, James, 26 Nov. 1686, Rebeckah Berry            8 SF-343
Rieslin, Matthias, 15 March 1737, Catherine Barber     4 AA-439
Rigbie, James, 1741, Elizabeth Harrison, dau. of
  Samuel and Sarah                                     9 SF
Rigbie, James, 5 day, 2 mo., 1761, Sarah Boulton
  Massey, widow of Aquilla Massey, and dau. of Isaac
  Boulton                                              7 SF-2
Rigdon, George, Jr., 12 Dec. 1734, Sarah Thompson      1 BA-288
Rigdon, John, 11 March 1740, Elizabeth Oachisson       1 BA-319
Rigdon, William, 10 Nov. 1748, Mary Pribble            1 BA-374
Riggan, Derby, 16 March 1752, Hannah Broughten         2 SO-67
Riggen, Charles, 25 March 1759, Rachel Cottingham      2 SO-70
Riggen, Dukes, 28 Jan. 1761, Martha Summors            2 SO-160
Riggen, John, 23 Feb. 1775, Charity Lankford           3 SO-71
Riggen, Joshua, 4 Dec. 1777, Sarah Stephenson, "rellex"
  of John Stephenson                                   3 SO-71
Riggen, Obed, 1 May 1755, Rebecca Matthews             2 SO-70
Riggen, Shadrah, 18 Sept. 1764, Comfort Cameron        2 SO-162
Riggen, Stephen, 5 Nov. 1764, Sarah Matthews           2 SO-161
Riggen, Teague, 2 Sept. 1753, Levinah Evens            2 SO-68
Riggen, Teege, 30 July 1667, Mary London               4 SO-679
Riggin, James, 10 March 1752, Betty Winright           2 SO-68
Riggin, Teague, 1667, Mary London                      5 SO-399
Riggin, Teague, 22 May 1749, Mary Shaw                 2 SO-69

Riggs, John, 16 Jan. 1721, Mary Davies                          4 AA-416
Right, Henry, 14 Jan. 1772, Eleanor Kitely                      3 AA-113
Right, Philbert, 3 Dec. 1712, Ester Bycraft                     2 PG-1
Right, William, 27 Dec. 1670, Frances Bloys                     5 SO-399
Rilby, John, 6 Sept. 1714, Elizabeth Silvester                 3 KE-315
Riley, Benja'n, 8 Jan. 1754, Hannah Smith                      2 KE-295
Riley, Joseph, 10 June 1744, Sarah Cornelius                   2 KE-270
Riley, Nicholas, 2 Dec. 1747, Sarah Smith                     2 KE-265
Rimel, John, 8 Sept. 1777, Mary Lewis                          1 MO-522
Rind, Alexander, 24 Aug. 1725, Abigail Green, alias
   Harvey, servant to Mr. Transum                               4 AA-425
Ringgold, (?), 11 May 1741, Rebecca Ringgold                   3 KE-321
Ringgold, Charles, 17 Jan. 1705, Elizabeth Park               3 KE-313
Ringgold, Elias, 15 April 1725, Mary Bordley                  3 KE-316
Ringgold, James, 2 Dec. 1726, Mary Lovey                      3 KE-318
Ringgold, Josias, 11 Aug. 1730, Sarah Smith                  3 KE-317
Ringgold, Thomas, 7 Sept. 1699, Mary Ringgold                3 KE-313
Ringgold, Thomas, 1 May 1712, Rebecca Wilmer                 3 KE-314
Ringgold, Thomas, 24 Oct. 1743, Anne Maria Earle            3 KE-320
Ringgold, William, Jr., 9 Jan. 1750, Sarah Jones            3 KE-321
Rion, John, 30 Nov. 1710, Mary Cobbey                         1 AA-77
Rippin, Henry, 30 Nov. 1723, Augustina Larramore,
   widow                                                       3 CE-11
Rippon, Henry, 26 Nov. 1727, Mary Sewell                     3 CE-14
Rise, William, 27 Aug. 1723, Rebecca Ashly                   3 KE-319
Risteau, George, 7 Aug. 1757, Frances Todd                   4 BA-71
Risteau, Isaac, 21 Feb. 1748, Elizabeth Reaven              2 BA-179
Risteau, Talbert, 20 June 1745, Mary Stokes                 2 BA-194
Ristien, Thos., 28 Nov. 1751, Marg'rt Sinkler               2 BA-204
Ristone, Abraham, 11 Nov. 1762, Elianor Farlow             2 BA-224
Ristone, Edward, Feb. 1723, Eleanor Neal                    3 BA-147
Ristone, John, 17 May 1747, Sarah Sinclair                 2 BA-241
Ristone, Jno., 21 May 1747, Sarah Sinkler                  2 BA-196
Riswicke, Thos., 27 July 1773, Mary Nottingham             1 SM-136
Ritsch, John, 13 Oct. 1762, Anna Cath. Berg                4 FR-1162
Rivirs, Charles, 26 Sept. 1704, Ann (?)                    3 AA-97
Rixon, John, 10 Jan. 1672, Ann Davis                       5 SO-399
Roach, Francis, 17 Sept. 1754, Mary Jarman                 2 BA-211
Roach, John, 2 Feb. 1726, Rozanna Dennis                   1 BA-246
Roach, Jonathan, 28 Feb. 1759, Ebe Lawson                  2 SO-70
Roach, Patrick, 8 Sept. 1746, Mary Hains                   3 TA-61
Roach, William, 5 Feb. 1767, Martha Just                   2 SO-161
Rob, James, 16 July 1737, Jane Gorden                      3 CE-21
Robenson, Rich'd, Jr., 15 Sept. 1749, Jemima Robertson     2 BA-197
Robenson, Thomas, "about the middle of" Nov. 1719,
   Mary Davis                                               3 AA-100
Roberson, Hampton, 5 Feb. 1752, Rebecca Jones              3 AA-111
Roberson, William, Jr., 21 Jan. 1768, Catherine Miles      2 BA-231
Roberts, Abraham, 4 Dec. 1758, Rebeckah Sands              1 QA-64
Roberts, Allen, 9 Oct. 1777, Ann Wilson                    1 CA-111a
Roberts, Andrew, 12 Feb. 1739, Margaret Connally           2 TA-168
Roberts, Ashell, 5 Dec. 1742, Mary Ingrum                  2 BA-238
Roberts, Benj., 7 Dec. 1746, Eliza Ray                     3 TA-63
Roberts, Benjamin, 12 Nov. 1749, Sophia Scott              1 QA-56
Roberts, Benjamin, 4 May 1754, Martha Cullison             2 BA-209
Roberts, Billingsley, 2 March 1758, Betty Manen            2 BA-49
Roberts, Evan, 1770, Margaret Plummer                      2 AA-409
Roberts, Francis, 23 Sept. 1771, Mary Pillsbrough          1 SM-136
Roberts, Henry, 10 Dec. 1699, Ann Hopkins                  2 AA-298
Roberts, Henry, 16 July 1724, Ruth Wilson                  1 AA-99
                                                             & 330
Roberts, James, 1 Jan. (?), Ann Rickets                    1 CE-330
Roberts, James, 19 July 1752, Sophia Thomas                1 QA-58
Roberts, John, (date not given), Susanna Berry             1 AA-96
Roberts, John, 17 Sept. 1704, Deborah Roberson             1 CA-111

| | |
|---|---|
| Roberts, Jno., 3 Sept. 1707, Grace Mannin | 1 CA-112 |
| Roberts, John, 5 Sept. 1709, Martha Aldridge | 1 AA-77 |
| 1 AA-258 gives date as 5 Nov. 1709. | |
| Roberts, John, 7 Feb. 1714, Ann Richardson | 2 BA-4 |
| Roberts, John, Jr., (date not given), Susanna Berry | 1 AA-321 |
| Roberts, John, 16 Jan. 1731, Mart Mortgaright | 2 TA-151 |
| Roberts, John, 9 Jan. 1734, Ann Swift | 2 PG-6 |
| Roberts, John, 15 July 1740, Dorety Morgain, dau. | |
| of John | 3 CE-22 |
| Roberts, Jno., Jr., 7 Dec. 1760, Mary Jones | 2 BA-220 |
| Roberts, John, c.Oct. 1775, Mary Horney | 1 CR-6 |
| Roberts, Jonathan, 13 Sept. 1730, Johanna Thomas | 3 BA-149 |
| Roberts, Rencher, 1 Aug. 1762, Mary Wallace, widow | |
| of Matthew Wallace | 3 SO-4 |
| Roberts, Richard, of Phila., son of Richard, late | |
| of Cal. Co., 29 day, 5 mo., 1770, Mary Harris, dau. | |
| of William | 6 SF |
| Roberts, Richardson, 5 Nov. 1755, Clorinda Leggatt | 2 BA-212 |
| Roberts, Robert, 15 Oct. 1706, Mrs. Parker | 1 BA-201 |
| Roberts, Robert, 16 Feb. 1728, Sarah Morgan | 3 CE-13 |
| Roberts, Roger, 23 Nov. 1693, Sarah Archer | 2 AA-294 |
| Roberts, Roger, 30 Nov. 1701, Anne Stanly | 2 AA-316 |
| Roberts, Roger, 2 Nov. 1752, Rebecca Crawford | 2 BA-84 |
| Roberts, Thomas, 8 Aug. 1676, Ann Webb | 9 SO-401 |
| Roberts, Thomas, 28 Oct. 1743, Elizabeth Renshaw | 1 WI-70 |
| Roberts, Thomas, 17 Oct. 1749, (?) Callahan | 3 TA-75 |
| Roberts, Thomas, Jr., 13 Oct. 1750, Eli Harvey | 3 TA-79 |
| Roberts, William, 12 Oct. 1704, Elizabeth Deane | 3 KE-313 |
| Roberts, William, 6 July 1705, Sarah Horn | 2 AA-328 |
| Roberts, William, 27 June 1713, Jane Squiers | 2 TA-71 |
| Roberts, William, 11 Dec. 1735, Ellinor Mayham | 3 BA-154 |
| Roberts, Will'm, 17 March 1736, Elis. Long | 1 QA-43 |
| Roberts, William, 12 April 1741, Sarah Davis | 3 TA-30 |
| Roberts, Wm., 12 Feb. 1747/8, Sarah St. Lee | 3 TA-68 |
| Roberts, Alexander, 3 Feb. 1755, Leah Dennis | 1 WI-44 |
| Robertson, Daniel, 18 day, 8 mo., 1768, Elizabeth | |
| Webster | 5 SF |
| Robertson, Edw'd, 21 April 1752, Marg'rt Standeford | 2 BA-205 |
| Robertson, Geo., 2 day, 2 mo., 1773, Susanna Waters | 6 SF |
| Robertson, James, 26 July 1746, Mary Dean, widow | 1 WI-66 |
| Robertson, John, 1 May 1711, Easter Mattucks | 4 AA-379 |
| Robertson, John, 9 Oct. 1755, Priscilla Wright | 1 WI-67 |
| Robertson, Joseph, 19 Jan. 1735, Mary Toby | 4 AA-437 |
| Robertson, Rich'd, 2 Aug. 1752, Mary Hall | 2 BA-205 |
| Robertson, Robert, 9 Nov. 1721, Sarah Taylor | 2 BA-19 |
| Robertson, Sam'l, 10 day, 2 mo., 1773, Eleanor Lewing | 6 SF |
| Robertson, William, 26 Dec. 1735, Alie Thompson | 2 BA-75 |
| Robertson, William, 21 May 1753, Sarah Dashiell | 1 WI-52 |
| Robertson, Wm., son of Samuel, 29 day, 3 mo., 1770, | |
| Elizabeth Crabb, dau. of Henry | 6 SF |
| Robeson, George, 20 May 1742, Anne Smith | 3 AA-106 |
| Robeson, James, 7 June 1752, Ann Ashor | 2 BA-205 |
| Robeson, John, 9 Jan. 1676/7, Tanzine Prideaux | 9 SO-402 |
| Robeson, Jno., 1 May 1711, Easter Mattocks | 3 AA-99 |
| Robeson, John, 10 April 1748, Lucy Murray | 3 BA-161 |
| Robeson, Oneall, 5 Nov. 1714, Martha Barns | 3 AA-106 |
| Robeson, Oneall, Jr., 13 Nov. 1740, Comfort Rowles | 3 AA-106 |
| Robeson, William, Jr., 21 Jan. 1768, Cathrine Miles | 2 BA-231 |
| Robins, Allen, 11 Feb. 1724, Martha Banner | 1 CE-335 |
| Robins, John, 9 July 1730, Mary Anne Turbutt | 2 TA-148 |
| Robins, Standly, 21 Jan. 1741, Sarah Goldsborough | 2 TA-174 |
| 3 TA-34 gives date as 6 Jan. 1741/2. | |
| Robins, Thomas, Jr., 3 Feb. 1696, Susanna Vaughan | 2 TA-5 |
| Robins, Thomas, 6 Dec. 1704, (?) Allin | 2 TA-42 |
| Robinson, Abraham, 24 Sept. 1744, Sarah Simpson | 1 BA-337 |

Robinson, Ahip, 28 Aug. 1697, Margrett Pryer, dau. of
   Thomas and Margaret                                    3 CE-1
Robinson, Charles, 26 May 1728, Ann Gentle                 1 PG-280
Robinson, Dan'l, 13 day, 11 mo., 1703, Sarah Neeves        6 SF
Robinson, Capt. Daniel, 18 July 1751, Susannah Brown       1 BA-366
                                                           & 385
Robinson, David, 17 Jan. 1711, Mrs. Judeth Combes          2 TA-70
Robinson, Jacob, 5 July 1714, Mary Whitaker, widow         2 BA-6
Robinson, John, 21 March 1666, Elizabeth Brown             3 CH
Robinson, John, Jr., 25 April 1703, Mary Donellan          2 TA-34
Robinson, John, 17 Sept. 1711, Grace Standley              2 TA-70
Robinson, John, June 1721, Haster Macklenane               1 PG-269
Robinson, John, 2 Sept. 1767, Elizabeth Buthaey            3 BA-168
Robinson, Joseph, 17 Sept. 1730, Eliza (?)                 1 AA-111
Robinson, Michael, 24 May 1733, Margaret McGumerry         3 CE-14
Robinson, Peter, Dec. 1740, Anne Athey                     1 PG-287
Robinson, Richard, 12 Jan. 1713, Elizabeth Slade           2 BA-4
Robinson, Richard, 22 Jan. 1718, Sarah Abbott              2 TA-89
Robinson, Richard, 15 Sept. 1749, Jemima Robertson         2 BA-197
Robinson, Rich'd Gurling, son of David, 6 April 1746,
   Judith Harrison                                        3 TA-58
Robinson, Solomon, 19 April 1720, Jane Martin              2 TA-92
Robinson, Solomon, 28 May 1741, Mary Fairhurst             2 TA-172
   3 TA-31 gives bride's name as Sarah Fairhurst.
Robinson, Mr. Thomas, 6 July 1697, Mrs. Sarah Frisby,
   dau. of James Frisby                                   3 CE-1
Robinson, Thomas, 30 Oct. 1714, Dorathy Williams           2 TA-74
Robinson, Thomas, 26 Nov. 1732, Rebecca Hony               1 QA-39
Robinson, Thomas, 13 Feb. 1734, Anne Godwin                1 QA-40
Robinson, Thomas, 22 Nov. 1737, Mary Beessley              2 TA-267
Robinson, Thomas, 22 Nov. 1737, Mary Beezley               2 TA-164
Robinson, Thomas, 26 Aug. 1752, Mary Ann Sheebrook         1 QA-59
Robinson, Thomas, 26 Oct. 1757, Henrietta Willen           1 QA-63
Robinson, Thomas, 1775, Sarah Tool                         1 CR
Robinson, William, 8 Jan. 1680, Elizabeth Hady             5 SO-399
Robinson, William, 11 Dec. 1703, Sarah Combest             1 BA-256
Robinson, William, 8 Dec. 1713, Sarah Combest              1 BA-213
Robinson, William, 21 Jan. 1729, Anne Elliott              1 QA-37
Robinson, Wm., 6 Dec. 1743, Judith Bullen                  3 TA-46
Robinson, William, Jr., 14 Nov. 1750, Mary Salisbury       1 QA-57
Robosson, Richard, 2 Sept. 1777, Mary Shrewer              7 AA-2
Robson, James, 18 Sept. 1720, Rebeckah Frith               2 TA-94
Robson, Richard, 7 Aug. 1701, Martha Roddry, dau. of
   Matthew and Sarah                                      1 AA-57
Robson, Rich., 7 Aug. 1701, Martha Rodriff                 1 AA-247
Robson, Thomas, 14 Nov. 1739, Easter Price                 3 TA-19
Robson, Wm., 4 May 1711, Hannah Maria Younger              2 TA-69
Roby, William, son of Richard, 12 Dec. 1762, Susannah
   Dement                                                 1 CH-205
Roch, John, 4 Feb. 1663, Sarah Williams                    5 SO-399
Rochester, Francis, 13 Feb. 1736, Sarah Edwards            1 QA-43
Rochester, Francis, 4 June 1758, Eliza Cassey              1 QA-63
Rochester, John, 11 Feb. 1734, Sarah Lambden               1 QA-40
Rochester, John, 9 April 1758, Mary Massey                 1 QA-63
Rochister, Francis, 8 Jan. 1740/1, Cathrin Johnson         1 QA-46
Rochister, Henry, 1 Sept. 1741, Eliz'h Massey              1 QA-47
Rock, Francis, 27 July 1759, Mary Pryer, widow, dau.
   of Robert and Elizabeth Cummings of North East         1 CE-312
Rock, George, 28 March 1743, Mary Story                    1 CE-290
Rock, "alias Old George," in the 64th yr. of life,
   "in the merry month of Apl, 16th day, 1772,"
   Katherine Simpers, age 40                              1 CE-315
Rocker, John, 14 Nov. 1771, Esabel Brown                   2 BA-263
Rockhold, Asall, 1749, Anne Rowe                           2 BA-243
   2 BA-198 gives date as 3 April 1749 and the bride's
   name as Ann Roe.

Rockhold, Asel, (banns pub.; date not given), Mary
  Rutledge                                              6 BA(1)
Rockhold, John, 13 April 1732, Mary Maynard         3 AA-103
Rockhold, John, 14 July 1771, Jemima Deeson         2 BA-262
Rockhold, Jos., 8 Dec. 1763, Eliz. Rutledge         2 BA-225
Rockhold, Reason, 31 Dec. 1754, Eliz. Sandy         2 BA-211
Rockhold, Thomas, 10 June 1757, Elizebeth Wright    3 AA-111
Rockwell, John, 25 May 1705, Elizabeth Morris       3 AA-97
Roct, George, 30 March 1767, Hanna Calcune          4 FR-1162
Rodderry, John, 13 June 1706, Mary Beckett          1 AA-72
Rodes, Henry, 15 Jan. 1697/8, Kathern Stockit       1 AA-39
Rodes, Richard, 16 March 1769, Susan Prosper        2 BA-258
Rodgers, William, 18 Aug.1726, Lucinda Thompson     1 AA-103
Rodwell, Thomas, 28 Aug. 1727, Anna Pennington      3 AA-102
Roe, Abner, 14 March 1744, Eliz'h Robards           1 QA-50
Roe, Abner, c.Aug. 1775, Julia Sylvester            1 CR-6
Roe, James, 14 Oct. 1746, Mary Anne Saile           3 TA-61
Roe, John, 13 Dec. 1735, Jane Eubanks               1 SF-69
Roe, John, 14 May 1757, Susanna Shepherd            1 QA-62
Roe, Joseph, June 1743, Eliz'h Wright               1 QA-48
Roe, Samuel, 13 July 1746, Ann Lamden               1 QA-52
Roe, Thomas, 15 April 1745, Mary Williams           3 BA-156
Roe, Thomas, 30 Jan. 1748, Mary Jones               3 BA-162
Roe, Thos. Parratt, 25 Aug. 1774, Jane Clark        1 CR
Roe, Thomas Richardson, 10 April 1748, Margarit Holton  1 QA-54
Roe, William, 15 May 1703, Sarah Wells              2 AA-321
Roe, William, 15 Jan. 1730, Mary Jones              2 BA-86
Rogars, Thomas, 23 Feb. 1746, Eliz'h Knotts         1 QA-53
Rogers, Abraham, 9 Jan. 1757, Margery Ripperth      1 QA-62
Rogers, Edward, 15 May 1722, Hannah Duffey          3 KE-315
Rogers, Hugh, 9 June 1720, Jane Anderson            2 PG-2
Rogers, John, 25 April 1714, Rebecca Stevens        2 BA-5
Rogers, John, 17 June 1744, Ann Butler              1 QA-49
Rogers, Joseph, 10 Feb. 1688, Mary Boker            8 SF-346
Rogers, Joseph, 15 Sept. 1730, Elizabeth McDaniel   2 TA-149
Rogers, Joseph, 5 Dec. 1756, Eliz. Campbell         2 BA-214
Rogers, Nicholas, 18 Aug. 1745, Henrietta Jones     3 BA-156
Rogers, Robert, Dec. 1723, Mary Preris; both servants
  to Capt. Larkin                                     4 AA-422
Rogers, Robert, 26 Dec. 1758, Ruth Williams         2 BA-218
Rogers, Roger, 16 Nov. 1726, Anne Write             2 TA-114
Rogers, Roger, 17 Dec. 1731, Mary Beadstead         2 TA-151
Rogers, Roger, 4 Oct. 1741, Sarah Kitts             2 TA-175
Rogers, Thom's, 5 Oct. 1724, Sarah Nelson; both servants
  to Henry Ridgely                                    4 AA-424
Rogers, Thomas, son of William and Grace, 15 April
  1762, Catherine Brown, dau. of Samuel and Elizabeth  9 SF
Rogers, William, 6 day, 3 mo., 1730, Elizabeth Harris
  Brown, widow of Samuel Brown, and dau. of William
  Harris                                              9 SF
Roial, Edward, 1 Oct. 1741, Rebecca Jones           1 QA-47
Rolle, Fideman, 14 Feb. 1745/6, Lydia Sherwood      3 TA-57
Rolls, John, 5 Oct. 1710, Sarah Goslinn             1 AA-77
Rolph, John, 20 July 1721, Mary Jones               3 KE-315
Rolston, Charles, 24 Aug. 1758, Mary Wells          1 QA-64
Rooke, Thomas, 6 Nov. 1770, Mary Flannigan          2 BA-261
Rookes, John, 8 Nov. 1733, Catherine Jacob          1 AA-116
Rooksbey, John, 20 Jan. 1705, Giles Kinedey         1 AA-72
Rooksby, Edward, 25 Sept. 1732, Hannah Smith        1 AA-114
Rooms, Jno., 12 Nov. 1760, Mary Walker              2 BA-220
Roos, Antony, 24 July 1738, Jane Miller             1 CE-285
Roose, James, 22 March 1773, Margret Kitely         2 BA-266
Roper, John, 23 Sept. 1701, Ellinour Carter         1 AA-57
                                                      & 248
Rose, Edward, 18 Dec. 1755, Hannah Frost            2 BA-213

```
Rose, Paulus, 28 July 1698, Mary Chilcott              2 AA-295
Rose, Peregrine, 31 Oct. 1760, Ellenor Potter          1 CE-310
Rose, Thomas, 23 Jan. 1702, Sarah Broadhead            1 AA-253
  1 AA-64 gives the bride's name as Sarah Broodhead.
Rose, Thomas, 27 Dec. 1725, Rachell Baxter             1 AA-101
Rose, Thomas, 17 Jan. 1736, Jean Bell, dau. of
  Richard Bell                                         3 CE-23
Rose, Thomas, 4 July 1765, Sarah Batt                  9 AA-250
Rose, Thomas, 22 Oct. 1777, Mary Smith                 3 PG-149
  2 AA-414 gives date as 10 Nov. 1777.
Rose, Wm., 12 Feb. 1744/5, Sarah Ridgway               3 TA-52
Rosebury, James, 19 Sept. 1752, Mary Wright            1 QA-59
Ross, Adam, 20 Nov. 1777, Jane Chambers                2 CE-1
Ross, Francis, 15 Aug. 1777, Mary Andrews              2 CE-1
Ross, John, son of Alexander and Katherine, 11 Dec.
  1735, Lydia Hollingsworth, dau. of Stephen           9 SF
Ross, John, 26 Feb. 1769, Sarah Smith                  2 BA-258
Ross, Reuben, 5 Dec. 1711, Elizabeth Harwood           1 AA-78
Ross, Samuel, 30 Nov. 1729 Rebecca Wood                1 BA-257
Ross, Samuel, 6 Jan. 1736, Eliz'th Lee                 1 BA-294
Roswell, Richard, c.Aug. 1775, Mary Davis              1 CR-6
Rothell, David, 8 Dec. 1742, Ann West                  2 TA-173
Rothell, John, 26 Aug. 1725, Elizabeth Rusinn?         2 TA-112
Rothell, John, 16 Jan. 1728, Sarah Lowder              2 TA-119
Rothwell, Thomas, 21 Feb. 1720, Ann Love               2 TA-95
Rotthell, Thomas, 24 Oct. 1727, Jeane Harper           2 TA-116
Rounsifie, Thomas, 26 May 1705, Rose Johnson           3 KE-313
Rous, Joseph, 12 Jan. 1740/1, Rebecca Blades           1 QA-46
Rouse, John, 8 Sept. 1744, Elizabeth Perryman          1 BA-337
Rouse, Thomas, 1728, Elizabeth Monk                    3 KE-316
Rouse, Thomas, 22 May 1759, Jane Maloyd                1 QA-65
Rouse, Zackariah, 28 Sept. 1736, Ann Adkinson          1 BA-289
Row, Jno., 17 Dec. 1761, Deb. Jones                    2 BA-222
Row, Thomas, 30 May 1721, Jane Row                     4 AA-414
Row, William, 12 Oct. 1758, Ann Wordsworth             2 BA-217
Rowe, John, 29 May 1751, Sarah Wharton                 2 BA-203
Rowe, John, 22 July 1755, Bridgett Moony               2 BA-212
Rowe, John, 23 Dec. 1777, Mary Ward                    2 CH(5)
Rowe, William, 12 Oct. 1758, Ann Wordsworth            2 BA-217
Rowell, John, 12 June 1677, Mary Owen                  9 SO-402
Rowell, John, May 1686, Margarett Gra-(?)              5 SO-399
Rowing, John, 14 Feb. 1751, Comfort Brown              2 BA-203
Rowins, William, 8 Dec. 1777, Rachel Dawson            1 CR-28
Rowland, Samuel, of Sussex Co., Del., 30 day, 1 mo.,
  1776, Hannah Turner                                  8 SF-153
Rowland, Thomas, 28 Sept. 1747, Eliza Lowe             3 TA-67
Rowles, Jacob, 27 Jan. 1723, Anne Lynch                3 BA-146
Rowles, Jacob, 4 Jan. 1727, Constance Sampson          3 BA-149
Rowles, Jacob, 28 Sept. 1746, Mary Scarff              3 BA-159
Rowles, Lacey, 21 May 1724, Mary Oldham, dau. of
  Thomas                                               9 SF
Rowles, Lacey, 31 Dec. 1734, Mary Allen, widow of
  James Allen                                          9 SF
Rowles, Richard, 30 Jan. 1753, Anne Gorswick           3 BA-166
Rowles, Thomas, 16 Oct. 1740, Sarah Joyce              3 AA-108
Rowls, Wm., 1707, Marth. Smith                         3 AA-99
Rownes, John, 1751, Comfort Brown                      2 BA-241
Royston, Abel, 2 March 1727, Eliza Robinson            2 CA-24
Rozenquist, Allix'r, 22 Dec. 1712, Hanna Smith         2 AA-345
Ruby, Thos., 27 May 1765, Charity Marsh                2 BA-228
Ruff, Daniel, 11 May 1740, Elizabeth Webster           1 BA-315
Ruff, Henry, 28 July 1757, Hannah Preston              1 BA-369
Ruff, John, March 1741, Mary Freeman                   2 BA-139
Rule, Geo., Jan. 1750/1, Grace Woodard                 3 TA-81
Rules, Cornelus, 11 Oct. 1739, Avis Harris             1 QA-45
```

```
Ruley, William, 9 Dec. 1725, Elizabeth Miller          1 AA-101
Ruliff, Gilbert, 31 Jan. 1777, Mary Carran             9 BA
Ruly, Anthony, 14 Feb. 1722, Elizabeth Cadle           1 AA-95
  1 AA-318 gives bride's name as Elizabeth Caddle.
Ruly, Mich'll, 21 June 1728, Anne Winterbury           3 CE-12
Rummage, George, 15 May 1754, Mary Noble               1 BA-353
Rumpley, James, 22 Sept. 1771, Sarah Gibson            2 BA-263
Rumsey, Benjamin, 24 May 1768, Mary Hall, dau. of Col.
  John and Hannah Hall of Balto. Co.                   1 CE-312
Rumsey, Edward, 10 July 1727, Margaret Rumsey          3 CE-16
Rumsey, William, son of Charles and Catherine of
  Bohemia River, 15 May 1725, Sabrinah Blaidenburgh,
  dau. of Benjamin and Margaret                        3 CE-16
Runton, Joseph, 25 April 1709, Mary Farmer             2 TA-59
Russam, Edward, 1 May 1740, Ann Erwine                 2 TA-168
Russel, Abraham, 26 July 1711, Jane Guildbert          2 AA-343
Russel, John, 18 June 1719, Sarah Cuningham, widow     4 AA-408
Russell, Alexander Thomas, 2 Sept. 1740, Ann Price?    1 WI-29
Russel, Elijah, 26 day, 1 mo., 1775, Esther Cranor     2 SF-288
Russel, G., 27 May 1774, Ann Draden Abell              1 SM-136
Russell, John, 6 Sept. 1770, Susan French              1 SM-135
Russell, Michael, 13 day, 11 mo., 1681, Elizabeth Shaw 8 SF-334
Russell, Thomas, 27 July 1702, Mary Cahill             1 BA-197
Russell, Thomas, 7 Nov. 1714, Mary Boxing              1 BA-215
Russell, Thomas, 17 Feb. 1774, Ann Thomas              1 CE-313
Russum, Edw'd, 30 April 1740, Anne Erwin               3 TA-22
Russum, James, 3 Dec. 1774, Anne Martindale            1 CR
Russum, Peter, 27 April 1721, Cathrine Dodds           2 TA-96
Ruston, Job, 6 July 1735, Mary Baker                   1 CE-283
Ruth, Jacob, 2 Sept. 1759, Sarah Airs                  2 BA-219
Ruth, Jno., (date not given), Jane Butler              1 QA-42
Ruth, Joseph, 14 Sept. 1772, Catherine Mansfield       1 BA-393
Rutherford, Richard, 1715, Margaret Baker              4 AA-393
Rutland, Thomas, 13 Jan. 1695, Jane Linsicom           1 AA-34
Rutland, Thomas, Jr., 12 Aug. 1764, Margaret Howard    1 AA-148
  9 AA-247 gives same information.
Rutledge, Benjamin, 28 April 1748, Mary Roe            2 BA-196
  2 BA-243 gives the bride's name as Mary Row.
Rutledge, Benj'n, 2 Feb. 1768, Eliz. Rockhold          2 BA-231
Rutledge, Ephr'm, 7 Feb. 1765, Ann Dallas              2 BA-227
Rutledge, Epr'm, 6 Feb. 1766, Susan Pocock             2 BA-229
Rutledge, John, 10 Dec. 1742, Eliz. Millhughes         2 BA-130
Rutledge, Mich'l, 17 Dec. 1765, Elinor Deason          2 BA-228
Rutlidge, Abraham, 13 Oct. 1747, Penelope Rutledge     3 BA-160
Rutlidge, John, 4 Feb. 1773, Ruth Standiford           2 BA-265
Rutt, William, 12 Oct. 1727, Anne Bean                 1 AA-105
Rutter, Jno., Jr., 19 July 1740, Catherin Jones        1 CE-289
Rutter, John, 4 May 1756, Mary Ricketts                1 QA-61
Rutter, Moses, 15 Jan. 1752, Ann Ricketts, dau. of
  Thomas and Mary                                      1 CE-313
Rutter, Richard, 3 June 1750, Mary Barney              3 BA-164
Rutter, William, 5 June 1766, Ann Rickets Roberts      1 CE-312
Ruvis, Thomas, 1 June 1770, Mary Connelly              2 BA-260
Ryan, Edward, 22 May 1743, Susannah Symmonds           3 CE-24
Ryan, Edward, 25 Oct. 1777, Sarah Demitt              10 BA-69
Rye, John, 9 Feb. 1710, Mary Clements, widow           3 CE-5
Ryle, Isaac, 15 July 1739, Hannah Tennant              2 KE-253
Ryley, Francis, 5 March 1738, Elizabeth England        1 BA-303
Ryley, John, 28 Jan. 1742, Ruth Anshor                 1 BA-328
Ryley, Jno., 3 April 1753, Mary Ruff                   2 BA-207
Ryley, Patrick, 24 Nov. 1725, Margert Standige         2 TA-112
Ryley, Philip, 6 June 1720, Mary Beckwith              4 AA-412
Ryn, Alexander, 11 Jan. 1730, Ann Cooke                4 AA-433
Ryon, Michael, 1 Feb. 1733, Mary Wright                2 TA-154
Ryon, Peter, 21 Dec. 1749, Mary Symson                 2 BA-199
```

| | |
|---|---|
| Ryston, Edward, 7 Dec. 1698, Margaret Singly | 2 AA-295 |
| Ryston, Thomas, Nov. 1751, Margaret Sinclair | 2 BA-241 |
| Sadler, Lawrence, 24 March 1705, Eliz'th Painter | 3 KE-323 |
| Sadlers, Joseph, 11 (Oct. 1768 ?), Ann Roberts | 2 BA-257 |
| Saffel, Joshua, 24 July 1777, Virlinda Prather | 1 MO-516 |
| Safford, Lawrence, 23 Oct. 1708, Alse King | 3 KE-324 |
| Sailes, George, 20 July 1730, Mary Earle | 2 TA-149 |
| Saintclair, Thomas, 9 Jan. 1748, Mary Huntingdon | 1 CH-178 |
| St.Clair, William, 26 July 1761, Mrs. Margaret Wilson | 2 KE-302 |
| St.John, Mich'l, June 1743, Margaret Pool | 1 QA-48 |
| Salisbury, Jam's, 4 Aug. 1730, Frances Hawkins | 1 QA-36 |
| Salsbury, William, 22 Aug. 1717, Mary Sheredine | 2 TA-80 |
| Salsbury, William, 24 April 1739, Jane Doring | 2 KE-226 |
| Salter, Sam'l, 26 Dec. 1753, Mary Pendergrass | 2 BA-209 |
| Sampson, Isaac, 17 April 1747, Mary Ristone | 2 BA-241 |
| Sampson, Richard, 15 May 1734, Ann Empey | 3 BA-152 |
| Samson, Benj., 11 Feb. 1766, Jemima Standeford | 2 BA-229 |
| Samson, Emanuel, 11 Nov. 1760, Sarah Rogers | 2 BA-220 |
| Samson, Isaac, 20 April 1747, Mary Risteau | 2 BA-196 |
| Samson, Rich'd, 17 Dec. 1758, Ann Wyle | 2 BA-218 |
| Sandage, John, 19 Sept. 1751, Sarah Grover | 2 BA-204 |
| Sanders, Edward, 29 Oct. 1728, Christiana Beardy | 1 BA-249 |
| Sanders, Francis, 12 July 1702, Susannah Eads | 2 AA-318 |
| Sanders, James, 21 Feb. 1725, Elizabeth Brewer | 1 AA-102 |
| Sanders, James, 2 April 1769, Susanah Rickets | 1 AA-149 |
| Sanders, John, 19 Nov. 1726, Mary Bullin | 2 TA-114 |
| Sanders, John, 2 Nov. 1747, Cassandra White | 2 TA-281 |
| Sanders, John, 27 June 1777, Martha Slate | 10 BA-68 |
| Sanders, John, 7 Nov. 1777, Mary Dunn | 7 AA-2 |
| Sanders, Nich's, 24 Dec. 1727, Mary Ridgely | 1 AA-106 |
| Sanders, Thomas, 6 May 1719, Rebecca Frith | 2 TA-90 |
| Sanders, William, 6 Oct. 1726, Elizabeth Johnson | 2 TA-114 |
| Sanders, William, 25 July 1740, Sarah White | 3 TA-23 |
|    2 TA-170 gives date as 28 July 1740. | |
| Sanders, William, 1 April 1742, Eliza White | 3 TA-37 |
|    2 TA-172 gives the date as 27 April 1742. | |
| Sanderson, Peter, 14 Jan. 1700, Hannah (?) | 2 TA-12 |
| Sandige, John, 25 Aug. 1751, Sarah Grover | 2 BA-241 |
| Sands, Alexander, 19 Sept. 1717, Frances Canman | 1 AA-279 |
| Sands, Robert, 11 April 1776, Sarah Norris | 2 AA-412 |
| Sands, Thomas, 31 Dec. 1730, Eliz'th Swift | 1 QA-37 |
| Sandsbury, John, 12 Dec. 1737, Ann Norris | 2 TA-164 |
| Sangster, James, 13 Nov. 1679, Mary Benston | 5 SO-399 |
| Sank, Zachius, 18 July 1771, Jemima Wickes | 2 BA-262 |
| Sankey, Thomas, 21 May 1723, Martha Marshall | 2 PG-3 |
|    1 AA-96 has the same information. | |
| Sapington, James, 4 March 17-(?), Ann Gray | 2 KE-236 |
| Sapinton, Nathaniell, 27 Dec. 1713, Margret Huntly | 3 CE-6 |
| Sapinton, Thomas, 30 Jan. 1717, Mary Rutland | 1 AA-79 |
| Sappinton, John, 17 April 1722, Sarah Sherbert | 1 AA-90 |
| Sappinton, Thomas, 30 Jan. 1717, Mary Rutland | 1 AA-281 |
| Sarde, John, 22 Dec. 1720, Eleanor Fisher | 1 AA-302 |
| Sargent, James, 9 Dec. 1735, Elianer Tayler | 3 AA-107 |
| Sargent, John, 2 Oct. 1692, Sarah Carne | 5 SO-399 |
| Sartain, Jno., 9 March 1736, Mable Collins | 1 QA-43 |
| Sarton, Robert, 6 April 1749, Elizabeth Cook | 1 QA-55 |
| Satchivell, George, 28 Aug. 1723, Elizabeth Grey | 1 AA-97 |
| Satterfield, Edward, 21 Feb. 1744, Mary Barkhurst | 1 QA-50 |
| Satterfield, Nathan'll, 22 Dec. 1739, Mary Tennent | 1 QA-45 |
| Satterfield, Nathan'l, 21 Oct. 1741, Sophia Yong | 1 QA-47 |
| Satterfield, William, 9 Sept. 1743, Mary Whitby | 1 QA-48 |
| Satterlee, James, 18 April 1756, Belvedera Davis | 1 QA-61 |
| Saunders, Benjamin, 25 May 1756, Susannah Jerman | 1 QA-61 |
| Saunders, James, son of James, 23 Sept. 1703, Jane | |
|    Cotter, widow | 1 AA-64 |

| | |
|---|---|
| Saunders, James, 25 June 1706, Elizabeth Jones, widow | 1 AA-72 |
| Saunders, John, 11 Nov. 1703, Rachell Davies | 1 AA-64 |
| Saunders, Rob't, 28 April 1765, Eliz. Andrews | 2 BA-228 |
| Saunders, Stephen, 15 May 1707, Rose Nelson | 1 AA-73 |
| Savage, Thomas, 13 Feb. 1759, Catharine Scotton | 1 QA-64 |
| Savin, William, 6 Oct. 1695, Sarah Hill, dau. of | |
| Samuell and Elizabeth | 3 CE-1 |
| Savory, John, 27 June 1699, Ann Reves | 1 BA-187 |
| Savory, John, 29 Aug. 1734, Mary Bucknal | 1 BA-276 |
| Sayth, John, 15 July 1735, Sarah Rich | 3 BA-154 |
| Saywell, James, 30 Jan. 1686, Mary Price | 2 TA-9 |
| Scaggs, Richard, Dec. (1727 ?), Mary Brushier | 2 PG-4 |
| Scandret, William, 1 April 1742, Anne Earle | 1 QA-47 |
| Scarff, Benj'n, 13 Sept. 1763, Ann Bayley | 2 BA-225 |
| Scarff, John, 29 July 1770, Hannah Talbott | 2 BA-260 |
| Scarlett, Stephen, 7 April 1740, Ruth Belshar | 1 BA-308 |
| Scharf,Henry, 28 Dec. 1758, Patty Hardisty | 2 BA-218 |
| Scheffer, George, 7 July 1761, Ursula Arnold | 4 FR-1167 |
| Scheffer, Henry, 19 June 1763, Elizabeth Keller | 4 FR-1167 |
| Scheidegger, John, 24 May 1757, Eva Mary Manz | 4 FR-1103 |
| Schellenbaum, Christ'n, 3 May 1757, Marg. Caselman | 4 FR-1103 |
| Scherer,John, 29 Dec. 1757, Mary Sus. Dentlinger | 4 FR-1103 |
| Schlegel, Ernst Carl, 9 Jan. 1770, Anna Margaretha | |
| Peifferni | 8 BA-176 |
| Schley, Geo. Thom., 16 May 1758, Mary Gietzendanner | 4 FR-1104 |
| Schmidt, George, 22 Jan. 1767, Catharine Sturm | 4 FR-1167 |
| Schmidt, William, 1 Dec. 1757, Agnes Mey | 4 FR-1103 |
| Schmitt, Phil, 20 Oct. 1761, Christin Sebastian | 4 FR-1167 |
| Schneberger, Antereus, 2 Dec. 1764, Cath. Gerber | 4 FR-1167 |
| Schneebeli, Leonhardt, 8 May 1758, Marg. Weisz | 4 FR-1104 |
| Schneider, Geo. Mich'l, 29 Nov. 1757, Judith Unsel | 4 FR-1103 |
| Schneider, Jacob, 1757, Maria Magdalena Bissinger | 5 FR-107 |
| Schnock, Simon, 9 Feb. 1768, Charlotte Keller | 4 FR-1167 |
| Schoenefeld, Frederick, 6 March 1763, M. El. | |
| Weschebach | 4 FR-1167 |
| Schoenfeld, Will'm, 26 Oct. 1761, Marg. Gessinger | 4 FR-1167 |
| Schoolfield, Henry, 27 Nov. 1746, Leah Addams | 2 SO-72 |
| Scholar, Robert, 17 Jan. 1756, Martha Bond | 1 QA-60 |
| Schollar, Robert, 8 Aug. 1732, Elizabeth Taylor | 1 QA-39 |
| Schonefeld, John, 23 March 1757, Mary Cath. Mezier | 4 FR-1103 |
| Schoomaker, Conrad, 17 Dec. 1733, Susanna Cheney | 1 AA-117 |
| Schotter, Christian, 3 Aug. 1762, A. M. Mueller | 4 FR-1167 |
| Schuemacher, Dan'l, 1 Feb. 1757, Elizab. Hoffman | 4 FR-1103 |
| Schur, Christ'n, 28 March 1758, M. Salome Bargett | 4 FR-1103 |
| Schuti, Jacob, 8 March 1762, Catherine Frey | 4 FR-1167 |
| Schyler, Ephraim, 17 Dec. 1777, Mary Guttery | 1 WA-534 |
| Scimmons, Thos., 6 Feb. 1753, Pricilla Maccomas | 2 BA-207 |
| Scochnessy, Patrick, 19 Nov. 1776, Catherine Cotter | 3 BA-669 |
| Scofield, Robert, 14 Oct. 1697, Mary Lewis | 2 AA-293 |
| Scolefield, John, 16 Nov. 1735, Mary (?) | 3 AA-109 |
| Scolefield, John, 4 Aug. 1744, Elizabeth (?) | 3 AA-109 |
| Sconderick, Thos. L., 29 May 1736, Esther Story | 1 QA-42 |
| Scot, James, 1 Feb. (1774 ?), Letitia Lewis | 6 BA(1) |
| Scot, John, 14 Nov. 1754, Sarah Edgar Wade | 1 CH-187 |
| Scotland, William, 15 July 1749, Eliz. Taylor | 2 BA-198 |
| Scott, Andrew, 28 April 1737, Anne Smith | 2 BA-73 |
| Scott, Aquilla, 13 Oct. 1743, Eliz. Puttee | 2 BA-133 |
| Scott, Aquilla, 16 Jan. 1770, Mary Preston | 2 BA-259 |
| Scott, Benjamin, 9 Nov. 1763, Mary Stevenson | 2 SO-174 |
| Scott, Charles, 17 Aug. 1732, Elizabeth Terry | 3 CE-14 |
| Scott, Charles, 8 Aug. 1733, Ann Williamson | 3 KE-329 |
| Scott, Daniel, 27 Jan. 1740, Hannah Butterworth | 2 BA-147 |
| Scott, Day, 20 Feb. 1728, Alice Ballard | 1 WI-15 |
| Scott, Day, 27 Aug. 1745, Esther Dashiell | 1 WI-35 |
| Scott, Edward, 17 April 1702, Martha Tildon | 3 KE-323 |

Scott, Col. Edward, 23 June 1724, Rachell Blay          3 KE-327
Scott, Edward, 7 Oct. 1725, Hannah Smith          3 KE-328
Scott, ffrancis, 7 June 1715, Elizabeth Lungle?          3 CE-7
Scott, George, 18 Feb. 1728/9, Catherine (?)          6 AA-201
Scott, George, 26 Jan. 1733, Izable Flemond          2 TA-154
Scott, George Day, 21 March 1760, Elizabeth Handy          1 WI-55
Scott, James, 18 Feb. 1741, Ann Wheeler          1 BA-322
Scott, James, Sept. 1749, Mary Martin          2 BA-244
    2 BA-199 gives date as 12 Nov. 1749.
Scott, Jas., 9 Feb. 1768, Ann Amoss          2 BA-231
Scott, James, 15 April 1770, Casandera Bond          2 BA-260
Scott, James, 1 Feb. 1774, Letitia Lewis          2 BA-253
Scott, James, 29 Oct. 1777, Anne Shaw          1 CR-28
    1 CR-10 has same information.
Scott, Joseph, son of Jacob and Hannah, 29 day, 10 mo.,
    1762, Ann Hawood          7 SF-8
Scott, Nathaniel, 6 Jan. 1746, Mary Godwin          1 QA-52
Scott, Nathaniel, 7 Aug. 1748, Mary Blades          1 QA-54
Scott, Richard, 28 June 1735, Mary Kean          1 BA-283
Scott, Rob't, 29 March 1749, Mary Carlile          2 BA-198
Scott, Samuel, June 1771, Sarah Benton          2 BA-51
Scott, Walter, 17 April 1707, Grace Rumsey          3 CE-3
Scott, Walter, 4 July 1733, Cathrin Burminham          3 CE-14
Scott, William, 16 Jan. 1747, Lucrese Hornton          1 QA-54
Scott, William, 2 July 1749, Elizabeth Tayler          2 BA-243
Scott, William, 4 Aug. 1754, Jane Hughs          2 BA-211
Scott, William, 28 Oct. 1755, Rachel Sparks          1 QA-60
Scott, William, 19 May 1757, Mary Smith          2 BA-215
Scotten, Richard, 14 (Feb. ?) 1728, Mary Spry          1 QA-36
Scotter, Devans, 19 July 1761, Mary Porrord          2 BA-222
Scotton, Richard, 26 Sept. 1758, Lydia Mereday          1 QA-64
Scotton, Thomas, 14 Sept. 1743, Sarah Hadly          1 QA-48
Scovee?, William, 15 June 1769, Hannah Hanson          3 BA-170
Screvener, Jno., 8 Nov. 1713, Eliz. Got          2 AA-348
Scrivener, Richard, 1 Sept. 1709, Mary Burck          2 AA-338
Scrivener, William, 27 Dec. 1773, Ann Batson          2 AA-411
Scrivin, Philip, 18 Sept. 1703, Mary Simmons          2 AA-322
Scroggan, John, 29 Oct. 1777, Ann Maslin or Mastin          2 CH(4)
Scyce, John, 1728, Sarah Dudley          3 KE-328
Seaborn, Edward, 5 Feb. 1722, Mary Cannon          1 AA-318
Seago, John, 17 April 1740, Margaret Birmingham          1 QA-46
Seamour, George, 9 Jan. 1750, Mary Ann Shepherd          1 QA-57
Seawell, Thomas, 8 Oct. 1677, Jeane Boist          5 SO-399
Seborn, Edw'd, 5 Feb. 1722, Mary Cannon          1 AA-94
Seddon, John, 3 Oct. 1745, Margaret Evans          3 BA-158
Sedgewicks, Elisha, 3 Oct. 1711, Grace Aman          1 AA-78
Sedgwick, Gabriell, 30 (Jan.?) 1713, Margarett (?)          4 AA-392
Sedgwick, Thomas, 21 Dec. 1777, Ann Rigby          1 CA-111a
Sedwick, John, 1 March 1764, Elizabeth Lauder or
    Sander Cook          2 CA-51
Seems, Francis, 14 Jan. 1733, Lucretia Chapman          1 CH-180
Seeny, Terrence, 2 May 1737, Rachell Poore          2 TA-163
Sefferson, John, 11 May 1725, Sarah Sapinton          3 CE-12
Seiney, Morgan, 4 Sept. 1703, Elizabeth Briant          3 KE-323
Selby, Benj., 4 Aug. 1757, Elizabeth Boone          3 AA-112
Selby, Ezekiel, 17 Dec. 1758, Isbell Denwood          2 SO-78
Selby, John, 24 Sept. 1750, Mary Atkinson          2 SO-77
Selby, John, 22 Oct. 1758, Grace Handy          2 SO-78
Selby, Joshua Wilson, 29 Jan. 1764, Sarah Fowler          9 AA-247
Selby, Parker, c.Aug. 1775, Priscilla Fountain          1 CR-6
Selby, Samuel, 12 Dec. 1717, Sarah Smith, dau. of
    Nathan          2 PG-2
Sellavin, William, 6 Dec. 1748, Bridget Phillips          2 SO-76
Sellman, Benjamin, 16 April 1733, Ann Powell          1 AA-118
Selman, John, 4 Dec. 1707, Martha Groce          1 AA-76

Selman, John, 18 June 1728, Eliza Taylor                      1 AA-107
Selman, William, 9 Oct. 1718, Anne Sparrow                   1 AA-287
Selman, William, 28 Jan. 1777, Priscilla Harwood             2 AA-413
Selvester, Benjamin, 19 May 1743, Mary Young                 1 QA-48
Seney, Solomon, 23 April 1732, Mary Nevill                   1 QA-38
Seney, Sollomon, 28 May 1747, Ann Nevel                      1 QA-53
Senhouse, John, 22 Dec. 1750, Anne Topping                   4 AA-453
Seon, Thomas, 28 Feb. 1737, Jean Handy                       2 SO-73
Serber, Jacob, 10 April 1768, Cath. Caufeld                  4 FR-1167
Sergant. John, 4 Feb. 1732, Elisabeth Gosstwick              3 BA-150
Sergeant, Jeremiah, son of Joseph and Frances, 11 day,
    5 mo., 1757, Ann Sidwell, dau. of Hugh and Ann           9 SF
Sergeant, John, son of Joseph, 25 April 1753, Rachel
    Kirk, dau. of Roger and Jane                             9 SF
Serviteer, John, 21 Sept. 1777, Elizabeth Smith             10 AA-69
Severn, John, 4 July 1756, Elinor Hayden                     1 QA-61
Sevill, Thomas, 21 Jan. 1730, Rebecca Dehorty                1 QA-38
Sewall, Harry, 28 Jan. 1770, Sarah Roach                     1 SM-135
Seward, Daniel, 17 Nov. 1748, Margaret Hines                 1 QA-55
Seward, George, 21 April 1737, Elianor Vandeford             1 QA-43
Seward, Isaac, 4 Nov. 1750, Milliston Vanderford             1 QA-57
Seward, John, 6 Nov. 1748, Sarah Offley                      1 QA-54
Seward, Thomas, 30 Dec. 1735, Eliza Johnson                  1 QA-41
Seward, William, 26 Sept. 1744, Mary Venderford              1 QA-49
Sewel, John, 17 Nov. 1719, Rachel Topping                    4 AA-410
Sewel, John, 2 May 1751, Mary Crouch                         2 KE-290
Sewell, John, 30 May 1721, Hannah Carroll                    4 AA-414
Sewell, Philip, 10 Feb. 1708, Sarah Floud                    4 AA-378
Sewell, Richard, 13 June 1699, Jane Ellis; the marriage
    was performed by Rev. Stephen Bordley, minister of
    St. Paul's Par., Kent Co.                                3 CE-2
Sewell, Thomas, 11 Feb. 1746, Mary Newnam                    1 QA-53
Seyler, Philip, 9 Dec. 1766, Christina Eberly                4 FR-1167
Seymore, Nicholas, 27 Feb. 1746, Eliz'h Mansfield            1 QA-53
Seymour, John, 2 Oct. 1729, Hannah Lawson                    1 QA-37
Shaaf, Casper, 12 Nov. 1759, Alice Charlton, dau. of
    Arthur and Elinor                                        1 FR-12
Shackles, John, 19 Oct. 1732, Deborah Symmons                1 AA-114
Shadows, David, 26 Dec. 1749, Ann Bozwell                    2 BA-199
                                                             & 244
Shafford, Robert, 17 (Dec. 1768 ?), Catherine (?)            2 BA-257
Shanahan, Jonathan, 15 April 1743, Margaret Catrope          3 TA-42
Shanahawn, Jonathan, 5 May 1743, Mary Catrop                 2 TA-174
Shanks, Joseph, 18 Feb. 1772, Susanna Goldsmith              1 SM-136
Shannahane, Peter, 25 Feb. 1717, Cathrine Pindergrass        2 TA-83
Shannem, Thomas, 26 Sept. 1750, Eliz. Kersey                 2 BA-202
Shannishshy, James, 14 Oct. 1736, Frances Pitchfork          2 TA-159
Sharp, George, 25 Feb. 1759,Hannah Baily                     1 WI-59
Sharp, John, 20 Nov. 1752, Hannah Cook                       2 BA-206
Sharp, Peter, 4 May 1704, Catharine Troth                    8 SF-422
Sharp, Sam'l, 2 June 1741, Anne Birckhead                    3 TA-31
    2 TA-172 gives date as 3 June 1741, and the bride's
    name as Ann Birkett.
Sharp, William, chirurgeon, 23 Oct. 1729, Ann Burkhead       8 SF-51
Sharpe, William, son of Peter, 4 July 1673, Elizabeth
    Thomas, dau. of Thomas Thomas                            1 TA-603
Sharpless, Benjamin, son of Benj. and Edith, of Phila.,
    4 day, 11 mo., 1774, Sarah Rigbie, dau. of James
    and Elizabeth                                            7 SF-32
Shaw, Dan'l, 14 April 1763, Prudence Bozley                  2 BA-225
Shaw, John, 26 July 1731, Catherine Abbott                   2 TA-151
Shaw, John, 2 July 1734, Frances Bays                        3 BA-152
Shaw, John, 20 Oct. 1737, Ann Eldrick                        2 TA-161
Shaw, John, 19 July 1777, Ann Welstead Pratt                 7 AA-1
Shaw, Matthew, 20 Feb. 1754, Susannah Barrat                 1 QA-59

Shaw, Richard, 2 Oct. 1706, Margrett Turnner          1 AA-72
Shaw, Richard, 17 May 1720, Elizabeth Parker          1 AA-299
Shaw, Thomas Nightsmith, 31 Dec. 1777, Sarah Stansbury  9 BA
Shaw, Weymoth, 23 April 1761, Ann Worthington         2 BA-221
Shaw, William, 17 July 1709, Jane Cox                 2 TA-61
Shaw, William, 21 Aug. 1722, Elizabeth Cursitor       2 TA-103
Shaw, William, 17 Sept. 1750, Ruth Harriman           3 BA-164
Shaw, William, 18 March 1759, Jane Bennet             1 WI-64
Shawhawn, Darby, 20 Nov. 1707, Sarah Meeks            3 KE-324
Shawhorn, John, 8 Oct. 1730, Elizabeth Peach          2 KE-220
Shea, William, 8 March 1770, Eliz. Willson            2 BA-260
Shealy, Daniel, 14 Aug. 1677, Elianor Harris          9 SO-402
Sheares, Robert, 1 Sept. 1747, Eliza Kersey           3 TA-66
Shearman, Thomas, 21 April 1728, Mary Shutten         2 KE-215
Shears, William, 20 Sept. 1744, Frances Shannassey    2 TA-184
Sheckels, Hezekiel, 1771, Hanna Dunn                  2 AA-411
Sheckels, Richard, 10 Feb. 1773, Sarah Simmons        2 AA-411
Sheckels, Samuel, 1771, Ann McSeney                   2 AA-410
Sheeld, John, 16 Jan. 1696, Elizabeth Bunn            1 BA-178
Sheepard, Francis, 21 Feb. 1748, Elizabeth Alesworth  3 AA-110
Sheepard, Nicholas, 25 March 1722, Anna Smith         3 AA-100
Sheers, John, 5 Jan. 1746, Tamar Ward                 1 QA-52
Sheffield, John, 17 Jan. 1710, Elizabeth Whittington  2 AA-341
Shehane, Cornelius, 6 Aug. 1723, Mary Stacy           2 TA-107
Shehawn, Daniel, 6 May 1760, Jane Roberts             2 TA-168
Shehawn, David, 1 Jan. 1738, Rose Parvis              2 TA-165
Shekel, Thomas, 11 Dec. 1701, Mary Budd               2 AA-317
Sheldon, Andrew, 30 Jan. 1769, Mary Fields            2 BA-257
Shelston, William, 25 Nov. 1739, Katherine Neall      1 PG-288
Shelton, Thomas, 6 Aug. 1777, Elizabeth Webb          3 PG-165
Shepard, Christopher, 5 Sept. 1733, Sarah Drew        1 BA-271
Shepard, James, 13 Nov. 1720, Mary Harrison           2 TA-95
Shepard, John, 14 Aug. 1753, Margrett Elliott         2 BA-208
Sheperd, John, 8 Oct. 1777, Mary Hudson               2 CE-1
Shephard, Rowland, 22 June 1727, Jane Taylor          1 BA-244
Shepherd, Henry, 1771, Sarah Dove                     2 AA-411
Sheppard, James, son of William, and Anne, 6 Nov.
   1746, Mary White, dau. of John and Mary            9 SF
Sheppard, Messer, son of William and Hannah, 10 Feb.
   1774, Susannah Redd, dau. of Adam and Miriam       9 SF
Sheppard, Robert, son of William and Ann, 8 Nov. 1744,
   Mary Slater, dau. of George and Sarah              9 SF
Shepperd, William, 18 Oct. 1757, Cathrine Linden      2 BA-216
Sherbutt, John, 14 Sept. 1697, Mary Fowler            2 AA-293
Sherelock, John, 30 Nov. 1737, Elizabeth Cheshire     2 BA-104
Shering, Jeames, 19 Dec. 1725, Catherin Edging        2 TA-112
Sherman, Job, 5 Feb. 1733, Abigail Hibble             1 WI-50
Shermon, Isaac, 28 May 1740, Sarah Linch              1 WI-53
Sherrard, William, 1 March 1757, Elizabeth Cornelius  2 KE-292
Sherwood, Dan'l, 8 Feb. 1745/6, Eliza Rice            3 TA-56
Sherwood, Edward Man, 19 Oct. 1722, Mary Skillington  2 TA-104
Sherwood, ffrancis, 21 July 1701, Mary (?)            2 TA-16
Sherwood, Francis, 10 May 1737, Johannah Neal         2 TA-163
Sherwood, Francis, 28 April 1742, Mary Lowry          3 TA-38
Sherwood, Henry, 29 day, 11 mo., 1765, Elizabeth
   Williams                                           8 SF-121
Sherwood, John, 28 Jan. (?), Elizabeth Berry          2 TA-31
Sherwood, John, 10 Sept. 1718, Penelope Skillington   2 TA-88
Sherwood, John, 19 Oct. 1724, Gemima Ryley            2 PG-4
Sherwood, John, Jr., 17 May 1738, Prudence Bozman     2 TA-165
Sherwood, John, Jr., 4 Jan. 1743/4, Catharine Cooper  3 TA-46
Shield, Bryan, 24 Sept. 1711, Jane Curtis             2 TA-70
Shield, Lambert, 25 April 1737, Mary Merchantt        2 TA-163
Shield, William, 17 Feb. 1723, Margrett Huff          3 KE-327
Shields, Caleb, 12 May 1777, Jane Brown               7 AA-1
   5 BA-12 gives date as 17 June 1777.

| | |
|---|---|
| Shields, Edmond, 23 Jan. 1724, Susanna Slyney | 4 AA-424 |
| Shields, James, 1 Aug. 1746, Eliz'h Griffin | 1 QA-52 |
| Shields, James, 17 July 1777, Henney Tarman | 1 CR-10 |
| Shields, James, 26 Aug. 1777, Henney Torman | 2 TA-28 |
| Shields, John, 16 Jan. 1696, Elizabeth Bunn | 1 BA-178 |
| Shields, Paul, 21 May 1761, Eliz. Brown | 2 BA-221 |
| Shiles, Edmund, 7 Feb. 1733/4, Elinor Hains | 1 WI-7 |
| Shiles?, John, Jr., 14 Sept. 1737, Ann Evains | 1 WI-30 |
| Shiletto, Thomas, 31 Jan. 1678, Mary Rogers | 5 SO-399 |
| Shipard, Francis, 21 Dec. 1766, Sarah Moss | 3 AA-112 |
| Shipley, Benjamin, 12 Dec. 1776, Agness Short | 5 BA-12 |
| Shipley, Richard, 22 Oct. 1728, Ketura Barnes | 4 AA-430 |
| Shipman, Nathaniel, 30 July 1757, Mary Pearce | 1 QA-62 |
| Shipton, John, Oct. 1757, Mary Speer | 2 BA-183 |
| Shirly, Ignatius, Nov. 1775, Mary Norris | 1 SM-137 |
| Shirman, Thomas, 20 Feb. 1736/7, Rachell Collins | 1 WI-16 |
| Shively, Bernard, 22 Sept. 1777, Eleanor Longford | 2 CH(1) |
| Shivers, John, 24 July 1722, Ellenor Howard | 4 AA-419 |
| Shoats, John, 27 Feb. 1772, Mary Kug | 2 BA-264 |
| Shockley, Robert, 4 Oct. 1674, Ann Boyden | 5 SO-399 |
| Shockly, Richard, 19 Oct. 1736, Sarah Todvine | 1 WI-19 |
| Shoebridge, John, 28 Oct. 1732, Mary Norris | 2 BA-75 |
| Shoebrook, Thomas, 3 March 1734, Margaret Fowler | 1 QA-40 |
| Shoemaker, Gideon, 12 May 1776, Eliza Whittington | 2 AA-413 |
| Shonahon, Justinian, 11 Feb. 1726/7, Elizabeth Hopkins | 2 TA-115 |
| Short, Abraham, 23 Jan. 1706, Naomy Thurman | 1 AA-73 |
| Short, Abraham, 9 Sept. 1764, Mary Chilcoat | 9 AA-248 |
| Short, George, 23 Dec. 1705, Susanna Darnell | 3 KE-323 |
| Short, Henry, 26 (July ?) 1733, Sarah Monsieur | 1 QA-40 |
| Short, John, 22 June 1732, Mary Miller | 1 AA-114 |
| Showdy, Francis, 13 Sept. 1754, Louzanna Taylor | 2 BA-211 |
| Showel, Thomas Roades, 29 Dec. 1760, Phillis Anna Baxter | 4 BA-72 |
| Shulivant, Owen, 11 Dec. 1709, Cathrine Whaley | 2 TA-64 |
| Siahs, John, 21 June 1736, Mary Chambers | 3 BA-155 |
| Sibbey, James, 28 Sept. 1777, Amelia Wiley | 1 MO-517 |
| Sibell, Henry, 28 May 1777, Elizabeth Henderson | 7 AA-1 |
| Sickelmore, Samuel, 8 Dec. 1713, Ruth Cammell | 2 BA-4 |
| Sickelmore, Samuel, 12 Sept. 1716, Katterne Herrington | 2 BA-9 |
| Sickelmore, Sutton, 29 July 1762, Prudence Hindon | 2 BA-223 |
| Sidewell, Hugh, son of John, 28 Oct. 1741, Hannah Berry, dau. of Samuel | 9 SF |
| Sidwell, Abraham, son of Hugh and Ann, 5 May 1756, Charity Harris, dau. of John and Phebe | 9 SF |
| Sidwell, Henry, son of Hugh and Ann, 26 Nov. 1746, Ellen Huff, dau. of Michael and Jennett | 9 SF |
| Sidwell, Henry, son of Hugh and Ann, 12 Sept. 1763, Margaret Hagan, dau. of Catherine | 9 SF |
| Sidwell, Hugh, son of Hugh and Ann, 7 March 1750/1, Anne Haines, dau. of Joseph | 9 SF |
| Sidwell, Isaac, son of Hugh and Ann, 2 Oct. 1755, Ann Brown, dau. of Thomas and Elinor | 9 SF |
| Sidwell, James, son of Richard and Margaret, 16 Oct. 1771, Hannah Allen, dau. of Wm. and Rachel | 9 SF |
| Sidwell, Joseph, son of Hugh and Ann, 30 Sept. 1762, Rachel Medcalf, dau. of James and Margaret | 9 SF |
| Sidwell, Richard, born in Letcomb Regis, Berks., (Eng.), 23 Jan. 1739/40, Margaret King, dau. of Francis | 9 SF |
| Sidwell, Richard, son of Hugh and Ann, 4 Oct. 1744, Ann Job, dau. of Thomas | 9 SF |
| Sillivane, Owen, 24 June 1703, Mary Dedman | 2 TA-36 |
| Sillson, Joseph, 1 July 1730, Sarah Longo | 2 TA-148 |
| Silver, Matthew, 30 Nov. 1721, Ann Cane? Woodall | 2 TA-97 |
| Silvero, Nicholas, 1676, Elizabeth Barnett | 9 SO-401 |

| | |
|---|---|
| Silvester, Benjamin, 12 Sept. 1733, Jane West | 1 QA-39 |
| Silvester, Benj., 1 Dec. 1733, Lucey Bradbury | 2 TA-154 |
| Silvester, James, 11 Sept. 1750, Sarah Climer | 1 QA-57 |
| Sim, Patrick, 11 July 1777, Mary Carroll | 3 PG-105 |
| Sim, William, 17 June 1750, Mary Low | 3 BA-165 |
| Simkins, John, 19 Aug. 1711, Sarah Bradley | 3 KE-324 |
| Simkins, John, 15 June 1744, Sarah Foreacres | 1 QA-49 |
| Simmonds, Richard, 30 July 1707, Alse Trew | 3 KE-323 |
| Simmons, Abra., 3 June 1764, Mary Garrett | 2 BA-226 |
| Simmons, Abraham, 1773, Priscilla Liles | 2 AA-411 |
| Simmons, Charles, 19 Oct. 1742, Eliz. Poteet | 2 BA-124 |
| | & 144 |
| Simmons, George, 7 Dec. 1736, Jemima Standiford | 2 BA-74 |
| Simmons, George, 24 Oct. 1738, Eliz. Fuller | 2 BA-112 |
| Simmons, Isaac, 19 Nov. 1777, Susanna Simmons | 3 PG-152 |
| Simmons, James, 1771, Rebeccah Sheckels | 2 AA-410 |
| Simmons, Jonathan, 20 June 1734, Elizabeth Swearingen | 2 PG-6 |
| Simmons, Jonathan, 1770, Elizabeth Child | 2 AA-410 |
| Simmons, Knighton, 1771, Elizabeth Saunders | 2 AA-410 |
| Simmons, Richard, Oct. 1713, Sara Thornbury | 2 AA-353 |
| Simmons, Richard, 22 June 1738, Susannah Rottenger | 9 AA-246 |
| Simmons, Thomas, 6 Feb. 1753, Pricilla McComas | 2 BA-207 |
| Simmons, Van, 5 May 1773, Mary Drury | 2 AA-411 |
| Simmons, William, 1 Sept. 1773, Beatridge Jones | 2 AA-411 |
| Simms, Joseph, 8 Sept. 1763, Elizabeth Dent | 1 CH-192 |
| Simons, John, 1 Dec. 1721, Rebecca Smith | 3 CE-11 |
| Simpers, Richard, 1 June 1751, Catherine Howell | 1 CE-314 |
| Simpson, John, 19 April 1733, Elizabeth Dehoff | 3 CE-14 |
| Simpson, Jos., 28 Jan. 1770, Mary Jarboe | 1 SM-135 |
| Simpson, Samuel, 25 Dec. 1777, Mary Osborn | 10 BA-70 |
| 9 BA has same information. | |
| Simpson, Thomas, 7 Aug. 1703, Rebecca Richardson | 3 KE-323 |
| Simpson, Thomas, 9 Feb. 1707, Esther Moggeridge | 3 KE-324 |
| Simpson, Thomas, 13 Feb. 1717, Mary Smith | 1 BA-286 |
| Sims, David, 15 July 1756, Henrietta Ridean | 1 QA-61 |
| Simson, Amos, 24 April 1716, Elizabeth Duvall | 1 AA-79 |
| Sin, Jacob, 31 Oct. 1756, Magd. Biber | 4 FR-1103 |
| Sin, Philip, 6 Nov. 1764, Elizab. Zimmerman | 4 FR-1167 |
| Sinclair, Mordecai, 31 Aug. 1765, Ann Due | 9 AA-249 |
| Sinclar, William, 8 April 1714, Rachel Denboe | 3 CE-6 |
| Sincler, James, 25 Dec. 1742, Mary Lester | 1 BA-332 |
| Sincler, Mechaell, 29 Oct. 1700, Hannah Hoff | 3 AA-96 |
| Sindall, Samuel, 21 Feb. 1744, Eliz. Carter | 2 BA-192 |
| Sinkler, Jas., 1 Dec. 1767, Jane McMar | 2 BA-231 |
| Sinkler, William, 26 Nov. 1730, Mary Hines | 3 BA-150 |
| Sinkler, William, March 1769, Mary Norris | 2 BA-258 |
| Sinn, Jacob, 2 Nov. 1766, Philippina Karner | 4 FR-1167 |
| Sinnet, Thomas, 7 Jan. 1737, Sarah Norris | 2 KE-221 |
| Sinnot, Garrett, 21 Nov. 1666. Alice Hunt | 3 CH |
| Sinnott, John, 28 Oct. 1755, Eliza Sparks | 1 QA-60 |
| Sinnott, Solomon, 9 Nov. 1752, Rebecca Obryon | 1 QA-59 |
| Sipple, Garrett, of Kent Co., Del., 29 day, 4 mo., | |
| 1763, Elizabeth Berry, Jr. | 8 SF-111 |
| Sisk, James, 15 Nov. 1744, Anne Gaining | 2 TA-197 |
| Sissill, John, 26 Aug. 1777, Eleanor Combs | 3 SM-535 |
| Sitton, John, 9 June 1729, Elizabeth Pindel | 2 PG-5 |
| Sizzarson, Isaac, 13 Nov. 1719, Jane Jacob | 2 TA-91 |
| Sizzarson, Rich'd, 9 Jan. 1717, Elizabeth Clifford | 2 TA-82 |
| Skarabon, Peter, 13 March 1745, Eliz. Scharf | 2 BA-194 |
| Skeen, George, 23 Oct. 1755, Sarah Hackett | 1 QA-60 |
| Skeen, George, 22 Feb. 1757, Elizabeth Bateman | 1 QA-62 |
| Skelington, Thomas, 30 Dec. 1732, Mary Cole | 2 TA-152 |
| Skidmore, Josias, 7 Aug. 1707, Rebecca Smith | 3 KE-324 |
| Skillington, Elijah, 16 Nov. 1739, Sarah Bozman | 3 TA-20 |
| 2 TA-168 gives the date as 21 Dec. 1739. | |

| | | |
|---|---|---|
| Skillington, Kenellam, 20 Oct. 1692, Lydia Croxtill, late of Barbadoes | 8 SF-391 | |
| Skinner, Andrew, 28 May 1669, Anne Snodon | 1 TA-601 | |
| Skinner, Daniel, 29 Sept. 1774, Mary Casson | 1 CR | |
| Skinner, Thos., 19 Jan. 1747/8, Mary Connakin | 3 TA-68 | |
| Skinner, Wm., 23 Oct. 1701, Elizabeth (?) | 2 TA-21 | |
| Skinner, William, 14 May 1744, Ruth Tanner | 3 TA-49 | |
| Skipen, James, 1753, Anne Warring | 2 BA-242 | |
| Skipper, James, 10 Nov. 1753, Ann Wareing | 2 BA-209 | |
| Skurrey, Thomas, 28 Feb. 1738, Mary Price | 3 CE-22 | |
| Sky, Thomas, 23 July 1706, Elizabeth Maryfield | 1 BA-201 | |
| Slad, Josias, 16 Jan. 1738, Mary Day | 3 AA-106 | |
| Slade, Ezekiel, 7 Jan. 1754, Ann Whitaker | 2 BA-209 | |
| Slade, Jno., 9 Feb. 1709, Elizabeth Crouch | 3 AA-98 | |
| Slade, Thomas, 29 Sept. 1748, Hannah Miles | 2 BA-197 | |
| Slade, William, 13 Aug. 1741, Eliz. Dulany | 2 BA-44 | |
| Slade, William, 16 Jan. 1770, Eliz. Stansbury | 2 BA-259 | |
| Slater, Ellis, 12 July 1729, Sarah Delamere | 2 CA-25 | |
| Slater, John, 15 Oct. 1704, Jane Richards | 2 TA-42 | |
| Slater, John, 11 April 1708, Margaret (?) | 4 AA-372 | |
| Slater, John, 11 April 1708, Margaret Pennington | 4 AA-378 | |
| Slater, John, 18 Aug. 1755, Roannah Pollard | 2 BA-212 | |
| Slater, Jonathan, 1771, Ann Robison | 2 AA-411 | |
| Slater, Timothy, 24 Dec. 1722, Mary Collins | 3 KE-326 | |
| Slater, William, 5 Nov. 1741, Marg't Lovet | 3 TA-33 | |
| Slaughter, Edward, 2 March 1756, Eve Harrington | 1 QA-60 | |
| Slaughter, James, 8 Nov. 1741, Mary Levett | 2 TA-175 | |
| Slaughter, William, 5 Dec. 1734, Eleanor Cannon | 2 TA-156 | |
| Slay, Edward, 19 Aug. 1755, Sophia Seymore | 1 QA-59 | |
| Slay, Thomas, 26 Aug. 1759, Frances Ricketts | 1 QA-65 | |
| Slemaker, James, 15 Sept. 1745, Elizabeth Giles | 3 BA-157 | |
| Slice, Samuel, 15 Oct. 1711, Mary Churce | 3 KE-324 | |
| Sligh, Thomas, 17 April 1734, Sophia Wilkisson | 3 BA-152 | |
| Slipper, Thomas, 20 Sept. 1703, Barbary Stuard | 3 KE-323 | |
| Slipper, William, Oct. 1729, Mary Hodgess | 3 KE-327 | |
| Sloan, Rev. Samuel, 21 Aug. 1780, Mrs. Elizabeth Moore | 2 SO-167 | |
| Slocum, Joseph, 26 Feb. 1749, Mary Horsley | 1 QA-56 | |
| Slone, John, 1 Aug. 1722, Sarah Rock | 2 TA-103 | |
| Sloss, Thomas, 23 Oct. 1750, Mary Stoughton, dau. of William and Ann | 3 SO-4 | |
| Slow, Wm., 19 Aug. 1735, Ann Dean | 2 TA-160 | |
| Slowin, John, 17 Oct. 1770, Eliz. Smith | 2 BA-261 | |
| Sluyter, Benjamin, Nov. 1777, (?) Thompson | 2 CE | |
| Slycer, John, son of Thomas and Mary, 6 June 1771, Elizabeth Wollaston, dau. of Joseph and Deborah | 9 SF | |
| Slycer, Thomas, son of Robert, of Tewkesbury, Glouc., (Eng.), 16 June 1737, Mary Harris, dau. of William | 9 SF | |
| Slye, Robert, 3 June 1773, Elizabeth Stoddart | 1 CH-204 | |
| Small, Charles, 27 Jan. 1763, Mary Ann Hammond | 3 AA-112 | |
| Small, John, 14 April 1738, Eliza Day | 2 TA-165 | |
| Small, John, 1 Oct. 1777, Ann Pettiboon | 7 AA-2 | |
| Small, Samuel, 29 May 1739, Sarah Banning | 3 TA-17 | |
| Smith, (?), 15 Oct. 17-(?), (wife's name not given) | 3 KE-309 | |
| Smith, Alexander, 24 Jan. 1758, Eliz. Guyton | 2 BA-217 | |
| Smith, Alexand'r, 6 Nov. 1764, Eliz. Smith | 2 BA-227 | |
| Smith, Alexand'r, 25 Dec. 1766, Martha Chalk | 2 BA-230 | |
| Smith, Anthony, 9 Jan. 1700, Johanna Hull | 1 AA-57 | |
| 1 AA-246 gives the bride's name as Joanna Hall. | | |
| Smith, Archibald, 1775, Sarah McCallum | 1 CR | |
| Smith, Casparus, 11 Oct. 1703, Ann Robinson, widow | 3 CE-4 | |
| Smith, Casparus, 13 Feb. 1728, Joan Lowther | 1 QA-36 | |
| Smith, Charles, 6 Nov. 1715, Martha Parker | 3 KE-326 | |
| Smith, Charles, 13 May 1726, Mary Cuninham | 2 KE-209 | |
| Smith, Charles, 28 Jan. 1747, Ann Connell | 3 BA-161 | |
| Smith, Charles, 2 Oct. 1760, Mary McClister, widow of Capt. Geo. McClister | 1 WI-96 | |

| | |
|---|---|
| Smith, Daniel, 13 Nov. 1735, Mary Wyat | 1 QA-41 |
| Smith, Daniel, 7 Sept. 1757, Mary Rolls | 1 QA-62 |
| Smith, Edward, 2 Aug. 1713, Mary Doulon | 4 AA-380 |
| Smith, Edward, 1775, Elizabeth Baxter | 1 CR |
| Smith, Ezekiel, 16 Sept. 1774, Ann Jacobs | 1 CR |
| Smith, Francis, 29 Nov. 1737, Eleanor Elbsby | 2 TA-164 |
| Smith, George, 3 Oct. 1671, Martha Gibbs | 5 SO-399 |
| Smith, George, 24 Dec. 1729, Mary Scrivener | 1 QA-37 |
| Smith, George, 10 Feb. 1730, Judah Turner | 1 WI-5 |
| Smith, George, 5 May 1752, Rebecca Chairs | 1 QA-58 |
| Smith, Gilbert, 9 June 1773, Lidia Kilty | 2 AA-411 |
| Smith, Henry, 24 Sept. 1734, Katherine Organ | 3 BA-152 |
| Smith, Henry, 3 May 1736, Katherine Dunn | 3 BA-155 |
| Smith, Henry, June 1738, Eliz. Druley | 2 BA-129 |
| Smith, Henry, 6 June 1738, Eliz. Dury | 2 TA-165 |
| Smith, Henry, 11 Oct. 1753, Mary Bell | 2 SO-75 |
| Smith, Jacob, mariner, 9 Dec. 1745, Lucy Coleman, spinster | 2 KE-269 |
| Smith, James, 19 Feb. 1703, Hannah Hurtt | 3 KE-323 |
| Smith, James, 21 Jan. 1705, Mary Hynson | 3 KE-323 |
| Smith, James, 6 Dec. 1708, Joyce Quinney | 3 KE-324 |
| Smith, James, 4 May 1710, Mrs. Susanna Crouch | 1 AA-77 & 259 |
| Smith, James, 18 May 1720, Rebecca Clark | 3 KE-326 |
| Smith, James, 24 Oct. 1734, Barbary Lanham | 3 KE-329 |
| Smith, James, 6 Oct. 1746, Charity Lett | 3 BA-159 |
| Smith, James, 25 Dec. 1749, Cislia Wilson | 2 AA-390 |
| Smith, Jas., 27 Jan. 1756, Mary Welling | 1 PG-302 |
| Smith, James, 2 Aug. 1777, Barbara White | 1 CA-111a |
| Smith, James, 23 Dec. 1777, Winnie Rogers | 2 CH(2) |
| Smith, Jesse, 25 Feb. 1762, Bettey Matthews | 2 SO-165 |
| Smith, John, 14 Feb. 1666, Margaret Barker | 3 CH |
| Smith, John, 24 Sept. 1699, Mary Davis | 3 KE-322 |
| Smith, John, 3 June 1704, Mary Coauch | 3 KE-323 |
| Smith, John, 7 April 1708, Mary Tornon | 1 AA-76 |
| Smith, John, 4 Dec. 1708, Mary Simpson | 1 CA-112 |
| Smith, John, 2 Feb. 1709/10, Mary Hedge | 1 BA-208 |
| Smith, John, 2 May 1710, Ellen Holt | 2 TA-68 |
| Smith, John, 1715, Isabellah Moore | 4 AA-392 |
| Smith, John, 6 June 1720, Mary Darrington | 4 AA-412 |
| Smith, John, son of John, 25 April 1721, Mary Rand | 1 PG-266 |
| Smith, John, 17 Jan. 1722, Eliza (?) | 2 TA-104 |
| Smith, John, 15 Sept. 1730, Eliza Bazill | 1 AA-111 |
| Smith, John, 3 Aug. 1736, Sarah Rowls | 3 AA-106 |
| Smith, John, 9 Jan. 1741/2, Eliz'th Fletcher | 1 QA-47 |
| Smith, John, 14 Nov. 1743, Sarah Dean | 1 QA-48 |
| Smith, John, 14 Feb. 1747, Wineford Hollings | 1 QA-54 |
| Smith, John, 14 day, 4 mo., 1750, Mary Milton | 1 SF-83 |
| Smith, John, 23 Nov. 1751, Mary Paremore | 2 SO-75 |
| Smith, Jno., 18 Dec. 1752, Margrett Scarf | 2 BA-206 |
| Smith, Jno., 3 Sept. 1764, Eliz. Davis | 2 BA-226 |
| Smith, John, 1 Oct. 1774, Eliz. Ford | 1 SM-136 |
| Smith, John, 28 July 1777, Mary Conaway | 10 BA-68 |
| Smith, John, 20 Aug. 1777, Elizabeth Rawlings | 3 PG-153 |
| Smith, John, 3 Sept. 1777, Elizabeth Rawlings | 2 CH(1) |
| Smith, Capt. John Addison, 17 Oct. 1765, Sarah Rogers, dau. of William | 3 BA-184 |
| Smith, John Moonger, 3 Sept. 1719, Mary Russel, widow | 4 AA-409 |
| Smith, Joseph, son of Nathan and Elizabeth, 4 day, 3 mo., 1710, Laurana Richardson, dau. of Dan'l and Eliza | 6 SF |
| Smith, Joseph, 11 April 1737, Mary Morgan | 3 BA-156 |
| Smith, Joseph, 5 July 1747, Mary Shepard 2 BA-194 gives the date as 15 Oct. 1747. | 2 BA-241 |
| Smith, Joseph, 16 May 1757, Deborah Onion | 2 BA-42 |

Smith, Jos., 13 Nov. 1773, Joanna Manning          1 SM-136
Smith, Joseph, 18 June 1777, Mary Toalson          1 HA-200
Smith, Josett, 12 Oct. 1714, Elenor Humfress       4 AA-392
Smith, Nathan, 1 June 1757, Blanch Dooley          1 BA-362
Smith, Nathaniel, 11 March 1752, Eliz'th Webster   1 BA-357
Smith, Mr. Nicholas, 14 April 1749, Ann Marr       2 KE-275
Smith, Oliver, 27 Aug. 1767, Elizabeth Saulsbury   2 KE-310
Smith, Richard, 10 June 1733, Margaret Williams    3 CE-17
Smith, Risdell, 26 Nov. 1755, Hanner Chattle       3 BA-165
Smith, Robert, 7 Aug. 1735, Mary Neall             2 TA-160
Smith, Samuel, of Kent Co., 2 April 17-(?), Judith
   Hoodt                                           1 SF-54
Smith, Samuell, 27 Jan. 1714, Elizabeth Wattkins   1 AA-78
Smith, Samuel, 28 July 1726, Anna Simpson          1 BA-241
Smith, Samuel, 3 Sept. 1727, Elisabeth Cox         3 BA-150
Smith, Samuel, 26 Sept. 1732, Grissel Locker       1 PG-286
Smith, Samuel, 18 June 1734, Elizabeth Gallion     1 BA-273
Smith, Samuel, 30 Aug. 1738, Avarilla Beck         2 BA-123
Smith, Samuel, 18 Dec. 1743, Jean Parish           2 BA-239
   2 BA-189 gives the date as 31 Dec. 1743, and the
   bride's name as Jane Parrish.
Smith, Thomas, 2 Feb. 1715, Eliza Rigden           2 PG-1
Smith, Thomas, 11 June 1724, Mary Diapper          1 AA-98
Smith, Thomas, 14 Feb. 1728, Mary Ann Ringgold     3 KE-327
Smith, Thomas, 9 Feb. 1729, Mary Slayfoot          3 KE-328
Smith, Thomas, 20 Jan. 1747, Mary Goldsmith        3 BA-161
Smith, Thomas, 25 Dec. 1755, Jane Pain             1 QA-60
Smith, Thomas, 31 May 1773, Dinah Blackburn        2 BA-266
Smith, Thomas, c.Aug. 1775, Deborah Pratt          1 CR-6
Smith, Thomas, 29 June 1777, Catherine Lewis      10 BA-68
Smith, Thomas, 18 Aug. 1777, Ruth Evans            3 PG-114
Smith, William, 2 Feb. 1696, Alice Gott            2 AA-293
Smith, William, 28 Jan. 1702, Elizabeth Seaborn    1 AA-64
   1 AA-253 gives bride's name as Eliz. Baborn.
Smith, William, 13 May 1711, Elizabeth Gardner     1 CA-114
Smith, William, 24 Dec. 1722, Ann Fowler           1 AA-94
Smith, William, 3 Aug. 1727, Elizabeth Mason       2 PG-4
Smith, William, 22 May 1729, Eilce Smith           3 BA-149
Smith, William, 29 July 1731, Ann Field            1 AA-112
Smith, William, 29 July 1732, Ann Fields           3 AA-105
Smith, William, 7 Oct. 1732, Catherine Everson     3 CE-15
Smith, William, 20 Jan. 1734, Sarah Pearson        1 CE-278
Smith, William, 23 Dec. 1743, Eliz. (?)            1 BA-349
Smith, William, Dec. 1751, Anne Peacock            2 BA-241
Smith, William, Jr., 19 Feb. 1759, Eliza Shaw      3 BA-166
Smith, William, 17 (Sept. 1768 ?), (wife's name not
   given)                                          2 BA-257
Smith, William, 7 Dec. 1769, Elizabeth Giles, dau.
   of Jacob                                        1 BA-393
Smith, William, 26 Nov. 1772, Rebecca Whelar       2 BA-265
Smith, William, 18 April 1776, Susanna Paca, dau. of
   Capt. John                                      1 BA-393
Smith, William, 14 Aug. 1777, Rebecca Sewell       1 HA-200
Smith, Winston, 5 Feb. 1740, Priscilla Paca        1 BA-319
Smith, Winstone, 18 July 1743, Mrs. Susanna Stokes 1 BA-337
Smithers, Richard, 14 Feb. 1700, Blanche Wells     1 BA-196
Smithers, Richard, 18 Aug. 1709, Philizanna Maxwell 1 BA-208
Smithson, Thos., Jr., 22 Jan. 1767, Sarah Bond     2 BA-230
Smithson, Wm., 11 Nov. 1766, Eliz. Scott           2 BA-229
Smithston, Wm. Eaton, 1 Sept. 1777, Rhoda Robey    2 CH(1)
Smyth, Charles, 16 Nov. 1703, Mary Bond            3 KE-323
Smyth, Levan, 31 Oct. 1703, Ezbell Reed            3 KE-323
Smyth, Thomas, 20 June 1734, Mary Frisby           3 KE-328
Smyth, Thomas, 12 March 1752, Sarah Gresham        3 KE-330
Smyth, Thomas, 11 Oct. 1764, Margret Hands, dau. of
   Bedingfield Hands, Esq.                         3 KE-300

| | |
|---|---|
| Smythers, William, 31 Oct. 1751, Mrs. Elizabeth Forester | 2 KE-276 |
| Snelson, William, 4 Feb. 1732, Margaret Hogg | 1 BA-261 |
| Snow, John, 16 Nov. 1740, Mary Westwood | 4 AA-442 |
| Snowden, Edward, 11 Feb. 1752, (wife's name not given) | 1 AA-132 |
| Snowden, Richard, son of Richard, Jr., and Mary, 19 day, 3 mo., 1709, Eliza Coale, Jr., dau. of Wm. and Eliza | 6 SF |
| Snowden, Richard, son of Richard and Mary, 19 day, 10 mo., 1717, Elizabeth Thomas, dau. of Samuel and Mary | 6 SF |
| Sockwell, Thomas, 25 Nov. 1718, Mary Barrett | 2 TA-89 |
| Sollars, Abraham, 1770, Rachel Owings | 2 AA-410 |
| Somervell, James, 1 Jan. 1722, Sarah Howe | 1 CA-114 |
| Somervell, Alexander, 2 Dec. 1759, Rebecca Dawkins | 2 CA-41 |
| Somervell, James, 5 Aug. 1755, Susanna Dare | 2 CA-37 |
| Sommers, Thomas, 4 Feb. 1762, Ann Boston | 2 SO-164 |
| Sommersill, Shechaniah, 19 Oct. 1752, Mary Haderick | 1 CE-311 |
| Soulegre, David, 25 Dec. 1721, Sarah Gemineau? | 2 TA-97 |
| Soullavin, John, 25 Dec. 1771, Kitty Grooves | 2 BA-263 |
| Southbee, William, 29 day, 1 mo., 1668, Elizabeth Read | 8 SF-314 |
| Southbee, William, 20 day, 4 mo., 1677, Jone Lee | 8 SF-317 |
| Southerland, John, 20 Nov. 1777, Nellie Fraser | 3 PG-116 |
| Southray, Samuel, 1 Feb. 1756, Mary Williams | 1 QA-60 |
| Spain, Beaven, 6 Jan. 1734, Elizabeth Rigdon | 1 BA-280 |
| Spadling, Andrew, 10 April 1709, Eliz'th Chaddock | 3 KE-324 |
| Sparkes, George, 3 Dec. 1730, Sarah Salisbury | 1 QA-37 |
| Sparkes, Joseph, 18 Nov. 1731, Elizabeth Kelley | 1 QA-38 |
| Sparks, Abner, 24 Aug. 1758, Mary Ann Bolton | 1 QA-64 |
| Sparks, Absolam, 17 Nov. 1748, Elizabeth Brown | 1 QA-55 |
| Sparks, Benjamin, 18 May 1738, Mary Baley | 1 QA-44 |
| Sparks, Caleb, 19 March 1745, Hanah O'Bryan | 1 QA-52 |
| Sparks, David, 20 Feb. 1759, Mary Tippins | 1 QA-64 |
| Sparks, Edward, 21 July 1752, Rebecca Banks | 1 QA-59 |
| Sparks, George, 14 Sept. 1729, Elizabeth Rickets | 1 QA-37 |
| Sparks, George, 6 Nov. 1755, Ann Bolton | 1 QA-60 |
| Sparks, James, 9 Feb. 1737/8, Elis. Barkhurst | 1 QA-43 |
| Sparks, John, Jr., 1 Jan. 1756, Catherine Hayse | 1 QA-60 |
| Sparks, Jonas, 4 Aug. 1731, Mary Sinnot | 1 QA-38 |
| Sparks, Josiah, 15 July 1749, Penelope Brown | 4 AA-451 |
| Sparks, Millinton, 9 Feb. 1740/1, Mabil Ruth | 1 QA-46 |
| Sparks, Nathan, 20 Feb. 1759, Eliza Bolton | 1 QA-64 |
| Sparks, William, 24 Aug. 1732, Mary Common | 1 QA-39 |
| Sparks, William, 30 Aug. 1738, Ellinor Brooks | 1 QA-44 |
| Sparrow, John, 3 Sept. 1728, Mary Knighton | 1 AA-107 |
| Sparrow, Solomon, son of Thomas and Elizabeth, 12 day, 6 mo., 1690, Sarah Smith, dau. of Thomas and Alice | 6 SF |
| Sparrow, Thomas, son of Thomas and Elizabeth, 8 June 1697, Ann BUrgess, dau. of Col. William and Ursula | 1 AA-37 |
| Sparrow, Thomas, son of Thomas, and Sophia (sic), 28 Nov. 1698, Sofia Richardson, dau. of William and Elizabeth | 1 AA-42 |
| Spear, Henry, 1711, Jane Calloway | 1 WI-11 |
| Spearman, Francis, 17 day, 4 mo., 1734, Jennet Corse | 1 SF-67 |
| Speed, Rich'd, 26 Feb. 1744, Jane Morgan | 1 QA-50 |
| Speer, Andrew, 10 March 1690, Priscilla (?) | 5 SO-399 |
| Spegle, John Cole, 19 May 1735, Deborah Cottrall | 1 BA-283 |
| Spence, Magna, 14 June 1703, Jane Whitehead | 2 TA-35 |
| Spence, Patrick, 24 Nov. 1712, Phebe Sizzarton | 2 TA-72 |
| Spencer, Alexander, 17 April 1737, Eliz'th Lee | 1 BA-295 |
| Spencer, Hugh, 28 April 1749, Eliza Money | 3 TA-73 |
| Spencer, James, 17 Aug. 1758, Batrix Dorney | 2 BA-217 |
| Spencer, John, 9 Aug. 1750, Mary Greenwood | 2 KE-281 |
| Spencer, Joseph, 14 Sept. 1749, Mary Deroachbroom | 3 TA-75 |
| Spencer, Phil., 12 Feb. 1750/1, Lucy Porter | 3 TA-81 |

```
Spencer, Rob't, 5 Oct. 1745, Mary Russell          3 TA-55
Spencer, Thomas, 30 Dec. 1740, Sarah Shanahan      3 TA-27
Spencer, William, son of William Spencer, of New Castle,
  30 June 1765, Mary Whitacker, dau. of Thomas Whit-
  acker of Inniskilling, Ireland                   3 BA-169
Spencer, William, 2 July 1776, Elizabeth Ward      2 AA-413
Spencer, Zachariah, 2 Feb. 1728, Christian Coob    1 BA-255
Spencer, Zachariah, 29 Sept. 1755, Ann Pogue       1 BA-373
Spense, Douglass, 20 June 1770, Catherine Mooney   3 BA-169
Spicer, John, 10 Nov. 1709, (?) Hawkins            2 AA-338
Spicer, John, 8 June 1777, Jesse Clay             10 BA-68
Spicer, Thomas, 1 Jan. 1735, Rebeckah Merryman     3 BA-154
Spicer, Wm., 28 Jan. 1724, Ann Disney              1 AA-100
Spindell?, Samuel, 30 Jan. 1752, Mary Taylor       1 QA-58
Spon, Johann Adam, 25 Sept. 1768, Anna Maria Kieffer  3 FR-105
Sprall, Jerimiah, 18 Jan. 1740/1, Naomi or Raomi
  Swift                                            1 QA-46
Spreaddex, William, 9 Sept. 1707, Elizabeth Hicks  1 AA-76
Sprigg, Edward, 26 April 1720, Eliza Pile, dau. of
  Dr. R'd. Pile                                    2 PG-2
Sprigg, Osborn, 11 July 1727, Rachel Belt, dau. of
  Col. Joseph Belt                                 2 PG-4
Sprigg, Thomas, 14 day, 12 mo., 1737, Elizabeth Gallo-
  way, dau. of Richard and Sophia                  6 SF
Sprignall, Caleb, 11 June 1719, Elizabeth Mills    2 TA-90
Spry, Christopher, 17 April 1735, Mary Wells       1 QA-40
Spry, Francis, 30 Dec. 1736, Elizabeth Hacket      1 QA-42
Spry, John, 11 Oct. 1744, Mary Massy               1 QA-49
Spry, Thomas, 24 Dec. 1747, Catherine Wells        1 QA-53
Spry, William, 17 Dec. 1743, Ruth McConnikin       1 QA-48
Spurr, James, 26 May 1735, Judeth Williams         3 BA-153
Spurrier, Wm., 7 Feb. 1702?, Elizabeth Turner      2 TA-31
Spurrier, William, 7 Feb. 1702, Elizabeth Fisher   2 TA-32
Squires, Daniel, 22 Nov. 1772, Rebecca Smith       3 AA-113
Stacy, William, 3 Aug. 1736, Rebecca Shield        2 TA-160
                                                   & 271
Stafford, Peter, 27 April 1772, Jane Lewis         2 BA-264
Stafford, Richard, 5 Dec. 1703, Mary Gaylor        1 AA-64
Stalkup, John, 30 Oct. 1752, Mary Treaderey        1 CE-293
Stallings, William, 23 Jan. 1728, Mary Harvey      1 AA-108
Standeford, Aq'a, 27 Dec. 1764, Sarah Clark        2 BA-227
Standeford, Arch'd, 25 June 1754, Eliz. Armstrong  2 BA-214
Standeford, Israel, 6 Jan. 1743, Cassandra Anderson 2 BA-189
Standeford, James, 6 Oct. 1737, Martha Watkins     2 BA-102
Standeford, Jno., 11 Jan. 1759, Jemima Robertson   2 BA-218
Standeford, Skelton, Jr., 4 Nov. 1755, Eliz. Pocock 2 BA-212
Standeford, William, 28 May 1731, Anne Hutchins    2 BA-89
Standeford, William, Nov. 1739, Christiana Wright  2 BA-155
  2 BA-116 gives the date as 8 Dec. 1740.
Standeford, William, 16 July 1750, Eliz. Carlile   2 BA-201
Standeford, William, Jr., 27 May 1767, Reb. Deason 2 BA-230
Standiford, Abraham, 8 Oct. 1769, Susan Chamberlane 2 BA-259
Standiford, Jacob, 29 (Sept. 1768?), Elizabeth
  Robinson                                         2 BA-257
Standiford, John, 1 Jan. 1726, Easther Fuller      2 BA-79
Standiford, John, 15 Dec. 1771, Ruthe Rutledge     2 BA-263
Standiford, Samuel, 30 Nov. 1732, Anne Rollo       2 BA-73
Standiford, Skelton, 5 Nov. 1772, Mary Richardson  2 BA-265
Standiford, Vincent, 4 April 1771, Prissilla Nearn 2 BA-262
Standiford, William, 31 Jan. 1769, Elinor Carlile  2 BA-257
Standley, John, 26 Aug. 1713, Elizabeth Thomas     2 TA-72
Standley, John, 6 May 1740, Eliza Eldrake          2 TA-168
Stanford, Jonathan, 28 June 1767, Grace Phillips   1 WI-97
Stanford, Richard, c.Aug. 1775, Hester Ann Russum  1 CR-6
Stanford, William, 1 June 1759, Mary Cooper, of
  Northampton Co., Va.                             1 WI-73
```

```
Stanley, William, 3 Oct. 1771, Margret Backhouse        2 BA-263
Stansbury, Cha., 25 April 1765, Eliz. Buck              2 BA-228
Stansbury, Daniel, 22 April 1748, Elizabeth Ashman      3 AA-111
Stansbury, Dixon, 4 Jan. 1740/1, Penelope Body          2 BA-170
Stansbury, John, 12 Feb. 1734, Ann Ensor                3 BA-153
Stansbury, Joseph, 12 Dec. 1773, Jane Long              3 BA-170
Stansbury, Richardson, 23 Feb. 1747, Mary Reaven        2 BA-196
Stansbury, Sam'l, 1 April 1761, Mary Harrod             2 BA-221
Stansbury, Sam'l, Sr., 24 May 1777, Anne Culleson       3 BA-173
Stansbury, Solomon, 27 Oct. 1743, Hannah Hix            2 BA-189
Stansbury, Thomas, 2 March 1735, Hannah Gorsuch         3 BA-155
Stansbury, Tobies, 27 April 1746, Mary Hammond          3 BA-166
Stansbury, William, 14 Feb. 1739/40, Elizabeth Ensor    3 BA-164
Stant (or Stout), John, c.Oct. 1775, Mary Carter        1 CR-6
Stanton, John, 15 July 1735, Mary Mason                 1 QA-41
Stanton, Thomas, 23 March 1743, Eliz'th McKnot          1 QA-49
Stanton, Thomas, 13 April 1749, Esther Perrey           1 QA-55
Stanton, Thos., 26 Sept. 1750, Sarah Atwell             3 TA-79
Stanton, Thomas, 2 day, 12 mo., 1776, Mary Carter       2 SF-288
Stanton, William, 11 Jan. 1736, Dorcas More             1 QA-42
Stanton, William, 7 Jan. 1746, Sarah Hollingsworth      1 QA-52
Stapleford, Barnaby, 27 Aug. 1718, Elizabeth Reader     2 TA-88
Stapleford, Daniel, 21 Dec. 1736, Susana Roberts        2 TA-158
Stapleford, John, 12 Jan. 1736, Rebecca Bullen          2 TA-158
Stapleton, George, Feb. 1722, Jane Black                4 AA-420
Stapleton, Thomas, 15 Jan. 1756, Sarah Crook            1 BA-373
Starkey, Edward, 18 Sept. 1742, Susanna Harper          3 TA-39
Starkey, Jacob, 22 Jan. 1744, Mary Turbel               2 BA-192
Starkey, John, 1 Jan. 1707, Elizabeth Boyle             1 AA-76
Starkey, John, 10 July 1738, Anne Greer                 2 BA-99
Starkey, John, 29 June 1758, Rachel Gossage             1 QA-63
Starkey, Jonathan, 23 June 1757, Mary Simmons           2 BA-215
Starkey, Joshua, 29 Sept. 1743, Hannah Meads            2 BA-126
Starkey, Will'm, 28 Nov. 1739, Catherin Voice           1 CE-287
Starkey, Will'm, 7 Jan. 1742/3, Susannah Cox            1 CE-289
Starling, Aron, 1 Aug. 1767, Sabra Moor                 2 SO-165
Starling, Henry, 9 Jan. 1755, Deborah Sommors           2 SO-77
Starling, Henry, 1 Feb. 1767, Elizabeth Vessels         2 SO-165
Starn, Bartholomew, 24 Aug. 1755, Cath'n Buckley        1 QA-60
Start, Benj., 27 Nov. 1741, Martha Smith                3 TA-34
Start, Richard, 4 Feb. 1740/1, Mary Hennessey           3 TA-28
Stavely, John, 15 April 1755, Margaret Redgrave         2 KE-292
Staycy, John, 5 July 1695, Martha Sockwell              8 SF-365
Steadman, James, 10 Oct. 1747, Mary Minson              2 BA-194
Steal, James, 1770, Mary Galloway                       2 AA-410
Steavenson, William, 21 June 1762, Rachel Crute, widow
   of Robert Crute                                      1 BA-383
Stedman, Richard, of Yeatley Parish, Co. Southampton,
   (Eng.), 29 Aug. 1744, Ann Kemson                     9 SF
Steedman, James, 23 Aug. 1747, Mary Misnon              2 BA-241
Steel, James, 12 (?) 1769, Mary Marr                    2 AA-409
Steel, James, 29 July 1777, Elizabeth Mahaffey          2 CE-1
Steel, John, 11 Nov. 1709, Mary Clark                   1 BA-208
Steel, John, 13 June 1720, Marg'tt Mercer               4 AA-412
Steel, Jos., 3 Feb. 1743, Eliz. Tomley                  2 BA-190
Steel, Joseph, 29 Jan. 1744, Elizab. Tomlin             2 BA-239
Steele, Francis, 26 Feb. 1705, Rebecca Pierce           3 CE-5
Steele, William, Nov. 1687, Frances Bowzer              5 SO-399
Steenson, John, 10 Feb. 1734, Mary Bailey               1 QA-40
Steiner, Jacob, 17 May 1758, Mary Anna Schley           4 FR-1104
Stenchcome, John, 23 July 1733, Katherine Maccleane     3 BA-151
Stenhouse, Dr. Alexander, 21 June 1761, Cordelia
   Christie, widow                                      1 BA-370
Stepenson, John, 1 May 1728, Grace Jones                2 KE-219
Stephan, Antereus, 30 Nov. 1761, Elizab. Kohler         4 FR-1167
```

| | | |
|---|---|---|
| Stephens, James, 2 Nov. 1752, Eliz. Cadle | 2 BA-206 | |
| Stephens, Jno., 19 Feb. 1704, Sarah Brown | 4 AA-390 | |
| Stephens, John, 31 Jan. 1741, Elizabeth Mercer | 4 AA-443 | |
| Stephens, Thomas, 28 April 1737, Mary Wright | 2 BA-89 | |
| Stephens, William, 23 Sept. 1724, Juliana Thomas | 2 TA-109 | |
| Stephens, Williams, 14 Feb. 1771, Margret Smith | 2 BA-261 | |
| Stephes, Francis, 4 Dec. 1739, Isabella Robertson | 1 QA-45 | |
| Sterling, Rev. James, 19 Sept. 1743, Rebecca Holt | 1 QA-48 | |
| Sterling, James, 7 Sept. 1749, Mary Smith; both of Kent Co. | 1 QA-56 | |
| Sterling, John, 28 May 1667, Alce Bassett | 4 SO-671 | |
| Stern, Bartholomew, 15 July 1750, Sarah Birch | 1 QA-57 | |
| Steuard, Isaac, 26 Oct. 1723, Ann Roe | 1 WI-15 | |
| Stevens, Edmondson, 3 Nov. 1720, Sidney Dickenson | 2 TA-94 | |
| Stevens, Edward, 23 Dec. 1718, Mary Yardsly | 3 KE-326 | |
| Stevens, Ephraim, 18 April 1773, Milcah Dashiell, dau. of Louther and Anna Dashiell of Wicomico Creek | 2 SO-167 | |
| Stevens, Epr'm, 28 Jan. 1768, Temperance Green | 2 BA-231 | |
| Stevens, George, c.Oct. 1775, Sarah Bayley | 1 CR-6 | |
| Stevens, Giles, 1722, Alice Gudgeon | 2 BA-22 | |
| Stevens, Giles, Jr., 13 Jan. 1757, Avarilla Pickett | 2 BA-214 | |
| Stevens, John, 6 July 1709, Elizabeth Allcock | 8 SF-439 | |
| Stevens, John, c.Aug. 1775, Ann Anderson | 1 CR-6 | |
| Stevens, Lewis, 1771, Mary Oliver | 2 AA-410 | |
| Stevens, Peter, 6 May 1739, Mary Thornton | 2 TA-166 | |
| Stevens, Richard, 25 Dec. 1730, Rachell Hacks | 1 WI-16 | |
| Stevens, Thomas, 14 Aug. 1734, Juliana Stevens | 2 TA-156 | |
| Stevens, Vachel, 15 March 1772, Ann Ramsey | 3 AA-113 | |
| Stevens, William, 15 Feb. 1687, Jane Atkinson, relict of Thomas Adkinson | 8 SF-344 | |
| Stevens, William, Jr., 5 Feb. 1695, Elizabeth Edmondson | 8 SF-369 | |
| Stevens, William, 6 day, 12 mo., 1700, Mary Pryor, late of Philadelphia | 8 SF-402 | |
| Stevens, William, 19 Nov. 1738, Mary Gray | 2 SO-73 | |
| Stevens, William, 25 Dec. 1750, Sarah Duke | 2 BA-202 | |
| Stevens, William, 15 May 1766, Winefred Whitmell, dau. of Col. Thos. Whitmell in Bertie Co., N. C. | 2 SO-166 | |
| Stevenson, Henry, 19 June 1735, Jemima Merryman | 3 BA-153 | |
| Stevenson, Hugh, 23 Feb. 1730, Eliza Swan | 1 AA-111 | |
| Stevenson, John, 13 Nov. 1735, Mary Tipton | 3 BA-153 | |
| Stevenson, Jno., 11 Aug. 1763, Anther Wyle | 2 BA-225 | |
| Stevenson, William, 29 Aug. 1735, Hannah Smith | 2 KE-224 | |
| Stevenson, Dr. William, of Annapolis, 28 Sept. 1735, Francina Augustina Frisby, dau. of James Frisby, late of Cecil Co., and his wife Ariana | 4 AA-437 | |
| Stevenson, William, 21 June 1762, Rachel Crute, widow of Robert Crute | 1 BA-383 | |
| Stevert, Alexander, 11 Dec. 1754, Mary M'Kinley | 2 BA-211 | |
| Steward, Cornelius, 1747, Mary Lowe | 2 BA-242 | |
| Steward, David, 1734, (wife's name not given) | 1 AA-118 | |
| Steward, George, 16 June 1758, Mary Barwick | 1 QA-63 | |
| Steward, James, 21 July 1710, Rachell Wicholl | 1 AA-77 | |
| Steward, James, 14 Aug. 1750, Mary Lang | 1 QA-57 | |
| Steward, John, 28 March 1703, Britchett Hughs | 2 TA-38 | |
| Steward, John, 3 day, 1 mo., 1723/4, Sarah Franklin, dau. of Robert and Artridge | 6 SF | |
| Steward, John, son of John, of A. A. Co., 9 day, 3 mo., 1769, Rebecca Hosier, dau. of Henry Hosier, dec. | 1 SF-102 | |
| Steward, Step'n, 12 Jan. 1730, Eliza Rutland | 1 AA-111 | |
| Steward, Stephen, Dec. 1734, Elizabeth Ward | 1 AA-118 | |
| Steward, Stephen, Jr., 7 Nov. 1777, Elizabeth Thomas 2 AA-414 gives the date as 8 Nov. 1777. 8 AA-13 has the same information as the latter source. | 7 AA-2 | |
| Steward, Thomas, 10 Jan. 1721, Elizabeth Carr | 2 TA-98 | |

Steward?, William, 1721, Katherine Donaldson                1 WI-7
Stewart, Anthony, of Annapolis, son of James Stewart,
  attorney, of Edinburgh, 15 March 1764, Jean Dick,
  dau. of James and Margaret Dick                          1 AA-146
  2 BA-226 has the same information.
Stewart, Cornelius, 25 Nov. 1747, Mary Low                 2 BA-194
Stewart, Cornelius, 13 April 1773, Ann Studart             2 BA-266
Stewart, Hugh, 6 Jan. 1761, Marg'r't Coldwell              2 BA-221
Stewart, James, 21 July 1710, Rachel Witchel               1 AA-260
Stewart, James, 24 Aug. 1739, Mary Meginney                3 TA-18
  2 TA-167 gives the date as 2 Oct. 1739, and the
  bride's name as Mary Meguiney.
Stewart, James, 10 Feb. 1741, Mary Wood                    1 BA-324
Stewart, James, 21 Dec. 1775, Alley Dove                   2 AA-412
Stewart, John, 7 Feb. 1760, Mary Selby                     2 SO-164
Stewart, Mordecai, 1770, Rachel Purnell                    2 AA-410
  1 AA-151 gives the date as 9 April 1771.
Stewart, Robert, 1 Jan. 1739, Eliz'h Thorp                 1 QA-45
Stewart, Thos., 31 Dec. 1737, Mary Glover                  2 TA-164
Stewart, William, 11 Dec. 1760, Sarah Dashiell, dau.
  of Charles and Eliza                                     1 WI-106
Stewnes (Stevens?), Robert, 17 Aug. 1668, Ann Nolton       5 SO-399
  The groom was formerly called Robert Lewin.
Stiffen, John, 18 Aug. 1709, Sarah Purdy                   1 AA-257
  1 AA-77 gives the groom's name as John Stiffinn.
Stiffin, John, 24 April 1701, Margaret Disney, dau. of
  William                                                  1 AA-57
                                                           & 247
Stigings, William, 13 July 1721, Mary Masters              1 BA-228
Stimpson, John, 11 Nov. 1730, Elizabeth Rawlings           3 AA-108
Stinchcomb, John, 6 Nov. 1742, Mary Davis                  3 AA-108
Stinchcomb, Lewis, 16 Nov. 1741, Anna Wright               3 AA-107
Stinchcomb, Nathaniel, 16 Aug. 1702, Elizabeth
  Chapell                                                  3 AA-97
  1 AA-58 & 251 give the date as 4 Sept. 1702, and
  the bride's name as Elizabeth Chappell.
Stinchcomb, Nathaniel, 15 Jan. 1733, Patience Rowles       3 BA-151
Stinchcomb, Nathaniel, 20 May 1735, Anna Burle             3 AA-104
Stinchcomb, Thomas, 13 Aug. 1777, Else Hilman?             7 AA-1
Stirling, Samuel, 28 Sept. 1721, Mary Harvey               1 AA-307
Sticthberry, Steven, 20 Aug. 1746, Jane Studholmes         3 TA-60
Stock, John Peter, 2 July 1765, Esther Alexander           4 FR-1167
Stockdell, Edward, 9 Aug. 1693, Jane (?)                   5 SO-399
Stockett, Mr. Lewis, 10 June 176-(?), Ann Ijams            1 AA-142
Stockett, Thomas, son of Capt. Thomas Stockett and
  Mary, born 17 April 1667, m. 12 March 1689, Mary
  Sprigg, dau. of Thomas Sprigg                            1 AA-54
Stockett, Thomas, 9 April 1700, Damaris Welsh, dau.
  of John and Mary                                         1 AA-54
Stockett, Thomas, Jr., 19 Aug. 1732, Eliza Larkin          1 AA-114
Stocksdale, Thomas, 5 day, 12 mo., 1776, Mary Patrick      4 SF-272
Stockton, John, 5 Nov. 1745, Elizabeth Alldredge           1 CE-290
Stockton, Benjamin, son of John and Elizabeth, 14
  Dec. 1769, Martha (?), dau. of Peter and Mary            1 CE-315
Stodart, James, 3 March 1708, Elizabeth Bishop             2 AA-336
Stogdon, John, 30 March 1703, Elizabeth Ford               2 AA-321
Stoker, John, 31 Oct. 1748, (wife's name not given)        3 TA-71
Stoker, Michael, 15 Jan. 1740/1, Dianah Booker             3 TA-28
Stokes, Humphrey Wells, son of Capt. John Stokes of
  Balto. Co., 31 Dec. 1730, Mary Knight, dau. of
  Stephen Knight of Cecil Co.                              3 CE-17
  2 BA-78 states that the groom was a son of John and
  Susanna Stokes, and the bride was a dau. of Stephen
  and Sarah Knight.
Stokes, Robert, 15 Aug. 1756, Rebecca Young                1 BA-351

| | |
|---|---|
| Stoll, Christoph, 20 Sept. 1761, Philippina Sthael | 4 FR-1167 |
| Stone, Edw., 27 Feb. 1770, Anna Joy | 1 SM-135 |
| Stone, Enoch, 11 Nov. 1773, Monica Goldsberry | 1 SM-136 |
| Stone, Henry, 2 July 1740, Constance James | 1 BA-313 |
| Stone, John, 1771, Sarah Taylor | 2 AA-410 |
| Stone, Joseph, 4 June 1770, Eliz. Mitchel | 2 BA-260 |
| Stone, Jos., 29 Dec. 1772, Dorothy Spink | 1 SM-136 |
| Stone, Joshua, 25 Feb. 1719/20, Mary Bechum | 2 AA-362 |
| Stone, Robert, 23 July 1700, Ann Smith | 2 AA-298 |
| Stone, Thomas, 14 April 1748, Mary Guy | 1 QA-54 |
| Stoop, Philip, 12 Oct. 1721, Mary Price | 3 CE-13 |
| Storey, Charles, 18 Aug. 1732, Martha Neale | 1 QA-39 |
| Storey, Thomas, 2 Feb. 1756, Rebeckah Silvester | 1 QA-60 |
| Story, Charles, 15 May 1733, Ann Britain | 1 BA-265 |
| Story, Henry, 4 July 1739, Hannah Cook | 1 QA-45 |
| Story, Joseph, 22 Jan. 1717, Jane Soper | 2 PG-1 |
| Story, Joshua, 14 Oct. 1762, Margarett Briscoe | 1 BA-379 |
| Story, Rich'd, 26 April 1740, Eliza Kemp | 3 TA-22 |
|    2 TA-168 gives the date as 27 April 1740. | |
| Story, Thomas, 13 Jan. 1743/4, Patience Richards | 1 FR-12 |
| Stotts, Abraham, 26 June 1760, Margret Johnson | 2 BA-220 |
| Stoughton, William, 20 Jan. 1767, Ann Catherwood, als. | |
|    Elzey | 3 SO-4 |
| Stout, James, 21 Feb. 1731, Ann Stout | 3 KE-328 |
| Stout?, John, 8 June 1759, Mary Ellers | 2 CR-272 |
| Stovell, Daniel, 1771, Mary Timms | 2 AA-410 |
| Stovell, Samuel, 1771, Elizabeth Marr | 2 AA-410 |
| Strachan, Capt. William, 6 July 1743, Mary Simpson | 1 AA-144 |
| Strand, Abraham, 25 day, 9 mo., 1677, in Salem, N. J., | |
|    Rachel Nicholson | 8 SF-318 |
| Strann, Abraham, 21 day, 9 mo., 1672, Mary Halbrook | 8 SF-315 |
| Stratton, Thomas, 18 Sept. 1733, Hannah Mannaring | 3 CE-18 |
| Street, Thomas, 1733, Sarah Feëler | 1 BA-275 |
| Street, Thos., 16 Dec. 1755, Mary Fox | 2 BA-213 |
| Street, Thomas, 7 July 1772, Sarah James | 2 BA-265 |
| Strickler?, Wendel, 8 Aug. 1758, Susanna Sax | 4 FR-1104 |
| Stringer, John, 2 July 1733, Mary Collier | 1 BA-266 |
| Stringer, Richard, son of Dr. Samuel, 16 Dec. 1672, | |
|    Ellinor Dorsey, dau. of John, son of Caleb | 6 AA-190 |
| Strong, Nathaniel, 17 Nov. 1738, Mary (?) | 2 PG-7 |
| Strong, Thomas, 24 Sept. 1711, Jane Phillips | 3 KE-324 |
| Strong, Thomas, 30 Jan. 1730, Mary Kelley | 3 KE-329 |
| Stuard, Robert, 26 Jan. 1698/9, Susan Wattes | 1 AA-44 |
| Stuart, Alexander, 15 Aug. 1708, Margaret Connor | 4 AA-378 |
| Stuart, James, 1 Aug. 1773, Cathreene Mathews | 3 BA-170 |
| Stuart, John, 24 Feb. 1741, Ann Fish | 9 AA-247 |
| Stuart, Patrick, 17 Nov. 1725, in London, Emma Chapman | 1 WI-39 |
| Stubbs, Daniel, son of Thomas, 20 March 1750/1, Ruth | |
|    Gilpin, dau. of Joseph and Mary | 9 SF |
| Stubs, Thos., 31 March 1752, Eliz. Davice | 2 BA-205 |
| Stuchberry, Peter, 7 Jan. 1760, Margret Moor | 2 SO-77 |
| Stud, Robert, 27 July 1734, Ann Mitchell | 2 TA-155 |
| Sturges, George, 22 April 1680, Frances Nicolls | 5 SO-399 |
| Sturm, Daniel, 7 April 1761, An. M. Stempel | 4 FR-1167 |
| Sturm, John, 13 Dec. 1756, Anna Barb. Hoffman | 4 FR-1103 |
| Sturm, Leonhardt, 29 Dec. 1761, Cath. Dail(yr) | 4 FR-1167 |
| Suit, Nathaniel, 24 June 1752, Mary Burch | 1 PG-376 |
| Suit, Walter, 26 Aug. 1777, Susanna Davis | 3 SM-536 |
| Sullavane, Daniel, 28 day, 1 mo., 1770, Marget Elvin; | |
|    both of Dor. Co. | 2 SF-288 |
| Sutton, Richard, of Phila., 12 Sept. 1698, Mary Howell | |
|    of Cecil Co. | 1 SF-40 |
| Sulgar?, David, 15 Aug. 1724, Mary Murphey | 2 TA-110 |
| Sulivane, James, 26 Aug. 1777, Margaret Wheatley | 1 CR-10 |
| | & 28 |

Sulivant, Owen, 27 June 1713, Elizabeth Mercer        2 TA-71
Sullavant, Darby, 30 Dec. 1714, Eliz'th Dunahoe       3 KE-326
Sullavant, Daniel, 27 Dec. 1697, Elizabeth Grotto     3 KE-322
Sullavant, David, 20 June 1731, Elizabeth Parker      3 KE-329
Sullivan, John, 25 Dec. 1771, Kitty Grooves           2 BA-263
Sullivan, Owan, 27 Sept. 1701, Dorothy Taylor, widow  1 BA-193
Sullivan, William, 28 March 1722, Margret Noble        1 WI-16
Sullivant, Owen, 7 Jan. 1736, Patience Mallitt        2 TA-162
Sullovan, John, 30 March 1733, Mary Small             1 QA-39
Sumaine, Samuel, 7 Sept. 1742, Susanna Minskie        4 AA-444
Sumbler, Benjamin, 29 Jan. 1666, Izabell Wale         4 SO-657
Summerlin, Francis, 24 Feb. 1772, Elizabeth Holoway   3 AA-113
Summers, Benjamin, 18 April 1676, Deborah Wooldridge  9 SO-401
Summers, Elias, 2 May 1776, Peggy Lankford            2 SO-168
Summers, Jacob, 28 Feb. 1773, Eleanor Quea            3 BA-169
Summers, James, c.Aug. 1775, Abisha French            1 CR-6
Summers, John, 28 Feb. 1773, Mary Lashford            3 BA-169
Summers, John, 10 Sept. 1775, Jemima Cullen           2 SO-168
Summers, Jno. Jacob, 27 April 1766, Araminta Roberts  2 BA-229
Summers, Lazarus, 2 Feb. 1755, Catherin Pellet        2 SO-174
Summers, Moses, 29 May 1765, Prissilla Lawson         2 SO-169
Summers, Thomas, 5 June 1709, Elizabeth Perry         2 TA-60
Sumner, William, 18 Sept. 1691, Margaret Butler       5 SO-399
Summers, David, 14 Dec. 1749, Mary Jurdin             2 SO-74
Sumpter, Robert, 2 Feb. 1720, Elisabeth Baily         1 AA-302
Sumpter, Robert, Sr., 19 July 1748, Sarah Benham      1 QA-54
Sunderland, John, 9 Sept. 1731, Susana Holland        3 AA-104
Sunderlon, Josiah, 18 Dec. 1718, Precilla Stockett    2 AA-360
Sunderman, Wm., 26 Sept. 1701, Margaret (?)           2 TA-21
Sunk, Geo., 23 Sept. 1766, Eliz. Pennington           2 BA-229
Surnam, Edward, 26 (?) 1664, Ann Frowin               5 SO-399
Suss, John George, 1 May 1753, Maria Catherina Dock   5 FR-113
Suter, James, 6 Oct. 1745, Grace Yearn                1 QA-51
Sutherland, David, 10 Sept. 1776, Eleanor Stockdell   5 BA-12
Sutton, Abraham, 3 July 1745, Martha Harrowsmith      3 BA-157
Sutton, Christopher, 12 Oct. 1746, Sarah League       2 BA-195
Sutton, Ellixander, 3 March 1746, Rachel Harris       1 QA-53
Sutton, Francis, 3 Nov. 1715, Elizabeth Armstrong     2 TA-76
Sutton, Henry, 15 April 1707, Mary Robinson           2 TA-47
Sutton, Henry, 20 July 1718, Mary Spiller             2 TA-87
Sutton, James, 9 Feb. 1734, Rebecca Spry              1 QA-40
Sutton, John, 3 Oct. 1746, Mary Beans                 1 PG-291
Sutton, John, 7 Aug. 1757, Elizabeth Keys             1 QA-62
Sutton, Joseph, 1 May 1748, Ruth Adams                2 BA-197
Sutton, Samuel, 25 Aug. 1757, Ruth Cantwell           1 BA-355
Sutton, Sam'l, 20 Nov. 1760, Ann Woodcock             2 BA-220
Sutton, Samuel, 15 May 1762, Sarah Lazell             1 BA-378
Swain, Nathan, 15 March 1764, Mary Drew               1 BA-383
Swallow, John, 11 Feb. 1696, Alice Cox                2 TA-6
Swan, Edward, 24 Jan. 1703/4, Elizabeth Griffith      1 BA-200
Swan, Henry, 29 Dec. 1777, Ann Dyson                  3 SM-536
Swan, James, 12 July 1734, Rebecca Larey              2 TA-155
Swan, John, 24 Jan. 1720/1, Eliza Foster              2 PG-2
Swan, Samuel, 25 Oct. 1763, Eliz. Demmett             2 BA-225
Swan, Thomas, 8 Jan. 1711, Sarah May                  2 TA-70
Swann, Jonathan, 22 Dec. 1767, Elioner Amery          1 CH-194
Swann, Thomas, 11 Jan. 1757, Ann Dent                 1 CH-187
Swearingen, Samuel, 28 May 1752, Anne Wickham, widow  1 FR-12
Sweatnam, Stephen, 20 Jan. 1728, Rachel Stanton       1 QA-36
Sweeting, Edward, 6 June 1756, Ruth Trotten           3 BA-166
Sweeting, Robert, 5 Dec. 1731, Sarah Laine            3 BA-150
Sweetting, Edward, 21 Dec. 1732, Mary Watts           3 BA-150
Sweney, Bryan, 1 Dec. 1720, Sarah Abbott              2 TA-94
Sweringen, John, 9 Feb. 1715, Mary Ray                2 PG-1
Sweringen, Samuel, 14 Feb. 1715, Eliza Farmer         2 PG-1

| | |
|---|---|
| Swift, Absolom, 17 April 1743, Ruth Webb | 1 QA-48 |
| Swift, Emanuel, 4 Sept. 1746, Rachel Hobbs | 1 QA-52 |
| Swift, Flower, 13 May 1725, Elizabeth Whitaker | 1 BA-234 |
| Swift, Gideon, 23 Feb. 1744, Esr Wells | 1 QA-50 |
| Swift, Gidion, 13 July 1749, Ann Johnson | 1 QA-55 |
| Swift, John, 11 Sept. 1703, Ann Hobbs | 2 TA-37 |
| Swift, John, 3 Nov. 1737, Martha Hobbs | 1 QA-43 |
| Swift, Lemon, 13 Feb. 1746, Frances Wright | 1 QA-53 |
| Swift, Luke, 28 Oct. 1758, Olydia Thrift | 2 BA-218 |
| Swift, Mark, 26 Dec. 1725, Ann Lockerd | 2 BA-28 |
| Swift, Moses, Jan. 1744, Rachal Chance | 1 QA-50 |
| Swift, Ralph, 14 April 1711, Ann Montique | 2 TA-69 |
| Swift, Richard, 16 Aug. 1716, Elizabeth Stacy | 2 TA-78 |
| Swift, Sam'l, 25 Dec. 1740, Rachel Hobs | 1 QA-46 |
| Swiggett, James, 3 July 1755, Elizabeth Priest | 2 CR-272 |
| Swillaven, Daniel, 24 April 1705, Priscilla Stirmey | 1 CA-111 |
| Swillawin, Owen, 30 Nov. 1723, Ann Millener | 1 BA-252 |
| Swinard, John, 12 April 1747, Sarah Wilson | 2 BA-241 |
|    2 BA-196 gives the date as 30 April 1747. | |
| Swinneck, John, 26 Jan. 1724, Mary Lippere | 1 AA-100 |
| Swinney, Terrence, 6 April 1730, Catherine Farrel | 2 TA-148 |
| Swoope, Benedick, Jr., 13 Dec. 1777, Margaret Keener | 9 BA |
| Sylvester, James, 10 Jan. 1737/8, Deborah Rowe | 1 QA-43 |
| Sylvester, William, 5 Feb. 1746, Alice Satterfield | 1 QA-53 |
| Syme, Nicholas, 25 July 1777, Elizabeth Johnson | 2 CH(4) |
| Symmonds, John, 30 March 1755, Eliz. Powell | 2 BA-212 |
| Sympers, Nathaniel, son of Thomas and Amey, 10 Oct. | |
|    1759, Ann Lewis, dau. of Richard and Amey | 1 CE-314 |
| Sympson, John, 12 Nov. 1730, Isbaella Rawlings | 1 AA-111 |
| Sympson, William, 12 Nov. 1739, Mary Larrissee | 1 BA-307 |
| Sympson, William, 18 Aug. 1742, Avarilla Perkins | 1 BA-329 |
| Syng, Philip, of Annapolis, goldsmith, 26 Feb. 1733/4, | |
|    Susanna Price, widow | 4 AA-436 |
| Talbee, Samuel, 1 Dec. 1736, Elizabeth Hitchcock | 2 BA-90 |
| Talbee, Zephaniah, 21 July 1763, Mary Woolling | 2 BA-225 |
| Talbot, Charles, 4 June 1713, Elizabeth Wood | 1 BA-213 |
| Talbot, John, 7 Jan. 1719/20, Ann Bockerdike | 4 AA-411 |
| Talbot, John, 17 Feb. 1723, Prudence Colegate | 1 AA-98 |
| Talbot, William, 31 Jan. 1729, Mary Roberts | 2 BA-40 |
| Talbott, Charles, 15 July 1754, Eliz. Young | 2 BA-211 |
| Talbott, Edmund, 26 Oct. 1749, Darcas Hall | 3 BA-165 |
| Talbott, Edmund, 18 June 1752, Rebecca Robinson | 3 BA-165 |
| Talbott, Edward, 7 April 1763, Marg't Slade | 2 BA-224 |
| Talbott, John, son of John and Mary, 22 Oct. 1741, | |
|    Margaret Webster, dau. of Isaac and Margaret | 9 SF |
| Talbott, John, son of Jos., 22 day 2 mo., 1760, | |
|    Mary Johns, dau. of Abraham and Eliza | 5 SF |
| Talbott, John, 1 Oct. 1777, Ann Davis | 3 PG-110 |
| Talbott, Joseph, III, 3 day, 3 mo., 1772, Anna Plummer | 6 SF |
| Talbott, Matthew, 5 June 1722, Mary Williamson | 3 BA-146 |
| Talbott, Thos., 21 Jan. 1766, Belander Slade | 2 BA-229 |
| Talbott, Vincent, 2 Feb. 1773, Eliz. Bosley | 2 BA-265 |
| Talburt, John, son of John, 15 Aug. 1722, Mary Rigges | 1 PG-261 |
| Talburt, John, son of Paul, of Pocklinton, Yorks., | |
|    (Eng.), 2 Feb. 1696, Sarah Lockyer, dau. of Thomas | |
|    Lockyer | 1 PG-264 |
| Talburt, Paul, son of John, 20 March 1719, Ann John- | |
|    stone, dau. of Robert Johnson (sic) | 1 PG-281 |
| Talour, Mathew, 26 Jan. 1743, Mary Thomasman | 1 QA-49 |
| Taney, Michael, 25 June 1771, Monica Brooke | 1 SM-136 |
| Tanquarry, Abraham, 30 (?) 1769, Wilhelminah Whitting- | |
|    ton | 2 AA-409 |
| Tarbutton, Edward, 8 Nov. 1744, Rachell Rattcliffe | 1 QA-50 |
| Tarleton, Richard, 18 July 1772, Eliz. Tiford | 1 SM-136 |
| Tasker, Benj., 31 July 1711, Anne Bladen, dau. of | |
|    William and Anne | 4 AA-380 |

```
Tasker, James, April 1776, Ann Stallions          2 AA-413
Tate, Da'd, 15 March 1768, Eliz. Sinklar          2 BA-231
Tate, George, 16 Aug. 1736, Catherine Munday      1 QA-42
Tate, Thomas, 23 Dec. 1735, Sarah Bermingham      1 QA-41
Tayler, Edward, May 1735, Mary (?)                1 CE-283
Tayller, Richard, 7 day, 6 mo., 1687, Ann Trasey  6 SF
Taylor, Abraham, 20 (?) (?), Dinah White          2 BA-5
Taylor, Abraham, 17 May 1751, Mary (?)            1 WI-108
Taylor, Abraham, 12 June 1777, Mary Foard         1 HA-200
Taylor, Ambrose, son of Peter and Elizabeth, 28 day,
   4 mo., 1773, Mary Sidwell, dau. of Henry and Ellen  9 SF
Taylor, Anthony, 27 Nov. 1666, Alce Bassett       5 SO-400
Taylor, Asa, 24 Dec. 1777, Hannah Kimble          1 HA-200
Taylor, Benjamin, 24 June 1737, Ann Hawkins       1 BA-297
Taylor, Brian, 7 May 1772, Barbara Dawkins        2 CA-49
                                                  & 53
Taylor, Caleb, 19 Jan. 1765, Elizabeth Denoone    9 AA-249
Taylor, Charles, 25 Dec. 1750, Eliz. Standeford   2 BA-202
Taylor, Dennis, 12 March 1767, Ann Addams         2 SO-177
Taylor, Elias, 19 Jan. 1764, Sarah Addams         2 SO-86
Taylor, Francis, 6 Oct. 1729, Eliz'th Whiteaker   1 BA-254
Taylor, George, 31 Jan. 1735/6, Mary Hutton       2 AA-391
Taylor, Gunby, 4 Jan. 1759, Naoma Carsly          2 SO-170
Taylor, Henry, 3 Oct. 1745, Sarah Armstrong       2 BA-193
Taylor, Hope, 5 Feb. 1683/4, Margaret Doricks or
   Daniels                                        9 SO-402
Taylor, James, 1 day, 8 mo., 1699, Isabel Adkison 8 SF-382
Taylor, James, 26 Nov. 1731, Mary Fossett         1 BA-256
Taylor, James, Jr., 26 Feb. 1741, Catherine Smith 3 CE-23
Taylor, James, 22 Aug. 1745, Elizabeth Ackworth   1 WI-67
Taylor, James, 9 May 1747, Sarah Kimball          1 BA-357
Taylor, Jeremiah, 15 June 1760, Mary Townsend     2 SO-170
Taylor, John, 9 Nov. 1713, Rachel Holmes          1 CA-114
Taylor, John, 29 Aug. 1721, Anne Hennel           4 AA-415
Taylor, John, 18 July 1723, Eliza Swift           2 TA-104
Taylor, John, April 1726, Rachel York, widow      2 BA-37
Taylor, John, 15 June 1742, Sarah Ward            2 BA-133
Taylor, John, 18 Oct. 1757, Eliz. Norris          2 BA-216
Taylor, Jno., 30 Nov. 1760, Martha Mayner         2 BA-220
Taylor, John, son of John, 21 Nov. 1767, Sarah Day 2 BA-158
Taylor, Jonathan, 31 Oct. 1706, Margaret Dowglass 1 AA-72
Taylor, Jonathan, 12 day, 9 mo., 1724, Elizabeth
   Sherwood                                       8 SF-40
Taylor, Joseph, 14 March 1675/6, Margaret Rollens 9 SO-401
Taylor, Joseph Gray, 15 Feb. 1777, Sarah Tilghman 2 SO-176
Taylor, Joseph Reed, 23 July 1751, Ann Bell Ballard,
   dau. of Jarvis                                 3 SO-4
Taylor, Lawrence, 5 Feb. 1699/1700, Mary Miles    1 BA-190
Taylor, Lawrence, 7 Feb. 1703/4, Agnes Montague   1 BA-200
Taylor, Lias, 19 Jan. 1736, Susannah Gunby        2 SO-80
Taylor, Michael, 24 May 1759, Mary Mitchell       1 BA-70
Taylor, Michael, 3 Sept. 1772, Salley Hall        2 BA-265
Taylor, Nathan, 15 May 1748, Elizabeth Leech      1 QA-54
Taylor, Richard, 21 Sept. 1706, Anne Tatloe       1 AA-72
Taylor, Richard, June 1716, Anne Perrey           3 CE-9
Taylor, Richard, 20 Feb. 1732, Jemima Godman      1 AA-115
Taylor, Richard, 23 Jan. 1749, Elizabeth Mounsieur 1 QA-56
Taylor, Richard, 6 Feb. 1777, Margaret Welsh      3 BA-172
Taylor, Robert, 17 March 1757, Sarah White        2 SO-85 ,
Taylor, Robert, 19 March 1771, Isabel Smith       2 BA-261
Taylor, Ruben, 11 Dec. 1729, Anne Smith           1 QA-37
Taylor, Sam'l, 12 April 1763, Patience Tipton     2 BA-225
Taylor, Snowden, Nov. 1734, Anne Godman           1 AA-119
Taylor, Thomas, 1 day, 2 mo., 1669, Elizabeth Marsh 8 SF-314
Taylor, Thomas, Jr., 1 Feb. 1696, Sarah (?)       2 TA-5
```

Taylor, Thomas, Sr., of Bullenbrooke, 12 Aug. 1701,
   Elizabeth (?)                                          2 TA-19
Taylor, Thomas, 21 Aug. 1701, Elizabeth Sharp          8 SF-368
Taylor, Thomas, of Fairfax Meeting, 28 day, 12 mo.,
   1750, Caleb Pierpoint, dau. of Charles and Sydney   4 SF
Taylor, Thomas, 21 May 1752, Ann Powell                1 QA-58
Taylor, Thomas, 4 June 1758, Jane Hanby                1 BA-70
Taylor, Thomas, 3 Nov. 1777, Elizabeth Evans          10 BA-69
Taylor, William, 14 Dec. 1752, Mary Prior              2 SO-79
Taylor, William, 20 day, 4 mo., 1757, Elizabeth
   Edmondson                                          8 SF-102
Tayman, Sabret, 16 Jan. 1742/3, Jemima Hitchcock       2 BA-238
Tayman, William, 25 Dec. 1750, Ann Nearn               2 BA-164
Tayman, William Cammell, 25 Dec. 1750, Ann Williams    2 BA-202
                                                      & 241
Teale, Emmanuel, 24 Dec. 1734, Katherine Johnson       3 BA-153
Teat, Nathan, 24 Feb. 1756, Elizabeth Hill             1 QA-60
Teatum, John, 21 Feb. 1720, Elizabeth Blisset          4 AA-414
Teauge, James, Nov. 1734, Mary Clark                   1 AA-119
Tedstell, Thomas, 28 Aug. 1707, Jane Eustace           1 AA-76
Temple, George, 5 Sept. 1757, Mary Lee                 1 QA-62
Temple, Thomas, 17 April 1699, Elenor Loreson          1 BA-186
Templeman, John, 12 June 1738, Mary Griffin            2 TA-165
Tenanly, Phil., 2 July 1720, Grace Thomas              1 PG-267
Terry, Benjamin, 26 Jan. 1743, Alifere Cosden, dau.
   of Alphonso                                        3 CE-26
Terry, Hugh, 28 Sept. 1727, Sarah Christian            3 CE-14
Tetley, Joseph, 8 Aug. 1777, Mary Wilkinson           10 BA-68
Teufferby, John, 8 May 1763, An. Marg. Kraemer         4 FR-1178
Tevis, Robert, 15 April 1707, Susanna Davies           1 AA-73
Thacker, William, 14 Feb. 1750/1, Hanner Cox           3 BA-165
Thackery, James, 16 Nov. 1777, Ann Hart                2 CE-1
Thackrel, Thomas, 9 April 1710, Mary Martin            4 AA-379
Tharp, Michael, 1 Jan. 1772, Eunice Cooper             1 WI-96
Tharp, William, 8 Jan. 1709, Jane Oistone              2 TA-65
Thayer, George, Nov. 1748, Katherine Graves            2 BA-243
Theis, John Henry, 7 Feb. 1764, Elizabeth Jons         4 FR-1178
Thesbord, Robart, 23 April 1772, Catheran Floud        2 BA-264
Thickpenny, Henry, 5 Jan. 1715, Rachel Dowden          2 PG-1
Thine, William, 5 June 1770, Sarah Davinne             2 BA-260
Thomas, Alexander, 1678, Cicell Shaw                   5 SO-399
Thomas, Benj'n, 6 Aug. 1746, Rebecca Kemp              1 QA-52
Thomas, Christopher, 13 Dec. 1757, Sus. Marg. Weisz    4 FR-1103
Thomas, David, Feb. 1732, Elizabeth Wheeler            1 BA-268
Thomas, Edward, 17 Dec. 1733, Sarah Herbert            3 BA-151
Thomas, Edward, 1770, Ann Murrey                       2 AA-409
Thomas, Evan, son of Samuel, 26 day, 12 mo., 1766,
   Rachel Hopkins, dau. of Gerrard                    6 SF
Thomas, Even, 8 March 1712/3, Mary Jones               2 AA-346
Thomas, Griffith, of Newcastle Co., Del., widower,
   9 day, 8 mo., 1739, Alse Brown                     1 SF-75
Thomas, Henry, 9 day, 9 mo., 1733, Rebekah Troth       8 SF-76
Thomas, Henry, 22 Jan. 1737, Jane Poteet               1 BA-303
Thomas, Hennery, 23 Feb. 1769, Eliz'th Piles           2 BA-258
Thomas, Isaac, July 1745, Blanch Jones, alias Hazlup   3 AA-109
Thomas, Israel, of Fairfax Co., Va., 2 day, 4 mo.,
   1754, Ann Richardson                               6 SF
Thomas, James, 13 April 1735, Mary Adams               3 BA-153
Thomas, Jno., 6 Nov. 1763, Sharlote Thrift             2 BA-225
Thomas, Jno., 22 Aug. 1777, Sarah Murray               7 AA-1
   6 SF gives the date as 23 Aug. 1777.
Thomas, Joseph, 4 Feb. 1732, Darkes Sutton             3 BA-150
Thomas, Philip, 11 day, 6 mo., 1724, Ann Chew, dau.
   of Samuel                                          6 SF
Thomas, Philip, 30 day, 4 mo., 1754, Ann Galloway      6 SF

```
Thomas, Phillomon, 5 March 1744, Sarah Scott          1 QA-50
Thomas, Reese, 5 Jan. 1734, Martha Gray               3 BA-153
Thomas, Richard, son of Philip and Ann, 29 day, 4 mo.,
  1760, Deborah Hughes, dau. of Thomas and Elizabeth  9 SF
Thomas, Richard, 7 Oct. 1767, Mary Waugh Baxter       1 CE-316
Thomas, Richard, c.Aug. 1775, Rhoda Porter            1 CR-6
Thomas, Rob't, 18 Jan. 1704, Jane ffreeborn           4 AA-389
Thomas, Robert, 13 Oct. 1756, Mary Sands              1 QA-61
Thomas, Sam'l, 15 day, 3 mo., 1688, Mary Hutchings    6 SF
  In another place in 6SF the date is given as 15
  day, 9 mo., 1688, and the bride's name as Mary
  Hutchins.
Thomas, Samuel, son of Richard, 31 day, 10 mo., 1775,
  Mary Cowman, dau. of John                           6 SF
Thomas, Samuel, c.Oct. 1775, Margaret Oldham          1 CR-6
Thomas, Simon, 18 Sept. 1738, Susanna Sands           1 QA-44
Thomas, Tristram, 19 Jan. 1732, Mary Watson           1 QA-39
Thomas, Trustram, 8 Dec. 1736, Mary Skinner           2 TA-158
Thomas, William, 22 day, 11 mo., 1707, Joanna Hosier  1 SF-51
Thomas, William, 7 Dec. 1721, Anne Jenkins            1 PG-268
Thomas, William, born 6 June 1729; m. 2 March 1762,
  Sarah Kennerly, b. 4 April 1742                     1 CE-309
Thomas, William, 11 May 1731, Elizabeth Allen         2 TA-151
Thomas, William, 27 day, 5 mo., 1738, Joannah Powell  8 SF-72
Thomas, William, Jr., 9 Feb. 1765, Rachel Leeds       2 TA-287
Thomas, Wm., 8 April 1765, Ichabard Thrift            2 BA-227
Thomas, William, 27 March 1770, Ann Colegate          2 BA-260
Thomas, William, 11 Oct. 1772, Mary Pardon            2 BA-265
Thomkins, Thomas, 19 May 1765, Esther Burch           2 BA-228
Thompson, Alexander, 30 April 1734, Sarah Smithson    1 BA-286
Thompson, Andrew, 13 May 1731, Mary Shaw              1 BA-266
Thompson, Aquilla, 20 Feb. 1753, Cathrine Whiteaker   2 BA-207
Thompson, Augustine, 17 Nov. 1729, Elizabeth Hall     1 QA-36
Thompson, Daniel, 3 Dec. 1719, Eliza Helsby           2 TA-92
Thompson, Dan'l, 24 Oct. 1758, Marg'rt Clark          2 BA-217
Thompson, Dowdal, 10 April 1740, Hester Baldwin, of
  Cecil Co.                                           1 QA-47
Thompson, Edward, 12 Aug. 1764, Jemima Groom          1 BA-383
Thompson, Henry, 24 July 1754, Hannah Baynard         2 CR-272
Thompson, James, 30 Oct. 1727, Elizabeth Gilbert      1 BA-252
Thompson, James, 28 June 1730, Sarah Miller           3 BA-149
Thompson, John, 27 Dec. 1726, Elizabeth Ward          4 AA-427
Thompson, John, 4 June 1730, Marg't Dunnefan          1 QA-36
Thompson, John, 19 Aug. 1734, Mary Julian             3 CE-21
Thompson, John, 12 March 1739 or 1740, Mary Griffith
  of Annapolis                                        3 CE-21
Thompson, John, 13 Nov. 1740, Mary Puttee             1 BA-313
  1 BA-375 gives the date as 14 Nov. 1740 and the
  bride's name as Mary Potee.
Thompson, Jno., 25 Dec. 1740, Sarah Blackwell         2 BA-161
Thompson, John, 26 March 1744, Mary Baldwin           4 AA-446
Thompson, John, 1748, Anne Petty                      2 BA-243
Thompson, John, 17 April 1748, Jane Houston           3 CE-25
Thompson, John, 18 July 1755, Margaret Gilbert        1 BA-375
Thompson, John, son of John, 4 May 1765, Mary Haly of
  Philadelphia                                        3 CE-26
Thompson, John, 18 Aug. 1772, Eliz. Rumsey            2 BA-265
Thompson, Ric., 20 Sept. 1735, Hester Miller          1 CE-282
Thompson, Richard, 19 June 1729, Eleanor Dudley       2 TA-120
Thompson, Richard, Jr., 12 Nov. 1739, Mary Alman, dau.
  of Abraham                                          3 CE-22
Thompson, Sam'l, 29 May 1766, Isabel Barns            2 BA-229
Thompson, Simon, 10 Nov. 1734, Savory Lett; both
  parties were negro                                  3 BA-152
Thompson, Thomas, 15 Jan. 1744, Sarah Durham          2 BA-192
```

Thompson, Thomas, 4 Dec. 1752, Ellinor Agon        1 BA-362
Thompson, Thomas, 9 Aug. 1759, Sarah Sparks        1 QA-65
Thompson, Thomas, 25 Feb. 1772, Henrietta Abel     1 SM-136
Thompson, Wilford, 11 Oct. 1774, Ann Shircliff     1 SM-136
Thompson, William, son of William and Mary, 11 April
  1681, Victoria Matthews, dau. of Thomas and Jane  3 CH
Thompson, William, 4 April 1704, Mary Hall         8 SF-419
Thomson, Jasper, 29 Aug. 1706, Ann Cleary          2 AA-330
Thomson, William, 28 Oct. 1762, Susanna Ross; they
  were married by Rev. Thomas Barton at Lancaster,
  Pa. William was born son to Rev. Samuel Thomson
  on 22 May 1735, and was ordained deacon and priest
  in the Church of England at the Bishop of London's
  Palace in Fullam, Dec. 1759; Susanna was born 17 Jan.
  1738, dau. of Rev. George Ross, Rector of North Elk
  alias St. Mary Ann's Parish.                     1 CE-316
Thorn?, Alexander, 10 Oct. 1726, Charrety Shirman  1 WI-17
Thornbury, John, 7 Aug. 1733, Elizabeth Stone      3 BA-151
Thornhill, Benjamin, 6 Dec. 1770, Ann Scott        2 BA-261
Thornhill, Jos., 22 Dec. 1772, Monica Brown        1 SM-136
Thornhill, Sam'll, 4 Feb. 1747, Mary Clybourn      2 BA-194
Thornhill, Samuel, 1748, Mary Clyburn              2 BA-242
Thornly, James, 25 Feb. 1741/2, Sarah Steen        2 KE-245
Thornton, John, 24 April 1739, Mary Davis          2 KE-226
Thornton, William (date not given), Cathe: Burchinall  2 KE-197
Thornton, William Lather, 9 Jan. 1745/6, Lettica Osborn  2 KE-259
Thorp, Edward, 6 Jan. 1731, Catherine Cullings     1 BA-259
Thorp, Edward, 31 May 1760, Mary Green             2 BA-220
Thorp, George, 18 Aug. 1724, Anne Noddes           1 AA-99
Thorp, Thomas, 1749, Hannah Horsley                1 QA-56
Thorpe, George, 8 Aug. 1724, Mrs. Anne Nodes, widow  4 AA-423
Thorpe, Dr. George, 4 Sept. 1729, Mrs. Mary Holmes  4 AA-431
Thorpe, Thomas, 1 Jan. 1731, Elizabeth Birmingham  1 QA-38
Thrap, Robert, 28 Feb. 1760, Eliz. Hilton          2 BA-219
Thrift, James, 16 May 1771, Ann Wilson             2 BA-262
Thrift, John, May 1728, Rebecca Blackledge         2 BA-29
Thrift, John, 1732, Sarah Dorney                   2 BA-205
Thurlow, Richard, 15 Nov. 1708, Ann Holdgate       4 AA-378
Thurston, George, 30 Jan. 1730, Frances Gibson     1 BA-254
Thyler, George, 1 Jan. 1748, Catherine Graves      2 BA-198
Tibbels, Abraham, 17 Sept. 1711, Rebekkah Standley  2 TA-69
Tibbett, James, 19 Feb. 1760, Rebecca Wordgworth   2 BA-219
Tidings, John, son of Richard and Charity, 16 day,
  6 mo., 1705, Mary Ellis                          6 SF
Tilghman, Mr. Edward, son of Col. Matthew, 25 April
  1759, Juliana Carroll, dau. of Dominick          3 CE-27
Tilghman, Gidden, 2 Aug. 1758, Tabitha Dormon      2 SO-170
Tilghman, James, III, Esq., of Annapolis, attorney,
  19 Jan. 1769, Susanna Stewart, dau. of George
  Stewart, Esq., of Annapolis                      5 AA-3
Tilghman, Matthew, 3 April 1741, Anne Lloyd        3 TA-29
Tilghman, Samuel, 9 Aug. 1774, Mary Dreaden        2 SO-173
Tilghman, Stephen, 12 July 1761, Franceis Paden    2 SO-170
Tilghman, William, 11 Sept. 1742, Sarah Townsand   2 SO-81
Tilghman, William, 13 Sept. 1774, Tabitha Welliss  2 SO-177
Tillard, Thomas, 20 Feb. 1776, Janet Hamilton      2 AA-412
Tillard, William, 22 Dec. 1741, Martha Simmons     2 AA-383
Tillard, William, Jan. 1776, Martha Hall           2 AA-412
Tilley, Thomas, 3 Nov. 1726, Rebecca Bateman       2 PG-4
Tillman, Gydeon, 15 Feb. 1681, Margaret Maneux     5 SO-399
Tillmon, Aaron, Sept. 1750, Hannah Broughton       2 SO-80
Tillotson, Baynard, 19 Jan. 1748, Margaret Chairs  1 QA-55
Tillotson, John, 6 Feb. 1742, Sarah Earle          1 QA-47
Timblin?, John, Nov. 1774, Elizabeth Johnson, dau. of
  Edward and Margaret                              3 BA-179

Timmons, John, 18 April 1745, Sarah Copland          2 BA-192
Timmons, Joseph, 30 May 1728, Eliz'th Hammond          1 WO-7
Timms, John, 25 Aug. 1776, Catherine Phipps          2 AA-413
Timms, Thomas, 18 Aug. 1747, Mary Stanton          3 TA-66
Tingle, Caleb, 11 Nov. (?), Elizabeth Forsch          1 WO-4
Tingle, Hugh, 22 Dec. 1683, Elizabeth Powell          5 SO-399
Tippens, William, 22 Dec. 1732, Dianna Layton          1 QA-39
Tipton, John, 18 Feb. 1747, Martha Murray          3 BA-161
Tipton, Jonas, 19 May 1772, Eliz. Ford          2 BA-264
Tipton, Jonathan, 15 Dec. 1709, Mary Chilcoat          2 AA-339
Tipton, Jonathan, 24 Sept. 1745, Eleanor Bryant          3 BA-157
Tipton, Luke, 26 Dec. 1749, Sarah Boston          3 BA-163
Tipton, Nicholas, son of William and Amphillis, 25 day,
   5 mo., 1775, Esther Price, dau. of Mordecai and
   Mary          4 SF-266
Tipton, Samuel, 16 Nov. 1777, Ruth Bowen          10 BA-69
Tipton, William, 25 Nov. 1736, Tabitha Wright          3 BA-155
Tipton, Wm., 26 Oct. 1765, Mary Miller          2 BA-228
Tivis, Robert, 28 Feb. 1723, Elizabeth Curry          1 AA-98`
Toadvin, Nicholas, 15 Nov. 1675, Sarah Lowry          5 SO-399
Toadvine, Nicholas, 24 Oct. 1676, Sarah Loury          9 SO-402
Toas?, John, of Kent Co., 14 day, 7 mo., 1699, Jone
   Queney of Cecil Co.          1 SF-44
Tobias, Curnelius, 24 Feb. 1712, Eleanor Shutten          3 CE-6
Tobin, Walter, 22 Dec. 1709, Mary Shea          4 AA-379
Tobitt, Walter, 22 Dec. 1709, Mary Shay          4 AA-378
Todd, Charles, 16 April 1761, Elizabeth Page          3 AA-112
Todd, David, 21 April 1753, Catherine Porter          2 BA-207
Todd, John, 1710, Keatien Smith          3 AA-100
Todd, John, 19 June 1756, Elizabeth Linstead          3 AA-111
Todd, Lance, 11 Oct. 1727, Anna Burle          3 AA-102
Todd, Lance, 13 Nov. 1735, Rachel Warfield, dau. of
   Alexander          6 AA-207
Todd, Lance, 10 April 1744, Elianer ffoard          3 AA-108
Todd, Nathan, 10 April 1766, Rebecca Boone          3 AA-112
Todd, Rezin, 2 Jan. 1772, Sarah Soward          3 AA-113
Todd, Richard, 3 March 1727, Mary Stinchecomb          3 AA-103
Todd, Samuel, 1 April 1755, Ann Aldridge          3 AA-111
Todd, Thomas, 25 Dec. 1777, Elizabeth Mills          9 BA
Todd, William, 4 May 1773, Presella Harryman          2 BA-266
Todvine, Thos., 6 Oct. 1745, Mary Baly          1 WI-40
Tofler, Peter, 17 April 1757, Anna Mary Sturm          4 FR-1103
Tolburt, John, 19 Oct. 1777, Ann Davis          2 CH(1)
Tolley, Walter, 20 Dec. 1735, Mary Garrettson          2 BA-127
Tolley, Walter, 22 Dec. 1751, Martha Hall          1 BA-349
Tollson, Thomas, 18 Feb. 1730, Elizabeth Noble          2 KE-234
Tolly, Thomas, 6 Nov. 1706, Catherine Howard          4 AA-372
Tolson, Francis, 22 Sept. 1707, Mary Clark, dau. of
   Robert; Francis Tolson was born at Wood Hall in
   Co. Cumberland (Eng.), Bright Church Parish, son
   of Henry Tolson.          1 PG-265
Tomkins, Thos., 19 May 1765, Esther Burch          2 BA-228
Tomlin, Robert, 23 Oct. 1701, Jeane (?)          2 TA-21
Tomlinson, Joseph, 26 Dec. 1723, Eliza Ross          2 TA-106
Tomlinson, Thomas, 3 June 1745, Elizabeth Wilkenson          3 BA-157
Tommes, Robert, (date not given), (wife's name not
   given)          1 AA-275
Tompkins, John, 21 Jan. 1768, Mary Brewer          4 SM-72
Tompkins, William, 7 Sept. 1758, Sarah Sandall          1 QA-64
Tompson, James, 30 Oct. 1727, Elizabeth Gilbert          1 BA-252
Tongue, John, 16 Nov. 1739, Elizabeth Welsh          9 AA-246
Tool, James, 17 Sept. 1777, Catharine O'Hara          10 BA-69
Toomy, John, 1 Dec. 1756, Bridgett Lyon          1 QA-61
Toomy, John, 10 Nov. (1768 ?), Salley Gouldsmith          2 BA-257
Tophouse, Francis, 1770, Ann Taylor          2 AA-409

```
Topping, Garrett, 28 June 1720, Sarah Duvall           4 AA-412
Touchstone, Henry, 12 Nov. 1749, Margret Mahen         1 CE-298
Touchstone, Richard, 25 Feb. 1717, Sarah Johnson       1 BA-256
Towgood, Josias, 3 Oct. 1698, Mary Purnell             2 AA-372
Townsand, William, 9 Dec. 1748, Sarah Cordrey          2 SO-80
Townsand, John, 5 Aug. 1764, Ann Cary                  2 SO-172
Townsend, George, 29 Jan. 1769, Mary Burnet            2 BA-257
Townsend, John, 31 Dec. 1741, Joana England, dau. of
   Joseph and Margaret                                 9 SF
Townsend, Solomon, 15 Feb. 1777, Mary Townsend         2 SO-176
Townsend, William, Aug. 1776, Mary Wonnel              2 SO-177
Towson, Abraham, 1 Jan. 1745, Elizabeth Mahorn         3 BA-158
Towson, Charles, 4 Sept. 1777, Betsy Ann Trapnal      10 BA-69
Towson, John, 29 Dec. 1771, Prunelfry Buck             2 BA-263
Towson, Richard, 26 Dec. 1758, Tabitha Rutledge        2 BA-218
Towson, William, 24 Feb. 1735, Ruth Gott               3 BA-155
Toy, Joseph, 29 May 1770, Frances Dallam               1 BA-286
Tracey, Tego, 5 Nov. 1694, Mary James                  2 AA-298
Tracy, Thomas, 15 Jan. 1701, Susannah Hawkins          2 AA-317
Tracy, William, 18 Sept. 1777, Mary Scissell           3 PG-150
Trainsworth, Joseph, 22 Oct. 1774, Sarah Ellis         3 BA-171
Tramell, Thos., 27 Dec. 1730, Mary Maccay              1 AA-111
Trapnell, Vincent, 20 Nov. (1768 ?), Martha Bozley     2 BA-257
Traquear?, Alexnader, Dec. 1727, Mary Cash             2 PG-4
Trasey, Benn, 13 May 1770, Tempy Edwards               2 BA-260
Traub, Adam, 12 April 1762, Cath. Muselman             4 FR-1178
Travers, Thomas, 20 Feb. 1774, Hannah Hutchins         6 BA(1)
Travis, John, 27 Nov. 1743, Anne Kelsey                2 BA-239
Traxel, Christian, 31 May 1761, Cath. Doerr            4 FR-1178
Trayman, James, 24 Aug. 1711, Elizabeth Banton         2 TA-69
Trayman, Thomas, 3 Aug. 1733, Mary Dutton              2 TA-153
Treagle, Christopher, 27 May 1734, Mary Rowles         3 BA-152
Treble, John, 21 Oct. 1755, Eliz. Logg                 2 BA-212
Tredway, Daniel, 2 Aug. 1744, Sarah Norris             2 BA-191
Tredway, John, 3 March 1761, Elizabeth Osborn, widow
   of Benjamin Osborn                                  1 BA-70
Tredway, John, 12 Jan. 1764, Sarah Griffith            1 BA-380
Tredway, Thomas, 27 Dec. 1734, Mary Ball               1 BA-281
Tredway, Thos., 26 Jan. 1761, Mary Gittings            2 BA-221
Tredwell, Richard, 7 June 1752, Maple Stevenson        2 BA-205
Treherne, George, 29 Aug. 1676, Anne Cammeday          5 SO-399
   9 SO-401 gives the bride's name as Cameday.
Trevis, James, 15 Jan. 1767, Ann Hutchins             2 BA-230
Trevis, John, 6 Dec. 1743, Ann Kelsey                  2 BA-189
Trew (or Crew), William, of Kent Co., 15 day, 2 mo.,
   1703, Martha Pope of Cecil Co.                      1 SF-47
Trew, William, 8 day, 1 mo., 1748/9, Mary George       1 SF-94
Trice, Alexander, Sept. 1687, Bridgett Eley            5 SO-399
Trickey?, Thos., 10 Feb. 1736, Mary Harrington         1 QA-43
Trimble, John, son of Joseph and Sarah, 10 day, 12
   mo., 1772, Catherine Wilson, dau. of Samuel and
   Catherine                                           9 SF
Trimble, Joseph, son of William and Mary, 31 Jan.
   1744/5, Sarah Churchman, dau. of John and Hannah    9 SF
Trimble, Joseph, son of William and Mary, 22 Feb.
   1753, Ann Chandler, dau. of William and Ann         9 SF
Trippe, Wm., 21 April 1744, Eliza Gibson               3 TA-48
Tripper, Edgar, 30 Oct. 1713, Elizabeth Pritchett      1 BA-213
Troth, George, 22 Dec. 1708, Rebecca Berry             2 TA-55
Troth, Henry, 31 March 1769, Elizabeth Neal            8 SF-134
Troth, James, 19 Nov. 1741, Sarah Harvey               2 TA-175
Troth, William, 20 April 1685, Isabel Harrison         8 SF-337
Troth, William, 11 Jan. 1704, Sarah Pratt              8 SF-432
Troth, William, Jr., 4 Feb. 1747, Ann Birkhead         8 SF-90
Trott, Henry, 1769, Sarah Frazier                      2 AA-409
```

Trott, John, Jr., 15 Sept. 1775, Luraner Wells        2 AA-412
Trott, Sabrett, 1771, Sarah Brown                     2 AA-410
Trotten, Luke, 15 Jan. 1744, Eliz. Body               2 BA-192
Trotten, Luke, 10 Feb. 1754, Susannah Long            3 BA-166
Trotter, James, 19 May 1719, Mary Feben, widow        4 AA-408
Trotton, Luke, 3 Oct. 1735, Elizabeth Lenox           3 BA-154
Truit, James, c.Oct. 1775, Sarah Williams             1 CR-6
Trulock, Joseph, 15 July 1726, Mary Noradick          2 KE-218
Truman, Thomas, 1 Oct. 1750, Elizabeth Dighton        3 BA-164
Trundle, Thomas, 22 Aug. 1738, Mary Farquson          9 AA-246
Tschudy, Nicolaus, 1 Aug. 1773, Barbara Burrer        8 BA-176
Tub (or Lub), William, 1 Jan. 1774, Martha Summerset  1 CH-201
Tubes. See Jubes.
Tuck, William, 24 Feb. 1738, Sarah Tavener            3 AA-105
Tucker, Charles, 16 Nov. 1741, Leah Abbott            2 TA-175
Tucker, James, 5 May 1709, Rebeckah Sewell            2 TA-59
Tucker, John, 23 Feb. 1708, Mary Lawson               2 TA-58
Tucker, Lewis, 26 Dec. (?), Katherine Partridge       1 BA-291
Tucker, Richard, 18 April 1705, Martha Thodam         2 AA-327
Tucker, Seaborn, 9 Nov. 1762, Eliz. Hitchcock         2 BA-224
Tucker, Seborn, 2 April 1730, Margaret Cob            1 BA-257
Tucker, William, 26 Dec. 1759, Ann Palmer             2 BA-219
Tucker, Wm., 9 Feb. 1762, Clement Beck                2 BA-223
Tucker, William, 1770, Sarah Gardinier                2 AA-409
Tuckin, Seaborn, 9 Nov. 1762, Eliz. Hitchcock         2 BA-224
Tuder, Jos., 20 June 1756, Eliz. Everett              2 BA-213
Tuder, Thomas, 15 Feb. 1758, Mary Edwards             2 BA-217
Tull, James, 24 Dec. 1750, Rachel White               2 SO-83
Tull, John, c.Oct. 1775, Catharine Merrell            1 CR-6
Tull, Richard, 9 Jan. 1671/2, Martha Rhoads           8 SO-401
Tull, Richard, 26 Jan. 1695/6, Elizabeth Turpin       5 SO-400
Tull, Stephen, (date not given), Sarah Hall           2 SO-81
Tull, Thomas, 4 Sept. 1666, Mary Mitchell (or Minshall) 6 SO-400
Tull, Thomas, Oct. 1666, Mary Minshall                5 SO-399
Tull, Thomas, 11 May 1769, Elizabeth Merrell          2 SO-172
Tull, William, 10 Nov. 1756, Mary Newbold             2 SO-83
Tull, William, 23 Dec. 1777, Mary Grace               1 CR-10
                                                        & 28
Tulley, Joseph, Dec. 1733, Sarah Jefferson            1 WI-10
Tulley, Richard, 23 May 1745, Mary Talor              1 WI-36
Tumbleson, William, 27 March 1770, Jane Hombledon     5 BA-14
Tumblestone, John, 16 Dec. 1717, Sarah Fish           2 TA-83
Tumlinson, Joseph, 21 Oct. 1738, Rebecca Sweringen    9 AA-246
Tunis, John, 21 Aug. 1755, Martha Hill                2 BA-212
Tunnell, William, 13 Jan. 1756, Arlanker Howard       1 WO-10
Turbell, Edward, 10 April 1727, Sarah Gay             3 BA-148
Turbutt, Rich'd, 16 Feb. 1750/1, Sarah Robins         3 TA-81
Turbutt, Samuel, 30 March 1714, Mrs. Rachel Golds-
    borough                                           2 TA-75
Turner, Abner, 29 Nov. 1740, Rebecca Troth            3 TA-26
    2 TA-171 gives the date as 15 Jan. 1740.
Turner, Edward, of Tal. Co., 12 Nov. 1730, Jane Kelly 2 KE-61
    1 SF-61 has the same information.
Turner, George, 31 Dec. 1777, Milcah Smith            1 CR-10
                                                        & 28
Turner, Hezekiah, 29 April 1764, Henrietta Chunn      1 CH-193
Turner, Jno., 6 Oct. 1706, Elizabeth Hodges           1 CA-111
Turner, Jno., Jr., 1 July 1718, Eliza Brushier,
    dau. of Samuel                                    2 PG-2
Turner, John, 16 Dec. 1756, Dorcas Ewen               1 QA-61
Turner, Jonathan, 29 Dec. 1743, Sarah Greenwood       2 KE-252
Turner, Joseph, 22 June 1729, Esther Lane             2 TA-120
Turner, Mathew, 14 Aug. 1734, Sarah Maybury           1 CE-279
    1 CE-284 gives the date as 15 Aug. 1734.
Turner, Richard, 8 Aug. 1671, Elizabeth Teague, widow 7 SO-401
    5 SO-399 gives the date as 8 March 1672.

Turner, Samuel, 18 Nov. 1762, Margaret Montgomery        1 CH-209
Turner, Solomon, 19 April 1734, Mary Crouch              3 AA-104
Turner, Thomas, 2 Dec. 1720, Sarah Register              2 TA-94
Turner, Thomas, 29 Sept. 1733, Mary Jones                1 AA-116
Turner, Thomas, 26 Oct. 1766, Mary Kimberley             2 BA-179
Turner, William, 27 Jan. 1718, Ann Maney                 2 PG-2
Turner, William, 1 July 1764, Rhoda Dent                 1 CH-193
Turner, Zachariah, Dec. 1777, Ann Brown                  2 AA-414
    8 AA-13 gives the date as 25 Dec. 1777.
Turnor, Robert, 3 May 1727, Mary Friend                  1 CE-281
Turpin, John, 23 Jan. 1695/6, Rebecca Bainton            5 SO-399
Turpin, Nehemiah, 14 July 1762, Orpha Brittingham        2 SO-176
Turpin, William, 6 Jan. 1668, Margaret Ivery             5 SO-399
Turpin, William, 3 March 1744/5, Elizabeth Williams      2 SO-79
Tutchstone, Richard, 25 Feb. 1717, Sarah Johnson         1 BA-256
Twilley, Robert, 9 April 1732, Ann Weatherly             1 WI-3
Twilly, James, 6 April 1759, Mary Phillips               1 WI-69
Tye, John, 11 Dec. 1735, Presiotia Hitchcock             3 BA-154
Tyferd, John, 14 Sept. 1670, Barbara Lawrence            7 SO-401
Tylar, Frederick, 29 Feb. 1733, Mary Dugwell             3 CE-21
Tyler, John, 8 March 1693/4, Alice Butter                5 SO-399
Tyler, Johnathan, 24 Dec. 1727, Sarah Shering            2 TA-117
Tyler, Robert, 10 June 1718, Mme. Mary Dodd              2 PG-2
Tyler, Robert, Gent., of P. G. Co., 12 June 1718,
    Mary Dodd, widow, of Annapolis                       4 AA-405
Tyler, Robert, Jr., 7 Jan. 1724/5, Mary Wade            2 PG-4
Tyler, Samuel, 11 July 1734, Susanna Duvall             2 PG-6
Tyler, Samuel, 21 Feb. 1762, Susannah Duvall            2 PG-7
Tyler, Thomas, 3 May 1702, Elizabeth Dane               8 SF-389
Tylor, Butler, 15 Jan. 1762, Rachel Bird                2 SO-171
Tylor, Elijah, 26 Oct. 1777, Ann Griffin                1 CR-10
                                                          & 28
Tylor, Thomas, 25 Jan. 1759, Jemima Cullen              2 SO-176
Typpings, Thos., 25 Nov. 1736, Lydia Hughbanks          1 QA-42
Tyre, Thomas, 4 Aug. 1730, Mary Hollingsworth           1 QA-36
Tyson, Elisha, son of Isaac and Esther, 5 day, 11 mo.,
    1776, Mary Amos, dau. of William and Hannah         4 SF-270
Ulmer, David, 2 July 1757, Rosina M. Hirschman          4 FR-1103
Underhill, John, 14 Jan. 1701, Sarah Lane               3 KE-332
Underhill, John, widower, 23 Nov. 1736, Anne Brown
    Dutton, widow of Robert Dutton, and dau. of
    William and Ann Brown                               9 SF
Underhill, Joseph, son of John, 11 Nov. 1736, Martha
    Oldham, dau. of Thomas and Susanna                  9 SF
Underhill, Thomas, 18 Nov. 1730, Rebecca Crowley        3 KE-332
Underhill, Thomas, son of John, 23 day, 4 mo., 1748,
    Elizabeth Norton, dau. of Richard                   9 SF
Underwood, Charles, 16 Feb. 1768, Ann Tartling          4 SM-72
Underwood, John, 8 Oct. 1733, Mary Brown                1 QA-40
Underwood, Thomas, 31 July 1743, Anne Petty             2 BA-239
Unick, Richard, 19 Oct. 170-(?), Katherine Bowdy        3 KE-332
Unkard, Laughlin, 13 Aug. 1703, Elizabeth Latum         3 KE-332
Upsal, Charles, 13 June 1769, Rylaid Wheatly            2 BA-258
Upton, Thomas, 26 Jan. 1729, Mary Heritage              1 QA-37
Urghvant, Alexander, April 1735, Mary Rees              1 BA-282
Uria, Thomas, 23 June 1751, Martha Clark                3 KE-332
Uriel, Capt. George, 24 July 1734, Elliner Welch        3 BA-152
Usher, Thomas, 15 Jan. 1702, Sarah Hicks                3 KE-332
Usher, Thomas, 10 Nov. 1703, Elizabeth Volentine        3 KE-332
Vain, John, 24 April 1709, Susannah Mulrain             2 TA-59
Vain, John, 27 Nov. 1734, Mary Cannady                  2 TA-156
Vake, John, 3 Oct. 1717, Mary Arrington                 2 TA-87
Valiant, Joseph, 17 Nov. 1741, Sarah Ray                3 TA-34
Valient, James, 15 Feb. 1747/8, Sarah Fairbank          3 TA-68
Valient, John, 16 Oct. 1749, Eliz. Cook                 3 TA-75

```
Van Bebber, James, son of Hendrick Van Bebber of
   Utrecht, 1730, Anna Laroun                          3 CE-17
Van Bebber, Matthias, 17 Nov. 1705, Haramontie Peter-
   son, dau. of Adam Peterson of Newcastle Co., Pa.    3 CE-3
Van Bibber, Isaac, son of James and Ann of Bohemia
   Manor, 27 Nov. 1768, Ann Chew, dau. of Benjamin
   and Sarah                                           1 CE-318
Van Burkeloo, Abell, 7 June 1715, Cathrin Herman       3 CE-13
Vanderford, Benjamin, 17 Aug. 1749, Ann Baley          1 QA-56
Vanderford, Charles, 11 Feb. 1749, Sarah Deleney       1 QA-56
Vanderford, James, 26 Feb. 1759, Sarah Calvin          1 QA-64
Vanderford, John, 21 July 1758, Mary Hines             1 QA-63
Vanderford, Thos., 9 Dec. 1740, Jane Emory             1 QA-46
Vandike, (?), 22 Jan. 1749/50, Mary Kirby              3 TA-76
Vanhorn, Barnett, 1 Nov. 1734, Elizabeth Ozier         3 CE-20
Vanhorne, Benj., 29 Aug. 1768, Martha Tunis            2 BA-232
Vannce, Andrew, 4 Jan. 1745, Sarah Low                 2 BA-193
Van Pool, Jacob, 23 Oct. 1726, Amy Cozine              1 CE-333
Vansant, Cornelius, 14 Aug. 1746, Elizabeth Doring     2 KE-265
Vansant, Ephraim, 22 Jan. 1746, Elizabeth Hall         2 KE-267
Vansant, Joshua, 10 day, 11 mo., 1749, Isabella Bowers 1 SF-81
Van Swaringen, Joseph, 26 July 1757, Eleanor Byrn      2 CE-39
                                                         & 42
Vaughan, Ephraim, 28 Feb. 1752, Elizabeth Cooper       1 WI-91
Vaughan, Thomas, 15 Dec. 1763, Mary Poteet             2 BA-225
Vaughn, Gist, 2 March 1769, Rachel Norris              2 BA-258
Vaughn, John, 30 Sept. 1714, Elizabeth Steapleford     2 TA-74
Vaughn, Levin, 23 March 1760, Betty Kershaw            1 WO-11
Vaughn, Thos., 15 Dec. 1763, Mary Poteet               2 BA-225
Veach, John, 2 Jan. 1716, Rebeka Dean                  2 TA-82
Veach, John, 29 Sept. 1731, Sarah Hodges               2 PG-5
Veal, Daniel, 15 Aug. 1726, Hannah Spencer             1 BA-245
Veazey, Edward, son of John, 19 June 1755, Elizabeth
   Coursey                                             3 CE-28
Veazey, George, 18 Nov. 1708, Alice Ward, dau. of
   William and Eliza                                   3 CE-3
Veazey, George, 3 April 1716, Kathrin Beard            3 CE-7
Veazey, James, 20 Nov. 1716, Mart Mercer               3 CE-10
Veazey, Robert L., 1 Jan. 1718, Luci Dermote           3 CE-9
Veazey, William, 16 May 1758, Mary Carr                1 CE-322
Veazey, William, 1 March 1771, Mary Rock               1 CE-322
Veeres, Jno., 30 July 1697, Ann Winn, widow            3 CE-2
Velin, Stephen, 7 Nov. 1776, Sarah Picket              3 BA-669
Venables, Benjamin, 9 June 1761, Betty Dashiell        1 WI-64
Venables, Joseph, 8 June 1756, Nelly Polk              1 WI-53
Vennem?, George, 27 Sept. 1771, Mary Hardesty          1 AA-151
Venum?, George, 29 Dec. 1736, Presselo Jones           3 AA-105
Vernon, William, 27 Nov. 1733, Mary Brown              1 AA-117
Vernum, John, 17 March 1757, Susannah Skipton          2 BA-215
Vernum, Oliver, 4 March 1738, Mary Brown               1 BA-295
Vershon, Charles, Aug. 1773, O'statia Oram             2 BA-266
Vertries, Hartmann, 10 Feb. 1744, (wife's name not
   given)                                              5 FR-118
Viccary, Hugh, 29 Dec. 1751, Margaret Phillips         1 QA-58
Vickars, Francis, 25 Feb. 1694, Mary (?)               2 TA-3
Vickers, Thomas, 14 Feb. 1726/7, Rebeckah Robinson     2 TA-115
Vickers, William Brown, 12 Nov. 1744, Eliza Millington 3 TA-50
Viers, Daniel, 2 May 1723, Dorothy Handley             1 AA-95
Villers, Samuel, 5 Feb. 1710, Anne Swinford            1 AA-77
Vine, Roland, 1727, Sarah (?)                          2 BA-76
Vines, John, 25 April 1723, Elisabeth Smith            1 AA-95
Vines, William, 27 Oct. 1720, Johannah Stone           4 AA-412
Vinson, Jethro, 28 June 1777, Mary Ann Letherton       1 CR-10
   1 CR-28 gives the bride's name as Mary Ann Leverton.
Vinson, Thomas, 18 Jan. 1724, Sarah Stanford           1 WI-1
```

Vowels, Jac., 19 Sept. 1771, Priscilla Payn          1 SM-136
Vowles, Thomas, 27 Dec. 1747, Susanna Chunn          2 SM-57
Voyseen, Francis, 28 Sept. 1699, Mary Meares         2 AA-297
Wade, Eli, 8 Feb. 1757, Elizabeth Horner             3 AA-112
Wade, Richard, 18 Feb. 1728, Elizabeth Edgar         1 PG-286
Wade, Zachariah, 3 Nov. (?), Nancy Noble             1 PG-312
Wadle, Robert, 26 Aug. 1736, Juliana James           2 TA-160
Wager, William, 18 Feb. 1704, Elizabeth Smith        1 AA-65
Wagner, Christopher, 9 Dec. 1767, Cath. Schneider    4 FR-1181
Wagster, Isaiah, 6 Nov. 1776, Mary Warrell           3 BA-669
Wailes, George, 25 Aug. 1754, Betty Taylor           1 WI-53
Wainewright, Thomas, 30 Nov. 1722, Pleasance Dorsey  3 BA-146
Wainright, James, 22 May 1774, Eliza Berry           1 CR
Wainwright, Thomas, 21 Jan. 1705/6, Ann (Susanna)
    Richardson                                       1 BA-201
                                                     & 203
Wait, Robert, 31 Dec. 1713, Anne Field               1 AA-269
Wakeling, Thomas, 4 Feb. 1731, Mary Henwood          1 AA-113
Walker, (?), 11 July 1731, (?) Thall                 1 AA-112
Walker, Charles, 1 Sept. 1772, Ann Cradock, dau. of
    Rev. Thomas                                      4 BA-74
Walker, Daniel, 2 Aug. 1743, Eliz'th Satterfield     1 QA-48
Walker, Daniel, 4 Oct. 1748, Sarah Gannon            1 QA-54
Walker, Davis, 9 Dec. 1746, Susan Knotts             1 QA-52
Walker, George, 14 Nov. 1728, Mary Hanson            3 BA-149
Walker, James, 25 March 1728, Eliza Peck             1 AA-106
Walker, James, 10 Feb. 1729, Rebecca Armstrong       2 TA-148
    2 TA-187 gives the date as 14 March 1729.
Walker, John, 10 Jan. 1670/1, Rachel Moody           7 SO-401
Walker, John, 19 ffeb. 1696, Violitt Watkins         1 AA-37
Walker, John, 28 Feb. 1699, Margarett (?)            2 TA-12
Walker, John, 12 May 1706, Deborah Jackson           2 AA-329
Walker, John, 12 June 1714, Mary Cox, widow          2 BA-6
Walker, John, 17 Aug. 1736, Cathe. Brin              2 TA-160
Walker, John, 29 Nov. 1737, Mary Caverly             2 TA-164
    2 TA-274 gives the date as 30 Nov. 1737 and the
    bride's name as Mary Cavillier.
Walker, John, 23 Jan. 1742/3, Rachel Boston          3 BA-164
Walker, John, 6 Jan. 1765, Easther Lyon              2 BA-227
Walker, John, 27 July 1777, Agnes Wagers             10 BA-68
Walker, Joseph, 30 Oct. 1746, Mary Starkey           1 QA-52
Walker, Nathan, 14 June 1744, Margaret Neighbours    2 TA-196
    3 TA-49 gives the date as 9 June 1744.
Walker, Samuell, 13 Nov. 1727, Susanah Michell       2 TA-116
Walker, Thomas, Dec. 1674, Jane Coppinhall           5 SO-400
Walker, Thomas, 13 Oct. 1748, Jane Scholar           1 QA-54
Walker, William, 27 April 1737, Sarah Gaskin         2 TA-163
Wallace, John, 24 Feb. 1730, Mary Hollins            3 CE-21
Wallar?, William, 18 Aug. 1744, Rachell Jones?       1 WI-38
Wallas, John, 2 Feb. 1719/20, Elizabeth Ross         3 CE-10
Waller, John, 8 Sept. 1735, Mary Polk                3 SO-4
Waller, John, 18 Aug. 1751, Mary Huffington          1 WI-60
Waller, Nathaniel, 22 Dec. 1756, Elizabeth Strobridge 1 WI-48
Waller, Richard, 28 Aug. 1740, Ann Collman           1 WI-30
Waller, Thomas, 6 Jan. 1728, Ann Jinkins?            2 TA-119
Waller, Thomas, Jr., 4 Feb. 1734/5, Jane Calloway    1 WI-8
Waller, William, 3 July 1760, Ann Laws, dau. of
    Thomas                                           3 SO-4
Wallis, James, 2 Feb. 1719, Sarah McKnight           3 CE-10
Wallis, John, son of Samuel, 3 day, 12 mo., 1761,
    Cassandra Coale, dau. of Skipwith and Margaret   7 SF-6
Wallis, Oliver, 9 Sept. 1723, Elisabeth Duckett      1 AA-97
Wallis, Samuel, son of Samuel, 23 day, 2 mo., 1730,
    Cassandra Talbott, dau. of John                  6 SF
    9 SF has the same information.

```
Wallis, Samuel, son of Samuel, 21 day, 4 mo., 1744,
   Grace Jacob, dau. of Thomas and Mary              9 SF
Wallox, John, 5 Aug. 1731, Eliz'th Jones             1 BA-263
Walmsley, William, Nov. 1740, Sarah Ward, dau. of John 3 CE-22
Walston, Joy, 24 March 1757, Betty Taylor            2 SO-97
Walston, William, 9 Nov. 1672, Ann Catlin            5 SO-400
Walter, Daniell, 25 Jan. 1730, Sarah Samuells        1 WI-24
Walter, Levin, 10 Jan. 1766, Sarah Nicholson, widow  1 WI-89
Walter, William, 24 Feb. 1703, Rebecca Markcum       3 KE-333
Walters, Christofir, 16 Feb. 1696/7, Elizabeth Powell 1 AA-36
Walters, Capt. Jacob, 20 June 1754, Sarah Dorsey     3 AA-112
Walters, Thomas, 13 July 1713, Elizabeth Stout       2 BA-2
Walters, Thomas, 25 July 1756, Alice Ward            1 QA-61
Walters, William, 25 July 1736, Mary Jones           1 BA-289
Waltham, John, 25 May 1681, Peerse Manlove           5 SO-400
Walton, Joseph, 23 March 1746, Sarah Matheny         2 BA-240
Walton, Joseph, 31 Dec. 1753, Mary Gibbins           2 BA-209
Walton, Thomas, 26 Oct. 1747, Elizabeth Williams     3 BA-160
Walton, Thos., 21 June 1750, Eliz. Maxwell           2 BA-201
Wamesley, John, 24 Feb. 1734, Eliza Ruley            1 AA-117
Wamsly, John, Aug. 1744, Sarah Anglen                3 AA-110
Wamsley, Robert, 20 Feb. 1734/5, Elizabeth Vanhorn   3 CE-20
Wane, John, 27 June 1771, Margret Allinder           2 BA-262
Wann, Edward, 23 July 1747, Prudence Marsh           3 BA-160
Wantland, James, 16 Sept. 1708, Mary Boyse           1 AA-76
Wantland, Thos., 20 Jan. 1763, Susanna Cullison      2 BA-224
Warain, John, 20 Feb. (?), Ann (?)                   1 AA-33
Ward, Cornelius, Jan. 1666, Margaret Franklin        5 SO-400
   6 SO-400 gives the date as 27 Nov. 1666 and the
   bride's last name as Frankling.
Ward, Daniel, 27 May 1733, Anne Boyed                3 BA-151
Ward, Daniel, 18 Nov. 1734, Mary Oldfield            2 TA-156
Ward, Edward, Jr., 5 April 1761, Mary Griffith       1 BA-370
Ward, George, 6 April 1729, Elizabeth Moore          2 TA-120
Ward, George, 24 Aug. 1760, Mary Oakley              2 BA-220
Ward, Mr. Henry, 9 May 1739, Mrs. Hannah Rickets     2 KE-229
Ward, Isaac, 1753, Anne Fields                       2 BA-242
Ward, John, 20 Feb. 1700, Elizabeth Gover, widow     1 AA-57
                                                      & 246
Ward, John, 17 Feb. 1701, Mary (?)                   3 CE-4
Ward, John, 11 Dec. 1706, Elizabeth Phillips         1 AA-72
Ward, John, 6 Nov. 1711, Eliza Smith                 2 PG-1
Ward, John, 25 March 1717, Susana Veazey             3 CE-8
Ward, John, 26 Dec. 1721, Susanna Gooby              1 BA-251
Ward, John, 17 Dec. 1737, Sarah Burrough             2 BA-103
Ward, John, 6 Feb. 1743, Catherin Baker              1 QA-49
Ward, John, 4 Dec. 1746, Jane Boys                   1 QA-52
Ward, John, 25 Aug. 1748, Alice Moor                 1 QA-54
Ward, John, 26 Dec. 1757, Eliz. Potter               2 BA-216
Ward, Jno., 6 Oct. 1766, Eliz. Sharp                 2 BA-229
Ward, John, 21 Dec. 1766, Mary Kelley                3 BA-168
Ward, John, 22 Jan. 1771, Sally Danton               2 BA-261
Ward, Jonathan, 28 Sept. 1712, Sarah Walston         1 BA-222
Ward, Jonathan, 8 Jan. 1717/8, Ann Hall              1 BA-222
Ward, Joseph, Jr., 7 Aug. 1743, Hannah Lee           2 BA-239
Ward, Joseph, 13 Feb. 1748, Mary Perkinson           2 BA-198
                                                      & 243
Ward, Joseph, 16 Jan. 1748/9, Elizabeth Long         2 SO-95
Ward, Joseph, 1749, Mary Parkinson                   2 BA-243
Ward, Joseph, 30 Jan. 1751/2, Mary Ward              2 SO-91
Ward, Matthias, 21 Jan. 1750, Margret Riggin         2 SO-91
Ward, Peregrine, 11 Oct. 1736, Mary Chew             3 CE-22
Ward, Ralph, 20 Nov. 1664, Elezabeth Bogges          1 KE-186
Ward, Richard, 15 Aug. 1739, Mary Gross              2 BA-149
Ward, Robert, Jr., 5 May 1706, Rebecca Cox           1 AA-72
```

```
Ward, Samuel, 31 Aug. 1762, Bettey Worthey          2 SO-182
Ward, Simon, 3 Sept. 1723, Margaret Lobb, widow of
  Joseph                                            3 BA-148
Ward, Stephen, 3 Dec. 1771, Mary Horsey             2 SO-185
Ward, Stephen, 30 May 1773, Leah Owens              2 SO-186
Ward, Thomas, 24 June 1729, Mary Caulk, widow of
  Jacob Caulk                                       3 CE-14
Ward, Thomas, 9 May 1744, Mary Palmer               3 TA-49
Ward, Thomas, 11 Nov. 1761, Hanah Starling          2 SO-184
Ward, William, 14 May 1718, Anne Douglas            3 CE-14
Ward, William, 27 Dec. 1723, Jane Prather           2 PG-3
Ward, William, 24 April 1750, Mary Godfrey          1 QA-57
Ward, William, 11 March 1757, Rebecca Davis, dau. of
  Thomas                                            3 CE-26
Ward, William, 5 Feb. 1765, Martha Doughety         2 SO-186
Ward, William, 27 July 1777, Verlinda Harrison      2 CH(3)
Warde, Callinwoode, 10 March 1694, Alies Laske      1 AA-37
Wardloe, Robert, 24 Nov. 1725, Catherine Hamon      2 TA-112
Wardlowe, Robert, 3 July 1732, Catherine Sick       2 TA-152
Ware, William, 21 Dec. 1710, Margaret Burges        1 AA-77
Warfield, Azel, son of Alexander, 26 Feb. 1751, Sarah
  Griffith, dau. of Charles                         6 AA-187
Warfield, Azel, 19 May 1768, Susanna Magruder       6 AA-188
Warfield, Edward, 6 Oct. 1741, Rachel Riggs         6 AA-217
Warfield, Dr. Joshua, 6 Aug. 1751, Rachel Howard    6 AA-191
Waring, Basil, 31 Jan. 1709, Martha Greenfield      2 PG-1
Waring, Basil, 1747, Fran.: Hambleton               3 TA-67
Waring, James Haddock, formerly of P. G. Co., 25 Dec.
  1735, Elizabeth Overard                           4 AA-437
Warman, Francis, 24 Feb. 1718, Frances Hanslap      1 AA-290
Warman, Stephen, 2 July 1704, Esther Gross          1 AA-64
Warman, Stephen, 16 March 1735, Mary Parish         1 AA-120
Warner, Cuthbert, 18 day, 11 mo., 1773, Rachel Hill,
  dau. of William                                   7 SF-28
Warner, Joseph, 6 day, 11 mo., 1725, Ann Coale      2 KE-59
Warner, Joseph, 11 June 1775, Ruth Trott            2 AA-412
Warner, Samuel, 15 Aug. 1715, Eliza Person          2 PG-1
Warner, William, 7 Sept. 1718, Alce Mullikin, widow 2 TA-257
Warner, William, 10 Sept. 1718, Alce Mullican       2 TA-88
Warrant, Jos., 25 Dec. 1760, Jane James             2 BA-221
Warrell, Samuel, 1 May 1742, Mary White             2 BA-117
Warren, John, 1751, Eliz'th Cane                    2 BA-241
Warren, John, 16 Feb. 1751, Eliz. Keen              2 BA-203
Warren, Leonard, 1770, Elizabeth Lane               2 AA-409
Warren, Peter, 9 Sept. 1758, Mary Chilcott          1 QA-64
Warrick, William, 17 Oct. 1756, Jennet Thaker       2 BA-214
Warrill, Henry, 30 (?) 1746, Juliatha Spicer        3 BA-159
Warring, Thomas, 12 Dec. 1734, Jane Orford          2 PG-6
Wasey, Nathaniel, 16 Nov. 1758, Sarah Forcom        1 QA-64
Wason, John, 1770, Dinah Pegerson                   2 AA-410
Waters, Arnold, 7 April 1773, Rachel Franklin       2 AA-411
Waters, George, 31 March 1767, Betty Handy, dau. of
  Robert and Ann                                    2 SO-188
Waters, Henry, 14 July 1748, Ann Beck               2 BA-197
Waters, Hezekiah, 20 July 1777, Elizabeth Pickett  10 BA-68
Waters, James, 29 Dec. 1754, Ann Dement             1 CH-186
Waters, John, 9 Jan. 1717, Ann Purnell              1 AA-79
                                                      & 281
Waters, John, 14 Feb. 1720, Mary Jiems (Ijams?)     1 AA-302
Waters, John, 28 Jan. 1724, Charity Ijams           1 AA-100
Waters, Jno., 22 Feb. 1767, Mary Horner             2 BA-230
Waters, John, 20 Sept. 1777, Eliza Carter           2 CH(3)
Waters, Joseph, son of James, 6 Aug. 1754, Katherine
  Carrico                                           1 CH-202
Waters, Joseph, son of James, 17 Feb. 1767, Chloe Dent  1 CH-202
```

Waters, Littleton, son of John and Mary Elizabeth,
  24 Dec. 1765, Esther Waters, dau. of Littleton      2 SO-180
Waters, Robert, 13 Dec. 1701, Anne Allen      1 BA-197
Waters, Robert, 11 July 1775, Mary Ireland      3 BA-172
Waters, Samuel, Jr., son of Samuel and Jane, 4 day,
  3 mo., 1732, Artridge Frankling, dau. of Robert
  and Artridge      6 SF
Waters, Samuel, son of Samuel and Artridge, 31 day,
  12 mo., 1772, Susannah Plummer, dau. of Joseph
  and Sarah      3 SF
Waters, William, 3 Nov. 1724, Rachell Duvall      1 AA-99
Waters, William, son of William and Rose, b. 11 Feb.
  1740; m. 29 March 1763, Sarah Hayward      2 SO-180
Waters, William, 4 Nov. 1762, Elizabeth Welch      1 CH-201
Wathan, Ricard, 28 Sept. 1773, Eleanor Mattingly      1 SM-136
Watkins, Christopher, 25 July 1751, Elinor Willson      1 QA-58
Watkins, Daniel, 3 May 1770, Sosia Biddeston      2 BA-260
Watkins, Dan'l Scott, 29 Dec. 1761, Eliz. Hatten      2 BA-223
Watkins, Esau, 11 April 1738, Sarah Johnson      3 KE-337
Watkins, Francis, 25 Sept. 1769, Eliz. Pines      2 BA-259
Watkins, James, 15 March 1757, Mary Johnson      1 QA-62
Watkins, John, (date not given), Mary Warman      1 AA-79
Watkins, John, 10 Feb. 1747, Eliz. Jones      2 BA-194
Watkins, John, 25 June 1750, Eliz. James      2 BA-201
Watkins, John, 9 Oct. 1754, Purify Greenfield      1 BA-355
Watkins, Nicholas, Jr., son of John, 12 Jan. 1764,
  Peggy Boyd      9 AA-248
Watkins, Rob't, 1 Aug. 1736, Marg't Phinnicum      1 QA-42
Watkins, Samuel, 12 Jan. 17-(?), Ann Chambers      1 AA-142
Watkins, Sam'll, 2 June 1757, Frances Hardesty      2 BA-215
Watkins, Solomon, 2 April 1749, Elizabeth Johnson      1 QA-55
Watkins, Stephen, son of John and Mary, b. 27 June
  1735; m. 1 Feb. 1757, Elinor Boyd, dau. of Benjamin  2 AA-402
Watkins, Thomas, 8 Sept. 1698, Mary Wells      2 AA-295
Watkins, Thomas, 19 Jan. 1738, Elizabeth Mead      2 BA-129
Watkins, Thomas, Jr., 24 Jan. 1767, Elizabeth Jones,
  dau. of Isaac      1 AA-148
Watkins, William, 9 Dec. 1741, Ann Barkabee      2 BA-205
Watkins, William, in the summer of 1742, Ann Blackaby;
  the marriage took place on Mr. Carbell's land; Mrs.
  Lawson and Mrs. Giddens were present.      2 BA-249
Watson, Abraham, 14 Feb. 1705, Margaret Jenkins      1 BA-201
Watson, Abron, 12 April 1733, Susannah Bishop      1 CE-277
Watson, Daniel, 6 May 1731. Isabella Finley      1 QA-38
Watson, David, 30 Oct. 1735, Hanna McCosh      1 QA-41
Watson, George, 28 July 1729, Ann Smith      1 AA-109
Watson, Hugh, 10 Jan. 1714, Mary (?)      3 CE-8
Watson, John, 18 Oct. 1705, Margrett Peterson      3 KE-334
Watson, John, 12 May 1729, Jean Scott, widow      2 BA-26
Watson, John, 17 Dec. 1730, Mary Young      1 QA-36
Watson, John, 24 May 1733, Mary Chenowith      2 BA-40
Watson, John, 9 June 1748, Esther Baley      1 QA-54
Watson, John Davis, 29 Aug. 1762, Ann Welsh      1 CE-321
Watson, Richard, 13 Oct. 1755, Margery Williams      1 QA-60
Watson, William, 12 Feb. 1731, Alicia Denlon      1 CE-280
Watson, William, 1 Jan. 1733, Rebecca Storey      1 QA-40
Watson, William, 5 May 1757, Bethiah Thornberry      2 BA-215
Watters, Godfrey, 3 Nov. 1726, Sarah White      3 AA-103
Watters, Henry, 13 Dec. 1757, Mary Ruff      2 BA-216
Watters, James, 13 March 1760, Lydia Guyton      2 BA-219
Watters, Jno., 5 Feb. 1756, Providence Baker      2 BA-213
Watters, John, 22 Feb. 1767, Mary Horner      2 BA-168
Watters, Samuell, 7 Jan. 1706/7, Jane Danster      4 AA-372
Watts, (?), 19 March 1695, Margrit Purdy      1 AA-34
Watts, Edward, 18 Feb. 1721, Mary Morgan, widow      3 BA-146

```
Watts, George, 7 Sept. 1745, Sarah Clark              3 TA-55
Watts, George, 8 Jan. 1758, Jane Connagoe             1 QA-63
Watts, John, 5 June 17-(?), Elizabeth Disney          1 AA-96
Watts, Jno., 31 Oct. 1700, Mary Moss, alias Katrick   1 AA-56
                                                        & 246
Watts, John, 14 Dec. 1703, Anne Jollett               1 AA-64
Watts, John, 3 July 1704, Elizabeth Hutson            3 KE-333
Watts, John, 3 Feb. 1714/5, Love Meeke                4 AA-392
Watts, John, 21 Feb. 1720, Susanna Stanton            2 TA-95
Watts, John, 5 June 1723, Elizabeth Disney            1 AA-320
Watts, John, 15 April 1743, Anne Body                 3 BA-166
Watts, John, 20 April 1756, Sarah Eaglestone          3 BA-166
Watts, John, 19 Sept. 1764, Mary Disney               9 AA-248
Watts, Rich'd, 14 Feb. 1731, Susanna Northcraft       1 AA-113
Watts, Robert, 10 Nov. 1709, Sarah Renell             2 AA-338
Watts, Thomas, 16 July 1721, Mary Dorrell, widow      3 CE-11
Watts, William, 11 Nov. 1694, Margaret (?)            2 TA-3
Wattson, Henry, 5 Jan. 1745, Margarit Cookson         1 QA-51
Wattson, Thos., 24 March 1761, Fra.: Hooper           2 BA-221
Waugh, James, 18 June 1733, Alice Green               1 AA-116
Wayman, Edmund, 13 Nov. 1716, Mary Lincicom           1 AA-274
Wayman, Francis, 5 Jan. 1764, Ruth Fowler             9 AA-248
Wayman, Leonard, 1 March 1719, Anne Rutland           1 AA-298
Wead, George, Sept. 1739, Hannah Pumphrey             3 AA-109
Wear, James, 19 July 1777, Sarah Smith                3 PG-165
Weatherburn, John Dixon, 10 Nov. 1776, Catherine
  Littlejohn                                          3 BA-669
Weatherby, Charles, 24 Feb. 1774, Marget Hillorn (or
  Killorn)                                            1 WI-111
Weatherly, William, 5 April 1719, Charrety Nicholson  1 WI-9
Weathers, Charles, 1 Sept. 1724, Margrett Peake       1 PG-282
Weathersbee, Thos., 12 Sept. 1745, Rachal Burroughs   1 QA-51
Weatherspool, Robert, 2 Dec. 1756, Lilly Lock         1 QA-61
Webb, James, 16 June 1756, Lydia Fisher               2 CR-273
Webb, John, 8 May 1740, Grace Harwood                 8 SF-78
Webb, Park, 4 Sept. 1774, Mary Fountain               1 CR
Webb, Peter, son of Parrington Webb of Little Baddow,
  Co. of Essex, Eng., Gent.,6 July 1704, at Choptank
  Quakers' Metting House, Sarah Stevens, dau. of
  William and Sarah                                   2 TA-237
  8 SF-425 describes the groom as a merchant, late
  of London, Eng.
Webb, Peter, 4 Nov. 1758, Sarah Anderson              8 SF-103
Webb, Richard, May 1672, Mary Jeferies                5 SO-400
  8 SO-401 gives the bride's name as Mary Jefferies.
Webb, Richard, 1 May 1700, Rebecca Parratt            8 SF-400
Webb, Rich'd, 1 March 1746, Susannah Williams         1 QA-53
Webb, Richard, son of James and Mary, of Fawn Twp.,
  York Co., Penna., 12 day, 2 mo., 1777, Elizabeth
  Burgess, dau. of Joseph and Deborah                 7 SF-37
Webb, Sam'l, 13 May 1764, Marg'rt Tuder               2 BA-226
Webb, Thomas, 13 Oct. 1723, Elizabeth Sivenack        1 AA-97
Webb, Thomas. 19 Nov. 1734, Elizabeth Child           2 PG-6
Webb, William, 1 day, 8 mo., 1753, Lydia Cogill       8 SF-97
Webb, William, 12 July 1758, Elizabeth Lee            1 BA-368
Webbat, Timothy, 11 Oct. 1743, Mary Nelson            1 QA-48
Webbe, George, 4 Feb. 1750, Margaret Adcocke          1 QA-57
Webber, John, 6 Aug. 1719, Sarah Cole                 4 AA-409
Weber, John, 30 Dec. 1756, Maria Elizab. Haas         4 FR-1103
Webster, Isaac, 1 day, 1 mo., 1761, Sarah Richardson,
  dau. of Joseph                                      6 SF
Webster, John, 2 Feb. 1714, Mary McDaniel             1 BA-215
Webster, Jno., 17 day, 2 mo., 1735, Mary Talbott      6 SF
  9 SF has the same information.
Webster, John, Jr., 26 June 1739, Hannah Gilbert      1 BA-314
```

Webster, Jno., 1 Jan. 1755, Mary Lynch                          2 BA-211
Webster, John, son of Samuel, 9 June 1761, Hannah Wood          1 BA-374
Webster, John, 13 Oct. 1764, Joanner C. Stevens                1 PG-375
Webster, Jno., 27 July 1765, Sarah Stevenson                    2 BA-228
Webster, Samuel, 2 Feb. 1726, Elizabeth Dallam                 1 BA-339
Webster, Samuel, son of Samuel, 19 July 1759,
    Margaret Stewart                                           1 BA-368
Webster, Thos., 5 Jan. 1752, Mary Guy                          1 PG-295
Webster, William, son of William and Sarah, 26 May
    1748, Ann Smith, dau. of John                              9 SF
Webster, William, Jr., 12 Sept. 1756, Ann Turner              1 PG-313
Webster, William, 12 Sept. 1756, Ann Turner                   1 PG-315
Webster, William, son of William and Sarah, 1 July
    1773, Margaret Coppock, dau. of John and Margaret          9 SF
Wedgwood, John, 8 Sept. 1733, Winnifredd Haines               1 AA-116
Weed, William, 19 Aug. 1732, Elizabeth Barnet                 1 QA-39
Weekes, Thomas, 12 Dec. 1742, Elizab. Enlowe                  2 BA-238
Weeks, Mathew, 2 Jan. 1743, Margarit Ponder                   1 QA-48
Weeks, Stephen, 13 May 1745, Ann Higgins                      1 QA-50
Weeks, Thomas, 12 July 1742; banns pub. three times;
    Elizabeth Enlowe                                           2 BA-238
Weel, John, 19 May 1726, Rachell Elstone                      2 TA-113
Weems, David, 5 Aug. 1742, Mrs. Easther Hill                  2 AA-383
Weems, David, 8 March 1777, Margaret Harrison                 2 AA-413
Weems, Richard, 7 April 1768, Mary Ward                       2 AA-400
Weems, Thomas, 27 July 1765, Mary Beckett                     9 AA-248
Ween, Jno., 8 Jan. 1760, Eliz. Godard                        2 BA-219
Weer, Thomas, 31 Oct. 1776, Mary Beerman                      5 BA-14
Weer, William, 9 March 1769, Catherine Osborne               5 BA-14
Weer, William, 20 May 1776, Elisabeth Blair                  5 BA-14
Wegley, Edw'd, 2 Jan. 1749/50, Jane Fisher                    3 BA-163
Weikes, Capt. Jos., 7 day, 5 mo., 1656, Marie Hartwell       1 KE-38
Weir, Thos., 7 Dec. 1756, Sarah Puttee                       2 BA-214
Weis, Peter, 31 Jan. 176-(?), Margaret Mayer                 4 FR-1181
Weisz, Henry, 9 Jan. 1759, Cath. Brunner                     4 FR-1104
Weisz, Jacob, 17 Jan. 1768, Mary Anna Hofman                 4 FR-1181
Weisz, John Valent, 18 April 1758, Cath. Froschauer          4 FR-1103
Welch, Benjamin, 20 Nov. 1701, Eliz. Nicholson               1 AA-57
                                                             & 249
Welch, John, 13 March 1700, Thomasin Hopkins                 1 AA-247
Welch, Laban, 3 Sept. 1761, Leah Corbin                      2 BA-222
Welch, Robert, 7 Oct. 1701, Mary (?)                         2 TA-21
Welch, Robert, 8 Aug. 1724, Eliz. Smith                      2 TA-110
Welch, Robert, 25 Sept. 1777, Ann Ferguson                   8 AA-13
Welch, Robert, 24 Nov. 1777, Eleanor Carr                    7 AA-2
Welch, William, Sr., 14 Jan. 1700, Rebecca (?)               2 TA-12
Welcher, John, 7 Aug. 1750, Unity Coffee                     2 BA-201
Welcher, Jno., 24 April 1764, Ann Foreasjute                 2 BA-226
Wellden, Nicholas, 1 July 1744, Mary McCherry                2 KE-253
Weller, Jacob, son of Daniel, March 1738, Maria
    Barbara Wilhide                                           5 FR-123
Weller, Jacob, son of Daniel, 13 Aug. 1755, Anna
    Elizabeth Krieger                                         5 FR-123
Weller, John, son of John (sic) and Maria Barbara
    Wilhide, 19 April 1768, Maria Barbara Krieger, dau.
    of Lorenz                                                 5 FR-123
Weller, John Jacob, son of Jacob and Maria Barbara,
    13 July 1762, Magdalena Krieger, dau. of Lorentz
    and Maria Elizabeth                                       5 FR-125
Weller, John Jacob, son of Jacob and Maria Barbara,
    23 Sept. 1766, Anna Margaret Harbaugh, dau. of
    George and Catherine                                      5 FR-125
Weller, Philip, son of Jacob and Maria Barbara, 30
    Sept. 1766, Juliana Wottring, dau. of John Daniel
    and Anna Maria                                            5 FR-126

Weller, Wm., 18 June 1729, Eliza Faith                 1 AA-108
Wells, Alexander, 12 July 1753, Leah Owings            4 BA-71
Wells, Benjamin, 16 April 1776, Rachel Atwell          2 AA-412
Wells, Daniel, 4 Dec. 1707, Sarah (?)                  4 AA-372
Wells, Davenport, 1 Sept. 1743, Mary Newnam            1 QA-48
Wells, Francis, 20 March 1757, Ann Tevis               4 BA-73
Wells, George, 16 June 1725, Susanna Ward              2 PG-4
Wells, John, 31 March 1709, Ann Powell                 2 AA-337
Wells, John, 12 Oct. 1715, Marg't Parsfield            2 PG-1
Wells, John, 11 Oct. 1761, Dinah Cromwell              4 BA-74
Wells, John, son of John, 26 Jan. 1773, Mary Riley,
  of Co. Donegal, Ireland                              1 CE-298
Wells, John, son of William and Anne, 29 day, 10 mo.,
  1776, Rachel Gassaway, dau. of Nicholas and
  Margaret                                             4 SF-270
Wells, Joseph, 11 April 1721, Margaret Swanson         1 AA-303
Wells, Jos., 30 Jan. 1748, Ann Carback                 2 BA-198
                                                       & 243
Wells, Jos., 24 Dec. 1754, Rebecca Melloy              2 BA-211
Wells, Nathan, 13 Dec. 1716, Mary Duckett              2 PG-1
Wells, Richard, 12 Aug. 1735, Mary Holliday            1 QA-41
Wells, Thomas, 9 Aug. 1705, Mary Hopkins               2 AA-328
Wells, Thomas, 17 Oct. 1721, Mary Disney               1 AA-97
Wells, Thomas, 16 Sept. 1736, Eliza Howard             3 BA-155
Wells, Thomas, 15 June 1772, Alice Wignall             3 BA-170
Wells, Thomas, Jr., 4 March 1773, Mary Major           4 BA-74
  5 BA-14 has the same information.
Wells, Toby, 20 Aug. 1665, Mary Richards               1 KE-186
Wells, William, 21 Sept. 1749, Mary Harner             1 QA-56
Wells, William, 7 Dec. 1769, Eliz. Wattson             2 BA-259
Wells, Zorobabel, 16 Feb. 1728, Mary Hollinsworth      1 QA-36
Welsh, John, 13 March 1700, Thomasin Hopkins           1 AA-57
Welsh, John, 4 July 1714, Ann Hollingsworth            1 BA-244
Welsh, Robert, 24 Feb. 1706, Catherine Lewis           1 AA-73
Welsh, Robert, 25 Sept. 1777, Ann Ferguson             7 AA-2
Welsh, Robert, 27 Nov. 1777, Eleanor Carr              8 AA-13
  2 AA-414 gives the date as 27 Nov. 1777.
Welsh, William, of Cecil Co., 3 Feb. 1700 or 1702,
  Downcabella Barker                                   1 SF-46
Wemset?, Robert, 31 Aug. 1727, Anne Harber             2 TA-116
Wessells, James, 10 Sept. 1707, Elizabeth Tolley       1 AA-76
West, Benjamin, 16 May 1728, Susanna Stockett, dau.
  of Thomas, of A. A. Co.                              2 PG-5
West, Benjamin, 29 April 1756, Hannah Parks            4 AA-213
West, Benjamin, 29 May 1777, Agness Varley             5 BA-14
West, Daniel, 12 Oct. 1741, Catherine Bustard          2 KE-242
West, David, 10 Oct. 1765, Hannah Thomson              2 BA-228
West, Francis, 10 Nov. 1696, Sarah Harry               2 AA-291
West, George, 14 Feb. 1727/8, Sarah Lowe               2 TA-117
West, George, 25 Oct?, 1740, Sarah Hurlock             2 TA-169
West, Henry, 9 Dec. 1736, Eliza Hurlock                2 TA-159
West, James, 3 Feb. 1755, Sarah Harris                 1 WI-69
West, John, 2 day, 3 mo., 1680, Joan Beerest, formerly
  of Salem on the Delaware                             8 SF-324
West, John, 26 Jan. 1735, Susannah Ozbourn             1 BA-287
West, Jonathan, Jr., 31 March 1758, Sophia Kimball     1 BA-359
West, Richard, 6 Oct. 1765, Mary Stead                 9 AA-249
West, Robert, 10 Nov. 1695, Sarah Spinks               1 BA-236
West, Robe: ., Jr., 22 Jan. 1730, Johanna Gash         1 BA-260
West, Stephen, 21 Aug. 1712, Eliza (?)                 2 AA-364
West, Stephen, 28 April 1726, Martha Hall              1 AA-107
West, Thos., 5 June 1739, Ann Tessie                   1 QA-45
West, Thomas, 8 Sept. 1757, Ann Pritchard              1 BA-363
West, William, 14 Aug. 1722, Susannah (?)              2 TA-103
Westal, George, 23 Oct. 1711, Anne Jacob               1 AA-78

Westall, John, 23 April 1739, Elizabeth Atkins          9 AA-246
Westcomb, William, 23 Sept. 1759, Elinor Maskell        2 BA-219
Westcombe, Samuel, 19 Jan. 1732, Sarah Thomas           1 BA-272
Westerman, Thos., 14 July 1750, Mary Tongue             2 BA-201
Westley, Francis, 26 April 1722, Mary Disney            1 AA-88
                                                        & 90
Weston, Joseph, 31 Dec. 1777, Rebecca Griffin          10 BA-70
Wetheral, Henry, 20 Dec. 1722, Mrs. Mary Chamberlain    2 BA-24
Wetheral, Henry, 20 Dec. 1724, Mrs. Ellen Presbury      2 BA-25
Wethers, Robert, 5 June 1726, Mary Hollingsworth        3 CE-16
Wethred, William, 25 Nov. 1761, Francina Hart           2 KE-303
Whaland, William, Nov. 1751, Mary Legoe                 2 BA-241
Whaley, Edward, 9 Jan. 1668, Elizabeth Ratcliffe        5 SO-400
Whaley, James, 13 July 1752, Mary Clannahan             1 QA-58
Whaley, John, 18 Sept. 1757, Mary Burkelow              1 QA-62
Whaley, Joseph, 5 Aug. 1729, Esther Lee                 1 QA-36
Whaley, William, 29 June 1758, Eliza Spencer            1 QA-63
Whall, John, 15 Sept. 1727, Margret Clark               2 KE-209
Wharfield, Alexand'r, 3 Dec. 1723, Dinah Davidge        4 AA-422
Wharfield, John, of Middle Neck Parish, 16 Feb. 1696,
   Ruthe Gather                                         1 AA-36
Wharfield, Samuel, 24 Oct. 1727, Sarah Welch            1 AA-105
Wharton, John, 28 Jan. 1744/5, Ann Brown                2 BA-192
                                                        & 244
Wharton, Joseph, 28 April 1746, Sarah Metheny           2 BA-195
Wharton, Robert, 5 Sept. 173-(?), Elizabeth Barrett     3 KE-336
Wharton, Robert, Jan. 1742, Rebecca Spry                1 QA-47
Wharton, William, 18 Aug. 1752, Martha Laurence         1 QA-59
Whealand, Henry, 27 Jan. 1736, Rebecca Legoe            2 BA-110
Whealand, Hen.; 21 July 1764, Isbell Willson            2 BA-226
Whealand, Patrick,26 Jan. 1749, Mary Cowdry             2 BA-200
   2 BA-244 gives the bride's name as Caudry.
Whealand, Pat., 6 Aug. 1767, Phebe Tunis                2 BA-231
Whealand, Soll., 18 Jan. 1761, Eliz. Copeland           2 BA-221
Whealand, Soll., 22 Feb. 1766, Eliz. Ward               2 BA-229
Whealand, Thos., 21 July 1767, Martha Dorney            2 BA-230
Whealand, William, 21 April 1752, Mary Lego             2 BA-205
Whealer, William, 3 Dec. 1747, Hanah Thomas             1 QA-53
Wheatley, Francis, 17 June 1771, Anastasia Cecil        1 SM-136
Wheatley, Sampson, 9 March 1731/2, Mary Lell            2 SO-184
Wheatley, Sylvester, 7 Sept. 1773, Eliz. Fraiser        1 SM-136
Wheatley, Thomas, 15 Dec. 1705, Elizabeth (?)           4 AA-390
Wheatley, William, 30 Jan. 1760, Marg'r't Elliott       2 BA-219
Wheeks, Daniel, 10 Sept. 1771, Nancy Lueester           2 BA-262
Wheeler, Clement, 5 Feb. 1732/3, Elizabeth Edelen       1 PG-283
Wheeler, Clement, 25 Feb. 1759, Jane Stonestreet        1 PG-322
Wheeler, Edward, 10 Feb. 1682, Margaret Hardy           5 SO-4-0
Wheeler, Francis, 19 Dec. 1775, Anna Birchmore          1 SM-137
Wheeler, Ignatius, 29 July 1753, Elizabeth Marbury      1 PG-373
Wheeler, Isaac, 28 June 1714, Sarah Stevens             3 SO-4
Wheeler, Leonard, 16 Feb. 1741, Ann Bond                1 BA-322
Wheeler, Moses, 23 Dec. 1748, Katherine Gardner         3 BA-162
Wheeler, Owen, 30 Sept. 1743, Ann Swift                 1 QA-48
Wheeler, Richard, 31 Oct. 1725, Rebecca (?)             3 BA-148
Wheeler, Robert, Jr., 23 Nov. 1732, Ann Duckett         2 PG-6
Wheeler, Roger, 16 April 1704, Elizabeth Gibson         1 CA-111
Wheeler, Solomon, 11 mo., 1745, Rachel Taylor           4 SF
Wheeler, Thomas, 6 March 1732/3, Susanna Duckett        2 PG-6
Wheeler, Thomas, 20 Oct. 1736, Ann Hawkins              3 BA-155
Wheeler, Thomas, 21 Dec. 1748, Elizabeth Hillen         3 BA-162
Wheeler, William, 14 Nov. 1706, Martha West             1 AA-72
Wheeler, William, 18 Sept. 1712, Margaret King          2 TA-72
Wheeler, William, 6 Feb. 1752, Jane Miller              2 BA-204
Wheeller, Isaac, 31 Oct. 1737, Mary Montegue            2 TA-162
Wheland, William, 24 Aug. 1752, Jessy Young             4 CE-261

Whelch, Rich'd, 14 April 1726, Charity Jacobs        1 AA-102
Whetts, Thomas, 13 April 1735, Rachel Floyd          3 BA-153
Whey, John, 2 July 1769, Salley Taylor               2 BA-259
Whichaley, Thomas, 25 April 1694, Elizabeth Ford, widow
  of Edward Ford; dau. of Thomas Allanson            3 CH
Whicks, Jno., 24 Jan. 1765, Mary Petstow             2 BA-227
Whicks, Thos., 20 Nov. 1766, Terriner Wilford        2 BA-230
Whidbey, Benjamin, 15 June 1756, Lydia Bell          2 CR-273
Whipps, John, 14 Nov. 1702, Margaret Theerston       2 AA-319
Whips, Samuel, 22 Jan. 1742, Mary McComas            2 BA-125
Whitaker, Abraham, 15 July 1725, Ann Poteet          2 BA-19
Whitaker, Abraham, 31 Dec. 1771, Eliz. Wheeler       2 BA-263
Whitaker, Abraham Isaac, 15 Dec. 1757, Mary Poteet   2 BA-215
Whitaker, Charles, 30 Jan. 1717/8, Mary Kembal       1 BA-221
Whitaker, Isaac, 13 Dec. 1759, Eliz. Hill            2 BA-219
Whitaker, Jas., 25 Aug. 1763, Cathrine Potee         2 BA-225
Whitaker, John, 27 April 1714, Ann Dadd              2 BA-5
Whitaker, Joseph, 8 May 1758, Ann Kelley             1 QA-63
Whitaker, Mark, 13 Feb. 1717, Elizabeth Emson        1 BA-220
Whitaker, Peter, 10 Jan. 1722, Frances Brown         1 BA-230
                                                       & 238
Whitaker, Peter, 12 Feb. 1744, Emelie Hitchcock      2 BA-192
Whitaker, Peter, 10 Feb. 1745, Amelia Hitchcock      2 BA-240
Whitby, Nathan, 20 June 1758, Mary Story             1 QA-63
White, Abraham, 15 Feb. 1773, Sarah Gather           2 AA-411
White, Andrew, 17 April 1710, Elinor Birk            4 AA-379
White, Benjamin, 1 Feb. 1722/3, Ann Hilliard         2 PG-3
White, Bernard, 11 April 1716, Elenor Norman         4 AA-397
White, Charles, 30 July 1777, Susanna Smith          3 PG-167
  8 AA-15 gives the date as 5 Aug. 1777.
White, Elias, 28 Feb. 1756, Sarah Dixon              2 SO-181
White, Erick, 19 April 1756, Rachael Bevens          2 BA-213
White, Francis, 1 Jan. 1732, Ann Wilkinson           1 BA-267
White, George, 25 Sept. 1732, Sarah Burras           1 AA-114
White, Henry, 11 May 1746, Abigall Boston            2 SO-89
White, James, 1 Oct. 1724, Sarah Cliff               2 TA-110
White, James, 28 Nov. 1777, Eleanor Litchfield       8 AA-15
  7 AA-2 gives the date as 22 Dec. 1777.
White, John, 7 June 1672, Sarah Keyser               5 SO-400
White, John, 6 June 1703, Elizabeth Bryan            2 TA-35
White, John, 23 April 1708, Eleanor Carty            1 AA-76
White, John, 4 Dec. 1711, Mary Griffin               3 CE-6
White, John, son of William, 31 day, 8 mo., 1717,
  Mary Job, dau. of Andrew and Elizabeth             9 SF
White, John, 1722, Mary Rencher                      3 BA-147
White, John, 27 Jan. 1725, Sarah Miller              1 AA-102
White, John, Jan. 1726, Mary Wood                    3 AA-103
White, John, 18 May 1726, Presilla Cobb              1 BA-257
White, John, 10 Dec. 1730, Rebecca Carman            1 QA-37
White, John, 2 Dec. 1733, Mary Ross                  2 AA-375
White, John, 20 May 1744, Rebekah Porter             2 SO-88
White, John, 23 Sept. 1744, Sarah Legoe              2 BA-239
  2 BA-135 gives the date as 4 Oct. 1744.
White, John, 27 Nov. 1745, Mary Maddux               2 SO-93
White, John, 1749, Mary Horton                       2 BA-243
White, John, 29 Jan. 1751, Eliz. Gott                2 BA-203
                                                       & 241
White, John, Jr., 12 May 1751, Henn. Yates           2 BA-203
White, John, son of John and Mary, 13 day, 1 mo.,
  1763, Sarah Murphy Wilson, widow of Thomas Wilson
  and dau. of Arthur and Margaret Murphy             9 SF
White, John, 16 Oct. 1771, Sarah White (sic) "his
  present wife"                                      1 CE-319
White, John, 21 Aug. 1777, Mary Sergant             10 BA-69
White, Joseph, 9 Feb. 1709, Mary Gater               4 AA-379

White, Jos., 7 Aug. 1766, Jane Watkins               2 BA-229
White, Joshua, 8 July 1740, Mary Ashly               3 AA-106
White, Luke, 17 Jan. 1762, Deborah Simmons           2 BA-223
White, Nicholas, 24 Nov. 1698, Grace Deviour, dau. of
    John                                             2 AA-372
White, Patrick, 4 March 1700, Elizabeth Pattison     2 TA-13
White, Richard, 6 Oct. 1742, Eliza Tucker            4 AA-444
White, Robert, 22 Sept. 1709, Anne Burges            1 AA-77
                                                     & 257
White, Robert, 28 Feb. 1726, Martha Bryan            3 KE-336
White, Samuell, 12 Aug. 1701, Clare (?)              2 TA-19
White, Samuell, 18 April 1706, Rachell Gaither       1 AA-72
White, Samuel, Jr., 1 Dec. 1736, Sarah Witchcoat     3 BA-156
White, Stephen, 1 Jan. 1751, Hannah Baker            2 BA-202
                                                     & 241
White, Tho.:, 6 Feb. 1704, Mary Lane                 1 CA-111
White, Thomas, 11 Feb. 1752, Ann Guinn               1 AA-132
White, Thomas, 6 March 1760, Sarah Lord              2 SO-87
                                                     & 97
White, William, of Rappahannock R., Va., 8 June
    1683, Martha Smith of the same place             8 SF-330
White, William, banns pub. in June 1699, Ann Baker,
    widow                                            1 BA-187
White, William, 12 Jan. 1715, Frances Boreiat        2 TA-77
White, William, 31 Jan. 1726/7, Margett Hambleton    2 TA-115
White, William, 14 May 1741, Cassa Brown             2 TA-171
White, William, son of John and Mary, 10 Nov. 1743,
    Sarah Pugh, dau. of John and Jane                9 SF
White, William, Jr., 27 Jan. 1744, Mary Brown        2 TA-198
    3 TA-51 gives the date as 3 Jan. 1744/5.
White, William, 1 Nov. 1744, Elizabeth Bratten       2 SO-94
White, William, 26 Oct. 1752, Hannah Baley           1 QA-59
White, William, 14 Jan. 1767, Molley Broughton       2 SO-184
White, William, 16 Feb. 1769, Mary Whitehead         2 BA-257
Whiteaker, Jas., 29 June 1749, Mary Saunders         2 BA-198
Whitecar, Mark, 6 Feb. 1743, Abigal Johnston         1 FR-12
Whitehead, George, 27 May 1705, Ezbell Stewartt      3 KE-334
Whitehead, Isaiah, 26 Sept. 1745, Sophia Lemar       1 QA-51
Whitehead, John, 19 Nov. 1733, Eliz'th Pryor         1 QA-39
Whitehead, Thomas, 11 Dec. (?), Eliz'th Smith        3 KE-334
Whitehead, Wm. Bond, 26 Feb. 1749, Susanna Wood      2 BA-200
                                                     & 244
Whitehead, Wm. Bond, 10 March 1766, Sarah Ingram     2 BA-229
Whitelock, Isaac, of Lancaster, Pa., 8 day, 7 mo.,
    1767, Sarah Rasin, widow of George Rasin         1 SF-99
Whitemore, Jos., 26 Feb. 1764, Hannah Hammelton      2 BA-226
Whiter, Henry, 29 Jan. 1727, Sarah Newman            3 CE-13
Whitington, Benjamin, 31 March 1749, Jane Ratcliffe  1 QA-55
Whitington, James, 21 Nov. 1752, Levina Marsh        2 BA-206
Whitley, John, 20 April 1749, Deborah Michael        1 QA-55
Whitmore, William, 10 May 1753, Mary Deall or Beall  1 PG-299
Whittaker, Rev. Nathaniel, 2 Nov. 1759, Sarah Roach  2 SO-96
Whittaker, Thomas, son of Robert and Mary, 2 Jan.
    1760, Elizabeth Rogers, dau. of Rowland and Ann  1 CE-317
Whittal, Francis, 6 Feb. 1724, Sarah Cole            1 AA-100
Whittby, Richard, 11 Nov. 1741, Deborah Frampton     2 TA-175
Whittington, James, 10 April 1773, Elizabeth Batson  2 AA-411
Whittington, Joseph, 12 Feb. 1735, Eliz'th Gould     1 QA-41
Whittington, Thomas, son of Jno., of Q. A. Co., 26
    April 1751, Rhoda Earle, dau. of James           1 QA-36
Whorton, Francis, 4 April 173-(?), Ann Harne         1 WO-2
Wiat, Richard, 10 May 1772, Dinah Corbin             2 BA-264
Wiatt, James, 3 Oct. 1,35, Mary Reading              2 KE-226
Wickam, Nathaniel, 19 Dec. 1723, Priscilla Tyler     2 PG-3
Wickersham, Thomas, son of Isaac, of Reading, Berks.
    Co., Penna., 27 day, 4 mo., 1776, Ann Bartlett   8 SF-156

```
Wickes, Benjamin, Feb. (?), Susanna Ringgold          3 KE-336
Wickes, Samuel, 13 Jan. 1706, Frances Wilmer          3 KE-334
Wicket, Joseph, 23 Nov. 1738, Mary Bush               2 TA-165
Wickham, Nathaniel, the 3rd, 1 Sept. 1755, Sarah Wood,
   dau. of Joseph and Sarah                           1 FR-12
Wickins, Robert, 3 June 1745, Jemima Holoway          3 BA-157
Wicks, Thomas, 15 Dec. 1742, Eliz. Enloe              2 BA-125
Widows, Robert, 17 Oct. 1765, Frances Hall            9 AA-250
Wiffin, Nathaniel, 22 April 1759, Elizabeth Knotts    1 QA-65
Wiggins, Charles, 22 Nov. 1739, Ann Calley            1 QA-45
Wiggins, Charles, 18 April 1759, Sarah Simkins        1 QA-65
Wiggins, Thomas, 15 Feb. 1759, Eliz. Moody            1 QA-64
Wiggons, Wm., 10 Feb. 1740/1, Eliz'h Collingwood      1 QA-46
Wight, Edward John, 20 June 1742, Alice Hood, widow
   of William Hood                                    3 CE-23
   3 CE-24 states that the bride was Elizabeth Hood,
   widow of William Hood.
Wilb, Andrew, 2 July 1769, Mary Matthews              2 BA-259
Wilborn, William, 21 Jan. 1731, Ann Crabtree          1 BA-256
Wilcocks, Henry, 19 day, 1 mo., 1669, Sarah Lewis,
   relict of William Lewis                            8 SF-315
Wild, John, 30 July 1714, Mary Clark                  3 KE-334
Wild, Jonathan, 30 Nov. 1738, Sarah Preble            1 BA-303
Wildey, John, 10 April 1701, Martha Carr              2 AA-315
Wiley, John, April 1748, Elizabeth Perdue             2 BA-243
Wiley, John, 28 Feb. 1749, Elizabeth Austin           1 QA-56
Wiley, William, 23 Dec. 1734, Margrett Sing           3 BA-152
Wilkins, Andrew, 29 Aug. 1719, Anne Jones             1 AA-295
Wilkins, Francis, 18 Feb. 1762, Frances Carback       2 BA-223
Wilkins, John, 3 May 1730, Esther Forty               1 AA-110
Wilkins, Thomas, 4 July 1716, Mary Comagys            3 KE-335
Wilkins, William, 19 April 1735, Deborah Palmer       4 AA-437
Wilkinson, Jethro Lynch, 29 Jan. 1761, Eliz. Marryman 2 BA-221
Wilkinson, Joseph, 18 Dec. 1755, Rebeckah Young       1 QA-60
Wilkinson, Joseph, 31 May 1757, Mary Thomas           1 QA-62
Wilkinson, Samuel, 3 Jan. 1748, Mary Asher            2 BA-242
   2 BA-196 gives the date as 14 April 1748.
Wilkinson, Sam'l, 12 Feb. 1759, Mary Wood             2 BA-218
Wilkinson, Thos., 21 Feb. 1747, Margarit Rigley       1 QA-54
Wilkinson, Thomas, 25 July 1755, Elizabeth Adcock     1 QA-59
Wilkinson, Thomas, 30 July 1757, Mary Whaley          1 QA-62
Wilkinson, William, 12 Feb. 1749, Mary Saunders       1 QA-56
Wilkinson, William, 6 April 1758, Mary Sparks         1 QA-63
Wilkisson, Robert, 8 June 1736, Rachel Lenox          3 BA-154
Wilks, Thomas, 24 June 1745, Sarah Manley             2 KE-259
Willard, John, 26 Dec. 1771, Mary Jones               2 BA-263
Willcockes, Henry, 9 Jan. 1669, Sarah Lewis, widow    1 TA-602
Willcocks, Daniel, 16 Oct. 1755, Damsell Paley        1 QA-60
Willcocks, Daniel, Jr., 16 May 1756, Mary Chairs      1 QA-61
   1 QA-55 gives the date as 23 Feb. 1748.
Willcox, Daniel, 14 Aug. 1750, Hannah Keys            1 QA-57
Willcox, Martin, 16 day, 2 mo., 1735, Dinah Heald,
   dau. of Samuel and Mary                            9 SF
Willess, Jabez, 23 Feb. 1774, Elizabeth Fleming       2 SO-187
Willett, Isaac, 10 Jan. 1764, Christany Nichols       9 AA-248
Williames, Henry, 20 Nov. 1664, Femety Albus          1 KE-186
Williams, (?), 25 Nov. 1702, Susanna Porter           3 KE-333
Williams, Abraham, Sept. (?), Eleanor Flemon          2 TA-274
Williams, Abraham, 25 Oct. 1732, Anne Oldson          1 QA-39
Williams, Andrew, 22 Dec. 1777, Jane Cunningham       7 AA-2
Williams, Baruch, late of P. G. Co., 7 May 1771,
   Rachel Baxter, dau. of Col. James and Elizabeth    1 CE-318
Williams, Basil, 6 April 1775, Jane Barret, dau.
   of Andrew                                          1 CE-318
Williams, Charles, 24 Sept. 1675, Mary Watson         5 SO-400
   8 SO-401 has the same information.
```

```
Williams, Charles, 13 July 1739, Judith Jones          1 BA-312
Williams, Chris'r, 23 Dec. 1744, Mary Spencer          1 QA-50
Williams, David, 26 Nov. 1667, Jane Covington          4 SO-689
Williams, David, 20 Aug. 1766, Matthew Houldbrook      1 WI-82
Williams, Edward, 21 Feb. 1737/8, Priscilla Walker     1 QA-43
Williams, Edward, 6 Dec. 1739, Margaret Hollyday       1 QA-45
Williams, Ennion, 3 Jan. 1721, Frances Bowes           8 SF-83
Williams, Esau, 15 April 1767, Mary Jones              1 WO-15
Williams, Evan, 9 Jan. 1676/7, Mary Periman            9 SO-402
Williams, George, 30 Nov. 1746, Hanah Scrivener        1 QA-52
Williams, George, 25 Jan. 1753, Mary Jarrett           2 BA-207
Williams, Henry, 6 July 1707, Mary Carrill             2 AA-332
Williams, Henry, 16 Jan. 1755, Rachael Williams        2 BA-211
Williams, Hugo, 21 March 1773, Lydia Stone             1 SM-136
Williams, Isaac, 7 Nov. 1744, Lydia Harwood            8 SF-86
Williams, Jacob, 8 June 1714, Mary Cox                 3 CE-6
Williams, James, 3 Nov. 1715, Fortune Henricks         2 TA-76
Williams, James, 24 Jan. 1720/1, Mary Webb             2 PG-2
Williams, James, 1 Nov. 1732, Mary Davis               1 QA-39
Williams, James, 20 July 1738, Eliza Bell              2 TA-165
Williams, James, 7 Oct. 1764, Grace Fleming            2 SO-183
Williams, Jerome, 7 April 1749, Anne Elliott           4 AA-451
Williams, John, 6 Dec. 1706, Mary Wheeler              1 BA-264
Williams, John, 21 Oct. 1708, Elizabeth Deal           2 TA-49
Williams, John, 16 Oct. 1717, Sarah Beauchamp          2 SO-89
Williams, John, 17 April 1720, Eliza Green             2 TA-92
Williams, John, 7 Oct. 1722, Grace White; both parties
    were servants to Rich'd Evans, innholder           4 AA-419
Williams, John, 12 Nov. 1724, Mary Fountain            2 SO-89
Williams, John, 12 Sept. 1731, Rachell Moore           1 WI-27
Williams, John, 10 April 1733, Elizabeth Polk          2 SO-90
Williams, John, 2 Dec. 1736, Margaret Clark            1 BA-290
Williams, John, 28 Aug. 1738, Anne Hix                 1 QA-44
Williams, John, 17 April 1749, Ruth Rockhold           2 BA-198
                                                         & 243
Williams, John, 26 June 1753, Sarah Davis              2 SO-95
Williams, John, son of John, 27 Dec. 1767, Betty Jones 2 SO-189
Williams, John, 23 July 1769, Ann Renshaw              2 BA-259
Williams, John, 1770, Elizabeth Taylor                 2 AA-409
Williams, John, 10 June 1770, Ann Seymer               3 BA-170
Williams, John, Jan. 1775, Elizabeth Person            3 BA-171
Williams, John, 27 July 1777, Anne Allen              10 BA-68
Williams, John Guy, 18 Oct. 1743, Rachel Ward          3 TA-45
    The groom's name is spelled Wms.
Williams, Joseph, 6 Oct. 1707, Easther Creed           1 CA-112
Williams, Joseph, 20 April 1710, Elisabeth Brewer      1 AA-77
                                                         & 259
Williams, Joseph, 1716, Ruth Clark                     1 AA-275
Williams, Joseph, 28 Feb. 1749, Abigail Clark          8 SF-93
Williams, Jos., 5 Feb. 1771, Ann Heard, dau. of Jac.   1 SM-135
Williams, Michael, 7 Feb. 1672, Ann Williams           5 SO-400
Williams, Morriss, 28 June 1748, Ann Du                1 BA-382
Williams, Moses, 1770, Catherine Wood                  2 AA-409
Williams, Owen, 21 July 1765, Mary White               2 BA-228
Williams, Planner, 1 Jan. 1760, Mary Robertson         2 SO-182
Williams, Richard, 14 Feb. 1709, Eleanor Stocket       1 AA-77
                                                         & 259
Williams, Richard, 12 June 1746, Anne Nairne           2 BA-240
    2 BA-195 gives the bride's name as Nearn.
Williams, Robert, age 28, (date not given), Jean Meek  1 CE-321
Williams, Robert, 7 Sept. 1714, Margret Edwards        2 TA-74
Williams, Robert, 6 Sept. 1777, Hannah Kenny          10 BA-69
Williams, Samuel, 3 Feb. (?), Rachel (?)               1 WO-2
Williams, Thomas, 10 June 1674, Frances Robinson       5 SO-400
Williams, Thomas, 21 April 1705, Mary Carr             2 TA-43
```

Williams, Thomas, 2 Jan. 1718, Catherine Dallas          4 AA-403
Williams, Thomas, 27 Dec. 1734, Ann Jacobs               2 TA-156
Williams, Thomas, 22 April 1742, Eliz'h Hollingsworth    1 QA-47
Williams, Thos., 9 June 1745, Rebecce White              1 QA-50
Williams, Thomas, 1 Feb. 1755, Elizabeth Gibbs           1 PG-311
Williams, Thomas, 24 Aug. 1758, Mary Wheatley            2 SO-97
Williams, Thos., 10 June 1759, Susannah Higgs            2 BA-218
Williams, William, 26 May 1716, Jean Asshe               2 BA-7
Williams, William, 22 May 1735, Lucy Ann Bayley          1 BA-282
Williams, William, 2 Feb. 1741, Elizabeth Harwood        8 SF-84
Williams, Wm., 8 Dec. 1748, Sarah Ellwood                2 BA-198
                                                         & 243
Williams, Wm., 30 Dec. 1750, Mary Austin                 3 TA-80
Williams, William, 6 (Oct. 1768?), Mary Rynoo            2 BA-257
Williams, William, 1770, Valinda Jones                   2 AA-409
Williamson, Geo., 15 June 1758, Keturah Durbin           2 BA-217
Williamson, John, 21 Aug. 1709, Mary Rurk                1 CA-112
Williamson, John, 13 Aug. 1713, Jane Weatherbourn        1 AA-268
Williamson, John, 3 May 1738, Eliza Holt                 1 QA-44
Williamson, Thomas, 14 Aug. 1739, Elizabeth Bois         1 BA-307
Williart, John, son of Peter and Elizabeth Magdalena,
  26 May 1775, Anna Margaret Protzman, dau. of
  Lorentz and Maria                                      5 FR-139
Willicomb, William, 18 June 1738, Susanna Betterswell    4 AA-439
Willion, Edward, 27 Feb. 1770, Sally Green               2 BA-260
Willion, Jno., 10 Nov. 1763, Rach'l Rigbee               2 BA-225
Willis, James, 13 March 1679, Rebecca Barnabe            5 SO-400
Willis, John, 10 July 1712, Margaret Cox                 8 SF-8
Willis, Joshua, 20 May 1774, Deborah Greenhawk           1 CR
Willis, Richard, 21 Feb. 1769, Hannah Bu-(?)             2 BA-258
Willis, Thomas, 11 Aug. 1726, Mary Neill                 2 TA-113
Willis, Thomas, 10 day, 7 mo., 1767, Siny Ricketts       2 SF-288
Willjahr, Elias, 6 April 176-(?), Rosina Gumbin          4 FR-1181
Willkinson, Anthony, 5 Nov. 1741, Lilly Manson           1 QA-47
Willkinson, Henry, 9 April 1748, Eliz'h Bruneniger       1 QA-54
Willoughby, John, 20 Dec. 1774, Anne Walker              1 CR
Willox, William, 2 March 1776, Dorcas Barratt            3 BA-172
Willmott, John, 1 Feb. 1721/2, Hannah Mayo               1 AA-89
Wills, Hugh, 25 Oct. 1737, Mary Richards                 1 QA-43
Willson, (?), 13 July 1724, Hannah Creswell              3 KE-335
Willson, Aq'a, 4 Dec. 1759, Kezia Everritt               2 BA-219
Willson, John, 10 Sept. 1740, Eloner Dasha               2 KE-236
Willson, John, 8 Sept. 1747, Susnanah Gittings           2 BA-193
Willson, John, 1 Dec. (1768?), Deliah Smith              2 BA-257
Willson, John, 22 July 1770, Margret Edy                 2 BA-260
Willson, Peter, 1 Sept. 1737, Cathrine Hern              2 KE-255
Willson, Robert, 4 Nov. 1777, Jean Elliott               1 WA-534
Willson, Wm., 18 Aug. 1745, Elisabeth Perkins            2 KE-260
Willson, William, 20 Feb. 1759, Esther Hollinsworth      1 QA-64
Willson, William, 15 Nov. 1759, Hannah Matthews          2 SO-181
Wilmer, Lambert, 8 Oct. 1767, Hannah Rickitts            2 BA-231
Wilmer, Simon, Jr., of Kent Co., 16 Sept. 1735, Mary
  Pryce, dau. of Mr. John Pryce, dec., of Comb, in
  the parish of Preston in the counties of Hereford
  and Radnor. The Rev. Theophilus Jones, father-in-
  law (i.e., step-father) of the bride, performed
  the wedding.                                           3 CE-19
Wilmot, Richard, 22 Dec. 1741, Mary Gittings             2 BA-151
                                                         & 168
Wilmo., Robert, 15 Dec. 1748, Sarah Merryman             3 BA-162
Wilson, Andrew, 16 July 1777, Elizabeth Graham          10 BA-68
Wilson, Benjamin, son of Thomas and Elizabeth, 7 day,
  12 mo., 1752, Lydia Job, dau. of Thomas and
  Elizabeth                                              9 SF
Wilson, Daniel, son of James, 29 day, 1 mo., 1768,
  Rebeckah Barnwell, dau. of James                       8 SF-130

Wilson, Garret, 21 Jan. 1745, Rosanna Smith          3 BA-158
Wilson, George, 4 April 1692, Jane Cooper          5 SO-400
Wilson, Henry, Jr., son of Henry, of Balto. Co.,
  3 day, 1 mo., 1771, Marg't Harris, dau. of William          6 SF
Wilson, James, Jr., 19 Dec. 1716, Mary Berry          8 SF-13
Wilson, James, 8 day, 10 mo., 1748, Jane Clark          8 SF-91
Wilson, James, 16 Oct. 1777, Ann Johnston          1 MO-521
Wilson, John, 28 April 1700, Frances Worsley          8 SF-385
Wilson, John, 16 Jan. 1704, Ann Jones          3 KE-334
Wilson, John, 3 Oct. 1733, Elianor Allen          1 AA-116
Wilson, John, 10 Oct. 1744, Sarah Gibson          3 TA-50
Wilson, John, 17 Sept. 1753, Mary Hedges, widow of
  Joseph Hedges          1 FR-11
Wilson, John, son of Christopher and Sarah, of Cumber-
  land, Eng., 14 day, 11 mo., 1764, Aliceanna Webs-
  ter, dau. of Isaac and Margaret          7 SF-14
Wilson, John, son of Samuel and Catherine, 2 May 1771,
  Deborah Rogers, dau. of William and Grace          9 SF
Wilson, Jonathan, 16 Nov. 1750, Mary Ray          3 TA-79
Wilson, Joseph, 4 Feb. 1729, Hannah Farmer          1 BA-255
Wilson, Joseph, 15 Dec. 1748, Mary Marthews          2 SO-91
Wilson, Joseph, 29 Aug. 1777, Ann S. Ferguson          3 PG-169
Wilson, Levin, 21 May 1771, Sarah Houghton Sloss,
  dau. of Thos. and Mary          3 SO-4
Wilson, Moses, 10 March (?), Ann Wildgoos          1 WO-4
Wilson, Peter, 6 day, 6 mo., 1682, Elizabeth Morgain,
  dau.-in-law of Bryan Omelia          8 SF-329
Wilson, Robert, 10 Nov. 1740, Lucy Collison          3 TA-26
Wilson, Solomon, 3 Aug. 1774, Hannah Bell          1 CR
Wilson, Thomas, 29 Aug. 1745, Ann King          2 KE-272
Wilson, Thomas, son of Thomas and Elizabeth, 7 May
  1747, Sarah Murphy, dau. of Arthur and Margaret          9 SF
Wilson, Thomas, 3 day, 3 mo., 1766, Lydia Regester          8 SF-123
Wilson, Thomas, son of William, 6 Aug. 1769, Eliza-
  beth Wood, dau. of Joseph and Catherine          1 FR-12
Wilson, William, 29 Oct. 1688, Mary Cotman          5 SO-400
Wilson, William, 8 Sept. 1705, Mary Williams          2 TA-44
Wilson, William, 24 June 1709, Mary Blades          2 TA-61
Wilson, William, 22 July 1728, Marabelle Esse          1 AA-107
Wilson, William, 20 Jan. 1732, Sarah Young          3 KE-337
Wilson, William, 5 Oct. 1757, Mary Killam          2 SO-95
Wilson, William, Jr., 27 Feb. 1770, Ann Kemp          8 SF-137
Wilson, William, 1 Oct. 1777, Rebecca Ferguson          3 PG-170
Wimple, Capt. Mangret, 22 Oct. 1730, Sarah Mills          2 TA-150
Wimsatt, Ignatius, 31 Dec. 1772, Mary Medley          1 SM-136
Wimsatt, Stephen, 25 Aug. 1770, Mary Low          1 SM-135
Winchester, John, 7 Sept. 1665, Janne Muntrose          1 KE-186
Windall, Edward, 29 April 1730, Cathrine Rain          2 KE-230
Windam.  See Windorn.
Winders, James, 9 May 1743, Elizabeth Sheerwood          1 FR-12
Windford, Richard, 19 July 1739, Roseanna Shepherd          1 QA-45
Windorn (Windam), William, 23 April 1747, Elizabeth
  Morris; the bride was born 17 Sept. 1726.          1 PG-319
Winford, Alexander, 19 Feb. 1730, Eliza Higgins          2 TA-150
Wingod, Thomas, 1 Jan. 1669, Elizabeth Cooper          5 SO-400
Winington, Robert, 30 May 1705, Elinor (?)          4 AA-390
Winks, Jos., 27 Nov. 1763, Mary Palmer          2 BA-225
Winn, John, 5 Feb. 1717, Anne Smallwood          1 PG-270
Winright, Steven, 30 Aug. 1737, Mary Evans          1 WI-27
Winsar, John, (1675?), Elizabeth Gager          8 SO-401
Winsor, Jacob, 27 Aug. 1738, Susanna Clemons          1 QA-44
Winsor, Samuel, 16 Dec. 1731, Sarah Stoker          2 TA-151
Winspear, William, 24 June 17-(?), Mary Duerty          3 KE-334
Winstandly, Peter, 22 July 1736, Mary Harris          2 TA-160
Winter, John, son of Walter, 6 Dec. 1736, Elizabeth
  Bruce          1 CH-183

| | |
|---|---|
| Winter, Laughlin, 14 Nov. 1734, Jennet McKentire | 1 CE-281 |
| Winterson, Joseph, 7 May 1775, Mary Taylor | 2 AA-412 |
| Wise, Richard, 13 Jan. 1711, Sarah Nichols | 2 AA-344 |
| Wise, Rich'd, 27 Dec. 1736, Margaret Nevil | 1 QA-42 |
| Wisely, John, 20 Oct. 1721, Mary Bond, widow | 2 BA-17 |
| Wiseman, Henry, alias Beeck, 29 April 1740, Jane Garvin | 1 BA-314 |
| Witchell, Thomas, 10 day, 3 mo., 1690, Mary Serson, widow | 6 SF |
| Withered, John, 3 Oct. 1695, Sarah Webb | 2 AA-293 |
| Witheret, John, 1 April 1711, Rebecca Ferris | 2 AA-342 |
| Witheret, John, 23 Oct. 1718, Mary Davis | 2 AA-360 |
| Witherhill, William, 27 May 1729, Mary Bucher | 1 AA-108 |
| Withgott, Henry, 25 Aug. 1703, Mary Delehay | 2 TA-37 |
| Wittain, William, 31 Jan. 1722, Elizabeth Smith | 3 CE-12 |
| Wittington, John, 20 Nov. 1709, Ellinor Clift | 2 TA-63 |
| Wivil, William, 22 June 1777, Sarah Burgess | 8 AA-13 |
| Wivill, Marmaduke, 14 March 1764, Harriott Wright | 9 AA-248 |
| Wodgworth, Thomas, Jan. 1741, Rebecca Pasmore | 2 BA-141 |
| Wolestain, Cornelias, 26 Dec. 1733, Mary Hapton | 3 CE-18 |
| Wolen, Dav., 16 Nov. 1767, Ann. M. Miller | 4 FR-1181 |
| Wolfe, John Lewis, 26 Dec. 1722, Anna Sartor; "both palatines" | 4 AA-420 |
| Wolff, Jacob, son of Paul, 28 Aug. 1769, Anna Maria Hof, dau. of Johan Wilhelm | 3 FR-106 |
| Wollaston, Joseph, son of Jeremiah, 2 Dec. 1742, Deborah Kirk | 9 SF |
| Wollox, John, 16 Dec. 1741, Elizabeth Yates | 1 BA-323 |
| Wolston, Thomas, 16 April 1677, Ruth London | 5 SO-400 |
| Wonnell, James, 17 Feb. 1746, Sarah Otwell | 2 SO-93 |
| Wood, David, 30 April 1747, Hannah Miles | 2 SO-88 |
| Wood, Henry, undated request to pub. banns, Susanah (Ramsey?) | 7 BA(1) |
| Wood, Henry, 3 Nov. 1766, Susannah (?) | 2 BA-229 |
| Wood, James, 27 Jan. 1762, Elizabeth Davidson | 3 BA-167 |
| Wood, Jepheniah, 14 Aug. 1777, Mary Lucas | 1 WO-517 |
| Wood, John, 1 July 1705, Sarah Gambill | 3 AA-97 |
| Wood, Dr. John, 16 Nov. 1709, Lydia (?) | 2 TA-63 |
| Wood, John, 19 Dec. 1737, Rebecca Eliason, dau. of Cornelias | 3 CE-23 |
| Wood, John, 20 Dec. 1737, Francis Flintom | 3 CE-22 |
| Wood, John, Nov. 1739, Elizabeth Bradford | 1 BA-323 |
| Wood, John, 20 Jan. 1755, Rachel Death | 1 CE-321 |
| Wood, John, 31 July 1758, Sarah Davidge | 1 BA-385 |
| Wood, John, 6 March 1776, Sarah Wood | 2 AA-413 |
| Wood, Joseph, 14 Oct. 1723, Eliz'th Pees | 2 KE-200 |
| Wood, Joseph, Jr., 17 Feb. 1734/5, Sarah Hodgson, dau. of Robert | 3 CE-19 |
| Wood, Joseph, 11 Sept. 1747, Catherine Julien | 1 FR-12 |
| Wood, Joseph, son of Thomas and Mary, 12 Jan. 1769, Katherine Daye, dau. of John and Lydia | 9 SF |
| Wood, Joseph, son of Joseph and Sarah, 9 April 1769, Anne Reed, dau. of James and Mary | 1 FR-12 |
| Wood, Joshua, 15 April 1729, Priscilla West | 1 BA-249 |
| Wood, Joshua, Sept. 1732, Mary Garrett | 1 BA-270 |
| Wood, Nathan, son of Nathan and Hannah, 13 Nov. 1744, Rebekah Trimble, dau. of John and Mary | 9 SF |
| Wood, Nich's, 30 June 1765, Mary Parker | 2 BA-228 |
| Wood, Richard, 9 June 1770, Mary Kun | 2 BA-260 |
| Wood, Robert, 23 July 1739, Ann Numbers, dau. of James | 3 CE-21 |
| Wood, Robert, 13 Oct. 1763, Catherine Dorsey, dau. of Nicholas | 1 FR-12 |
| Wood, Thomas, 26 Oct. 1732, Mary Lashly | 2 PG-6 |
| Wood, Warnell, 28 May 1754, Thamer Smith | 3 BA-165 |
| Wood, William, 6 May 1705, Ann Hill | 2 AA-327 |

```
Wood, William, 1 Jan. 1715, Elizabeth Lowe              2 TA-77
Wood, William, 18 Dec. 1731, Elizabeth Lambeth          1 QA-38
Wood, William, 27 Dec. 1736, Grace Rowdin               1 QA-42
Wood, Wm., 3 Oct. 1754, Ann Watkins                     2 BA-211
Wood, Wm., 7 Jan. 1762, Eliz. Davice                    2 BA-223
Wood, Zebeda, 10 Sept. 1776, Ann Drury                  2 AA-413
Woodall, John Allen, 18 Nov. 1748, Mary Commegys        1 QA-55
Woodall, Robert, 6 Feb. 1721, Sarah Hill                2 TA-98
  2 TA-100 gives the bride's name as Mary Hill.
Woodall, William, 15 Dec. 1757, Mary Man or Marr        2 KE-299
Woodbury, Jonathan, Jr., oldest son of Samuel Wood-
  bury who was brother to Jonathan Woodbury, late
  of Bristol, New Eng., 4 Sept. 1750, Lydia Lyndsey
  of Bristol                                            3 CE-26
Woodcock, William, 24 Dec. 1713, Mary Amboy             1 BA-213
Wooden, John, 27 Jan. 1716, Mary Gill                   3 BA-148
Wooden, Sollomon, 17 Aug. 1726, Sarah Gresham           1 AA-103
Woodey, John, 27 Dec. 1738, Mary Lynsey                 1 BA-310
Woodfield, Anthony, 28 Aug. 1773, Mary Ford             2 AA-411
Woodfield, Thomas, 16 Jan. 1777, Jeane Calman           2 AA-413
Woodhouse, George, 25 Dec. 1777, Ann Keith              9 BA
Woodhouse, George, 25 Dec. 1777, Ann Keith             10 BA-70
Woodland, Blackledge, 20 April 1760, Eliz. Jackson      2 BA-220
Woodland, James, 28 Feb. 1738/9, Sarah Hall             2 KE-225
Woodland, Joseph, July 1772, Cassandra Massey           2 BA-265
Woodland, William, Feb. 1703, Sarah Blackleach          3 KE-333
Woodland, Mr. William, 17 Jan. 1744/5, Mrs. Kathrine
  Freeman                                               2 KE-255
Woodlow, John, 23 April 1771, Ruth Tower                2 BA-262
Woods, Henry, 13 Dec. 1726/7, Sarah Turner              2 TA-114
Woodward, Abraham, 7 Nov. 1707, Elizabeth Finloe        1 AA-76
Woodward, Abraham, 25 (?) 1715, Priscilla Orr-(?)       4 AA-393
Woodward, Mr. Amos, 3 April 1728, Mrs. Acca Dorsey,
  dau. of Mrs. Caleb Dorsey                             4 AA-429
Woodward, John, 6 Aug. 1741, Grace Webb                 3 TA-32
Woodward, John, 2 Dec. 1745, Ann Pathy                  1 QA-51
Woodward, Thomas, son of Richard and Mary, 26 Dec.
  1745, Elizabeth Kirk Jacob, widow of John Jacob,
  and dau. of Roger and Elizabeth Kirk                  9 SF
Woolcot, James, 28 Dec. 1749, Susanah Parrot            3 TA-76
Wooler, John, 4 April 1768, Frances Brannan             2 BA-231
Woolf, Garret Hance, 21 Nov. 1742, Mary Cope            4 AA-444
Woolfe, Francis, 26 March 1733, Mary St. Laurence       1 AA-115
Woolford, James, 3 Nov. 1698, Grace Stevens             8 SF-394
Woolhead, Thomas, 25 May 1777, Caroline Hill            3 BA-173
Wooller, Jno., 3 April 1768, Fanny Brammer              2 BA-101
Woolling, Major, 5 Nov. 1756, Frances Johnson           2 BA-214
Woolling, Richard, 5 Feb. 1758, Eliz. Buchanan          2 BA-217
Woolling, R'd, 8 July 1762, Mary Mulling                2 BA-223
Woollon (Wootton), John, 10 March 1726/7, Margrit
  Davis                                                 1 WI-19
Woolman, Henry, 27 June 1713, Prudence Errington        2 TA-71
Wooten, Edward, 5 Jan. 1679, Cullett Southern           5 SO-400
Wooters, Jacob, 20 May 1774, Mary Jump                  1 CR
Wooters, Shadrach, 9 Aug. 1757, Hannah Dunbar           2 CR-273
Wootton, (?), 23 May 1727, Elizabeth Bridges            1 AA-105
Wootton, Turner, 1 Jan. 1723, Agnes Chambers            1 AA-98
Wordsworth, Thos., 18 Aug. 1768, Mary Wyle              2 BA-232
Worrinton, George, 29 Sept. 1739, Agnes Truitt          1 WO-8
Worrilow, William, 6 March 1691, Margaret Pinner        8 SF-357
Worrilow, William, 10 Feb. 1700, Sarah Mackee           8 SF-403
Worsly, Samuel, 21 April 1720, Elizabeth Setton         1 AA-299
Worthington, John, son of Charles, of Deer Creek,
  7 day, 11 mo., 1769, Priscilla Willson, dau.
  of Henry                                              4 SF-255
```

Worthington, Samuel, 17 Jan. 1759, Mary Tolley          2 BA-218
Worthington, Thomas, 23 July 1711, Elizabeth Redgly     3 AA-98
Worthington, Vachel, 17 Nov. 1757, Pressilla Bond       2 BA-216
  4 BA-71 has the same information.
Worthington, Vornol, 10 Dec. 1745, Anna Hammond         3 AA-110
Worthington, William, 5 Nov. 1717, Sarah Homewood       3 AA-111
                                                          & 281
Worthington, William, 30 June 1734, Hannah Cromwell     3 BA-152
Worthington, William, 2 March 1769, Sarah Ristow        2 BA-258
Wottring, John, Jr., son of John Daniel, Sept. 1763,
  Elizabeth Glatt                                       5 FR-144
Wottring, John Daniel, 1744, Anna Maria Rebmann         5 FR-145
Wright, Abell, 12 Jan. 1695/6, Katherine Clarke         5 SO-400
Wright, Abraham, 14 April 1745, Dorcas Toder            2 BA-240
  2 BA-193 gives the date as 23 May 1745 and the
  bride's name as Darkes Tudor.
Wright, Abraham, 20 Feb. 1759, Avarilla Harryman        2 BA-218
Wright, Benjamin, 4 March 1735, Elizabeth Ledore        3 AA-104
Wright, Bloyce, 26 Nov. 1757, Mary Talbott              2 BA-216
Wright, Christopher, 1 June 1673, Isabel Gradwell       5 SO-400
Wright, Dawson, 28 July 1743, Elizabeth Wales           3 AA-107
Wright, Edward, 15 Nov. 1720, Margret Booth             2 TA-95
Wright, Edward, 1 Jan. 1730, Abigail Connor             1 QA-37
Wright, Edward, 28 Nov. 1749, Anna Chairs               1 QA-56
Wright, Edward, 10 Dec. 1750, Mary Reed                 1 QA-57
Wright, Fairclough, 15 May 1735, Frances Roe            1 QA-40
Wright, Geo., 8 June 1766, Sarah Scoles                 2 BA-229
Wright, Henry, 23 June 1723, Sarah Hopkins              3 AA-100
Wright, Isaac, 19 May 1761, Mary Richardson             2 BA-221
Wright, Jacob, 9 Dec. 1756, Betty Baily                 1 WI-69
Wright, Jacob, 4 Aug. 1765, Prissilla Ingram            2 BA-228
Wright, James, 3 May 1738, Martha Hynson                1 QA-44
Wright, James, 7 Jan. 1777, Ann Cassey                  3 BA-173
Wright, John, 12 June 1677, Mary Fox                    9 SO-402
Wright, John, 27 Oct. 1706, Mary Paggett                3 KE-334
Wright, John, 15 Oct. 1707, Hannah Darling              3 CE-15
Wright, John, 22 Nov. 1729, Rachel Godwin               1 QA-37
Wright, Jno., 4 May 1762, Jemima Hendon                 2 BA-223
Wright, Joseph, Jr., 8 Jan. 1740, Jane Wooden           2 BA-74
Wright, Joseph, 1750, Margaret James                    2 BA-241
Wright, Levin, 24 Sept. 1760, Elizabeth Darby           1 WI-69
Wright, Levin, 11 day, 7 mo., 1773, Mary Rumbly; both
  of Dor. Co.                                           2 SF-288
Wright, Nathan, 15 day, 3 mo., 1746, Mary Tillotson     1 SF-79
Wright, Nathanael, 29 March 1719, Elizabeth Navarre     4 AA-407
Wright, Nathaniel, 11 April 1769, Sophia Rutledge       2 BA-258
Wright, Richard, 22 Dec. 1726, Mary Ijams               1 AA-317
Wright, Samuell, 28 Dec. 1719, Ann Bellard              3 KE-335
Wright, Samuel, 2 March 1730, Sarah Merriken            3 AA-104
Wright, Samuel, 26 Oct. 1738, Sarah Conaway             3 AA-104
Wright, Solomon, son of Solomon and Mary, 20 Sept.
  1750, Mary Tidmarsh, dau. of William and Martha       1 QA-65
Wright, Thomas, 15 July 1708, Diana Evans               4 AA-378
Wright, Thomas, 5 May 1735, Christian Enloes            2 BA-77
Wright, Thomas, 5 July 1757, Ann Evans                  2 BA-215
Wright, William, 7 Dec. 1669, Frances Bloys             5 SO-400
Wright, William, 27 Dec. 1670, Frances Bloys            5 SO-399
Wright, William, 5 Sept. 1714, Juliana Benbow           2 BA-6
Wright, William, 2 Dec. 1719, Sarah Adair               4 AA-411
Wright, William, Jr., 4 Sept. 1721, Ann Howles          2 BA-17
Wright, William, 7 May 1727, Elizabeth Barton           2 BA-26
Wright, William, son of Bloice, 28 Feb. 1738, Sarah
  Day                                                   2 BA-136
Wright, Wm., 28 Sept. 1762, Sarah Childs                2 BA-224
Wright, Wm., 3 Feb. 1767, Mary Heathcut Pickitt         2 BA-230

Wrightson, James, (c.March 1750/1), Eliza Porter    3 TA-82
Wroth, James, 18 Feb. 1723, Anne Walmsley    3 CE-13
Wroth, John, 3 Feb. 1705, Katherine Conaway    3 KE-334
Wroth, Thomas, 12 Jan. 1747, Mary Penington, widow
   of John Penington    3 CE-26
Wurtenbecker, John Bernh't, 22 March 1757, Mary Eva
   Hein    4 FR-1103
Wyat, John, 8 April 1742, Hannah Deaverix    1 QA-47
Wyatt, Edward, 9 Aug. 1772, Margarit Riggen    2 SO-185
Wyatt, John, 9 Oct. 1739, Fortune Foster    3 AA-105
Wyatt, Solomon, 8 July 1741, Margaret Wyes    1 QA-46
Wyet, Thomas, 28 Jan. 1730, Mary Ann Forbes    1 QA-38
Wyet, Thomas, 25 May 1732, Esther Wharton    1 QA-39
Wyle, Abel, 25 Jan. 1759, Sarah Samson    2 BA-218
Wyle, Aquila, 10 April 1770, Pine Sparks    2 BA-260
Wyle, Benjamin, 30 Oct. 1755, Elinor Samson    2 BA-212
Wyle, John, 12 May 1748, Eliz'th Perdue    2 BA-197
Wyle, Vincent, 24 Jan. 1769, Sarah Sutton    2 BA-257
Wyle, Walt, 29 Dec. 1763, Susannah Norris    2 BA-226
Wyle, William, 1 Jan. 1753, Eliz. Little    2 BA-207
Wyleye, George, 21 June 1724, Ann Martiall    1 AA-98
Wynn, John, Jr., 24 Aug. 1738, Sarah Robey    1 PG-309
Wyre, James, 4 Nov. 1748, Ann Reed    1 QA-54
Wyvill, Edward Hall, 1770, Susanna Hilla Cambden    2 AA-409
Wyvill, Marmaduke, 15 Oct. 1755, Susanna Burgess    2 AA-398
Wyvill, Marmaduke, 15 March 1764, Harriett Rate    2 AA-397
Wyvill, William, 14 Feb. 173-(?), Elinor Boyd    2 PG-6
Wyvill, William, 17 June 1777, Sarah Burgess    7 AA-1
Yackly, Robert, 3 June 1735, Sarah Mitchel    2 PG-6
Yalding, William, 5 Feb. 1676/7, Mary Wilson    9 SO-402
Yardsley, John, 23 July 1745, Ann Buttlon    1 QA-51
Yarnons?, Andrew, 10 Jan. 1728, Ann Gillbird    2 TA-119
Yarnsheire, John, 9 Nov. 1729, Eliza Colson    1 AA-109
Yate, John, 5 Dec. 1721, Martha Jadwin    2 TA-97
Yates, Joseph, 5 Nov. 1712, Mary Cowdrey    1 BA-244
Yates, Joseph, 30 June 1729, Mary Evans    1 BA-250
Yates, Joseph, 30 July 1730, Alice Smith    1 AA-111
Yates, Joseph, 15 Sept. 1735, Catharine Herrett    1 BA-284
Yates, William, 24 April 1748, Anne Dorney    2 BA-243
Yealdhall, Will'm, 13 Feb. 1704, Mary Stephens    4 AA-390
Yearks, Sam'l, 3 Sept. 1761, Sarah Mortimer    2 BA-222
Yearly, John, 14 March 1754, Margaret Philips    3 BA-168
Yearly, Nath'l, 12 Feb. 1767, Rachel Edy    2 BA-230
Yeates, William, 28 April 1748, Ann Dorney    2 BA-197
Yeats, Joseph, 14 Sept. 1736, Catherine Turret    2 BA-117
Yeats, Thomas, 17 June 1744, Elizab. Martin    2 BA-239
Yeats, Thos., 21 June 1744, Eliz. Martin    2 BA-190
Yeats, William, 5 Aug. 1744, Anne Thornbury    2 BA-239
   2 BA-191 gives the date as 8 Sept. 1744.
Yeats, William, 28 April 1748, Ann Dorney    2 BA-197
Yeo, James, 25 May 1755, Rebecca Rollo    2 BA-212
Yoe, Stephen, 24 Dec. 1730, Mary Earle, mother of
   Alice Murphey    1 QA-36
Yoe, Stephen, 26 June 1759, Eliza Box    1 QA-65
Yoe, William, 18 May 1756, Sarah Bostock    1 QA-61
Yong, William, 26 Dec. 1740, Elis. Cocklin    1 QA-46
Yonge, Will, 14 April 1670, Frances (?)    1 TA-601
Yonguer, William, 15 Sept. 1709, Hannah Moriah
   Cratcherwoodlayer    2 TA-62
York, Edward, 21 Oct. 1742, Anne Dorney    2 BA-238
York, George, 7 May 1721, Lettice Doddridge    2 BA-17
York, George, Feb. 1738, Eliner Meads    2 BA-136
York, Geo., 30 Nov. 1766, Cathrine Gardner    2 BA-230
York, John, 16 Oct. 1752, Sarah Horner    2 BA-204
York, John, 16 Oct. 1777, Hannah Deaver    1 HA-200

| | |
|---|---|
| York, William, 1 Jan. 1733, Eliz. Debruler | 2 BA-76 |
| Yostain, Henry, 24 Jan. 1730, Jane Rider | 3 BA-150 |
| Young, Charles, 23 Dec. 1750, Margaret Marsh | 1 QA-57 |
| Young, David, 7 Nov. 1714, Margret Porter | 3 CE-7 |
| | & 13 |
| Young, Edward, 26 Jan. 1736, Hanna Hamer | 1 QA-42 |
| Young, George, 16 Dec. 1777, Mary Hellen | 1 CA-111a |
| Young, Henry, 19 Nov. 1772, Delila Harryman | 2 BA-265 |
| Young, Jacob, 31 Dec. 1713, Mary Price | 3 CE-5 |
| Young, Jacob, 10 Dec. 1729, Margaret Carmack | 1 CE-282 |
| Young, John, Jr., (date not given), (?) Atkinson | 1 QA-40 |
| Young, John, 10 Feb. 1714/5, Elizabeth Frances | 4 AA-392 |
| Young, Joseph, 24 Dec. 1732, Ann Johnson | 1 CE-279 |
| Young, Joseph, 27 Aug. 1758, (?) Beal | 1 QA-64 |
| Young, Nathaniel, 25 Dec. 1733, Anne Buttler | 3 BA-151 |
| Young, Paul, 20 May 1733, Rosehannah Mash | 3 BA-151 |
| Young, Paul, 24 April 1743, Mary Davis | 3 BA-156 |
| Young, Richard, 28 Feb. 1714, Margrett Prindewell | 1 AA-78 |
| Young, Richard, banns pub. on 25 March 1725, Mrs. | |
| Mary Browne | 2 CA-24 |
| Young, Robert, 27 Jan. 1757, Jane Mortimer | 2 BA-214 |
| Young, Robert, 11 July 1769, Sarah Matthews | 1 BA-388 |
| Young, Robert, 1771, Hanna Gardiner | 2 AA-411 |
| Young, Robert, 19 June 1777, Elizabeth Norvell | 2 AA-414 |
| Young, Samuell, 14 July 1687, Mary (?) | 4 AA-372 |
| Young, Samuel, 2 Feb. 1730, Elenor Johnson | 1 CE-280 |
| Young, Sam'l, 9 April 1765, Reb. Stokes | 2 BA-227 |
| Young, Suel, 13 Jan. 1736, Margrett Acton | 3 BA-156 |
| Young, William, 8 Jan. 1706, Mary Bishop | 2 AA-331 |
| Youngblood, John Miles, 21 Jan. 1729, Mary Coal | 1 BA-254 |
| Youngblood, Peter, 26 Nov. 1750, Mary Wheals | 2 BA-202 |
| Younger, John, 30 June 1733, Mary Price | 2 TA-153 |
| Ziegler, Hy., 27 Jan. 1768, Elizab. Schuhmacher | 4 FR-1187 |
| Zimmerman, George, 15 Nov. 1763, Cath. Christ | 4 FR-1187 |
| Zimmerman, John, 28 March 1763, Hansi Hurtig | 4 FR-1187 |
| Zurkel, George, 23 Nov. 1763, Elizab. Reithernner | 4 FR-1187 |

## ADDENDA

| | |
|---|---|
| Beckett, Humphrey, 31 Oct. 1777, Lydia Sunderland | 3 CA |
| Dasheel, Benjamin, 25 Dec. 1777, Ann Yoe | 3 CA |
| Dorothy (sic), Moses, 27 Aug. 1777, Sidney Mackinnel | 3 CA |
| Fowler, John, 10 Oct. 1777, Susannah Phillips | 3 CA |
| Games, Robert, 12 Aug. 1777, Ann Bowen | 3 CA |
| Lee, Charles, 28 July 1777, Mary Leach | 3 CA |
| MacGuire, John, 16 Nov. 1727, Alice Maccay | 1 AA-106 |
| Mackhon, Robert, 27 Aug. 1749, Ann Amery | 1 CH-183 |
| Mackinnie, John, 26 Dec. 1777, Mary (Henshaw ?) | 3 CA |
| Mills, Leonard, 4 Dec. 1777, China Fraser | 3 CA |
| Owens, Charles, Oct. 1777, Betty Barton | 3 CA |
| Page, Daniel, 10 Nov. 1777, Leonora Piles | 3 CA |
| Roberts, Allen, 9 Oct. 1777, Ann Wilson | 3 CA |
| Sedgwick, Thomas, 21 Dec. 1777, Anne Rigby | 3 CA |
| Smith, James, 12 Aug. 1777, Barbara White | 3 CA |
| Young, George, 16 Dec. 1777, Mary Hillen | 3 CA |

APPENDIX

The following marriage records and marriage references have
been included in an attempt to fill at least partially the gap
between the founding of the colony of Maryland in 1634 and the
beginning of church records in the latter quarter of the seventeenth century. The entries have been taken from the published
Archives of Maryland, including selected volumes of Proceedings
of the General Assembly, the Council, the Provincial Court, the
Chancery Court, and certain county courts. The volumes used in
compiling the information in this section are: I, II, III, IV,
X, XLI, LI, LIII, LIV, and LX. After each entry is given the volume number followed by the page number. It should be noted that
in many cases the exact date of the marriage is not given, but
only a date by which the marriage had already occurred.

Abrahams, Isaac, m. by Dec. 1660, Elizabeth, relict of Thomas
  Reade. 41:379
Adams, Henry, of Chas. Co., m. by Jan. 1671/2, Margaret, admini-
  stratrix of Oliver Balse. 60:361
Andrews, Christopher, of Kent Co., m. by 7 Oct. 1672, Mary, widow
  of William Stanley. 51:86
Arnold, Lawrence, m. by 10 April 1674, Ann, dau. of Andrew
  Ellenor, a Spaniard. 51:113
Atkins, George, m. by 12 March 1666/7, the relict of Richard
  Pinner. 60:63
Baisey, Michael, m. by 29 Jan. 1652, the widow of Anthony Raw-
  lings. 10:213
Ballard, Charles, of Som. Co., m. by 29 Jan. 1666, Sarah, relict
  of John Elzey. 54:656
Banks, Lieut. Richard, m. by 10 April 1653, Margaret, widow of
  Richard Hatton who was brother to Thomas Hatton, Secretary
  of the Province. 10:259
Beckwith, George, m. by Oct. 1657, Frances, dau. of Nicholas
  Harvey. 10:548
Beedle, Henry, m. by 26 June 1673, Sophia, extx. of Richard
  Wells. 51:427
Besson, Capt. Thomas, m. by 27 March 1679, Hester, widow of
  Henry Caplin of A. A. Co. 51:262
Bland, Thomas, m. by 1675, Damaris, widow and executrix of Nicho-
  las Wyatt. 51:153
Blangy, Lewis, m. by 4 Dec. 1677, Mary, administratrix of Dis-
  borah Bennett. 51:205
Blomfield, John, m. by 25 Aug. 1669, Elizabeth, administratrix
  of Luke Barbier. 51:334
Bonner, Henry, m. by Dec. 1670, Eliza Storey, administratrix of
  Walter Storey. 51:37, 44
Bonner, Henry, m. by 1 Sept. 1674, Elizabeth, widow of John Tay-
  lor. 60:579
Boughton, Richard, of Chas. Co., "about to marry" in June 1668,
  Verlinda (Eaton), widow of Thomas Burdit. 60:133
Bowles, John, m. by 1 Feb. 1671/2, Margery, widow of William
  Batten. 51:70

Breed, John, m. by 24 April 1679, the mother of Ignatius
    Mathews.  51:242
Brooke, John, m. by Feb. 1688/9, Katherine, administratrix of
    Robert Stevens.  51:327
Brookes, Francis, m. by 19 Jan. 1652, Mrs. Ann Boulton.  10:215
Brown, Gerrard, m. by Oct. 1674, Martha, relict of William Allen
    of Chas. Co.  60:588
Burdit, Thomas, m. by June 1668, Verlinda Eaton, sister of
    Nathaniel and Samuel Eaton.  60:133
Burgess, John, m. by 20 April 1678, Amy, widow of John Tucker.
    51:259
Buttram, Nicholas, m. by 13 Nov. 1679, Elizabeth, widow of Andrew
    Henderson, and mother of Roger Moore.  51:303
Cady, Robert, of Chas. Co., m. by March 1670/1, Ellenor, widow
    of (?) Corner or Conner.  60:328
Chadbourne, William, m. by May 1675, Susanna, relict of Richard
    Foxon.  51:475
Chandler, Job, m. by May 1659, Ann, sister of Simon Overzee.
    53:460
Clark, (?), m. by 26 July 1658, Jane, relict of Nicholas Cawsine
    and mother of Mary Adams and Jane Cockshutt.  41:171
Clawe, William, m. by 27 May 1677, Sarah, widow of William Cole.
    51:498
Clocker, Daniel, m. by Oct. 1658, Mary, relict of James Courtney.
    41:185
Coates, Leonard, m. by 16 Oct. 1679, Martha, administratrix of
    William Russell.  51:539
Colclough, Maj. George, m. by Jan. 1660/1, Elizabeth, widow of
    Simon Overzee.  41:403
Courtney, James, license dated 23 May 1639, Mary Lawne.  4:52
Cox, Henry, m. by 22 April 1652, the widow of Robert Ward of
    St. M. Co.  10:161
Cressy, Samuel, m. by 1 June 1676, Susanna, widow of William
    Robinson.  51:184
Dabb, John, m. by 10 April 1674, the widow of 1) Andrew Ellinor,
    and 2) Macom Mehenny.  51:113
Delahay, Thomas, m. by 9 July 1681, Eve, dau. of William Rich of
    Island Creek.  54:602
Dobson, Samuel, m. by April 1662, the mother of Mary Stratton.
    53:214
Drury, William, m. by 4 July 1679, Christian, widow of John
    Merriken.  51:300
Dunn, (?), m. by 1 June 1653, Joan, dau. of William Porter.
    54:17
Eaton, Jeremy, m. by 17 Nov. 1673, Mary, administratrix of Jona-
    than Sybry.  51:106
Edwin, William, license dated 26 March 1637/8, Mary Whitehead.
    4:24
Elenor, Andrew, of Kent Co., 5 day, 3 mo., 1656, Anicake Hanson.
    54:38
Ellery, Henry, m. by April 1659, the widow of William Stephenson.
    41:283
Elliott, Henry, m. by 10 July 1678, Jane, widow of John Halfhead.
    51:221
Elliott, William, of Kent Co., m. by 1 June 1653, the widow of
    William Porter.  54:16, 17
Eltonhead, William, m. by Nov. 1649, the widow of Capt. Philip
    Taylor.  4:527
Emerson, Nicholas, m. by 16 Oct. 1679, Elizabeth, mother of
    Richard Beck.  51:536
Evans, Lieut. William, m. by 21 June 1650, the widow and execu-
    trix of William Thompson.  10:23
Fenwick, Cuthbert, antenuptial contract dated 1 Aug. 1649, Mrs.
    Jane Moryson, widow of Robert Moryson of the county of Ke-
    coughtan, in Virginia.  41:262

Fouckes, Richard, m. by 6 April 1664, Anne, relict of Humphrey
   Haggett. 53:481
Fowke, Gerard, Feb. 1661/2, about to marry, Anne, widow of Job
   Chandler. 53:222
Frissell, Thomas, of Chas. Co., m. by Nov. 1658, Hannah Glossing-
   ton; both servants of Simon Oversee. 53:28
Galey, Thomas, of Chas. Co., m. by Nov. 1673, Martha, administra-
   trix of John Lewger. 60:512; 65:251
Gerard, Thomas, m. by March 1659/60, Susan, heir at law to her
   bro. Abel Snow. 41:372
Godson, Peter, 6 July 1654, "intending to marry," Jane, widow of
   Richard Moore of Cal. Co. 10:396
Goodrick, George, m. by April 1658, Ursula, widow of Capt.
   William Lewis. 41:58
Granger, Benja., m. by 17 Oct. 1678, the dau. of John Avery.
   51:527
Gray, Francis, license dated 26 Nov. 1638, Alice Morman. 4:51
Greene, Thomas, 2 April 1643 swore there was no impediment to
   his marrying Millicent Browne. 4:192
Greene, Thomas, m. by 2 March 1658/9, the widow of Nicholas
   Harvey. 41:249
Greene, William, m. by Jan. 1660/1, Elizabeth, executrix of
   Henry Potter. 41:394
Gutridge (or Goodricke), George, m. by June 1658, the widow of
   Capt. William Lewis. 10:523
Hall, (?), of Kent Co., m. by 1 June 1661, Margaret, executrix
   of Thomas Hill. 54:205
Hall, Edward, m. by 25 Jan. 1652, Rebecca, widow of George
   Manners. 10:216
Hall, Walter, m. by 30 April 1658, the relict of Henry Fox.
   41:79
Hambleton, John, m. by 26 Dec. 1655, Temperance, dau. of Richard
   Moore. 10:433
Haslewood, John, 25 March 1679, Ann, executrix of John Avery.
   51:237
Hatton, Richard, m. by 11 Dec. 1674, Ann, daughter and heir of
   John Price. 51:445
Head, William, m. by 5 June 1679, the widow of Henry Carline.
   51:278
Head, William, m. by 5 June 1679, as his second wife, Elizabeth
   Cash. 51:278
Helmes, John, m. by March 1669/70, the widow of John Mills, of
   Chas. Co. 60:249
Henderson, Andrew, m. by 23 Jan. 1671, Elizabeth, mother of
   Roger Moore. 51:315
Hill, Thomas, m. by April 1661, Elizabeth Robinson. 54:216-217
Hills, Thomas, m. by 28 April 1661, Elizabeth, widow and execu-
   trix of John Deere. 54:217
Hills, William, of Chas. Co., m. by June 1667 at Mr. Montague's,
   Idy Hadlowe. 60:116
Hollis, Henry, m. by 10 Dec. 1679, Elizabeth, widow of John
   Grammer. 51:305
Hollis, John, 2 June 1639, Restituta Tue. 4:52
Holt, Robert, m. by 28 June 1662, Christian Bonfield. 3:463
   This may have been a bigamous marriage as Holt already had
   a wife named Dorothy. 41:150
Howell, Humphrey, m. by 7 Oct. 1648, Blanch Oliver. 4:424
   Blanch had married 1) John Harrison, and 2) Roger Oliver.
   10:108
Hussey, Thomas, m. by Aug. 1666, Johanna, widow of John Nevill.
   60:27
James, Charles, m. by 20 Nov. 1674, Elizabeth, dau. of Leonard
   Strong. 51:142
Jenifer, Daniel, m. by Sept. 1669, Mary, executrix of William
   Smythe, late of St. M. Co. 51:327

Jenkins, John, m. by 27 May 1658, the widow of Thomas Bachelor.
   41:96
Johns, Richard, m. by 18 June 1678, Elizabeth, widow of Thomas
   Sparrow.  51:228
Johnson, Frederick, m. by 25 Feb. 1642, the widow of Richard
   Stevens.  4:185
Johnson, James, m. by 31 May 1651, Barbara Hatton, kinswoman of
   Thomas Hatton, Secretary of the Province.  10:12
Jordain, Capt. Jno., m. May 1669, Elizabeth, widow of Col.
   William Evans.  51:284
Joyner, William, m. by 10 April 1674, Sarah, dau. of Andrew
   Ellenor.  51:113
Kanery, Richard, 22 Aug. 1655, about to marry, Mary, executrix
   of John Hodger.  10:419
Kilbourne, Francis, of Chas. Co., m. by March 1670/1, Eliza,
   administratrix of Daniel Johnson.  60:333 Eliza was widow
   of Daniel Johnson.  51:66
King, Samuel, of Kent Co., m. by Jan. 1668, the widow of Nicholas
   Pickard.  54:255
Ladd, Richard, m. by 6 May 1676, Rosamond, widow of Joseph Hors-
   ley.  51:190
Lambert, John, of Chas. Co., m. by Nov. 1666, Ellinor, dau. of
   John Nevill.  60:49, 278
Lee, Hugh, m. by 16 Oct. 1651, Hannah, widow of Richard Heuett.
   Lee was dead by 30 July 1663, and his widow married William
   Price.  49:35;  54:22;  57:177
Lewis, William, license dated 2 Nov. 1638, Ursula Gifford.  4:50
Lunn, Thomas, m. by 27 March 1679, Dianah, relict of Oliver
   Hollaway.  51:269
Mackmere, Jeremiah, m. by Jan. 1670/1, Philise, mother of John
   Howard.  60:281
Mackmillion, George, of Chas. Co. m. by Jan. 1669, Grace Carr.
   60:221
Maddookes, Rice, m. by 1 Jan. 1657/8, Anne, relict of John
   Dandy.  41:13
Mehenny, Macom, m. by 10 April 1674, the widow of Andrew Ellenor.
   51:113
Mitchell, George, banns pub. 29 Sept. 1668, Izabell Higgens.
   54:729
Mitchell, Henry, by Oct. 1659, Grace Molden.  41:338
Morris, John, of Chas. Co., m. by March 1661/2, Eleanor, widow
   of William Empson.  53:196
Moy, Roger, license dated 24 Nov. 1638, Ann Phillipson.  4:51
Munkister, (?), of Chas. Co., m. by Sept. 1671, Elizabeth, widow
   of John Charman.  60:346
Nash, Richard, m. by 28 June 1670, Ann, widow of Richard Blunt.
   54:289
Neale, James, m. by 2 Aug. 1658, the dau. of Benjamin Gill.
   41:238
Nicholls, John, m. by 19 May 1651, the widow of William Evans.
   10:87
Oliver, Roger, m. by 29 Sept. 1649, the mother of Henry Harrison.
   4:506  His wife was Blanche, widow of John Harrison.  10:108
O'Neale, Hugh, m. by 26 Sept. 1661, Mary, widow of (?) Van der
   Donk.  53:326
Orley, Thomas, m. by 15 May 1657, Rebecca, widow of 1) George
   Manners, and 2) Edward Hall.  10:505
Ormsby, John, m. by 16 Oct. 1641, Frances Griffen.  4:67
Pagett, William, m. by 12 May 1679, Amy, sister of James Pascall.
   51:263
Paine, John, of Chas. Co., 23 Sept. 1667, Marie White.  60:116
Peake, George, m. by 4 Nov. 1657, the relict of Robert Parr.
   10:554
Pope, Henry, m. by 10 Jan. 1663, Anne, widow of Thomas Bulmear
   of Patuxent.  10:307

Price, Edward, of Chas. Co., m. by June 1673, the relict of John
    Thompkinson. 60:495
Price, William, m. by 10 Jan. 1664, Hannah, relict of Hugh Lee.
    53:542
Rawles, William, m. by 5 June 1679, Elizabeth Cash, widow of
    William Head. 51:278
Record, (Benjamin?), m. by 11 March 1679, Elizabeth, widow of
    Thomas Hall. 51:267
Rialls, Edward, swore there was no impediment to marrying, Anne
    Chapman. 4:272
Ringgold, Thomas, of Kent Co., by Nov. 1657, Christian, admini-
    stratrix of Thomas Hill, Sr. 54:121, 126
Robinson, John, of Chas. Co., 21 March 1666, Elizabeth Brown.
    60:116
Rowse, Gregory, m. by 13 May 1679, Bridgett, widow of Robert
    Sheale. 51:274
Sallers, John, m. by 7 June 1679, Ann, relict of Jeremiah Shuli-
    vant of A. A. Co. 51:248
Salter, John, m. by Jan. 1655, Jane, widow of Francis Lumbar.
    54:47
Scott, Cuthbert, 28 Oct. 1678, Elizabeth, widow of Col. William
    Evans, and 2) Capt. Jno. Jordain. 51:284
Scott, William, m. by 22 April 1650, Sarah, widow of Wm. Bruff
    of St. M. Co. 10:162
Sharp, Peter, chirurgeon, 6 March 1651, Judith, widow of John
    Garey. 10:139
Sharpe, William, son of Peter, 4 July 1673, Elizabeth, dau. of
    Thomas Thomas. 54:603
Shells, (Robert ?), m. by 19 Feb. 1661/2, Judith, widow of John
    Greenhill or Greenwell. 41:563
Smith, Robert, 23 Nov. 1638, license dated, Rose Gilbert. 4:51
Smoot, William, m. by 1651, the mother of Elizabeth Wood. 53:343
Smyth, John, of Chas. Co., m. by 14 Feb. 1666/7, Margaret Barker.
    60:116
Stearman, Richard, m. by Dec. 1662, the widow of Edmond Brent.
    53:304
Stevens, John, m. by 20 April 1671, Margaret, widow of Edward
    Jolly. 51:193
Stone, Francis, license dated 28 June 1642, Deborah Paulus.
    4:67
Streeter, Capt. Edward, m. by 20 Oct. 1656, the relict of Col.
    Thomas Burbage. 10:469
Synnett, Garrett, of Chas. Co., 21 Nov. 1666, Alice Hunt. 60:116
Taylor, John, m. by 16 Jan. 1651, Sarah, mother of Richard
    Bennett of Poplar Hill. 10:84
Thompson, Richard, m. by 24 June 1641, Ursula Bish. 4:66
Tilly, Joseph, m. by 26 April 1675, Mary, widow and executrix of
    John Little of Cal. Co. 51:159
Trueman, Thomas, m. by 20 April 1671, Mary, widow of John Bogue.
    51:364
Utie, Nathaniel, marriage contract dated 18 Jan. 1667, Elizabeth,
    dau. of John Carter of Lancaster Co., Va. 51:4
Van Swearingen, Garrett, m. by May 1669, Barbara de Barrette.
    2:205
Ward, Thomas, chirurgeon, m. by March 1649/50, Eliza, widow of
    Edward Commins. 10:43, 63
Warren, Humphrey, m. by 29 March 1651, Susan, dau. of William
    Smith. 10:174
Warren, Ignatius, m. by 3 March 1673, dau. of Robert Cole.
    51:457
Watkins, Thomas, of A. A. Co., m. by 27 March 1679, Elizabeth,
    dau. of Henry Caplin. 51:261
Williams, Lodowick, m. by 23 Aug. 1674, Mary, dau. of James
    Stringer of A. A. Co. 51:135
Williamson, David, of Som. Co., m. by 1 March 1678, the eldest
    sister of John Covington. 51:302

Wright, John, m. by 29 Dec. 1675, Mary, administratrix of
    Bartholomew Glevin.    51:165
Young, (?), m. by 5 April 1676, Elizabeth, mother of Edward
    Packer or Parker.    51:192, 311